Lecture Notes in Computer Science   9504

Commenced Publication in 1973
Founding and Former Series Editors:
Gerhard Goos, Juris Hartmanis, and Jan van Leeuwen

Editorial Board

David Hutchison
  Lancaster University, Lancaster, UK
Takeo Kanade
  Carnegie Mellon University, Pittsburgh, PA, USA
Josef Kittler
  University of Surrey, Guildford, UK
Jon M. Kleinberg
  Cornell University, Ithaca, NY, USA
Friedemann Mattern
  ETH Zurich, Zürich, Switzerland
John C. Mitchell
  Stanford University, Stanford, CA, USA
Moni Naor
  Weizmann Institute of Science, Rehovot, Israel
C. Pandu Rangan
  Indian Institute of Technology, Madras, India
Bernhard Steffen
  TU Dortmund University, Dortmund, Germany
Demetri Terzopoulos
  University of California, Los Angeles, CA, USA
Doug Tygar
  University of California, Berkeley, CA, USA
Gerhard Weikum
  Max Planck Institute for Informatics, Saarbrücken, Germany

More information about this series at http://www.springer.com/series/7407

Grzegorz Rozenberg · Arto Salomaa
José M. Sempere · Claudio Zandron (Eds.)

Membrane Computing

16th International Conference, CMC 2015
Valencia, Spain, August 17–21, 2015
Revised Selected Papers

 Springer

Editors
Grzegorz Rozenberg
LIACS, Leiden University
Leiden, Zuid-Holland
The Netherlands

Arto Salomaa
Turku Center for Computer Science
Turku
Finland

José M. Sempere
Universidad Politécnica de Valencia
Valencia
Spain

Claudio Zandron
University of Milan-Bicocca
Milano
Italy

ISSN 0302-9743 ISSN 1611-3349 (electronic)
Lecture Notes in Computer Science
ISBN 978-3-319-28474-3 ISBN 978-3-319-28475-0 (eBook)
DOI 10.1007/978-3-319-28475-0

Library of Congress Control Number: 2015958549

LNCS Sublibrary: SL1 – Theoretical Computer Science and General Issues

Printed on acid-free paper

This Springer imprint is published by SpringerNature
The registered company is Springer International Publishing AG Switzerland

Preface

The present volume contains the invited contributions and a selection of papers presented at the 16th International Conference on Membrane Computing (CMC16), which was held in Valencia, Spain, August 17–21, 2015 (website: http://users.dsic.upv.es/workshops/cmc16/), as well as three selected papers from the Asian Conference on Membrane Computing (ACMC) 2015, held in Anhui University, Hefei, Anhui, China, November 12–15, 2015 (website: http://2015.asiancmc.org/).

The CMC series started with three workshops organized in Curtea de Argeş, Romania, in 2000, 2001, and 2002. The workshops were then held in Tarragona, Spain (2003), Milan, Italy (2004), Vienna, Austria (2005), Leiden, The Netherlands (2006), Thessaloniki, Greece (2007), and Edinburgh, UK (2008).

The 10th edition was organized again in Curtea de Argeş, in August 2009, where it was decided to continue the series as the Conference on Membrane Computing (CMC). Subsequent editions were held in Jena, Germany (2010), Fontainebleau, France (2011), Budapest, Hungary (2012), Chişinău, Moldova (2013), and Prague, Czech Republic (2014).

A regional version of CMC, the Asian Conference on Membrane Computing, ACMC, started in 2012 in Wuhan (China), and continued in Chengdu, China (2013) and Coimbatore, India (2014).

CMC16 was organized, under the auspices of the European Molecular Computing Consortium (EMCC), by the Research Group on Computation Models and Formal Languages of the Universitat Politècnica de València and it was supported by the Escuela Técnica de Ingeniería Informática (ETSINF, UPV).

CMC16 consisted of three different parts: the first day was organized as a tutorial day, with lectures by Gheorghe Paun, Rudolf Freund, Claudio Zandron, Gyorgy Vaszil, and Agustín Riscos-Núñez. From Tuesday to Thursday the conference continued with standard sessions; invited lectures were given by Ion Petre (Abo Akademi University, Finland), Andrés Moya (Universitat de València, Spain), and Vincenzo Manca (University of Verona, Italy). The last day of the conference was devoted to the presentation of extended abstracts and to interaction between participants. Based on the votes of the CMC16 participants, the Best Paper Award of this edition was given to Rudolf Freund and Petr Sosík for their paper "On the Power of Catalytic P Systems with One Catalyst."

The editors express their gratitude to the Program Committee, the invited speakers, the authors of the papers, the reviewers, and all the participants for their contributions to the success of CMC16.

November 2015

Grzegorz Rozenberg
Arto Salomaa
José M. Sempere
Claudio Zandron

Organization

Steering Committee

Artiom Alhazov	Chişinău, Moldova
Bogdan Aman	Iasi, Romania
Matteo Cavaliere	Edinburgh, UK
Erzsébet Csuhaj-Varjú	Budapest, Hungary
Rudolf Freund	Wien, Austria
Marian Gheorghe	Bradford, UK - Honorary Member
Thomas Hinze	Cottbus, Germany
Florentin Ipate	Bucharest, Romania
Alberto Leporati	Milan, Italy
Linqiang Pan	Wuhan, China
Gheorghe Păun	Bucharest, Romania and Seville, Spain - Honorary Member
Agustín Riscos-Núñez	Seville, Spain
Petr Sosik	Opava, Czech Republic
Gyorgy Vaszil	Debrecen, Hungary
Sergey Verlan	Paris, France
Claudio Zandron	Milan, Italy - Chair

Organizing Committee

Marcelino Campos	Valencia, Spain
Guillem Pitarch	Valencia, Spain
María Samblás	Valencia, Spain
José M. Sempere	Valencia, Spain - Co-chair
Claudio Zandron	Milan, Italy - Co-chair

Program Committee

Artiom Alhazov	Chişinău, Moldova
Matteo Cavaliere	Edinburgh, UK
Ludek Cienciala	Opava, Czech Republic
Gabriel Ciobanu	Iasi, Romania
Erzsébet Csuhaj-Varjú	Budapest, Hungary
Giuditta Franco	Verona, Italy
Rudolf Freund	Wien, Austria
Marian Gheorghe	Bradford, UK
Thomas Hinze	Cottbus, Germany
Florentin Ipate	Bucharest, Romania

Shankara Narayanan Krishna	Bombay, India
Alberto Leporati	Milan, Italy
Vincenzo Manca	Verona, Italy
Maurice Margenstern	Metz, France
Giancarlo Mauri	Milan, Italy
Radu Nicolescu	Auckland, New Zealand
Linqiang Pan	Wuhan, China
Gheorghe Păun	Bucharest, Romania and Seville, Spain
Mario de Jesús Pérez Jiménez	Seville, Spain
Dario Pescini	Milan, Italy
Agustín Riscos-Núñez	Seville, Spain
José M. Sempere	Valencia, Spain - Co-chair
Petr Sosík	Opava, Czech Republic
Gyorgy Vaszil	Debrecen, Hungary
Sergey Verlan	Paris, France
Claudio Zandron	Milan, Italy - Co-chair
Gexiang Zhang	Chengdu, Sichuan, China

Additional Reviewers

Bogdan Aman	Iasi, Romania
Raluca Lefticaru	Bucharest, Romania
Alin Stefanescu	Bucharest, Romania
Álvaro Romero Jiménez	Seville, Spain
Andrei Alexandru	Iasi, Romania
Miguel Á. Martínez-Del-Amor	Seville, Spain

Contents

Contents XI

Invited Papers

Information Theory in Genome Analysis

Vincenzo Manca[(✉)]

Dipartimento di Informatica, Centro di BioMedicina Computazionale,
Università degli Studi di Verona, Verona, Italy
vincenzo.manca@univr.it

Abstract. Classical concepts of Information Theory are quickly summarized and their application to the computational analysis of genomes is outlined. Genomes are long strings, and this open the possibility of considering them as information sources. From this viewpoint, it turns out that information entropy, mutual information, entropic divergences, codes, and dictionaries (finite formal languages) are fundamental tools for extracting the biological information on which biological functionalities are based on. The importance of random genomes is also motivated, and some genomic distributions are presented and discussed.

1 Introduction

Genomes are containers of biological information that direct the functions of the organisms and transmit biological information along their generations. Recently, concepts from algorithms, formal languages, computer science, and linguistics [2,5–7,10,12–14,17,19,23–25,28,29,31,32] were applied to the mathematical and computational analysis of DNA and genomes. Moreover, *alignment free* methods emerged [15,16,32,33], where genomes are investigated, in the whole, rather than by means of local similarities deduced by classical methods of string alignment. Here we show that many aspects of genomic information are related to concepts of information theory, which can be fruitfully applied when genomes are considered as information sources in the original sense developed by Shannon in his seminal work on the mathematical theory of communication [30] (see [20–22] for short introductions to related subjects).

2 Basic Notation

Let us recall basic concepts and notation. For basic concepts on strings and formal languages, the reader can refer to classical textbooks (see for example [27]). Strings will be denoted by Greek letters (possibly with subscripts). In particular, λ denotes empty string. The length of a string α is denoted by $|\alpha|$, $\alpha[i]$ denotes the symbol occurring at position i of α, and $\alpha[i,j]$ denotes the substring of α starting at position i and ending at position j (all the symbols between these positions in the order they have in α). The most important operation over strings is **concatenation** of α, β, usually denoted by the juxtaposition $\alpha\beta$. The

© Springer International Publishing Switzerland 2015
G. Rozenberg et al. (Eds.): CMC 2015, LNCS 9504, pp. 3–18, 2015.
DOI: 10.1007/978-3-319-28475-0_1

overlap concatenation of two strings $\alpha\gamma, \gamma\beta$, is $\alpha\gamma\beta$ where γ is the maximum substring that is suffix of the first string and prefix of the second one.

The **genomic alphabet** of symbols representing nucleotides is $\Gamma = \{a, c, g, t\}$ (and $\Gamma^\star$ is the set of all possible words over Γ). A genome $\mathbb{G}$ is a "long" string over Γ (its symbols are written in a linear order, from left to right, according to the chemical orientation $5' - 3'$ of DNA molecules). All the substrings of a genome $\mathbb{G}$ define the finite language $D(\mathbb{G})$, while all the substrings of length k provide the language $D_k(\mathbb{G})$. Any subset of $D(\mathbb{G})$ is a **dictionary** of $\mathbb{G}$. Elements of $D(\mathbb{G})$ are also called **words, factors, k-mers, k-grams**) of $\mathbb{G}$ (k prefix is used when we want explicitly mention the length of strings). The set of positions where (the first symbol of) a factor α occurs in $\mathbb{G}$ is denoted $pos_{\mathbb{G}}(\alpha)$, and the multiplicity of a factor α in $\mathbb{G}$, that is, the number of times it occurs in G, is denoted by $mult_{\mathbb{G}}(\alpha)$.

It is very important to distinguish two kinds of words of a genome $\mathbb{G}$: repeat and hapaxes. A **hapax** of $\mathbb{G}$ is a word occurring in G once, while a **repeat** of $\mathbb{G}$ is a word occurring in $\mathbb{G}$ at least twice. Any string that includes a hapax is a hapax too, while any string included in a repeat is a repeat too. A repeat is maximal if it is not substring of another repeat. A hapax is minimal if any substring of it is a repeat. From the given definitions, elongating a maximal repeat α with a symbol $x \in \Gamma$, both αx and $x\alpha$ are minimal hapaxes. However, the converse implication does not hold, because if αx (or $x\alpha$), is a minimal hapax, this does not imply that α is a maximal repeat (even if it is surely a repeat).

A dictionary L of a genome $\mathbb{G}$ (completely) covers $\mathbb{G}$ if, when we arrange the words of L in all the position intervals of $\mathbb{G}$ where they occur, then any position of $\mathbb{G}$ belongs to some interval where a word α of L occurs. When L does not cover $\mathbb{G}$, the fraction of positions covered by the words of L is the *sequential coverage* of L, while the number of words covering a position is the *positional coverage* of L in that position.

Important **genomic indexes** for a genome G are: (i) $mrl(\mathbb{G})$ denoting the *maximal repeat length*, (ii) $mhl(\mathbb{G})$ denoting the *minimal hapax length*, (iii) $mfl(\mathbb{G})$ denoting the shortest length m such that for all $k < m$, all k-mers over γ occur in G.

3   A Glimpse in Information Theory

Information theory "officially" begins with Shannon's booklet [30] published in 1948. The main idea of Shannon is linking information with probability. In fact, the starting definition of this seminal work is that of **information source** as a pair (X, p), where X is a finite set of objects (data, signals, words) and p is a probability function assigning to every $x \in X$ the probability $p(x)$ of occurrence (emission, reception, production). The perspective of this approach is the mathematical analysis of communication processes, but its impact is completely general and expresses the probabilistic nature of information. Information is an inverse function of probability, because it is a sort of *a posteriori* counterpart of the *a priori* uncertainty represented by probability, measuring the gain of knowledge when an event occurs. For this reason the more an event is rare, the more it is informative. However, if event E has probability p_E, for several technical reason it is better to define $inf(E)$ as $1/\lg(p_E) = -\lg(p_E)$ than $1/p_E$. The logarithm guarantees the information additivity for a joint event (E, E') where components are independent, giving $inf(E, E') = inf(E) + inf(E')$. However, in passing, it is important to remark that the relationship between information and probability is in both verses, because as Bayesian approaches make evident, information can change the probability evaluation (conditional probability, on which Bayes theorem is based, defines how probability changes when we know that an event occurred). A famous example of this phenomenon is the famous three-doors (or Monty Hall) dilemma [26], which can be fully explained by using Bayes theorem.

In the following of this section we give a quick overview of the basic concepts in Information theory. The reader is advised to refer to [9, 11, 30] for more details in Information and Probability theory.

3.1 Entropy

As a consequence of the probabilistic approach, the average quantity of information, for an information source (X, p) is given by

$$H(X, p) = -\sum_{x \in X} p(x) \lg p(x). \tag{1}$$

Information entropy corresponds (apart multiplicative and additive constants) to H function defined by Ludwig Boltzmann when he founded statistical mechanics as microscopical representation of thermodynamical entropy. This is the reason for which physics entropy and information entropy share a common name. Mathematically, they are the same thing, and this equivalence has a deep common probabilistic basis with consequences so far not completely understood (a belief common to many physicists claims that information could explain some of unsolved puzzles of modern physics): *It from bit* is one of the last speculations of John Archibald Wheeler, a founder of quantum gravity, suggesting that information is fundamental to the physics of the universe.

Entropy allows us to discover theorems connecting the probabilistic measure of information with the digital quantity of information. The digital quantity of information is always related to a given code, that is, a function from a set C, a finite language over a finite alphabet, of strings (words, signals, ...) to a set X of data. In order to simplify our discussion, assume that a code is 1-to-1, or that it is represented by a function $\gamma : X \to C$ (codes where more than an encoding in C are associated to one datum, are called redundant, but are not considered here). The digital quantity of datum d, with respect to the code is the length of string α encoding it. Usually, codes are required to have some basic properties ensuring simple sequential decoding. Namely, a code is *univocal* if any string over the alphabet of the code can be factorized in a unique way as concatenation of strings of the code.

Let p a probability defined on set of pairs (a cartesian product) $X \times Y$. The joint entropy extends naturally to:

$$H(X \times Y, p) = - \sum_{x \in X y \in Y} p(x,y) \lg p(x,y). \tag{2}$$

Conditional entropy is defined by using conditional probability:

$$p(y|x) = p(x,y)/p(x) \tag{3}$$

where

$$p(x) = \sum_{y \in Y} p(x,y) \tag{4}$$

by setting:

$$H(Y|X, p) = - \sum_{x \in X, y \in Y} p(x,y) \lg p(y|x). \tag{5}$$

It can be shown that:

$$H(X \times Y, p) = H(X, p_X) + H(Y|X, p) - \sum_{x \in X y \in Y} p(x,y) \lg p(x,y)$$

where p_X is the marginal probability assigning to x the value $p(x)$ defined in (4).

3.2   Entropic Divergence

After the definition of entropy for an information source (X, p) other two key concepts are the entropic divergence and the mutual information. Shannon defines directly the second one, but after Kullback and Leibler [18] now it seems more appropriate to define mutual information by means of the entropic divergence KL. It is a sort of distance measuring how much two probability distributions defined on the same domain differ each other. This value is always positive, apart the case of two identical distribution (in this case $D(p,q) = 0$), However KL is nor symmetric neither transitive. The formula is the following:

$$KL(p,q) = \sum_{x \in X} p(x) \lg(p(x)/q(x)). \tag{6}$$

Similar divergences can be defined, in particular a symmetric version of divergence of KL, due to Jeffreys [9] is given by:

$$JKL(p,q) = \sum_{x \in X} [p(x) - q(x)] \lg(p(x)/q(x)) \tag{7}$$

It is easy to realize that $JKL(p,q) = KL(p,q) + KL(p,q)$.

3.3   Mutual Information

Let p a probability defined over $X \times Y$, where p_X, p_Y are the two marginal probabilities over X, Y respectively, the mutual information $I(X,Y)$ is given by:

$$I(X,Y) = KL(p, (p_X \cdot p_Y)). \tag{8}$$

It can be shown that (probabilities over X, Y are not indicated):

$$I(X,Y) = H(X) + H(Y) - H(X,Y) \tag{9}$$

and

$$I(X,Y) = H(X) - H(X|Y). \tag{10}$$

Shannon's booklet proves three fundamental theorems. The first Shannon's theorem provides a lower bound to the optimality of codes. *Given an information source no code can exist having a average length (with respect to a given probability distribution of data) shorter that the entropy of the source.*

Mutual information is the basis of Shannon's second theorem: *even if symbols of an information source are transmitted with some noise along a channel, then it is possible to encode them in such a way that transmission could become safe, in the sense that, the longer are the transmission encodings, the more error probability, along the channel, approaches to zero.* In more precise terms, the theorem establishes quantitative notions giving the possibility of avoiding error transmission if the rate of transmission is lower that the capacity of transmission channel, where notions of transmission rate and of capacity channel are formally defined in terms of transmission codes and in terms of mutual information (between the transmitter information source and the receiver information source).

Third Shannon's theorem concerns with signals. To this end, the entropic notions are extended to the case of continuous information sources, then, by using these continuous notions, quantitative evaluation about safe communication by means of continuous signals are proven.

3.4   Univocal and Prefix-Free Codes

A code C with n words is minimal if no code of n words exist having a shorter average length. A lexicographic code of n words consists of the first n words in the lexicographic ordering of strings. A lexicographic code is minimal.

A code $\gamma : X \to C$, encoding a set of data X, where $\gamma(x)$ is the encoding of datum x, is optimal with respect to an information source (X, p) if no other code exists having a smaller average length:

$$\sum_{x \in X} |x| p(x).$$

The *Kraft norm* associated to a code $\gamma : X \to C$ is defined by in the following way (for the sake of simplification let us identify a code with the set C of its encodings), where k is the cardinality of the alphabet of the code.

$$\|C\| = \sum_{\alpha \in C} k^{|\alpha|}. \tag{11}$$

A theorem tell us that a code C is univocal iff $||C|| \leq 1$ [9]. Moreover, for any C satisfying this inequality it is possible to construct a code C' with the same Kraft norm, that is *prefix free* (no encoding of C is prefix of another encoding). Prefix freeness of a code guarantees an efficient way for reconstruct the sequence of data associated to the concatenation of their encodings (in the same order as data are arranged). Therefore, when encodings of data are transmitted with a prefix-free code, we do not need to separate encodings in order to avoid ambiguity. Other more complex properties can be defined on codes, which ensure other efficiency properties of decoding processes. Of course, no ambiguity is present if codes are fixed-length codes where all the encodings have the same length. However this requirement is often too strong in many cases of encoding processes. In fact, assume that we want to optimize the global length of a string encoding a sequence of data. In this case, it is reasonable to have codes where data more frequent are encoded by shorter strings, while data seldom appearing are encoded by longer strings.

In general a code is optimal with respect to a probability of occurrences of its data, when its probabilistic *average length* $\sum_{\alpha \in C} |\alpha| p(\alpha)$ is minimal. Simple algorithms exist providing codes that are optimal for a given probability distribution (the famous Huffman encoding [9] is one of them).

3.5   Compression

An issue related to optimal encodings is the compression of strings. In general terms, a compression algorithm is a way of representing a string α by a string β shorten than α (let us assume β to belong to the same alphabet of α) such that the original string α can be completely and univocally recovered from β by a *decompression* algorithm (partial forms of compression where sone loss of original string are tolerated, are also useful in some cases). The compression ratio is given by the fraction $|\beta|/|\alpha|$, and the smaller it is, the more the compression algorithm gains space when it compress the original string. Of course, this gain is usually paid by a computational cost in the compression and/or in the decompression. It is easy to realize that a compression algorithm cannot be universal. In fact it can give a small ratio for some strings, but it cannot do the same for all the strings over the alphabet, because otherwise by the compression algorithm we could represent all the strings of a given length by means of shorter strings, but this is impossible because the cardinality of longer strings is greater than that of shorter strings, therefore all the strings of a given length could not be uniquely determined from their compressed corresponding strings. Nevertheless, it is often interesting that compression could really compress some classes of strings for which a more compact way is required in some circumstances. Methods of compression are usually based on three different principles (in many aspects related). The first is based on a known distribution of probabilities of some words occurring in the string. In this case, it is enough to define short encodings for words with high occurrence probabilities and longer encodings for those with low probabilities. The second method is based on dictionaries. If we know a dictionary of words occurring in a string, then we memorize this dictionary, and replace in the text the words by the corresponding encodings. This provides a space gain when we have for example one thousand binary words of length 20. In fact, one thousand objects need only binary strings of length 10, therefore we gain 10 bits for each word. In a text of 100.000 binary symbols we have $100.000/20 = 5000$ word occurrences of length 10, giving an encoding string of 500.000 binary symbols, therefore if the dictionary memorization requires 10.000 binary symbols, we obtain a representation of the original string with an encoding string of 50.000 symbols plus a dictionary of 10.000, with a compression ratio of $60.000/100.000$. The third method is based on a rearrangement of a string from which the original string can uniquely be recovered, in such a way that in the rearranged string similar substrings are contiguous. If this happen, an element of type α^n can be encoded by encoding α and n, that need $|\alpha|$ symbols plus $O(\lg n)$ symbols instead than $n|\alpha|$ symbols (the n copies of α scattered in the original sequence).

3.6 Entropic Paradox

It is important to remark an aspect that highlights an intrinsic paradoxical nature of information. An initial section of Shannon's fundamental booklet (Sect. 6), devoted to introduce the notion of entropy is entitled "Choice, Uncertainty and Entropy". What sounds strange in this title is a sort of identification between Entropy and uncertainty, where the first was already defined as an average measure of the information quantity emitted by an information source. It reasonable to identify notions that seem to be opposite? This impression of contradiction continues when Shannon proves that the maximum value reached by entropy is realized when the probability distribution of an information source is the uniform distribution where all the events (emitted symbols) have the same probability. In this sense, a completely random source reaches the maximum entropy. This means that a random symbol emission process is more informative than a process where symbols are generated according to a precise rule. Why Shannon does found its theory on such a kind of conceptual ambiguity? Of course, Shannon is not interested in philosophical issues, but surely he is conscious of this problem. Is it safe to identify information with uncertainty? Is it not something like to identify knowledge with ignorance? A possible answer to this position is related to the intrinsic relative nature of information. It is not really important to quantify information, but the gain/loss of information in the passage between two different states. In this sense it is only matter of the orientation we choose, because a gain of information corresponds exactly to the same loss of uncertainty, or equivalently, what is the information quantity that we gain, after a passage of state, corresponds to the uncertainty that we lose with respect to the previous state. Information is oriented in time, or better, time arrow is a consequence of information orientation along a dynamical process. When we put gas molecules inside a volume, each of them having an initial position and speed, if collisions are elastic (with no energy loss, that implies constancy of speed distribution variance), then in colliding they exchange information, by tending to a limit distribution (which can be proved to be the gaussian speed distribution). Information theory tell us that Gaussian distribution is the distribution having the maximum entropy among those having a fixed variance. This means that the thermodynamical low of maximum entropy is a consequence of large numbers laws and information theory laws (this is an extreme simplification of the phenomenon, but centers its main point).

4 Genomic Distributions and Dictionaries

For the following discussion it is important to recall explicitly the notion of **discrete distribution**. It is a function assigning to any value x of a finite or enumerable subset B of real numbers a real value $f(x)$ in such a way that $\sum_{x \in B} f(x)$ is a finite value b. When $b = 1$ the distribution is called a (discrete) probability distribution, because $f(x)$ can be seen as the probability of occurrence of the value $x \in B$. When B is a set of values expressing quantities defined on genomes, then the distribution is called a genomic distribution. In the following, we consider some genomic distributions that result important in the perspective of informational analyses of genomes. Of course, any genomic distribution f, when is normalized (by considering $f(x)/b$), it becomes a probability distribution, therefore it determines an information source, to which all concepts outlined above can be applied. Many important genomic distributions are based on the notion of genomic dictionary, and genomic distributions are the key for applying information theoretic concepts to genomes. Here we will give only a succinct list of distributions and related concepts. We want to stress that by using them we can extract and analyze information from real genomes, by deciding if some parts of a genome are almost casual or if their information content is telling us that possibly some biological functions are related to their "information density". In this regard, an aspect that is outside the classical approach of Shannon is the comparison with randomness. This comparison can be developed by generating (pseudo) random genomes and comparing directly them with real genomes, or indirectly, by comparing distributions observed over genomes with those that probability theory tell us to rule random processes. This is an amazing aspect, almost paradoxical, of probability theory (related to the laws of large numbers): purely random phenomena follow perfect mathematical laws. When you extracted balls from an urn where you are completely ignorant about what can be the result of your extraction, in this case, we know that the probability of extracting k white balls in n extraction is $\binom{n}{k} 1/2^n$, and that for n going to infinite, the distribution of these probabilities approximates to the Gaussian curve (Moivre-Laplace's theorem, that Gauss discovered as the law according to which errors are distributed). The apparent contradiction of such rule comes when we consider "random" as equivalent to "chaos" (to be precise, the two concepts are not equivalent, but a deep analysis of this distinction would be out the scope of the present discussion). In fact, if chaos is, in some sense, the lack of any rule how it is possible that chaotic/random phenomena can be described by precise mathematical laws? The nature of this paradox is informational (as the previous use of the term "ignorance" suggests) and only a deep discrimination between the causes acting over an observed phenomenon, and the knowledge of their nature and realization (what happens and what I know about what happens), can conciliate some intrinsic aporias underlying facts and conjectures about them (Jacob Bernoulli's "Ars Conjectandi" is the title of the first systematic treatise about probability). Now, we can generate (pseudo) random strings with deterministic algorithms. This is one of the most exciting success of twentieth century (Universal Computability and Deterministic Chaos among the top scientific achievements of the century, and they are related). If we can generate random strings over alphabet of four symbols, we can generate random genomes, and these genomes are probably the origins of real genomes. Therefore a key point, that we do not touch here, for understanding life evolution is just based in methods comparing real genomes with random genomes. But let us stop abruptly here this discussion and go back to the list of some genomic distributions.

4.1   Distributions of k-mer Cardinality

Given a genome $\mathbb{G}$ the distribution:

$$k \mapsto |D_k(\mathbb{G}|$$

is a characteristic of $\mathbb{G}$. Important values of k, related to $\mathbb{G}$, are the value for which $|D_k(\mathbb{G}|$ is maximum and the value for which the possible k-words are more than k-words occurring in the genome (corresponding to $mfl(\mathbb{G})$). Of course, these values are strongly related to the length of $\mathbb{G}$, but their exact determination is related to specific aspect of the genome.

4.2   Multiplicity and Co-multiplicity Distributions

Let $\mathbb{G}$ a genome and L be a genomic dictionary of $\mathbb{G}$. Let us consider the multiplicity $mult_{\mathbb{G}}(\alpha)$ for every $\alpha \in L$. If we set:

$$\|L\| = \sum_{\alpha \in L} mult_{\mathbb{G}}(\alpha)$$

then $mult_{\mathbb{G}}(\alpha)/\|L\|$ is a probability distribution. Let $M = max\{mult_{\mathbb{G}}(\alpha) \mid \alpha \in L\}$. A distribution directly related to multiplicity is the co-multiplicity $comult$, assigning to any value k in $\{1, 2, \ldots M\}$ the number of words of L having multiplicity k, that is:

$$k \mapsto |\{\alpha \in L \mid mult_{\mathbb{G}}(\alpha) = k\}|.$$

Also co-multiplicity can be normalized if co-multiplicities are divided by $|L|$, the cardinality of L. Particular cases of multiplicity and co-multiplicity distributions are based on the k-mer of $\mathbb{G}$, for some k. These distributions, especially multiplicity, are well studied especially for small values of k ($k < 12$). The empirical entropy $E_k(\mathbb{G})$ of length k of a genome $\mathbb{G}$ is the entropy associated to the information source $(D_k(\mathbb{G}), mult_\mathbb{G}(\alpha)/||L||)$, that is:

$$E_k(\mathbb{G}) = \sum_{\alpha \in D_k(\mathbb{G})} (mult_\mathbb{G}(\alpha)/||D_k(\mathbb{G}||)) \lg(mult_\mathbb{G}(\alpha)/D_k(\mathbb{G}||)).$$

It is easy to verify that $D_k(\mathbb{G}||) = |\mathbb{G}| - k + 1$.

4.3   Distributions Relating Word Length and Multiplicity

These kinds of genomic distributions answer to the following questions. (i) What is the average, minimum, or maximum length of words occurring k times in a genome $\mathbb{G}$? (ii) How many times do the words of length k occur in a genome $\mathbb{G}$ (on average, minimum, or maximum value)?

4.4   Spectra of Genomic Dictionaries

When a word occurs in a genome $\mathbb{G}$, we say that it occurs at the position where its first symbol occurs. The set $pos_\mathbb{G}(\alpha)$, also called the spectrum of word α in $\mathbb{G}$, provides all the positions of $\mathbb{G}$, where α occurs (if α does not occur in $\mathbb{G}$ its spectrum in $\mathbb{G}$ is empty). Of course, if a dictionary L covers completely $\mathbb{G}$, then from the spectra of its words it is possible to reconstruct uniquely $\mathbb{G}$. Moreover, the following equation derives directly from the definitions of $mult$ and pos:

$$mult_\mathbb{G}(\alpha) = |pos_\mathbb{G}(\alpha)|.$$

Representations of genomes by means of word spectra may be very redundant, and the redundancy level can be measured in terms of average positional coverage. However, this redundancy is a positive aspect when we want recover the genome from a dictionary that covers completely it. The set of all k-mers occurring in a genome is a completely covering dictionary, therefore spectra of k-mers uniquely determines genomes. However, an important question concerns the search for minimal dictionaries that, almost completely, cover a given genome. In fact, in this case, their spectra identify (almost completely) the entire genome by reducing the representation redundancy. For example, in human chromosomes, we found [3] that around a third of all possible 6-mers has a coverage near to 98 %, but these 6-mers are specific of each chromosome, even if, in groups of four, their intersections are very consistent (around one thousand).

4.5   Hapax Overlap Factorizations

Given a genome $\mathbb{G}$ there exist a non trivial dictionary L of $\mathbb{G}$ such that $\mathbb{G}$ is completely determined by L? The following algorithm provides an answer to this question, by generating a dictionary of m-**forward overlap factors** having this property of univocal identification of $\mathbb{G}$. Before giving a pseudo-code of the algorithm, let us explain the main idea. Let fix a length m amd factorize $\mathbb{G}$ in the following manner, where w_j for $j = 1, 2, \ldots n$, are substrings of $\mathbb{G}$ of length m, while h_j are the shortest hapaxes between the w substrings, h_n is the rightmost hapax of $\mathbb{G}$, and w_{n+1} is the string following h_n up to the end of $\mathbb{G}$:

$$\mathbb{G} = w_1 h_1 w_2 h_2 w_3 h_3 \ldots h_{n-1} w_n h_n w_{n+1}.$$

Given the representation above of $\mathbb{G}$, we define a dictionary L by setting:

$$L = \{w_1 h_1, h_1 w_2 h_2, h_2 w_3 h_3, \ldots h_{n-1} w_n h_n, h_n w_{n+1}\}.$$

The algorithm generating L is given by the following procedure.

1 Set $i := 1, j := 1$;
2 Move m positions forward from position i of $\mathbb{G}$;
3 From position $i + m$ go forward and set h_j as the first position of $\mathbb{G}$ such that factor $\mathbb{G}[i + m, h_j]$ is a hapax of $\mathbb{G}$. If such a hapax does not exist, set $g := j - 1$ and go to step 5;
4 Set $i := h_j + 1$ and go to step 2;
5 Set $F_1 = \mathbb{G}[1, h_1]$;
6 For $j = 1, \ldots, g - 1$ Set $F_j = \mathbb{G}[h_j, h_{j+1}]$;
7 Set $F_g = \mathbb{G}[h_{g-1}, |\mathbb{G}|]$.

It can easily be shown that the factors $F_1, F_2, \ldots$ given from the previous algorithm are exactly the dictionary L as defined above, and directly from their construction (they share hapaxes at most with other two factors) they can be concatenated (with overlap) in a unique way and their overlap concatenation is exactly $\mathbb{G}$. These factors are very useful in the analysis of $\mathbb{G}$. Researches in progress are using these factors in some analyses of genomes that are relevant to the identification of genome pathological situations (in human genome). Of course, changing the value of m, we get different factorizations. According to the cases of interest, a suitable trade-off between the length of m and the average length of hapaxes can be required. Moreover, a variable forward length can be used for optimize some aspects of the factorization. In [2] a more complex algorithm generating hapax overlap factorization is given, aimed at realizing some minimality principles.

4.6   Recurrence Distance Distributions

Let us consider the spectrum $pos_{\mathbb{G}}(\alpha)$ of a given word α in a given genome $\mathbb{G}$, and enumerate the positions of this set in their increasing order: $p_1, p_2, \ldots, p_m$. Then the values $d_1 = p_2 - p_1, \ldots, d_i = p_{i+1} - p_i, \ldots, d_{m-1} = p_m - p_{m-1}$ are called recurrence distances of α in $\mathbb{G}$. Distribution $RDD_{\mathbb{G}}(\alpha)$ associates to any recurrence distance the number of times it appear in the above enumeration. It can be shown that in Bernoullian genomes RDD distributions are exponential distributions ($\lambda e^{-\lambda x}$ for some real parameter λ). This fact is very important, because the entropic divergence between the observed $RDD(\alpha)$ of a genome and the exponential $RDD(\alpha)$ in a Bernoullian genome of the same length is a sort of measure of the non-randomness of α in $\mathbb{G}$ (parameter λ can be evaluated by searching the exponential with the minimum error with respect to the observed distribution). In [4] RDD distributions were used for introducing a new method for discovering DNA encoding regions (inclusive of transcribed region that are not translated into proteins).

4.7   Genome Representations

The three preceding subsections determine in a natural way forms of genome representations that are alternative to the standard sequence representation over Γ^*. The reader is invited to provide the details of this. However, other unconventional genome representations can be defined, which could suggest new ways to consider and analyze genomes. Let us shortly mention some of them.

1. **Hapax Permutation**. Let us factorize $\mathbb{G}$ as:

$$\mathbb{G} = \mathbb{G}[1, p_1]\mathbb{G}[p_1, p_2]\mathbb{G}[p_2, p_3]\ldots\mathbb{G}[p_{m-1}, p_m]$$

   where all factors above are hapaxes, then the set of these factors (enumerated in some order, for example, in lexicographic order) plus a permutation of $\{1, 2, \ldots, m\}$ identifies $\mathbb{G}$.
2. **Characteristic vectors**. $\mathbb{G}$ is identified by three boolean vectors: vector X of length $|\mathbb{G}|$ where 1 is placed in all the positions where a is in $\mathbb{G}$, vector Y of length $|\mathbb{G}| - \sum X$ where 1 is placed in all the positions where c is in $\mathbb{G}$, vector Z of length $|X| - \sum Y$ where 1 is placed in all the positions where g is in $\mathbb{G}$ (in the positions of X which do not correspond to 1 in Y and Z, surely t is placed in $\mathbb{G}$).
3. **Random Exceptions**. Let us generate a random sequence R of length $|\mathbb{G}|$ over the symbols of Γ (by means of some algorithm of random generation, where some parameters of the adopted random generation seed identify completely the generated sequence). Then, consider a boolean vector B of length $|\mathbb{G}|$ having 1 in the positions where $\mathbb{G}$ differs from R. If m is the number of the different positions, we can associate to B other two vectors X and Y. Vector X of length m has 1 in the positions i where the order distance $\mathbb{G}(i) - B(i)$ is 1, according the circular order $a < c < g < t < a$ (for example, $d(a, c) = 1, d(a, g) = 2, d(a, t) = 3$), while vector Y of length $m - \sum X$ (value $\sum X$ corresponds to the number of 1 of X) has 1 in the positions j where the order distance $\mathbb{G}(j) - B(j)$ is 2. Of course, in the remaining positions k of B the distance $\mathbb{G}(k) - B(k)$ is 3.
4. **Word Elongations**. Consider a dictionary of L of all possible k-words (for some length k, for example $k = 6$). If for every word w in L we give the sequence $Elong_{\mathbb{G}}(w)$ of the words L following all the occurrence of w, then $\mathbb{G}$ is completely identified by the set $Elong_{\mathbb{G}}(L) = \{Elong_{\mathbb{G}}(w) \mid w \in L\}$ of elongations of w, and from the word w_1 of L occurring in the first k positions of $\mathbb{G}$ (a simple algorithm can be given for reconstructing univocally $\mathbb{G}$ from $Elong_{\mathbb{G}}(L)$ and w_1). Other kinds of representations can be developed, where the idea of elongation is elaborated in similar, but different, ways (for

example, elongations of some "seeds", located in suitable positions of G, until the elongations do not reach the position before the beginning of another seed).

5. **Lexicographic Gaps.** Let us factorize G by words of a given length. Each of them represents the number $||w||$ corresponding to the position of w in the lexicographic order of strings. Then, given the first word of G, the sequence of integer numbers $||w|| - ||w'||$, where w' is the word following w, identifies completely G.

6. **Alphabetic Transcription.** The usual string representation of a genome over the alphabet Γ can be transformed into a string in a different alphabet by encoding k-mers into suitable characters (letters, ciphers, colors, . . .). These kinds of representations are more properly "visualizations" of genomes, but can be very useful for a better reading of recurrent pattern that become more evident for specific inspections of genomic regions [3].

4.8   Complete Segmentations and Segment Dictionaries

A Segmentation $S(G)$ of a genome G is given by a sequence of substrings of G, of factors, or segments $G_1, G_2, \ldots, G_m$ such that their concatenation provides G. Given a genomic dictionary L of G, the segmentation $S(G)$ is L-complete when $D(G_i) = L$ for $1 \leq i \leq m$. In real genomes, very often, complete segmentations consist of factors with very different lengths. This means that words of a dictionary are usually distributed in a non homogeneous way. Symmetrically, we can consider a segmentation where all the factors have the same length and for each of them we consider the words of L occurring in that factor. In this case, very often, we get very different set of words in the different factors. Segmentation distributions can associate to each factor the cardinality of its dictionary, or to each value of k the minimal lengths $l_1, l_2, \ldots, l_m$ such that:

$$G[1, l_1], G[l_1 + 1, l_2], \ldots G[l_{m-1} + 1, l_m]$$

results to be a L-complete segmentation of G. Given a segmentation of factors of the same length and a word α, how much are the segments where α occurs k times? In a Bernoullian genome this distribution follow a Poisson law $\lambda^k e^{-\lambda}/k!$ (parameter λ depends on the genome length and on the segment length).

4.9   Occurrence Order and Context Dictionaries

Given a genome G and a word α of a dictionary L of G, we say that at position h word α has *occurrence order* j, and write $occur_G(\alpha, h) = j$, if α occurs in G at position h (its first symbol occurs in h) and $mult_{G[1,h-1]}(\alpha, h) = j - 1$. In this case, the context dictionary of α in G, around its occurrence of order j, within radius m, is the set of words of L that are in G within m positions before and after h:

$$L_{j,k}(\alpha)\{\beta \in L \mid occur_G(\alpha, h) = j, \ \beta = G[l_1, l_2], h - m < l_1 < l_2 < h + m\}.$$

For some suitable m, the following language:

$$L_m(\alpha) = \cap_{j \in pos_\mathbb{G}(\alpha)} L_{j,m}$$

defines the words of $\mathbb{G}$ that are related to α in $\mathbb{G}$. These kind of languages are very important in the analyses of functions that some words play in a given genome.

5   Conclusions

The previous discussion was mainly of mathematical (and philosophical) nature. However, in closing we want avoid to give the impression that these two aspects cover all the aspects of genomes viewed as information sources. The main interest in defining informational concepts over genomes, is the computational aspect that here was not presented. The interested reader is advised to consult the papers given in reference for realizing the kind of results that can be obtained when informational measures, dictionaries, and distributions are computed in real genomes. After computing them, we compare them, and extract regularities and characteristics related to particular genomes or classes of genomes. In this kind of activity, the most critical point is the computational efficiency. For example, when we consider human genome, and its dictionary of 30-mers, you reach a dictionary size of billions of words (near to the length of the whole genome). If you want use it for computing the empirical entropy at length 30, your computer almost surely crashes and you cannot conclude your computation. This means that suitable data structure have be used for avoiding these computational limits. In this specific case, if you represent dictionaries in terms of suffix arrays [1], you can obtain your result in two hours with a normal laptop. This strategy was systematically implemented in [3] that supports a number of functionalities for computing almost all the formulas that were presented in this paper. Presently, we analyzed more than two hundreds genomes of several types (virus, archea, prokaryotes, eukaryotes, multicellular organisms of different types up to many type of mammalians). Two main research lines, only mentioned in the discussion above, are: (i) the extraction of dictionaries, based only of informational analyses that could integrate analogous analyses developed according to biochemical aspects (see The project ENCODE (ENCyclopedia Of DNA Elements) [8], http://nature.com/encode, http://epd.vital-it.ch); (ii) the analysis of evolution of genomes on the basis of their genomic complexity (according to suitable definitions of this notion) [3,20]. The field of investigation is very rich and the challenges are very ambitious, but what is encouraging and exciting is that results obtained so far seem to confirm that genomes obey to the laws of information theory, the same rules that nowadays allows us to communicate in a so integrate and pervasive way (transmitting data that obey to Shannon's theorems).

References

1. Abouelhoda, M.I., Kurtz, S., Ohlebusch, E.: Replacing suffix trees with enhanced suffix arrays. J. Discrete Algorithms **2**(1), 53–86 (2004)
2. Bonnici, V.: Informational and Relational Analysis of Biological Data. Ph.D. Thesis, Department of Computer Science, University of Verona (2015)
3. Bonnici, V., Manca, V.: Infogenomics tools: a computational suite for informational analysis of genomes. Bioinform. Proteomics Rev. **1**(1), 7–14 (2015)
4. Bonnici, V., Manca, V.: Recurrence distance distributions in computational genomics. Am. J. Bioinformat. Comput. Biol. **1**, 7–14 (2015)
5. Brendel, V., Busse, H.: Genome structure described by formal languages. Nucleic Acids Res. **12**(5), 2561–2568 (1984)
6. Castellini, A., Franco, G., Manca, V.: A dictionary based informational genome analysis. BMC Genomics **13**(1), 485 (2012)
7. Castellini, A., Franco, G., Milanese, A.: A genome analysis based on repeat sharing gene networks. Nat. Comput. **14**, 403–420 (2015)
8. ENCODE Project Consortium: An integrated encyclopedia of DNA elements in the human genome. Nature **489**(7414), 57–72 (2012)
9. Cover, T.M., Thomas, J.A.: Elements of Information Theory. John Wiley & Sons, New York (1991)
10. Deonier, R.C., Tavaré, S., Waterman, M.: Computational Genome Analysis: An Introduction. Springer, New York (2005)
11. Feller, W.: An Introduction to Probability Theory and its Applications, vol. 1. Wiley, New York (1968)
12. Franco, G., Manca, V.: Algorithmic applications of XPCR. Nat. Comput. **10**, 805–819 (2011)
13. Franco, G., Milanese, A.: An investigation on genomic repeats. In: Bonizzoni, P., Brattka, V., Löwe, B. (eds.) CiE 2013. LNCS, vol. 7921, pp. 149–160. Springer, Heidelberg (2013)
14. Gimona, M.: Protein linguistics–a grammar for modular protein assembly? Nat. Rev. Mol. Cell Biol. **7**(1), 68–73 (2006)
15. Hampikian, G., Andersen, T.: Absent sequences: nullomers and primes. In: Pacific Symposium on Biocomputing, vol. 12, pp. 355–366 (2007)
16. Hao, B., Qi, J.: Prokaryote phylogeny without sequence alignment: from avoidance signature to composition distance. J. Bioinform. Comput. Biol. **2**(01), 1–19 (2004)
17. Head, T.: Formal language theory and DNA: an analysis of the generative capacity of specific recombinant behaviors. Bull. Math. Biol. **49**(6), 737–759 (1987)
18. Kullback, S., Leibler, R.A.: On information and sufficiency. Ann. Math. Stat. **22**, 79–86 (1951)
19. Manca, V.: Infobiotics: Information in Biotic Systems. Springer, Heidelberg (2013)
20. Manca, V.: Infogenomics: genomes as information sources. In: Emerging Trends in Computational Biology, Bioinformatics, and Systems Biology, pp. 1–10. Morgan Kauffman (2015)
21. Manca, V.: Outlines of an informational approach to computational genomics. In: Gheorghe Paun's 65th Birthday Festschrift Volume, pp. 1–12 (2015)
22. Manca, V.: Research lines in infogenomics. Bioinform. Proteomics Rev. **1**(1), 1–4 (2015)
23. Manca, V., Franco, G.: Computing by polymerase chain reaction. Math. Biosci. **211**(2), 282–298 (2008)

24. Păun, G., Rozenberg, G., Salomaa, A.: DNA Computing, New Computing Paradigms. Springer, Heidelberg (1998)
25. Puglisi, A., Baronchelli, A., Loreto, V.: Cultural route to the emergence of linguistic categories. Proc. Nat. Acad. Sci. U.S.A. **105**(23), 7936–7940 (2008)
26. Rosenhouse, J.: The Monty Hall Problem. John Wiley & Sons, New York (2009)
27. Rozenberg, G., Salomaa, A.: Handbook of Formal Languages: Beyonds Words, vol. 3. Springer, Heidelberg (1997)
28. Searls, D.B.: The language of genes. Nature **420**(6912), 211–217 (2002)
29. Searls, D.B.: Molecules, languages and automata. In: Sempere, J.M., García, P. (eds.) ICGI 2010. LNCS, vol. 6339, pp. 5–10. Springer, Heidelberg (2010)
30. Shannon, C.E.: A mathematical theory of communication. Bell Syst. Tech. J. **27**, 379–423, 623–656 (1948)
31. Vinga, S.: Information theory applications for biological sequence analysis. Briefings Bioinform. **15**(3), 376–389 (2013)
32. Vinga, S., Almeida, J.: Alignment-free sequence comparison–a review. Bioinformatics **19**(4), 513–523 (2003)
33. Yin, C., Chen, Y., Yau, S.S.T.: A measure of DNA sequence similarity by Fourier transform with applications on hierarchical clustering. J. Theoret. Biol. **359**, 18–28 (2014)

Towards a Theory of Life

Andrés Moya[1,2]([⊠])

[1] Unidad Mixta de Investigación en Genómica y Salud de la Fundación
para el Fomento de la Investigación Sanitaria y Biomédica de la Comunidad
Valenciana (FISABIO), Instituto Cavanilles de Biodiversidad y Biología Evolutiva,
Universitat de València, Valencia, Spain
[2] CIBER en Epidemiología y Salud Pública (CIBERESP), Madrid, Spain
andres.moya@uv.es

Abstract. In this paper, I set out the contributions made by some
European biologists, as well as other more heterodox ones, to the recent
development of theoretical thinking in biology. Theoretical biology is a
relatively new discipline when compared with theoretical physics, in part
because the formal languages of logic and computing which it uses have
only emerged recently. Finally, I suggest that in order to build a theory
of life we need to combine a cell theory based on a proper description
of the laws that map the genotype in the phenotype and vice versa with
the laws of evolution. Only then will we be able to properly explain the
transformation and complexity of living things.

1 Introduction

A biologist presenting their ideas on logic and computing at a conference of
experts in computing - computing with membranes to be precise - is surprising for
two reasons: firstly, because it reflects the intellectual openness of the computer
scientists who invited me, and then secondly because I think they sense, like me,
that there is a very close relationship between biology and computing. Hence I
believe that my audaciousness in presenting my ideas in such a special forum is
justified.

The purpose of this paper is to describe my own path to discovering what
I can now put forward as an early thesis statement: that logic and computing
are the natural abstract languages of biology, in the same way that calculus
was in its day for physics. I do not mean that other formal languages are not
appropriate for biology, but rather that computing is the most appropriate one.
I have reached this conclusion by way of some fairly tortuous thinking which I
am going to set out in this paper, a paper which, in a nutshell, is a condensed
version of my recent book "The Calculus of Life" [1]. The logic in its development
has a certain historical chronology involving three periods. The first relates to
the relevance which particular biologists, who can in some way be considered
recent pioneers of theoretical biology, have had for me. Although admittedly,
they are just some of the scientists and intellectuals who have influenced me.
The second period coincides with my search for ways of approaching biology

© Springer International Publishing Switzerland 2015
G. Rozenberg et al. (Eds.): CMC 2015, LNCS 9504, pp. 19–24, 2015.
DOI: 10.1007/978-3-319-28475-0_2

from logic and computing. Computing is a recent science, as is modern logic, even though it precedes computing. Some of the reasons why it has been so difficult to develop theoretical biology, in the same way as we have theoretical physics that is almost as old as physics itself, are internal to biology, mainly the complexity of its many objects of study. However, here I will look at the late development of languages, namely logic and computing, which are appropriate for biology. Biology has been waiting for them, and when we have begun to apply them, biological theorising has soared to levels of explanatory depth of biological entities which were barely imaginable beforehand. Finally, the third period is my own thinking in the field of new biology, the field of systems. This modern biology is the one that Goethe would have dreamed of, and probably other later vitalist authors too. Theoretical biology is arranged around the biology of (computable) systems. We can model and compare biological phenomena and we are on track to improve this even more. This modern biology means that theoretical biology is not a purely speculative field that is excessively conceptual and abstract and unconnected with biologists empiricist interests.

2   Biology

There is a fine tradition of recent theoretical thought in biology which, in some ways, has been buried by the subsequent emergence of biology popularisation literature, mainly about biological evolution, which has been promoted by British or American authors such as Gould and Dawkins to mention just two great icons in the field. They are authors, scientists themselves, who also wrote and thought about biology. I consider them as important forerunners for the establishment of theoretical biology. The list is skewed by my own interests but their names are well known: Jacob and Monod, pioneers of molecular biology, von Bertalanffy, a pioneer of the systemic conception of entities including biological ones, and Waddington, a pioneer of theoretical biology. There are other authors worthy of attention who go back even further than the four I have just mentioned and whose logical-mathematical training and willingness to address biology as a whole were very significant. Here I am talking about Woodger, Turing, Rosen and von Neumann. Although I briefly discuss the work of these latter four, in my book I focus on the four I mentioned previously, probably because they are scientists involved in the research of life.

Monod poses a key problem in biology, one which hovers over its entire history. It is the confrontation or the relative weight that contingency and chance have had in the evolution of life compared with necessity. In fact, contemporary biology is strongly influenced by the idea that new biological developments of any kind appear by chance and are selected. Necessity has a teleological aftertaste to the extent that if you examine the tree of life and the time when these fresh developments have emerged, you get the impression that the most recent ones are more complex than the oldest ones. Put in another way, the evolution of life is an evolution in complexity. However, we do not have much experience with which to test this. The ideal experiment would be to see the dynamics of life on other planets where it has emerged.

Jacob is important for his theories about reductionism, particularly in its ontological variant. As a pioneer in molecular biology he confers full powers on genes to map the phenotype. He does not deny that properties not written in the genes may emerge, but he claims that these properties appear because the genes are there. Genes are the basic units that are transmitted from generation to generation and it is their products which, in broad interaction between them and with the environment, make it possible to create that entire functional superstructure which we call a living being.

von Bertalanffy is the father of the general systems theory. If anyone could be credited with the idea that the whole is greater than the sum of its parts, that person would be von Bertalanffy. von Bertalanffy is the most theoretical of all my favourite theoretical biologists. Living organisms are systemic conglomerates at all their levels. Cells, multicellular organisms, populations, ecosystems; all these hierarchies of biological organisation are systems formed by the most basic unit components from which properties emerge. von Bertalanffys systems contrast with Jacobs ontological reductionism. Yet that is biology, in which there is always a vigorous debate between the analytical-reductionist and synthetic-systemic traditions.

Finally, Waddington is the great conceptual father of modern theoretical biology. We owe the concept of epigenetics to him, and like few others he was prescient in seeing that the big problem of biology lies in the discovery and integration of the laws governing the relationship between genotypes and phenotypes. Biology requires the development of a phenotype theory which combines the laws that map the genotype in the phenotype and the phenotype in the genotype. Although Waddington, and anyone at this time, recognises the enormous contribution that genetics has made to verifying the tree of life proposed by Darwin, i.e. confirmation of the unit and the genealogical relationship between all living beings, it is still an insufficient and gene-centric contribution to the origin and transformation of living beings. For Waddington, I would repeat, we need an evolutionary theory of the phenotype.

3   Logic and Computing

Modern logic was born with Frege and Boole and its history is recent when we consider the Aristotelian origins of traditional logic, which is as old as reasoning in the West. I mention the youth of modern logic to stress that the science of computing has largely drawn on these authors, particularly Boole, for the advent of computing which, obviously, is even younger than modern logic. What does computing have that makes it so familiar to biology and means I venture to claim that it is a very appropriate formal language for it? Consider the extraordinary analogy of hardware (machinery) and software (algorithm) in computing with cellular machinery, proteins or the phenotype as biological hardware and DNA or genes as biological software, program or algorithm. As far as biology is concerned, the twin concepts of hardware/software (machinery/program) have permeated it to such an extent that much of the deep reasoning underlying modern biology, particularly in molecular biology, uses concepts drawn from computing. Hence we can say that DNA - at least, because there may be other informational levels - is an informational program or algorithm run at the cellular level by the protein machinery. The relationship between computing and biology is deeper than this, because if we admit the algorithmic nature of DNA then we can assess whether, for example, it is feasible to measure its complexity or whether the cell is a Turing machine.

However, I would now like to stress one aspect of computing which in my view is fundamental to biology; the simulation of biological phenomena. In my book, I use two examples, which can now be seen as historical, and which explore and contrast the properties of living beings. They are the cellular automaton called 'Life' by the mathematician Conway and 'Algorithmic Chemistry' by Fontana and Buss.

'Life' is a cellular automaton playing with the fundamental property of life; its ability to persist. In fact, a cell of the grid (which would be the equivalent of an organic cell) is defined as living or dead by the status of its eight neighbours. It starts from an initial set of live or active cells which are arranged in a certain way in the grid. Rules are applied to them in order to assess in successive rounds (generations) what the map of living cells will be, continuing the process for as long as they exist. Though the rules are simple, indeed disdainfully simple, they show properties on the grid that are reminiscent of the behaviour of living beings such as cooperation, competition, multiplication or the indefinite survival of some of the structures formed by these cells, etc. The rules are as follows: (a) if two neighbouring cells are alive, the reference cell maintains its status: dead if it was dead and alive if it was alive; (b) if there are three live neighbours, the reference cell will be alive regardless of whether it was alive or dead before applying the rule; and (c) if the number of neighbouring live cells is zero, one, four, five, six, seven or eight, the reference cell will die after applying the rule.

'Life' is an example of life dynamics under deterministic rules that make up a closed evolution. The dynamic is the same whenever we begin with the same number of cells, including their location, as well as the same starting grid size (the environment). However, in spite of this and as noted above the simulation captures many properties of living entities.

Another computational approach to biological phenomena which intrigued me at the time is Fontana and Busss 'Algorithmic Chemistry'. It is essentially a reactor consisting of a set of initial objects which are structures that follow the rules of lambda calculus, well known in computational theory. The total set of objects remains constant and in each cycle or generation they are allowed to interact or collide with each other to reconfigure the population in terms of composition. A general observation in all the experiments conducted in these reactors was the invariable appearance after a reasonably high number of cycles of new objects, usually much more complex than any of the initial ones, which exhibited properties typical of biological entities such as self-maintenance and multiplication. They also observed emergent properties. Indeed, they identified the emergence of new complex objects due to the joining together of others which, in turn, already had a degree of complexity and exhibited new properties with respect to those presented by the combined objects. These behaviours emulated the hierarchical organisation of biological entities where, for example, cells which exhibit specific properties are grouped into tissues or organs that collectively present other properties.

These computational experiments by Fontana and Buss show behaviour typical of the evolutionary dynamics of open systems. Although the rules or axioms are defined, the interactions between the objects are not, and instead are random, and the simulation itself allows the incorporation of mutations (random alteration of objects in the reactor at any time during the experiment). However, the amazing thing was the systematic emergence and persistence of complex structures with emergent properties and organisational hierarchy in spite of the contingency introduced by the chance factor of the random combination of the objects and mutations. It would be something like a kind of necessity inherent in the dynamics of the living entities which evolved towards greater complexity.

4   Cell and Evolution

The development of a theory of life would involve a suitable combination of two sets of sub-theories which unfortunately have been unevenly developed. They are the theories of the cell and of evolution. It is almost a platitude now to say that the fundamental unit of life is the cell, and this is a key finding of biology which has been well accepted for centuries. Indeed, it predates evolutionary theory itself, which has only been consolidated after much time and effort. Yet taking the cell as the basic unit of life is not the same as saying that we thoroughly grasp all the processes that occur within it. Molecular biology has been the science that has taken the most important steps in examining the structure and function of cellular components in depth. However, we still need to draw up a catalogue of the laws that govern it. To a great extent, and going back once more to the twin concepts of (genetic) information and (metabolic) cellular machinery, the phenotype of a cell is far from fully understood on the basis of its primary genetic information (genotype). In fact, the laws of transformation that enable us to infer the phenotype (or mapping) from the informational genotype as well as possible additional epigenetic laws are the big problem of modern biology. Nevertheless, we should not think that as a result we have not made great strides. Quite the reverse is the case. We are in a very sweet spot in research into the cell as a fundamental unit in which we are close to learning as never before about its collective behaviour (as a whole) based on real-time knowledge of all its fundamental components and processes. In the history of biology, ridicule has been heaped on vitalist authors, some of them distinguished biologists, who refused to accept that the essence of life - for example the essence of a cell - can be captured by studying its parts. This vitalist tradition began with Goethe and continued with Bergson and Driesch. Their intention would probably be not so much resorting to a non-physical principle in which to site the essence of living things, but rather the unavailability of methodological and conceptual procedures to address living entities as a whole. These authors would be reconciled with modern biology if, as Mayr says, we showed them that relationships between the parts of an entity, which we can now measure, are as important as the parts themselves. It would be like Goethes dream come true.

As I noted above, modern evolutionary theory confirms without a shadow of a doubt the union of all organisms in their evolution from the moment that life appeared on Earth. Nevertheless, deeper understanding of this transformation and the gradual emergence of more complex forms calls for the addition of thorough knowledge of the laws of genotype-phenotype transformation of the cell. The combination of the two sub-theories would provide a unified theory of life.

Acknowledgements. This paper has been supported by the European Union's ST-FLOW and SYMBIOMICS projects, the Ministry of Economy and Competitiveness's SAF2012-31187 project and the Regional Government of Valencia's Prometeo II/2014/065 project.

Reference

1. Moya, A.: The Calculus of Life. Springer, New York (2015)

An Excursion Through Quantitative Model Refinement

Sepinoud Azimi[1,3], Eugen Czeizler[1,3], Cristian Gratie[1,3], Diana Gratie[1,3],
Bogdan Iancu[1,3], Nebiat Ibssa[2], Ion Petre[1,3]([✉]), Vladimir Rogojin[1,3],
Tolou Shadbahr[1], and Fatemeh Shokri[1]

[1] Department of Computer Science, Åbo Akademi University, Turku, Finland
[2] Department of Information Technology, University of Turku, Turku, Finland
[3] Turku Centre for Computer Science (TUCS), Turku, Finland
ipetre@abo.fi

Abstract. There is growing interest in creating large-scale computational models for biological process. One of the challenges in such a project is to fit and validate larger and larger models, a process that requires more high-quality experimental data and more computational effort as the size of the model grows. Quantitative model refinement is a recently proposed model construction technique addressing this challenge. It proposes to create a model in an iterative fashion by adding details to its species, and to fix the numerical setup in a way that guarantees to preserve the fit and validation of the model. In this survey we make an excursion through quantitative model refinement – this includes introducing the concept of quantitative model refinement for reaction-based models, for rule-based models, for Petri nets and for guarded command language models, and to illustrate it on three case studies (the heat shock response, the ErbB signaling pathway, and the self-assembly of intermediate filaments).

1 Introduction

Building and analysing large-scale models has attracted much attention recently as shown, e.g., by building whole-cell models [24] or organ models [2,34]. This is supported by advancement of biotechnologies, especially in terms of growing amounts of experimental data leading to a deeper understanding of the functions of a cell. On the other hand, the computational techniques for building biomodels have seen in contrast more modest progress. The most commonly used technique today is to compile a collection of submodels and to focus the computational effort on the communication and compatibility between them. This is a rather ad-hoc approach, highly sensitive to availability of existing submodels and vulnerable even to minor changes in them.

We discuss in this paper an approach for building large-scale models based on the idea of iteratively building the model through adding details to it step-by-step so that its experimental fit and validation is preserved in each step. This allows the modeler to start with an abstract view of the model and to add details

G. Rozenberg et al. (Eds.): CMC 2015, LNCS 9504, pp. 25–47, 2015.
DOI: 10.1007/978-3-319-28475-0_3

to it as they become available; it also allows the modeler to deal with a hierarchy of models and to easily zoom-in and -out to various levels of detail as needed in various applications. Several methods have been proposed to facilitate model refinement in different frameworks, e.g., ODE-based models [9,19], rule-based models [29], Petri nets [37], biochemical reaction networks [21], π-calculus [33].

This paper is thought of as an excursion through quantitative model refinement, introducing briefly the concept of fit-preserving refinement in several modeling frameworks and demonstrating it on three case-studies. It is only partially self-contained due to space restrictions; instead it indicates in many places references for further reading on each topic. The paper is structured as follows. In Sect. 2 we introduce reaction-based models and their associated ODE-based mass-action semantic. In Sect. 3 we introduce the main concept of this paper, that of quantitative model refinement; we also formulate a necessary and sufficient condition for how the numerical details of a refined model should be set so that it preserves the fit and the validation of the initial model. In Sect. 4 we introduce our three case studies: the heat shock response, the ErbB signaling pathway, and the self-assembly of intermediate filaments. In Sect. 5 we discuss two software implementations of the quantitative model refinement. In Sect. 6 we discuss the concept of model refinement in the context of rule-based, Petri nets, and guarded command language modeling. We conclude the paper with a short discussion in Sect. 7.

2   Preliminaries

We recall in this section some of the basic notions and definitions we need throughout the paper. For more details we refer to [5,9,11,20].

2.1   Reaction-Based Models

In this section we briefly introduce the notion of *reaction-based models* following the notations in [9,11].

A reaction-based model $N = (\mathscr{S}, \mathscr{R})$ consists of a set of species $\mathscr{S} = \{S_1, S_2, ..., S_m\}$ and a set of *reactions* $\mathscr{R} = \{r_1, \ldots, r_n\}$. A *reaction* r_j is of the form:

$$r_j : \sum_{i=1}^{m} c_{ij} S_i \rightarrow \sum_{i=1}^{m} d_{ij} S_i,$$

where $c_{i,j}, d_{i,j} \in \mathbb{N}$, $1 \leq i \leq m$, $1 \leq j \leq n$. A reaction can also be described as:

$$r_j : \mathbf{c_j} \rightarrow \mathbf{d_j},$$

where $\mathbf{c_j} = (c_{1j}, c_{2j}, ..., c_{mj})^T$ and $\mathbf{d_j} = (d_{1j}, d_{2j}, ..., d_{mj})^T$ are called the left- and right-*complex* of reaction r_j, resp.

The *stoichiometric coefficient* of species S_i in reaction r_j is denoted by s_{ij} and defined as $s_{ij} = d_{ij} - c_{ij}$. We say a species S_i is *produced* in reaction r_j of N, if If $s_{ij} > 0$, and that it is *consumed* otherwise.

A mass-action reaction-based model is described as $M = (\mathscr{S}, \mathscr{R}, \mathbf{k})$ where $N = (\mathscr{S}, \mathscr{R})$ is a reaction-based model and $\mathbf{k} = (k_{r_1}, \ldots, k_{r_n}) \in \mathbb{R}_{\geq 0}^{\mathscr{R}}$. We call $k_{\mathbf{c} \to \mathbf{d}}$ the reaction rate constant of reaction $\mathbf{c} \to \mathbf{d}$.

2.2 ODE-based Mass-Action Model

We introduce here the *ODE-based mass-action model* corresponding to a reaction-based model; for details we refer to [13,25]. In an ODE the dynamics of a system is expressed in terms of the time-dependent evolution of each species' concentration. We assume that the concentrations of the species is only affected by the reaction. In the case of an ODE model the time evolution of any S_i concentration can be considered as a function $s_i : \mathbb{R}_{\geq 0} \to \mathbb{R}_{\geq 0}$. We define s_i in the case of mass-action kinetics, through the following system of ODEs:

$$\dot{s}_i = \sum_{j=1}^{n} (d_{ij} - c_{ij}) k_j \prod_{q=1}^{m} s_q^{c_{qj}},$$

where $\dot{s}$ denotes the differential of s. We define the system of ODE for all species in a compact form as:

$$\dot{\mathbf{s}} = \sum_{\mathbf{c} \to \mathbf{d} \in \mathscr{R}} k_{\mathbf{c} \to \mathbf{d}} \mathbf{s}^c (\mathbf{d} - \mathbf{c}),$$

where $\mathbf{s} = (s_1, s_2, \ldots, s_m)^T$, $\dot{\mathbf{s}} = (\dot{s}_1, \dot{s}_2, \ldots, \dot{s}_m)^T$ and $\mathbf{s}^c = \prod_{i=1}^{m} s_i^{c_i}$.

Note that we only consider irreversible reactions since any reversible reaction in the form of

$$r_j : \sum_{i=1}^{m} c_{ij} S_i \rightleftarrows \sum_{i=1}^{m} d_{ij} S_i$$

can also be written as two different irreversible reactions:

$$r_j^{(1)} : \sum_{i=1}^{m} c_{ij} S_i \to \sum_{i=1}^{m} d_{ij} S_i, \quad r_j^{(2)} : \sum_{i=1}^{m} d_{ij} S_i \to \sum_{i=1}^{m} c_{ij} S_i.$$

3 Quantitative Model Refinement

The top-down development of large biological models starts with an initial abstraction of the considered biological phenomena, which can then iteratively extended by adding details to it. In the context of reaction-based models relying on mass-action kinetics, one can distinguish *data refinement*, which consists in the replacement of one (or more) species with several variants, i.e. *subspecies*, and *process refinement*, where a generic reaction is replaced with a set of reactions that captures the process in more details by providing intermediary steps. We focus here on data refinement.

Building models via refinement becomes increasingly difficult as the model size grows. Generating the refined reactions manually is both tedious and error prone. To address this, one can rely on *structural refinement*, which provides a generic and systematic approach for generating refined reactions based on the desired refinement of species. Furthermore, fitting a large model is a computationally expensive process and thus it becomes critical that, to the extent possible, the computational effort spent on fitting previous versions of the model is not completely wasted, but instead the obtained parameter values are reused for the initialization of the refined model. This can be accomplished via *fit-preserving refinement*, where the parameters of the refined model are set up so as to capture the same dynamics with respect to the species of the original model.

3.1 Structural Refinement

In this subsection we discuss structural data refinement, as introduced in [9]. We start with the definition of species refinement, which aims to capture the replacement of species from the original model with subspecies in the refined one.

Definition 1 ([9]). *Let $\mathscr{S}$ and $\mathscr{S}'$ be two sets of species. A relation $\rho \subseteq \mathscr{S} \times \mathscr{S}'$ is a* species refinement relation *if and only if it satisfies the following conditions:*

1. *for each $S \in \mathscr{S}$, $\rho(S) \neq \varnothing$;*
2. *for each $S' \in \mathscr{S}'$ there exists exactly one $S \in \mathscr{S}$ such that $S' \in \rho(S)$.*

For each $S \in \mathscr{S}$ we denote $\rho(S) = \{S \in \mathscr{S}' \mid (S, S') \in \rho\}$. Intuitively, the constraints from the definition ensure that each species from the original model is refined to at least one subspecies (more than one in the case of nontrivial refinements) and each species of the refined model corresponds to exactly one "parent" species from the original model. A species refinement ρ can also be written as an $(\mathscr{S} \times \mathscr{S}')$-matrix with $\{0, 1\}$ entries, referred to as the *characteristic matrix* of ρ, defined as follows:

$$M_\rho = (m_{S,S'})_{S \in \mathscr{S}, S' \in \mathscr{S}'}, \qquad m_{S,S'} = \begin{cases} 1, & \text{if } S' \in \rho(S); \\ 0, & \text{otherwise.} \end{cases}$$

Note that each column of the matrix has exactly one 1-entry.

The species refinement relation induces the structural refinement of complexes, reactions and reaction networks.

Definition 2 ([11]). *Let $\mathscr{S} = \{S_1, \ldots, S_m\}$ and $\mathscr{S}' = \{S'_1, \ldots, S'_{m'}\}$ be two sets of species and $\rho \subseteq \mathscr{S} \times \mathscr{S}'$ a species refinement relation.*

1. *Let $\mathbf{c} = [c_1, \ldots, c_m]^T \in \mathbb{N}^{\mathscr{S}}$ and $\mathbf{c}' = [c'_1, \ldots, c'_{m'}] \in \mathbb{N}^{\mathscr{S}'}$ be two complexes over $\mathscr{S}$, respectively $\mathscr{S}'$. We say that $\mathbf{c}'$ is a ρ-refinement of $\mathbf{c}$, denoted $\mathbf{c}' \in \rho(\mathbf{c})$, if*

$$\sum_{\substack{1 \leq j \leq m' \\ S'_j \in \rho(S_i)}} c'_j = c_i, \quad \text{for all } 1 \leq i \leq m$$

or, equivalently, if $\mathbf{c} = M_\rho \mathbf{c}'$.

2. Let $r : c \to d$ be a reaction over $\mathscr{S}$ and $r' : c' \to d'$ a reaction over $\mathscr{S}'$. We say that r' is a ρ-refinement of r, denoted $r' \in \rho(r)$, if $c' \in \rho(c)$ and $d' \in \rho(d)$.
3. Let $N = (\mathscr{S}, \mathscr{R})$ and $N' = (\mathscr{S}', \mathscr{R}')$ be two reaction-based models. We say that N' is a ρ-refinement of N, denoted $N' \in \rho(N)$, if

$$\mathscr{R}' \subseteq \bigcup_{r \in \mathscr{R}} \rho(r) \quad \text{and} \quad \rho(r) \cap \mathscr{R}' \neq \varnothing, \text{ for all } r \in \mathscr{R}.$$

In case $\mathscr{R}' = \bigcup_{r \in \mathscr{R}} \rho(r)$, we say that N' is the full ρ-refinement of N.
4. Let $M = (\mathscr{S}, \mathscr{R}, \boldsymbol{k})$ and $M' = (\mathscr{S}', \mathscr{R}', \boldsymbol{k}')$ be two mass-action reaction-based models. We say that M' is a ρ-refinement of M, denoted $M' \in \rho(M)$, if $(\mathscr{S}', \mathscr{R}') \in \rho(\mathscr{S}, \mathscr{R})$. We say that M' is a full ρ-refinement of M if $(\mathscr{S}', \mathscr{R}')$ is the full ρ-refinement of $(\mathscr{S}, \mathscr{R})$.
5 Let $\boldsymbol{\sigma} \in \mathbb{R}^{\mathscr{S}}$ and $\boldsymbol{\sigma}' \in \mathbb{R}^{\mathscr{S}'}$ (thought of as the initial values for the system of ODEs associated to M and M'). We say that $\boldsymbol{\sigma}'$ is a ρ-refinement of $\boldsymbol{\sigma}$, denoted $\boldsymbol{\sigma}' \in \rho(\boldsymbol{\sigma})$, if $\boldsymbol{\sigma} = M_\rho \boldsymbol{\sigma}'$.

Example 1. Consider the reaction $A + B \xrightarrow{k} 2B$. We refine the reaction to include two different subtypes of species A, A_1 and A_2; species B remains unchanged but for the lack of clarity we denote it in the refined model by a new variable, say B_1. The corresponding species refinement relation is given by $\rho = \{(A, A_1), (A, A_2), (B, B_1)\}$. The two possible refinements of the considered reaction are $A_1 + B_1 \xrightarrow{k_1} 2B_1$, $A_2 + B_1 \xrightarrow{k_2} 2B_1$.

Note that this reaction is part of the Lotka-Volterra model; for a complete discussion of the refinement of this model we refer to [5, 10].

3.2   Fit-Preserving Refinement

In this subsection we define the fit-preserving refinement, as introduced in [5], with the notations and formal definition from [9]. Given an initial value problem, i.e. an ODE $\dot{x} = \boldsymbol{F}(\boldsymbol{x})$ with the initial condition $\boldsymbol{x}(0) = \boldsymbol{x_0}$, we use $\boldsymbol{x}[\boldsymbol{x_0}]$ to denote its (unique) solution.

The problem we investigate in this section is the following:

What is the numerical setup (kinetic rate constants and initial values) of a refined model ensuring that for each species of the basic model, its corresponding function in the mathematical model is the sum of the functions corresponding to its subspecies in the refined model?

The problem is strongly motivated by the need to preserve the numerical fit of an already validated model, while allowing its extension with additional details through quantitative model refinements. We give this problem a solution in this section and we use this solution in several different frameworks and case-studies in the remaining of the paper.

Definition 3. Let $M = (\mathscr{S}, \mathscr{R}, \boldsymbol{k})$ and $M' = (\mathscr{S}', \mathscr{R}', \boldsymbol{k}')$ be two mass-action reaction networks and $\rho \subseteq \mathscr{S} \times \mathscr{S}'$ a species refinement relation. For any $\boldsymbol{\sigma} \in$

$\mathbb{R}_{\geq 0}^{\mathscr{S}}$ and $\boldsymbol{\sigma}' \in \mathbb{R}_{\geq 0}^{\mathscr{S}'}$ we denote by $\boldsymbol{s}[\boldsymbol{\sigma}] : [0, \tau) \to \mathbb{R}_{\geq 0}^{\mathscr{S}}$ $(\boldsymbol{s}'[\boldsymbol{\sigma}'] : [0, \tau') \to \mathbb{R}_{\geq 0}^{\mathscr{S}'})$ the vector of the real functions obtained as solutions of the ODE system associated to M (to M', resp.) with initial values $\boldsymbol{\sigma}$ ($\boldsymbol{\sigma}'$, resp.).

We say that M' is a ρ-fit-preserving refinement of M if $M' \in \rho(M)$ and, for all $\boldsymbol{\sigma} \in \mathbb{R}_{\geq 0}^{\mathscr{S}}$ and $\boldsymbol{\sigma}' \in \mathbb{R}_{\geq 0}^{\mathscr{S}'}$ such that $\boldsymbol{\sigma} = \boldsymbol{M}_\rho \boldsymbol{\sigma}'$, we have that

$$\boldsymbol{s}[\boldsymbol{\sigma}](t) = \boldsymbol{M}_\rho \boldsymbol{s}'[\boldsymbol{\sigma}'](t),$$

for all values of t in a suitable right-neighborhood of 0.

Note that, for the same set of reactions, it is sometimes possible that two different assignments of kinetic rate constants lead to exactly the same ODE. For such models it is shown in [4] that the values of the rate constants can not be computed even from exact and complete experimental data for the system's dynamics. As such, the requirement that a model has uniquely identifiable rate constants will be regarded as reasonable and desirable even outside the refinement framework.

What we are looking for is an effective procedure for assigning the values of the kinetic rate constants of the refined model so that a fit-preserving refinement is obtained. An (implicit) assignment that achieves this is given in Definition 4.

Definition 4. Let $M = (\mathscr{S}, \mathscr{R}, \boldsymbol{k})$ and $M' = (\mathscr{S}', \mathscr{R}', \boldsymbol{k}')$ be two mass-action reaction networks and $\rho \subseteq \mathscr{S} \times \mathscr{S}'$ a species refinement relation. We say that M' is a canonical ρ-refinement of M if M' is a full ρ-refinement of M and, for every $\boldsymbol{c} \to \boldsymbol{d} \in \mathscr{R}$ and every $\boldsymbol{c}' \in \rho(\boldsymbol{c})$, we have that

$$\sum_{\boldsymbol{d}' \in \rho(\boldsymbol{d})} k'_{\boldsymbol{c}' \to \boldsymbol{d}'} = \binom{\boldsymbol{c}}{\boldsymbol{c}'} k_{\boldsymbol{c} \to \boldsymbol{d}} \ , \ where \ \binom{\boldsymbol{c}}{\boldsymbol{c}'} = \frac{\prod_{i=1}^{|\mathscr{S}|} c_i!}{\prod_{j=1}^{|\mathscr{S}'|} c_j'!} \ .$$

It is shown in [9] that any canonical ρ-refinement is also a fit-preserving refinement. We provide here the stronger result of [11].

Theorem 1 ([11]). Let $M = (\mathscr{S}, \mathscr{R}, \boldsymbol{k})$ and $M' = (\mathscr{S}', \mathscr{R}', \boldsymbol{k}')$ be two reaction networks such that M' is a full ρ-refinement of M.

1. If M' is a canonical ρ-refinement of M, then M' is a fit-preserving ρ-refinement of M.
2. If M has uniquely identifiable rate constants, then M' is a fit-preserving ρ-refinement of M if and only if M' is a canonical ρ-refinement of M.

Note that Theorem 1 provides a complete characterization of fit-preserving refinement in the context of mass-action models. What is remarkable in this characterization is the linear dependency between the rate constants of the refined model and those of the original model.

Example 2. Consider again the reaction from Example 1 and its refinements. In this case, canonical refinement translates to having $k_1 = k$ and $k_2 = k$, since the left hand sides of the two refined reactions are distinct.

For a more comprehensive discussion of fit-preserving refinement, see [11], where several distinct fit-preserving refinements of the Brusselator [30] are presented and compared.

3.3   Refinement Induced by the Composition of Species

In this subsection we rely on the initial refinement ideas proposed in [5], where a distinction is made between complex species (which consist of several, smaller, units, e.g. molecules composed of atoms) and atomic species, which can not be divided into smaller parts, within the current resolution of the model. For example, consider the following chemical reaction: $A + B{:}C \xrightarrow{k} A{:}B + C$.

The definition of refinement presented in Sect. 3 does not consider the composition of species. However, this information may be relevant, particularly in cases when the subspecies distinguished in the refined model are in fact induced by the data refinement of one (or several) atomic species. For the chosen reaction, note that there are three atomic species, namely A, B and C, and two complex species, $A{:}B$ and $B{:}C$. For uniformity, we assume that the reactants and products of a reaction are all complex species, thus we allow a complex species to be composed of a single atomic species.

Assume that in the refined model we can distinguish two types of B. We can write this as an *atomic refinement relation*:

$$\rho_{\text{atomic}} = \{(A, A_1), (B, B_1), (B, B_2), (C, C_1)\}.$$

This induces a refinement of all complex species of the model where, just as in the case of reaction refinement, we aim to capture all possible combinations of subspecies which are meaningful with respect to the composition of the species from the original model. In this case, the species refinement relation for complex species becomes

$$\rho = \{(A, A_1), (B{:}C, B_1{:}C_1), (B{:}C, B_2{:}C_1), (A{:}B, A_1{:}B_1), (A{:}B, A_1{:}B_2), (C, C_1)\}.$$

Given the species refinement relation ρ, structural refinement can proceed as in Sect. 3.1. The advantage of defining an atomic refinement is its compactness. Moreover, as we show in Sect. 5, this is enough for enabling the automated computation of the structural refinement of a model.

4   Case-Studies

We introduce in this section the three case studies discussed in this paper: the heat shock response, the ErbB signaling pathway, and the self-assembly of intermediate filaments.

4.1   The Heat Shock Response

The eukaryotic heat shock response is a conserved regulatory network that acts as a defence mechanism against proteotoxicity arising from environmental stressors such as: elevated temperature, toxins, infections, etc. Elevated temperatures induce protein misfolding leading to the formation of aggregates which hinder protein homeostasis, eventually bringing about apoptosis. The deleterious effects of elevated temperature upon proteins are counterbalanced by a family of molecular chaperones, called heat shock proteins, which bind to misfolded proteins, facilitating their recovery process so as to prevent apotosis. We consider the following basic molecular model for the heat shock response, introduced in [32].

Heat shock proteins (hsp's) play a key role in the process of protein refolding, chaperoning misfolded proteins in the recovery process and facilitating the degradation of severely damaged proteins. Heat shock proteins possess an affinity towards misfolded proteins and, hence, they sequester them, form hsp: mfp complexes, helping them recover to their original conformation (prot). The hsp-encoding genes transactivation controls the cell's response to environmental stressors. Gene transcription is regulated by a family of proteins, called heat shock factors (hsf's). Heat shock factors are found predominantly in the cell in a monomeric state when the cell does not withstand any stress from the environment, extensively bound to heat shock proteins (hsp: hsf). Elevated temperatures lead to the breakage of hsp: hsf, causing the release of hsf's. Heat stress induces the dimerization of heat shock factors (hsf$_2$) and their consequent trimerization (hsf$_3$), bringing them to a conformation which enables their binding with the promoter elements of the hsp-encoding gene, heat shock element (hse). This promotes hsp synthesis. However, once the expression level of hsp is elevated enough for the cell to endure the effects of environmental stressors, hsp synthesis is turned off. Heat shock proteins, thus, sequestrate the free hsf's, break dimers and trimers and impel DNA unbinding, by the formation of hsp: hsf complexes. Consequently, the production of trimers is impeded. Temperature elevation causes proteins to misfold, as a consequence heat shock proteins are detached from heat shock factors, hsp: hsf complexes being broken. Now free hsf's dimerize and trimerize, thus promoting the synthesis of hsp's. We list the complete set of reactions in Table 1.

Table 1. The molecular model for the eukaryotic heat shock response proposed in [32].

Reaction	Description
2 hsf $\rightleftarrows$ hsf$_2$	Dimerization (1)
hsf + hsf$_2$ $\rightleftarrows$ hsf$_3$	Trimerization (2)
hsf$_3$ + hse $\rightleftarrows$ hsf$_3$: hse	DNA binding (3)
hsf$_3$: hse $\rightarrow$ hsf$_3$: hse + hsp	hsp synthesis (4)
hsp + hsf $\rightleftarrows$ hsp: hsf	hsf sequestration (5)
hsp + hsf$_2$ $\rightarrow$ hsp: hsf + hsf	Dimer dissipation (6)
hsp + hsf$_3$ $\rightarrow$ hsp: hsf +2 hsf	Trimer dissipation (7)
hsp + hsf$_3$: hse $\rightarrow$ hsp: hsf +2 hsf + hse	DNA unbinding (8)
hsp $\rightarrow$ $\emptyset$	hsp degradation (9)
prot $\rightarrow$ mfp	Protein misfolding (10)
hsp + mfp $\rightleftarrows$ hsp: mfp	mfp sequestration (11)
hsp: mfp $\rightarrow$ hsp + prot	Protein refolding (12)

Various post-translational modifications can affect heat shock factors (phosphorylation, acetylation, sumoylation) and influence DNA-binding activity. The heat shock response is attenuated as a result of the acetylation of heat shock factors (hsf's). We introduce here the refinement of hsf molecules as shown in [19], by considering the acetylation status of the hsf molecule at its $K80$ residue.

The species in the refined model are classified in two categories: *atomic* or *complex*. Atomic species refer to *self-contained* species, autonomous in their structure, see [12]. The structure of a complex however consists in at least two atomic species bound together. All species to be refined, previously mentioned above are atomic.

The refined model includes two types of heat shock factors: one to represent the acetylation of the lysine residue ($K80$) of hsf's and one for the non-acetylated hsf's. As a consequence, the $\mathsf{hsf_3 : hse}$ complex, for example, is to be refined into 4 subtypes conforming to the status of its every hsf molecule, considering the symmetry in the acetylation sites distribution: $\mathsf{rhsf_3 : rhse}$, $\mathsf{rhsf_3}^{(1)} : \mathsf{rhse}$, $\mathsf{rhsf_3}^{(2)} : \mathsf{rhse}$, $\mathsf{rhsf_3}^{(3)} : \mathsf{rhse}$. We denote by $\mathsf{rhsf_3}^{(i)} : \mathsf{rhse}$ the complex where i of the 3 hsf's are acetylated at site $K80$.

The refinement described above can be formalized through the species refinement relation below (one row for each species of the basic model):

$$\rho = \{(\mathsf{hse, rhse}), (\mathsf{hsp, rhsp}), (\mathsf{prot, rprot}), (\mathsf{mfp, rmfp}), (\mathsf{hsp : mfp, rhsp : rmfp}),$$
$$(\mathsf{hsf, rhsf}), (\mathsf{hsf, rhsf}^{(1)}),$$
$$(\mathsf{hsf_2, rhsf_2}), (\mathsf{hsf_2, rhsf_2}^{(1)}), (\mathsf{hsf_2, rhsf_2}^{(2)}),$$
$$(\mathsf{hsf_3, rhsf_3}), (\mathsf{hsf_3, rhsf_3}^{(1)}), (\mathsf{hsf_3, rhsf_3}^{(2)}), (\mathsf{hsf_3, rhsf_3}^{(3)}),$$
$$(\mathsf{hsp : hsf, hsp : rhsf}), (\mathsf{hsp : hsf, rhsp : rhsf}^{(1)}),$$
$$(\mathsf{hsf_3 : hse, rhsf_3 : rhse}), (\mathsf{hsf_3 : hse, rhsf_3}^{(1)} : \mathsf{rhse}), (\mathsf{hsf_3 : hse, rhsf_3}^{(2)} : \mathsf{rhse}),$$
$$(\mathsf{hsf_3 : hse, rhsf_3}^{(3)} : \mathsf{rhse})\}.$$

The refined model in [19] comprises 20 reactants and 55 irreversible reactions, while the initial model in [32] consists of 10 reactants and 17 irreversible reactions. The numerical details of the refined model, set in accordance with Theorem 1, can be found in [19]. Through refinement, the model preserves its fit and validation, even though its size increases considerably, both in number of reactants, and in number of reactions.

4.2   The ErbB Signalling Pathway

The ErbB signalling pathway is an evolutionary regulatory pathway, which plays a key role in the regulation of diverse cellular processes (growth, differentiation, motility, etc.) and whose anomalous behaviour is associated with cancer development in humans. The ErbB signalling pathway involves a number of cellular ligands, among which we are interested in this survey in EGF and HRG, and four receptor tyrosine kinases: ErbB1, ErbB2, ErbB3, ErbB4.

The Initial ErbB Signalling Pathway Model. The activation of the pathway commences with the binding of the epidermal growth factor (EGF) to the epidermal growth factor receptor EGFR (ErbB1), which brings about a dimerization of the newly formed complex and subsequently a rapid auto-phosphorylation of its tyrosine residues. The signal is propagated through two distinct pathways: Shc-dependent and Shc-independent, both of which lead to the activation of Ras-GTP. The Shc-dependent pathway is activated by the Shc protein, which binds to the dimerized, phosphorylated, ligand-bound receptor and then subsequently to Grb2. The Shc-independent pathway is in turn activated by the direct binding with Grb2. Both the aforementioned pathways require Sos to be recruited to the membrane. The pathway sustains an elaborate internalization process along with the degradation of several complexes. However, the recruitment of Sos impels an association with protein Ras which causes the activation of Ras in a GTP-dependent manner. Subsequent to its formation and activation, the inactivation of Ras-GTP is a consequence of the dissociation from the receptor complex involving protein GAP. It is not clear so far however what is the responsible kinase for the phosphorylation of Raf, but the model in [17] considers protein Raf to be phosphorylated by free Ras-GTP. Then in turn, subsequent to its phosphorylation, Raf is able to phosphorylate MEK. Doubly phosphorylated MEK sucessively phosphorylates ERK, see [17]. The initial model in [17] acknowledges the negative feedback loop from doubly phosporylated ERK to Sos, promoting as a result, the unbinding between Grb2-Sos and the receptor complex. Without any stimulation from EGF, the system is in a steady-state. The initial model described in [17] distinguishes between two pools of dually phosphorylated ERK (ERK-PP), first of which is identified in the cytoplasm and the latter in association to the internalized receptor. As described in [17], the model consists of 13 chemical processes: the activation of EGFR , the recruitment of the following proteins: Shc, Grb2 and Sos, the activation and the inactivation of Ras, the activation of Raf, the MEK phosphorylation/dephosphorylation, the dephosphorylation of ERK , the negative feedback from ERK to Sos, the internalization of receptor complexes and degradations reaction. A more elaborate discussion about the model can be found in [17]. The model has 103 species and 148 reactions.

The Refined ErbB Signaling Pathway Model. This subsection briefly describes the expansion of the EGFR signalling pathway model from [17] by means of fit-preserving data refinement, taking into account four members of the ErbB family: ErbB1 (EGFR), ErbB2 (HER2), ErbB3, ErbB4, and two ligands: EGF and HRG. The resulting model has 421 species and 928 reactions.

We consider only the following two refinements of two atomic species:

$$\text{EGFR} \rightarrow \{\text{ErbB1}, \text{ErbB2}, \text{ErbB3}, \text{ErbB4}\}; \quad \text{EGF} \rightarrow \{\text{EGF}, \text{HRG}\}.$$

Obviously, these refinements cascade to other refinements of complex species. We discuss this in the following.

Consider first the receptor activation reaction:

$$\text{EGF} + \text{EGFR} \overset{k_{lb}^+}{\underset{}{\leftrightarrow}} \text{EGF-EGFR}. \tag{1}$$

We refine it to include both ligands $L_1, L_2 \in \{\text{EGF}, \text{HRG}\}$ and the receptors $R_1, \ldots, R_4 \in \{\text{ErbB1}, \text{ErbB2}, \text{ErbB3}, \text{ErbB4}\}$ as follows:

$$L_i + R_j \overset{k_{i,j}^+}{\underset{k_{i,j}^-}{\longleftrightarrow}} L_i\text{–}R_j, \text{ for all } i = \overline{1,2}, j = \overline{1,4}.$$

We aim to set the kinetic rate constants of the refined model in concordance to the sufficient conditions for fit-preserving refinement in Sect. 3. Let's consider the ligand-binding reaction (1); its corresponding kinetic rate constants are set as follows: $k_{i,j}^- = k_{lb}^-$ and $k_{i,j}^+ = k_{lb}^+$, for all $i = \overline{1,2}, j = \overline{1,4}$.

Consider now the dimerization of the ligand-bound receptor reaction:

$$2\,\text{EGF-EGFR} \overset{k_d^+}{\underset{k_d^-}{\longleftrightarrow}} (\text{EGF-EGFR})^2.$$

In the refined model we considered all possible combinations of ligand-bound receptor monomers, found on the *left-hand side* of the dimerization reactions. Since we have two types of ligands and four types of receptors, this gives us eight types of combinations ligand-receptors. Accordingly, the dimerization of the ligand-bound receptor is refined in the following manner:

$$C_i + C_j \overset{k_{i,j,l}^+}{\underset{k_{i,j,l}^-}{\longleftrightarrow}} (C_l)^2,$$

where $C_i, C_j, C_l \in \{\text{EGF} - \text{ErbB}p, \text{HRG} - \text{ErbB}q \,|\, p, q \in \overline{1,4}\}$. Note that we only consider the formation of homo-dimers in our considerations; hetero-dimers may also be included, with the consequence of drastically increasing the model size.

According to Theorem 1, the kinetic rate constants of the refined dimerization reaction are set as follows:

$$k_{i,j,l}^+ = \begin{cases} 0, & \text{if } l \neq i; j \\ k_d^+, & \text{otherwise.} \end{cases} \, ; \quad k_{i,j,l}^- = \begin{cases} 0, & \text{if } l \neq i; j \\ \dfrac{k_d^-}{8}, & \text{otherwise.} \end{cases}$$

Consider now the receptor production $\overset{k_p}{\longrightarrow} \text{EGFR}$, refined as $\overset{k_i}{\longrightarrow} R_i$, $i = \overline{1,4}$, where $R_i \in \{\text{ErbB1}, \text{ErbB2}, \text{ErbB3}, \text{ErbB4}\}$. The corresponding kinetic rate constants are set so as to comply with the condition in Theorem 1: $k_i = \dfrac{k_p}{4}$.

Finally, complex species of the initial model of [17] were refined taking into account all combinations of receptor-ligand binding. Let's take, for instance, a species $(\text{EGF-EGFR}^*)^2\text{-AC}$, where AC represents a so-called *chain of bound atomic species* (such as GAP-Grb2-Sos-Ras-GDP-Prot). According to our method, species $(\text{EGF-EGFR}^*)^2\text{-AC}$ was refined into the subspecies below:

$$(\text{EGF-EGFR}^*)^2\text{-AC} \rightarrow \{(C_i^*)^2 - AC\}, \quad 1 \leq i \leq 8,$$

with $C_i \in \{\text{EGF} - \text{ErbB}p, \text{HRG} - \text{ErbB}q \,|\, p, q = \overline{1,4}\}$ and with "$*$" character denoting the phosphorylation status the molecule.

4.3   Intermediate Filaments Self-assembly

Intermediate filaments (IF), together with actin filaments and microtubules, are the three types of protein filaments forming the cytoskeleton of eukaryotic cells [35]. IF in particular have an important role in the structural reinforcement of the cells and their organization into tissues, and in distributing the tensile forces across cells within a tissue [27]. IF sub-units are α-helical rods which assemble both laterally and using end-to-end interactions into rope-like filaments [15]. The emerging filaments range in length from hundreds of nm to micro-meter values, while their width (when in mature state) is preserved at 11 nm.

In the following we choose vimentin filaments as a representative for the class of intermediate filaments proteins, and we analyze their in-vitro assembly principles. Based on the recent studies in [6] and [28] we present both a well validated molecular and computational model of the in vitro vimentin assembly into filaments, as well as a refined model distinguishing between the different lengths of the emerging filaments.

The in-vitro vimentin assembly process follows four stages. In the first stage, monomers associate laterally into dimers and then into tetrameres (denoted as T). The tetramer sub-units are the first chemically stable compounds in the IF assembly process, and, moreover, the assembly can be blocked/freezed before continuing further. This is why when modelling the in-vitro IF assembly this first stage is omitted, and the IF assembly is assumed to be starting from tetramer level. The second assembly phase consist of a series of further lateral associations: two tetrameres merge into an octamer (O), two octamers merge into a hexadecamer (H), and two hexadecamer merge into a unit length filament (ULF). ULFs (denoted as U) are the basic units of the emerging filament structures. In the third assembly phase the filaments start forming and elongating, by sub-sequent end-to-end associations of both ULFs and of shorter filaments. In the final assembly phase the filaments undergo a radial compaction, from an ULF diameter of about 15 nm to a filament diameter of about 11 nm [15]. Since within this last assembly phase the ULF per filament ratio does not suffer any further modifications, this stage does not bring any changes within the molecular model itself.

Depending on the number n of constituent ULF's within one filament, we can differentiate between the emergent assemblies based on their "size" n. A common problem in modelling self-assembly systems is dealing with the combinatorial explosion of all possible emergent assemblies as possible different species. In case of the IF model above, this translates into the problem of representing and reasoning about all the emergent filaments of size 1, 2, 3, etc. In [6], the authors introduce a well validated molecular and numerical model for in-vitro vimentin assembly. Within this model, see Table 2 (a), the emerging filaments consisting of at least two ULFs are treated in a homogenous manner, and are captured within the same generic species F. With this assumption in place, the authors succeed to validate several experimental data sets on the time dependent mean length of the emerging vimentin IFs. The model however is not able to capture the time distribution of a particular length filament, say the time distribution of filaments containing exactly 3 ULFs.

Using the refinement method described in Sect. 3 we can refine the generic filament species F according to any desired (finite) resolution level. For example, for introducing a model distinguishing between all filaments of lengths 1 to 5 ULFs, as well as filaments containing at least 6 ULFs, we can use the species refinement relation below; the entire refined molecular model is described in Table 2(b):

$$\rho = \{(T, rT), (O, rO), (H, rH), (U, rF_1), (F, rF_2), (F, rF_3), (F, rF_4), (F, rF_5), (F, rF_{\geq 6})\}.$$

Moreover, by setting the kinetic rate constants of the refined model as in Theorem 1, we can ensure that the newly generated refined model is preserving its predictions for mean filament length. This implies that the refined models is indeed also validating the experimental data sets used in [6]. The kinetic rate constants of the refined model may be chosen as described in Table 2(b).

5 Software Support

We discuss in this section two software tools for implementing quantitative model refinement in practice.

5.1 ModelRef

We have developed a software tool called *ModelRef* [22] implementing fit-preserving model refinement for atomic-only species as described in Sect. 3. The

Table 2. The molecular models of the basic (a) and the refined (b) representations of the IF assembly process.

(a) Basic model		(b) Refined model	
Reaction	Rate constant	Reaction	Rate constant
$T + T \rightarrow O$	k_t	$rT + rT \rightarrow rO$	$k_t' = k_t$
$O + O \rightarrow H$	k_o	$rO + rO \rightarrow rH$	$k_o' = k_o$
$H + H \rightarrow U$	k_h	$rH + rH \rightarrow rF_1$	$k_h' = k_h$
$U + U \rightarrow F$	k_u	$rF_1 + rF_1 \rightarrow rF_2$	$k_{(1,1)}' = k_u$
$U + F \rightarrow F$	k_{uf}	$rF_1 + rF_i \rightarrow rF_{i+1}, \, 1 \leq i \leq 4$	$k_{(1,i)}' = k_{uf}$
$F + F \rightarrow F$	k_{ff}	$rF_1 + rF_j \rightarrow rF_{\geq 6}, \, j \in \{5, \geq 6\}$	$k_{(1,j)}' = k_{uf}$
		$rF_2 + rF_2 \rightarrow rF_4$	$k_{(2,2)}' = k_{ff}$
		$rF_i + rF_i \rightarrow rF_{\geq 6},$ $\quad , i \in \{3, 4, 5, \geq 6\}$	$k_{(i,i)}' = k_{ff}$
		$rF_2 + rF_3 \rightarrow rF_5$	$k_{(2,3)}' = 2\,k_{ff}$
		$rF_i + rF_j \rightarrow rF_{\geq 6},$ $\quad , 2 \leq i < j \leq 5, i + j \geq 6$	$k_{(i,j)}' = 2\,k_{ff}$
		$rF_i + rF_{\geq 6} \rightarrow rF_{\geq 6} \; 2 \leq i \leq 5$	$k_{(i, \geq 6)}' = 2\,k_{ff}$

user provides as the input a numerical model as well as the refinement criteria. The numerical model in the input contains a set of chemical species, their initial concentrations, set of chemical reactions and their reaction kinetic rates. In the refinement criteria one indicates the correspondence between original and the refined species.

ModelRef generates the refined model as follows:

- Every species from the original model that should be refined is substituted with the corresponding set of the refinement species.
- Every reaction from the original model that includes species being refined either as reactants or products is substituted with the set of reactions including the respective refinement species. The resulting set of reactions and their kinetic rates are calculated as defined in Sect. 3.

ModelRef handles models in both *SBML* and *CPS* file formats. The *Systems Biology Markup Language (SBML)* is one of the most wide-spread open interchange formats for computer models of biological processes [18]. *CPS* is a native file format of *Complex Simulator Pathway (COPASI)* [16] for storing and exchanging biological models.

The refinement criteria should be provided in *CSV (Comma Separated Values)* table, where the first column contains names of the original biochemical species, while the right column contains a set of species that should substitute/refine the respective original species from the left column.

ModelRef is implemented as a Java library and it is deployed as a stand-alone Java console application, as an Anduril [31] component and as a web-based service. Anduril is an open source component-based workflow framework for scientific data analysis developed at the Computational Systems Biology Laboratory, University of Helsinki. Anduril provides and API that allows to integrate rapidly various existing software tools and algorithms into a single data analysis pipeline. An Anduril pipeline comprises a set of interconnected executable programs (called components) with well-defined I/O ports, where an output port of a component may be connected to the input ports of some number of other components.

The web-service allows for a user to upload on our web-server a numerical model in either *SBML* or *CPS* formats, the refinement criteria as *CSV* table, and then, it sends back to the user the resulting refined model in either *SBML* or *CPS* format.

Since *ModelRef* is implemented as a Java class library, its functionality can be extended by other developers and it can be directly incorporated into other Java programs. As an Anduril component, *ModelRef* can be easily incorporated into data analysis pipelines.

5.2 StructRef

StructRef relies on the data refinement induced by an atomic refinement relation, as described in Sect. 3.3. The software is thought of as an interactive tool allowing the modeler to specify the initial atomic refinement relation, but also to intervene and alter intermediary results to better fit prior knowledge about the model that is refined.

The software takes as input a model represented in the SBML format. Intermediary results are saved as XML files. The final output, the structural refinement of the input model, is represented as SBML, with the intermediary results inserted as annotations, to allow for their reuse.

The software works as follows:

- Species are read from the input model and their composition is inferred from their names. Currently, the software assumes that the atomic components of a complex species are separated by colons, but this can easily be extended in future versions. Moreover, at the end of this step, an XML is generated with the composition information. The modeler can inspect this file and make changes as needed.
- The (possibly updated) composition information is used for inferring the names of all atomic species from the model. A template XML file is produced for the atomic refinement relation. The template contains a trivial refinement, namely the renaming of all atomic species by prepending "r" to their original names. The modeler must edit this file in order to describe a nontrivial refinement.
- The composition information and the atomic refinement relation are used for generating the refinement of complex species, using the approach presented in Sect. 3.3. The result is presented in XML format and contains the name and composition information for each of the refined species. The modeler can update this file to rename species, or to remove some of them, so as to match prior knowledge about the system that is modeled (some of the automatically generated combinations of refined atomic species may be impossible).
- The refinement of complex species is used to generate the refined reactions of the model, as described in Sect. 3.1. Again, the modeler can alter the results to remove some of the reactions.
- The refined model is generated as an SBML file, including all the intermediary information that was generated by the software.

The software was implemented in Python and uses Qt4 for the graphical user interface. It can be found at [36]

6   Quantitative Refinement in Other Formalisms

Quantitative refinement is by no mean restricted to the reaction-based and ODE-based models. In this section we discuss the refinement in three other formalisms, namely rule-based models, Petri net models and guarded command based models. In each part we briefly introduce the modeling in that specific framework and we also give a short explanation on how to apply the refinement in each formalisms. The structural part of the refinement has a different solution in each approach, in some cases leading to a compact representation of the refined models. For a more detailed discussion we refer to [21].

6.1   Rule-Based Models Refinement

A model within a a rule-based modelling framework is described by the molecules of interest, their components (i.e. a post-translational modification site) and the states corresponding to each component. The interaction between the components are captured through graph-rewriting rules, where a rule can refer to either a certain type of reactions or a class of reactions. We refer to [8] for a detailed presentation of this framework.

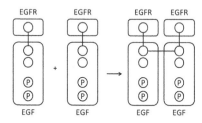

Fig. 1. A graphical representation of the species EGF-EGFR and of the rule showing the dimerization of EGF-EGFR through a binding site. Note that the sites denoted by letter P represent phosphorylation sites, while the other sites represent binding sites.

Rule-based languages are used to characterize the dynamics of the system at hand. Rules produce reactants introducing classes of reactions, which express classes of reactions describing specific interactions between atomic and/or complex species. In practice, a rule specifies *group rules*, which characterize interactions between species through regular expressions. The conversion from reactants to products is enabled through a rate law.

A graphical representation of the dimerization of EGF-EGFR is in Fig. 1.

In case one would need to refine either of the species to include two types of ligands or four types of receptors as discussed in Sect. 4.2, the only required adjustment needed is adding a site for EGF (with two possible vlaues) and one for EGFR (with four possible values). Note that the rule illustrated in Fig. 1 remains unchanged, in stark contrast with the combinatorial explosion discussed in Sect. 4.2.

6.2   Refinement of Petri Net Models

The *Petri nets* formalism is used to represent systems with concurrency and resource sharing, which makes it suitable for modeling biological systems. In this formalism each species is represented by a *place* with as many *tokens* as the number of instances of the species present in the system, and each reaction by a *transition* whose *pre-* and *post-places* correspond to the species on the left and the right hand side of the reaction, respectively, where arc multiplicities represent the stoichiometric coefficients of species involved in the reaction. For more information on modeling biological systems in the framework of Petri nets

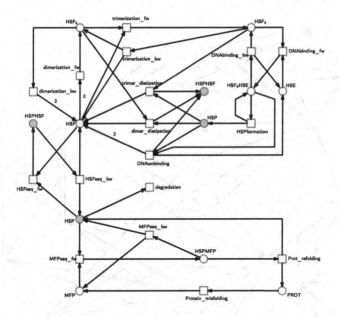

Fig. 2. Petri net representation of the initial HSR model.

we refer to [26]. A Petri net model of the heat shock response case study is presented in Fig. 2.

Coloured Petri nets are an extension of Petri nets where places are assigned data types called color sets, and each place may host tokens of different colors (values in the place's color set). Transitions can have additional constraints on the colors of the tokens traversing them, in the form of *guards*, and arc multiplicities are replaced by expressions containing variables and/or values from the color set of the place connected to the arc. For more information on modeling with colored Petri nets, see [23].

Refinement of a model in the sense of Sect. 3 can be implemented in the framework of Petri nets by creating a new model where each refined species is represented as a place, and each refined reaction as a transition, which results in a model explosion of the same magnitude as in the case of reaction-based models. In the framework of colored Petri nets, the initial model can be transformed in the refined model via coloring. All subspecies of a species may be modeled using the same place as the parent species, having a color set with as many colors as the desired number of subspecies. New reactions can be represented with the same transition as the parent reaction, with possible constraints expressed via transition guards. It can also happen that the coloring scheme chosen for the refinement of species prompts to adding new transitions in the refined model to account for some of the refined reaction, in case the modeler wants to avoid too complex transition guards.

For the case study of the heat shock response, one coloring strategy is to consider integer color sets with as many colors as the number of subspecies

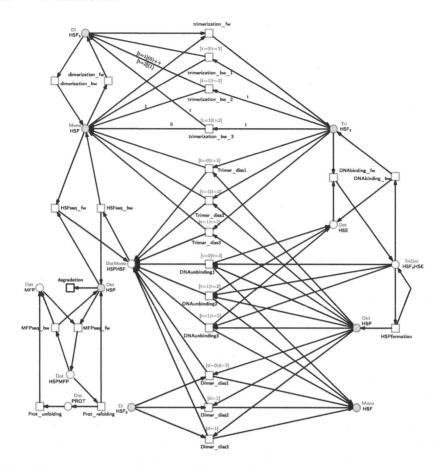

Fig. 3. Representation of the refined HSR model as a colored Petri net, using as few colors as possible (Color figure online).

for the species refining to at least two subspecies. A possible resulting model is depicted in Fig. 3. Compared to the network for the initial HSR model, this refined version contains several additional transitions. They account for reactions that have the same left hand side, but different right hand sides, e.g. a trimer with one acetylated molecule can produce either a non-acetylated monomer and a single-acetylated dimer, or an acetylated monomer and a non-acetylated dimer. The same model could be implemented while preserving the network structure by using variables on each adjacent arc and a guard on the trimerization_bw transition that accounts for all valid variable bindings at once.

A different coloring strategy is to consider the color set of places representing complex species to be the cartesian product of the color sets of the places representing the components of the complex. In this case, there is a distinction between e.g. one-acetylated dimers, depending on which of the two composing monomers is acetylated. This results in an adjustment of the kinetic constants of some reactions, but the resulting colored Petri net has exactly the same structure as the initial one. We refer to [14,21] for all details of this construction. Note that both colored Petri net representations of the refinement are smaller in size than the fully expanded model, showing that the framework of colored Petri nets can be successfully used to obtain compact models upon refinement.

6.3   Guarded Command-Based Models Refinement

The *guarded command-based models*, inspired by the guarded command languages first introduced in [7], is a modelling framework to capture the dynamics of alternative and repetitive constructs with a non-deterministic component in which the enabled activity is not utterly dependent on the initial input.

Table 3. Basic guarded command-based model for intermediate filaments self-assembly.

Guarded command	
$[r_2]\, T \geq 2 \rightarrow T^2 * k_t : T' = T - 2 \wedge O' = O + 1;$	(2)
$[r_3]\, O \geq 2 \rightarrow O^2 * k_o : O' = O - 2 \wedge H' = H + 1;$	(3)
$[r_4]\, H \geq 2 \rightarrow H^2 * k_h : H' = H - 2 \wedge U' = U + 1;$	(4)
$[r_5]\, U \geq 2 \rightarrow U^2 * k_h : U' = U - 2 \wedge F' = F + 1;$	(5)
$[r_6]\, U \geq 1 \wedge F \geq 1 \rightarrow U * F * k_{uf} : U' = U - 1 \wedge F' = F - 1 \wedge F' = F + 1$	(6)
$[r_7]\, F \geq 2 \rightarrow F^2 * k_{ff} : F' = F - 2 \wedge F' = F + 1.$	(7)

A guarded command-based model comprises a set of variables and a set of guarded commands. A guarded command consists of a *guard*, an *update* and a corresponding *rate* to the guarded command. The guard is a Boolean predicate over all the variables in the model and the update describes a transition which the system can make if the guard is true. To obtain the guarded command corresponding to a reaction of a reaction network we use the approach proposed in [1], for example the guard corresponding to the reaction $F + F \rightarrow F$ of Table 2 is obtained as follows:

- the reaction can be enabled whenever there are at least two F in the system to bind and form an F, therefore, we define the corresponding *guard* to be "$F \geq 2$", i.e. the guarded command can be enabled whenever $F \geq 2$;
- we define the *rate* corresponding to the guarded command to be "$F^2 * k_{ff}$" which is in correspondence with the definition of a reaction rate of a mass-action ODE-based model, see [25];
- we define the *update* corresponding to the guarded command to be "$F' = F - 2 \wedge F' = F + 1$", i.e. whenever the guard is enable two F are consumed and one F is produced.

Table 4. Refined guarded command-based model for intermediate filaments self-assembly.

Guarded command	
$[r_8]\, rT \geq 2 \rightarrow rT^2 * k_t' : rT' = rT - 2 \wedge rO' = rO + 1;$	(8)
$[r_9]\, rO \geq 2 \rightarrow rO^2 * k_o' : rO' = rO - 2 \wedge rH' = rH + 1;$	(9)
$[r_{10}]\, rH \geq 2 \rightarrow rH^2 * k_h' : rH' = rH - 2 \wedge rF_1' = rF_1 + 1;$	(10)
$[r_{11}]\, rF_1 \geq 2 \rightarrow rF_1^2 * k_{(1,1)}' : rF_1' = rF_1 - 2 \wedge rF_2' = rF_2 + 1;$	(11)
for $1 \leq i \leq 4$:	
$[r_{12}]\, rF_1 \geq 1 \wedge rF_i \geq 1 \wedge \rightarrow rF_1 * rF_i * k_{(1,i)}' : rF_1' = rF_1 - 1 \wedge$ $rF_i' = rF_i - 1 \wedge rF_{i+1}' = rF_{i+1} + 1;$	(12)
for $j \in \{5, \geq 6\}$:	
$[r_{13}]\, rF_1 \geq 1 \wedge rF_j \geq 1 \wedge \rightarrow rF_1 * rF_j * k_{(1,i)}' : rF_1' = rF_1 - 1 \wedge$ $rF_j' = rF_j - 1 \wedge rF_{\geq 6}' = rF_{\geq 6} + 1;$	(13)
$[r_{14}]\, rF_2 \geq 2 \rightarrow rF_2^2 * k_{(2,2)}' : rF_2' = rF_2 - 2 \wedge rF_4' = rF_4 + 1;$	(14)
for $i \in \{3, 4, 5, \geq 6\}$:	
$[r_{15}]\, rF_i \geq 2 \rightarrow rF_1 * rF_j * k_{(1,i)}' : rF_i' = rF_i - 2 \wedge rF_{\geq 6}' = rF_{\geq 6} + 1;$	(15)
$[r_{16}]\, rF_2 \geq 1 \wedge rF_3 \geq 1 \wedge \rightarrow rF_2 * rF_3 * k_{(2,3)}' : rF_2' = rF_2 - 1 \wedge$ $rF_3' = rF_3 - 1 \wedge rF_5' = rF_5 + 1;$	(16)
for $2 \leq i < j \leq 5, i + j \geq 6$:	
$[r_{17}]\, rF_i \geq 1 \wedge rF_j \geq 1 \wedge \rightarrow rF_i * rF_j * k_{(i,j)}' : rF_i' = rF_i - 1 \wedge$ $rF_j' = rF_j - 1 \wedge rF_{\geq 6}' = rF_{\geq 6} + 1;$	(17)
$[r_{18}]\, rF_i \geq 1 \wedge rF_{\geq 6} \geq 1 \wedge \rightarrow rF_i * rF_{\geq 6} * k_{(i,\geq 6)}' : rF_i' = rF_i - 1 \wedge$ $rF_{\geq 6}' = rF_{\geq 6} - 1 \wedge rF_{\geq 6}' = rF_{\geq 6} + 1.$	(18)

The list of all guarded commands corresponding to the basic intermediate filaments self-assembly is presented in Table 3.

Refinement in guarded command-based models is similar to the one of reaction-based models. In this approach whenever there is a refined variable in a guard we replace that guard with a set of guards considering to all possible refinements whereas in the refinement of reaction networks we would replace each reaction involving any refined reactant by the corresponding set of all possible refined reactions, for more information we refer to [1].

The list of all guarded commands corresponding to the refined intermediate filaments self-assembly is presented in Table 4.

7   Discussion

We discussed in this paper quantitative model refinement, an algorithmic approach for building large biomodels in an iterative fashion, while ensuring that the fit and the validation of the model is preserved throughout the construction. This allows the computational modeler to avoid repeating parameter estimation in each step of the model construction, even as the model size increases in each step; rather, the modeler may choose a setup that allows the model to preserve its fit to existing data in each step. Quantitative refinement also allows the modeler to deal with partial information about some of the parameters of the model, including such numerical values of the parameters whenever available, checking their consistency with the other parameters and with the data, and compensating for lack of information about parameters with an algorithmic solution. We investigated the versatility of the fit-preserving refinement method with respect to four broadly used frameworks: reaction models, rule-based models, Petri net models, and guarded command-based models.

The computational advantages of the refinement-driven top-down approach as opposed to the bottom-up approach based on collection of submodels is most evident in the case study on the ErbB signaling pathway. For instance, the ErbbB model of [3], consisting of 828 reactions and 499 reactants, was fit to experimental data by running about 100 times annealing methods, over 24 hours on a cluster consisting of 100 nodes. The refinement-driven approach starts from an initial model of [17] consisting of 103 reactants and 148 reactions, and leading to a refined model consisting of 421 reactants involved in 928 reactions; the refined model has a good numerical behavior, avoiding any supplementary model fit.

An interesting challenge that remains open to investigate is the scalability of the quantitative model refinement approach on larger case studies.

Acknowledgments. This work was partially supported by the Academy of Finland under project 267915. Bogdan Iancu's current affiliation is at Department of Mathematics and Statistics, University of Turku, Finland.

References

1. Azimi, S., Petre, I.: Quantitative model refinement for guarded command models. To appear (2015)
2. Bassingthwaighte, J.B.: Strategies for the physiome project. Ann. Biomed. Eng. **28**(8), 1043–1058 (2000)
3. Chen, W.W., Schoeberl, B., Jasper, P.J., Niepel, M., Nielsen, U.B., Lauffenburger, D.A., Sorger, P.K.: Input-output behavior of erbb signaling pathways as revealed by a mass action model trained against dynamic data. Mol. Syst. Biol. **5**, 239 (2009)
4. Craciun, G., Pantea, C.: Identifiability of chemical reaction networks. J. Math. Chem. **44**(1), 244–259 (2008)
5. Czeizler, E., Czeizler, E., Iancu, B., Petre, I.: Quantitative model refinement as a solution to the combinatorial size explosion of biomodels. In: Proceedings of the 2nd International Workshop on Static Analysis and Systems Biology (SASB 2011), Electronic Notes in Theoretical Computer Science, vol. 284, pp. 35–53 (2012)
6. Czeizler, E., Mizera, A., Czeizler, E., Back, R.J., Eriksson, J.E., Petre, I.: Quantitative analysis of the self-assembly strategies of intermediate filaments from tetrameric vimentin. IEEE/ACM Trans. Comput. Biol. Bioinf. (TCBB) **9**(3), 885–898 (2012)

7. Dijkstra, E.W.: Guarded commands, nondeterminacy and formal derivation of programs. Commun. ACM **18**(8), 453–457 (1975)
8. Faeder, J.R., Blinov, M.L., Goldstein, B., Hlavacek, W.S.: Rule-based modeling of biochemical networks. Complexity **10**(4), 22–41 (2005)
9. Gratie, C., Petre, I.: Fit-Preserving data refinement of mass-action reaction networks. In: Beckmann, A., Csuhaj-Varjú, E., Meer, K. (eds.) CiE 2014. LNCS, vol. 8493, pp. 204–213. Springer, Heidelberg (2014)
10. Gratie, C., Petre, I.: Fit-preserving data refinement of mass-action reaction networks. Technical Report, Turku Centre for Computer Science (2014)
11. Gratie, C., Petre, I.: Complete characterization for the fit-preserving data refinement of mass-action reaction networks. Technical Report 1128, Turku Centre for Computer Science (2015)
12. Gratie, D.E., Iancu, B., Azimi, S., Petre, I.: Quantitative model refinement in four different frameworks, with applications to the heat shock response. Technical Report 1067, TUCS (2013)
13. Gratie, D.-E., Iancu, B., Petre, I.: ODE analysis of biological systems. In: Bernardo, M., de Vink, E., Di Pierro, A., Wiklicky, H. (eds.) SFM 2013. LNCS, vol. 7938, pp. 29–62. Springer, Heidelberg (2013)
14. Gratie, D.E., Petre, I.: Hiding the combinatorial state space explosion of biomodels through colored petri nets. Annals of University of Bucharest LXI, pp. 23–41 (2014)
15. Herrmann, H., Aebi, U.: Intermediate filaments: molecular structure, assembly mechanism, and integration into functionally distinct intracellular scaffolds. Annu. Rev. Biochem. **73**(1), 749–789 (2004)
16. Hoops, S., Sahle, S., Gauges, R., Lee, C., Pahle, J., Simus, N., Singhal, M., Xu, L., Mendes, P., Kummer, U.: Copasi–a complex pathway simulator. Bioinformatics 22(24), 3067–3074 (2006). http://bioinformatics.oxfordjournals.org/content/22/24/3067.abstract
17. Hornberg, J., Binder, B., Bruggeman, F., Schoeberl, B., Heinrich, R., Westerhoff, H.: Control of MAPK signalling: from complexity to what really matters. Oncogene **24**(36), 5533–5542 (2005)
18. Hucka, M., et al.: The systems biology markup language (sbml): a medium for representation and exchange of biochemical network models. Bioinformatics 19(4), 524–531 (2003). http://bioinformatics.oxfordjournals.org/content/19/4/524.abstract
19. Iancu, B., Czeizler, E., Czeizler, E., Petre, I.: Quantitative refinement of reaction models. Int. J. Unconventional Comput. **8**(5–6), 529–550 (2012)
20. Iancu, B.: Quantitative Refinement of Reaction-Based Biomodels. Ph.D. thesis, Turku Centre for Computer Science (2015)
21. Iancu, B., Gratie, D.-E., Azimi, S., Petre, I.: On the implementation of quantitative model refinement. In: Dediu, A.-H., Martín-Vide, C., Truthe, B. (eds.) AlCoB 2014. LNCS, vol. 8542, pp. 95–106. Springer, Heidelberg (2014)
22. Ibssa, N.: Quantitative model refinement (2015). http://combio.abo.fi/research/quantitative-model-refinement/
23. Jensen, K., Kristensen, L.M.: Coloured Petri Nets. Springer-Verlag, Berlin Heidelberg (2009)
24. Karr, J.R., Sanghvi, J.C., Macklin, D.N., Gutschow, M.V., Jacobs, J.M., Bolival, B., Assad-Garcia, N., Glass, J.I., Covert, M.W.: A whole-cell computational model predicts phenotype from genotype. Cell **150**(2), 389–401 (2012)
25. Klipp, E., Herwig, R., Kowald, A., Wierling, C., Lehrach, H.: Systems Biology in Practice: Concepts, Implementation and Application. John Wiley & Sons, New York (2008)

26. Koch, I., Reisig, W., Schreiber, F.: Modeling in Systems Biology: The Petri Net Approach, vol. 16. Springer Science & Business Media, London (2010)
27. Lazarides, E.: Intermediate filaments as mechanical integrators of cellular space. Nature **283**(5744), 249–256 (1980)
28. Mizera, A., Czeizler, E., Petre, I.: Self-assembly models of variable resolution. In: Priami, C., Petre, I., de Vink, E. (eds.) Transactions on Computational Systems Biology XIV. LNCS, vol. 7625, pp. 181–203. Springer, Heidelberg (2012)
29. Murphy, E., Danos, V., Feret, J., Krivine, J., Harmer, R.: Rule Based Modelling and Model Refinement, Elem. Comput. Syst. Biol. pp. 83–114. Wiley Book Series on Bioinformatics, John Wiley & Sons, Inc. (2010)
30. Nicolis, G., Prigogine, I.: Self-Organizationin Nonequilibrium Systems: From Dissipative Structures to Order Through Fluctuations. Wiley, New York (1977)
31. Ovaska, K., et al.: Large-scale data integration framework provides a comprehensive view on glioblastoma multiforme. Genome Med. 2(9), 65+, 2010. http://dx.doi.org/10.1186/gm186
32. Petre, I., Mizera, A., Hyder, C., Meinander, A., Mikhailov, A., Morimoto, R., Sistonen, L., Eriksson, J., Back, R.: A simple mass-action model for the eukaryotic heat shock response and its mathematical validation. Natural Comput. **10**(1), 595–612 (2011)
33. Pistore, M., Sangiorgi, D.: A partition refinement algorithm for the π-calculus. In: Alur, R., Henzinger, T.A. (eds.) CAV 1996. LNCS, vol. 1102, pp. 38–49. Springer, Heidelberg (1996)
34. Rudy, Y.: From genome to physiome: integrative models of cardiac excitation. Ann. Biomed. Eng. **28**(8), 945–950 (2000)
35. Schliwa, M.: The Cytoskeleton, Cell Biology Monographs, vol. 13. Springer-Verlag, Vienna, Austria (1986)
36. Shokri, F.: Structref (2015). https://github.com/fshokri/StructRef
37. Suzuki, I., Murata, T.: A method for stepwise refinement and abstraction of petri nets. J. Comput. Syst. Sci. **27**(1), 51–76 (1983)

Regular Papers

Polarizationless P Systems
with One Active Membrane

Artiom Alhazov[1] and Rudolf Freund[2]([⊠])

[1] Institute of Mathematics and Computer Science, Academy of Sciences of Moldova,
Academiei 5, 2028 Chişinău, Moldova
artiom@math.md

[2] Faculty of Informatics, TU Wien, Favoritenstraße 9-11, 1040 Vienna, Austria
rudi@emcc.at

Abstract. The aim of this paper is to study the computational power of P systems with one active membrane without polarizations. For P systems with active membranes, it is known that computational completeness can be obtained with either of the following combinations of features: (i) two polarizations, (ii) membrane creation and dissolution, (iii) four membranes with three labels, membrane division and dissolution, (iv) seven membranes with two labels, membrane division and dissolution. Obviously, in polarizationless P systems with only one active membrane only object evolution rules and send-out rules are possible. We consider two variants here – external output and internal output – and show how the choice of the output region influences the generative power. Moreover, we illustrate the connection between (polarizationless) P systems with one active membrane and catalytic P systems with one catalyst in the skin region.

1 Introduction

Membrane computing is a theoretical framework of parallel distributed multiset processing. It has been introduced by Gheorghe Păun in 1998, and since then it has been an active research are, see [11] for the comprehensive bibliography and [7,9] for a systematic survey. Membrane systems are also called P systems.

It has been shown in [4] (some results being improvements of the results from [1,3]) that the following P systems with active membranes are computationally complete:

(i) P systems with one membrane and two polarizations, as acceptors,
(ii) polarizationless P systems with membrane creation and dissolution,
(iii) polarizationless P systems starting with four membranes and three labels,
(iv) polarizationless P systems starting with seven membranes and two labels.

In this paper we investigate the family of P systems with one active membrane without polarizations. Similar questions have been addressed in [2] for non-cooperative transitional P systems without any additional features.

© Springer International Publishing Switzerland 2015
G. Rozenberg et al. (Eds.): CMC 2015, LNCS 9504, pp. 51–62, 2015.
DOI: 10.1007/978-3-319-28475-0_4

2   Definitions

We assume the reader to be familiar with the basic notions from formal language theory, e.g., see [10], and for the area of P systems we refer to [6,7,9] as well as to [11] for actual news.

2.1   Formal Language Prerequisites

The set of all positive integers is denoted by $\mathbb{N}_1$, and the set of all non-negative integers by $\mathbb{N}$. For a finite set V, the set of all strings over V is denoted by V^*. The concatenation operation for strings is denoted by $\bullet$ (which is only written when necessary) and the empty string is denoted by λ. Any set $L \subseteq V^*$ is called a (string) language. For a string $w \in V^*$ and a symbol $a \in V$, the number of occurrences of a in w is written as $|w|_a$. The set of permutations of a string $w \in V^*$ is denoted by $\mathrm{Perm}(w) = \{x \in V^* : |x|_a = |w|_a$ for all $a \in V\}$. We denote the set of all permutations of the strings in L by $\mathrm{Perm}(L)$, and we extend this notation to families of languages. We use FIN, REG, LIN, CF, MON, RE to denote the families of finite, regular, linear, context-free, monotone, and recursively enumerable languages, respectively. The family of languages generated by matrix grammars without appearance checking and with erasing rules and the family of extended [tabled] interactionless L systems is denoted by MAT and $E[T]0L$, respectively. The family of sets of numbers generated by forbidden random context multiset grammars is denoted by $NfRC$.

Throughout this paper we use the string notation to denote multisets, although in membrane systems, the order in which symbols are written is irrelevant, unless we speak about the symbols sent to the environment. In particular, speaking about the contents of some membrane, when we write $a_1^{n_1} \cdots a_m^{n_m}$ (or any permutation of it), we mean a multiset consisting of n_i instances of symbol a_i, $1 \le i \le m$.

2.2   P Systems with One (Active) Membrane

We present the definition of a *P system with active membranes*, simplified for studying the generative power in case of systems with only one membrane, i.e., with the simplest membrane structure $\mu = [\ ]_1$:

$$\Pi = \left(O, [\ ]_1, w_1, R_1, i_0\right), \text{ where}$$
O is a finite set of objects,
w_1 is the initial multiset in membrane region 1,
R_1 is the set of rules associated to membrane 1,
i_0 is the output region; $i_0 = 0$ is assumed for languages.

The rules of a membrane system have the forms $(a_0)\ [\ a \to u\ ]_1$ (*evolution rules*, evolving an object), and $(c_0)\ [\ a\ ]_1 \to [\ ]_1 b$ (*send-out rules*, sending an object out, possibly renaming it), where $a, b \in O$ and $u \in O^*$.

The rules are applied in the maximally parallel way: no further rule should be applicable to the idle objects, except that rules of type (c_0) may be applied to at most one object in any step.

A *catalytic P system* (with one membrane) is a construct

$$\Pi = (O, C, [\ ]_1, w_1, R_1, i_0), \text{ where}$$

O is a finite set of objects,

C is a special subset of O whose elements are called *catalysts*,

w_1 is the initial multiset in membrane region 1,

R_1 is the set of rules associated to membrane 1,

i_0 is the output region; $i_0 = 0$ is assumed for languages.

The rules in R are either of the form $a \rightarrow (b_1, tar_1) \cdots (b_k, tar_k)$ (non-cooperative rules) with a and the b_i, $1 \leq i \leq k$, $k \geq 0$, being from $O \setminus C$ and the $tar_i \in \{here, out\}$ being the targets for the corresponding symbols b_i, or of the form $ca \rightarrow c(b_1, tar_1) \cdots (b_k, tar_k)$ (catalytic rules) with $c \in C$.

A *configuration* of a P system is a construct which contains the information about the contents of the skin membrane as well as the sequence of objects sent out. A sequence of transitions between the configurations is called a *computation*. The computation *halts* when a configuration is reached such that no rules are applicable. In case of external output ($i_0 = 0$), as the result of a (halting) computation we may consider the strings obtained by the *sequence* of objects sent to the environment; we denote it by $L(\Pi)$. Both in case of internal output ($i_0 = 1$) and in case of external output, we may consider as the result the vector of multiplicities of objects in region i_0, which we denote by $Ps(\Pi)$, or the total number of objects in region i_0, which we denote by $N(\Pi)$.

The family of P systems with one polarizationless active membrane is denoted by $OP_1(a_0, c_0)$. The class of sets of numbers/vectors/strings generated by a family $\mathcal{F}$ of P system is denoted by $N\mathcal{F}$, $Ps\mathcal{F}$ and $L\mathcal{F}$, respectively. We use the superscript *int* or *ext* when speaking about internal and external output, respectively, and we may omit superscript *ext* in the case of generating languages, i.e., external output always has to be assumed for $L\mathcal{F}$.

Moreover, we may use a subscript T to denote terminal filtering of the result; in this case, a subset $T \subset O$ is additionally specified for Π, and the objects not belonging to T are not considered in the result. For example, the family of sets of vectors of non-negative integers generated internally by P systems with one polarizationless active membrane with terminal filtering is denoted by $Ps_T^{int}OP_1(a_0, c_0)$.

Example 1. To illustrate generation, consider the following P system:

$$\Pi = (O = \{S, a, b, c, d, f\}, [\ ]_1, w_1 = S, R_1, i_0),$$
$$R_1 = \{\, [\ S \rightarrow Sabcd\,]_1, \ [\ S \rightarrow f\,]_1,$$
$$[\ a\,]_1 \rightarrow [\ ]_1 a, \ [\ b\,]_1 \rightarrow [\ ]_1 b, \ [\ c\,]_1 \rightarrow [\ ]_1 c\,\}.$$

Object S produces objects a, b, c, d in arbitrary but equal amounts. Objects a, b, c are sent out in arbitrary order. Hence, if $i_0 = 1$ then $N(\Pi) = \mathbb{N}_1$ (i.e., the set of all positive integers), and if $i_0 = 0$ then $L(\Pi) = \bigcup_{n \geq 0} Perm(a^n b^n c^n) = \{w \in \{a,b,c\}^* : |w|_a = |w|_b = |w|_c\}$.

P systems can be also viewed as acceptors. In that case, an input subalphabet Σ is additionally specified in the tuple defining P system before μ, and $i_0 = 1$ is the input region. An input multiset over Σ is additionally placed inside the membrane before the computation starts, and it is accepted if and only if the computation halts; the result $Ps_{acc}(\Pi)$ is the set of all accepted inputs, and the family of vector sets accepted by P systems with one active membrane is denoted by $Ps_{acc}OP_1(a_0, c_0)$.

3   Comparison with a Transitional Model: Catalytic P Systems with One Catalyst

The model of P systems with active membranes, for the case of one membrane, can be compared with the following case of transitional P systems: non-distributed P systems with one catalyst. Indeed, for each P system with one active membrane, there exists a 1-catalytic non-distributed P system with the same behavior, as non-cooperative rules work equivalently in both models: $[A \to u]_h$ is equivalent to $A \to u$, and sending out corresponds to particular rules with one catalyst, i.e., $[A]_h \to [\ ]_h a$ corresponds with $cA \to c(a, out)$, or, if without restricting generality we assume the set of symbols that may appear inside the system to be disjoint from the set of symbols that may be sent to the environment, simply with $cA \to c(a, here)$.

Notice that for P system with external output, we may ignore the objects remaining inside the system when it halts (as explained in the next section), while for P systems with internal output, we should ignore the objects sent out. In this way, for the case of internal output, sending out corresponds to a catalytic erasing, while for the case of external output sending out corresponds to a catalytic renaming of a non-terminal symbol into a terminal symbol.

Hence, we can immediately conclude that

$$X_\beta^\alpha OP_1(a_0, c_0) \subseteq X_\beta OP_1(ncoo, cat_1)$$

for $X \in \{N, Ps, L\}$, $\alpha \in \{int, ext\}$, $\beta \in \{-, T\}$, where $\beta = -$ stands for not specifying a subscript.

One-catalytic P systems were investigated in [5], where some subclasses of P systems with one catalyst are defined and certain results on their generative power are presented. In particular, it was shown in [5] that

$$N_{-c}OP_1(wsepcat_1) = NREG \text{ and } N_{-c}OP_1(complcat_1) \subseteq NfRC.$$

Clearly, the corresponding restrictions might also be considered for polarizationless P systems with one active membrane, and such results can be claimed as upper bounds for the corresponding restrictions, e.g.,

$$NOP_1(wsep(a_0, c_0)) = NREG,$$

where the restriction of the *weak separation* can be reformulated for the model with active membranes as follows: the set O of objects is divided into three **disjoint** subsets O', O'' and O''', such that

- objects $a \in O'$ have no associated rules (they cannot evolve or be sent out, so if they are produced, they remain idle inside the system),
- objects $a \in O''$ have associated send-out rules, but no evolution rules,
- objects $a \in O'''$ have associated evolution rules, but no send-out rules.

It is worth mentioning that the additional requirement from [5] that the objects produced by a catalytic rule cannot undergo a non-cooperative rule is *automatically* satisfied after translation into the active membrane case, so the only restriction remaining in the case of weak separation is that a rule of type (a_0) and a rule of type (c_0) are not allowed to compete for the same object. This restriction means, for instance, that all objects that have associated send-out rules cannot evolve inside the system, they simply wait there until they are chosen to be sent out.

A different restriction considered in [5] is *complete* P systems (mentioned above as $complcat_1$). It can be reformulated in the model of polarizationless P systems with active membranes as follows: there is no object having associated rules of type (c_0) and no rules of type (a_0). This restriction means that no object is allowed to be temporarily idle; if it is not sent out, then it either evolves immediately, or remains idle throughout the computation. It follows that

$$NREG \subseteq NOP_1 \left(compl \left(a_0, c_0 \right) \right) \subseteq NfRC.$$

It is interesting to note that weak separation and completeness are, in some sense, two opposite requirements. While the latter one requires that *all* objects which can be sent out must evolve if they are not chosen to be sent out, the first special case requires that *no* objects which can be sent out are allowed to evolve. Of course, in the most general case there can be both kinds of objects which can be sent out.

4 External Output

The first goal of this section is to present a reduction of any P system with one active membrane without polarizations and external output to an equivalent normal form. Then we will use this normal form to prove an upper bound result. For this the normal form, without loss of generality we assume the output symbols appearing in the environment to be disjoint from the symbols used inside the skin membrane; in this case we write $\Pi = (O, T, [\ ]_1, w_1, R_1, 1)$ with $T \subset O$ being the output alphabet:

Theorem 1. *For any P system $\Pi = (O, T, [\ ]_1, w_1, R_1, 1)$ with one active membrane without polarizations and external output (where we assume the output symbols appearing in the environment to be disjoint from the symbols used inside the skin membrane) we can effectively construct an equivalent P system*

$\Pi'\left(O', T, [\ ]_1, w'_1 = S, R'_1, 1\right)$ *with one active membrane without polarizations and external output (where again the output symbols appearing in the environment are disjoint from the symbols used inside the skin membrane) in the* normal form *fulfilling the following conditions:*

1. *The initial multiset in Π' is a single symbol S which does not appear on the right side of any other rule in R'_1.*
2. *The only erasing rule allowed is $\ll S \to \lambda]_1$ for the initial object S.*
3. *Every symbol in O' appears on the left side of some rule in R'_1 and can be reached from S by using the evolution rules in Π'.*

Proof. We approach this normal form in several stages, thereby constructing O' and R'_1 step by step.

1. First, we remark that we can guarantee that in Π' no objects remain inside the skin region when Π' halts. Indeed, let O_λ be the set of all objects that do not have associated rules. Starting with R_1 for R'_1, we now add the rule set $R_\lambda = \{[\ a \to \lambda]_1 \mid a \in O_\lambda\}$ to R'_1, thus making sure that there are no objects that can remain idle at the end of a halting computation. On the other hand, adding the rules from R_λ does not affect the results obtained by the original P system Π with external output, since preserving/erasing objects from O_λ has no alternatives, and it does not affect the environment.
2. Second, starting with $O' = O$, we can use a new symbol $S \notin O$ and add it to O' as the new initial multiset w'_1; moreover, we add $R_S = \{[\ S \to w_1]_1\}$ to R'_1.
3. Third, we eliminate all symbols which cannot be obtained by using evolutions rules when starting with S: In fact, we start with the set $M_0 = \{S\}$ and iteratively, for $i \geq 1$, construct the sets

$$M_i := M_{i-1} \cup \{X \mid X \in w \text{ for some } w \text{ with}$$
$$[\ v\ ]_1 \Longrightarrow [\ w\ ]_1 \text{ and } v \in M_{i-1}\},$$

where the derivation steps $[\ v\ ]_1 \Longrightarrow [\ w\ ]_1$ use evolution rules from the rule set R'_1 constructed so far. Obviously, these iterations end after at most $n := |O \backslash T| + 2$ steps, in fact, as soon as $M_i = M_{i-1}$. Then we take $O' := M_n$ and eliminate from R'_1 all rules containing a symbol from $(O \backslash T) \backslash M_n$ on the left or on the right side. Hence, now O' and R'_1 only contain symbols which can be reached from S.
4. We now claim that we can eliminate the λ-rules $[\ a \to \lambda]_1$ in the rule set R'_1 constructed so far, eventually except for $[\ S \to \lambda]_1$. For this purpose, we first compute the set of objects from which the empty multiset λ can be obtained: We start with $M_0^\lambda = \{a \mid [\ a \to \lambda]_1 \in R'_1\}$ and iteratively, for $i \geq 1$, construct the sets

$$M_i^\lambda := M_{i-1}^\lambda \cup \{a \mid [\ a \to u\ ]_1 \text{ for some } u \in M_{i-1}^*\}.$$

Obviously, these iterations end after at most $n := |O \backslash T| + 2$ steps, in fact, as soon as $M_i^\lambda = M_{i-1}^\lambda$. Then we take M_n^λ and replace each rule $[\ a \to u\ ]_1$ by all possible rules $[\, a \to u' \,]_1$ where the u' are obtained from u by removing, in all possible combinations, some objects from M_n^λ. This will again yield an equivalent system, because instead of eliminating a symbol in the next step we just do not produce it. Hence, we now can just eliminate the λ-rules $[\, a \to \lambda \,]_1 \in R'_1$ for all $a \in O \backslash (T \cup \{S\})$ from $\in R'_1$ without affecting the results, yet with one exception – if there is a rule $[\, a \,]_1 \to [\ ]_1 b \in R_1$ for some $b \in T$, but no other rule for a except $[\, a \to \lambda \,]_1$, in which case only one copy of a can be sent out to the environment, whereas all other copies of a would have been eliminated by the rule $[\, a \to \lambda \,]_1$; to cope with this subtle detail, we finally have to add the set of rules

$$R_t = \{[\, a \to \# \,]_1 \mid [\, a \to \lambda \,]_1 \in R_1,$$
$$[\, a \,]_1 \to [\ ]_1 b \in R_1 \text{ for some } b \in T, \text{ and}$$
$$[\, a \to \lambda \,]_1 \text{ is the only evolution rule for } a \text{ in } R_1\}$$
$$\cup \{[\, \# \to \# \,]_1\}$$

to the rule set R'_1 constructed so far; $\#$ is a new symbol to be added to O', and if it appears in a configuration, the system will never halt and therefore will not produce any result. The introduction of $\#$ is only enforced in case we non-deterministically generate more than one copy of a symbol a for which the only rules are the evolution rule $[\, a \to \lambda \,]_1$ and some send-out rules of the form $[\, a \,]_1 \to [\ ]_1 b \in R_1$ for some $b \in T$, from which only one can be used in one derivation step.

In that way, from the original P system Π we finally have obtained an equivalent P system Π' fulfilling all normal form conditions.   □

Corollary 1. $LOP_1(a_0, c_0) \subseteq MON$.

Proof. Indeed, the total number of objects (inside and outside the membrane) never decreases throughout the computation (except, possibly, for the empty string, generated in one step), and the length of the result matches the total number of objects when the system halts.   □

Obviously, similar results hold for the corresponding sets of (vectors of) numbers generated by $OP_1(a_0, c_0)$ systems with external output:

Corollary 2. *For any* $Y \in \{N, Ps\}$, $Y^{ext}OP_1(a_0, c_0) \subseteq YMON$.

We now proceed with a lower bound result.

Theorem 2. $LOP_1(a_0, c_0) \supseteq REG \bullet \mathrm{Perm}(REG)$.

Proof. Consider an alphabet T and two arbitrary regular languages over T. Then there exist reduced regular grammars $G_1 = (N_1, T, P_1, S_1)$ and $G_2 =$

(N_2, T, P_2, S_2) generating them, such that $N_1 \cap N_2 = \emptyset$. We construct the following P system:

$$\Pi = \left(O = N_1 \cup N_2 \cup T \cup T', [\ ]_1, w_1 = S_1, R_1 \right),$$
$$T' = \{ a' \mid a \in T \},$$
$$R_1 = \{ [\ A \to aB\ ]_1 \mid (A \to aB) \in P_1 \} \cup \{ [\ A \to S_2\ ]_1 \mid (A \to \lambda) \in P_1 \}$$
$$\cup \{ [\ A \to a'B\ ]_1 \mid (A \to aB) \in P_2 \} \cup \{ [\ A \to \lambda\ ]_1 \mid (A \to \lambda) \in P_2 \}$$
$$\cup \{ [\ a' \to a'\ ]_1 \mid a \in T \}$$
$$\cup \{ [\ a\ ]_1 \to [\ ]_1 a, [\ a'\ ]_1 \to [\ ]_1 a \mid a \in T \} .$$

The P system constructed above generates $L(G_1) \bullet L(G_2)$, except that the symbols generated by the second grammars are first produced in a primed form, and may undergo trivial rewriting for an arbitrarily long time before they are sent out, which ensures that after generating a string from $L(G_1)$, any permutation of a string from $L(G_2)$ can be generated. □

We have to mention that for the sets of (Parikh vectors of) natural numbers generated by $OP_1(a_0, c_0)$ systems, the preceding lower bound result does not help at all, since obviously $Ps(REG \bullet \mathtt{Perm}(REG)) = Ps(REG)$, i.e.,

$$Y(REG) \subseteq YOP_1(a_0, c_0), Y \in \{ N^{ext}, Ps^{ext} \} .$$

We now present a few closure properties for the families $YOP_1(a_0, c_0)$, $Y \in \{ L, N^{ext}, Ps^{ext} \}$.

Theorem 3. *For any* $Y \in \{ L, N^{ext}, Ps^{ext} \}$, *the families* $YOP_1(a_0, c_0)$ *are closed under renaming morphisms.*

Proof. The statement follows from applying the renaming morphism to the send-out rules. □

Theorem 4. *For any* $Y \in \{ L, N^{ext}, Ps^{ext}, N^{int}, Ps^{int} \}$, *the families* $YOP_1(a_0, c_0)$ *are closed under union.*

Proof. The closure under union follows from adding a new axiom and productions for the non-deterministic choice between multiple axioms. □

5   Internal Output

In this case the environment is no longer relevant: it does not matter which symbol is written on the right side of a send-out rule. The object sent out no longer affects the result, so sending out is equivalent to a sequential version of erasing.

Of course, we can generate $PsREG$ with rules of type (a_0) corresponding to the rules of a reduced regular grammar. Hence,

$$Ps^{int}OP_1(a_0, c_0) \supseteq PsREG.$$

Is it an *open question* whether non-semilinear number sets can be generated, see also the partial results transferred from the one-catalytic model, recalled in Sect. 3.

6   P Systems with Internal Input

In this section we show that, not very surprisingly, for P systems with one polarizationless active membrane, their accepting power is even smaller than their generative power. More exactly, unless such a P system accepts all allowed inputs, it only accepts specific finite sets. We start by establishing some useful facts (we remind that we use $\subseteq$ to denote the submultiset relation, $\cup$ to denote the union of multisets, and $\setminus$ to denote the difference of multisets).

Lemma 1. *Let Π be an $OP_1(a_0, c_0)$ system with alphabet O and let $[\, u\,]_1 \Rightarrow [\, v\,]_1\alpha$ be a derivation in Π, with $\alpha \in O \cup \{\lambda\}$. Then for every multiset $u' \subseteq u$, either $[\, u'\,]_1$ is already a halting configuration, or there exist a multiset $v' \subseteq v$ and a $\beta \in O \cup \{\lambda\}$ such that $[\, u'\,]_1 \Rightarrow [\, v'\,]_1\beta$ in Π.*

Proof. In a transition $[\, u\,]_1 \Rightarrow [\, v\,]_1\alpha$, one of three possible cases happens for every (copy of) object a in u:

- a is rewritten by some rule of Π into a (possibly empty) multiset γ, with γ contributing to v;
- a is sent out by some rule of Π as α;
- a remains idle, contributing to v.

Note that v consists exactly of the resulting objects from the first case and the objects of the third case. More precisely, let the union of multisets of the right side rules for all copies of rewritten objects be v_r, and let the multiset of idle objects be v_i; then, $v = v_r \cup v_i$. By definition of the model, the second case was applied to at most one (copy of) an object in u. Also by definition of the model, for each object in the third case, there exist no rules to evolve it, except, possibly, send-out rules, in which case $\alpha \neq \lambda$.

We recall that u' may be obtained from u by erasing some (copies) of objects. Fix some correspondence of (copies of) objects in u' to objects in u, and consider a transition from u' by the same behavior of objects in u' as of objects in u:

- rewritten objects will yield some submultiset v'_r of v_r;
- β will be produced in the environment, with $\beta = \alpha$ or $\beta = \lambda$;
- idle objects will yield some submultiset v'_i of v_i.

It is obvious that these rules are applicable, and that $v'_r \cup v'_i \subseteq v$. Maximality also holds, except in one special situation: in case $\alpha \neq \lambda$, α was produced from a (copy of) an object not in u', and there exists at least one object b that was idle in the transition $[\, u\,]_1 \Rightarrow [\, v\,]_1\alpha$. In this situation, one such object b, instead of staying idle, has to be sent out as β, and the resulting multiset in the skin is $v' = v'_r \cup v'_i \setminus b$.

Therefore, $[\, u'\,]_1 \Rightarrow [\, v'\,]_1\beta$ in Π if at least one (copy of) object from u' falls into the first or the second case, and otherwise $[\, u'\,]_1$ is already a halting configuration. □

Lemma 2. *If $n \in N(\Pi)$, then also $n' \in N(\Pi)$ for any non-negative integer $n' \leq n$.*

Proof. Let the alphabet of Π be O, let the initial contents of the skin membrane of Π be w_1, and let the input subalphabet of Π be Σ. By definition of acceptance, a number n is accepted if and only if there exists a halting computation in Π starting from configuration $[\, u \,]_1$, for some $u \in \{w_1\} \Sigma^n$.

Consider the "sub-input" of only n' objects, i.e., $u' \in \{w_1\} \Sigma^{n'}$ such that $u' \subseteq u$. If $[\, u \,]_1$ is already halting, then so is $[\, u' \,]_1$, hence, the statement of the lemma holds. Now we assume the contrary: $[\, u \,]_1 \Rightarrow [\, v \,]_1 \alpha$. By the previous lemma, in one step, either the computation with u' in the skin will immediately halt (and the statement of the lemma again holds), or there is a one-step transition $[\, u' \,]_1 \Rightarrow [\, v' \,]_1 \beta$ with $v' \subseteq v$.

Iterating the application of the previous lemma, by induction, we conclude that there exists a computation starting from $[\, u' \,]_1$ that will halt in at most as many steps as the halting computation starting from $[\, u \,]_1$ that we considered. Hence, $n' \in N(\Pi)$. $\qquad\square$

It follows that the accepted set of numbers is either $\mathbb{N}$, or empty, or it contains all integers less than or equal to the maximal accepted number, so accepting P systems with one polarizationless active membrane cannot be computationally complete, and P systems with one polarizationless active membrane are obviously weaker as acceptors than as generators:

$$N_{acc}OP_1\,(a_0, c_0) \subseteq \{\emptyset, \mathbb{N}\} \cup \{\{k \mid 0 \le k \le n\} \mid n \in \mathbb{N}\}\,.$$

In the rest of the section we show, by all necessary examples, that this inclusion is an equality:

$$\Pi_\emptyset = \big(O = \{a\}, \Sigma = \{a\}, [\ ]_1, w_1 = a, R_1, i_0 = 1\big)\,, \text{ where}$$
$$R_1 = \big\{[\, a \to a \,]_1\big\}\,.$$
$$\Pi_\mathbb{N} = \big(O = \{a\}, \Sigma = \{a\}, [\ ]_1, w_1 = \lambda, R_1, i_0 = 1\big)\,, \text{ where}$$
$$R_1 = \big\{[\, a \to \lambda \,]_1\big\}\,.$$
$$\Pi_n = \big(O, \Sigma = \{a_0\}, [\ ]_1, w_1 = \lambda, R_1, i_0 = 1\big)\,, \text{ where}$$
$$O = \{a_i \mid 0 \le i \le n\}\,,$$
$$R_1 = \big\{[\, a_i \to a_{i+1} \,]_1, \ [\, a_i \,]_1 \to [\ ]_1 a_0 \mid 0 \le i < n\big\} \cup \big\{[\, a_n \to a_n \,]_1\big\}\,.$$

Clearly, $\Pi_\emptyset$ accepts nothing, since with any input it starts with at least one object, and then carries out an infinite computation. On the other end of the spectrum, system $\Pi_\mathbb{N}$ accepts any input, with erasing it in one step and then halting. Finally, we claim that system Π_n accepts exactly the set $\{k \mid 0 \le k \le n\}$. Indeed, any object increments its index every step, unless the object is sent out, or the index reaches n (forcing an infinite computation). It is easy to see that at most n input objects may be sent out in this way; the system with input $(a_0)^k$ has a halting computation if and only if $k \le n$.

Overall, we have established the following results (with $\alpha \in \{int, ext\}$):

$$REG \bullet \mathtt{Perm}\,(REG) \subseteq LOP_1\,(a_0, c_0) \subseteq MON,$$
$$PsREG \subseteq Ps^\alpha OP_1\,(a_0, c_0)\,,$$
$$N^\alpha OP_1\,(wsep\,(a_0, c_0)) = NREG \subseteq N^\alpha OP_1\,(compl\,(a_0, c_0)) \subseteq NfRC,$$
$$N_{acc}OP_1\,(a_0, c_0) = \{\{k \mid 0 \le k \le n\} \mid n \in \mathbb{N}\} \cup \{\emptyset, \mathbb{N}\}.$$

7 Conclusions

In this paper we have considered the family of languages generated by polarizationless P systems with one active membrane. A normal form was given for the case of external output. It was then shown that the family of languages generated by polarizationless P systems with one active membrane lies between $REG \bullet \text{Perm}(REG)$ and MON, and that it is closed under union and renaming morphisms. The exact characterization is an *open question*, but polarizationless P systems with one active membrane can be simulated by (and are, therefore, *at most* as powerful as) P systems with one catalyst in the skin membrane, transferring two results on the generative power of two restricted classes, independently from the output region.

Then we also considered sets of vectors or numbers generated internally, as well as sets of (vectors of) numbers accepted by polarizationless P systems with one active membrane. Several questions about the families of these sets are still *open*, too.

Another possible generalization to be considered is to allow rules of type (b_0) to bring objects from the environment into the skin region. Note that such systems would still correspond to a subclass of 1-catalytic P systems, but some definitions would have to be revised, as well as all related results.

We have proved that accepting P systems with one polarizationless active membrane are not computationally complete, unlike those with two polarizations or like those with membrane creation and dissolution, or with multiple membranes and membrane dissolution.

The questions about the computational power of polarizationless P systems with active membranes with 2 and 3 membranes in the initial configuration are still *open*, as well as of polarizationless systems with less than 7 membranes and two labels, or of all polarizationless systems with only one label.

References

1. Alhazov, A.: P systems without multiplicities of symbol-objects. Inf. Process. Lett. **100**(3), 124–129 (2006)
2. Alhazov, A., Ciubotaru, C., Ivanov, S., Rogozhin, Y.: The family of languages generated by non-cooperative membrane systems. In: Gheorghe, M., Hinze, T., Păun, Gh., Rozenberg, G., Salomaa, A. (eds.) CMC 2010. LNCS, vol. 6501, pp. 65–80. Springer, Heidelberg (2010)
3. Alhazov, A., Freund, R., Păun, Gh.: Computational completeness of P systems with active membranes and two polarizations. In: Margenstern, M. (ed.) MCU 2004. LNCS, vol. 3354, pp. 82–92. Springer, Heidelberg (2005)
4. Alhazov, A., Freund, R., Riscos-Núñez, A.: Membrane division, restricted membrane creation and object complexity in P systems. Int. J. Comput. Math. **83**(7), 529–548 (2006)
5. Freund, R.: Special variants of P systems with one catalyst in one membrane. In: Leung, H., Pighizzini, G. (eds.) Proceedings of the 8th International Workshop on Descriptional Complexity of Formal Systems - DCFS 2006, Las Cruces, New Mexico, pp. 250–258 (2006)

6. Păun, Gh.: Computing with membranes. J. Comput. Syst. Sci. **61**(1), 108–143 (2000). Turku Center for Computer Science-TUCS report 208, November 1998. http://www.tucs.fi
7. Păun, Gh.: Membrane Computing: An Introduction. Springer, Heidelberg (2002)
8. Păun, Gh, Rozenberg, G., Salomaa, A.: Membrane computing with an external output. Fundamenta Informaticae **41**(3), 313–340 (2000)
9. Păun, Gh., Rozenberg, A., Salomaa, A. (eds.): The Oxford Handbook of Membrane Computing. Oxford University Press, New York (2010)
10. Rozenberg, G., Salomaa, A. (eds.): Handbook of Formal Languages, 3 Volumes. Springer, Heidelberg (1997)
11. The P Systems Website: www.ppage.psystems.eu

Bridging Deterministic P Systems
and Conditional Grammars

Artiom Alhazov[1], Rudolf Freund[2]($\boxtimes$), and Sergey Verlan[3]

[1] Institute of Mathematics and Computer Science,
Academy of Sciences of Moldova, Academiei 5, 2028 Chişinău, Moldova
artiom@math.md
[2] Faculty of Informatics, TU Wien, Favoritenstraße 9-11, 1040 Vienna, Austria
rudi@emcc.at
[3] LACL, Département Informatique, Université Paris Est,
61, av. Général de Gaulle, 94010 Créteil, France
verlan@u-pec.fr

Abstract. We continue the line of research of deterministic parallel non-cooperative multiset rewriting with control. We here generalize control, i.e., rule applicability context conditions, from promoters and inhibitors, which are checking presence or absence of certain objects up to some bound, to regular and even stronger predicates, focusing on predicates over the multiplicity of one symbol at a time.

1 Introduction

As shown in [18], non-cooperative P systems with atomic promoters have $PsET0L$ as lower bound and with atomic inhibitors even characterize $PsET0L$, while when in addition using one catalyst, see [7,12], or else promoters or inhibitors of weight 2, see [8], leads to the computational completeness of non-cooperative P systems. A question about the power of deterministic systems was posed in [10], inspired by the fact that all identical objects have the same behavior in the same context. This question was answered in [2]: deterministic non-cooperative P systems have weak power, namely, only accepting finite number sets and their complements, even using generalized context conditions (except for the sequential case, when they keep computational completeness).

Generalized context conditions for rule applicability are defined as a list of pairs (p_i, F_i), $1 \leq i \leq k$, applicable to a rule if at least one condition applies, in the following way: p_i, called promoter, must be a submultiset of the current configuration (or the contents of the current region), and none of the elements of F_i, called inhibitors, is allowed to be a submultiset of the current configuration (or the contents of the current region). A subsequent paper, [5], precisely characterized the power of priorities alone, as well as established how much power of promoters and inhibitors is actually needed to reach $NFIN \cup coNFIN$. Already in [2] it has been shown that generalized context conditions are equivalent to arbitrary predicates on boundings, i.e., all boolean combinations over conditions

© Springer International Publishing Switzerland 2015
G. Rozenberg et al. (Eds.): CMC 2015, LNCS 9504, pp. 63–76, 2015.
DOI: 10.1007/978-3-319-28475-0_5

$< m$ (and, hence, also $\geq m$, $> m$, $\leq m$, $= m$ and $\neq m$) for multiplicities of symbols. In other words, generalized context conditions are able to check exactly the multiplicities of symbols up to an arbitrary fixed bound m. In this paper we consider stronger context conditions.

The model we study is very closely related to the model called *conditional grammars*, see [9], where a context-free rule is applicable if the current sentential form belongs to a specified language. The main differences are that here we consider multisets instead of strings and that the computation is maximally parallel and deterministic. Actually, since the scope of this paper is limited to non-cooperative rules, maximal parallelism simply means that *all* objects that can evolve must do so, and since we only focus on determinism, it follows that all copies of the same object in a configuration have to evolve by the same rule.

This paper is a revised version of [3], with improved presentation and extended with new results.

2   Definitions

For an alphabet V, by V^* we denote the free monoid generated by V under the operation of concatenation, i.e., containing all possible strings over V. The *empty string* is denoted by λ.

In this paper we will not distinguish between a multiset, its string representation (having as many occurrences of every symbol as its multiplicity in the multiset, the order in the string being irrelevant), and a vector of multiplicities (assuming that the order of enumeration of symbols from V is fixed). By V° we denote the set of all multisets over V.

For further notions and concepts from formal language theory we refer the reader to textbooks as [17], and for the area of P systems we refer to [14–16] as well as to [19] for actual news.

2.1   Register Machines

Register machines are well-known universal devices for computing (generating or accepting) sets of (vectors of) natural numbers.

Definition 1. *A* register machine *is a construct*

$$M = (m, B, l_0, l_h, P)$$

where

- *m is the number of registers,*
- *P is the set of instructions bijectively labeled by elements of B,*
- *$l_0 \in B$ is the initial label, and*
- *$l_h \in B$ is the final label.*

The instructions of M can be of the following forms:

- $p : (ADD(r), q, s)$, with $p \in B \setminus \{l_h\}$, $q, s \in B$, $1 \leq r \leq m$.
  Increase the value of register r by one, and non-deterministically jump to instruction q or s.
- $p : (SUB(r), q, s)$, with $p \in B \setminus \{l_h\}$, $q, s \in B$, $1 \leq r \leq m$.
  If the value of register r is not zero then decrease the value of register r by one (decrement case) and jump to instruction q, otherwise jump to instruction s (zero-test case).
- $l_h : HALT$.
  Stop the execution of the register machine.

A configuration *of a register machine is described by the contents of each register and by the value of the current label, which indicates the next instruction to be executed. M is called* deterministic *if the ADD-instructions all are of the form $p : (ADD\,(r)\,, q)$.*

In the accepting case, a computation starts with the input of a k-vector of natural numbers in its first k registers and by executing the first instruction of P (labeled with l_0); it terminates with reaching the $HALT$-instruction. Without loss of generality, we may assume all registers to be empty at the end of the computation.

2.2 P Systems

In this paper, we only consider membrane systems with the simplest membrane structure $\mu = [\ ]_1$, i.e., with even omitting μ, we consider a (cell-like) *P system* as a construct

$$\Pi = (O, \Sigma, w_1, R_1)$$

where O is the alphabet of *objects*, $\Sigma \subseteq O$ is the alphabet of *input symbols*, w_1 the multiset of objects present in the skin region at the beginning of a computation, and R_1 is a finite set of *evolution rules*, associated with the skin region.

If a rule $u \rightarrow v$ has at least two objects in u, then it is called *cooperative*, otherwise it is called *non-cooperative*.

3 Context Conditions

Let $\Pi = (O, \Sigma, w_1, R_1)$ be a P system.

By a *strong context* in this paper we mean a language of multisets, i.e., a subset of O°. Let $a \in O$ and $u \in O^\circ$, then $a \rightarrow u$ is a non-cooperative rule. The rules are applied in the maximally parallel way, which in the case of our interest, i.e., for deterministic non-cooperative P systems, correspond to replacing every occurrence of each symbol a by the corresponding multiset u from the right side of the applicable rule (if there is any; no competition between different rules can happen due to determinism).

Now let w be a multiset in the skin region. Then rule $a \rightarrow u$ with a strong context condition $C \subset O^\circ$ (written $a \rightarrow u|C$) is applicable if and only if $|w|_a > 0$ and $w \in C$. We especially consider the following variants:

- $+(s) = \{w \in O^\circ \mid |w|_s > 0\}$: a singleton atomic promoter $s \in O$ represents the context condition;
- $-(s) = \{w \in O^\circ \mid |w|_s = 0\}$: a singleton atomic inhibitor $s \in O$ represents the complementary context condition;
- $+(p) = \{w \in O^\circ \mid p \subseteq w\}$: a singleton promoter $p \in O^\circ$ of a higher weight represents the context condition;
- $-(q) = \{w \in O^\circ \mid q \not\subseteq w\}$: a singleton inhibitor $q \in O^\circ$ of a higher weight corresponds to the complementary context condition;
- $+(P) = \bigcup_{p \in P} +(p)$: a (finite) promoter-set $P \subset O^\circ$ is specified, i.e., at least one promoter out of P must be satisfied;
- $-(Q) = \bigcap_{q \in Q} -(q)$: a (finite) inhibitor-set $Q \subset O^\circ$ corresponds to the complementary context condition, i.e., any inhibitor from Q can forbid the rule to be applied;
- $+(P) \cap -(Q)$: a promoter-set P and an inhibitor-set Q together are called a *simple context condition*, written (P, Q);
- $\bigcup_{1 \leq i \leq m} (+(P_i) \cap -(Q_i))$: a finite union of simple context conditions is specified (these context conditions were considered in [2,5] and shown to be equivalent to predicates on boundings[1]);
- $\{w \in O^\circ \mid b_k(w) \in M\}$: a bounding b_k is an operation on a multiset, for any symbol preserving its multiplicity up to k, or "cropping" it down to k otherwise; a predicate on bounding can be specified by a finite set M of multisets with multiplicities not exceeding k; it can express precisely all Boolean combinations of conditions $|w|_a < j$, $a \in O$, $1 \leq j \leq k$;
- $ctxt(REG)$: a regular strong context condition can be specified by a regular multiset language or as a Parikh image of a regular string language; e.g.,

$$\mathsf{Eq}(a, b) = \{w \in O^\circ \mid |w|_a = |w|_b\};$$

- $ctxt^k$: if a strong context condition only depends on the multiplicities of k symbols from O (and all other symbols do not affect the applicability), we represent this property by a superscript k of $ctxt$; for instance, if we denote the symbols mentioned above by $S = \{s_1, \cdots, s_k\}$, then

$$ctxt^k(REG) = \{\{u \cup v \mid u \in L, \ v \in (O \setminus S)^\circ\} \mid L \subseteq S^\circ, \ L \in PsREG\};$$

hence $\mathsf{Eq}(a, b) \in ctxt^2(REG)$; by $ctxt(\mathsf{Eq})$ we denote being able to compare the multiplicities of two symbols (for different pairs of symbols separately) for being equal, together with the complementary condition;
- $ctxt(REC)$: to stay within Turing computability of the resulting P systems, in this paper we at most consider recursive context conditions, i.e., multiset languages with decidable membership; for example, $ctxt(CS)$ means that we use Parikh images of context-sensitive languages;

---

[1] The meaning of a promoter-set in [7] is different, but the results on the computational power are equivalent up to the descriptional complexity parameters such as number of promoters/inhibitors and their weights.

– if a one-symbol strong context condition only depends on the multiplicity of one symbol, it can be specified by a predicate over $\mathbb{N}$; for example,

$$\mathsf{Sq}(a) = \{w \in O^\circ \mid |w|_a = k^2, \ k \geq 0\} \text{ and}$$
$$\mathsf{Sq}'(a) = \{w \in O^\circ \mid |w|_a = k^2, \ k \geq 1\}$$

are examples; hence, $\mathsf{Sq}, \mathsf{Sq}' \in ctxt^1(CS) \subseteq ctxt^1(REC)$; by $ctxt(\mathsf{Sq})$ or $ctxt(\mathsf{Sq}')$ we denote being able to test the multiplicities (of different symbols separately) for squares (including zero or not, respectively), together with the complementary condition.

Remark 1. Take an arbitrary context condition $Z \subseteq O^\circ$. It is not difficult to see that any rule $a \to u$ without a context condition can be replaced by two rules $a \to u|Z$ and $a \to u|(O^\circ \setminus Z)$, yielding an equivalent system preserving determinism.

It was already mentioned that context conditions as considered in [2,5] are equivalent to predicates on boundings. We would like to note that such checking up to bounded multiplicities precisely corresponds to the predicates that can be specified by first-order logic.

For the rest of the paper we need some additional definitions. Let $R_1 \in T_1^\circ$, $R_2 \in T_2^\circ$ be multiset languages. The *direct product* of R_1 and R_2, denoted by $R_1 \times R_2$, is the multiset language $\{u \cup v \mid u \in R_1, \ v \in R_2\}$. Equivalently, we may say that $R_1 \times R_2$ consists of all multisets w such that $pr_{T_1}(w) \in R_1$ and $pr_{T_2}(w) \in R_2$, where pr_T is the projection on the subalphabet T ($pr_T(a) = a$ if $a \in T$ and $pr_T(a) = \lambda$ otherwise). A direct product of multiset languages is similar to language concatenation or language shuffle in the string case, but there is no linear order in multisets (for our purposes, the case of disjoint subalphabets suffices).

We now can explain more formally what we mean when we say that a strong condition only depends on multiplicities of k symbols: it is any multiset language of the form $L \times (O \setminus S)^\circ$, where $L \subseteq S^\circ$ and $|S| = k$. Although $L \times (O \setminus S)^\circ$ is itself a multiset language over O, not over S, we informally call it a condition *over k symbols*, because $w \in L \times (O \setminus S)^\circ$ if and only if $pr_S(w) \in L$.

Finally, we introduce a special class of regular multiset languages, let us call them *separated regular multiset languages*, denoted by $sepREG$, which are finite unions of direct products of unary regular multiset languages.

Remark 2. Let $\mathbb{C}$ be a separated regular multiset language over the alphabet $\Sigma = \{a_i \mid 1 \leq i \leq k\}$, i.e., a finite union of direct products of unary regular multiset languages; let us write $\mathbb{C}$ as

$$\mathbb{C} = \bigcup_{s=1}^{m} U_1^{(s)} \times \cdots \times U_k^{(s)}.$$

The $U_i^{(s)}$, $1 \leq i \leq k$, $1 \leq s \leq m$, are regular unary languages over the symbol a_i, i.e., each of them is the union of a finite set over a_i and a finite union of infinite sets of the form $\{a_i^{n''(i)^{(s)}+m(i)^{(s)}j} \mid j \geq 0\}$. As is well known, we can take the least common multiple (lcm) $M(i)^{(s)}$ of the $m(i)^{(s)}$ and thus obtain each $U_i^{(s)}$ as the union of a finite set over a_i and a finite union of infinite sets of the form $\{a_i^{n'^{(s)}(i)+M(i)^{(s)}j} \mid j \geq 0\}$. Now taking again the lcm M of all the $M(i)^{(s)}$, we obtain a representation of the $U_i^{(s)}$, $1 \leq i \leq k$, $1 \leq s \leq m$, as the union of a finite set over a_i – with all elements therein $< M$ – and a finite union of infinite sets of the form $\{a_i^{n^{(s)}(i)+Mj} \mid j \geq 1\}$ with $0 \leq n^{(s)}(i) < M$.

4   Regular Context Conditions

As expected, computational completeness can easily be obtained with specific regular context conditions.

Theorem 1. $Ps_a DOP_1\big(ncoo, ctxt^2(REG)\big) =$
$$Ps_a DOP_1\left(ncoo, ctxt(\texttt{Eq})\right) = PsRE.$$

Proof. Consider an arbitrary register machine $M = (m, B, l_0, l_h, P)$ with m registers. For each register i, $1 \leq i \leq m$, we represent its value by the difference of the multiplicities of associated objects a_i and b_i. Hence, increment can be performed by producing one copy of a_i, decrement can be performed by producing one copy of b_i, and zero can be distinguished from non-zero by the following regular conditions:

$$Z_i = \{w \in O^\circ \mid |w|_{a_i} = |w|_{b_i}\} = \texttt{Eq}\,(a_i, b_i),\ 1 \leq i \leq m;$$
$$P_i = \{w \in O^\circ \mid |w|_{a_i} \neq |w|_{b_i}\} = O^\circ \setminus \texttt{Eq}\,(a_i, b_i),\ 1 \leq i \leq m.$$

We now construct the following P system:

$$\Pi = (O, \Sigma, w_1, R_1),\ \text{where}$$
$$O = Q \cup \{a_i, b_i \mid 1 \leq i \leq m\},$$
$$\Sigma \subseteq \{a_i \mid 1 \leq i \leq m\},$$
$$w_1 = q_0,$$
$$R_1 = \{q \to a_i q' \mid q : (ADD(i), q') \in P\}$$
$$\cup \{q \to b_i q'|P_i,\ q \to q''|Z_i \mid q : (SUB(i), q', q'') \in P\}.$$

Using the regular context conditions P_i and Z_i, the P system Π can simulate the SUB-instructions on register i in an obvious way and thus simulate the computations of the given register machine M. $\square$

A natural question arises – what can P systems do if each of their context conditions only depends on the multiplicity of *one* symbol? We address this important issue in the following subsection.

4.1   One-Symbol Regular Context Conditions

It turns out that with regular context conditions over *one* symbol, P systems can only accept subregular multiset languages, namely exactly the separated regular multiset languages.

Theorem 2. $Ps_a DOP_1\left(ncoo, ctxt^1(REG)\right) = sepREG.$

Proof. We first show that every separated regular multiset language over an alphabet $\Sigma = \{a_i \mid 1 \leq i \leq k\}$ can be accepted by a P system with one-symbol regular context conditions in a deterministic way. For establishing this inclusion, we first consider arbitrary unary regular multiset languages U_i over a_i, $1 \leq i \leq k$, as well as the following P system.

$$\Pi = (O = \Sigma \cup \{p_i \mid 1 \leq i \leq k+1\}, w_1 = p_1, R_1),$$
$$R_1 = \{p_i \to p_{i+1}|C_i,\ p_i \to p_i|C_i' \mid 1 \leq i \leq k\},$$
$$C_i = U_i \times (\Sigma \setminus \{a_i\})^\circ,\quad C_i' = \Sigma^\circ \setminus C_i,\ 1 \leq i \leq k.$$

The work of Π is simple. We start with p_1 and check if the multiplicity $n(1)$ of a_1 is in C_1 or not; in case $a_1{}^{n(1)} \notin C_1$, we enter an infinite loop with the rule $p_1 \to p_1|C_1'$, otherwise we proceed to p_2 using the rule $p_1 \to p_2|C_1$. In general, for each symbol a_i with multiplicity $n(i)$, we enter an infinite loop with the rule $p_i \to p_i|C_i'$ in case $a_i{}^{n(i)} \notin C_i$, whereas otherwise, in case $a_i{}^{n(i)} \in C_i$, we proceed to p_{i+1} using the rule $p_i \to p_{i+1}|C_i$. After having checked $a_i{}^{n(i)} \in C_i$ successfully for all i, $1 \leq i \leq k$, the P system finally reaches p_{k+1} and halts. Hence, Π accepts precisely the multiset language $\mathbb{C} = U_1 \times \cdots \times U_k$.

It remains to show how an arbitrary finite union of such sets $\mathbb{C}$ can be accepted in a deterministic way. Let

$$\mathbb{C} = \bigcup_{s=1}^m U_1^{(s)} \times \cdots \times U_k^{(s)}.$$

Instead of the objects p_i we now use the control symbols $p_i^{(s)}$, $1 \leq s \leq m$, $1 \leq i \leq k$, where the s are the indices of the sets $\mathbb{C}_s = U_1^{(s)} \times \cdots \times U_k^{(s)}$ the given separated regular multiset language consists of. Then R_1 contains the following rules:

$$R_1 = \{p_i^{(s)} \to p_{i+1}^{(s)}|C_i^{(s)},\ p_i^{(s)} \to p_1^{(s+1)}|C_i'^{(s)} \mid 1 \leq s \leq m,\ 1 \leq i \leq k\}$$
$$\cup\ \{p_1^{(m+1)} \to p_1^{(m+1)}\}.$$

These rules now control the checking procedure as follows: for each s, $s = 1, \cdots, m$, sequentially we check whether the multiplicity n_i of symbol a_i is in $C_i^{(s)}$ and as before proceed to $i+1$ in the positive case, whereas in case of failure, i.e., if $a_i{}^{n(i)} \notin U_i^{(s)}$, which means that the input cannot be in $\mathbb{C}^{(s)}$, instead of entering an infinite loop we proceed to checking whether the input is in $\mathbb{C}^{(s+1)}$. Only in the case we have not found any s such that the input is in $\mathbb{C}^{(s)}$, we obtain $p^{(m+1)}$ and thus enter an infinite loop with the rule $p_1^{(m+1)} \to p_1^{(m+1)}$. Hence, any separated regular multiset language can be accepted by a P system with one-symbol regular context conditions in a deterministic way.

We now prove the other inclusion, i.e., for any arbitrary P system Π with regular context conditions over one symbol and with the input subalphabet Σ we effectively construct the separated regular multiset language over Σ accepted by Π.

Consider the P system

$$\Pi = (O = \Sigma \cup N, w_1, R_1).$$

According to Remark 2, any rule $a \to w|C$ in R_1 with a regular context condition C can be split into a finite number of rules of the form $a \to w|C'$ where C' either is a singleton set containing one unary multiset $\{b^n\}$ over some $b \in O$ or an infinite multiset over b of the form $\{b^{n+Mj} \mid j \geq 1\}$ such that $0 \leq n < M$.

Now let M be this constant from Remark 2, computed from all the one-symbol regular context conditions appearing in the rules of R_1. We partition the space O° of all possible multisets over O into $2M^{|O|}$ disjoint classes, such that each class is represented by the information about the multiplicities $n(a)$ of each symbol $a \in O$: either $M \leq n(a) < 2M$, which then also represents all multisets with multiplicities $n(a) + jM$, $j \geq 1$, or $0 \leq n(a) < M$. Hence, each class can thus be represented by some multiset over O where each symbol has multiplicity less than $2M$. In fact, in our derivation sequences we have to take into account the multiplicities of the symbols in N as well as of the symbols in the input alphabet Σ.

As inputs we only have to consider multisets with multiplicities $n(a)$ of the input symbols a obeying either the condition $M \leq n(a) < 2M$, which then also represent all inputs with multiplicities $n(a) + jM$, $j \geq 1$, or the condition $0 \leq n(a) < M$. Hence, each class can thus be represented by some input over Σ where each symbol has multiplicity less than $2M$. In fact, in our derivation sequences we never need to take into account multiplicities of symbols which exceed $2M$ – if this happens after the application of a maximal multiset of rules, then we reduce the corresponding numbers by multiples of M to again obtain numbers in the range between M and $2M - 1$ and proceed with this reduced configuration. The reason why we can do this is simple - multiples of M symbols again evolve into multiples of M symbols, hence, they would not lead outside the corresponding class obtained after this reduction process. For any such input as described above, we either reach a halting configuration or else, according to the pigeon hole principle, we inevitably end up in an infinite loop and never halt. Each of these accepted inputs describes a separated regular multiset language $\mathbb{C} = U_1 \times \cdots \times U_k$, where for every i, $1 \leq i \leq k$, either $U_i = \{a_i^n\}$ or $U_i = \{a_i^{n+Mj} \mid j \geq 1\}$. Therefore, the (finite) union of all these accepted classes $\mathbb{C}$ is a separated regular multiset language, too. $\qquad\square$

5   Stronger Context Conditions

We now consider one-symbol context conditions that are slightly stronger than regular. It is expected that with recursively enumerable context conditions over one symbol we get something like $PsRE \cup coPsRE$, so we are interested in intermediate cases. We look at ways of obtaining $PsRE$ by encoding a number by a multiplicity of *one* object, say, a_i, in such a way that increment and decrement are reasonably simple to be performed with non-removable objects.

We propose the following encoding: "ignoring the greatest square", i.e., a number $t \geq 0$ is encoded by $n = k^2 + t$ where $k > (t-1)/2$. The latter inequality is equivalent to $t < 2k + 1$, which is equivalent to $k^2 + t < (k+1)^2$, so k is the greatest square not exceeding n, hence, $n - \left(\max \left\{ k \mid k^2 \leq n \right\} \right)^2$ is indeed a correct decoding of t.

In this way, a zero-test becomes a test whether the encoding number is a perfect square. Increment is performed as increment of the encoding number, followed by the addition of $2k + 1$ if the next perfect square, i.e., $(k+1)^2$, has been reached. On the other hand, a decrement can be done by adding $2k$ to the encoding number. The value k can be stored as the multiplicity of another non-removable object, say, b_i, whose multiplicity is to be incremented each time the encoding number is increased by $2k$ or by $2k + 1$. Hence, while knowing n is enough to be able to find t, to implement increment and decrement in a P system, number t is represented by $a_i^n b_i^k$.

Note that we start with one copy of a_i and b_i for every i, and these objects are not erased until the end of a computation. While $n = 1$ and $k = 1$ encode $t = 0$, there is no need to consider 0 in the testing for perfect squares, so we can use $\mathsf{Sq'}$ instead of Sq. On the other hand, for symbols $q \in O$ which never appear in the computation in more than one copy, $\mathsf{Sq'}(q)$ can also serve in the role of a promoter q.

Putting all that together, with taking

$$Z_i = \{ w \in O^\circ \mid |w|_{a_i} = k^2, \ k \geq 1 \} = \mathsf{Sq'}\left(a_i \right), \ P_i = O^\circ \setminus Z_i, \ 1 \leq i \leq m,$$

we construct the following deterministic accepting P system:

$$\Pi = (O, \Sigma, w_1, R_1), \text{ where}$$
$$O = Q \cup \{ a_i, b_i \mid 1 \leq i \leq m \},$$
$$\Sigma \subseteq \{ a_i \mid 1 \leq i \leq m \},$$
$$w_1 = q_0 a_1 b_1 \cdots a_m b_m,$$
$$R_1 = \{ q \to a_i \tilde{q}, \ \tilde{q} \to q' | P_i, \ \tilde{q} \to \hat{q} | Z_i, \ \hat{q} \to a_i b_i q', \ b_i \to a_i a_i b_i | \mathsf{Sq'}(\hat{q})$$
$$\mid q : (ADD(i), q') \in P \}$$
$$\cup \{ q \to q'' | Z_i, \ q \to \hat{q} | P_i, \ \hat{q} \to b_i q', \ b_i \to a_i a_i b_i | \mathsf{Sq'}(\hat{q})$$
$$\mid q : (SUB(i), q', q'') \in P \}$$
$$\cup \{ a_i \to \lambda | \mathsf{Sq'}(q_f), \ b_i \to \lambda | \mathsf{Sq'}(q_f) \mid 1 \leq i \leq m \} \cup \{ q_f \to \lambda \}.$$

The rules in the last line of the description of R_1 are not needed for acceptance, but can be used in the case of computing functions to remove all objects representing the contents of the decrementable registers when the simulated register machine reaches the final state q_f.

Yet there is a major drawback of this result established above in comparison with the result from Theorem 1, as the input has to be encoded: given a number n_i for input register i, we have to compute the numbers $n_i + k_i^2$ and k_i such that $k_i^2 \leq n_i \leq k_i^2 + 2k_i$. But this is an algorithm which is not difficult to be implemented; also our context condition for testing a number to be a perfect square does not require a difficult algorithm.

Hence, we have just shown the following result, where the subscript wa instead of a in $Ps_{wa}DOP_1\,(ncoo, ctxt(\mathsf{Sq}'))$ indicates weak computational completeness as for having to encode the input:

Theorem 3. $Ps_{wa}DOP_1\left(ncoo, ctxt^1(CS)\right) =$
$Ps_{wa}DOP_1\left(ncoo, ctxt(\mathsf{Sq}')\right) = PsRE.$

We can strengthen the claim of Theorem 3 by showing **strong** computational completeness, in the sense of deterministic acceptance. Yet the same construction as given above even works for computing functions: without restricting the computing power of register machines, we assume that in the simulated register machine, the output registers are never decremented. For the additional output registers, we then simulate each increment instruction $q : (ADD(i), q') \in P$ on the output register i by a single rule $q \to a_i q'$. In this way, the output is produced without encoding.

It remains to show that P systems with strong context conditions over one symbol can simulate register machines where also the **input** is not encoded. We use the following idea. To represent the input N of a register in the way the P system constructed in the proof of Theorem 3 needs it, we first describe how to get two numbers x_N and y_N such that N is a function of x_N and y_N, and, moreover, by computing these two numbers from N, we get their representation in the form we need them as for the P system constructed in Theorem 3.

First we explain the algorithm how to obtain x_N and y_N: Starting with N represented by N copies of an object c_N, the multiplicity of these input objects is incremented until it becomes a perfect positive square (counting the increments, thus finally obtaining x_N), and then incrementing it (again counting the increments, thus finally obtaining y_N) until it again becomes a perfect square. From these two numbers x_N and y_N we can regain N by the formula computed in the following:

Given input N, the next positive perfect squares are $k_N^2 = N + x_N\ (x_N \geq 0)$ and $(k_N + 1)^2 = N + x_N + y_N$, then $y_N = 2k_N + 1$, so $k_N = (y_N - 1)/2$, and $N = k_N^2 - x_N = (y_N - 1)^2/4 - x_N$. Of course, the function $f(x_N, y_N) = (y_N - 1)^2/4 - x_N$ decoding N from x_N and y_N can be implemented by a register machine and simulated by a P system as described in Theorem 3. In the following example we specify more formally the precomputing block mentioned above.

Example 1. Encoding the input number N. Let the input N be given as a multiplicity of symbol c_i, and we want to obtain values x_N and y_N described above in auxiliary registers j and l, respectively, but represented already in the way we need their contents x_N and y_N implemented with the corresponding number of symbols a_j and b_j as well as a_l and b_l. We also use an additional starting object s_i and in sum the following rules:

$$s_i \to c_i a_j \tilde{s}_i | P_i', \quad \tilde{s}_i \to s' | P_j, \quad \tilde{s}_i \to \hat{s}_i | Z_j, \quad \hat{s}_i \to a_j b_j s', \quad b_j \to a_j a_j b_j | \mathsf{Sq}'(\hat{s}_i),$$
$$s_i \to c_i t_i | Z_i',$$
$$t_i \to c_i a_l \tilde{t}_i | P_i', \quad \tilde{t}_i \to t_i' | P_l, \quad \tilde{t}_i \to \hat{t}_i | Z_l, \quad \hat{t}_i \to a_l b_k t', \quad b_k \to a_l a_l b_l | \mathsf{Sq}'(\hat{t}_i),$$
$$t_i \to q_0^{(i)} | Z_i', \text{ where}$$
$$Z_i' = \{ w \in O^\circ \mid |w|_{c_i} = k^2, \ k \geq 1 \} = \mathsf{Sq}'(c_i), \quad P_i' = O^\circ \setminus Z_i'.$$

Essentially, the rules above are exactly like increment instructions from Theorem 3, tracking how many times the multiplicity of the input object c_i has to be incremented to reach a positive perfect square and the next perfect square.

In the next phase of the encoding procedure, the P system should simulate a register machine which starts in state $q_0^{(i)}$ and computes the function $f(x_N, y_N) = (y_N - 1)^2/4 - x_N$, given x_N in register j and y_N in register l, producing the result (i.e., the value N of the input register i to be represented) in register i, represented by symbols a_i and b_i and thus in a suitable way to be the input for the P system constructed in Theorem 3.

Theorem 4. $Ps_a DOP_1 \left(ncoo, ctxt^1 (CS) \right) = Ps_a DOP_1 \left(ncoo, ctxt(\mathsf{Sq}') \right) = PsRE.$

Proof. Clearly, any input vector can be processed accordingly in the way described in Example 1, and then a simulation of the register machine on these inputs as outlined in Theorem 3 completes the explanation of the stated result. $\square$

6   Bridging P Systems and Indian Parallel Grammars

Most of the upper bound results for deterministic controlled P systems heavily rely on determinism. A closer look at the proofs reveals that it is not determinism itself which is important, but rather the requirement that in any derivation, if some object evolves, then also all identical objects evolve by means of the same rule. Hence, we would like to consider relaxing determinism to this property.

A similar property has been considered in [13] already in 1980, for the case of L systems, calling them $0LIP$ systems: like in Indian parallel grammars, all identical symbols simultaneously evolve by the same rule, but like in Lindenmayer systems, all symbols evolve in parallel. In the area of P systems, such a requirement may be viewed as a special case of the *label agreement* feature (label selection, target selection, and target agreement have extensively been studied, for example, see [4,6]).

For non-cooperative P systems, we define the *rule agreement* derivation mode (denoted by *ra*) as follows: the evolution is maximally parallel and non-deterministic with the single restriction that in one derivation step, the same rule must be used for all identical objects.

Obviously, deterministic controlled P systems are a subclass of controlled P systems with rule agreement. With enough consideration, it should not be difficult to see that such coordinated non-determinism does not increase the power of controlled P systems, e.g., in case of Theorem 2, which also should stay valid in this case, so $Ps_aOP_1^{ra}\left(ncoo, ctxt^1(REG)\right) = sepREG$. Similarly, the accepting power with generalized context conditions also should not be increased, remaining $NFIN \cup coNFIN$. However, we now have enough non-determinism to be able to consider the generative case, too.

Lemma 1. $PsOP_1^{ra}(ncoo) \supseteq PsREG$.

Proof. No context conditions are needed to generate a set from $PsREG$. Moreover, the rule agreement feature is not essential for this inclusion, as the construction below does not rely on parallelism. Indeed, for an arbitrary reduced regular grammar $G = (N, T, P, S)$, consider the P system

$$\Pi = (O = N \cup T, w_1 = S, R_1),$$
$$R_1 = \{A \to aB \mid A \to aB \in P\} \cup \{A \to \lambda \mid A \to \lambda \in P\},$$

which generates $Ps\left(L\left(G\right)\right)$.   □

Using the rules $A \to (a, out)$ instead of the rules $A \to a$ we could even generate the regular languages themselves in the usual way by concatenating the symbols sent out to the environment into strings. However, the case of generating languages is known to be complicated even in the weakest case, see [1]. We do not go into these details here, and instead concentrate on generating vectors for the rest of this section; we also do not use any other communication with the environment, noticing that this does not influence the computational power of non-cooperative systems.

The rule agreement feature is known to increase the generative power of non-cooperative P systems: while it is folklore that $PsOP(ncoo) = PsREG$, with the rule agreement feature the famous non-regular set of powers of two can be generated already with two rules:

$$\Pi = (O = \{a, b\}, w_1 = a, R_1 = \{a \to aa, \ a \to b\}).$$

It is worth noting that already with R_1 being a finite subset of

$$\{a \to a^k \mid k \geq 0\} \cup \{a \to b\}$$

the entire class of languages generated by $DTU0L$ systems is covered. Inspecting more carefully the way P systems with rule agreement work, we realize a strong connection with the $[E]0LIP$ systems introduced in [13], but we cannot claim equality since with rule agreement alone we are not able to synchronize for different symbols when we stop evolving them and take the result.

7 Conclusions

It is known that generalized context conditions are equivalent to predicates on boundings, and that using them in deterministic maximally parallel non-cooperative P systems still leaves their accepting power as low as $NFIN \cup coNFIN$. We have shown that regular context conditions over two symbols yield computational completeness of deterministic maximally parallel non-cooperative P systems. We have characterized the power of P systems with regular context conditions over one symbol by some restricted subclass of regular multiset languages. On the other hand, we have shown computational completeness using a simple stronger one-symbol context condition, namely

$$\mathsf{Sq}'(a) = \{w \in O^\circ \mid |w|_a = k^2,\ k \geq 1\}.$$

Finally, we have considered a relaxation of the determinism requirement to the so-called *rule agreement*. The obtained P systems often have the same accepting power as the deterministic ones, while their generative power is of separate interest.

Some interesting questions remain open for future research:

- What kind of additional context conditions is necessary and sufficient for generating some set of vectors that cannot be generated without context conditions?
- What kind of additional context conditions is necessary and sufficient for obtaining computational completeness of non-cooperative P systems with rule agreement?

References

1. Alhazov, A., Ciubotaru, C., Ivanov, S., Rogozhin, Y.: The family of languages generated by non-cooperative membrane systems. In: Gheorghe, M., Hinze, T., Păun, Gh., Rozenberg, G., Salomaa, A. (eds.) CMC 2010. LNCS, vol. 6501, pp. 65–80. Springer, Heidelberg (2010)
2. Alhazov, A., Freund, R.: Asynchronous and maximally parallel deterministic controlled non-cooperative P systems characterize *NFIN* and *coNFIN*. In: Csuhaj-Varjú, E., Gheorghe, M., Rozenberg, G., Salomaa, A., Vaszil, G. (eds.) CMC 2012. LNCS, vol. 7762, pp. 101–111. Springer, Heidelberg (2013)
3. Alhazov, A., Freund, R.: Deterministic non-cooperative P systems with strong context conditions. In: 13th Brainstorming Week on Membrane Computing (2015, to appear)
4. Alhazov, A., Freund, R.: P Systems with toxic objects. In: [11], pp. 99–125
5. Alhazov, A., Freund, R.: Priorities, promoters and inhibitors in deterministic non-cooperative P systems. In: [11], pp. 86–98
6. Alhazov, A., Freund, R.: Small P systems defining non-semilinear sets. In: Adamatzky, A. (ed.) Automata, Universality, Computation. ECC, vol. 12, pp. 183–217. Springer, Heidelberg (2015)
7. Alhazov, A., Freund, R., Verlan, S.: Promoters and inhibitors in purely catalytic P systems. In: [11], pp. 126–138

8. Alhazov, A., Sburlan, D.: Ultimately confluent rewriting systems. Parallel multiset–rewriting with permitting or forbidding contexts. In: Mauri, G., Păun, Gh., Jesús Pérez-Jímenez, M., Rozenberg, G., Salomaa, A. (eds.) WMC 2004. LNCS, vol. 3365, pp. 178–189. Springer, Heidelberg (2005)
9. Dassow, J., Păun, Gh.: Regulated Rewriting in Formal Language Theory. Monographs in Theoretical Computer Science. An EATCS Series, vol. 18. Springer, Heidelberg (1989)
10. Gheorghe, M., Păun, Gh., Pérez-Jiménez, M.J., Rozenberg, G.: Research frontiers of membrane computing: open problems and research topics. Int. J. Found. Comput. Sci. **24**(5), 547–624 (2013)
11. Gheorghe, M., Rozenberg, G., Salomaa, A., Sosík, P., Zandron, C. (eds.): CMC 2014. LNCS, vol. 8961. Springer, Heidelberg (2014)
12. Ionescu, M., Sburlan, D.: On P systems with promoters/inhibitors. J. Univers. Comput. Sci. **10**(5), 581–599 (2004)
13. Klejn, H.C.M., Rozenberg, G.: A study in parallel rewriting systems. Inf. Control **44**, 134–163 (1980)
14. Păun, Gh.: Computing with membranes. J. Comput. Syst. Sci. **61**(1), 108–143 (2000). and Turku Center for Computer Science-TUCS Report 208, November 1998, www.tucs.fi
15. Păun, Gh.: Membrane Computing. An Introduction. Springer, Heidelberg (2002)
16. Păun, Gh., Rozenberg, G., Salomaa, A. (eds.): The Oxford Handbook of Membrane Computing. Oxford University Press, New York (2010)
17. Rozenberg, G., Salomaa, A. (eds.): Handbook of Formal Languages, vol. 3. Springer, Heidelberg (1997)
18. Sburlan, D.: Further results on P systems with promoters/inhibitors. Int. J. Found. Comput. Sci. **17**(1), 205–221 (2006)
19. The P Systems Website: ppage.psystems.eu

Automated Verification of Stochastic Spiking Neural P Systems

Bogdan Aman$^{(\boxtimes)}$ and Gabriel Ciobanu

Institute of Computer Science, Romanian Academy, Iaşi, Romania
bogdan.aman@gmail.com, gabriel@info.uaic.ro

Abstract. In this paper we consider stochastic spiking neural P systems, a class of distributed parallel neural-like computing models. We translate a restricted variant of the stochastic spiking neural P systems using uniform distribution into a network of timed automata, proving that such a translation preserves faithfully their behaviours. This relationship allows the verification of several kinds of properties (both qualitative and quantitative) using the statistical model checking extension of the complex software tool UPPAAL.

1 Introduction

Membrane computing [13] is a known branch of natural computing that aims to abstract computing ideas and formal models from the structure and functioning of living cells, as well as from the organization of cells in tissues, organs (brain included) or other higher order structures such as colonies of cells (e.g., of bacteria) [1]. A structure is represented by a set of regions, each delimited by a surrounding membrane, and arranged in a tree or a graph form. Multisets of objects are distributed inside these regions, and they can be modified or moved between adjacent/connected compartments. Objects represent the formal counterpart of the molecular species (spikes, ions, proteins, etc.) floating inside cellular compartments, and are described by means of strings over a given alphabet. Evolution rules represent the formal counterpart of chemical reactions, and are given in the form of rewriting rules that operate on objects. The models considered, called membrane systems (P systems), are parallel, distributed computing models, processing multisets of symbols in cell-like compartmental architectures. These models have been applied to the description of biological systems [10,11].

Spiking neural (SN) P systems represent a class of distributed parallel computing models inspired from the way neurons communicate with each other by means of electrical impulses (see Fig. 1), where there is a synapse between each pair of connected neurons. Roughly, a spiking neural P system consists of a set of neurons placed in the nodes of a directed graph, where neurons send signals (spikes, denoted by the symbol a) along synapses (arcs of the graph). Stochastic spiking neural P systems are obtained from spiking neural P systems by associating to each spiking rule a firing time that indicates how long an enabled rule

© Springer International Publishing Switzerland 2015
G. Rozenberg et al. (Eds.): CMC 2015, LNCS 9504, pp. 77–91, 2015.
DOI: 10.1007/978-3-319-28475-0_6

waits before it is executed. Such firing times are random variables (abstractions for the concept of chance) whose probability distribution functions have domain contained in $\mathbb{R}^+$.

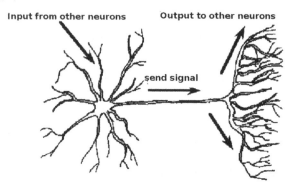

Fig. 1. Communication between neurons

The presence of unreliable components in spiking neural P system can be considered in many different aspects (e.g., in the form of a stochastic delays of the spiking rules [8], or the stochastic loss of spikes [15]). The presence of unreliable components pose an important constrains on the possible modelling and verification of spiking neural P system. In this paper we provide a formally correct algorithm for translating systems described in stochastic spiking neural P systems of [8] into a class of timed safety automata. This connection allows the verification of several kinds of properties, both qualitative and quantitative, using the statistical model checking extension of the UPPAAL software tool.

2 Stochastic Spiking Neural P Systems

Some notations and basic definitions are shortly presented.

The set of non-negative integers is denoted by $\mathbb{N}$. Given a finite alphabet $V = \{a_1, \ldots, a_n\}$, the free monoid generated by V under the operation of concatenation is denoted by V^*. The elements of V^* are called strings, and the empty string is denoted by λ. The set of all non-empty strings over V is denoted by V^+. When $V = \{a\}$ is a singleton, then we write simply a^* and a^+ instead of $\{a\}^*$ and $\{a\}^+$, respectively.

A regular expression E over an alphabet V is defined as follows:

$$E = \lambda \mid a \mid (E)(E) \mid (E) \cup (E) \mid (E)^+, \text{where } a \in V.$$

$E^* = (E)^+ \cup \{\lambda\}$. We associate a language $L(E)$ to each expression E:

$$L(E) = \begin{cases} \{\lambda\} & \text{if } E = \lambda; \\ \{a\} & \text{if } E = a; \\ L(E_1)L(E_2) & \text{if } E = (E_1)(E_2); \\ L(E_1) \cup L(E_2) & \text{if } E = (E_1) \cup (E_2); \\ L((E_1)^+) & \text{if } E = (E_1)^+. \end{cases}$$

Some parentheses can be omitted when writing a regular expression. More details can be found in [14].

We use a restricted version of the stochastic spiking neural P system presented in [8], considering only uniform distribution up to a given bound.

Definition 1. *A stochastic spiking neural P system of degree $m \geq 1$ is defined by $\Pi = (O, \sigma_1, \ldots, \sigma_m, syn, out)$, where:*

- *$O = \{a\}$ is the singleton alphabet (a is called spike);*
- *$\sigma_1, \ldots, \sigma_m$ are neurons, of the form*

$$\sigma_i = (n_i, R_i), 1 \leq i \leq m, where:$$

   (a) $n_i \geq 0$ is the initial number of spikes contained in σ_i;
   (b) R_i is a finite set of rules of the following two forms:
      (1) $E/a^c \to a; F(d)$, where E is a regular expression over a, and $c \geq 1$, and F is a probability distribution function with domain $[0, d]$;
      (2) $a^s \to \lambda; F(d)$, for $s \geq 1$, with the restriction that for each rule $E/a^c \to a; F'$ of type (1) from R_i, we have $a^s \notin L(E)$, and F is a probability distribution function with domain $[0, d]$;
- *$syn \subseteq \{1, 2, \ldots, m\} \times \{1, 2, \ldots, m\} \times \mathbb{N}$ with $i \neq j$ for each $(i, j, r) \in syn$, $1 \leq i, j \leq m$ (synapses between neurons);*
- *$out \in \{1, 2, \ldots, m\}$ indicates the output neuron.*

The rules of type (1) are called *spiking rules*, and are applied as follows: if the neuron σ_i contains k spikes, and $a^k \in L(E)$, $k \geq c$, then the rule $E/a^c \to a; F'$ can be applied. This means removing c spikes from neuron σ_i, and producing 1 spike. The rules of type (2) are called *forgetting rules* and are applied as follows: if the neuron σ_i contains exactly s spikes, then the rule $a^s \to \lambda; F''$ from R_i can be used, meaning that s spikes are removed from neuron σ_i.

From the moment in which a rule is enabled up to the moment when the rule fires, a random amount of time elapses, whose probability distribution is specified by a function F associated to the rule (different rules may have associated different distributions). Once the rule fires, the update of the number of spikes in the neuron, the emission of spikes and the update of spikes in the receiving neurons are all simultaneous and instantaneous events. Multiple rules may be simultaneously enabled in the same neuron. Whenever multiple enabled rules in a neuron have the same random firing time, the order of firing is randomly chosen, with a uniform probability distribution across the set of possible firing orders.

The initial configuration of the system is $C_0 = \{n_1, \ldots, n_m\}$, where $n_1, \ldots, n_m$ are the numbers of spikes present in each neuron. During the computation, a configuration $C = \{n'_1, \ldots, n'_m\}$ is described by the number of spikes n'_i present in each neuron σ_i, for $1 \leq i \leq m$. Using the rules described above, we can define transitions among the configurations of a system. Notice that, because of the way the firing of the rules has been defined, in general there is no upper bound on how many rules fire for each transition. For two configurations

C_1, C_2 of Π we denote by $C_1 \overset{r_j}{\to} C_2$ the effect of applying a rule r_j of a neuron. Also $C_1 \Rightarrow C_2$ denotes the fact that there is a direct transition from C_1 to C_2 in Π in which at most one rule was applied in each neuron, followed by moving to the next time step. The reflexive and transitive closure of the relation $\Rightarrow$ is denoted by $\Rightarrow^*$. Any sequence of transitions starting in the initial configuration C_0 is called a computation. A computation halts if it reaches a configuration C_i where no rule can be used.

Example 1. In what follows we present a graphical form of stochastic spiking neural P systems. Here we just introduce the example without emphasizing on its behaviour (we will consider latter this aspect). In Fig. 2, each neuron is represented by an oval marked with a label and having inside both its current number of spikes and its rules. The synapses linking the neurons are represented by directed arrows, while a short directed arrow pointing to (from) the environment identifies the output (input) neuron. In the following example we consider only an output neuron (and so the input synapse is not drawn).

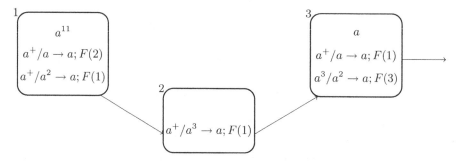

Fig. 2. A simple example of a stochastic SN P system

The system consists of three neurons labelled by 1, 2, 3 in which neuron 3 is the output one. In an initial configuration C_0, neurons 1 and 3 are ready to fire. The spike of neuron 3 leaves it empty, and unable to spike again before receiving a new spike. Neuron 2 cannot fire until it succeeds to collect exactly 3 spikes. The computation continues until consuming all spikes from all neurons.

3   Networks of Timed Automata

Timed automata [2] extended with integer variables, structured data types, user defined functions, broadcast, urgent channels and channel synchronization have been used by several software tools for simulation and verification of various systems with time.

Syntax. We assume a finite set of real-valued variables $\mathcal{C}$ ranged over by x, y standing for clocks, a set of clock resets ranged over by r, r_i, and a finite alphabet Σ ranged over by a, b standing for actions. A clock constraint g is a conjunctive formula of constraints of the form $x \sim m$ or $x - y \sim m$, for $x, y \in \mathcal{C}$, $\sim \in \{\leq, <, =, >, \geq\}$, and $m \in \mathbb{N}$. The set of clock constraints is denoted by $\mathcal{B}(\mathcal{C})$.

Definition 2. *A* **timed safety automaton** *$\mathcal{A}$ is a tuple $\langle N, n_0, E, I \rangle$, where*

- *N is a finite set of nodes;*
- *n_0 is the initial node;*
- *$E \subseteq N \times \mathcal{B}(\mathcal{C}) \times \Sigma \times 2^\mathcal{C} \times N$ is the set of edges;*
- *$I : N \to \mathcal{B}(\mathcal{C})$ assigns invariants to nodes.*

$n \xrightarrow{g,a,r} n'$ is a shorthand notation for $\langle n, g, a, r, n' \rangle \in E$. Node invariants are restricted to constraints of the form $x \leq m$ or $x < m$, where $m \in \mathbb{N}$.

A simple example of a timed safety automaton is depicted in Fig. 3.

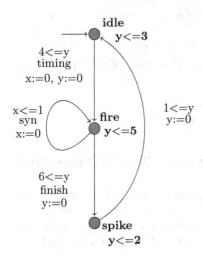

Fig. 3. Timed safety automata

A timed safety automata is a graph having a finite set of nodes and a finite set of labelled transitions, using real time clocks. The clocks are initialized with zero when the system starts, and then increased synchronously with the same rate. The behaviour of the automaton is restricted by using clock constraints, i.e. guards on transitions, and *node invariants* (e.g., see Fig. 3). An automaton is allowed to stay in a node as long as the timing conditions of that node are satisfied. A transition can be taken when the transition guards are satisfied. When a transition is taken, clocks may be reset to zero.

Networks of Timed Automata. A network of timed automata is the parallel composition $\mathcal{A}_1 \mid \ldots \mid \mathcal{A}_n$ of a set of timed automata $\mathcal{A}_1, \ldots, \mathcal{A}_n$ combined into a single system using the CCS-like parallel composition operator and with all internal actions hidden. Synchronous communication inside the network is by handshake synchronization of input and output actions. In this case, the action alphabet Σ consists of a? symbols (for input actions), a! symbols (for output actions), and τ symbols (for internal actions). A detailed example is found in [12].

A network can perform both delay and action transitions. An action transition is enabled if the clocks and variables assignment satisfies all guards on the corresponding edges. In synchronization transitions, the resets on the edge with an output label are performed before the resets on the edge with an input label. To model urgent synchronization transitions that have priority with respect to the delay transitions, a notion of urgent channels is used. On urgent channels it is not possible to delay an execution whenever such an execution is possible. One-to-many synchronizations are possible using broadcast channels: an edge with synchronization label a! emits a broadcast and any enabled edge with synchronization label a? synchronizes with the emitting automata.

Let $u, v, \ldots$ denote clock assignments mapping $\mathcal{C}$ to $\mathbb{R}_+$ of non-negative real numbers. $g \models u$ means that the clock values u satisfy the guard g. For $d \in \mathbb{R}_+$, the clock assignment mapping all $x \in \mathcal{C}$ to $u(x) + d$ is denoted by $u + d$. Also, for $r \subseteq \mathcal{C}$, the clock assignment mapping all clocks of r to 0 and agreeing with u for the other clocks in $\mathcal{C} \backslash r$ is denoted by $[r \mapsto 0]u$. Let n_i stand for the ith element of a node vector n, and $n[n_i'/n_i]$ for the vector n with n_i being substituted with n_i'.

A network state is a pair $\langle n, u \rangle$, where n denotes a vector of current nodes of the network (one for each automaton), and u is a clock assignment storing the current values of all network clocks and integer variables.

Definition 3. *The operational semantics of a timed automaton is a transition system where states are pairs $\langle n, u \rangle$ and transitions are defined by the rules:*

- $\langle n, u \rangle \xrightarrow{d} \langle n, u + d \rangle$ *if $u \in I(n)$ and $(u + d) \in I(n)$, where $I(n) = \bigwedge I(n_i)$;*
- $\langle n, u \rangle \xrightarrow{\tau} \langle n[n_i'/n_i], u' \rangle$ *if $n_i \xrightarrow{g,\tau,r} n_i'$, $g \models u$, $u' = [r \mapsto 0]u$ and $u' \in I(n[n_i'/n_i])$;*
- $\langle n, u \rangle \xrightarrow{\tau} \langle n[n_i'/n_i][n_j'/n_j], u' \rangle$ *if there exist $i \neq j$ such that*

  1. $n_i \xrightarrow{g_i, a?, r_i} n_i'$, $n_j \xrightarrow{g_j, a!, r_j} n_j'$, $g_i \wedge g_j \models u$,
  2. $u' = [r_i \mapsto 0]([r_j \mapsto 0]u)$ *and $u' \in I(n[n_i'/n_i][n_j'/n_j])$.*

4   Relating Stochastic SN P Systems to Timed Automata

In this section we present an algorithmic translation of stochastic spiking neural P systems into timed safety automata, and prove that such a timed safety automata has a bisimilar behaviour with the initial stochastic spiking neural P system. This allows the use of existing tools such as UPPAAL for the verification of complex systems of neurons.

Building a Timed Safety Automaton for each Neuron: Given a neuron $\sigma_i = (n_i, R_i)$ of a stochastic spiking neural P system Π, we associate to it several timed safety automata.

- For each rule $r_{ij} : E/a^c \to a; F(d) \in R_i$ we associate an automaton $\mathcal{A}_{ij} = \langle N_i, n_{ij}, E_{ij}, I_{ij} \rangle$, where the components are as follows:
  - $N_i = \{n\_ij, n\_ij\_fired\}$
    The node n_ij denotes that in neuron i exists a rule r_{ij}, while the node n_ij_fired illustrates that the neuron i fired the rule r_{ij}.
  - $I(n\_ij) = \{x <= d\}$, $I(n\_ij\_fired) = \{x <= 0\}$
    The nodes n_ij and n_ij_fired should be exited before a maximum of d and 0, respectively, units of time have elapsed.
  - $E_{ij} = \{n_{ij}, E, r[i][j]?, \{n_i = n_i - c, x = 0\}, n_{ij\_fired}\}$
    The transition $\{n_{ij}, E, r[i][j]?, \{n_i = n_i - c, x = 0\}, n_{ijc}\}$ illustrates the fact that when a rule r_{ij} is executed in neuron i (denoted by the synchronization on urgent channel $r[i][j]?$ and the fulfilment of expression E), then c spikes are removed from n_{ij} and the local clock x is reset to 0 in order to model the delay according to the distribution $F(d)$. Using urgent

channels illustrates the fact that from all rules of a neuron one will be
selected nondeterministically.

To simulate the continuation of the rule we have three cases:

(1) $E_{ij} = E_{ij} \cup \{n_{ij\_fired}, , syn[i][1]?, , n_{ij}\}$

The transition $\{n_{ij\_fired}, , syn[i][1]?, , n_{ij}\}$ illustrates the fact that the
spike created by rule r_{ij} is sent on all outgoing synapses (illustrated by
the broadcast channel $syn[i][1]$). Graphically the obtain automaton
can be represented as in Fig. 4.

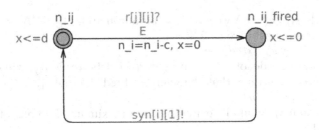

Fig. 4. An automaton associated to a rule $r_{ij} : E/a^c \rightarrow a; F(d)$

(2) $E_{ij} = E_{ij} \cup \{n_{ij\_fired}, , , , n_{ij}\}$

This case is similar with the previous case, except that there is no
outgoing synapse (illustrated by the missing of the broadcast channel
$syn[i][1]$) as illustrated in Fig. 5.

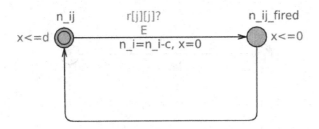

Fig. 5. An automaton associated to a rule $r_{ij} : E/a^c \rightarrow a; F(d)$

(3) $E_{ij} = E_{ij} \cup \{n_{ij\_fired}, , output = output + 1, , n_{ij}\}$

This case is similar with the case (1), except that there is no outgoing
synapse (illustrated by the missing of the broadcast channel $syn[i][1]$)
but the current neuron is the output neuron (illustrated by the update
$output = output + 1$). Graphically this case can be represented as in
Fig. 6.

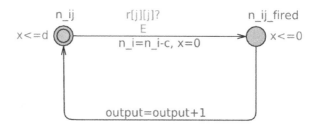

Fig. 6. A transition associated to a rule $r_{ij} : E/a^c \rightarrow a^p; d$

- for each rule $r_{ij} : a^s \rightarrow \lambda$ we associate an automaton $\mathcal{A}_{ij} = \langle N_i, n_{ij}, E_{ij}, I_{ij} \rangle$, where the components are as follows:
  - $N_i = \{n\_ij, n\_ij\_fired\}$
    The node n_ij denotes that in neuron i exists a rule r_{ij}, while the node n_ij_fired illustrates that the neuron i fired the rule r_{ij}.
  - $I(n\_ij) = \{x <= d\}$
    The node n_ij should be exited before a maximum of d units of time have elapsed.
  - $E_{ij} = \{n_{ij}, n_i == s, r[i][j]?, \{n_i = n_i - s, x = 0\}, n_{ij\_fired}\}$
    $\cup \{n_{ij\_fired},,, n_{ij}\}$
    The transition $\{n_{ij}, n_i == s, r[i][j]?, \{n_i = n_i - s, x = 0\}, n_{ij\_fired}\}$ describes that s spikes are removed from n_i, if n_i contains exactly s spikes, and the local clock x is reset to 0 whenever a forgetting rule r_{ij} is executed in neuron i (denoted by the synchronization on urgent channel $r[i][j]?$). The transition $\{n_{ij\_fired},,, n_{ij}\}$ illustrates that in the next step the neuron will be able to fire again. Graphically the automaton is represented in Fig. 7.

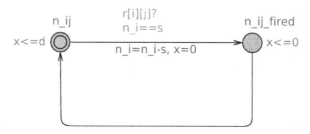

Fig. 7. A transition associated to a rule $r_j : a^s \rightarrow \lambda$

- For each neuron n_i we associate an automaton $\mathcal{A}_i = \langle N_i, n_i, E_i, I_i \rangle$, where $N_i = \{n_i\}$, $E_i = \emptyset$, $I_i = \emptyset$. The components N_i, E_i and I_i are updated depending on the structure of σ_i and the incoming/outgoing synapses:
  - for each incoming synapse (z, i) we have:
    * $E_i = E_i \cup \{n_i,, syn[z][pzi]!, n_i = n_i + pzi, n_i\}$;
      If on synapse (z, i) are received pzi spikes on the broadcast channel syn, then the number of spikes from neuron n_i is incremented with pzi. Graphically this transition can be represented as in Fig. 8.

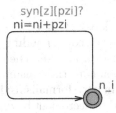

Fig. 8. A transition associated to an incoming synapse (z, i, w_{zi})

- for each rule $r_{ij} \in R_i$ we have:
  * $E_i = E_i \cup \{n_i, , r[i][j]!, , n_i\}$;
    This transition signifies the fact that a rule r_{ij} of neuron n_i will be executed if it synchronizes on the urgent channel $r[i][j]$. Graphically this transition can be represented as in Fig. 9.

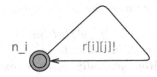

Fig. 9. An automaton associated to a rule r_{ij}

Building a timed automaton for each neuron leads to the next result about the equivalence between a stochastic spiking neural P systems Π with the initial configuration C_0 and its corresponding timed safety automaton $\mathcal{A}_\Pi$ in the initial state $\langle n_{C_0}, u_{C_0} \rangle$ (i.e., $(\mathcal{A}_\Pi, \langle n_{C_0}, u_{C_0} \rangle)$). Their transition systems differ not only in transitions, but also in states. Thus, we adapt the notion of bisimilarity.

Definition 4. *A symmetric relation $\sim$ over stochastic spiking neural P systems and the corresponding timed safety automata, is a bisimulation if whenever $(C, (\mathcal{A}_\Pi, \langle n_C, u_C \rangle)) \in \sim$:*

- *if $C \xrightarrow{r_j}_c C'$, then $\langle n_C, u_C \rangle \xrightarrow{\tau} \langle n_{C'}, u_{C'} \rangle$ and $(C', (\mathcal{A}_\Pi, \langle n_{C'}, u_{C'} \rangle)) \in \sim$ for some C'.*
- *if $C \xrightarrow{r_j}_p C'$, then $\langle n_C, u_C \rangle \xrightarrow{\tau} \langle n_{C'}, u_{C'} \rangle$ and $(C', (\mathcal{A}_\Pi, \langle n_{C'}, u_{C'} \rangle)) \in \sim$ for some C'.*
- *if $C \xrightarrow{d} C'$, then $\langle n_C, u_C \rangle \xrightarrow{d} \langle n_{C'}, u_{C'} \rangle$ and $(C', (\mathcal{A}_\Pi, \langle n_{C'}, u_{C'} \rangle)) \in \sim$ for some C', where $u_{C'} = u_C + d$.*

Having defined bisimulation, we can state our main theorem as follows.

Theorem 1. *Given a stochastic spiking neural P system Π with initial configuration C_0, there exists a timed safety automaton $\mathcal{A}_\Pi$ with a bisimilar behaviour. Formally, $C_0 \sim (\mathcal{A}_\Pi, \langle n_{C_0}, u_{C_0} \rangle)$.*

Proof (Sketch). The construction of the timed safety automaton simulating a given stochastic spiking neural P system is presented above.

A bisimilar behaviour is given by:

- when execution starts, the global clock of the stochastic spiking neural P system and the local clocks of the corresponding timed automata are set to 0;
- the application of a rule in a neuron is matched by two τ edges obtained by translation (a τ edge corresponds to the consumption/production of spikes);
- the passage of time is similar in both formalisms: in stochastic spiking neural P system the global clock is used to decrement by d all timers in the configuration when no rule is applicable, while in the timed automata all local clocks are decremented synchronously with the same value d when no edge can be taken.

Thus, the size of a timed safety automata $\mathcal{A}_\Pi$ is polynomial with respect to the size of a stochastic spiking neural P system Π, and the state spaces have the same number of states.

Reachability Analysis. One of the most useful question to ask about a timed automaton is the reachability of a given set of final states. Such final states may be used to characterize safety properties of a system.

Definition 5. *We write* $\langle n, u \rangle \to \langle n', u' \rangle$ *whenever* $\langle n, u \rangle \xrightarrow{\sigma} \langle n', u' \rangle$ *for* $\sigma \in \Sigma \cup \mathbb{R}_+$. *For an automaton with initial state* $\langle n_0, u_0 \rangle$, $\langle n, u \rangle$ *is reachable if and only if* $\langle n_0, u_0 \rangle \to^* \langle n, u \rangle$. *More generally, given a constraint* $\phi \in \mathcal{B}(\mathcal{C})$ *if* $\langle n, u \rangle$ *is reachable for some* u *satisfying* ϕ *then a state* $\langle n, \phi \rangle$ *is reachable.*

Invariant properties can be specified using clock constraints in combination with local properties on nodes. The reachability problem is decidable [7].

The reachability problem can be also defined for stochastic SN P systems.

Definition 6. *We write* $C \to C'$ *if* $C \xrightarrow{r_j}_c C'$ *or* $C \xrightarrow{r_j}_p C'$ *or* $C \xrightarrow{d} C'$. *Starting from a configuration* C_0, *a configuration* C_1 *is reachable if and only if* $C_0 \to^* C_1$.

The following result is a consequence of Theorem 1.

Corollary 1. *For a stochastic spiking neural P system, the reachability problem is decidable.*

Bisimulation. Two timed automata are defined to be timed bisimilar in [7] if and only if they perform the same action transitions and reach bisimilar states.

Definition 7. *A symmetric relation* $\mathcal{R}$ *over the timed automata and the alphabet* $\Sigma \cup \mathbb{R}_+$, *is a bisimulation if:*

- *for all* $(s_1, s_2) \in \mathcal{R}$, *if* $s_1 \xrightarrow{\sigma} s_1'$ *for* $\sigma \in \Sigma \cup \mathbb{R}_+$ *and* s_1', *then* $s_2 \xrightarrow{\sigma} s_2'$ *and* $(s_1', s_2') \in \mathcal{R}$ *for some* s_2'.

Proposition 1. [9] *Timed bisimulation is decidable.*

In a similar way we define the bisimulation over configurations of stochastic spiking neural P systems.

Definition 8. *A symmetric relation* $\mathcal{R}$ *over configurations of stochastic spiking neural P systems, is a bisimulation if:*

– for all $(C_1, C_2) \in \mathcal{R}$, if $C_1 \xrightarrow{r_j}_c C_1'$ for some C_1', then $C_2 \xrightarrow{r_j}_c C_2'$ and $(C_1', C_2') \in \mathcal{R}$ for some C_2'.

– for all $(C_1, C_2) \in \mathcal{R}$, if $C_1 \xrightarrow{r_j}_p C_1'$ for some C_1', then $C_2 \xrightarrow{r_j}_p C_2'$ and $(C_1', C_2') \in \mathcal{R}$ for some C_2'.

– for all $(C_1, C_2) \in \mathcal{R}$, if $C_1 \xrightarrow{t} C_1'$ for $t \in \mathbb{N}$ and some C_1', then $C_2 \xrightarrow{t} C_2'$ and $(C_1', C_2') \in \mathcal{R}$ for some C_2'.

The following result is a consequence of Theorem 1.

Corollary 2. *For two configurations of stochastic spiking neural P systems, timed bisimulation is decidable.*

5   Verification of Stochastic Spiking Neural P Systems

In this section we present the automated verification of the stochastic spiking neural P system by using the software tool UPPAAL (http://www.uppaal.org/). Such a verification is possible due to the translation of stochastic spiking neural P systems into timed safety automata presented in the previous section.

We start from the stochastic spiking neural P system described in Example 1, and translate it into the timed safety automata described in Fig. 10.

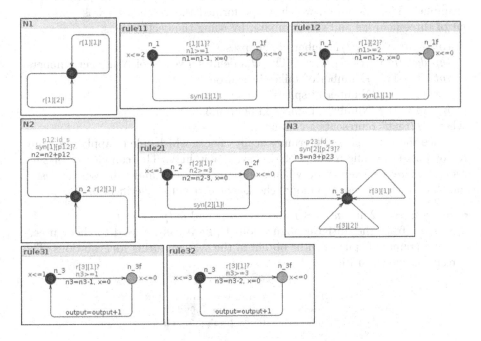

Fig. 10. A simple example modelled in UPPAAL

UPPAAL allows the automated verification of several properties involving several thousands of possible states, very difficult to be validated by any experimental effort. In this way we show how it is possible to prove/verify certain complex properties of complex biological systems modelled by stochastic spiking neural P systems. This can be done without the high expenses required by the experimental work in laboratories leading sometimes to wrong conclusions.

The model checking approach uses various techniques to automatically and efficiently check a given system against specified formulas. The formulas can be of two types path formulae (quantify over paths or traces of the model) and state formulae (individual states). Path formulae can be classified into reachability ($E \langle \rangle \phi$), safety ($A [ ] \phi$ and $E [ ] \phi$) and liveness ($A \langle \rangle \phi$ and $\phi \rightsquigarrow \psi$), where ϕ and ψ are boolean expressions over predicates on nodes and integer variables.

Reachability properties are used to check whether there exist a path starting at an initial state, such that ϕ is eventually satisfied along that path. Safety properties are used to verify that something bad will never happen, while liveness properties check whether the system always progresses.

We present various properties that could be analyzed and verified for the running example. We have used an Intel PC with 8 GB memory, 2.50 GHz × 4 CPU and 64-bit Ubuntu 14.04 LTS to run the experiments. The results are presented for each analyzed property.

Example 2. Using reachability and safety properties, and some given initial values we performed some verifications in UPPAAL for the system presented in Example 1. The system on which we performed the verification was composed out of three neurons and six automata, by using the declarations:

$const\ int\ N = 2$; //Number of synapses
$typedef\ int[0, N - 1]\ id\_s$; //The id_s defines a vector of N integer numbers.
$int\ n1 = 11$; //Number of spikes in neuron 1
$int\ n2 = 0$; //Number of spikes in neuron 2
$int\ n3 = 1$; //Number of spikes in neuron 3
where "//text" represents a comment.

Since the neurons nondeterministically choose which rule to apply, the number of possible configurations of this system is high. The complexity of such systems increases even more when additional neurons and synapses are used, and that is why we use the model checker of UPPAAL for verification.

- $E <> n1 == 2$ and $n2 == 1$ and $n3 == 1$ and $output == 2$
  Starting from the initial configuration, UPPAAL can be used to check if certain amounts of spikes can be obtain in the system during its evolutions. The result is shown in Fig. 11.

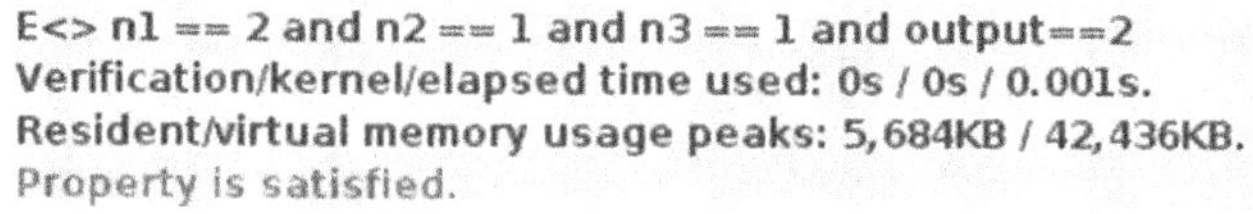

> E<> n1 == 2 and n2 == 1 and n3 == 1 and output==2
> Verification/kernel/elapsed time used: 0s / 0s / 0.001s.
> Resident/virtual memory usage peaks: 5,684KB / 42,436KB.
> Property is satisfied.

Fig. 11. Verification of reachability of a given configuration

If our constructed systems is correct, we should not be able to reach configurations in which the amount of certain spikes does not respect the evolution of the model. Considering such an impossible to reach configuration: $n1 == 2$

and $n2 == 0$ and $n3 == 1$ and $output == 4$ we obtain, as expected, a negative response as shown in Fig. 12.

```
E<> n1 == 2 and n2 == 0 and n3 == 1 and output==4
Verification/kernel/elapsed time used: 0.01s / 0s / 0.014s.
Resident/virtual memory usage peaks: 5,684KB / 42,436KB.
Property is not satisfied.
```

Fig. 12. Verification of reachability for a given configuration

- $A <> output == i$, for $i \in \{1, 2, 3, 4, 5\}$
  Starting from the initial configuration, UPPAAL can be used to check if certain amounts of spikes can be obtain as the output of the system. In this case we check which can be the output of the system and, depending on the applied rules, the output can be different. The results are shown in Fig. 13.

```
E<> output==1
Verification/kernel/elapsed time used: 0s / 0.01s / 0.001s.
Resident/virtual memory usage peaks: 5,684KB / 42,436KB.
Property is satisfied.
E<> output==2
Verification/kernel/elapsed time used: 0s / 0s / 0.001s.
Resident/virtual memory usage peaks: 5,684KB / 42,436KB.
Property is satisfied.
E<> output==3
Verification/kernel/elapsed time used: 0.01s / 0s / 0.001s.
Resident/virtual memory usage peaks: 5,684KB / 42,436KB.
Property is satisfied.
E<> output==4
Verification/kernel/elapsed time used: 0s / 0s / 0s.
Resident/virtual memory usage peaks: 5,684KB / 42,436KB.
Property is satisfied.
E<> output==5
Verification/kernel/elapsed time used: 0.01s / 0s / 0.014s.
Resident/virtual memory usage peaks: 5,684KB / 42,436KB.
Property is not satisfied.
```

Fig. 13. Verification that always its output is between 1 and 4

- $A[\ ]$ *not deadlock*
  A deadlock is a state in which no further evolution is possible. The existence of the deadlock means that the systems stops after some steps. For the above system, the result of the deadlock verification is depicted in Fig. 14.

```
A[] not deadlock
Verification/kernel/elapsed time used: 0s / 0s / 0.005s.
Resident/virtual memory usage peaks: 4,500KB / 41,348KB.
Property is not satisfied.
```

Fig. 14. Verification of deadlock

- $Pr[\# <= 100](<> output == 4)$ Estimates the probability of the *output* to be equal to 4 within 100 model time steps. The result of the verification is depicted in Fig. 15.

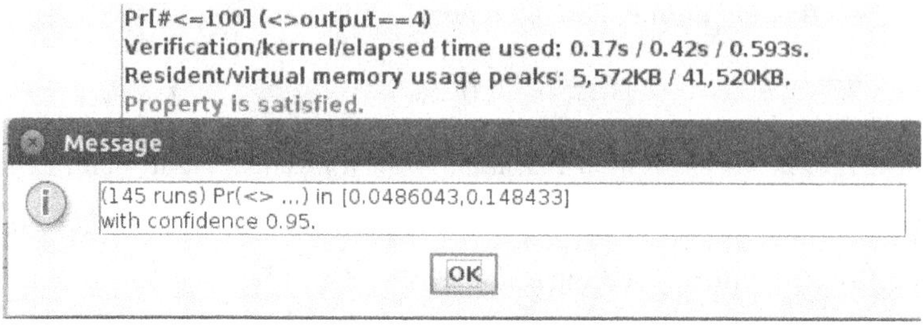

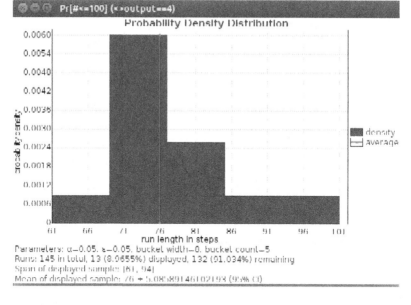

Fig. 15. Probability of reaching *output* $== 4$ in less than 100 steps

The tool can produce a number of histograms over model time, like probability density distribution (Fig. 16) that is useful for comparison of various distributions.

Fig. 16. Probability density distribution

6 Conclusion

Over the years we provided several connections between membrane systems and Petri nets for simulation and automated verification of the properties of membrane systems: enhanced mobile membranes [3,4] are verified in [5], while mobile membrane with delays are verified in [6].

In this paper we provide a formally correct algorithm for translating stochastic spiking neural P systems into a network of timed automata, and so suitable to be verified by using UPPAAL. This allows the verification of several kinds of properties, both qualitative and quantitative, involving also the UPPAAL statistical model checking. This approach could be related to a previous attempt of modelling complex neural systems by using stochastic spiking neural P systems [8]. Due to the large number of possible reachable configurations of such a neural system, it makes sense to use various model checking capabilities of a complex software tool as UPPAAL to verify several properties: reachability of desired configurations, the fact that the system does not stop, whether the amount of resources is constant and which is the probability of some events happening.

Acknowledgements. Many thanks to the reviewers for their useful comments. The work was supported by a grant of the Romanian National Authority for Scientific Research, project number PN-II-ID-PCE-2011-3-0919.

References

1. Alberts, B., Johnson, A., Lewis, J., Morgan, D., Raff, M., Roberts, K., Walter, P.: Molecular Biology of the Cell, 6th edn. Garland Science, New York (2014)
2. Alur, R., Dill, D.L.: A theory of timed automata. Theor. Comput. Sci. **126**, 183–235 (1994)
3. Aman, B., Ciobanu, G.: Describing the immune system using enhanced mobile membranes. Electron. Notes Theor. Comput. Sci. **194**, 5–18 (2008)
4. Aman, B., Ciobanu, G.: Simple, enhanced and mutual mobile membranes. In: Priami, C., Back, R.-J., Petre, I. (eds.) Transactions on Computational Systems Biology XI. LNCS, vol. 5750, pp. 26–44. Springer, Heidelberg (2009)
5. Aman, B., Ciobanu, G.: Properties of enhanced mobile membranes via coloured Petri nets. Inf. Process. Lett. **112**, 243–248 (2012)
6. Aman, B., Ciobanu, G.: Verification of membrane systems with delays via Petri nets with delays. Theor. Comput. Sci. **598**, 87–101 (2015)
7. Bengtsson, J., Yi, W.: Timed automata: semantics, algorithms and tools. Lect. Notes Comput. Sci. **3098**, 87–124 (2004)
8. Cavaliere, M., Mura, I.: Experiments on the reliability of stochastic spiking neural P systems. Nat. Comput. **7**(4), 453–470 (2008)
9. Cerans, K.: Decidability of bisimulation equivalences for parallel timer processes. Lect. Notes Comput. Sci. **663**, 302–315 (1992)
10. Ciobanu, G., Păun, Gh., Pérez-Jiménez, M.J. (eds.) Applications of Membrane Computing. Springer, Heidelberg (2006)
11. Frisco, P., Păun, Gh., Pérez-Jiménez, M.J. (eds.) Applications of Membrane Computing in Systems and Synthetic Biology. Springer, Heidelberg (2014)
12. Henzinger, T.A., Nicollin, X., Sifakis, J., Yovine, S.: Symbolic model checking for real-time systems. Inf. Comput. **111**, 192–224 (1994)
13. Păun, Gh., Rozenberg, G., Salomaa, A. (eds.) Handbook of Membrane Computing. Oxford University Press, New York (2010)
14. Rozenberg, G., Salomaa, A. (eds.): Handbook of Formal Languages, vol. 3. Springer, Heidelberg (1997)
15. Xu, Z., Cavaliere, M., An, P., Vrudhula, S., Cao, Y.: The stochastic loss of spikes in spiking neural P systems: design and implementation of reliable arithmetic circuits. Fundamenta Informaticae **134**(1–2), 183–200 (2014)

Dynamically Changing Environment
for Generalized Communicating P Systems

Ákos Balaskó[1], Erzsébet Csuhaj-Varjú[2]([✉]), and György Vaszil[3]

[1] Computer and Automation Research Institute, Hungarian Academy of Sciences,
Kende u. 13-17, H-1111, Budapest, Hungary
balasko@sztaki.hu
[2] Department of Algorithms and Their Applications, Faculty of Informatics,
Eötvös Loránd University, Pázmány Péter sétány 1/c, 1117, Budapest, Hungary
csuhaj@inf.elte.hu
[3] Department of Computer Science, Faculty of Informatics,
University of Debrecen, Kassai út 26, Debrecen 4028, Hungary
vaszil.gyorgy@inf.unideb.hu

Abstract. We define a modified concept of a generalized communicating P system, where the environment is represented by a finite multiset of objects which is allowed to dynamically change during the computation. We demonstrate the computational completeness of three restricted variants of this model, the cases when the system uses only split rules, or only join rules, or only parallel-shift rules. We discuss the relation between the original and the new model, and propose classifications of the environment.

1 Introduction

Among computational complete subclasses of P systems, there are purely communicating variants, i.e., membrane systems which work without any change of their objects but only with importing/exporting objects from and/or to the environment and communicating objects between their regions. The possible large computational power of these constructs is due to the fact that some types of the objects are supposed to be found in an unbounded number in the environment. That is, whenever the P system needs some extension of its "workspace", i.e., to complete a transition it needs more (a finite number of new) objects than it has inside, then these objects are always available. This property implies the question how the computational power (and the behavior) of membrane systems change if there is only a finite number of objects in the environment that changes from time-to-time. Such model is where the objects in the environment are provided by a multiset rewriting system which starts its work from an initial finite multiset. Thus, at any computational step, the current environment is represented by a finite multiset of objects that is allowed to dynamically change during the computation.

This question is especially interesting in the case when the membrane system represents a complex service system, thus any type of the objects corresponds

G. Rozenberg et al. (Eds.): CMC 2015, LNCS 9504, pp. 92–105, 2015.
DOI: 10.1007/978-3-319-28475-0_7

to a service and/or an application. Generalized communicating P systems are such models. These constructs were introduced in [8], originally with the aim of providing a common generalization of various purely communicating models.

A generalized communicating P system, or a GCPS for short, is a tissue-like P system (a hypergraph) where each node represents a cell and each edge is represented by a rule. Every node contains a multiset of objects which can be communicated, that is, it may move between the cells according to interaction (communication) rules. The form of an interaction rule is $(a, i)(b, j) \rightarrow (a, k)(b, l)$ where a and b are objects and i, j, k, l are labels identifying the input and the output cells. Such a rule means that an object a from cell i and an object b from cell j move synchronously to cell k and cell l, respectively. The system is embedded in an environment, represented by cell 0, which may have certain objects in an infinite number of copies and certain objects only in a finite number of copies. The GCPS and the environment interact by using the communication (interaction) rules given above, with the restriction that at every computation step only a finite number of objects is allowed to enter in any cell from the environment. The rules are applied in a maximally parallel manner, possibly implying changes in the configuration of the GCPS, i.e., changing the multisets representing the contents of the cells. A computation in a GCPS is a sequence of configurations directly following each other, starting from the initial configuration and ending in a halting configuration. The result of the computation is the number of objects found in a distinguished cell, the output cell.

GCPSs have been studied in details, with special emphasis on their generative (computational) power. It has been shown that even restricted variants of these constructs (with respect to the form of rules) are able to generate any recursively enumerable set of numbers. Furthermore, several of them even with relatively small numbers of cells and with simple underlying (hypergraph) architectures are computationally complete [2,3]. It is also shown that the maximal expressive power can also be obtained with GCPSs where the alphabet of objects is a singleton [1].

One other important property of GCPSs is their strong similarity with Petri nets, and thus they can be used for behavioral investigation of complex service and/or application compositions (e.g. scientific workflows) as well. Since workflows are usually executed in heterogeneous and distributed environments, to achieve automated enactment of workflows in these remote and complex systems, adaptation, i.e., reacting to unpredictable changes of the conditions is highly recommended. This observation was one more inspiration for us to introduce a modified version of generalized communicating P systems where the objects of the environment are provided by a multiset rewriting system which starts its work from an initial finite multiset.

In the paper, after introducing the new model, we demonstrate the computational completeness of its three restricted variants, the cases where the system uses only split, or only join, or only parallel-shift rules. We also discuss the relation between the basic and the new model of GCPSs, and propose classifications of the environment.

2   Preliminaries

We first recall some basic notions and notations from membrane computing, formal language theory and computability theory; for further details consult [5–7].

2.1   Some Basic Notions

An alphabet is a finite non-empty set of symbols. For an alphabet V, we denote by V^* the set of all strings over V, including the empty string, λ.

A finite multiset over V is a mapping $M : V \longrightarrow \mathbb{N}$; $M(a)$ is said to be the multiplicity of a in M ($\mathbb{N}$ denotes the set of non-negative integers). A finite multiset M over an alphabet V can be represented by all permutations of a string $x = a_1^{M(a_1)} a_2^{M(a_2)} \ldots a_n^{M(a_n)} \in V^*$, where $a_j \in V$, $M(a_j) \neq 0$, $1 \leq j \leq n$; x represents M in V^*. The size of a finite multiset M, represented by $x \in V^*$ is defined as $\Sigma_{a \in V} |x|_a$. We note that if no confusion arises, we also use the customary set notation for denoting multisets. Thus, we denote the set of finite multisets over V by V^*.

A pair $M = (O, P)$ is said to be a multiset rewriting scheme, if O is an alphabet, the alphabet of objects, and P is a finite set of rules of the form $u \to v$, where u, v are finite multisets over O and u is non-empty. P is called the set of multiset rewriting rules of M.

Let x, y be two finite multisets over O. We say that y can be directly derived from x by M, written as $x \Longrightarrow_M y$ if y can be obtained from x by a maximally parallel application of rules in P; i.e., there is a multiset R of rules of elements of P such that y is obtained from x by parallel application of elements of R and there is no multiset R' properly including R such that y can be obtained from x by applying elements of R' in parallel.

The reflexive and transitive closure of $\Longrightarrow_M$ is denoted by $\Longrightarrow_M^*$.

2.2   Register Machines

Now we recall the notion of a register machine; for further details the reader is referred to [4].

A register machine is a 5-tuple $RM = (Q, \mathcal{R}, q_0, q_f, I)$, where Q is a finite non-empty set, called the set of states, $\mathcal{R} = \{A_1, \ldots, A_k\}$, $k \geq 1$, is a set of registers, $q_0 \in Q$ is the initial state, and $q_f \in Q$ is the final state. I is a set of instructions of the following forms: $(p, A+, r, s)$, where $p, r, s \in Q, p \neq q_f, A \in \mathcal{R}$, called an increment instruction or $(p, A-, r, s)$, where $p, r, s \in Q, p \neq q_f, A \in \mathcal{R}$, called a decrement instruction. Furthermore, for every $p \in Q$, $(p \neq q_f)$, there is exactly one instruction of the form either $(p, A+, r, s)$ or $(p, A-, r, s)$.

A configuration of a register machine RM, defined above, is given by a $(k+1)$-tuple $(q, m_1, \ldots, m_k)$, where $q \in Q$ and $m_1, \ldots, m_k$ are non-negative integers, q corresponds to the current state of RM and $m_1, \ldots, m_k$ are the current numbers stored in the registers (in other words, the current contents of the registers or the value of the registers) $A_1, \ldots A_k$, respectively.

A transition of the register machine consists in updating the number stored in a register and in changing the current state to another one, according to an instruction.

An increment instruction $(p, A+, r, s) \in I$ is performed if RM is in state p, the number stored in register A is increased by 1, and after that RM enters either state r or state s, chosen non-deterministically.

A decrement instruction $(p, A-, r, s) \in I$ is performed if RM is in state p, and if the number stored in register A is positive, then it is decreased by 1 and then RM enters state r, and if the number stored in A is 0, then the contents of A remains unchanged and RM enters state s.

We say that a register machine $RM = (Q, \mathcal{R}, q_0, q_f, I)$, with k registers, given as above, generates a non-negative integer n if starting from the initial configuration $(q_0, 0, 0, \ldots, 0)$ it enters the final configuration $(q_f, n, 0, \ldots, 0)$.

The set of non-negative integers generated by RM is denoted by $N(RM)$.

Register machines generate all recursively enumerable sets of non-negative integers [4]; the family of these sets of numbers is denoted by NRE.

3 Generalized Communicating P Systems with a Dynamically Changing Environment

One important characteristics of generalized communicating P systems is that certain environmental objects are available in an infinite number of copies at each computational step, thus, if needed, the GCPS can freely use an arbitrary number of them. A reasonable restriction is, if the environment is supposed to be a dynamically changing supply of a finite number of objects at every step of the computation. In the following, we define the concept of a generalized communicating P system with a dynamically changing environment, a deGCPS for short, where the number of objects present in the environment is finite at every step of the computation and it is determined by the interaction of a multiset rewriting system representing the environment and the "core" GCPS. In other words, a computation step consists of two substeps: at first, using its rewriting rules the multiset rewriting system generates the contents of the environment, i.e., changes the multiset of objects present in the environment. Then, the communication rules of the "core" GCPS are applied to its cells, possibly involving objects of the environment in these actions, in a maximal parallel manner.

Definition 1. *A generalized communicating P system with dynamic environment (a deGCPS, for short) of degree n, where $n \geq 1$, is an $(n + 5)$-tuple*

$$\Pi = (O, M, w_0, w_1, \ldots, w_n, R, h)$$

where

1. *O is a finite alphabet, called the set of objects of Π;*
2. *$M = (O, P)$ is a multiset rewriting scheme;*
3. *w_0 is a finite multiset representing the initial environment and $w_i \in O^*$, for every i, $1 \leq i \leq n$, is a finite multiset of objects initially associated to cell i;*

4. R is a finite set of interaction rules of the form $(a, i)(b, j) \rightarrow (a, k)(b, l)$, where $a, b \in O$, $0 \leq i, j, k, l \leq n$;
5. $h \in \{1, \ldots, n\}$ is the output cell.

The $n + 3$-tuple $(O, w_1, \ldots, w_n, R, h)$ is said to be the core (core GCPS) of Π.

Now we define the functioning of deGCPSs.

We start with the semantics of the interaction rules.

The cells and the environment interact with each other by means of the rules, having the form $(a, i)(b, j) \rightarrow (a, k)(b, l)$, with $a, b \in O$ and $0 \leq i, j, k, l \leq n$, given above. For simplicity, we consider the environment as the cell labeled by 0. Such an interaction rule may be applied if there is an object a in cell i and an object b in cell j. As the result of the application of the rule, the object a moves from cell i to cell k and b moves from cell j to cell l.

Let $\Pi = (O, M, w_0, w_1, \ldots, w_n, R, h)$, $n \geq 1$, be a deGCPS.

A configuration of Π is an $(n + 1)$-tuple $(z_0, z_1, \ldots, z_n)$ with $z_0, z_i \in O^*$, for all $1 \leq i \leq n$; z_0 is the multiset of objects present in the environment, whereas, for all $1 \leq i \leq n$, z_i is the multiset of objects present inside cell i.

The initial configuration of Π is $(w_0, w_1, \ldots, w_n)$.

Generalized communicating P systems with dynamically changing environment work by performing transitions. A transition in Π consists of two steps: first, the current multiset of the environment is changed by applying the rules of M in maximally parallel, and then rules of R are applied in a maximally parallel manner.

Formally, for a configuration $c = (z_0, z_1, \ldots, z_n)$ of Π, a new configuration $c'' = (z_0'', z_1'', \ldots, z_n'')$ of Π is obtained by a transition as follows: $c' = (z_0', z_1', \ldots, z_n')$ is obtained from $c = (z_0, z_1, \ldots, z_n)$ by the maximally parallel application of rules in M, denoted by $c \Longrightarrow_P c'$, and then c'' is obtained from c' by a maximally parallel application of rules in R, denoted by $c \Longrightarrow_R c'$.

A successful generation in Π is a sequence of transitions starting from the initial configuration and ending in a final configuration, i.e., in a configuration of the form $c_f = (u_0, u_1, \ldots, u_n)$, where no rule of R can be applied to c_f and no rule of P can be applied to u_0. Notice, that in this case neither the environment, nor the system is able to continue its work.

The result of a successful generation in a deGCPS Π is the number of objects present in the output cell, cell h.

We say that Π generates a non-negative integer n if there is a successful generation by Π such that n is the size of the multiset of objects present inside the output cell in the final configuration.

The set of non-negative integers generated by a deGCPS Π in this way is denoted by $N(\Pi)$.

Analogously to generalized communicating P systems, possible restrictions on the interaction rules (modulo symmetry) can be introduced: Let O be an alphabet and let us consider an interaction rule $(a, i)(b, j) \rightarrow (a, k)(b, l)$ with $a, b \in O$, $i, j, k, l \geq 0$. Then, the following cases can be distinguished:

1. $i = j = k \neq l$: the *conditional-uniport-out rule* sends b to cell l provided that a and b are in cell i (rule of type *uout*, for short);
2. $i = k = l \neq j$: the *conditional-uniport-in rule* brings b to cell i provided that a is in that cell (rule of type *uin*, for short);
3. $i = j$, $k = l$, $i \neq k$: the *symport2 rule* corresponds to the minimal symport rule [6], i.e., a and b move together from cell i to k (rule of type *sym2*, for short);
4. $i = l$, $j = k$, $i \neq j$: the *antiport1 rule* corresponds to the minimal antiport rule [6], i.e., a and b are exchanged in cells i and k (rule of type *anti1*, for short);
5. $i = k$ and $i \neq j$, $i \neq l$, $j \neq l$: the *presence-move rule* moves the object b from cell j to l, provided that there is an object a in cell i and i, j, l are pairwise different cells (rule of type *presence*, for short);
6. $i = j$, $i \neq k$, $i \neq l$, $k \neq l$: the *split rule* sends a and b from cell i to cells k and l, respectively (rule of type *split*, for short);
7. $k = l$, $i \neq j$, $k \neq i$, $k \neq j$: the *join rule* brings a and b together to cell i (rule of type *join*, for short);
8. $i = l$, $i \neq j$, $i \neq k$ and $j \neq k$: the *chain rule* moves a from cell i to cell k while b is moved from cell j to cell i, i.e., to the cell where a was previously (rule of type *chain*, for short);
9. i, j, k, l are pairwise different numbers: the *parallel-shift rule* moves a and b from two different cells to another two different cells (rule of type *shift*, for short).

$NOdetP_k(x)$ denotes the set of numbers generated by generalized communicating P systems with dynamically changing environment of degree k and with rules of type x where $k \geq 1$ and $x \in \{uout, uin, sym2, anti1, presence, split, join, chain, shift\}$.
$NOdetP_*(x)$ is the notation for $\bigcup_{k=1}^{\infty} NOdetP_k(x)$.

4   Power of deGCPS Systems

In the following we show that any recursively enumerable set of numbers can be obtained with a deGCPS system with four cells, using rules only of type *split* or *join*.

Theorem 1. $NOdetP_4(split) = NRE$.

Proof. Let $RM = (Q, \mathcal{R}, q_0, q_f, I)$ be an arbitrary register machine, where Q is the set of states, $\mathcal{R} = \{A_1, \ldots, A_k\}$, $k \geq 1$, is a set of registers, $q_0 \in Q$ is the initial state, $q_f \in Q$ is the final state, and I is a set of instructions. To prove the statement, we construct a dePCGS Π with only split rules and four cells such that $N(RM) = N(\Pi)$ holds.

Let us assume, without the loss of generality, that there are no two decrement instructions $(i, A-, j, k)$ and $(l, A-, m, n)$ in I such that $j = n$, that is, there is no instruction label which appears in two different decrement instructions in such a way that in one instruction it is the label which follows the decrement of a non-empty register (j in the first instruction above), and in another one it is the label which follows the successful zero check of the register (n in the second instruction above). To see why this assumption can be made, consider the following: if two such instructions $(p, A-, r, s)$ and $(q, A-, s, t)$ exist, then we relabel the second one to $(q, A-, s', t)$, and for all $(s, A\pm, k, l) \in P$, we also add $(s', A\pm, k, l)$ to P.

To help the easier reading, we first show how instructions of RM can be simulated, the components of Π then easily can be inferred from the constructions.

Now we show how to construct rules simulating an increment instruction (p, A_i+, r, s): at the beginning of the simulation of any instruction, cell 1 contains objects X and Y, cell 2 contains as many occurrences of c_i as the number stored in register A_i, and cells 3 and 4 are empty. The environment contains symbol Q_p.

The rules in R are as follows:

1. $(p, 0)(c_i, 0) \rightarrow (p, 2)(c_i, 3)$,
2. $(X, 1)(Y, 1) \rightarrow (X, 2)(Y, 3)$,
3. $(Y, 3)(c_i, 3) \rightarrow (Y, 1)(c_i, 2)$,
4. $(X, 2)(p, 2) \rightarrow (X, 1)(p, 0)$,

and corresponding rules in M are:

$$(a): Q_p \rightarrow pc_iQ'_p, \ (b): Q'_p \rightarrow Q''_p, \ (c): pQ''_p \rightarrow Q_r, \ (d): pQ''_p \rightarrow Q_s.$$

Π works as follows: First the environment rewrites Q_p to $pc_iQ'_p$. Then symbol X moves to cell 2, and Y moves to to cell 3, while by rule 1., p moves to cell 2 and c_i to cell 3. Then M rewrites Q'_p to Q''_p and using rules 3. and 4., objects X and Y return to cell 1, c_i moves to cell 2 (thus, the contents of register A_i is incremented by one) and p returns to the environment. After this, the environment rewrites Q''_p either to Q_r or Q_s, non-deterministically chosen and erases p. Thus, the next instruction can be executed.

Rules simulating a decrement instruction (p, A_i-, r, s) are as follows: at the beginning of the simulation of any instruction, cell 1 contains objects X and Y, cell 2 contains as many occurrences of c_i as the number stored in register A_i, and cell 3 and cell 4 are empty. The rules in R are given as follows:

1. $(p, 0)(\bar{c}_i, 0) \rightarrow (p, 4)(\bar{c}_i, 2)$,
2. $(X, 1)(Y, 1) \rightarrow (X, 3)(Y, 4)$,
3. $(\bar{c}_i, 2)(c_i, 2) \rightarrow (\bar{c}_i, 3)(c_i, 0)$,
4. $(p, 4)(Y, 4) \rightarrow (p, 0)(Y, 1)$,
5. $(p, 4)(Y, 4) \rightarrow (p, 3)(Y, 2)$,
6. $(X, 3)(\bar{c}_i, 3) \rightarrow (X, 1)(\bar{c}_i, 0)$,
7. $(\bar{c}_i, 2)(Y, 2) \rightarrow (\bar{c}_i, 0)(Y, 1)$,
8. $(X, 3)(p, 3) \rightarrow (X, 1)(p, 0)$.

The corresponding rules in M are the following:

$$
\begin{aligned}
&(a): Q_p \rightarrow Q'_p\bar{c}_ip, \ (b): Q'_p \rightarrow \bar{Q}_r, \quad (c): Q'_p \rightarrow \bar{Q}_s, \\
&(d): \bar{Q}_rc_ip \rightarrow \bar{Q}'_r, \ (e): \bar{Q}_r \rightarrow \#, \quad (f): p \rightarrow \#, \\
&(g): c_i \rightarrow \#, \qquad (h): \bar{Q}'_r\bar{c}_i \rightarrow Q_r, \ (i): \bar{Q}_s \rightarrow \bar{Q}'_s, \\
&(j): \bar{Q}'_s\bar{c}_ip \rightarrow Q_s, \ (k): \# \rightarrow \#.
\end{aligned}
$$

Notice that because of our assumption on the register machine RM, for any instruction label l, either $Q_l \to \#$ or $Q_l \to \bar{Q}'_l$, is present in I.

Π simulates the execution of the instruction as follows: At the beginning the environment contains Q_p and there is no other symbol in it. The environment rewrites Q_p to $p\bar{c}_i Q'_p$, and then, by rule 2. of R, symbols X and Y leave cell 1 and move to cell 3 and 4, respectively, and by rule 1. of R, p moves to cell 4 and $\bar{c}_i$ moves to cell 2. The computation now may continue in two directions, depending on whether the simulated register supposed to store zero or not, thus Q'_p will be rewritten to $\bar{Q}_r$ (the register is not empty), or $\bar{Q}_s$ (the register is empty). Suppose that the simulated register A_i is not empty. Then in cell 2 there should exist at least one c_i. This implies that rules 3. and 4. or rules 3. and 5. of can be applied in parallel.

Suppose that rules 3. and 4. are applied in parallel. Then symbol $\bar{c}_i$ moves to cell 3, symbols c_i and p leave to the environment and symbol Y moves to cell 1. Then the environment uses its rule $\bar{Q}_r c_i p \to \bar{Q}'_r$. If rules 3. and 5. are used together, then only c_i leaves to the environment. Then the environment uses its rules $\bar{Q}_r \to \#, c_i \to \#, p \to \#$. Thus, the computation terminates without any success. Notice, that the same happens if the latter rules are used after performing rules 3. and 4., thus the computation continues only if the correct choice of the environmental rules takes place. Having $\bar{Q}'_r$ in the environment, rule 6. of R is performed, thus $\bar{c}_i$ leaves to the environment. The procedure ends with the application of the environmental rule $\bar{Q}'_r \bar{c}_i \to Q_r$. Now suppose that after introducing $\bar{Q}_r$ in the environment, rule 3. cannot be applied, i.e., A_i is empty. Then either rule 4. or rule 5. can be applied, but none of them introduces c_i in the environment. Then the environment introduces $\#$, thus the computation ends unsuccessfully.

Suppose now that the simulated register, A_i, should be empty. Then $\bar{Q}_s$ should be introduced in the environment. Then either rule 4. or rule 5. of R can be applied. If rule 4. is applied then p leaves to the environment. Let the environment have rules $\bar{Q}_s \to \bar{Q}'_s$ and $p \to \#$. Then the only correct choice is rule 5. Then, in the next step Π uses its rules 7. and 8., thus $\bar{c}_i$ and p leave to the environment and x and Y return to cell 1. Then the environment uses rule $\bar{Q}'_s \bar{c}_i p \to Q_s$ and the computation successfully ends. Suppose that after introducing $\bar{Q}_s$ in the environment, register A_i is not empty. But then either rules 3. and 4. or rules 3. and 5. can be applied in parallel. If the environment has rule $c_i \to \#$, then the environment, which is of the form $\bar{Q}_s c_i$ or $\bar{Q}_s p c_i$ will be rewritten to $Q'_p \#$ or $Q'_p \# \#$, thus, the computation will not successfully terminate.

Notice that the rules in P and in R, together, simulate the instructions of RM, and they are given in such way that the simulation of every instruction does not interfere with the simulation of any other instruction.

The initial state of the environment in Q_{q_0}. If Q_{q_f}, i.e., the counterpart of state q_f in Π appears in the environment, after then no rule of P will be applicable. In the next step, R performs a rule, i.e., moves objects X and Y, but after then no rule of R is applicable. Thus, the end of the generation process in RM

corresponds to the end of the computation in Π. Notice, that the number generated by RM is the number stored in register 1, and this is exactly the number of objects c_1 that can be found in cell 2, which is the output cell. By the explanations and arguments given above, it can be seen that Π correctly simulates RM and $N(\Pi) = N(RM)$ holds. Since any recursively enumerable set of numbers can be generated by a register machine, and reversely, any register machine generates a recursively enumerable set of numbers, we proved the statement.

In the following we deal with deGCPSs with join operation.

Theorem 2. $NOdetP_4(join) = NRE$.

Proof. As in the previous case, we will simulate the work of register machines. Suppose that $RM = (Q, \mathcal{R}, q_0, q_f, I)$ is an arbitrary register machine. To prove the statement, we construct a dePCGS Π such that $N(RM) = N(\Pi)$ holds and Π has four cells. As in the previous case, we assume that there are no two decrement instructions $(p, A-, r, s)$ and $(q, A-, s, t)$ in I, that is, there is no instruction label which appears in two different decrement instructions in such a way that in one instruction it is the state which follows the decrement of a non-empty register (s in the second instruction above), and in another one it is the label which follows the successful zero check of the register (s in the first instruction above).

As in the previous proof, to help the easier reading, we first show how instructions of RM can be simulated. Then, the reader may easily infer the components of Π from the constructions.

The rules simulating an increment instruction (p, A_i+, r, s) are given as follows: at the beginning of the simulation of any instruction, cell 1 contains objects X and Y, cell 2 contains as many occurrences of c_i as the number stored in register A_i, and cells 3,4 are empty. The environment contains symbol Q_p.

The rules in R are as follows:

1. $(p, 0)(X, 1) \rightarrow (p, 3)(X, 3)$,
2. $(c_i, 0)(Y, 1) \rightarrow (c_i, 2)(Y, 2)$,
3. $(p, 3)(Y, 2) \rightarrow (p, 0)(Y, 0)$,
4. $(X, 3)(Y, 0) \rightarrow (X, 1)(Y, 1)$.

The corresponding rules in M are as follows:

$$(a): Q_p \rightarrow Q'_p c_i p, \ (b): Q'_p \rightarrow Q''_p, \ (c): Q''_p p Y \rightarrow Q'''_p Y,$$
$$(d): Q'''_p \rightarrow Q_r, \quad (e): Q'''_p \rightarrow Q_s.$$

Π simulates the instruction as follows: At the beginning the only symbol in the environment is Q_p. At the first step, M rewrites Q_p to $Q'_p p c_i$. At the next step, by rules 1. and 2. of R, symbols p and X move to cell 3 and symbols c_i and Y move to cell 2. After then the environment rewrites Q'_p to Q''_p. Then rule 3. of R is applied, moving p and Y to the environment. The environment then uses its rule $Q''_p p Y \rightarrow Q'''_p Y$. After then rule 4. of R is applied and Y and X move to cell 1. At the next step the environment changes Q_p''' either to Q_r or to Q_s. Thus the instruction is simulated.

Next we show how a decrement instruction (p, A_i-, r, s) is simulated: at the beginning of the simulation of the instruction, cell 1 contains objects X and Y, cell 2 contains as many occurrences of objects c_i as the number stored in register A_i, and cells 3 and 4 are empty. The environment contains symbol Q_p.

The corresponding rules in R are as follows:

1. $(p, 0)(X, 1) \to (p, 3)(X, 3)$,
2. $(c_i, 2)(Y, 1) \to (c_i, 4)(Y, 4)$,
3. $(p, 3)(c_i, 4) \to (p, 0)(c_i, 0)$,
4. $(X, 3)(Y, 4) \to (X, 1)(Y, 1)$,
5. $(p, 3)(Y, 1) \to (p, 0)(Y, 0)$,
6. $(X, 3)(Y, 0) \to (X, 1)(Y, 1)$.

The corresponding rules in M are the following:

$$(a) : Q_p \to Q_p'p, \ (b) : Q_p' \to Q_p'', \ (c) : Q_p''pc_i \to Q_r,$$
$$(d) : Q_p \to \bar{Q}_pp, \ (e) : \bar{Q}_p \to \bar{Q}_p', \ (f) : \bar{Q}_p'pY \to \bar{Q}_p''Y,$$
$$(g) : \bar{Q}_p'' \to Q_s, \ (h) : Q_p'' \to \#, \ (i) : \bar{Q}_p' \to \#,$$
$$(j) : \# \to \#.$$

Suppose that A_i is not empty. At the first step, the environment rewrites Q_p to $Q_p'p$. Then, by parallel application of rules 1. and 2. of R, objects p and X move to cell 3 and objects Y and c_i move to cell 4. After then, Q_p' will be rewritten to Q_p''. In the next step, rules 3. and 4. of R are used in parallel, moving p and c_i to the environment, and objects X and Y return to cell 1. Then the environment will use its rule $Q_p''pc_i \to Q_r$, thus the instruction was correctly simulated. Suppose now that no c_i was present in cell 2, thus, the guess about the simulated register A_i being non-empty was wrong. Then rule 2. was not applicable, and objects p and X moved to cell 3. After the next step by R, the environment will have the form $Q_p''pY$, but only the rule $Q_p'' \to \#$ is applicable to this word, thus the computation does not terminate successfully.

Let us consider the case when the simulated register A_i is empty. At the first step, the environment rewrites Q_p to $\bar{Q}_pp$. Then by rule 1. of R, objects p and X move to cell 3. In the next step, the environment rewrites $\bar{Q}_p$ to $\bar{Q}_p'$. By rule 5. of R, objects p and Y move to the environment. Then the actual environment, $\bar{Q}_p'pY$ will be rewritten to $\bar{Q}_p''Y$, and then by rule 6. of R objects X and Y move to cell 1. In the next step, the environment will be rewritten to Q_s. Suppose now that although A_i was guessed to be empty, cell 2 contained at least one c_i. Then, after the second step by R, the environment will be of the form $\bar{Q}_p'pc_i$. Since only the rule $\bar{Q}_p' \to \#$ is applicable, the computation does not terminate successfully. Thus the instruction was correctly simulated.

The rules in P and R, together, simulate the instructions of RM, and the simulation of every instruction does not interfere with the simulation of any other instruction.

The initial state of the environment in Q_{q_0}. If Q_{q_f}, i.e., the counterpart of state q_f in Π appears in the environment, after then no rule of P and R. Thus, the end of the generation process in RM corresponds to the end of the computation in Π. Notice, that the number generated by RM is the number stored in register 1, and this is exactly the number of objects c_1 that can be found in cell 2, which is the output cell. By the arguments given above, it can be seen that Π correctly simulates RM and $N(\Pi) = N(RM)$ holds. Since any recursively enumerable set of numbers can be generated by a register machine, and reversely, any register machine generates a recursively enumerable set of numbers, we proved the statement.

Next we investigate deGCPSs with only parallel-shift rules.

Theorem 3. $NOdetP_5(shift) = NRE$.

Proof. The proof follows the same way as we did in the previous cases, based on simulation the work of register machines, hence we hold the same assumptions supposing that $RM = (Q, \mathcal{R}, q_0, q_f, I)$ is an arbitrary register machine; a dePCGS Π such that $N(RM) = N(\Pi)$ holds, but now Π has five cells. Moreover we assume that there are no two decrement instructions $(p, A-, r, s)$ and $(q, A-, s, t)$ in I.

As in the previous proofs, to help the easier reading, we first show how instructions of RM can be simulated. Then, the reader may easily infer the components of Π from the constructions.

The rules simulating an increment instruction (p, A_i+, r, s) are given as follows: at the beginning of the simulation of any instruction, cell 1 contains objects X, cell 2 contains as many occurrences of c_i as the number stored in register A_i, and cells 3,4 and 5 are empty. The environment contains symbol Q_p.

The rules in R are as follows:

1. $(p, 0)(X, 1) \rightarrow (p, 1)(X, 2)$,
2. $(c_i, 0)(X, 2) \rightarrow (c_i, 2)(X, 3)$,
3. $(X, 3)(p, 1) \rightarrow (X, 1)(p, 0)$.

The corresponding rules in M are as follows:

$$(a): Q_p \rightarrow Q'_p p, \ (b): Q'_p \rightarrow Q''_p c_i, \ (c): Q''_p \rightarrow Q'''_p,$$
$$(d): Q'''_p p \rightarrow Q_r, \ (e): Q'''_p p \rightarrow Q_s.$$

The instruction is simulated by Π as follows: At first, M rewrites Q_p to $Q'_p p$ introducing a new p instruction symbol. Then rule 1 is applied, which moves symbol p from the environment to cell 1 while symbol X is moved from cell 1 to cell 2. Next, as symbol p is disappeared from the environment, rewriting rule b can be applied in M, hence symbol Q'_p is rewritten to $Q''_p c_i$. Therefore in the next step rule 2 of R can be applied that moves c_i to cell 2, and symbol X from cell 2 to cell 3. By applying rule c in M, symbol Q''_p will be rewritten to Q'''_p. Next symbol X is moved to cell 1 while p leaves cell 1 and moves to the environment. Finally M rewrites its content nondeterministically to Q_s or Q_r. Thus the instruction is simulated.

Next we show how a decrement instruction (p, A_i-, r, s) is simulated: at the beginning of the simulation of the instruction, cell 1 contains object Y_p for all $p \in Q$, cell 3 contains Z_1 and Z_2, cell 2 contains as many occurrences of objects c_i as the number stored in register A_i, and cells 4, 5 are empty. The environment contains symbol Q_p.

The corresponding rules in R are as follows.

1. $(p, 0)(Y_p, 1) \rightarrow (p, 1)(Y_p, 2)$,
2. $(Y_p, 2)(Z_1, 3) \rightarrow (Y_p, 3)(Z_1, 4)$,
3. $(c_i, 2)(Y_p, 3) \rightarrow (c_i, 3)(Y_p, 4)$,
4. $(Z_1, 4)(Z_2, 3) \rightarrow (Z_1, 3)(Z_2, 2)$,
5. $(Z_2, 2)(c_i, 3) \rightarrow (Z_2, 3)(c_i, 0)$,
6. $(Y_p, 4)(p, 1) \rightarrow (Y_p, 1)(p, 0)$,
7. $(Z_2, 2)(Y_p, 3) \rightarrow (Z_2, 3)(Y_p, 5)$,
8. $(Y_p, 5)(p, 1) \rightarrow (Y_p, 1)(p, 0)$.

The corresponding rules in M are the following:

$$(a): Q_p \rightarrow Q'_p p, \ (b): Q'_p \rightarrow Q''_p, \ (c): Q''_p \rightarrow Q'''_p,$$
$$(d): Q'''_p \rightarrow \bar{Q}_p, \ (e): \bar{Q}_p \rightarrow \bar{Q}'_p, \ (f): \bar{Q}_p c_i p \rightarrow Q_r,$$
$$(g): \bar{Q}'_p p \rightarrow Q_s, \ (h): p \rightarrow \#, \ \ \ (i): c_i \rightarrow \#,$$
$$(j): \# \rightarrow \#.$$

At the first step, the environment rewrites Q_p to $Q'_p p$. Then, by application of rule 1 of R, object p moves to cell 1 in parallel with Y_p which moves from cell 1 to cell 2. After this, Q'_p will be rewritten to Q''_p. In the next step, rule 2 is applied moving symbol Y_p and Z_1 from cell 2 and cell 3 to cell 3 and cell 4 respectively. In the next step the environment rewrites it content to symbol Q'''_p.

Let us suppose first that A_i is not empty. It means that at least one occurrence of c_i is in cell 2. Now rule 3 and rule 4 is applied in parallel, moving c_i and Z_1 to cell 3, symbol Y_p to cell 4 and Z_2 to cell 2. Now the environment rewrites Q'''_p to $\bar{Q}_p$. In the last communication step rule 5 and rule 6 are applied returning symbol Y_p and Z_2 to their original cell, and moving c_i and p to the environment. Now c_i and p appeared in the environment, therefore rule f is applied by M that rewrites the content to Q_r.

Now we suppose that A_i is empty. As above, the environment contains Q'''_p, symbol p is in cell 1, Y_p is in cell 3 and symbol Z_1 is in cell 4. Now symbols Z_1 and Z_2 are moved to cell 3 and cell 2 respectively by application of rule 4. The environment rewrites its content to $\bar{Q}_p$, and then - as rule 3 cannot be applied in the previous step - application of rule 7 returns Z_2 to cell 3, while Y_p is moved to cell 5. In the environment rewriting rule e is applied that replaces $\bar{Q}_p$ with $\bar{Q}'_p$. Next, rule 8 moves Y_p to cell 1 while p returns to the environment. This indicates the application of rule g rewriting $\bar{Q}'_p p$ to Q_s.

As in the previous proofs, the rules in P and R, together, simulate the instructions of RM, and the simulation of every instruction does not interfere with the simulation of any other instruction.

The initial state of the environment in Q_{q_0}, the final state is Q_{q_f}, i.e., the counterpart of state q_f. When the final state appears in the environment, no rule of P (and R) is applicable, thus, the end of the computation in RM corresponds to the end of the computation in Π. Also, the number generated by RM (the number stored in register 1) is exactly the number of objects c_1 that can be found in cell 2, which is the output cell. By the arguments given above, it can be seen that Π correctly simulates RM and $N(\Pi) = N(RM)$ holds. Since any recursively enumerable set of numbers can be generated by a register machine, and reversely, any register machine generates a recursively enumerable set of numbers, our statement is proved.

4.1 Discussion

In the generic model, in GCPSs a subset of objects is distinguished, elements of which are allowed to occur in an infinite number of copies in the environment. Thus, the environment serves an infinite supply of certain objects. In some sense, this environment could be considered as a static one, since whenever the GCPS needs such an object from the environment, the object is available. This might not be the case for deGCPSs. Therefore, according to their effect on the computation process, we may distinguish different types of environments: how much extent the computed set of numbers and the computation processes differ from each other in a certain deGCPSs and a GCPS obtained from its core. Some other research direction is to study the robustness of a deGCPS: the system is robust if it computes the same set of numbers for any environment M, sensitive with respect to the environment if there exists at least two different environments M and M' which lead to different sets of computed numbers, and hypersensitive if there exists infinitely many pairwise different environments M_n, $n = 1, 2, \ldots$ such that any two of them results in different sets of computed numbers. We plan study these problems in the future.

The interesting fact that both "infinite" and finite environments turn out to be universal is due to that in the "infinite" case in any computation step the necessary number of objects that should be/can be imported from the environment is a finite number. Thus, by a suitable multiset rewriting system, the necessary environmental objects for the core GCPS can be provided.

In other words, in the previous sections we showed that the core GCPS in cooperation with a rewriting system as environment has the same generative power as the general model that requires the possibility of symbols in infinite occurrences contained by the environment.

Considering that real-life situations e.g. workflow enactment on a dynamic and heterogeneous distributed infrastructure has no control on the change of the environment. In addition it must prevent its execution and adapt itself to the unpredictable environmental changes. Therefore in the following we consider the case when the environment is not created just for supporting correctness of the computation, but it may cause harmful exceptions in the course of the execution of the core GCPS.

References

1. Csuhaj-Varjú, E., Vaszil, G., Verlan, S.: On generalized communicating P systems with one symbol. In: Gheorghe, M., Hinze, T., Păun, G., Rozenberg, G., Salomaa, A. (eds.) CMC 2010. LNCS, vol. 6501, pp. 160–174. Springer, Heidelberg (2010)
2. Csuhaj-Varjú, E., Verlan, S.: On generalized communicating P systems with minimal interaction rules. Theoret. Comput. Sci. **412**, 124–135 (2011)
3. Krishna, S.N., Gheorghe, M., Dragomir, C.: Some classes of generalised communicating P systems and simple kernel P systems. In: Bonizzoni, P., Brattka, V., Löwe, B. (eds.) CiE 2013. LNCS, vol. 7921, pp. 284–293. Springer, Heidelberg (2013)
4. Minsky, M.: Finite and Infinite Machines. Prentice Hall, Englewood Cliffs (1967)
5. Păun, G.: Membrane Computing. An Introduction. Springer, Heidelberg (2002)
6. Păun, G., Rozenberg, G., Salomaa, A. (eds.): The Oxford Handbook of Membrane Computing. Oxford University Press, Oxford (2010)
7. Rozenberg, G., Salomaa, A. (eds.): Handbook of Formal Languages, vol. 1–3. Springer, Heidelberg (1997)
8. Verlan, S., Bernardini, F., Gheorghe, M., Margenstern, M.: Generalized communicating P systems. Theoret. Comput. Sci. **404**(1–2), 170–184 (2008)

Spiking Neural P Systems with Structural Plasticity: Attacking the Subset Sum Problem

Francis George C. Cabarle[1]([⊠]), Nestine Hope S. Hernandez[1],
and Miguel Ángel Martínez-del-Amor[2]

[1] Algorithms and Complexity Lab, Department of Computer Science,
University of the Philippines Diliman, Diliman, 1101 Quezon City, Philippines
fccabarle@up.edu.ph, nshernandez@dcs.upd.edu.ph
[2] Department of Computer Science and AI, University of Sevilla,
Avda. Reina Mercedes s/n, 41012 Sevilla, Spain
mdelamor@us.es

Abstract. Spiking neural P systems with structural plasticity (in short, SNPSP systems) are models of computations inspired by the function and structure of biological neurons. In SNPSP systems, neurons can create or delete synapses using *plasticity rules*. We report two *families of solutions*: a *non-uniform* and a *uniform* one, to the **NP**-complete problem Subset Sum using SNPSP systems. Instead of the usual rule-level non-determinism (choosing which rule to apply) we use synapse-level nondeterminism (choosing which synapses to create or delete). The nondeterminism due to plasticity rules have the following improvements from a previous solution: in our non-uniform solution, plasticity rules allowed for a normal form to be used (i.e. without forgetting rules or rules with delays, system is simple, only synapse-level nondeterminism); in our uniform solution the number of neurons and the computation steps are reduced.

Keywords: Membrane computing · Spiking neural P system · Structural plasticity · **NP**-complete · Subset Sum

1 Introduction

Membrane computing, [18] a branch of *natural computing*, aims to abstract and obtain computing ideas, data structures and operations from the function and structure of living cells. Several introductory and advanced books [8,19] (including a handbook [21]) have been produced for this branch, as well as a recent collection of applications to systems and synthetic biology [9]. As early as 2006, *membrane algorithms* [16] have been introduced for approximation inspired by *P systems* (the model of computations in membrane computing). The P systems webpage [1] includes an updated list of workshops, conferences, and books on or related to membrane computing (including a collection of PhD theses). The Thomson Reuters Institute for Scientific Information (in short, ISI) has identified

© Springer International Publishing Switzerland 2015
G. Rozenberg et al. (Eds.): CMC 2015, LNCS 9504, pp. 106–116, 2015.
DOI: 10.1007/978-3-319-28475-0_8

membrane computing as a "fast emerging research front" as early as October 2003, see e.g. [2].

In this work, the specific P systems we consider are *spiking neural P systems* (in short, SNP systems) first introduced in [12]. In particular, we focus on a variant of SNP systems known as *spiking neural P systems with structural plasticity* (in short, SNPSP systems), recently introduced in [4] and improved and extended in [7]. We do not go into the details of SNP systems here, including their neuroscience inspirations, computing power (i.e. what a model can or cannot compute) and computational complexity (i.e. time and space efficiency in solving problems). We refer the reader instead to good introductions in [12, 20] and the SNP systems chapter in the membrane computing handbook [21]. In SNPSP systems, *neurons* are placed on the vertices of a directed graph, and the edges between neurons are called *synapses*. Aside from *spiking rules* (more details below) which are used to consume and produce spikes, SNPSP systems have *plasticity rules*. Plasticity rules allow a neuron σ_i to create or delete synapses from itself (i.e. outgoing edges of σ_i) but cannot create or delete synapses towards itself (incoming edges of σ_i). The plasticity rules in SNPSP systems are inspired by actual structural plasticity in biological neurons [3].

In this work we use SNPSP systems to provide *families of solutions* to the **NP**-complete problem Subset Sum. The hardness of the Subset Sum problem is applied to practical and important use in order to secure many systems requiring encryption, e.g. in [11]. Of course, when we refer to solutions to a problem, we mean to say that we provide an *algorithm* solving the problem, where the algorithm in this case is the constructed SNPSP system.

This paper is organized as follows: some preliminaries for the rest of this work are given in Sect. 2. Syntax and semantics of SNPSP systems in Sect. 3. The Subset Sum problem as well as some existing solutions using SNP systems are provided in Sect. 4. Complexity classes of SNPSP systems, with respect to the type of solution, are also provided in Sect. 4. A non-uniform family of solutions is given in Sect. 5. A uniform family of solution is provided in Sect. 6. Lastly, Sect. 7 provides some final remarks and future research directions.

2   Preliminaries

Before proceeding to the syntax (i.e. elements that constitute a model) and semantics (i.e. the meaning and use of elements of a model) of SNPSP systems, we briefly recall *regular expressions*. Regular expressions will be used by neurons to check which spiking or plasticity rules to apply. We denote the set of natural (counting) numbers as $\mathbb{N} = \{0, 1, 2, \ldots\}$, where $\mathbb{N}^+ = \mathbb{N} - \{0\}$. Let V be an alphabet, V^* is the set of all *finite* strings over V with respect to *concatenation* and the *identity element* λ (the empty string). The set of all non-empty strings over V is denoted as V^+, so $V^+ = V^* - \{\lambda\}$.

A language $L \subseteq V^*$ is *regular* if there is a regular expression E over V such that $L(E) = L$. A regular expression over an alphabet V is constructed starting from λ and the symbols of V using the operations union, concatenation, and $+$.

Specifically, (*i*) λ and each $a \in V$ are regular expressions, (*ii*) if E_1 and E_2 are regular expressions over V then $(E_1 \cup E_2)$, $E_1 E_2$, and E_1^+ are regular expressions over V, and (*iii*) nothing else is a regular expression over V. With each expression E we associate a *language* $L(E)$ defined in the following way: (i) $L(\lambda) = \{\lambda\}$ and $L(a) = \{a\}$ for all $a \in V$, (ii) $L(E_1 \cup E_2) = L(E_1) \cup L(E_2)$, $L(E_1 E_2) = L(E_1)L(E_2)$, and $L(E_1^+) = L(E_1)^+$, for all regular expressions E_1, E_2 over V. Unnecessary parentheses are omitted when writing regular expressions. If $V = \{a\}$, we simply write a^* and a^+ instead of $\{a\}^*$ and $\{a\}^+$. If $a \in V$, we write $a^0 = \lambda$.

3   Spiking Neural P Systems with Structural Plasticity

In this section we define SNP systems with structural plasticity. Motivations and recent results in SNPSP systems are included in a series of papers in [5–7]. A spiking neural P system with structural plasticity (SNPSP systems) of degree $m \geq 1$ is a construct of the form $\Pi = (O, \sigma_1, \ldots, \sigma_m, syn, out)$, where:

- $O = \{a\}$ is the singleton alphabet (a is called spike);
- $\sigma_1, \ldots, \sigma_m$ are neurons of the form (n_i, R_i), $1 \leq i \leq m$; $n_i \geq 0$ indicates the initial number of spikes in σ_i; R_i is a finite rule set of σ_i with two forms:
  1. Spiking rule: $E/a^c \rightarrow a$, where E is a regular expression over O, $c \geq 1$;
  2. Plasticity rule: $E/a^c \rightarrow \alpha k(i, N)$, where E is a regular expression over O, $c \geq 1$, $\alpha \in \{+, -, \pm, \mp\}$, $k \geq 1$, and $N \subseteq \{1, \ldots, m\} - \{i\}$;
- $syn \subseteq \{1, \ldots, m\} \times \{1, \ldots, m\}$, with $(i, i) \notin syn$ for $1 \leq i \leq m$ (synapses between neurons);
- $in, out \in \{1, \ldots, m\}$ indicate the input and output neuron labels.

Given neuron σ_i (we also say neuron i or simply σ_i) we denote the set of neuron labels with σ_i as their presynaptic (postsynaptic, respectively) neuron as $pres(i)$, i.e. $pres(i) = \{j|(i, j) \in syn\}$ (as $pos(i) = \{j|(j, i) \in syn\}$, respectively). Essentially, $|pres(i)|$ and $|pos(i)|$ is the out- and in-degree of the neuron (i.e. vertex) σ_i, respectively. Spiking rules are applied as follows: If neuron σ_i contains b spikes and $a^b \in L(E)$, with $b \geq c$, then a rule $E/a^c \rightarrow a \in R_i$ can be applied. Applying such a rule means consuming c spikes from σ_i, thus only $b - c$ spikes remain in σ_i. Neuron i sends one spike to every neuron with a label in $pres(i)$ at the same step as rule application. A *writing convention* we adopt is as follows: if a rule $E/a^c \rightarrow a$ has $L(E) = \{a^c\}$, we simply write this as $a^c \rightarrow a$.

Plasticity rules are applied as follows. If at step t we have that σ_i has $b \geq c$ spikes and $a^b \in L(E)$, a rule $E/a^c \rightarrow \alpha k(i, N) \in R_i$ can be applied. The set N is a collection of neurons to which σ_i can create a synapse to, or remove a synapse from, using the applied plasticity rule. The rule consumes c spikes and performs one of the following, depending on α:

- If $\alpha := +$ and $N - pres(i) = \emptyset$, or if $\alpha := -$ and $pres(i) = \emptyset$, then there is nothing more to do, i.e. c spikes are consumed but no synapses are created or removed. The former case corresponds to the case when σ_i has a synapse to all neurons with labels in N, while the latter corresponds to the case when σ_i has no more outgoing synapses to delete.

- for $\alpha := +$, if $|N - pres(i)| \leq k$, deterministically create a synapse to every σ_l, $l \in N_j - pres(i)$. If however $|N - pres(i)| > k$, *nondeterministically* select k neurons in $N - pres(i)$, and create one synapse to each selected neuron.
- for $\alpha := -$, if $|pres(i)| \leq k$, deterministically delete all synapses in $pres(i)$. If however $|pres(i)| > k$, *nondeterministically* select k neurons in $pres(i)$, and delete each synapse to the selected neurons.

If $\alpha := \pm$ ($\alpha := \mp$, respectively), create (delete, respectively) synapses at step t and then delete (create, respectively) synapses at step $t+1$. Only the application priority of synapse creation or deletion is changed, but the semantics of synapse creation and deletion remain the same as when $\alpha \in \{+, -\}$. Neuron i can receive spikes from t until $t + 1$, but σ_i can only apply another rule at time $t + 2$.

An important note is that for σ_i applying a rule with $\alpha \in \{+, \pm, \mp\}$, creating a synapse always involves a sending of one spike when σ_i connects to a neuron. This single spike is sent at the time the synapse creation is applied, i.e. whenever synapse (i, j) is created between σ_i and σ_j during synapse creation, we have σ_i immediately transferring one spike to σ_j.

SNPSP systems are *locally sequential* (at each step, at most one rule is applied per neuron) but *globally parallel* (neurons operate in parallel). Note that the application of rules in neurons are *synchronized*, i.e. a global clock is assumed and if a neuron can apply a rule then it must do so. A *configuration* of an SNPSP system is based on (a) distribution of spikes in neurons, and (b) neuron connections based on syn. For some step t, we can represent: (a) as $\langle s_1, \ldots, s_m \rangle$ where s_i, $1 \leq i \leq m$, is the number of spikes contained in σ_i; for (b) we can derive $pres(i)$ and $pos(i)$ from syn, for a given σ_i. The initial configuration therefore is represented as $\langle n_1, \ldots, n_m \rangle$, with the possibility of a disconnected graph.

Rule application (as defined above) allows for *transitions* from one configuration to another. A *computation* is defined as a *sequence of transitions*, from an initial configuration, and following rule application semantics. A computation halts if the system reaches a halting configuration, i.e. a configuration where no rules can be applied. The *output* neuron applying a rule (we also say *firing*) triggers an output of the system, which will be defined below. The output neuron sends spikes to the *environment*, and $pres(out) = \emptyset$. The *input* neuron receives spikes from the environment and $pos(in) = \emptyset$.

An example of an SNPSP system is $\Pi = (\{a\}, \sigma_l, \sigma_m, \sigma_n, syn, n)$ where $\sigma_l = (1, \{a \to \pm 1(l, \{m, n\})\})$, $\sigma_m = \sigma_n = (0, \{a \to a\})$, $syn = \{(m, n)\}$, and the output neuron is σ_n. However and in what follows, for the sake of brevity we omit formally defining the SNPSP system construct. We instead provide a graphical representation as in Fig. 1. A computation of Π is as follows: the initial

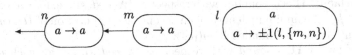

Fig. 1. An SNPSP system Π.

configuration is $\langle 1, 0, 0 \rangle$ representing the corresponding spike distribution in the neuron order $\sigma_l, \sigma_m, \sigma_n$.

Since $a \in L(a)$, the plasticity rule of σ_l can be applied (we denote this as step t). Since $\alpha := \pm$ and $k = 1 < |\{m, n\}|$, σ_l must nondeterministically choose to create either synapse (l, m) or (l, n) at t. At t therefore we have either the synapse set $syn' = syn \cup \{(l, m)\}$ or $syn'' = syn \cup \{(l, n)\}$. Also at t we have σ_l immediately sending a spike to σ_m if (l, m) is created, and the spike distribution is now $\langle 0, 1, 0 \rangle$. If (l, n) is created, the spike distribution is $\langle 0, 0, 1 \rangle$, since σ_n immediately receives a spike from σ_i during synapse creation. At step $t + 1$ the created synapse at t is deleted, since $\alpha := \pm$, so we have $syn = \{(m, n)\}$ again. Notice that if (l, m) was created, the single spike is sent out to the environment (i.e. σ_n spikes) at step $t + 2$. Otherwise the spike is sent to the environment at $t + 1$ (if (l, n) was created).

4 Solving Subset Sum with SNPSP systems

SNP systems have been used to solve many **NP**-complete problems, see e.g. [13–15,17,22]. These solutions are usually categorized as either *non-uniform* or *uniform* solutions. A problem Q is solved in a non-uniform way if for each specified instance I of Q we build an SNPSP system $\Pi_{Q,I}$, whose structure and initial configuration depend on I. Furthermore, $\Pi_{Q,I}$ halts and the output neuron spikes at a specified time interval if and only if I is a positive instance of Q. A uniform solution to Q consists of a family $\{\Pi_Q(n)\}_{n \in \mathbb{N}}$ of SNPSP systems such that, given an instance $I \in Q$ of size n, we introduced a polynomial (in n) number of spikes in specified (set of) input neuron(s) of $\Pi_Q(n)$. Again, $\Pi_Q(n)$ halts and the output neuron spikes at a specified time, if and only if I is a positive instance.

More formally, let $X = (I_X, \Theta_X)$ be a decision problem, and $g : \mathbb{N} \to \mathbb{N}$ a computable function, where I_X is a set of instances and Θ_X is a predicate over I_X. We say X is solvable by a family $\mathbf{\Pi} = \{\Pi(n) | n \in \mathbb{N}\}$ of SNPSP systems, in time bounded by g, in a *nondeterministic* and *uniform way* (denoted as $X \in \mathbf{NSNP}(g)$) if the following hold:

- The family $\mathbf{\Pi}$ is polynomially uniform by Turing machines, i.e. there exists a deterministic Turing machine working in polynomial time which constructs $\Pi(n), n \in \mathbb{N}$.
- There exist polynomial time computable functions, *cod* and s, over I_X, such that
  - For each instance $w \in I_X$, $s(w)$ is a natural number, and $cod(w)$ is a valid input (using some encoding) of the SNPSP system $\Pi(s(w))$.
  - The family $\mathbf{\Pi}$ is g-bounded with respect to (X, cod, s), i.e. for each instance $w \in I_X$, the minimum length of an accepting computation of $\Pi(s(w))$ with input $cod(w)$ is bounded by $g(|w|)$.
  - The family $\mathbf{\Pi}$ is *sound* with respect to (X, cod, s), i.e. for each $w \in I_X$, if there exists an accepting computation of $\Pi(s(w))$ with input $cod(w)$, then $\Theta_X(w) = 1$.

- The family Π is *complete* with respect to (X, cod, s), i.e. for every $w \in I_X$, if $\Theta_X(w) = 1$ then there exists a computation of $\Pi(w)$ with input $cod(w)$ which is an accepting computation.

We say $X = (I_X, \Theta_X)$ is solvable in polynomial time by a family $\Pi = \{\Pi(n) | n \in \mathbb{N}\}$ of SNPSP systems, in a nondeterministic and uniform way (denoted as $X \in \mathbf{NPSNP}$) if there exists a $k \in \mathbb{N}$ such that X is solvable by the family Π in time bounded by a polynomial, in a nondeterministic and uniform way.

The preference of uniform solutions over non-uniform solutions is given by the fact that the former are more strictly related to the structure of the problem, instead of specific instances of the problem. For non-uniform solutions, input neurons are not needed since the problem instance is embedded in the system structure (e.g. number of spikes, neurons, or rules) while in uniform solutions, at least one input neuron is needed to introduce the instance into the system.

Deterministic and nondeterministic solutions (both for non-uniform and uniform solutions) can be found in [13–15, 17, 22]. Note that nondeterministic solutions allow for more "compact" solutions, in terms of the number of neurons in the system. Unless $\mathbf{P} = \mathbf{NP}$, we need exponential space (i.e. neurons) to deterministically solve hard problems in polynomial time.

The $\mathbf{NP}$-complete problem considered here, Subset sum, can be defined as follows:

Problem: Subset Sum [10]

- Instance: S, and a (multi)set $V = \{v_1, v_2, \ldots, v_n\}$, with $S, v_i \in \mathbb{N}$ and $1 \leq i \leq n$;
- Question: Is there a sub(multi)set $B \subseteq V$ such that $\sum_{b \in B} b = S$?

In [15], the Subset sum problem was also solved in a nondeterministic and non-uniform way using SNP systems with *extended rules*: extended rules, as compared to spiking rules, are of the form $E/a^c \rightarrow a^p$ with the meaning that each step a neuron can produce $p \geq 1$ spikes instead of only one spike. Additionally, [15] used some neurons that applied rules sequentially, while some neurons applied their rules in an *exhaustive* manner (i.e. it is possible to apply a rule more than once in one step). A follow-up and improved (uniform) solution was then given in [14]. There are several ways of encoding an instance of Subset Sum as the input to the system. Two common ways (used in this work, and as [15] and [14]) involve either (i) starting with an initial configuration where each σ_i stores v_i number of spikes, $1 \leq i \leq n$ (for the non-uniform solution), or (ii) each σ_{in_i} receives a number of spikes from the environment equal to non-zero multiples of $v_i, 1 \leq i \leq n$ (for the uniform solution).

5   A Non-uniform Solution to Subset Sum

We begin by providing a family Π of nondeterministic and non-uniform SNPSP systems solving Subset Sum in constant time, as given in [7]. Actually, the non-uniform solution provided in this section fixes a "bug" in the non-uniform solution given in [7]. The non-uniform solution provided in [7] indeed solves the Subset Sum problem, but it is possible for the solution to produce false positive results. The size of each $\Pi \in \mathbf{\Pi}$ is dependent on the value of n and each $v_i, 1 \leq i \leq n$. The number of neurons is a function of the magnitude of each v_i.

The construct of each SNPSP system $\Pi_{\text{ss},I}, \Pi_{\text{ss}} \in \mathbf{\Pi}$, that solves instance I of the Subset Sum problem is as follows:

$$\Pi_{\text{ss},I} = \left(\{a\}, \left\{\sigma_i, \sigma_{i_{(Y)}}, \sigma_{i_{(N)}}, \sigma_{i_{(j)}}, \sigma_{out} \,\middle|\, 1 \leq i \leq n, 1 \leq j \leq v_i\right\}, syn, out\right)$$

where $V = \{v_1, v_2, \ldots, v_n\}$ and we need to check for the value S. We refer to Fig. 2 for a graphical representation of Π_{ss}. Compared to the non-uniform solution in [15], each Π_{ss} has the following *normal form* (i.e. a simplifying set of restrictions): (i) *simple*, i.e. each neuron has exactly one rule; (ii) only *synapse-level nondeterminism*, i.e. nondeterministic choice exists only in choosing which synapse to create and not which rule to apply (known as *rule-level nondeterminism*; (iii) no forgetting rule or rule with a delay is used.

The initial configuration is where every σ_i has one spike, and every other neuron has none. In step 1, each neuron σ_i nondeterministically chooses to create either synapse $(i, i_{(Y)})$ or $(i, i_{(N)})$. If $(i, i_{(N)})$ is created, neuron $\sigma_{i_{(N)}}$ consumes a spike but has $pres(i_{(N)}) = \emptyset$, hence no more computations can proceed. If $(i, i_{(Y)})$ is created, then at step 2, $\sigma_{i_{(Y)}}$ then it sends one spike each to $\sigma_{i_{(1)}}$ to $\sigma_{i_{(v_i)}}$, i.e. v_i number of spikes are produced since $|pres(i_{(Y)})| = v_i$.

Once neurons $\sigma_{i_{(1)}}$ to $\sigma_{i_{(v_i)}}$ receive one spike each, they send one spike each to σ_{out} at step 3. If exactly S number of spikes are received by σ_{out} then σ_{out} will send a spike to the environment. Therefore if an affirmative answer to the problem instance exists, a spike would be sent to the environment in four steps since the initial configuration. Otherwise, no spike sent to the environment in four steps indicates a negative answer to the instance. Whether σ_{out} sends a spike or not, the system still halts in four steps. This ends the description of the non-uniform solution.

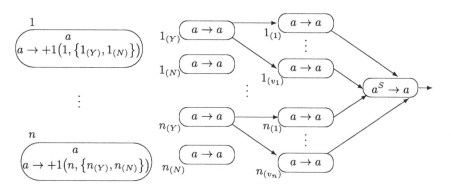

Fig. 2. The non-uniform SNPSP system Π_{ss} solving Subset Sum.

In Π_{ss} the computation time is constant (four steps) but the number of neurons is dependent on the individual values of the input numbers $v_i, 1 \leq i \leq n$. In this case, our non-uniform solution using exactly one (plasticity) rule in some neurons is enough to replace the functions of rules with delays and forgetting rules in the non-uniform solution in [15]. At the price of extending the computation time, we obtain a uniform solution in the following section.

6   A Uniform Solution to Subset Sum

Next, we provide a family Π solving Subset Sum in a nondeterministic and uniform way in constant time. In this case, the system only "knows" the value of n, while S and each $v_i, 1 \leq i \leq n$ must be introduced into the system using $n+1$ input neurons. This uniform family of solutions improves the solution provided in the previous section and the uniform solution in [15].

Each SNPSP system $\Pi_{us}(n), \Pi_{us} \in \Pi$, that solves instance I of size n of the problem is illustrated in Fig. 3. We introduce $2v_i, 1 \leq i \leq n$ spikes into the corresponding input neuron in_i, while we introduce $2S$ spikes into in_{n+1}. Figure 3 shows these spikes already present in the $n+1$ input neurons. These even number of spikes cannot be used by σ_{in_i} until a spike is received from σ_{c_i}. Neurons $\sigma_{c_i}, 1 \leq i \leq n$ are the only neurons with nondeterminism (synapse-level). These neurons nondeterministically allow their corresponding σ_{in_i} neurons to spike (if σ_{c_i} creates synapse (c_i, in_i)) or not (if σ_{c_i} creates synapse (c_i, x)). Note that there is no σ_x so that (c_i, x) is never actually created.

Neurons σ_{c_i} apply their rules at step 1, and at step 3 neurons $e_{i,1}$ spike if they become activated from their corresponding in_i neuron. It also takes 3 steps before σ_{h_3} and σ_{h_4} begin to spike, starting with the spiking of σ_{h_1} at step 1. Neurons σ_{h_3} and σ_{h_4} "feed" a spike to each other starting at step 3. A spike is also sent from σ_{h_4} to σ_{t_1} (the "comparison trigger" neuron). At step 4 the odd number of spikes in σ_{t_1}, sent by the activated $e_{i,1}$ neurons and σ_{h_4}), allows the use of its forgetting rule to remove all of its spikes.

At step 5 only σ_{h_4} sends a spike to σ_{t_1}. At step 6, σ_{t_1} sends one spike each to σ_{h_4} and σ_{t_2}, while σ_{t_1} receives one more spike from σ_{h_4}. At step 7, σ_{h_4} stores two spikes so it can never spike again, while σ_{t_1} sends one more spike to σ_{t_2}. At step 8, σ_{t_2} sends a spike to σ_{acc} and $\sigma_{n_{n+1}}$ which become activated with an odd number of spikes now. Both σ_{acc} and $\sigma_{n_{n+1}}$ empty their spikes (removing two spikes each step) while sending one spike each to σ_{out}.

If the number of spikes accumulated in σ_{acc} equals the $2S$ number of spikes in $\sigma_{n_{n+1}}$, then the system will halt without producing a spike to the environment. Otherwise, σ_{out} will receive one spike from either σ_{acc} or $\sigma_{n_{n+1}}$ and send one spike to the environment. Halting without σ_{out} producing a spike, and halting with σ_{out} producing a spike, corresponds to a positive and negative answer to the problem instance, respectively. This ends the description of the uniform solution.

The number of neurons is constant, with $4n + 9$ neurons. The system halts in at most $2 \sum_{i=1}^{n} v_i + 6$ steps: we have one initial step; at most $max\{v_i | 1 \leq i \leq n\} + 1$ to move the spikes from σ_{in_i} to σ_{t_1}; one step for σ_{t_1} to send its first (out of two) spike; σ_{acc} and $\sigma_{in_{n+1}}$ become activated after two steps, once σ_{t_1} has sent two spikes; at most $\sum_{i=1}^{n} v_i$ steps for comparison between the spikes of σ_{acc} and $\sigma_{in_{n+1}}$; the last step is for σ_{out} to send one spike to the environment. Since $max\{v_i | 1 \leq i \leq n\} \leq \sum_{i=1}^{n} v_i$, we obtain the upper bound for the halting time.

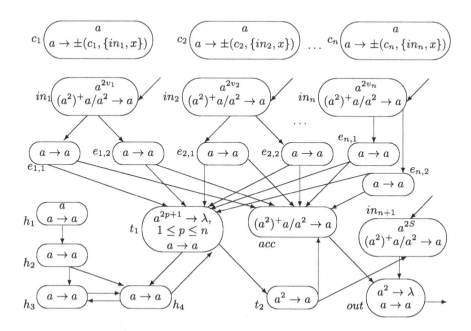

Fig. 3. The uniform SNPSP system Π_{us} solving Subset Sum.

Actually, the forgetting rules in Π_{us} can be removed by using a plasticity rule that functions like a forgetting rule, which is done by the σ_{c_i} neurons (synapse (c_i, x) is never created). The number of neurons and the halting time will still remain the same. In comparison, the non-uniform system in [15] solving Subset Sum (using forgetting rules, rules with delays, and standard rules) computes in four steps, while their uniform solution halts in at most $3 \sum_{i=1}^{n} v_i + 6$ steps using $5n + 13$ neurons (also using delays, forgetting rules, and standard rules). Thus, one benefit of using synapse-level nondeterminism in this case is decreasing the needed neurons by a linear amount. Also in this case, fewer number of neurons helped improve the computation time: spikes have fewer neurons to pass through, so the spike of σ_{out} is sent to the environment sooner rather than later.

7   Final Remarks

In this work, we fixed the non-uniform solution to Subset Sum in [7] using SNPSP systems. We also provided a uniform family of solutions to Subset Sum using SNPSP systems. The use of plasticity rules in this case allowed for a simplifying set of requirements (i.e. normal form) to be applied to our non-uniform solution, compared to the non-uniform solution in [15]. In particular, in our non-uniform solution the plasticity rules could replace forgetting rules and rules with delays. Our uniform solution decreased the number of neurons compared to a uniform solution to **Subset Sum** using SNP systems in [15]. A clear research direction of interest is to show how to solve other hard problems using plasticity rules. Also, how do we make better use of the nondeterminism at the synapse level due to plasticity rules, to perhaps encode problem instances?

Synapse-level nondeterminism in this work provided a reduction in the number of neurons, but perhaps we can also use plasticity rules to further reduce system parameters, e.g. number of neurons, number of rules in neurons, or synapses in the system. As an extension and future work, we also plan to use SNPSP systems to solve other hard problems, in particular, combinatorial problems come to mind: since plasticity rules can (non)deterministically try to create connections (i.e. synapses), one natural use of such rules is to try different combinations of connections in order to solve problems. These work extensions will provide further complexity classes (e.g. semi- or non-uniform) and members of these classes.

Acknowledgements. F.G.C. Cabarle is grateful for the support of the HRIDD HRDP grant I-15-0626-06 of the DOST PCIEERD, Philippines. N. H. S. Hernandez is supported by the UPAA San Francisco & Mely & Rick Ray foundation professorial chair, and the HRIDD HRDP grant I-15-1006-19 of the DOST PCIEERD, Philippines. M.A. Martínez-del-Amor acknowledges the support of the Alain Bensoussan Fellowship programme of ERCIM, and of the project TIN2012-37434 of the "Ministerio de Economía y Competitividad" of Spain, co-financed by FEDER funds.

References

1. P systems web page. http://ppage.psystems.eu/
2. ISI emerging research front, October 2003. http://esi-topics.com/erf/october2003.html
3. Butz, M., Wörgötter, F., van Ooyen, A.: Activity-dependent structural plasticity. Brain Res. Rev. **60**(2), 287–305 (2009)
4. Cabarle, F.G.C., Adorna, H.N., Ibo, N.: Spiking neural P systems with structural plasticity. In: Proceedings of Asian Conference on Membrane Computing (ACMC), Chengdu, China, 4–7 November 2013 (2013)
5. Cabarle, F.G.C., Adorna, H.N., Pérez-Jiménez, M.J.: Asynchronous spiking neural P systems with structural plasticity. In: Calude, C.S., Dinneen, M.J. (eds.) UCNC 2015. LNCS, vol. 9252, pp. 132–143. Springer, Heidelberg (2015)
6. Cabarle, F.G.C., Adorna, H.N., Pérez-Jiménez, M.J.: Sequential spiking neural P systems with structural plasticity based on max/min spike number. Neural Comput. Appl., 1–11 (2015)
7. Cabarle, F.G.C., Adorna, H.N., Pérez-Jiménez, M.J., Song, T.: Spiking neural P systems with structural plasticity. Neural Comput. Appl. **26**(8), 1905–1917 (2015)

8. Ciobanu, G., Păun, G., Pérez-Jiménez, M.J. (eds.): Applications of Membrane Computing. Springer, Heidelberg (2006)
9. Frisco, P., Gheorghe, M., Pérez-Jiménez, M.J. (eds.): Applications of Membrane Computing in Systems and Synthetic Biology. Springer, Heidelberg (2014)
10. Garey, M.R., Johnson, D.S.: Computers and Intractability: A Guide to the Theory of NP-Completeness. W. H. Freeman & Co., New York (1979)
11. Impagliazzo, R., Naor, M.: Efficient cryptographic schemes provably as secure as subset sum. J. Cryptology $9(4)$, 199–216 (1996)
12. Ionescu, M., Păun, G., Yokomori, T.: Spiking neural P systems. Fundamenta Informaticae $71(2$–$3)$, 279–308 (2006)
13. Leporati, A., Gutiérrez-Naranjo, M.A.: Solving subset sum by spiking neural P systems with pre-computed resources. Fundamenta Informaticae 87, 61–77 (2008)
14. Leporati, A., Mauri, G., Zandron, C., Păun, G., Pérez-Jiménez, M.J.: Uniform solutions to sat and subset sum by spiking neural P systems. Nat. Comput. $8(4)$, 681–702 (2009)
15. Leporati, A., Zandron, C., Ferretti, C., Mauri, G.: Solving numerical NP-complete problems with spiking neural P systems. In: Eleftherakis, G., Kefalas, P., Păun, G., Rozenberg, G., Salomaa, A. (eds.) WMC 2007. LNCS, vol. 4860, pp. 336–352. Springer, Heidelberg (2007)
16. Nishida, T.Y.: Membrane algorithms. In: Freund, R., Păun, G., Rozenberg, G., Salomaa, A. (eds.) WMC 2005. LNCS, vol. 3850, pp. 55–66. Springer, Heidelberg (2006)
17. Pan, L., Păun, G., Pérez-Jiménez, M.J.: Spiking neural P systems with neuron division and budding. Sci. China Inf. Sci. $54(8)$, 1596–1607 (2011)
18. Păun, G.: Computing with membranes. J. Comput. Syst. Sci. $61(1)$, 108–143 (2000)
19. Păun, G.: Membrane Computing. An Introduction. Springer, Heidelberg (2002)
20. Păun, G., Pérez-Jiménez, M.J.: Spiking neural P systems recent results, research topics. In: Condon, A., Harel, D., Kok, J.N., Salomaa, A., Winfree, E. (eds.) Algorithmic Bioprocesses, pp. 273–291. Springer, Heidelberg (2009)
21. Păun, G., Rozenberg, G., Salomaa, A. (eds.): The Oxford Handbook of Membrane Computing. Oxford University Press, New York (2010)
22. Wang, J., Hoogeboom, H.J., Pan, L.: Spiking neural P systems with neuron division. In: Gheorghe, M., Hinze, T., Păun, G., Rozenberg, G., Salomaa, A. (eds.) CMC 2010. LNCS, vol. 6501, pp. 361–376. Springer, Heidelberg (2010)

P Systems with Generalized Multisets Over Totally Ordered Abelian Groups

Rudolf Freund[1]($\boxtimes$), Sergiu Ivanov[2], and Sergey Verlan[2]

[1] Faculty of Informatics, TU Wien, Favoritenstraße 9-11, 1040 Vienna, Austria
rudi@emcc.at
[2] LACL, Université Paris Est – Créteil Val de Marne,
61, av. Général de Gaulle, 94010 Créteil, France
{sergiu.ivanov,verlan}@u-pec.fr

Abstract. In this paper we extend the definition of a multiset by allowing elements to have multiplicities from an arbitrary totally ordered Abelian group instead of only using natural numbers. We consider P systems with such generalized multisets and give well-founded notations for the applicability of rules and for different derivation modes. These new definitions raise challenging mathematical questions and we propose several solutions yielding models sometimes having quite unexpected behavior. Another interesting application of our results is the possibility to consider complex objects and to manipulate them directly in a P system instead of their numerical encodings.

1 Introduction

Recent developments in the P systems area consider objects which can have a kind of negative quantities. The notions of anti-spike [9] and antimatter [2] introduce dual objects that "annihilate" if they are present at the same moment in the configuration. Motivated by these results, the paper [14] asks for a "negative" extension of multisets in P systems, i.e. replacing the multiset multiplicity function $f : O \to \mathbb{N}$ by the function $f : O \to \mathbb{Z}$. The question of multisets with negative and more generally with real coefficients is not new, for example, in [4,5] a first-order two-sorted theory for such generalized multisets is developed, and it "contains" the classical ZFC set theory (Zermelo-Fraenkel set theory with the axiom of choice). Another approach is used in [1] where some properties of multisets with integer coefficients are obtained. An overview of other attempts to generalize the concept of multisets can be found in [3].

The challenging part in the definition of a P system working with generalized multisets is to properly define the notion of the applicability of a rule. In order to be able to solve this problem we restrict the model to generalized multisets over Abelian groups with total order and a recursive description. Thus, our multiset multiplicity function will be of the form $f : O \to G$, where G is such a group. The recursive description condition allows us to claim that the power of the obtained model does not go beyond the power of Turing machines. As in ordinary P systems, the definition of the applicability of rules and multisets of rules takes into

© Springer International Publishing Switzerland 2015
G. Rozenberg et al. (Eds.): CMC 2015, LNCS 9504, pp. 117–136, 2015.
DOI: 10.1007/978-3-319-28475-0_9

account the existence of some resources that cannot be over-consumed. However, the richer underlying group structure allows us to define several variants for the applicability of individual rules and multisets of rules which do not always have an equivalent in the traditional model of P systems. We define three possibilities: the *free mode* which does not impose any restriction, the $\exists - mode$ which requests that at least one resource decreases, and the $\forall - mode$ which requests that all resources decrease. The application of multisets of rules can be also defined in several ways. Together with the traditional interpretation, it becomes possible to define other variants, for example, allowing multisets of rules to be applicable even though not all the individual rules contained there are applicable themselves. Another interesting question is the definition of the maximally parallel derivation mode, which is a rather complex task, because we also have to deal with negative coefficients. We also remark that traditional P systems are obtained as a particular case of our model using generalized multisets with multiplicities from the group $(\mathbb{Z}, +)$, additionally restricted to positive values.

An important consequence of our results is that they permit to define P systems manipulating more complex objects directly. For example, a point (x, y) in a 2-dimensional plane can be represented directly as $a^{(x,y)}$ and manipulated directly with rewriting rules, e.g., consider the rule $a^{(1,0)} \rightarrow a^{(2,2)}$, which moves the point marked by a from the coordinate (x, y) to the coordinate $(x+1, y+2)$. Of course, this can be done in traditional P systems by using four objects (for each half-coordinate) and the corresponding rules, but we think that a direct representation is more concise and better reflects the computational process.

The paper is organized as follows. Section 2.1 contains the notions we use from group theory and Sect. 3 defines the concept of generalized multisets over totally ordered Abelian groups. Section 4 introduces P systems over such generalized multisets and gives sufficient conditions for the finiteness of the set of applicable multisets of rules in each step. Section 5 contains several examples using a direct manipulation of group objects.

2   Definitions

In this section, we first recall some well-known notations. We assume the reader to be familiar with the underlying notions and concepts from formal language theory, e.g., see [13], as well as from the area of P systems, e.g., see [10–12]; we also refer the reader to [15] for actual news in this area. In the second subsection, we introduce some notions from group theory, e.g., see [7].

2.1   Preliminaries

The set of integers is denoted by $\mathbb{Z}$, and the set of non-negative integers by $\mathbb{N}$.

For an alphabet V, by V^* we denote the free monoid generated by V under the operation of concatenation, i.e., containing all possible strings over V. The *empty string* is denoted by λ. A *multiset* M with underlying set A is a pair (A, f) where $f : A \rightarrow \mathbb{N}$ is a mapping. If $M = (A, f)$ is a multiset then its *support* is defined as $supp(M) = \{x \in A \mid f(x) > 0\}$. A multiset is empty (respectively finite) if its support is the empty set (respectively a finite set).

A relation over a set A is any subset $R \subseteq A \times A$. We will also use the infix notation aRb for $(a, b) \in R$.

Given a set A, a total function $f : A \times A \to A$ is called a *binary operation* over A. As for relations, we will also use the infix notation afb to refer to $f(a, b)$, for $a, b \in A$.

A relation $\leq \subseteq A \times A$ is a called a *total order* if the following statements hold for every three elements $a, b, c \in A$:

- *antisymmetry:* if $a \leq b$ and $b \leq a$ then $a = b$,
- *transitivity:* if $a \leq b$ and $b \leq c$ then $a \leq c$,
- *totality:* either $a \leq b$ or $b \leq a$.

For $a, b \in A$ and a total order $\leq$ on A, we will sometimes write $b \geq a$ as equivalent to $a \leq b$, and use $a < b$ $(a > b)$ to denote that $a \leq b$ and $a \neq b$ $(a \geq b$ and $a \neq b)$.

2.2   Groups and Group Presentations

Groups. Let $G = (G', \circ)$ be a group with group operation $\circ$ being a binary operation. As is well-known, the group axioms are

- *closure:* for any $a, b \in G'$, $a \circ b \in G'$,
- *associativity:* for any $a, b, c \in G'$, $(a \circ b) \circ c = a \circ (b \circ c)$,
- *identity:* there exists a (unique) element $e \in G'$, called the *identity*, such that $e \circ a = a \circ e = a$ for all $a \in G'$, and
- *invertibility:* for any $a \in G'$, there exists a (unique) element a^{-1}, called the *inverse* of a, such that $a \circ a^{-1} = a^{-1} \circ a = e$.

Moreover, the group is called *commutative* or *Abelian*, if for any $a, b \in G'$, $a \circ b = b \circ a$.

For any element $b \in G'$, the order of b is the smallest number $n \in \mathbb{N}$ such that $b^n = e$ provided such an n exists, and then we write $ord\,(b) = n$; if no such n exists, $\{b^n \mid n \geq 1\}$ is an infinite subset of G' and we write $ord\,(b) = \infty$.

In the following, we will not distinguish between G' and G if the group operation is obvious from the context.

A *subgroup* of the group $(G, \circ)$ is any group $(H, \circ)$ with $H \subseteq G$ and the same group operation $\circ$.

Representation of Groups. For representing group elements we can use strings; the definitions and examples from group theory we exhibit now follow the exposition given in [2], based on the notions in [7].

For any set B, B^{-1} is defined as the set of symbols representing the inverses of the elements of B, i.e., $B^{-1} = \{b^{-1} \mid b \in B\}$. We now consider the strings in $(B \cup B^{-1})^*$ and two strings as different unless their equality follows from the group axioms, i.e., for any $a, b, c \in (B \cup B^{-1})^*$, $a \circ b \circ b^{-1} \circ c = a \circ c$; using these reductions, we obtain a set of irreducible strings from those in $(B \cup B^{-1})^*$, the set of which we denote by $I(B)$. Then the *free group* generated by B is $F(B) = (I(B), \circ)$ with the elements being the irreducible strings over $B \cup B^{-1}$ and the group operation to be interpreted as the usual string concatenation, yet, obviously, if we concatenate two elements from $I(B)$, the resulting string eventually has to be reduced again. The identity in $F(B)$ is the empty string.

In general, B (not containing the identity) is called a *generator* of the group G if every element a from G can be written as a finite product/sum of elements from B, i.e., $a = b_1 \circ \cdots \circ b_m$ for $b_1, \ldots, b_m \in B$. In this paper, we restrict ourselves to finitely presented groups, i.e., having a finite presentation $\langle B \mid R \rangle$ with B being a finite generator set and moreover, R being a finite set of relations among these generators. In a similar way as in the definition of the free group generated by B, we here consider the strings in B^* to be reduced according to the group axioms and the relations given in R. Informally, the group $G = \langle B \mid R \rangle$ is the largest one generated by B subject only to the group axioms and the relations in R. Formally, we will restrict ourselves to relations of the form $b_1 \circ \cdots \circ b_m = c^{-1}$ with $b_1, \ldots, b_m, c \in B$, which equivalently may be written as $b_1 \circ \cdots \circ b_m \circ c = e$; hence, instead of such relations we may specify R by strings over B yielding the group identity, i.e., instead of $b_1 \circ \cdots \circ b_m = c^{-1}$ we take $b_1 \circ \cdots \circ b_m \circ c$ (these strings then are called *relators*).

Example 1. The free group $F(B) = (I(B), \circ)$ can be written as $\langle B \mid \emptyset \rangle$ (or even simpler as $\langle B \rangle$) because it has no restricting relations.

Example 2. The *cyclic group* of order n has the presentation $\langle \{a\} \mid \{a^n\} \rangle$ (or, omitting the set brackets, written as $\langle a \mid a^n \rangle$); it is also known as $\mathbb{Z}_n$ or as the quotient group $\mathbb{Z}/\mathbb{Z}_n$.

Example 3. $\mathbb{Z}$ is a special case of an Abelian group generated by (1) and its inverse (-1), i.e., $\mathbb{Z}$ is the free group generated by (1). $\mathbb{Z}^d$ is an Abelian group generated by the unit vectors $(0, \ldots, 1, \ldots, 0)$ and their inverses $(0, \ldots, -1, \ldots, 0)$. It is well known that every finitely generated Abelian group is a direct sum of a torsion group and a free Abelian group where the torsion group may be written as a direct sum of finitely many groups of the form $\mathbb{Z}/p^k\mathbb{Z}$ for p being a prime, and the free Abelian group is a direct sum of finitely many copies of $\mathbb{Z}$.

Example 4. A very well-known example for a non-Abelian group is the hexagonal group with the finite presentation $\langle a, b, c \mid a^2, b^2, c^2 \rangle$. All three generators a, b, c are self-inverse.

Remark 1. Given a finite presentation of a group $\langle B \mid R \rangle$, in general it is not even decidable whether the group presented in that way is finite or infinite. Hence, in this paper we restrict ourselves to infinite groups where the word equivalence problem $u = v$ is decidable, or equivalently, there is a decision procedure telling us whether, given two strings u and v, $u \circ v^{-1} = e$. In that case, we call $\langle B \mid R \rangle$ a *recursive* or *computable* finite group presentation.

Remark 2. In general, as long as we have given the group by a computable finite presentation, for a mechanism having the full power of Turing computability, we can require that the "strings" computed are irreducible ones. Hence, for a given recursively enumerable set L of elements over the computable finite presentation $\langle B \mid R \rangle$ of a group, such a mechanism can generate the irreducible string representations of the elements in L and also compute recursive relations on them.

For an additive group $(G, +)$, where the group operation can be interpreted as addition, the sum $a + (-b)$ is often written as $a - b$, and e is replaced by 0, whenever no ambiguity arises. The following shortcut notations are also frequently used, for $a \in G$ and $z \in \mathbb{Z}$ defining the *scalar product* of a group element a with an integer number z:

$$za = \begin{cases} a^z = \sum_{i=1}^n a, & z > 0, \\ a^0 = 0 \text{ (group identity)}, & z = 0, \\ (-a)^{-z} = \sum_{i=1}^n (-a), & z < 0. \end{cases}$$

A *linearly* or *totally ordered group* is construct $(A, +, \leq)$ where $(A, +)$ is a group, $\leq \subseteq A \times A$ is a total order on A and, for any triple $a, b, c \in A$, the fact that $a \leq b$ implies that $c + a \leq c + b$ and $a + c \leq b + c$.

A linearly ordered group $(A, +, \leq)$ is said to be *Archimedean*, if for every $a, b \in A$ there exists an $n \in \mathbb{N}$ such that $b \leq na$ holds.

Remark 3. An equivalent definition is that an Archimedean group is a linearly ordered group without any bounded cyclic subgroup (i.e., there does not exist a cyclic subgroup S and an element x with x greater than all elements in S).

Remark 4. As is well known, an Archimedean group is isomorphic to a subgroup of the field of real numbers, and therefore any Archimedean group is an Abelian group, too.

Example 5. A typical example for an Archimedean group (with a computable finite presentation) is $(\mathbb{Z}, +, \leq)$ with the normal order relation $\leq$; on the other hand, for $n > 1$, $(\mathbb{Z}^n, +, \leq)$ with the lexicographic ordering $\leq$ is a totally ordered Abelian group, but not Archimedean.

3   Generalized Multisets over an Abelian Group

Given an Abelian group $(G, +)$, a *generalized multiset over G* or a $G - multiset$ over a finite alphabet V is a mapping $h : V \to G$. For any $a \in G$, $h(a)$ denotes the coefficient of a in h considered as a formal power series $\Sigma_{x \in V} h(x)x$, and in the sense of multisets, $h(a)$ will also be called the multiplicity of a in h. The support of h is defined as the set of objects which have nonzero multiplicity in h: $supp(h) = \{a \in V \mid h(a) \neq 0\}$, where $0 \in G$ is the identity in G. We will denote the empty G-multiset by o, i.e., $o(a) = 0$, for all $a \in V$. The set of all G-multisets over the alphabet V will be denoted by V^G.

The union of two G-multisets h_1 and h_2 over the same alphabet V is defined as the G-multiset $h_1 + h_2$ with the property that $(h_1 + h_2)(a) = h_1(a) + h_2(a)$, for all $a \in V$. Symmetrically, the difference of h_1 and h_2 is defined as the G-multiset $h_1 - h_2$ such that $(h_1 - h_2)(a) = h_1(a) - h_2(a)$, for all $a \in V$. Thus, all G-multisets over V form the Abelian group $(V^G, +)$ with the identity element o and $-h$ as the inverse of h. By fixing an enumeration of the elements of V, each G-multiset over V can be represented as a vector of size $|V|$ containing elements of G as components, i.e., an element $h \in (V^G, +)$ can also be written as a vector $(h(a_1), \ldots, h(a_n))$ where $\langle a_1, \ldots, a_n \rangle$ is an ordered version of the alphabet $V = \{a_1, \ldots, a_n\}$. In that sense, $(V^G, +)$ is a vector space over V with scalar multiplication over $\mathbb{Z}$. If G is totally ordered, $(V^G, +)$ is also totally ordered with respect to the lexicographical ordering.

Conventional multisets can be seen as $(\mathbb{Z}, +)$-multisets additionally restricted to non-negative multiplicities. With this constraint, the submultiset relation can be defined in the usual way, and submultiset difference $h_1 - h_2$ can be restricted to the cases in which h_2 is a submultiset of h_1.

4   P Systems with Multisets over a Totally Ordered Abelian Group

Given a totally ordered Abelian group G and a finite alphabet V, we first define three variants for *rewriting a G-multiset w over V by a V^G − multiset rewriting rule $u \to v$*, where $u, v \in V^G$:

Definition 1. *Let G be a totally ordered Abelian group G and V a finite alphabet, then a V^G − multiset rewriting rule $u \to v$, where $u, v \in V^G$, is said to be*

- *$\forall$ − applicable to $w \in V^G$ if and only if for all $a \in V$ such that $u(a) \neq 0$, the following holds:*

$$u(a) > 0 \text{ and } u(a) \leq w(a) \quad or \quad u(a) < 0 \text{ and } -u(a) \leq -w(a).$$

- *$\exists$ − applicable to $w \in V^G$ if and only if there exists an $a \in V$ such that $u(a) \neq 0$, the following holds:*

$$u(a) > 0 \text{ and } u(a) \leq w(a) \quad or u(a) < 0 \text{ and } -u(a) \leq -w(a).$$

- *freely applicable to $w \in V^G$.*

The result of the application of the rule $u \to v$ to w in any variant of applicability is $w - u + v$.

We remark that the conditions for the $\forall$-applicability and for the $\exists$-applicability of a rule are identical, except for the objects against which they are checked.

4.1   P Systems

In order to keep definitions more readable, we here only define P systems with only one membrane region, i.e., we need not define the membrane structure and the communication of multisets through membranes.

Definition 2. *For a totally ordered Abelian group $(G, +)$, a P system with generalized multisets is a tuple*

$$\Pi_G = (O, T, w_0, R) \text{ where}$$

- *O is a finite alphabet of objects,*
- *$T \subseteq O$ is the alphabet of terminal objects,*
- *w_0 is the initial contents of the skin region of the system, and*
- *R is a finite set of O^G-multiset rewriting rules of the form $u \to v$, where $u \neq o$ and v are O^G-multisets.*

Definition 3. *For a multiset of O^G-multiset rewriting rules R, we define the following shortcut notations:*

$$LHS(R) = \sum_{u \to v \in R} u \quad and \quad RHS(R) = \sum_{u \to v \in R} v.$$

A configuration of Π_G is described by the O^G-multiset contained in the skin region. Applying a multiset P of rules from R to a configuration w leads to a new configuration w' defined as

$$w' = w - LHS(P) + RHS(P)$$

for all the three variants for the application of the rule $LHS(P) \to RHS(P)$ as defined in Definition 1, i.e., we take the multiset of rules to get one bigger rule to be applied in these three ways, with the applicability in the $\forall$- and $\exists$-case being constrained by the conditions on all elements or on one element from O as defined there.

Example 6. In this example we will show that in the $\forall$-mode and the $\exists$-mode the applicability of a multiset of rules can differ from the applicability of individual rules. Consider the following P system Π over $(\mathbb{Z}, +, \leq)$:

$$\Pi = (\{a, b, c\}, \{a, b, c\}, ac, R), \text{ where } R = \{r_1 : ab \to c; r_2 : cb^{-1} \to a\}.$$

Then it is clear that neither r_1 nor r_2 is $\exists$- or $\forall$-applicable to ac. At the same time, the multiset of rules $r_1 r_2$ is both $\exists$- and $\forall$-applicable to ac as b and b^{-1} will reduce to zero.

Definition 4. *A derivation in Π_G is a sequence of configurations $w_0, w_1, \ldots, w_n$ with $w_i \in O^G$ and in which w_{i+1} is obtained from w_i by applying a subset of rules $P_i \subseteq R$ according to the strategy for choosing the subsets P_i which is called the derivation mode, variants of which will be defined and discussed later. The* *last configuration of a derivation that also fulfills the* halting condition *is called a* halting configuration. *We remark that usually the total halting condition is considered checking that no multiset of rules taken according to the derivation mode is applicable any more. The result of a halting derivation is the projection of the contents of the skin in the halting configuration on T, i.e., if $w_n \in O^G$, then the result w_T in T^G is obtained by taking $w_T(a) = w_n(a)$ for $a \in T$ and $w_T(a) = 0$ for $a \in O \setminus T$.*

The set of T^G-multisets computed by Π_G as results of halting derivations using the α-mode of rule application in the derivation mode δ with the halting condition τ is denoted by $L_{\alpha,\delta,\tau}(\Pi_G)$, where $\alpha \in \{free, \forall, \exists\}$ are the three variants of rule application as defined in Definition 1. In the case of the total halting condition we will omit τ.

4.2   Derivation Modes

In general, no applicability conditions would be required for G-multiset rewriting rules to be applied, because multiset difference is defined for any pair of G-multisets, which is reflected by the variant of free rule application. Yet without any applicability condition, every rule is applicable to any configuration of a P system. Generalizing the idea of limited resources usually employed in conventional P systems, the two rule applicability variants $\alpha \in \{\forall, \exists\}$ have been defined in Definition 1.

In the case of conventional multisets restrained to non-negative numbers exclusively, the $\forall$-applicability translates to the usual applicability condition requiring the sum of the left-hand sides of a rule to be a submultiset of the current contents of the skin region, whereas the $\exists$-applicability is very much different.

Definition 5. *Let $(G, +)$ be a totally ordered Abelian group and let $\Pi_G = (O, T, w_0, R)$ be a P system with G-multisets over O; then for any configuration C of Π the set of applicable multisets of rules taken from R in the α-mode of rule applicability, $\alpha \in \{free, \forall, \exists\}$, is denoted by $Asyn_\alpha(C)$. The asynchronous derivation mode then is defined by applying any multiset of rules from $Asyn_\alpha(C)$ in a derivation step in Π from C.*

Definition 6. *The* sequential derivation *mode is defined as the mode in which exactly one rule is applied in every derivation step – according to the α-mode of rule application, $\alpha \in \{free, \forall, \exists\}$.*

The sequential mode of conventional P systems is generalized by the $\forall$-sequential mode in P systems with generalized multisets.

The three different approaches to defining rule application can be directly used to generalize even other derivation modes in which the size of multisets of rules applied in every configuration is statically bounded, like the k-restricted minimal parallelism.

On the other hand, for the maximally parallel mode further constraints on the choice of rules are necessary, because otherwise, even with $\forall$-applicability, the number of multisets of rules applicable to a given configuration may be infinite:

Example 7. Consider the two-letter alphabet $O = \{a, b\}$, the Archimedean group $(\mathbb{Z}, +, \leq)$, and the following three $\mathbb{Z}$-multisets over O: w, u_1, and u_2, with $w(a) = 1$, $u_1(a) = 1$, $u_2(a) = -2$, and $w(b) = u_1(b) = u_2(b) = 0$. Take two $O^{\mathbb{Z}}$-multiset rewriting rules r_1 and r_2 having u_1 and u_2 as left-hand sides, respectively. Then any multiset of rules from the infinite set $\{r_1^i r_2^j \mid i = 2j + 1, j \in \mathbb{N}\}$ will be $\forall$-applicable to w, i.e., even $Asyn_\forall(w)$ is infinite and thus there will be no multiset of rules which cannot be extended.

In fact, we want to avoid such a situation during a computation, and so our first approach for getting a maximality condition on applicable multisets of rules is what we call *dynamic maximality*, defined as follows:

(a) only consider such $\forall$-applicable multisets of rules in R so that, for any non-empty submultiset R', $LHS(R') \neq o$, and

(b) whenever the set of $\forall$-applicable multisets is infinite, no rules are applied and the system halts.

In our previous example with the configuration w and the rules r_1 and r_2, we would not be able to consider any multiset of rules which includes $r_1^2 r_2$, because $LHS(r_1^2 r_2) = o$. The number of applicable multisets of rules in this case would be finite. We also remark that dynamic maximality does not statically forbid rules which may lead to a lock-up of the system. So, for example, if the P system is in configuration w with $w(a) = 0$ and $w(b) \neq 0$ and has a rule acting on the object b, the rules r_1 and r_2 will not be $\forall$-applicable and the system can evolve.

Condition (a) from above makes sense in general, so all derivation modes could be defined with requiring this condition for all multisets of rules called to be applicable:

Definition 7. *Let $(G, +)$ be a totally ordered Abelian group and let $\Pi_G = (O, T, w_0, R)$ be a P system with G-multisets over O; then for any configuration C of Π the set of applicable multisets of rules taken from R and also fulfilling the condition that for any non-empty submultiset $R' \subseteq R$, $LHS(R') \neq o$, in the α-mode of rule applicability, $\alpha \in \{free, \forall, \exists\}$, is denoted by $Asyn_\alpha^+(C)$. The asynchronous$^+$ mode of derivation then is defined by applying any multiset of rules from $Asyn_\alpha^+(C)$ in a derivation step in Π from C.*

We can even put stronger conditions on the applicability of rules:

Definition 8. *Let $(G, +)$ be a totally ordered Abelian group and let $\Pi_G = (O, T, w_0, R)$ be a P system with G-multisets over O; then for any configuration C of Π the set $Asyn_\alpha^{++}(C) \subseteq Asyn_\alpha^+(C)$ contains all rules $u \to v$ from $Asyn_\alpha^+(C)$, $\alpha \in \{free, \forall, \exists\}$, such that for all $a \in O$, $u(a) \geq 0$ if $C(a) \geq 0$ and $u(a) < 0$ if $C(a) < 0$. The asynchronous^{++} mode of derivation then is defined by applying any multiset of rules from $Asyn_\alpha^{++}(C)$ in a derivation step in Π from C.*

Based on this definition of $Asyn_\alpha^+(C)$ and $Asyn_\alpha^{++}(C)$, our second approach to getting a maximality condition which guarantees that in any case we can get a finite set of rules applicable in the maximally parallel way, is to require an additional feature for the underlying group.

We first define a partial order relation on vectors over a totally ordered Abelian group based on comparing the values of each component.

Definition 9. *Let $(G, +, \leq)$ be a totally ordered Abelian group. Then we define the partial order relation $\leq_c$ on vectors over G as follows: Let u and v be two non-zero n-dimensional vectors over G with all components being non-negative, i.e., $u = (u_1, \ldots, u_n)$, $v = (v_1, \ldots, v_n)$, $u_j \geq 0$ and $v_j \geq 0$, $1 \leq j \leq n$, $\sum_{i=1}^{n} u_i > 0$ and $\sum_{i=1}^{n} v_i > 0$, then we say that $(u_1, \ldots, u_n) \leq_c (v_1, \ldots, v_n)$ if and only if $u_j \leq v_j$ for all $1 \leq j \leq n$.*

This componentwise comparison of two vectors which are non-negative can be extended to arbitrary vectors having in mind the typical concept of reducing resources, but now from any side of zero in each component.

Definition 10. *For a totally ordered Abelian group $(G, +, \leq)$ we define the signum function $sg : G \to \{-1, 0, 1\}$ as follows:*

$$sg(x) = \begin{cases} 1, & \text{if } x > 0, \\ 0, & \text{if } x = 0, \\ -1, & \text{if } x < 0. \end{cases}$$

We extend this function to n-dimensional vectors over G as follows: for an n-dimensional vector $v = (v_1, \ldots, v_n)$ over G, we define $sg((v_1, \ldots, v_n)) = (sg(v_1), \ldots, sg(v_n))$.

Definition 11. *Let $(G, +, \leq)$ be a totally ordered Abelian group. Then we define the partial order relation $\leq_{sg-c}$ on vectors over G as follows: Let u and v be two arbitrary n-dimensional vectors over G, $u = (u_1, \ldots, u_n)$, $v = (v_1, \ldots, v_n)$; then we say that $(u_1, \ldots, u_n) \leq_{sg-c} (v_1, \ldots, v_n)$ if and only if for all $1 \leq j \leq n$,*

$$sg(u_j)sg(v_j) \geq 0 \text{ and } sg(u_j)u_j \leq sg(v_j)v_j.$$

Remark 5. We observe that, in the preceding definition, $sg(u_j)u_j \leq sg(v_j)v_j$ can also be written as $|u_j| \leq |v_j|$. Moreover, using the Hadamard product $\odot$, i.e., multiplying vectors component-wise, $u \leq_{sg-c} v$ can also be defined by the conditions $sg(u) \odot sg(v) \geq 0$ and $sg(u) \odot u \leq sg(v) \odot v$.

Definition 12. *Let $(G, +, \leq)$ be a totally ordered Abelian group. G is called a $P-group$ if and only if the following condition holds:*

- *Let $r_1, \ldots, r_k$ be any non-empty set of non-zero n-dimensional vectors over G with all components being non-negative and let r be any arbitrary n-dimensional vector over G with all components being non-negative. Then the inequality*

$$\sum_{i=1}^{k} x_i r_i \leq_c r$$

only has a finite number of solutions $(x_1, \ldots, x_k)$ in $\mathbb{N}^k$.

Example 8. Consider $(\mathbb{Z}^n, +, \leq)$ with $\leq$ being the following order relation: For two vectors $u, v \in \mathbb{Z}^n$, $u \neq v$, $u \leq v$ if and only if $||u|| < ||v||$ or $||u|| = ||v||$ and $u < v$ with respect to the lexicographic ordering $<$. Then $(\mathbb{Z}^n, +, \leq)$ is a P-group. As norm $||u||$ of a vector $u = (u_1, \ldots, u_n)$ we can take the *maximum norm* defined as $||u|| = \max\{u_1, \ldots, u_n\}$.

Lemma 1. *Let $(G, +, \leq)$ be a P-group. Then G is Archimedean.*

Proof. Consider $w, v \in G$ with both being positive. Then according to the P-condition for G, the inequality $xw \leq v$ only has finitely many solutions for $x \in \mathbb{N}$. Let n be the maximal solution; then $(n + 1)w > v$, which proves that G is Archimedean. $\qquad\square$

Yet for totally ordered Abelian groups, also the converse of this lemma is true.

Lemma 2. *Let $(G, +, \leq)$ be an Archimedean group. Then G is a P-group, too.*

Proof. Let $r_1, \ldots, r_k$ be any set of non-zero n-dimensional vectors over G with all components being non-negative and let r be any arbitrary n-dimensional vector over G with all components being non-negative. If a component j of r is zero, then any solution with $x_i > 0$ implies $r_i(j) = 0$. Now let $r(j) > 0$. If $r_i(j) = 0$ for all $1 \leq i \leq k$, then obviously for this component the desired order relation will always be fulfilled. Yet as all the vectors r_i are non-zero, there must be a component j_i such that $r_i(j_i) > 0$, and let $r(j_i) > 0$. Due to the Archimedean property of the group G, there must exist a natural number m_i such that $m_i r_i(j_i) > r(j_i) > 0$. Hence, for every solution $(x_1, \ldots, x_k)$ in $\mathbb{N}^k$ of the inequality

$$\sum_{i=1}^{k} x_i r_i \leq_c r$$

we must have $0 \leq x_i < m_i$ for all $1 \leq i \leq k$. As the number of such vectors obviously is finite, we conclude that G is a P-group. $\qquad\square$

Lemma 3. *Let $(G, +, \leq)$ be a P-group and $\Pi_G = (O, T, w_0, R)$ be a P system with G-multisets over O. Then for any configuration C of Π the set $Asyn_\forall^{++}(C)$ is finite.*

Proof. Consider a configuration C of Π_G and a multiset of rules P. Then construct the corresponding G-multiset C' with $C'(a) = C(a)$ for $C(a) \geq 0$ and $C'(a) = -C(a)$ for $C(a) < 0$, i.e., we take $C' := sg(C) \odot C$. For any rule r_i from P we construct the corresponding rule r_i' in the same way, i.e., we take $r_i' := sg(r_i) \odot r_i$. According to the definition of a P-group, the inequality $x_1 r_1' + \ldots + x_n r_n' \leq_c C'$ has only finitely many solutions over $\mathbb{N}$, which themselves constitute the $-$ finite $-$ set $Asyn_\forall^{++}(C)$. We observe that taking $Asyn_\forall^{++}(C)$ guarantees that all the r_i are approaching each component of C from the same side of the zero element, hence, summing up the left-hand sides of the rules yields the same effect as summing up the absolute values of them. $\qquad\square$

As according to Lemma 3 the set $Asyn_\forall^{++}(C)$ must be finite, the set of non-extendable rules in $Asyn_\forall^{++}(C)$ must be finite, too; hence, it is a well-defined finite set.

Definition 13. *Let* $(G, +, \le)$ *be a P-group and* $\Pi_G = (O, T, w_0, R)$ *be a P system with G-multisets over O. Then for any configuration C of* Π*, the set of all non-extendable multisets from* $Asyn_\forall^{++}(C)$ *is denoted by* $Maxpar_\forall^{P++}(C)$*. The* maximally parallel *derivation mode* $maxpar_\forall^{P++}$ *then is defined by applying any multiset of rules from* $Maxpar_\forall^{P++}(C)$ *in a derivation step in* Π *from C.*

Remark 6. If we only consider non-negative components in the vectors representing rules and configurations, then our model with $Asyn_\forall^{++}(C)$ in a P system over a P-group directly corresponds to the usual concept of P systems, except that now we are dealing with generalized multisets. Moreover, the derivation mode $maxpar_\forall^{P++}$ corresponds to the "classical" maximally parallel derivation mode.

Remark 7. In some sense, Lemma 3 corresponds to the representation of negative multiplicities by using antimatter. In fact, for any rule either positive or negative components can be used, but not both at the same time. This is equivalent to having two non-negative components encoding the positive and the negative part of the original component (of course, both of them cannot be positive at the same time).

As we want to deal with negative multiplicities directly, we want to consider $Asyn_\forall^+(C)$ and not $Asyn_\forall^{++}(C)$ and therefore need a stricter variant of P-groups:

Definition 14. *Let* $(G, +, \le)$ *be a totally ordered Abelian group* $(G, +, \le)$*. G is called a GP* − *group if and only if the following condition holds:*

- *Let* $r_1, \ldots, r_k$*,* $k > 0$*, be any set of n-dimensional vectors over G and let r be any arbitrary n-dimensional vector over G. Then the inequality*

$$\sum_{i=1}^{k} x_i r_i \le_{sg-c} r$$

only has a finite number of solutions $(x_1, \ldots, x_k)$ *in* $\mathbb{N}^k$ *fulfilling the condition that*

for all non-zero vectors $(y_1, \ldots, y_k)$ *over G with*
$$(0, \ldots, 0) \le_c (y_1, \ldots, y_k) \le_c (x_1, \ldots, x_k) \text{ we have}$$
$$\sum_{i=1}^{k} y_i r_i \ne 0. \qquad (*)$$

We immediately observe that for non-negative vectors the condition for the GP-group reduces to the condition in the P-group, as in this case $\le_c$ coincides with $\le_{sg-c}$.

Lemma 4. *Let* $(G, +, \le)$ *be a GP-group. Then G is a P-group, too.*

Proof. Let $r_1, \ldots, r_k$ be any set of non-zero n-dimensional vectors over G with all components being non-negative and let r be any arbitrary n-dimensional vector over G with all components being non-negative. The inequality

$$\sum_{i=1}^{k} x_i r_i \leq_{sg-c} r$$

then can also be written as

$$\sum_{i=1}^{k} x_i r_i \leq_{c} r$$

and, moreover, condition $(*)$ must also be fulfilled, as the sum $\sum_{i=1}^{k} x_i r_i$ is always non-negative. Hence, from the GP-condition being fulfilled we immediately infer that the P-condition must be fulfilled, too, i.e., the inequality only has finitely many solutions. □

Lemma 5. *Let $(G, +, \leq)$ be a GP-group and $\Pi_G = (O, T, w_0, R)$ be a P system with G-multisets over O, then for any configuration C of Π the set $Asyn_{\forall}^{+}(C)$ is finite.*

Proof. Let $|O| = n$ and $|R| = k$. We define $L_i := LHS(r_i)$, $1 \leq i \leq k$, for some enumeration of rules of R. Obviously, C and each L_i, $1 \leq i \leq k$, can be seen as members of the n-dimensional vector space over G. From the definition of the GP-group we conclude that the inequality

$$\sum_{i=1}^{k} x_i L_i \leq_{sg-c} C$$

has only a finite number of solutions $(x_1, \ldots, x_k)$ satisfying condition $(*)$. We remark that the multiplicities of elements for any multiset of rules $R' \in Asyn_{\forall}(C)$ can be seen as a vector $(v_1, \ldots, v_k) \in \mathbb{N}^k$. Using the previous inequality we obtain that there are only a finite number of elements in $Asyn_{\forall}(C)$ that satisfy condition $(*)$. The remaining elements in $R' \in Asyn_{\forall}(C)$ do not satisfy it, so for each such element R' there must exist a vector $(y_1, \ldots, y_k) \in \mathbb{N}^k$ such that $\sum_{i=1}^{k} y_i L_i = 0$. But this implies that there exists a submultiset $R'' \subseteq R'$ such that $LHS(R'') = o$. Now consider $Asyn_{\forall}^{+}(C)$. Since it contains only multisets of rules R' such that there are no submultisets $R'' \subseteq R'$ having $LHS(R'') = o$ we immediately obtain that $Asyn_{\forall}^{+}(C)$ is finite. □

Definition 15. *Let $(G, +, \leq)$ be a GP-group and $\Pi_G = (O, T, w_0, R)$ be a P system with G-multisets over O. Then for any configuration C of Π, the set of all non-extendable multisets from $Asyn_{\forall}^{+}(C)$ is denoted by $Maxpar_{\forall}^{GP+}(C)$. The maximally parallel derivation mode $maxpar_{\forall}^{GP+}$ then is defined by applying any multiset of rules from $Maxpar_{\forall}^{GP+}(C)$ in a derivation step in Π from C.*

As according to Lemma 5 the set $Asyn_{\forall}^{+}(C)$ must be finite, the set of non-extendable rules in $Asyn_{\forall}^{+}(C)$ must be finite, too; hence, this set $Maxpar_{\forall}^{P+}(C)$ is a well-defined finite set.

We now prove that the "standard" example of an Archimedean group, namely $(\mathbb{Z}^n, +, \leq)$, is a GP-group.

Lemma 6. $(\mathbb{Z}^n, +, \leq)$ *is a GP-group.*

Proof. Consider arbitrary d-dimensional vectors $r_1, \ldots, r_k, r$ over $\mathbb{Z}^n$. Consider the polytope $\mathcal{P}$ delimited by r and the hyperplanes parallel to the coordinate axes. Since $\mathcal{P}$ is closed, it only contains a finite number of points. Denote $P(x_1, \ldots, x_n) = \sum_{i=1}^{k} x_i r_i$. Let $S \subseteq \mathbb{N}^k$ be the set of vectors such that any $(x_1, \ldots, x_n) \in S$ satisfies the inequality $\sum_{i=1}^{k} x_i r_i \leq_{sg-c} r$ and the condition $(*)$. Then it is clear that $P(x_1, \ldots, x_n)$ must belong to $\mathcal{P}$. We claim that S is finite. We shall prove this statement by contradiction:

Assume that S is infinite. Since $\mathcal{P}$ is finite, by the pigeonhole principle there exists an infinite number of vectors $v_1, v_2, \cdots \in S$ such that $P(v_1) = P(v_2) = \ldots = P(v)$. Now by the pigeonhole principle applied to the vector components there must be infinitely many of them with the same signum vector $sg(u)$. Let us list these vectors as $u_1, u_2, \ldots$. Then, again using the pigeonhole principle applied to the vector components, we obtain that for any vector u_i there exists a vector u_j such that $u_i(m) < u_j(m)$ for some m, $1 \leq m \leq k$. As we only have a finite number of components, among all those vectors there must exist some u_i and u_j such that $u_i \leq_{sg-c} u_j$. Hence, we obtain that there exist two vectors $u_i, u_j \in S$ such that $P(u_i) = P(u_j)$ and $u_i \leq_{sg-c} u_j$. But in this case $P(u_j - u_i) = 0$ contradicts condition $(*)$. □

5   Examples

In this section we will give some examples of how P systems with generalized multisets can directly manipulate complex objects. We will model the movement of a chess knight on an infinite two-dimensional plane. To represent the position of the knight, we will use two-component integer tuples from the Archimedean group $(\mathbb{Z}^2, +, \leq)$ as defined in Example 8.

We explicitly define the set of coordinate offsets corresponding to the eight possible knight moves as follows:

$$J = \{(i, j) : |i| = 3 - |j|, \ j \in \{1, 2\}\}.$$

For illustration purposes only, we will allow rules with empty left-hand sides in our first example. In such a rule the multiplicity of every symbol in the left-hand side is the zero element of the group. Recall that usually such rules are not allowed in our model.

Example 9. Consider the following P system with $\mathbb{Z}^2$-multisets:

$$\Pi_1 = (\{a\}, \{a\}, a^{(0,0)}, R_1),$$
$$R_1 = \{a^{(0,0)} \to a^v \mid v \in J\},$$

working in the sequential derivation mode and an α-mode of rule applicability, with $\alpha \in \{free, \forall, \exists\}$. The multiplicity of a in a configuration represents the current position of the knight. Any of the rules in R_1 is applicable to any configuration of Π_1, and an application of any one of them corresponds to a knight move. Unconditional halting can be employed to assure that the system stops.

Remark that in the case of rules with empty left-hand sides, $\exists$- and $\forall$-applicability conditions essentially reduce to free applicability. To avoid such rules, we can rely on a special object which behaves similarly to a catalyst in conventional P systems.

Example 10. Consider the following P system with $\mathbb{Z}^2$-multisets:

$$\Pi_2 = (\{a, c\}, \{a\}, c^x a^{(0,0)}, R_2),$$
$$R_2 = \{c^x a^{(0,0)} \to c^x a^v \mid v \in J\},$$

where $x \in \mathbb{Z}^2$ and $x \neq (0,0)$. With $\forall$-applicability, at most one rule from R_2 can be applied to any configuration, because every rule from R_2 consumes and reproduces c^x. Thus, even in a parallel derivation mode, the activity of Π_2 will be sequential. Halting can be achieved by adding the rule $c^x a^{(0,0)} \to c^{(0,0)} a^{(0,0)}$, which may "erase" c whenever the knight reaches the origin (the multiplicity of a is $(0,0)$).

It also is possible to stay off empty left-hand sides without adding the "catalyst", by specifying the coordinate offsets for all four elements of $I = \{(1,0), (0,1), (-1,0), (0,-1)\}$.

Example 11. Consider the following P system with generalized multisets:

$$\Pi_3 = (\{a\}, \{a\}, a^{u_0}, R_3),$$
$$R_3 = \{a^{(x,y)} \to a^{(z,t)} \mid (x,y) \in I, (z-x, t-y) \in J\},$$

where $u_0 \in \mathbb{Z}^2$, and $u_0 \neq (0,0)$. The set R_3 contains a rule per each element of I, per each possible knight movement. This is necessary to allow the knight to move throughout the whole plane under $\exists$- and $\forall$-applicability: indeed, with these conditions, the rules with $a^{(1,0)}$ in the left-hand side will only be applicable when the knight is in the half-plane to the right of the vertical axis, and will not be applicable when the knight is to the left of the vertical axis or right on it, because in these two cases the configuration of Π_3 will have the form $a^{(u,0)}$, with $u \leq 0$.

Since Π_3 does not employ a "catalyst", its behaviour in a parallel mode with $\forall$-applicability is very different from that of Π_2. Suppose that the knight is at position (i,j), with $i > 0$ and $j > 0$; the corresponding configuration of Π_3 will be $a^{(i,j)}$. The rules for R_3 which are $\forall$-applicable in this configuration are of the forms $a^{(1,0)} \to a^{(z,t)}$ and $a^{(0,1)} \to a^{(z,t)}$; the multiset of rules to be applied can therefore contain i rules of the first type and j rules of the second. But since each rule corresponds to a knight move, this means that, in a parallel mode with $\forall$-applicability, the knight may make up to $i+j$ moves in a single evolution step. In other words, the farther the knight is from origin, the faster it can move.

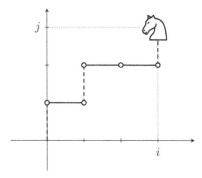

Fig. 1. A possible choice of the multiset of rules to be applied in configuration $a^{(i,j)}$. The segments —o correspond to the left-hand sides of the form $a^{(1,0)}$, while the segments --o correspond to the left-hand sides of the form $a^{(0,1)}$.

Figure 1 illustrates the way in which the position of the knight relative to the origin influences the form of applicable multisets of rules.

We remark that in the case of one-symbol alphabets, like that of Π_3, the $\exists$- and $\forall$-applicability conditions are effectively equivalent. This means that all of the arguments about Π_3 from the previous paragraph are valid for a parallel derivation mode with $\exists$-applicability as well.

In the case of a P system over a GP-group and a parallel mode in which $\forall$-applicability is required for the whole multiset of rules, but not for each rule individually, the simulation of knight movement can be done in a yet different way. Instead of having four rules per each move, it is possible to only have one rule per move, and to make use of special compensation rules.

Example 12. Consider the following P system with generalized multisets:

$$\Pi_4 = (\{a\}, \{a\}, a^{u_0}, R_4),$$
$$R_4 = \{a^{(1,0)} \rightarrow a^{(z,t)} \mid (z-1, t) \in J\} \cup R'_4,$$
$$R'_4 = \{a^v \rightarrow a^v \mid v \in \{(-2,0), (-1,1), (-1,-1)\}\},$$

working in a parallel mode with $\forall$-applicability, where $u_0 \in \mathbb{Z}^2$, and $u_0 \neq (0,0)$. Remember that the rules of the form $r : a^{(1,0)} \rightarrow a^{(z,t)}$ are not applicable when the knight is in the second quadrant, for example. However, in this case it is possible to consider the multiset of rules containing an instance of r and of the compensation rule $a^{(-2,0)} \rightarrow a^{(-2,0)}$. The total left-hand side of this two-element multiset will be $a^{(-1,0)}$, so this multiset will be applicable whenever the knight is to the left of the vertical axis. On the other hand, the total right-hand side will be $a^{(z-2,t)}$, and the total effect of applying these two rules at the same time will be displacing the knight by $(z-1, t)$, which is precisely the effect of r when it is applied alone.

While the rules of the form $a^{(1,0)} \rightarrow (z,t)$ together with the compensation rule $a^{(-2,0)} \rightarrow a^{(-2,0)}$ can simulate knight moves in both the half-planes delimited by the vertical axis, they cannot handle the situations in which the knight is on the axis itself, because in those situations the configuration of Π_4 has the form $a^{(0,y)}$. The compensation rules $a^v \to a^v$ with $v \in \{(-1,1),(-1,-1)\}$ are meant to handle precisely these cases. Indeed, when the knight is at the coordinates $(0,y)$ with $y > 0$, one may consider the multiset of rules including an instance of $a^{(1,0)} \to a^{(z,t)}$ and an instance of $a^{(-1,1)} \to a^{(-1,1)}$. The total left-hand side will be $a^{(0,1)}$, so the multiset of rules will be applicable to $a^{(0,y)}$, while the cumulative effect will amount to doing the move $(z-1,t)$. Similarly, the compensation rule $a^{(-1,-1)} \to a^{(-1,-1)}$ helps to handle the situations in which the knight is at the coordinates $(0,y)$ for $y < 0$.

We stress once again the fact that in Π_4 it is the rules of the form $a^{(1,0)} \to a^{(z,t)}$ that actually modify the configurations of the system. Compensation rules only matter when multisets of applicable rules are picked and do not by themselves cause any displacement of the knight.

Besides structural dissimilarities between Π_3 and Π_4, we remark that the dynamic characteristics of the two systems working in parallel modes are quite different as well. In Π_3, the number of rules applied in one step depends on the distance of the knight from the origin. In Π_4, however, the condition that no submultisets of the applied multiset of rules are allowed to have zero total left-hand side comes into play. It means that not more than one rule $r : a^{(1,0)} \to a^{(z,t)}$ can be applied in one step if the compensation rule $a^{(-2,0)} \to a^{(-2,0)}$ is used. Indeed if this compensation rule is combined with two instances of r, the total left-hand side of the group will be $a^{(0,0)}$. This issue does not affect the other two compensation rules, because, when put together with instances of r, they always yield a non-zero total left-hand side.

Therefore, in Π_4 working in the maximally parallel mode with $\forall$-applicability, the knight performs "supermoves" in the right half-plane and on the vertical axis, just like in Π_3, while in the left half-plane it may only do one movement per evolution step of the system.

Due to the restriction that no multiset of rules which has zero total left-hand side can be applied in a parallel mode, both the systems Π_3 and Π_4 from the previous two examples halt whenever the knight reaches the origin. This can be avoided by adding "catalytic" rules, similar to those shown in the definition of Π_2.

Example 13. Consider the following P system with generalized multisets:

$$\Pi_5 = (\{a,c\}, \{a\}, c^x a^{(0,0)}, R_5),$$
$$R_5 = \{c^{(0,0)} u \to c^{(0,0)} v \mid u \to v \in R_4\} \cup R_5',$$
$$R_5' = \{c^x a^{(0,0)} \to c^x a^v \mid v \in J\},$$

working in a parallel mode with $\forall$-applicability. The rules of the form $c^{(0,0)} u \to c^{(0,0)} v$ are essentially the rules from R_4 lifted to employ the "catalyst". Remark that these rules do not actually use c: it appears with multiplicity $(0,0)$ in both the left-hand and in the right-hand sides, and it has therefore no effect on the way in which these rules are picked for application. This means that these lifted rules assure precisely the same behavior of the system as those from R_4. The rules from R_5', on the other hand, do make use of the catalyst to allow the knight to leave the origin. By putting the lifted rules together with those from R_5', we assure that the knight can move throughout the plane unhindered.

The side effect of having the additional rules from R_5' in Π_5 is that, in the maximally parallel mode, these rules will be applicable once to any configuration. Thus, in Π_5 with maximal parallelism, the knight always makes one move more than in Π_4.

We will now give a more complex example of a P system with generalized multisets which simulates the simultaneous movement of two knights, and which halts when the two knights reach the same position in the plane. We will employ maximal parallelism with $\forall$-applicability, and will prefer to allow the two knights to make multiple moves in a single evolution step. To achieve proper synchronization, we will use rules with priorities, defined as in the case of conventional P systems.

For reasons of readability, we will omit the symbols which have the multiplicity $(0,0)$ when writing the rules. We will also need the notations $E = \{(1,0),(0,1)\}$ and $z \in \mathbb{Z}^2$, $z \neq (0,0)$.

Example 14. Consider the P system $\Pi_6 = (V, T, w_0, R_6)$ with generalized multisets over the GP-group $\mathbb{Z}^2$, with the alphabet $V = \{a, b, \bar{a}, \bar{b}, c, t_1, t_2, t_3, \#\}$, the set of terminal symbols $T = \{c\}$, and the initial configuration $w_0 = t_1^z a^{u_1} b^{u_2}$, where $u_1, u_2 \in \mathbb{Z}^2$ are the initial positions of the two knights. The set of rules of Π_6 is defined as follows:

$$R_6 = R_6^{move} \cup R_6^{comp} \cup R_6^{time} \cup R_6^{trap}, \text{ where}$$
$$R_6^{move} = \{a^u \to a^v, b^u \to b^v \mid a^u \to a^v \in R\},$$
$$R_6^{comp} = \{x^u \to \bar{x}^u \mid x \in \{a,b\}, u \in E\} \cup \{\bar{a}^u \bar{b}^u \to c^u \mid u \in E\},$$
$$R_6^{time} = \{t_1^z \to t_1^z, t_1^z \to t_2^z, t_2^z \to t_3^z\},$$
$$R_6^{trap} = \{t_1^z \bar{x}^u \to \#^z, t_2^z x^u \to \#^z, t_3^z \bar{x}^u \to \#^z, \#^z \to \#^z \mid x \in \{a,b\}, u \in E\},$$

where the rules from R_6^{trap} have priority over all other rules, and R is a set of rules simulating knight movement in a parallel mode without a "catalyst", like, for instance, R_3 or R_4. The rules from R_6^{move} therefore assure the parallel and independent movement of the knights. The rules from R_6^{comp} compare the positions by first rewriting a and b to their barred variants, and by then transforming the pairs of $\bar{a}$ and $\bar{b}$ into instances of c. The rules from R_6^{time} implement a timer which waits for some number of steps by using the rule $t_1^z \to t_1^z$ and which is then successively transformed into t_2 and t_3. The rules from R_6^{trap} control the whole process: if some a or b are rewritten into $\bar{a}$ or $\bar{b}$ while t_1 is still present in the system, the trap symbol $\#$ is added; the trap symbol can never be erased and forces the system to loop indefinitely. Similarly, if not all of a or b have been rewritten to $\bar{a}$ and $\bar{b}$ when t_2 appears in the system, the trap symbol is added. Finally, if after the rules from R_6^{comp} have rewritten some pairs of $\bar{a}$ and $\bar{b}$ into instances of c, there are still some $\bar{a}$ or $\bar{b}$ in the system, the rule $t_3^z \bar{x}^u \to \#^z$, with $x \in \{a,b\}$, will introduce the trap symbol as well.

The rules of Π_6 therefore ensure that the system evolves in two phases: the movement phase, during which the knights are allowed to move, and the comparison phase, during which the knights are no longer allowed to move and their positions are compared one to the other. The multiplicity of c in the halting configuration indicates the position in the plane where the two knights met.

6 Conclusions

In this paper we have considered the challenging problem of defining P systems using generalized multisets that can have multiplicities taken from a totally ordered Abelian group. This definition rises several interesting mathematical questions concerning the applicability and the definition of unbounded group modes. We gave a partial answer to these questions defining some sufficient conditions that allow for defining a behavior similar to the one in the traditional case. Moreover, by considering generalized multisets with multiplicities from the group $(\mathbb{Z}, +)$ restricted to positive values, we obtain the exact behavior of P systems.

Another interesting point is the ability to represent and manipulate the objects directly, without encoding them using natural numbers. This approaches the idea of numerical P systems [12], as our model can be considered as a set of variables updated by rewriting rules.

References

1. Alexandru, A., Ciobanu, G.: Algebraic properties of generalized multisets. In: Proceedings of the 15th International Symposium on Symbolic and Numeric Algorithms for Scientific Computing (SYNASC), pp. 367–374. IEEE (2013)
2. Alhazov, A., Aman, B., Freund, R., Păun, Gh.: Matter and anti-matter in membrane systems. In: Macías-Ramos, L.F., Martínez-del-Amor, M.Á., Păun, Gh., Riscos-Núñez, A., Valencia-Cabrera, L. (eds.) Proceedings of the Twelfth Brainstorming Week on Membrane Computing, pp. 1–26. Fénix Editora, Sevilla (2014)
3. Blizard, W.D.: Multiset theory. Notre Dame J. Formal Logic **30**(1), 36–66 (1989)
4. Blizard, W.D.: Real-valued multisets and fuzzy sets. Fuzzy Sets Syst. **33**, 77–97 (1989)
5. Blizard, W.D.: Negative membership. Notre Dame J. Formal Logic **31**(1), 346–368 (1990)
6. Dassow, J., Păun, Gh.: Regulated Rewriting in Formal Language Theory. Springer, Heidelberg (1989)
7. Holt, D.F., Eick, B., O'Brien, E.A.: Handbook of Computational Group Theory. CRC Press, Boca Raton (2005)
8. Minsky, M.L.: Computation: Finite and Infinite Machines. Prentice Hall, Englewood Cliffs (1967)
9. Pan, L., Păun, Gh.: Spiking neural P systems with anti-matter. Int. J. Comput. Commun. Control **4**(3), 273–282 (2009)
10. Păun, Gh.: Computing with membranes. J. Comput. Syst. Sci. **61**(1), 108–143 (2000). Turku Center for Computer Science-TUCS Report 208, November 1998. http://www.tucs.fi
11. Păun, Gh.: Membrane Computing: An Introduction. Springer, Heidelberg (2002)

12. Păun, Gh., Rozenberg, G., Salomaa, A. (eds.): The Oxford Handbook of Membrane Computing. Oxford University Press, Oxford (2010)
13. Rozenberg, G., Salomaa, A. (eds.): Handbook of Formal Languages. Springer, Heidelberg (1997). 3 Volumes
14. Păun, Gh.: Some quick research topics. http://www.gcn.us.es/files/OpenProblems_bwmc15.pdf
15. The P Systems Website. http://www.ppage.psystems.eu

On the Power of Catalytic P Systems
with One Catalyst

Rudolf Freund[1]([✉]) and Petr Sosík[2]

[1] Faculty of Informatics, TU Wien, Favoritenstraße 9-11, 1040 Vienna, Austria
rudi@emcc.at
[2] Faculty of Philosophy and Science, Research Institute of the IT4Innovations
Centre of Excellence, Silesian University in Opava, Opava, Czech Republic
petr.sosik@fpf.slu.cz

Abstract. We show that catalytic P systems with one catalyst can simulate partially blind register machines and partially blind counter automata. To demonstrate their capability, we also present an example of a P automaton with one catalyst accepting a language with non-semilinear Parikh image as well as an example of a P system with one catalyst generating a non-semilinear vector set.

1 Introduction

Catalytic P systems represent the original model of P systems introduced in the seminal papers [12]. Its key ingredient is a hierarchical structure of membranes μ embedded in the outermost *skin* membrane. Every membrane encloses a *region* possibly containing other membranes and also specific objects (used in the multiset sense). The objects evolve, alone or together with other objects, due to *evolution rules*, being transformed into new objects, eventually also passing through a membrane. The objects evolve in the maximally parallel way, i.e., only non-extendable multisets of rules are applied in each derivation step in every membrane. If the evolution rules only allow the objects to evolve alone, then the system is said to be *non-cooperative*; if there are rules which specify the evolution of several objects together at the same time, then the system is called *cooperative*; an intermediate case is that where a certain object which cannot be changed itself (and therefore is called a *catalyst*) appears together with another object in an evolution rule, then such a rule is called *catalytic*, and P systems using catalytic rules together with non-cooperative rules are called *catalytic P systems*; if only catalytic rules appear, we speak of a *purely catalytic P system*. As it was finally shown in [6], catalytic P systems with two and purely catalytic P systems with three catalysts are computationally complete, i.e., they are able to generate any recursively enumerable set of vectors of natural numbers.

It is a long-standing open problem how to characterize the families of (vectors of) natural numbers generated by catalytic P systems with only one catalyst and by purely catalytic P systems with only two catalysts. In this paper we establish a lower bound for the family of (vectors of) natural numbers generated by catalytic

© Springer International Publishing Switzerland 2015
G. Rozenberg et al. (Eds.): CMC 2015, LNCS 9504, pp. 137–152, 2015.
DOI: 10.1007/978-3-319-28475-0_10

P systems with only one catalyst by showing that such systems can at least simulate partially blind register machines. We also give an example of a P automaton with one catalyst and 165 rules accepting a language with non-semilinear Parikh image. The proof techniques presented in Sects. 3 and 4 imply that the corresponding non-semilinear set of vectors of non-negative integers can be accepted or generated by a catalytic P system with one catalyst in an analogous way. Moreover, we even exhibit an example of a P system with one catalyst generating a non-semilinear vector set, namely $\{(n, m) \mid 0 \leq n, n \leq m \leq 2^n\}$, with only 19 rules, which nicely relates to the result shown in [1], where a P system with two catalysts was exhibited generating this non-semilinear vector set with 14 rules, and the result proved in [2], where a P system with two catalysts generating a more complicated non-semilinear number set, namely $\{2^n \mid n \geq 1\}$, with only 20 rules was constructed.

2 Definitions

For an alphabet V, by V^* we denote the free monoid generated by V under the operation of concatenation, i.e., containing all possible strings over V. The *empty string* is denoted by λ. A *multiset* M with underlying set A is a pair (A, f) where $f : A \to \mathbb{N}$ is a mapping. If $M = (A, f)$ is a multiset then its *support* is defined as $supp(M) = \{x \in A \mid f(x) > 0\}$. A multiset is empty (respectively finite) if its support is the empty set (respectively a finite set). If $M = (A, f)$ is a finite multiset over A and $supp(M) = \{a_1, \ldots, a_k\}$, then it can also be represented by the string $a_1^{f(a_1)} \ldots a_k^{f(a_k)}$ over the alphabet $\{a_1, \ldots, a_k\}$, and, moreover, all permutations of this string precisely identify the same multiset M.

2.1 Register Machines and Multi-Counter Automata

Register machines are well-known universal devices for computing (generating or accepting) sets of vectors of natural numbers.

Definition 1. *A* register machine *is a construct*

$$M = (m, B, l_0, l_h, P)$$

where

- *m is the number of registers,*
- *P is the set of instructions bijectively labeled by elements of B,*
- *$l_0 \in B$ is the initial label, and*
- *$l_h \in B$ is the final label.*

The instructions of M can be of the following forms:

- *$l_1 : (ADD\,(r)\,, l_2, l_3)$, with $l_1 \in B \setminus \{l_h\}$, $l_2, l_3 \in B$, $1 \leq r \leq m$.*
  Increase the value of register r by one, and non-deterministically jump to instruction l_2 or l_3.

- $l_1 : (SUB\,(r)\,,l_2,l_3)$, with $l_1 \in B \setminus \{l_h\}$, $l_2,l_3 \in B$, $1 \leq r \leq m$.
  If the value of register r is not zero then decrease the value of register r by one
  (decrement case) and jump to instruction l_2, otherwise jump to instruction l_3
  (zero-test case).
- $l_h : HALT$.
  Stop the execution of the register machine.

A configuration of a register machine is described by the contents of each
register and by the value of the current label, which indicates the next instruction
to be executed.

In the accepting case, a computation starts with the input of a k-vector of
natural numbers in its first k registers and by executing the first instruction of P
(labeled with l_0); it terminates with reaching the $HALT$-instruction. Without
loss of generality, we may assume all registers to be empty at the end of the
computation.

In the generating case, a computation starts with all registers being empty
and by executing the first instruction of P (labeled with l_0); it terminates with
reaching the $HALT$-instruction and the output of a k-vector of natural numbers
in its first k registers. Without loss of generality, we may assume all registers
$> k$ to be empty at the end of the computation.

Definition 2. A multi-counter automaton is a construct

$$M = (m, T, B, l_0, l_h, P)$$

where

- m is the number of registers,
- T is the input alphabet,
- P is the set of instructions bijectively labeled by elements of B,
- $l_0 \in B$ is the initial label, and
- $l_h \in B$ is the final label.

The instructions of M can be of the following forms:

- $l_1 : (read(a), l_2)$, $l_1 \in B \setminus \{l_h\}$, $l_2 \in B$, $a \in T$. The symbol a is read from the
  input tape, and the computation continues with the instruction labeled by l_2.

- $l_1 : (ADD\,(r)\,,l_2,l_3)$, with $l_1 \in B \setminus \{l_h\}$, $l_2,l_3 \in B$, $1 \leq r \leq m$.
  Increase the value of register r by one, and non-deterministically jump to
  instruction l_2 or l_3.
- $l_1 : (SUB\,(r)\,,l_2,l_3)$, with $l_1 \in B \setminus \{l_h\}$, $l_2,l_3 \in B$, $1 \leq r \leq m$.
  If the value of register r is not zero then decrease the value of register r by one
  (decrement case) and jump to instruction l_2, otherwise jump to instruction l_3
  (zero test case).
- $l_h : HALT$. Stop the execution of the multi-counter automaton.

A multi-counter automaton works with its registers in the same way as a register machine, yet the input now is a string over the input alphabet T, which is read symbol by symbol from the input tape by using the read-operations $l_1 : (read(a), l_2)$. With the accepting computations a set of strings is defined.

We can also generate a set of strings by using write operations which symbol by symbol write the string to be generated on the output tape:

- $l_1 : (read(a), l_2)$, $l_1 \in B \setminus \{l_h\}$, $l_2 \in B$, $a \in T$.

The symbol a is written on the output tape.

2.2   Partially Blind Register Machines and Multi-Counter Automata

We now consider one-way nondeterministic machines which have registers or counters allowed to hold positive or negative integers and which accept by final state with all registers or counters being zero. Such machines are called *blind* if their actions depend on state and input alone and not on the register or counter configuration. They are called *partially blind* if they block when any register or counter is negative (i.e., only non-negative register or counter contents are permissible) but do not know whether or not any of the registers or counters contains zero. Blind multi-counter automata are equivalent in power to the reversal bounded multi-counter machines of Baker and Book [4].

Definition 3. *A partially blind register machine is a construct*

$$M = (m, B, l_0, l_h, P)$$

where

- *m is the number of registers,*
- *P is the set of instructions bijectively labeled by elements of B,*
- *$l_0 \in B$ is the initial label, and*
- *$l_h \in B$ is the final label.*

   The instructions of M can be of the following forms:

- *$l_1 : (ADD\,(r), l_2, l_3)$, with $l_1 \in B \setminus \{l_h\}$, $l_2, l_3 \in B$, $1 \leq r \leq m$.*
  Increase the value of register r by one, and non-deterministically jump to instruction l_2 or l_3.
- *$l_1 : (SUB\,(r), l_2)$, with $l_1 \in B \setminus \{l_h\}$, $l_2 \in B$, $1 \leq r \leq m$.*
  If the value of register r is not zero then decrease the value of register r by one and jump to instruction l_2, otherwise abort the computation.
- *$l_h : HALT$.*
  Stop the execution of the register machine.

Again, a *configuration* of a partially blind register machine is described by the contents of each register and by the value of the current label, which indicates the next instruction to be executed.

A computation works as for a register machine, yet with the restriction that a computation is aborted if one tries to decrement a register which is zero. Moreover, acceptance or generation now also requires all registers (except output registers) to be empty at the end of the computation.

Definition 4. *A partially blind multi-counter automaton is a construct*

$$M = (m, T, B, l_0, l_h, P)$$

where

- *m is the number of registers,*
- *T is the input alphabet,*
- *P is the set of instructions bijectively labeled by elements of B,*
- *$l_0 \in B$ is the initial label, and*
- *$l_h \in B$ is the final label.*

The instructions of M can be of the following forms (with $read(a)$ for acceptance of strings and $write(a)$ for the generation of strings):

- *$l_1 : (read(a), l_2)$, $l_1 \in B \setminus \{l_h\}$, $l_2 \in B$, $a \in T$.*
  The symbol a is read from the input tape, and the computation continueswith the instruction labeled by l_2.
- *$l_1 : write(a)$, $l_1 \in B \setminus \{l_h\}$, $a \in T$.*
  The symbol a is written on the output tape.
- *$l_1 : (ADD(r), l_2, l_3)$, with $l_1 \in B \setminus \{l_h\}$, $l_2, l_3 \in B$, $1 \le r \le m$.*
  Increase the value of register r by one, and non-deterministically jump to instruction l_2 or l_3.
- *$l_1 : (SUB(r), l_2)$, with $l_1 \in B \setminus \{l_h\}$, $l_2 \in B$, $1 \le r \le m$.*
  If the value of register r is not zero, then decrease the value of register r by one and jump to instruction l_2, otherwise abort the computation.
- *$l_h : HALT$.*
  Stop the execution of the register machine.

A computation works as for a multi-counter automaton, yet with the restriction that a computation is aborted if one tries to decrement a counter which is zero. Moreover, acceptance or generation now also requires all counters to be empty at the end of the computation.

2.3 Catalytic P Systems

The following definition cites Definition 4.1 in Chap. 4 of [14].

Definition 5. *An extended catalytic P system of degree $m \ge 1$ is a construct*

$$\Pi = (O, C, \mu, w_1, \ldots, w_m, R_1, \ldots, R_m, i_0) \text{ where}$$

1. *O is the alphabet of objects;*
2. *$C \subseteq O$ is the alphabet of catalysts;*

3. μ is a membrane structure of degree m with membranes labeled in a one-to-one manner with the natural numbers $1, 2, \ldots, m$;

4. $w_1, \ldots, w_m \in O^*$ are the multisets of objects initially present in the m regions of μ;

5. R_i, $1 \le i \le m$, are finite sets of evolution rules over O associated with the regions $1, 2, \ldots, m$ of μ; these evolution rules are of the forms $ca \rightarrow cv$ or $a \rightarrow v$, where c is a catalyst, a is an object from $O \setminus C$, and v is a string from $((O \setminus C) \times \{here, out, in\})^*$;

6. $i_0 \in \{0, 1, \ldots, m\}$ indicates the output region of Π.

The membrane structure and the multisets in Π constitute a *configuration* of the P system; the *initial configuration* is given by the initial multisets $w_1, \ldots, w_m$. A transition between configurations is governed by the application of the evolution rules, which is done in the maximally parallel way, i.e., only applicable multisets of rules which cannot be extended by further rules are to be applied to the objects in all membrane regions.

The application of a rule $u \rightarrow v$ in a region containing a multiset M results in subtracting from M the multiset identified by u, and then in adding the multiset identified by v. The objects can eventually be transported through membranes due to the targets *in* and *out*. We refer to [14] for further details and examples.

The P system continues with applying multisets of rules in the maximally parallel way until there remain no applicable rules in any region of Π. Then the system halts. We consider the number of objects from $O \setminus C$ contained in the output region i_0 at the moment when the system halts as the *result* of the underlying computation of Π. The system is called *extended* since the catalytic objects in C are not counted to the result of a computation. The set of results of all computations possible in Π is called the set of natural numbers *generated by* Π and it is denoted by $N(\Pi)$ if we only count the total number of objects in the output membrane; if we distinguish between the multiplicities of different objects, we obtain a set of vectors of natural numbers denoted by $Ps(\Pi)$.

The problem how to count the catalysts in the case of generating catalytic P systems can be avoided if using external output, i.e., the output is sent to the environment, indicated by $i_0 = 0$.

When the sequence of symbols sent out to the environment from the skin membrane is interpreted as a string, a catalytic P system constitutes a device to generate a string language. If in one computation step of a catalytic P system (with only one catalyst) more than one symbol is sent out to the environment, any permutation of the symbols sent out in this step is considered for building up a final string as a result of a computation.

For the input being taken from the environment, we need an additional target indication *come* as, for example, used in a special variant of communication P systems introduced by Petr Sosík (e.g., see [16]) where no objects are generated or deleted, but the objects may only pass through membranes; $(a, come)$ on the right-hand side of a rule applied in the skin membrane means that the object a is taken into the skin membrane from the environment (all objects there are assumed to be available in an unbounded number). The multiset of all objects taken from the environment during a halting computation then is the multiset accepted by this accepting P system, which in this case we shall call a *P automaton*; the idea of *P automata* was first published in [5] and considered at the same time under the notion of *analysing P systems* in [8]. The set of non-negative integers and the set of (Parikh) vectors of non-negative integers accepted by halting computations in Π are denoted by $N_{aut}(\Pi)$ and $Ps_{aut}(\Pi)$, respectively.

Moreover, a P automaton can also be considered as a device to accept string languages by considering the sequence of symbols taken in during a successful computation as the accepted string. If in one computation step of a catalytic P system (with only one catalyst) more than one symbol is taken in from the environment, any permutation of the symbols taken in during this step is considered for building up a final string as a result of a computation.

Remark 1. As in this paper we only consider catalytic P systems with only one catalyst, without loss of generality, also taking into account the well-known flattening process, e.g., see [7], we can restrict ourselves to one-membrane catalytic P systems with the single catalyst in the skin membrane and with external output, i.e., for obtaining the set of vectors of natural numbers or sets of strings the needed objects are sent out from the skin membrane to the environment; on the other hand, for accepting strings in the automaton case, the input anyway has to be taken from the environment.

Remark 2. Finally, we make the convention that a one-membrane catalytic P system with the single catalyst in the skin membrane and with external output throughout the rest of the paper will be described without specifying the trivial membrane structure or the output region (assumed to be the environment), i.e., we will just write

$$\Pi = (O, \{c\}, T, w, R)$$

where O is the set of objects, c is the single catalyst, T is the input alphabet in case of generating or accepting string languages (and omitted if we only deal with natural numbers), w is the initial input specifying the initial configuration, and R is the set of rules.

3   One-Membrane Catalytic P Systems with One Catalyst Can Simulate Partially Blind Register Machines

We now prove our main result, i.e., we show how the computations of a partially blind register machine can be simulated by a one-membrane P system with one catalyst.

Theorem 1. *Any partially blind register machine can be simulated by a one-membrane catalytic P system with one catalyst.*

Proof. We prove this result for a partially blind register machine accepting sets of vectors of natural numbers. Hence, consider a partially blind register machine

$$M = (m, B, l_0, h, P)$$

with the input vector $(n_1, \ldots, n_k)$ being given in the first $k \leq m$ registers. We divide the set B into disjoint sets, i.e.,

$$B = \bigcup_{1 \leq r \leq m} B_{ADD(r)} \cup \bigcup_{1 \leq r \leq m} B_{SUB(r)} \cup \{h\},$$

where $B_{ADD(r)}$ exactly contains the labels of ADD-instructions and $B_{SUB(r)}$ exactly contains the labels of SUB-instructions on register r.

We now construct a one-membrane catalytic P system with one catalyst

$$
\begin{aligned}
\Pi &= (O, \{c\}, w, R),\\
O &= \{o_r \mid 1 \leq r \leq m\} \cup \{\#, c, d, d'\}\\
&\quad \cup \{o_{r,j} \mid 1 \leq r \leq m,\ 0 \leq j \leq r\}\\
&\quad \cup B \cup \{p_j \mid p \in B,\ 0 \leq j \leq m+1\} \cup \{h_{m+2}\},\\
w &= l_0 c d o_1{}^{n_1} \ldots o_k{}^{n_k},\\
R &= R_s \cup R_\#,
\end{aligned}
$$

where $(n_1, \ldots, n_k)$ is the input vector.

The set of rules R consists of the simulation rules in R_s and the trap rules in $R_\#$; R_s contains both catalytic and non-cooperative rules:

$$
\begin{aligned}
R_s = &\ \{co_r \rightarrow co_{r,0} \mid 1 \leq r \leq m\}\\
&\cup \{cp \rightarrow cp_0 o_r \mid p \in B_{ADD(r)}, 1 \leq r \leq m\}\\
&\cup \{cp_i \rightarrow cp_{i+1} \mid p \in B_{ADD(r)}, 1 \leq r \leq m, 0 \leq i \leq m\}\\
&\cup \{cp_{m+1} \rightarrow cq, cp_{m+1} \rightarrow cs \mid p : (ADD(r), q, s) \in P, 1 \leq r \leq m\}\\
&\cup \{p \rightarrow p_0 \mid p \in B_{SUB(r)}, 1 \leq r \leq m\}\\
&\cup \{co_r \rightarrow co_{r,0}, co_{r,r} \rightarrow c \mid 1 \leq r \leq m\}\\
&\cup \{cp_i \rightarrow cp_{i+1}, o_{r,i} \rightarrow o_{r,i+1} \mid p \in B_{SUB(r)}, 1 \leq r \leq m, 0 \leq i < r\}\\
&\cup \{p_r \rightarrow p_{r+1} \mid p \in B_{SUB(r)}, 1 \leq r \leq m\}\\
&\cup \{cp_i \rightarrow cp_{i+1} \mid p \in B_{SUB(r)}, 1 \leq r \leq m, r+1 \leq i \leq m\}\\
&\cup \{cp_{m+1} \rightarrow cq \mid p : (SUB(r), q) \in P, 1 \leq r \leq m\}\\
&\cup \{h \rightarrow h_0, h_0 \rightarrow h_1, h_1 \rightarrow h_2, cd \rightarrow cd', cd' \rightarrow c\}\\
&\cup \{ch_i \rightarrow ch_{i+1} \mid 2 \leq i \leq m+1\} \cup \{ch_{m+2} \rightarrow c\}
\end{aligned}
$$

$R_\#$ only contains non-cooperative rules:

$$R_\# = \{o_{r,r} \to \# \mid 1 \le r \le m\}$$
$$\cup \{p \to \# \mid p \in B_{ADD(r)}, 1 \le r \le m\}$$
$$\cup \{p_i \to \# \mid p \in B_{ADD(r)}, 1 \le r \le m, 0 \le i \le m+1\}$$
$$\cup \{p_i \to \# \mid p \in B_{SUB(r)}, 1 \le r \le m, 0 \le i \le m+1, i \ne r\}$$
$$\cup \{h_i \to \# \mid 2 \le r \le m+2\}$$
$$\cup \{d' \to \#, \# \to \#\}$$

For all o_r, $1 \le r \le m$, we use the rules

$$co_r \to co_{r,0} \text{ and } o_{r,j} \to o_{r,j+1}, \ 1 \le r \le m, 0 \le j < r,$$

i.e., we count up the second index from 0 to r until we reach $o_{r,r}$.

The simulation of ADD- and SUB-instructions runs through a cycle of $m+3$ steps which allow the catalyst to eliminate one copy of the symbol o_r (whose copies represent the number in register r) in step $r+2$ when simulating a SUB-instruction.

Simulation of $p : (ADD(r), q, s)$, with $p \in B \setminus \{l_h\}$, $q, s \in B$, $1 \le r \le m$:

- $cp \to cp_0 o_{r,1}$, $p \to \#$;
  in the first step, a new copy of o_r is generated;
- $cp_i \to cp_{i+1}$, $p_i \to \#$, $0 \le i \le m$;
  the index i is counted up from 0 to $m+1$;
- $cp_{m+1} \to cq$, $cp_{m+1} \to cs$, $p_{m+1} \to \#$;
  finally, the new label q or s is introduced.

In every step, the catalyst c is kept busy with the program symbols p_i, as otherwise the rules $p_i \to \#$ would enforce the introduction of the trap symbol $\#$.

Simulation of $p : (SUB(r), q)$, with $p \in B \setminus \{l_h\}$, $q \in B$, $1 \le j \le m$:

- $p \to p_0$, $co_r \to co_{r,0}$;
  in the first step, one copy of o_r is marked; the choice is non-deterministic, hence, we have to guarantee that at the end, only the corresponding symbol $o_{r,r}$ can be erased in step $r+2$, whereas any other symbol $o_{x,x}$, $x \ne r$ will be trapped by the rule $o_{x,x} \to \#$; moreover, if no register, even none of the others, is non-empty, the additional symbol d has to be used, which in the next step will be trapped, i.e., the rules $cd \to cd'$ and then $d' \to \#$ would have to be used in the first two steps;
- $cp_i \to cp_{i+1}$, $o_{r,i} \to o_{r,i+1}$, $p_i \to \#$, $0 \le i < r$;
  the indices i of both the program symbol and the object symbol are incremented in every step until r is reached, with the program symbol p_i keeping the catalyst busy;
- $p_r \to p_{r+1}$, $co_{r,r} \to c$, $o_{r,r} \to \#$;
  in step $r+2$ of the cycle, the catalyst c is left free from the program symbol p_r for erasing $o_{r,r}$, which otherwise would have to be trapped, which also happens if the catalyst is misused for another rule $co_x \to co_{x,0}$, $1 \le x \le m$;

- $cp_i \to cp_{i+1}$, $p_i \to \#$, $r+1 \leq i \leq m$;
  the index of the program symbol p_i is incremented until $m+1$ is reached;
- $cp_{m+1} \to cq$, $p_{m+1} \to \#$;
  finally, the next program symbol q is obtained.

In the moment the halt label h has been generated, we have to check that all registers are empty, as the computation should halt if and only if all registers are empty and no wrong guess has been made during the whole computation causing an infinite computation with the trap rule $\# \to \#$.

Final procedure when the halt label h has been generated:

- $h \to h_0$, $cd \to cd'$;
  $h_0 \to h_1$, $cd' \to c$, $d' \to \#$;
  in the first two steps, the additional symbol d is erased;
- $h_1 \to h_2$;
  in the third step, due to maximal parallelism, the catalyst would have to be used with any register symbol o_r using the rule $co_r \to co_{r,0}$;
- $ch_i \to ch_{i+1}$, $h_i \to \#$, $2 \leq i \leq m+1$;
  during the next m steps, any register object $o_{r,r}$ introduced in one of the first three steps has got the chance to be trapped;
- $ch_{m+2} \to c$, $h_{m+2} \to \#$;
  with erasing the final program symbol, the computation in the P system now stops if and only if all registers have been empty at the end and if during the whole simulation no wrong guess has been made.

In sum, we conclude that the P system with its successful computations exactly simulates the successful computations of the given partially blind register machine and therefore accepts the same set of vectors of natural numbers. □

4   One-Membrane Catalytic P Systems with One Catalyst Can Simulate Partially Blind Multi-counter Machines

As an immediate consequence of our main theorem established in Sect. 3, we can easily show the corresponding result for partially blind multi-counter automata:

Theorem 2. *Any partially blind multi-counter automaton can be simulated by a one-membrane catalytic P system with one catalyst.*

Proof. Consider a partially blind multi-counter automaton

$$M = (m, T, B, l_0, l_h, P)$$

with the inputs being strings over T.

A one-membrane catalytic P automaton with one catalyst

$$\Pi = (O, \{c\}, T, w, R)$$

simulating the computations of M can be constructed as in the proof of Theorem 1; the input now is taken in by rules using $(a, come)$, $a \in T$.

The simulation of $p : (read(a), q) \in P$ works like the simulation of an ADD-instruction, yet now starting with $cp \to cp_0(a, come)$.

In that way we accept the string read in with the rules having $(a, come)$ on the right-hand side, which exactly mimics the acceptance of the corresponding string accepted by the underlying partially blind multi-counter automaton.   □

5   Examples

We first construct a one-membrane P automaton with one catalyst accepting the language

$$L = \{a^n b^m \mid 0 \le n, 1 \le m \le 2^n\}$$

whose Parikh image is the corresponding non-semilinear set of vectors of integers

$$Ps(L) = \{(n, m) \mid 0 \le n, 1 \le m \le 2^n\}.$$

The language L is accepted by the partially blind multi-counter automaton

$$M = (2, \{a, b\}, B, l_0, l_h, P)$$

with the set P containing the instructions

$l_0 : (ADD(1), l_1, l_8)$ $l_8 : (read(b), l_9)$
$l_1 : (read(a), l_2)$ $l_9 : (SUB(1), l_{10})$
$l_2 : (SUB(1), l_3)$ $l_{10} : (ADD(2), l_8, l_{11})$
$l_3 : (ADD(2), l_4, l_4)$ $l_{11} : (ADD(2), l_{12}, l_{14})$
$l_4 : (ADD(2), l_2, l_5)$ $l_{12} : (SUB(2), l_{13})$
$l_5 : (SUB(2), l_6)$ $l_{13} : (SUB(2), l_{11})$
$l_6 : (ADD(1), l_5, l_7)$ $l_{14} : (SUB(2), l_h)$
$l_7 : (SUB(1), l_0)$ $l_h : HALT$

A string from $\{a^n b^m \mid 0 \le n, 1 \le m \le 2^n\}$ is accepted as follows:

(a) Instruction l_0 non-deterministically guesses whether all symbols a have been already read from the input tape; in the affirmative case the program continues with step (c).

(b) Instructions l_1 to l_7 read the symbol a and then try to double the contents of counter 1 into counter 2 and copy the contents of counter 2 back to counter 1. Since M is partially blind, it can only guess when the whole contents of counter 1 has been doubled and when the whole contents of counter 2 has been copied back to counter 1. In any case, the program loops back to step (a), with counter 1 now containing any value between 1 and 2^k where k is the number of cycles executed so far.

(c) After n repetitions of the loop formed by instructions l_0 to l_7, after the last execution of instruction l_0, counter 1 contains a randomly guessed value m between 1 and 2^n. Instructions l_8 to l_{10} cyclically read symbols b from the input tape and simultaneously decrement counter 1. Counter 2 serves as an

auxiliary counter only needed for using non-deterministic ADD-instructions to guess when all symbols b have been read and when all counters are empty. On the other hand, we note that if the automaton attempts to decrement counter i, $i \in \{1, 2\}$, after having emptied it, the computation crashes.
(d) If both guesses mentioned in step (c) have been correct, then the whole tape contents has been read and counter 1 is zero. Instructions l_{11} to l_{14} empty counter 2 and the program halts.

The description given above explains that only strings from the language L are accepted by the machine M. Now we can construct a one-membrane catalytic P automaton with one catalyst

$$\Pi = (O, \{c\}, T, w, R),$$
$$O = \{o_1, o_2, \#, c, d, d'\}$$
$$\cup \{o_{1,0}, o_{1,1}, o_{1,2}, o_{2,0}, o_{2,1}, o_{2,2}\}$$
$$\cup B \cup \{p_j \mid p \in B,\ 0 \le j \le 3\} \cup \{h_4\},$$
$$T = \{a, b\},$$
$$w = l_0 c d,$$
$$R = R_s \cup R_{\#}.$$

In accordance with the notation in Sect. 3, we have

$$B_{ADD(1)} = \{l_0, l_6\},$$
$$B_{ADD(2)} = \{l_3, l_4, l_{10}, l_{11}\},$$
$$B_{SUB(1)} = \{l_2, l_7, l_9\},$$
$$B_{SUB(2)} = \{l_5, l_{12}, l_{13}, l_{14}\},$$
$$B = B_{ADD(1)} \cup B_{ADD(2)} \cup B_{SUB(1)} \cup B_{SUB(2)} \cup \{l_1, l_8, l_h\}.$$

Then the set of rules R is exactly constructed as in Sect. 3, except that there are also rules simulating instructions $(read(a), l_2)$ and $l_8 : (read(b), l_9)$ as explained in Sect. 4. Following the description, we obtain that R_s contains 97 rules (35 to simulate ADD-instructions, 10 to simulate $read$-instructions, 44 to simulate SUB-instructions, and 8 for miscellaneous purposes). The set $R_{\#}$ contains 68 rules, altogether it sums up to 165 rules for the whole P automaton. By Theorems 1 and 2, the P automaton Π accepts exactly the language L.

Now we show how we can obtain the vector set

$$S = \{(n, m) \mid 0 \le n, n \le m \le 2^n\}$$

generated by a P system with only one catalyst and 19 rules. In fact, we are simulating a generalized version of partially blind register machines, where each SUB-instruction also allows for a non-deterministic choice as well as for including arbitrary ADD-instructions with each continuing label, e.g., compare with the corresponding model in [2]:

The vector set S is generated by the generalized partially blind register machine

$$M = (4, B, l_0, l_h, P)$$

with the set P containing the generalized instructions:

$l_0 : \left(SUB(1), \{l_0 ADD(2)^2, l_1 ADD(2)^2, l_2 ADD(4)\}\right)$
$l_1 : \left(SUB(2), \{l_1 ADD(1) ADD(4), l_0 ADD(3) ADD(4)\}\right)$
$l_2 : \left(SUB(2), \{l_2, l_h\}\right)$
$l_h : HALT$

We also assume that M already starts with 1 in register 1 and in register 4, thus avoiding to have initial instructions $ADD(1)$ and $ADD(4)$. With instruction l_0, we double the contents of register 1 into register 2, and as we cannot check for zero, we non-deterministically either jump back to l_0 to continue this process or else jump to l_1, where we recopy the contents of register 1 into register 2, and again, as we cannot check for zero, we non-deterministically either jump back to l_1 to continue this process or else jump to l_0 The registers 3 and 4 are the output registers for the first and second component of the output vector (n, m). In order to assure correct halting with zero registers 0 and 1 we have to assume that in the last round register 1 is emptied with l_0 and finally register 2 is emptied with using instruction l_2.

Looking carefully into the proof constructions given in the preceding section we realize that the final cleaning is not necessary to be implemented, because after the elimination of the auxiliary symbol d we may immediately may stop the simulation, as checking the registers 1 and 2 for zero is not a constituting element of the construction in the generating case. Hence, in that case we can save a lot of rules at the end, and in fact are simulating the following program for M instead:

$l_0 : \left(SUB(1), \{l_0 ADD(2)^2, l_1 ADD(2)^2, \lambda ADD(4)\}\right)$
$l_1 : \left(SUB(2), \{l_1 ADD(1) ADD(4), l_0 ADD(3) ADD(4)\}\right)$

Instead of l_h we simply use λ, i.e., we just omit all the symbols and productions involving variants of the halting label. We now implement this reduced program using the proof construction given in the proof of Theorem 1 taking into account the simplifications discussed above, i.e., we can construct the following one-membrane catalytic P system with one catalyst:

$$\Pi = (O, \{c\}, T, w, R),$$
$$O = \{o_1, o_2, o_3, o_4, \#, c, d, d'\}$$
$$\cup \{o_{1,0}, o_{1,1}, o_{1,2}, o_{2,0}, o_{2,1}, o_{2,2}\}$$
$$\cup \{l_{i,j} \mid i \in \{0, 1\}, j \in \{0, 1, 2, 3\}\},$$
$$T = \{o_3, o_4\},$$
$$w = l_0 c d o_1 o_4.$$

R only contains the following 32 rules:

$$R = \{l_0 \to l_{0,0}, l_1 \to l_{1,0}, co_1 \to co_{1,0}, co_2 \to co_{2,0}\}$$
$$\cup \{cl_{0,0} \to cl_{0,1}, o_{1,0} \to o_{1,1}, cl_{1,0} \to cl_{1,1}, o_{2,0} \to o_{2,1}\}$$
$$\cup \{l_{0,1} \to l_{0,2}, co_{1,1} \to c, cl_{0,2} \to cl_{0,3}\}$$
$$\cup \{cl_{0,3} \to cl_0 o_2 o_2, cl_{0,3} \to cl_1 o_2 o_2, cl_{0,3} \to co_4\}$$
$$\cup \{cl_{1,1} \to cl_{1,2}, o_{2,1} \to o_{2,2}, l_{1,2} \to l_{1,3}, co_{2,2} \to c\}$$
$$\cup \{cl_{1,3} \to cl_1 o_1 o_4, cl_{1,3} \to cl_0 o_1 o_3 o_4, cd \to cd', cd' \to c\}$$
$$\cup \{x \to \# \mid x \in \{l_{0,0}, l_{0,2}, l_{0,3}, l_{1,0}, l_{1,1}, l_{1,3}, o_{1,1}, o_{2,2}, d', \#\}\}.$$

The P system constructed above still can be reduced in a considerable way, as we observe that during the whole simulation of the program of the generalized partially blind register machine the situation that both registers are empty can never happen, hence, we do not need the auxiliary symbol d and its derivative d'. Moreover, this also allows us to reduce the length of the cycles from 5 to 3, which yields the much smaller P system only needing 19 rules:

$$\Pi = (O, \{c\}, T, w, R),$$
$$O = \{o_1, o_2, o_3, o_4, o_{1,1}, o_{2,1}, o_{2,2}\#, c\} \cup \{l_{i,j} \mid i \in \{0,1\}, j \in \{1,2\}\},$$
$$T = \{o_3, o_4\},$$
$$w = l_0 co_1 o_4,$$
$$R = \{l_0 \to l_{0,1}, l_1 \to l_{1,1}, co_1 \to co_{1,1}, co_2 \to co_{2,1}\}$$
$$\cup \{l_{0,1} \to l_{0,2}, co_{1,1} \to c, o_{1,1} \to \#, \# \to \#\}$$
$$\cup \{cl_{0,2} \to cl_0 o_2 o_2, cl_{0,2} \to cl_1 o_2 o_2, cl_{0,2} \to co_4, l_{0,2} \to \#\}$$
$$\cup \{cl_{1,1} \to cl_{1,2}, l_{1,1} \to \#, o_{2,1} \to o_{2,2}\}$$
$$\cup \{co_{2,2} \to c, o_{2,2} \to \#, l_{1,2} \to l_1 o_1 o_4, l_{1,2} \to l_0 o_1 o_3 o_4\}.$$

We finally observe that the final configuration of a halting computation only contains terminal symbols, i.e., as common in usual P systems generating sets of (vectors of) numbers we need not specify T. Moreover, we can save all trap rules generating the trap symbol $\#$ if we take the model of toxic objects, see [3]; in this case only 14 rules remain.

6   Conclusion

In this paper we have shown a lower bound for the computational power of catalytic P systems with only one catalyst – at least, these systems are able to simulate partially blind register machines and partially blind multi-counter automata. Yet the proof technique we have applied here so far could not be applied to purely catalytic P systems with two catalysts. The reason is the following: inspecting carefully the proof of Theorem 1, one can observe that non-cooperative rules are essential especially during the simulation of SUB-instructions. Simultaneously, when a wrong rule is chosen non-deterministically, again non-cooperative rules are used to generate the trap symbol # in the same computational step. In the case of purely catalytic system with two catalysts, all these non-cooperative rules have to be replaced by catalytic rules with the second catalyst. Hence, there would be no guarantee of producing the trap symbol # due to the existence of two rules using the second catalyst, while only one of them (randomly chosen) can be executed.

The problem of the upper bound for the computational power of catalytic P systems with one catalyst, as well as that for purely catalytic P systems with two catalysts, still remains open.

Acknowledgements. This work was supported by the European Regional Development Fund in the IT4Innovations Centre of Excellence project (CZ.1.05/1.1.00/02.0070), and by the Silesian University in Opava under the Student Funding Scheme, project SGS/6/2014.

References

1. Alhazov, A., Freund, R.: Small P systems defining non-semilinear sets. In: Adamatzky, A. (ed.) Automata, Universality, Computation. ECC, vol. 12, pp. 185–221. Springer, Heidelberg (2015)
2. Alhazov, A., Freund, R.: Small catalytic P systems. In: Workshop on Membrane Computing at UCNC, Auckland (2015)
3. Alhazov, A., Freund, R.: P systems with toxic objects. In: Gheorghe, M., Rozenberg, G., Salomaa, A., Sosík, P., Zandron, C. (eds.) CMC 2014. LNCS, vol. 8961, pp. 99–125. Springer, Heidelberg (2014)
4. Baker, B.S., Book, R.V.: Reversal-bounded multipushdown machines. J. Comput. System Sci. **3**, 315–332 (1974)
5. Csuhaj-Varjú, E., Vaszil, Gy.: P automata or purely communicating accepting P systems. In: Păun, Gh., Rozenberg, G., Salomaa, A., Zandron, C. (eds.) WMC 2002. LNCS, vol. 2597, pp. 219–233. Springer, Heidelberg (2003)
6. Freund, R., Kari, L., Oswald, M., Sosík, P.: Computationally universal P systems without priorities: two catalysts are sufficient. Theor. Comput. Sci. **330**(2), 251–266 (2005)
7. Freund, R., Leporati, A., Mauri, G., Porreca, A.E., Verlan, S., Zandron, C.: Flattening in (Tissue) P systems. In: Alhazov, A., Cojocaru, S., Gheorghe, M., Rogozhin, Y., Rozenberg, G., Salomaa, A. (eds.) CMC 2013. LNCS, vol. 8340, pp. 173–188. Springer, Heidelberg (2014)
8. Freund, R., Oswald, M.: A short note on analysing P systems. Bull. EATCS **78**, 231–236 (2002)
9. Gheorghe, M., Rozenberg, G., Salomaa, A., Sosík, P., Zandron, C. (eds.): CMC 2014. LNCS, vol. 8961. Springer, Heidelberg (2014)
10. Sheila, A.: Greibach: remarks on blind and partially blind one-way multicounter machines. Theor. Comput. Sci. **7**, 311–324 (1978)
11. Minsky, M.L.: Computation: Finite and Infinite Machines. Prentice Hall, Englewood Cliffs (1967)
12. Păun, Gh.: Computing with membranes. J. Comput. Syst. Sci. **61**, 108–143 (2000). also see TUCS Report 208, 1998, www.tucs.fi
13. Păun, Gh.: Membrane Computing. An Introduction. Springer, Heidelberg (2002)

14. Păun, Gh., Rozenberg, G., Salomaa, A. (eds.): The Oxford Handbook of Membrane Computing. Oxford University Press, New York (2010)
15. Rozenberg, G., Salomaa, A. (eds.): Handbook of Formal Languages, vol. 3. Springer, Heidelberg (1997)
16. Sosík, P., Matýsek, J.: Membrane computing: when communication is enough. In: Calude, C.S., Dinneen, M.J., Peper, F. (eds.) UMC 2002. LNCS, vol. 2509, pp. 264–275. Springer, Heidelberg (2002)
17. The P Systems Website: ppage.psystems.eu

An Integrated Model Checking Toolset
for Kernel P Systems

Marian Gheorghe[1]([⊠]), Savas Konur[1], Florentin Ipate[2,3], Laurentiu Mierla[2,3],
Mehmet E. Bakir[4], and Mike Stannett[4]

[1] School of Electrical Engineering and Computer Science,
University of Bradford, Bradford BD7 1DP, UK
{m.gheorghe,s.konur}@bradford.ac.uk
[2] Department of Computer Science, University of Bucharest,
Street Academiei nr. 14, 010014 Bucharest, Romania
[3] Department of Computer Science, University of Pitesti,
Street Targul din Vale, nr.1, 110040 Pitesti, Arges, Romania
florentin.ipate@ifsoft.ro, laurentiu.mierla@gmail.com
[4] Department of Computer Science, University of Sheffield, Sheffield S1 4DP, UK
mebakir1@sheffield.ac.uk

Abstract. *P* systems are the computational models introduced in the
context of membrane computing, a computational paradigm within the
more general area of unconventional computing. *Kernel P (kP)* systems
are defined to unify the specification of different variants of P systems,
motivated by challenging theoretical aspects and the need to model different
problems. kP systems are supported by a software framework,
called kPWORKBENCH, which integrates a set of related simulation and
verification methodologies and tools. In this paper, we present an extension
to kPWORKBENCH with a new model checking framework supporting
the formal verification of kP system models. This framework supports
both LTL and CTL properties. To make the property specification an
easier task, we propose a property language, composed of natural language
statements. We demonstrate our proposed methodology with an
example.

1 Introduction

Membrane computing is a computational paradigm, within the more general
area of unconventional computing [29], inspired by the structure and behaviour
of eukaryotic cells. The formal models introduced in this context are called
membrane systems or P systems. After their introduction [27], membrane systems
have been widely investigated for computational properties and complexity
aspects, but also as a model for various applications [28]. The introduction of
different variants of P systems has been motivated by challenging theoretical
aspects, but also by the need to model different problems. An account of the
theoretical developments is presented in [28], a set of general applications can be
found in [6], whereas specific applications in systems and synthetic biology are

© Springer International Publishing Switzerland 2015
G. Rozenberg et al. (Eds.): CMC 2015, LNCS 9504, pp. 153–170, 2015.
DOI: 10.1007/978-3-319-28475-0_11

provided in [11,20,24] and some of the future challenges are presented in [15]. More recently, applications in optimisations and graphics [16] and synchronisation of distributed systems [9] have been developed.

In many cases the specification of a certain system requires features, constraints or types of behaviour which are not always provided by a single formal model. It is very helpful to have some flexibility with modelling approaches. This flexibility might come from the way new features can be added or old ones are redefined. This approach might lead to a proliferation of various variants of the model. Software tools supporting the most used P system models have been conceived. They come with a set of specification languages, known generically as P–Lingua [26]. P–Lingua aims to keep the syntax as close as possible to the original models and provides a simulation platform for all these models and a consistent user interface environment, called MeCoSim [25].

An alternative approach has been considered, by defining a specification language that allows to relatively easily specify the most utilised P system models. The newly defined concept of *kernel P systems* (*kP systems*) has been introduced in order to provide a theoretical support for this language. A revised version of the model and the specification language can be found in [12] and its usage to specify the 3-colouring problem and a comparison to another solution provided in a similar context [8], is described in [14]. The kP systems have been also used to specify and analyse, through formal verification, synthetic biology systems, e.g. genetic gates [21,22].

Kernel P systems are supported by a software framework, kPWORKBENCH, which integrates a set of related simulation and verification methodologies and tools. In this paper, we present a new model checking framework that we have developed in support of formal verification of kernel P system models. The framework supports both LTL and CTL properties by making use of the SPIN and NuSMV model checkers. To make the property specification an easier task, we propose a property language, composed of *natural language* statements. We demonstrate our proposed methodology on the subset sum problem.

The paper consists of five sections. Section 2 introduces the basic concepts related to kP systems. Section 3 discusses the previous model checking approach, and presents the new model checking methodology. Section 4 applies our proposed methodology to an instance of the subset sum problem. Section 5 briefly discusses the applicability of our approach to the analysis of biological systems. Finally, Sect. 6 draws conclusions and provides some future research directions.

2   Kernel P Systems

A kernel P system is a formal model that uses some well-known features of existing P systems and also includes some new concepts and, more importantly, it provides a coherent framework integrating all these elements. So, it can be considered as a unifying framework allowing to express different variants of P systems within the same formalism [2,10,12].

2.1   KP–Lingua

The kP system models are described in a machine readable language, called *kP–Lingua* [10]. Below, we illustrate the kP systems concepts with an example, which is slightly adjusted from [2,10].

Example 1. A type definition in kP–Lingua.

```
type C1 {
    choice {
        > 2b : 2b -> b, a(C2) .
          b ->  2b .
    }
}
type C2 {
    choice {
        a -> a, {b, 2c}(C1) .
    }
}
m1 {2x, b} (C1) - m2 {x} (C2) .
```

Above, C1, C2 denote two compartment types, which are instantiated as m1, m2, respectively. m1 starts with the initial multiset 2x, b and m2 starts with x. The rules of C1 are chosen non-deterministically, only one at a time – this is achieved by the use of the key word choice. The first rule is fired only when its guard becomes true; in other words, only when the current multiset has at least three b's. This rule also sends an a to the instance of C2 that is linked. In the type C2, there is only one rule to be fired, which happens only when there is an a in the compartment C1.

2.2   kPWorkbench

The specifications written in kP–Lingua are supported by a software platform, kPWORKBENCH, which integrates a set of tools and translators that bridge several target specifications that we employ for kP system models, written in kP-Lingua. kPWORKBENCH permits *simulation* and *formal verification* of kP system models using several simulation and verification tools and methods.

The framework features a native simulator [3,23], allowing the simulation of kP system models. In addition, it also integrates the FLAME simulator [7], a general purpose large scale agent based simulation environment, based on a method that allows to express kP systems as a set of communicating X-machines [17].

kPWORKBENCH's model checking environment permits the formal verification of kernel P system models. The framework supports both *Linear Temporal Logic (LTL)* and *Computation Tree Logic (CTL)* properties by making use of the SPIN [18] and NuSMV [5] model checkers. In order to facilitate the formal specification, kPWORKBENCH features a property language, called *kP-Queries*, comprising a list of natural language statements representing formal property patterns, from which the formal syntax of the SPIN and NuSMV formulas are automatically generated.

3   Verification of kP Systems

The application scope of P systems has recently broadened from contextual grammars to synthetic biology. This has unsurprisingly increased the efforts for establishing formal verification, in particular model checking, methods and methodologies for various P systems [4,13,19]. These successful attempts were mainly concerned with specific variants bound to an array of constraints, e.g. a limited feature set and a basic set of properties.

However, the efforts for a comprehensive, integrated and automated verification approach for general and unified languages, e.g. kP systems, are limited. This is mainly due to the computational challenges imposed by such formalisms. These bring in a lot of complications as they feature a dynamic structure by preserving the structure changing rules such as membrane division, dissolution and link creation/destruction. A state defined in this expansive context is consequently variable in size. It is, however, a challenging task to find the proper projections of such complex abstractions in model checking tools, as they require a fixed sized pre-allocated data model.

Table 1. The LTL and CTL property constructs currently supported by the kP-Queries file

Property pattern	Language construct	LTL formula	CTL formula
Next	next p	X p	EX p
Existence	eventually p	F p	EF p
Absence	never p	$\neg(F\ p)$	$\neg(EF\ p)$
Universality	always p	G p	AG p
Recurrence	infinitely-often p	G F p	AG EF p
Steady-State	steady-state p	F G p	AF AG p
Until	p until q	p U q	A $(p\ U\ q)$
Response	p followed-by q	G $(p \rightarrow F\ q)$	AG $(p \rightarrow EF\ q)$
Precedence	q preceded-by p	$\neg(\neg p\ U\ (\neg p \wedge q))$	$\neg(E\ (\neg p\ U\ (\neg p \wedge q)))$

3.1   Previous Approach

In [10] we presented our initial efforts towards an integrated model checking approach, which permits formal properties to be verified against kP system models, specified in kP-Lingua, using the SPIN model checker. The kP-Lingua representations of the models are automatically translated into the SPIN's modelling language PROMELA. In order to ease the intricate and complex process of building logical formulas, the approach also features a *natural language query (NLQ)* tool, automatically converting predefined natural language queries into the corresponding PROMELA representation of temporal logic (LTL) formulas, through graphical user interface (GUI) elements.

In this approach, a strategy is devised to find a projection and mapping between a kP-Lingua model and the PROMELA representation. For some entities, e.g. multiset of objects, compartments, guards, rules, etc., finding a direct correspondence is possible. However, concepts such as maximal parallelism and membrane division are more difficult to deal with. To handle such cases, the following solution is devised [10]: "We collapse individual instructions (to atomic blocks) to the highest degree permitted by SPIN, minimizing the so-called intermediate state space which is irrelevant to a P system computation; and secondly, we appoint the states relevant to our model explicitly, using a global flag (i.e. a Boolean variable), raised when all processes have completed a computational step. Hence, we make a clear distinction between states that are pertinent to the formal investigation and the ones which should be discarded. This contrast is in turn reflected by the temporal logic formulae, which require adjustment to an orchestrated context where only a narrow subset of the global state space is pursued."

Although this approach employs useful strategies for both automatic translation of models and properties, it has some drawbacks: (i) It reformulates LTL properties into their corresponding PROMELA specifications. The translation requires introducing some special predicates into the state expressions. This results in long and complex state expressions, and hence formulas, which require manual manipulation of the corresponding translation in order to build complex queries with nested temporal operators. (ii) It only considers the use of SPIN model checker and hence only focuses on verifying LTL properties. Since there is no CTL model checker, e.g. NUSMV, integrated into the tool, we cannot verify CTL properties. (iii) According to some user feedbacks, the use of the NLQ tool has not been very practical. The tool has two user interfaces: one for constructing state expressions and one for constructing the actual properties. A property building task requires traversing between two interfaces, causing usability inconveniences.

Table 2. The LTL and CTL property constructs currently supported by the kP-Queries file

Pattern	Spin – LTL Translation	NuSMV – LTL Translation	NuSMV – CTL Translation
Next	ltl p1 { X (!pInS U (p && pInS)) }	LTLSPEC X p	SPEC EX p
Existence	ltl p1 { <> (p && pInS) }	LTLSPEC F p	SPEC EF p
Absence	ltl p1 { !(<> (p && pInS)) }	LTLSPEC !(F p)	SPEC !(EF p)
Universality	ltl p1 { [] (p || pInS) }	LTLSPEC G p	SPEC AG p
Recurrence	ltl p1 { [] (<> (p && pInS) || !pInS) }	LTLSPEC G (F p)	SPEC AG (EF p)
Steady-State	ltl p1 { <> ([] (p || !pInS) && pInS) }	LTLSPEC F (G p)	SPEC AF (AG p)
Until	ltl p1 { (p || !pInS) U (q && pInS) }	LTLSPEC p U q	SPEC A [p U q]
Response	ltl p1 { [] ((p -> <> (q && pInS)) || !pInS) }	LTLSPEC G (p -> F q)	SPEC AG (p -> EF q)
Precedence	ltl p1 { !((!p || !pInS) U (!p && q && pInS)) }	LTLSPEC !(!p U (!p & q))	SPEC !(E [!p U (!p & q)])

3.2   The New Approach

To tackle these drawbacks, a new model checking environment for kPWORKBENCH has been developed, including a property language (with an editor) for the specification of queries[1] to be verified against kP-Lingua models. An EBNF grammar for this language is defined for the most common property patterns and a parser supporting the new property specification language has been implemented.

The property language editor interacts with the kP-Lingua model in question and allows users to directly access the native elements in the model, which results in less verbose and shorter state expressions, and hence more comprehensible formulas. These features and the natural language like syntax of the language make the property construction much easier compared to our previous approach.

The new model checking environment supports both SPIN and NUSMV model checkers. The translations from a kP-Lingua representation to the corresponding SPIN and NUSMV inputs are automatically performed. The property language allows specifying the target logical formalism (i.e. LTL and CTL) for the different properties, without placing a requirement on a specific model checker, the same set of properties being able to be reused in various model checking experiments.

Targeting flexibility, expressivity and model checking language independence, the new verification approach for kP-Lingua models enriches kPWORKBENCH with a mechanism for defining *kP-Queries* files, which are especially designed for the purpose of being used to verify kP-Lingua models. The format of kP-Queries file is supported by an intuitive, coherent and integrated property specification language, allowing the construction of queries involving kP-Lingua model entities and targeting the LTL and CTL formalisms.

The new introduced property specification language aims to be independent from any target model checking language, yet integrating elements from LTL and CTL logical formalisms in a uniform way, such that property patterns from a set of most commonly used ones are considered in conjunction with two special keywords, *ltl* and *ctl*, giving the queries a formal context to be represented in. This approach also addresses one other limitation of the previous one, allowing the specification of nested properties in constructing more complex queries. Complex state expressions can be formulated by using relational and Boolean operators, while the only currently supported atomic operands are the object multiplicities of kP-Lingua model membranes. Table 1 summarizes the currently considered property patterns, together with the corresponding language construct, LTL and CTL representations.

Aiming for a generic and reusable property language, kP-Queries files do not embody any constructs that pertain to specific model checking languages, nor do they specify the target translation language the queries will be represented in. kP-Queries can be associated with kP-Lingua models, in conjunction with them serving as input for the translation engines defined in kPWORKBENCH. The properties specified in a formalism which is not supported by the target model checking language are simply discarded, only the appropriate ones being considered for translation.

---

[1] In the paper, we use the terms property and query interchangeably.

kPWORKBENCH currently integrates translation mechanisms for two targets: PROMELA and SMV, the modeling languages of the model checkers SPIN and NuSMV, respectively. While both PROMELA and SMV allow the specification of LTL properties, the latter also supports the CTL formalism.

As kP systems modelled in kP-Lingua are automatically translated into a computationally equivalent representation targeting a model checking language, the verification procedure should take into account one subtle difference concerning the modelling procedure and the underlying formalism of the two computationally equivalent models. The translation of queries specified into the kP-Queries files needs to be formulated in such a way that we target only P system states (i.e. the states in which the computational step of the P system is completed), regardless of the various intermediate states required by the formalism of the translated model. This is the case for the translations targeting the SPIN model checker, as the translated model and properties are required to accommodate a special variable and state expressions over it, respectively. Namely, each LTL formula should be translated to SPIN using a special predicate, $pInS$, showing that the current SPIN state represents a P system configuration (the predicate is true when a SPIN configuration reaches a P system state on the execution path) or represents an intermediate state (it is false if intermediary steps are executed) – see [19] for the theoretical validation of this translation. On the other hand, the translations targeting NuSMV does not require a special treatment from the point of view of differentiating between source and destination model states. Table 2 depicts the translations of the above considered property patterns, targeting both SPIN and NuSMV, emphasizing also the use of the special Boolean variable $pInS$.

The implementation of the domain specific language used by kP-Queries files relies on ANTLR (ANother Tool for Language Recognition) [1] for its state of the art parser generator capabilities. The EBNF grammar of the property specification language serves as input for ANTLR in order to automatically generate the corresponding syntactical and semantic analyzers, together with the necessary data structures for representing the resulted *abstract syntax tree* (AST) and the underlying functionality of traversing it.

As the abstract syntax tree resulted from the parsing process directly reflects the structure of the grammar and its semantic model, a well defined domain model layer was introduced for supporting the internal representation of the data, thus decoupling the functionality relying on this data structure from the underlaying components of the parsing framework. By projecting the abstract syntax tree representation into a semantically equivalent internal data structure, a separation of concerns is achieved with the benefit of gaining greater flexibility in being able to independently change the parsing strategy from the property translation functionality. The projection of the abstract syntax tree to the internal data structure representation is achieved by the implementation of a model builder mechanism which is able to traverse the hierarchical representation of the AST, having at the same time the responsibility of semantically validating the kP-Queries files.

The new model checking module for kPWORKBENCH is especially designed around the concepts of maintainability and extensibility, following the SOLID programming principles [31] in achieving this goal. The entities composing the internal data representation, besides of playing the role of *data transfer objects* (DTO), are augmented with a minimal yet very powerful functionality for allowing them to be treated in an uniform way. The internal data structure is a tree-like hierarchical representation, augmented with the behavior required by the *Visitor design pattern* [32], aiming for *separation of concerns* (i.e. separating the translation strategies form the internal data structure they operate on) and following the *open/closed principle* (i.e. the set of translation strategies is open to be extended while the internal data structure is closed to further modifications).

The design pattern used in the model checking module implementation treats the nodes from the internal data representation as *visitable entities*, capable of accepting *visitors* and requests to visit them. Each *visitor* implementation holds specific functionality for visiting every single node. The model checking module implements its property translation strategies as visitors, being capable of translating every node of the internal representation of the properties into the corresponding form required by the target model checking language. By using this mechanism, each translation strategy implementation is independent, localized and coherent. Furthermore, a Singleton [30] implementation of a translation manager is able to receive an internal representation of a property together with a translation target and to perform the translation of the property by instantiating the corresponding visitor and delegate it to visit the property data structure.

4   Case Studies

4.1   The Subset Sum Problem

This case, the subset sum problem, will illustrate most of the features of the kP–Lingua, the presence of compartments, guarded rules and flexible execution strategies. The subset sum problem is stated as follows [2]:

Given a finite set $A = \{a_1, \ldots, a_n\}$, of n elements, where each element a_i has an associated weight, w_i, and a constant k, it is requested to determine whether or not there exists a subset $B \subseteq A$ such that $w(B) = k$, where $w(B) = \sum_{a_i \in B} w_i$. The following kP-Lingua code represents a model, where $n = 7$, $w(A) = \{3, 25, 8, 23, 5, 14, 30\}$ and $k = 55$.

```
type Main {

choice {
= 55x: a -> {yes, halt} (Output) .
> 55x: a -> # .
        }

choice {
```

```
!r1: a -> [a, r1][3x, a, r1] .
!r2: a -> [a, r2][25x, a, r2] .
!r3: a -> [a, r3][8x, a, r3] .
!r4: a -> [a, r4][23x, a, r4] .
!r5: a -> [a, r5][5x, a, r5] .
!r6: a -> [a, r6][14x, a, r6] .
!r7: a -> [a, r7][30x, a, r7] .
        }
}

type Output {
step -> 2step .
!yes: 9step -> no, halt .
}

main {a} (Main) - output {step} (Output) .
```

The model has two compartment types, **Main** and **Output**, and two compartments **output**, and **main**. The first rule of **Main** is a rewrite communication rule, which is guarded by {= 55x}. If this guard is satisfied, it will produce a **yes** and a **halt** object in **Output**, which is a positive answer for the problem. The second rule is a structure changing rule which results in the compartment dissolution. These two rules are encapsulated within a **choice** block, which means that at each step only one of the rules is selected and executed, and the selection is non-deterministic. The second **choice** block consists of seven division rules, each of which is guarded with !r_i, which aims to prevent any of the successor compartment to execute the same rule. Each rule divides the active compartment into two new compartments of the type **Main**. New compartments will inherit the multiset objects of their parent. In addition, the multiset objects on the right hand side of the rule will pass to the corresponding child compartment. For example, if the first division rule is selected, then the compartment will be divided into two new compartments and both will inherit their parent objects. In addition, one of them will have the {a, r1} objects, while the other one will have {3x, a, r1}.

The compartment type **Output** has been added just to collect the results. We have extended the model to be able to produce a negative answer, **no**, if the system reaches its maximum number of steps and has not produced a positive answer, **yes**, so far. **Output** has two rewriting rules: the first rule increments the multiplicity of the **step** counter by one at each step, and the second rule produces a **halt** and a **no** object, if a **yes** object has not been produced so far, and the **step** counter is 9. In this case, both rules are executed (or at least the system attempts to execute both), in the given order.

kPWORKBENCH automatically converts the kP-Lingua model into the corresponding input languages of SPIN, and NuSMV. In order to verify that the Subset Sum problem works as desired, we have constructed a set of properties specified in kP-Queries, listed in Table 3. A subset of these properties are verified

Table 3. List of properties derived from the property language and their representations in different formats.

Prop.	Pattern	(i) Informal, (ii) Formal, (iii) Spin – LTL, (iv) NuSMV – LTL and (v) NuSMV – CTL Representations
1	Response	(i) *The execution of the computation will be followed by a halt* (ii) output.halt = 0 **followed-by** output.halt >0 (iii) ltl prop1 { [] ((m1[0].x[2] == 0 -><>(m1[0].x[2] >0 && state == step_complete) || state != step_complete) || state != step_complete) } (iv) LTLSPEC G (output.halt = 0 ->F output.halt >0) (v) SPEC AG (output.halt = 0 ->EF output.halt >0)
2	Existence	(i) *The computation will eventually halt* (ii) **eventually** output.halt >0 (iii) ltl prop1 {<>(m1[0].x[2] >0 && state == step_complete)} (iv) LTLSPEC F output.halt >0 (v) SPEC EF output.halt >0
3	Until	(i) *The computation will eventually halt with either a 'yes' or 'no' result* (ii) output.halt = 0 **until** (output.halt >0 and (output.yes >0 or output.no >0)) (iii) ltl prop1 { (m1[0].x[2] == 0 || state != step_complete) U ((m1[0].x[2] >0 && (m1[0].x[3] >0 || m1[0].x[1] >0)) && state == step_complete) } (iv) LTLSPEC output.halt = 0 U (output.halt >0 & (output.yes >0 | output.no >0)) (v) SPEC A [output.halt = 0 U (output.halt >0 & (output.yes >0 | output.no >0))]
4	Until	(i) *The computation will halt within n+2 steps (for n=7)* (ii) output.halt = 0 and output.step <= 9) **until** (output.halt >0 and output.step <=9) (iii) ltl prop1 { ((m1[0].x[2] == 0 && m1[0].x[0] <= 9) || state != step_complete) U ((m1[0].x[2] > 0 && m1[0].x[0] <= 9) && state == step_complete) } (iv) (output.halt = 0 & output.step <= 9) U (output.halt >0 & output.step <= 9) (v) A [(output.halt = 0 & output.step <= 9) U (output.halt > 0 & output.step <= 9)]
5	Steady-state	(i) *The system will halt in the steady-state with a 'yes' or 'no' result* (ii) **steady-state** ((output.yes >0) or (output.no >0) implies (output.halt >0)) (iii) ltl prop1 { <>([] (((m1[0].x[3] >0 || m1[0].x[1] >0) ->m1[0].x[2] >0) || state != step_complete) && state == step_complete) } (iv) LTLSPEC F (G ((output.yes >0 | output.no >0) ->output.halt >0)) (v) SPEC AF (AG ((output.yes >0 | output.no >0) ->output.halt >0))
6	Absence	(i) *The computation will never halt with a 'no' result* (ii) **never** (output.halt >0 and (output.no >0)) (iii) ltl prop1 { !(<>((m1[0].x[2] >0 && (m1[0].x[3] == 0 && m1[0].x[1] >0)) && state == step_complete)) } (iv) LTLSPEC !(F (output.halt >0 & (output.yes = 0 & output.no >0))) (v) SPEC !(EF (output.halt >0 & (output.yes = 0 & output.no >0)))
7	Existence	(i) *A 'yes' result is eventually observed within no more than three steps* (ii) **eventually** (output.yes >0 and output.step <= 3) (iii) ltl prop1 { <>((m1[0].x[3] >0 && m1[0].x[0] <= 3) && state == step_complete) } (iv) LTLSPEC F (output.yes >0 & output.step <= 3) (v) SPEC EF (output.yes >0 & output.step <= 3)
8	Existence	(i) *A 'yes' result is eventually observed after more than three steps* (ii) **eventually** (output.yes >0 and output.step >3) (iii) ltl prop1 { <>((m1[0].x[3] >0 && m1[0].x[0] >3) && state == step_complete) } (iv) LTLSPEC F (output.yes >0 & output.step >3) (v) SPEC EF (output.yes >0 & output.step >3)
9	Precedence	(i) *A 'yes' result is always observed before a 'no' result* (ii) output.yes >0 **preceded-by** output.no >0 (iii) ltl prop1 { !((!(m1[0].x[3] >0) || state != step_complete) U (!(m1[0].x[3] >0) && m1[0].x[1] >0 && state == step_complete)) } (iv) LTLSPEC !(!(output.yes >0) U (!(output.yes >0) & output.no >0)) (v) SPEC !(E [!(output.yes >0) U (!(output.yes >0) & output.no >0)])

in [10] using the model checker SPIN using the old verification approach. Here, we use the new procedure of verifying kP-Lingua models for investigating the validity of a set of properties.

The applied pattern types are given in the second column of the table. For each property we provide the following information; **(i)** informal description of each kP-Query, **(ii)** the formal kP-Query, **(iii)** the translated form of the kP-Query into the SPIN modelling language, PROMELA, and into the **(iv)** CTL, and **(v)** LTL forms of the NuSMV specification. The results of all queries are positive.

In the following, we briefly describe why all properties listed in the Table 3 are true. After all division rules are applied, $2^7 = 128$ compartments of the type Main are generated. The contents of each compartment are determined by their ancestors. Here, we try to find out if any of the child compartments includes 55 x objects. Since there are more than one compartment with exactly 55 x objects, the output produces a yes and a halt object. If none of the compartments included 55 x objects, then the output would produce a no and a halt object (without producing a yes object). Hence, a halt object is always produced. This explains why Properties 1, 2, 3, and 5 are true. Property 4 is also true, since the algorithm is a faithful linear time solution and the computation ends at most within $n + 2$ steps. Property 6 tests that there will never be a no object before a yes object is produced. Since there is at least one child compartment which has 55 x, a yes will be triggered first. Thus, a no object is never produced before it. In other words, a yes object is always produced before a no object. Hence, Properties 6 and 9 are true. Property 7 is also true, because after the first step, the division rules will be applied and a child compartment will be created. Then, the child compartments that have 55 x will trigger a yes object in the output. After the production of a yes object, it will remain inside the output compartment. This explains why Property 8 returns true.

As illustrated in Table 3, the intuitive and coherent form of kP-Queries lead to relatively short, yet natural language-like property specifications, which are independent from any specific model checking language. This approach brings the flexibility of independently considering the particularities of each model checker when translating properties, without the need to embody any of the required aspects into the specification language of kP-Queries. Being associated to kP-Lingua models, kP-Queries facilitates the construction of queries against the entities of the model and automatically considering the translation of these entities without user interaction.

Furthermore, unlike the previous one, the new verification approach is not bound to the usage of a graphical user interface. Although by using a GUI the property specification process is more intuitive, it is considered more tedious by most users aiming to script and automate a verification task. In order to address this usability problem, the process of using the new kPWORKBENCH verification approach is also assisted by a simple GUI, guiding non-expert users through the entire procedure, while empowering experienced users with a flexible and expressive mechanism for using the verification framework from a command line interface or shell scripts.

4.2 Generating Square Numbers

We present below a kernel P systems model that generates square numbers (starting with 1) each step. The multiplicity of object "s" is equal to the square number produced each step.

Table 4. List of properties derived from the property language and their representations in different formats.

Prop.	Pattern	(i) Informal, (ii) Formal, (iii) Spin (LTL) Representations
1	Universality	(i) *No more than one termination signal will be generated*
		(ii) **always** m.t <= 1
		(iii) ltl prop { [] (c[0].x[t_] <= 1 || state != step_complete) }
2	Absence	(i) *The system will never generate 15 as a square number*
		(ii) **never** m.s = 15
		(iii) ltl prop { !(<> (c[0].x[s_] == 15 && state == step_complete)) }
3	Steady-state	(i) *In the long run, the system will converge to a state in which, if the termination signal is generated, no more a objects will be available*
		(ii) **steady-state** (m.a = 0 implies m.t = 1)
		(iii) ltl prop { <> ([] ((c[0].x[a_] == 0 -> c[0].x[t_] == 1) || state != step_complete) && state != step_complete) }

Prop.	Pattern	(i) Informal, (ii) Formal, (iii) NuSMV (CTL) Representations
4	Existence	(i) *The system will eventually consume all a objects, on some runs*
		(ii) **eventually** m.a = 0
		(iii) SPEC EF m.a = 0
5	Existence	(i) *On some runs the system will eventually halt*
		(ii) **eventually** m.t = 1
		(iii) SPEC EF m.t = 1
6	Universality	(i) *No more than one termination signal will be generated*
		(ii) **always** m.t <= 1
		(iii) SPEC AG m.t <= 1
7	Absence	(i) *The system will never generate 15 as a square number*
		(ii) **never** m.s = 15
		(iii) SPEC !(EF m.s = 15)
8	Precedence	(i) *The consumption of all a objects will always be preceded by a halting signal*
		(ii) m.a = 0 **preceded-by** m.t = 1
		(iii) SPEC !(E [!(m.a = 0) U (!(m.a = 0) & m.t = 1)])
9	Response	(i) *By starting the computation with at least one a object, on some runs the system will eventually consume all of them*
		(ii) m.a >0 **followed-by** m.a = 0
		(iii) SPEC AG (m.a > 0 -> EF m.a = 0)
10	Response	(i) *A halting signal will always be followed by the consumption of all a objects*
		(ii) m.t = 1 **followed-by** m.a = 0
		(iii) SPEC AG (m.t = 1 -> EF m.a = 0)

```
type main {
max {
= t: a -> {} .
< t: a -> a, 2b, s .
< t: a -> a, s, t .
< t: b -> b, s .
      }
}

m {a} (main).
```

An execution trace for this model can be visualised as follows:

```
a
a 2b s
a 4b 4s
a 6b 9s
. . .
```

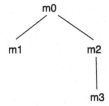

Fig. 1. The structure.

kPWORKBENCH automatically converts the kP-Lingua model into the corresponding input languages of the SPIN, and NuSMV model checkers. In order to verify that the problem works as desired, we have constructed a set of properties specified in kP-Queries, listed in Table 4. The applied pattern types are given in the second column of the table. For each property we provide the following information; (i) informal description of each kP-Query, (ii) the formal kP-Query, (iii) the translated form of the kP-Query into the LTL specifications written in SPIN modelling language, and CTL specifications written in the NuSMV language. The results of all queries are positive, as expected (Fig. 1).

4.3   Broadcasting with Acknowledgement

In this case study, we consider broadcasting with acknowledgement in ad-hoc networks. Each level of nodes in the hierarchy has associated a unique type with communication rules to neighbouring (lower and upper) levels. This is the only way we can simulate signalling with kP systems such that we do not hard-wire the target membranes in communication rules, i.e. assume we do not know how many child-nodes are connected to each parent as long as we group them by the same type; evidently, this only applies to tree structures. The kP Systems model written in kP–Lingua is given as follows:

```
type L0 {
max {
a -> b, a (L1), a (L2) .
    }
}
type L1 {
max {
a, c -> c (L0) .
    }
}

type L2 {
max {
a -> b, a (L3) .
b, c -> c (L0) .
```

```
    }
}

type L3 {
max {
a, c -> c (L2) .
    }
}


m0 {a} (L0) .

m1 {c} (L1) - m0 .
m2 {} (L2) - m0.
m3 {c} (L3) - m2 .
```

In order to verify that the model works as desired, we have verified some properties, presented in Table 5. The results are positive, except Properties 1 and 5, as expected. These results confirm the desired system behaviour.

Table 5. List of properties derived from the property language and their representations in different formats.

Prop.	Pattern	(i) Informal, (ii) Formal, (iii) Spin (LTL) Representations
1	Existence	(i) *The terminal nodes will receive the broadcast message at the same time*
		(ii) **eventually** (m1.a >0 and m3.a >0)
		(iii) ltl prop { <> ((c[1].x[a_] > 0 && c[3].x[a_] > 0) && state == step_complete) }
2	Absence	(i) *The root node will never receive an acknowledgement without sending a broadcast*
		(ii) **never** m0.a >0 and m0.c >0
		(iii) ltl prop { !(<> ((c[0].x[a_] > 0 && c[0].x[c_] > 0) && state == step_complete)) }
3	Response	(i) *The node m2 will always receive the broadcast message before its child node (m3)*
		(ii) m2.a $= 1$ **followed-by** m3.a $= 1$
		(iii) ltl prop { [] ((c[2].x[a_] == 1 -> <> (c[3].x[a_] == 1 && state == step_complete)) || state != step_complete) }

Prop.	Pattern	(i) Informal, (ii) Formal, (iii) NuSMV (CTL) Representations
4	Existence	(i) *The node m1 will eventually receive the broadcast message*
		(ii) eventually m1.a >0
		(iii) SPEC EF m1.a > 0
5	Existence	(i) *The terminal nodes will receive the broadcast message at the same time*
		(ii) **eventually** m1.a >0 and m3.a >0
		(iii) SPEC EF (m1.a > 0 & m3.a > 0)
6	Absence	(i) *The root node will never receive an acknowledgement without sending a broadcast*
		(ii) **never** m0.a >0 and m0.c >0
		(iii) SPEC !(EF (m0.a > 0 & m0.c > 0))
7	Response	(i) *The node m2 will always receive the broadcast message before its child node (m3)*
		(ii) m2.a $= 1$ **followed-by** m3.a $= 1$
		(iii) SPEC AG (m2.a = 1 -> EF m3.a = 1)
8	Steady-state	(i) *In the long run, the system will converge to a state in which the root node will have been received the acknowledgement from the all terminal nodes and no more broadcasts will occur*
		(ii) **steady-state** (m0.c $= 2$ implies m0.a $= 0$)
		(iii) SPEC AF (AG (m0.c = 2 -> m0.a = 0))
9	Steady-state	(i) *In the long run, the system will converge to a state in which the root node will have been received the acknowledgement from all the terminal nodes and no more acknowledgements will occur*
		(ii) **steady-state** (m0.c $= 2$ implies (m1.c $= 0$ and m3.c $= 0$))
		(iii) SPEC AF (AG (m0.c = 2 -> (m1.c = 0 & m3.c = 0)))

5   Discussion

kP systems (and P systems in general) are a suitable formalism for modelling biological systems, especially multi-cellular systems and molecular interactions taking place in different locations of living cells. These non-deterministic models facilitate the *qualitative* analysis of such systems. Namely, they allow one to describe all chains of reactions, observe various interactions between species and determine various dependencies between molecules. In [22], two biological systems, the quorum sensing in *P. aeruginosas* and the synthetic pulse generator, and in [21] some genetic Boolean gates have been qualitatively analysed using the NuSMV and SPIN model checkers. However, the ideas and methodology presented in these papers were not fully automated. Our work presented in this paper tackles this issue. The model checking framework now works in a fully automated fashion and is integrated into the kPWORKBENCH platform. Thus, this work can be considered progress on the conceptually presented methodology introduced in [21,22].

6   Conclusions and Future Work

In this paper, we have presented a new model checking framework that we have developed in support of formal verification of kP system models. It supports both LTL and CTL properties by making use of the SPIN and NuSMV model checkers. The new framework for kP-Lingua models enriches kPWORKBENCH with a mechanism for defining kP-Queries files, which are especially designed for the purpose of being used to verify kP-Lingua models. The format of kP-Queries file is supported by an intuitive, coherent and integrated property specification language, allowing the construction of queries involving kP-Lingua model entities and targeting the LTL and CTL formalisms. We have demonstrated our proposed methodology on the subset sum problem, by verifying a set of properties constructed in kP-Queries.

Recently, in addition to the properties presented in the paper, we have investigated and proved more complex and interested properties for the three examples provided. For example, in the square numbers generator, by introducing a new symbol to denote the iteration step and modifying the rules so that this is incremented whenever s is incremented from a (in rules (2) and (3) of type Main), we can verify that s equals the square of the iteration step. In the subset sum example, we cannot verify anything related to newly created compartments as we cannot refer to them. One way of addressing this problem would be to map somehow the compartment creation into a corresponding symbol in the Output compartment. For example, when a new compartment of type Main is created and this contains 3 elements (the first rule of the second choice of compartment Main), a rule which will send a r1 into Output whenever a compartment with 3 elements is created (has both 3 x and r1) will be added. We can then verify that there is a path for which output.r1 > 0 (this means in Output an r1 has been received after the compartment Main with 3 elements has been created).

We aim to extend the current implementation by considering more complex queries over kP-Lingua model entities, offering the verification tool greater power and expressivity, and also by investigating how properties involving the active membranes can be formulated and proved. We also aim to evaluate the methodology with several other case studies to better understand its potential and limitations more generally. In this respect, we will expand the synthetic biology investigations [21,22] and develop verification strategies for some synchronisation [9] and graphics [16] problems.

Acknowledgements. SK and MG acknowledge the support provided for synthetic biology research by EPSRC ROADBLOCK (project number: EP/I031812/1). The work of FI and LM was supported by a grant of the Romanian National Authority for Scientific Research, CNCS-UEFISCDI (project number: PN-II-ID-PCE-2011-3-0688). MB is supported by a PhD studentship provided by the Turkey Ministry of Education.

References

1. ANTLR website. http://www.antlr.org
2. Bakir, M.E., Ipate, F., Konur, S., Mierla, L., Niculescu, I.: Extended simulation and verification platform for kernel P systems. In: Gheorghe, M., Rozenberg, G., Salomaa, A., Sosík, P., Zandron, C. (eds.) CMC 2014. LNCS, vol. 8961, pp. 158–178. Springer, Heidelberg (2014)
3. Bakir, M.E., Konur, S., Gheorghe, M., Niculescu, I., Ipate, F.: High performance simulations of kernel P systems. In: Proceedings of the 2014 IEEE 16th International Conference on High Performance Computing and Communication, HPCC 2014, France, Paris pp. 409–412 (2014)
4. Blakes, J., Twycross, J., Konur, S., Romero-Campero, F., Krasnogor, N., Gheorghe, M.: Infobiotics workbench: A P systems based tool for systems and synthetic biology. In: Frisco, P., Gheorghe, M., Pérez-Jiménez, M.J. (eds.) Applications of Membrane Computing in Systems and Synthetic Biology. Emergence, Complexity and Computation, vol. 7, pp. 1–41. Springer, Switzerland (2014)
5. Cimatti, A., Clarke, E., Giunchiglia, E., Giunchiglia, F., Pistore, M., Roveri, M., Sebastiani, R., Tacchella, A.: NuSMV 2: an opensource tool for symbolic model checking. In: Brinksma, E., Larsen, K.G. (eds.) CAV 2002. LNCS, vol. 2404, pp. 359–364. Springer, Heidelberg (2002)
6. Ciobanu, G., Pérez-Jiménez, M.J., Păun, G. (eds.): Applications of Membrane Computing. Springer, Heidelberg (2006)
7. Coakley, S., Gheorghe, M., Holcombe, M., Chin, S., Worth, D., Greenough, C.: Exploitation of high performance computing in the FLAME agent-based simulation framework. In: Proceedings of the IEEE 14th International Conference on High Performance Computing and Communication, HPCC 2012, Liverpool, UK, pp. 538–545 (2012)
8. Díaz-Pernil, D., Gutiérrez-Naranjo, M.A., Pérez-Jiménez, M.J.: A uniform family of tissue P systems with cell division solving 3-COL in a linear time. Theor. Comput. Sci. **404**, 76–87 (2008)
9. Dinneen, M.J., Yun-Bum, K., Nicolescu, R.: Faster synchronization in P systems. Nat. Comput. **11**(4), 637–651 (2012)

10. Dragomir, C., Ipate, F., Konur, S., Lefticaru, R., Mierla, L.: Model checking kernel P systems. In: Alhazov, A., Cojocaru, S., Gheorghe, M., Rogozhin, Y., Rozenberg, G., Salomaa, A. (eds.) CMC 2013. LNCS, vol. 8340, pp. 151–172. Springer, Heidelberg (2014)
11. Frisco, P., Gheorghe, M., Pérez-Jiménez, M.J. (eds.): Applications of Membrane Computing in Systems and Synthetic Biology. Springer, Berlin (2014)
12. Gheorghe, M., Ipate, F., Dragomir, C., Mierlă, L., Valencia-Cabrera, L., García-Quismondo, M., Pérez-Jiménez, M.J.: Kernel P systems - version 1. In: 11th Brainstorming Week on Membrane Computing, pp. 97–124. Fénix Editora (2013)
13. Gheorghe, M., Ipate, F., Lefticaru, R., Dragomir, C.: An integrated approach to P systems formal verification. In: Gheorghe, M., Hinze, T., Păun, G., Rozenberg, G., Salomaa, A. (eds.) CMC 2010. LNCS, vol. 6501, pp. 226–239. Springer, Heidelberg (2010)
14. Gheorghe, M., Ipate, F., Lefticaru, R., Pérez-Jiménez, M.J., Ţurcanu, A., Valencia-Cabrera, L., García-Quismondo, M., Mierlă, L.: 3-Col problem modelling using simple kernel P systems. Int. J. Comput. Math. 90(4), 816–830 (2012)
15. Gheorghe, M., Păun, G., Pérez-Jiménez, M.J., Rozenberg, G.: Research frontiers of membrane computing: open problems and research topics. Int. J. Found. Comput. Scence 24, 547–624 (2013)
16. Gimel'farb, G.L., Nicolescu, R., Ragavan, S.: P system implementation of dynamic programming stereo. J. Math. Imaging Vis. 47(1–2), 13–26 (2013)
17. Holcombe, M.: X-machines as a basis for dynamic system specification. Softw. Eng. J. 3(2), 69–76 (1988)
18. Holzmann, G.J.: The model checker SPIN. IEEE Trans. Softw. Eng. 23(5), 275–295 (1997)
19. Ipate, F., Lefticaru, R., Tudose, C.: Formal verification of P systems using spin. Intern. J. Found. Comput. Sci. 22(1), 133–142 (2011)
20. Konur, S., Gheorghe, M.: A property-driven methodology for formal analysis of synthetic biology systems. IEEE/ACM Trans. Comput. Biol. Bioinf. 12, 360–371 (2015)
21. Konur, S., Gheorghe, M., Dragomir, C., Ipate, F., Krasnogor, N.: Conventional verification for unconventional computing: a genetic XOR gate example. Fundamenta Informaticae 134(1–2), 97–110 (2014)
22. Konur, S., Gheorghe, M., Dragomir, C., Mierlă, L., Ipate, F., Krasnogor, N.: Qualitative and quantitative analysis of systems and synthetic biology constructs using P systems. ACS Synth. Biol. 4(1), 83–92 (2015)
23. Konur, S., Kiran, M., Gheorghe, M., Burkitt, M., Ipate, F.: Agent-based high-performance simulation of biological systems on the Gpu. In: Proceedings of the 2015 IEEE 15th International Conference on High Performance Computing and Communication, HPCC 2015, New York, USA (2015)
24. Konur, S., Ladroue, C., Fellermann, H., Sanassy, D., Mierlă, L., Ipate, F., Kalvala, S., Gheorghe, M., Krasnogor, N.: Modeling and analysis of genetic boolean gates using the infobiotics workbench. In: Proceedings of Verification of Engineered Molecular Devices and Programs. VEMDP 2014, pp. 26–37. Austria, Vienna (2014)
25. MeCoSim website. http://www.p-lingua.org/mecosim/
26. P-Lingua website. http://www.p-lingua.org
27. Păun, G.: Computing with membranes. J. Comput. Syst. Sci. 61(1), 108–143 (2000)
28. Păun, G., Rozenberg, G., Salomaa, A. (eds.): The Oxford Handbook of Membrane Computing. Oxford University Press, New York (2010)
29. Rozenberg, G., Bäck, T., Kok, J.N. (eds.): Handbook of Natural Computing. Springer, Heidelberg (2012)

30. Singleton. http://en.wikipedia.org/wiki/Singleton_pattern
31. SOLID. http://en.wikipedia.org/wiki/SOLID_(object-oriented_design)
32. Visitor design pattern. http://en.wikipedia.org/wiki/Visitor_pattern

A New Strategy to Improve the Performance of PDP-Systems Simulators

Carmen Graciani[✉], Miguel A. Martínez-del-Amor, and Agustín Riscos-Núñez

Department of Computer Science and Artificial Intelligence,
Research Group on Natural Computing, Universidad de Sevilla, Seville, Spain
{cgdiaz,mdelamor,ariscosn}@us.es

Abstract. One of the major challenges that current P systems simulators have to deal with is to be as efficient as possible. A P system is syntactically described as a membrane structure delimiting regions where multisets of objects evolve by means of evolution rules. According to that, on each computation step, the applicability of the rules for the current P system configuration must be calculated. In this paper we extend previous works that use Rete-based simulation algorithm in order to improve the time consumed during the checking phase in the selection of rules. A new approach is presented, oriented to the acceleration of Population Dynamics P Systems simulations.

Keywords: Rete algorithm · P systems · Membrane computing · Rule applicability · Simulator performance

1 Introduction

In Membrane Computing it is relatively common to find in the literature designs of P systems where a collection of rules is described by means of a single template (usually using indexed objects). P-Lingua standard allows the definition of rule patterns with parameters, thus getting closer to the usual syntax used in the papers. For example, the following rule pattern represents one thousand evolution rules acting over different objects:

$$[o_i \rightarrow x_i], 1 \leq i \leq 1000.$$

Nevertheless, when designing simulator software, we commonly assume that the rules will be handled individually. For instance, all built-in simulators in the *pLinguaCore* library (even those from *PMCGPU project* [27]) always unwrap any rule pattern within the .pli file, and then they load in memory every single rule obtained. Therefore, in the previous example, our simulators would handle those 1000 rules separately. It seems clear that, if we were able to process rule patterns without unwrapping them, then the performance would improve dramatically.

This paper provides a step forward in this direction, proposing an improvement of the first phase of the simulation loop based on a Rete network: checking which rules are applicable (an how many times).

© Springer International Publishing Switzerland 2015
G. Rozenberg et al. (Eds.): CMC 2015, LNCS 9504, pp. 171–184, 2015.
DOI: 10.1007/978-3-319-28475-0_12

The paper is structured as follows. First, some preliminary notions about production systems and the classical Rete algorithm are recalled. Then, Sect. 3 discusses how to bring a Rete-like approach into the pseudocode of simulation engines used in membrane computing software tools. Some further details are given for the case of PDP systems in Sect. 4. Finally, the paper concludes with some final remarks and future work.

2   Production Systems

A rule-based production system is a model of computation that has been widely used in the field of Artificial Intelligence for a wide range of tasks in many domains. It is classically defined by a set of *rules* (rulebase), a set of *facts* (working memory), and a *rule engine* that controls the execution.

Each rule consists of a conjunction of *condition elements* and a set of *actions*. The general form is

if [condition]* then [action]*

Usually the condition part is known as the *left-hand side (LHS)* of the rule and each condition is called a *pattern*. The action part is known as the *right-hand side (RHS)* and describe the *effects* of applying the rule.

The rule engine repeatedly performs the operations described in Algorithm 1 until no more rule is applicable (or an action element stops it).

---

applicable ← ∅;
foreach *rule* **do**
    | Test LHS of the rule against the working memory;
    | **if** *it matches* **then**
    | | add rule to *applicable*
    | **end**
end
Choose one rule from *applicable* (if any);
Perform the actions of the RHS of the selected rule;

Algorithm 1. Match-act cycle

The actions produce, in most cases, the inclusion and/or deletion of facts within the working memory. Because of those changes, some rules may become applicable while, conversely, some other rules may stop being applicable.

It is well known that a large part of the time and memory consumed by a ruled-based production system is due to the matching phase; that is, determining which rules are applicable at any given instant, according to the current facts in the working memory. Thus, the main challenge of match algorithms is to update this information in an efficient way.

2.1   The Rete Algorithm

The Rete algorithm [8] is a classic and widely used algorithm for checking rule
satisfaction. It takes advantage of two empirical observations:

- *Temporal redundancy:* The application of the rules does not change all the
  working memory. Only some facts are affected and the remaining ones (probably, most of them) stay unchanged. Rete maintains state information across
  cycles and performs incremental matching.
- *Structural similarity:* Several rules can (partially) share the same (or similar)
  conditions in the LHS. Rete recognises those identical features in order to
  avoid making the same tests multiple times.

Before the match-act cycles take place, the set of rules is preprocessed yielding
a network (a directed acyclic graph). During the match-act cycles, tokens associated with facts flow through this network each time that they are added/deleted
to the working memory. At any given point, the contents of the network correspond to the conditions that have already been checked against the current
facts.

We will use the set of rules in Fig. 1(a), and the network associated to it
(displayed below the set of rules) in order to illustrate the description of the
different components of such a network and the process followed to construct
it. Figure 1(b) shows how tokens, corresponding to different facts added to the
working memory, pass through the network during a match-act cycle.

The network constructed for a given set of rules has two roots and three
kinds of nodes:

- **Root** α is the entry to the α-nodes subnetwork. During the match-act cycles
  this root receives the changes in the working memory (added or removed facts)
  and pass those tokens to its successors (α-nodes).

  In the figure, root α is represented as a squared node with a symbol α
  inside.
- α-**nodes**, children of the root α. They are included in the network for each
  different pattern appearing in any of the LHS of the rules. α-nodes perform
  the checking for the associated condition to all the tokens they receive. Only
  when the test is successful, the token passes to the successors (β-nodes).

  In the figure, α-nodes are represented as rectangles, showing their associated
  condition inside them. For example, in order to match the first condition of
  rule R1, an object must verify p1 relation, and its first argument must be equal
  to number 3, as described in the corresponding α-node. Since in this small
  example there are only three different patterns in the LHS of R1 and R2, the
  network contains only three different α-nodes.
- **Root** β is the entry to the β-nodes subnetwork.

  In the figure, root β is the double squared node with a symbol β inside.
- β **-nodes** perform inter–patterns conditions. β-nodes receive tokens from two
  nodes (an α-node and a β-node) and have two different memories to store
  the tokens that arrive from each parent. Every time a new token arrives,
  the condition will be checked for all possible combinations of this token with

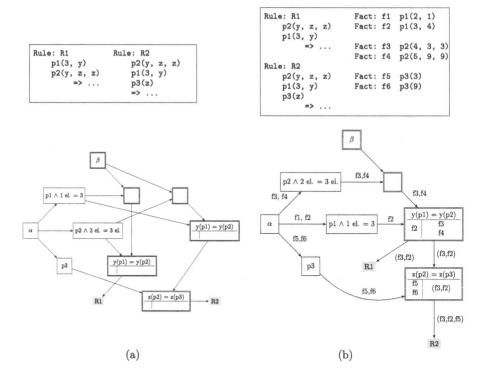

Fig. 1. Two different Rete networks for R1 and R2. The one on the right also illustrates the flow of tokens for a given working memory f1, ..., f6.

tokens from the local memory of the other parent. Successful combinations (if any) are passed on to successor nodes (either terminal or β-nodes).

β-nodes directly connected to the root β are a particular case; they do not use any local memory, they just let tokens pass trough them.

In the figure, β-nodes are the double squared ones where the associated inter–pattern condition is displayed inside them. Below the condition there are two cells, where the tokens stored in each local memory are shown.

For the given example, the first non-elementary β-node is associated to the following condition: the second argument of the token verifying the p1 relation must be the same as the first argument of the token that verifies the p2 relation (we denote this as $y(p1) = y(p2)$).

– **Terminal-nodes** receive tokens which match all the conditions of the LHS of a rule (including inter–patterns conditions), and produce the output of the network. The set of applicable rules is composed by the rules whose terminal-node are not empty.

In the figure, terminal-nodes are the grey ones.

The path from the root β, through different β-nodes, down to a terminal-node defines the complete LHS of a rule. Unless otherwise indicated, inter–pattern conditions are checked in the same order as they occur in the rule.

Note that a very simple change in the order of R1 conditions yields a very different network, as shown in Fig. 1(b). Now, the set of rules not only share conditions p2(y, z, z) and p1(3,y), but also that they occur at the beginning of the LHS, and moreover in the same order. Therefore, they continue sharing the α-nodes for those conditions (like in Fig. 1(a)), but now they also share the first β-nodes.

Algorithm 2 describes the general process that constructs the network for a given set of rules.

NET $\leftarrow$ graph ($\{\alpha, \beta\}, \emptyset$);
foreach *rule, R* **do**
    $C \leftarrow$ first condition of R;
    $A \leftarrow \alpha$-node in NET associated to C;
    `// if it does not exist, then add it to NET as an` α `child`
    $B \leftarrow \beta$-node in NET child of A and β;
    `// if it does not exist, then add it to NET`
    foreach *condition D in R (in order of occurrence after C)* **do**
        $A \leftarrow \alpha$-node in NET associated to D;
        `// if it does not exist, then add it to NET as an` α `child`
        $B \leftarrow \beta$-node in NET, child of A and B, associated to inter-pattern condition between D and previous conditions in R;
        `// if it does not exist, then add it to NET`
    end
    $T \leftarrow$ terminal-node in NET, child of B;
    `// if it does not exist, then add it to NET as child of` B
    Add R to T memory;
end

Algorithm 2. Network construction

The most important issue regarding performance is the order of the conditions in the LHS of the rules. This leads to consider the following strategies to improve the efficiency.

- Most specific to most general. If the rule activation can be controlled by a single data, place it first.
- Data with the lowest number of occurrences in the working memory should go near the top.
- Volatile data (ones that are added and eliminated continuously) should go last, particularly if the rest of the conditions are mostly independent.

Those strategies try to minimise (in general), not only the number of β-nodes that will exist in the network (and, therefore, the number of checks performed until a token arrives into a terminal node), but also the number of β-nodes that must be updated each time that a fact flows through their memories.

In resume, the key advantage of Rete is that rule conditions are only re-evaluated when a fact is asserted or deleted. In this way, asserting a new fact is simply a case of passing a token through the network, and a smaller number of matching operations are performed. In a naive implementation, each new fact would be compared against every single pattern of every rule, which means a greater time complexity. Retracting a fact is identical to assertion, but items are removed from node memories.

3   Rete and P System Simulation

In this section we explore how the Rete algorithm and the strategies described in the previous section can be adapted to Membrane Computing simulators. We assume that the reader is familiar with basic concepts related to this area, for an extensive bibliography and documentation please refer to the handbook [23] and the P systems webpage [25].

Since there is no implementation *in vivo* nor *in vitro* of P systems, the development of *in silico* simulators has been one of the most active research lines in the area [7,12]. In [9], a specification language for membrane systems called P-Lingua has been presented. This language aims to be a standard to define P systems. The P-Lingua framework also includes a Java library called *pLinguaCore*, which is able to parse (plain-text) files in P-Lingua format defining P systems from a number of different models [6,14,18], checking whether they contain any syntax or semantics errors. P-Lingua files can also be exported into xml or binary formats, so that the converted files can then be used as the input for simulation tools. Moreover, the library includes several built-in simulators for each supported model. It is an Open Source software tool available at [26].

We will now discuss about the functioning of such simulator engines provided by *pLinguaCore*. After parsing the P system defined in the input P-Lingua (`.pli`) file, the simulation process of each computation step is carried out in two phases: selection and execution of rules. In the first phase, the checking of the applicability of the rules is made sequentially. Such method only simulates one possible computation, so it is used for confluent P systems (that is, systems for which all the computations with the same input lead to the same result).

Checking the applicability of rules normally consumes plenty of time in *pLinguaCore* simulators, and in fact, it is mainly in this checking subroutine where the complexity of the simulation algorithm resides. For P systems where the rules have an associated probability, there is an additional difficulty: deciding how to implement the semantics, which informally indicate that rules should be applied in a "maximally parallel way, according to their probabilities". In particular, *pLinguaCore* includes a variety of simulation algorithms for PDP systems: *Binomial Block Based* (BBB) algorithm [1] does a random loop over blocks of rules (i.e. rules having the same LHS), and assigns a maximal number of applications to each one; *Direct Non Deterministic distribution with Probabilities* (DNDP) algorithm [6] does also a random loop, but over the rules, and assigning a probabilistic number of applications; and *Direct distribution based on Consistent Blocks Algorithm* (DCBA) [16] performs a proportional distribution of objects among blocks of rules before assigning a maximal, but probabilistic number of applications to each rule. The main difference among these three approaches is not their performance, but the fact that they produce significantly different behaviours. DCBA is the one that tries to perform the selection of rules to be applied in a more realistic or accurate way, from an ecological point of view. Since it is the most common choice for PDP systems simulation, in what follows we will focus particularly on it.

It is worth stressing the fact that the Rete-based algorithm that we introduce in this paper is completely independent from the computation mode of the considered P-system model (sequential, maximal/minimal parallelism, distributed, etc.). Indeed, the Rete network contains information about which rules are "individually" applicable. When calculating applicable multisets of rules, the computation model comes into play.

For a first approximation to the study of how to use Rete algorithm ideas within Membrane Computing we have chosen to focus on rules handling polarisation, which can be written in the following form

$$u_1^{n_1} \cdots u_k^{n_k} [v_1^{m_1} \cdots v_1^{m_1}]_s^c \to \cdots$$

(k and/or l can be 0) with $u_1, \ldots, u_k, v_1, \ldots, v_1 \in \Gamma$.

Also, on many occasions the symbols of the alphabet have subscripts (generally numerical) used to describe rulesets. In general, the following possibilities occur:

– Subscripts belong to a fixed set of possibilities:

$$u_i [v_j]_s^c \to \cdots \quad \text{such that } 1 \leq i, j \leq 10$$

– The value of a subscript of an object is determined by other subscripts values:

$$u_{i,i+1} []_s^c \to \cdots \quad \text{such that } 1 \leq i \leq 10$$

– Subscripts from different symbols may also be related:

$$u_{i,j} [v_{i+1,j-1}]_s^c \to \cdots \quad \text{such that } 1 \leq i, j \leq 10$$

Generalising the above, rulesets schemes would be something of the form:

$$u_{j_1:\Gamma_1}^{n_1} \cdots u_{j_k:\Gamma_k}^{n_k} : \gamma_k [v_{i_1:\theta_1}^{m_1} : \theta_1 \cdots v_{i_{k'}:\theta_{k'}}^{m_{k'}} : \theta_{k'}]_s^c \to \cdots$$

where each Γ is a relation over the symbol subscripts and each γ is a relation over the symbol subscripts and all the subscripts of the previous symbols. In such a scheme we can distinguish three kinds of conditions:

– A membrane labelled with s must have charge c : $[]_s^c$
– Outside the membrane there must be at least n_j copies of element u_j and its subscripts must verify Γ_j: $u_{j:\Gamma_j}^{n_j} : \gamma_j$.

This condition is interrelated with the previous one as the membrane has to be the same as in the previous conditions. Also, the object subscripts are related in terms of γ_j with the subscripts of the objects in the former conditions.

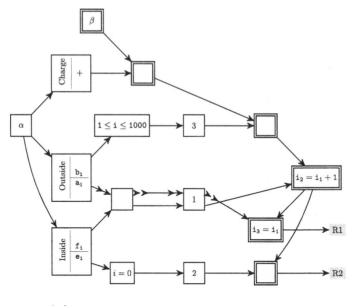

R1. $[]_2^+ b_{i_1:1 \leq i_1 \leq 1000}^3 [f_{i_2} : i_2 = i_1 + 1] a_{i_3} : i_3 = i_1 \rightarrow \ldots$
R2. $[]_2^+ b_{i_1:1 \leq i_1 \leq 1000}^3 [f_{i_2} : i_2 = i_1 + 1][e_{i_3:i_3=0}^2] \rightarrow \ldots$

Fig. 2. Rete network for P systems

– Inside the membrane there must be at least m_i copies of element v_i and its
  subscripts must verify θ_i: $[v_{i:\theta_i}^{m_i} : \theta_i]$.

  Equivalent interrelation to those listed above have to be taken into account.

So, for each symbol in a given P system configuration, the token passing
trough the network must contain information about the number of copies and
its subscripts. As the symbol is, at the same time, inside a membrane and,
probably, outside of one or more membranes a different token is sent for each
symbol situation.

Following the work introduced in [10], α-nodes can be divided into several
nodes, one for each condition over the arguments of a pattern. Moreover, we
consider here a strategy to reduce the amount of redundant information in the
network. We will allow these new detailed α-nodes to be used by several patterns,
in such a way that each pattern will not be associated to a single α-node, but
to a path from root α to a β-node.

For example, let us consider the following rules

1. $a_i b_i^3 [f_{i+1}]_2^+ \rightarrow \ldots$ for $1 \leq i \leq 1000$
2. $b_i^3 [f_{i+1} e_0^2]_2^+ \rightarrow \ldots$ for $1 \leq i \leq 1000$

It is important to highlight that this strategy allows us to handle only two
templates of LHS, instead two thousand different (but similar) individual rules.

First of all, we can rewrite them as in Sect. 2.1, in order to put at the beginning common conditions. Figure 2 shows the new syntax, together with the constructed network. Note that there are specific detailed α-nodes for conditions about the membrane charge, about the region where the objects should be, about the index of the objects, and about their multiplicity.

Considering that, in a given configuration, several membranes may have the same label, all β-nodes (including those directly connected to root β) and terminal-nodes have different slots to distinguish between them.

In production systems, the changes in the working memory correspond mainly to adding or removing facts. In membrane computing, the modifications caused by the application of the rules mainly refer to polarization of the membranes or their associated multisets of objects. Each time that something is modified on a configuration, the corresponding tokens go trough the network, and in β-nodes the inter–relations between them are checked. Moreover, the checking does not yield a Boolean answer, but instead, the maximum number of times that the related rules could be used is updated.

4   Population Dynamics P Systems and DCBA Algorithm

Population Dynamics P systems are a variant of multienvironment P systems with extended active membranes [5]. As discussed before, the simulation of PDP systems has been a research topic for years. In total, up to 4 simulation algorithms were defined, each trying to improve both in accuracy and in performance for their predecessor. The latest defined algorithm is called DCBA [16], which implements a proportional distribution of objects among rules with overlapping LHS (i.e. competing for objects). Rules having the same LHS are arranged into blocks, and these are also restricted to the consistency condition: rules within a block must have the same LHS and the same charge in the RHS [16].

DCBA consists of 3 phases for the selection of rules: phase 1 (distribution), phase 2 (maximality) and phase 3 (probabilistic). The general scheme is the following:

1. Initialization of the algorithm: *static distribution table* (**columns:** blocks, **Rows:** (objects,membrane))
2. **Loop over Time**
3.   **Selection** stage:
4.   **Phase 1** (Distribution of objects along rule blocks)
5.   **Phase 2** (Maximality selection of rule blocks)
6.   **Phase 3** (Probabilistic distribution, blocks to rules)
7.   **Execution** stage

As analysed in [17], Phase 1 is the bottleneck of the simulation in sequential mode, taking more than the half of the run time. Whereas Phase 2 performs a random loop over remaining blocks of rules to achieve maximality, and Phase 3 carries out a random multinomial distribution from blocks to rules, Phase 1 has to deal with all the defined blocks of rules, and distribute the objects among

foreach *environment* $e_j, 1 \le j \le m$ **do**

> Apply filters 1 and 2 to $\mathcal{T}_j$ using configuration C_t, obtaining the dynamic table $\mathcal{T}'_j$;
>
> Check *mutual consistency* for the blocks remaining in $\mathcal{T}'_j$. Launch an error if at least one inconsistency is found. Optionally, select a maximal subset of consistent blocks, and continue;
>
> Apply filter 3 to $\mathcal{T}'_j$ (delete empty rows);
>
> **repeat**
>
> > Add all non-null values in the rows of $\mathcal{T}'_j$;
> >
> > Normalize the values of $\mathcal{T}'_j$ by using the total sum of rows;
> >
> > Multiply each row by the number of copies of the corresponding object in C_t;
> >
> > Calculate the minimum of the previous values per column;
> >
> > Select the block corresponding to the column with that minimum value;
> >
> > Delete the number of copies of the objects in the LHS according to that selection;
> >
> > Apply filters 2 and 3 to $\mathcal{T}'_j$;
>
> **until** *(Reached a maximum number of iterations)* $\vee$ *(All the column minimums are 0)*;

end

Algorithm 3. DCBA selection (Phase 1)

them. Algorithm 3 shows a brief overview of Phase 1 (more details can be seen in [16]).

Essentially, the proportional distribution of objects is carried out by using a table which implements the relationship between rules and their LHS as follows: each column corresponds to each rule block, each row to a pair (object, membrane), and the value in position (i, j) is $1/k$, if the object of row i appears k times in the LHS of block of j, or 0 otherwise. The algorithm always starts with a static table, that will be the same for each transition step. The checking of applicability of rules is carried by applying two filters to the static table, and generating a dynamic table in turn. Depending on the current configuration of the PDP system, the table is dynamically modified by deleting columns related to non-applicable blocks: due to the charge associated to the membrane in the LHS (filter 1), and due to the availability of objects in the LHS according to the configuration (filter 2).

Finally, there is a further restriction within phase 1: if two non-consistent blocks (having different associated right-hand charge) can be selected at the same time given a configuration, then the simulation algorithm will return an error, or optionally non-deterministically choose a subset of consistent blocks.

Evolution rules in PDP systems follow the scheme presented in previous section. Moreover, each environment contains a P system. Since they do not share objects directly, a separate Rete *evolution network* for each P system can be considered.

foreach *environment* $e_j, 1 \leq j \leq m$ **do**
> **repeat**
>> Add all non-null values in the rows of T_j;
>> Normalize the values of T_j by using the total sum of rows;
>> Multiply each row by the number of copies of the corresponding object in C_t;
>> Calculate the minimum of the previous values per column;
>> Select the block corresponding to the column with that minimum value;
>> Delete the number of copies of the objects in the LHS according to that selection and send the corresponding tokens to the networks;
>
> **until** *(Reached a maximum number of iterations)* $\vee$ *(All the column minimums are 0)*;

end

Algorithm 4. Phase 1 reduction due to the use of Rete networks

Environments can send (receive) objects to (from) other environments, by means of a set of communication rules of the following form.

$$(x)_{e_j} \rightarrow (y_1)_{e_{j_1}} \cdots (y_h)_{e_{j_h}}$$

A new network for the set of communication rules has to be constructed, but this is quite simple as their LHS include just one single condition, the existence of an object in an specific environment.

These *communitation network* must be synchronised with the evolution networks for an accurate simulation. When the initial configuration is included, for each object in the environments, a token is sent to the evolution network associated to that environment and to the communication network. If during a computation step of a simulation, an evolution rule of any P system sends out to its environment an object, then a token removing it is sent to the corresponding evolution network and, also, a token adding it to the corresponding environment has to be sent to the communication network. Moreover, when a communication rule is used during a computation step, in addition to tokens sent trough the communication network, a token has to be sent to the evolution network associated to each receiving P system.

As mentioned before, each time that a token passes through the network the maximum number of times that any rule affected by this change in a configuration is updated. With this information, T_j is dynamically updated and there is no need to use an initial static distribution table (step 1 in DCBA is replaced by the construction of the networks). Indeed, it would not be necessary to apply any filter to T_j. This updating includes checking mutual consistency launching an error if an inconsistency is found. Algorithm 4 briefly describes new Phase 1.

5   Conclusions and Future Work

In this paper we have presented how to use Rete-based checking for applicability to improve the time consuming by DCBA. For further work new simulators have to be added to *pLinguaCore* (and also to *PMCGPU project*), not unwrapping rules and constructing Rete-based networks instead, and adapting selection phase. The basic lines shown should be adapted to each specific model in order to improve the efficiency of the designed simulator.

As is well known, one of the key points of the efficiency of the Rete algorithm is the proper order in the conditions of the LHS of the rule. On the other hand, one of its disadvantages is the memory consumed by β-nodes, what has led to modified algorithms for production systems as [19] and the more recent Rete* [24]. It will be interesting to study the impact of this drawback within Membrane Computing framework. In order to test the performance, it is desirable to work on a battery of examples as diverse and demanding as possible (e.g. in [17] a random generator of systems was used to stress the simulators).

On the other hand, the adaptation of the Rete algorithm has been made by considering that the computer where the software runs has only one processor and, in this way, the software simulation of the P systems is made sequentially in a one-processor machine. Nonetheless, new hardware architectures are being used for simulating P systems [2–4,15,17,20–22], so the parallel versions of the Rete algorithm [11,13] and their relations with parallel simulators of P systems will be considered in the future.

Acknowledgements. The authors acknowledge the support of the project TIN2012-37434 of the Ministerio de Economía y Competitividad of Spain, cofinanced by FEDER funds.

References

1. Cardona, M., Colomer, M.A., Margalida, A., Palau, A., Pérez-Hurtado, I., Pérez-Jiménez, M.J., Sanuy, D.: A computational modeling for real ecosystems based on P systems. Nat. Comput. **10**(1), 39–53 (2011). Springer, Netherlands
2. Cecilia, J.M., García, J.M., Guerrero, G.D., Martínez-del Amor, M.Á., Pérez-Hurtado, I., Pérez-Jiménez, M.J.: Simulating a P system based efficient solution to SAT by using GPUs. J. Log. Algebr. Program. **79**(6), 317–325 (2010). Membrane computing and programming
3. Cecilia, J.M., García, J.M., Guerrero, G.D., Martínez-del-Amor, M.Á., Pérez-Hurtado, I., Pérez-Jiménez, M.J.: Simulation of P systems with active membranes on CUDA. Briefings Bioinformatics **11**(3), 313–322 (2010)
4. Cecilia, J.M., García, J.M., Guerrero, G.D., Martínez-del Amor, M.Á., Pérez-Jiménez, M.J., Ujaldón, M.: The GPU on the simulation of cellular computing models. Soft Comput. **16**(2), 231–246 (2012)
5. Colomer, M.A., Martínez-del Amor, M.A., Pérez-Hurtado, I., Pérez-Jiménez, M.J., Riscos-Núñez, A.: A uniform framework for modeling based on P systems. In: 2010 IEEE Fifth International Conference on Bio-Inspired Computing: Theories and Applications (BIC-TA), pp. 616–621, September 2010
6. Colomer, M.A., Pérez-Hurtado, I., Pérez-Jiménez, M.J., Riscos-Núñez, A.: Comparing simulation algorithms for multienvironment probabilistic P systems over a standard virtual ecosystem. Nat. Comput. **11**(3), 369–379 (2012)

7. Díaz-Pernil, D., Graciani, C., Gutiérrez-Naranjo, M.A., Pérez-Hurtado, I., Pérez-Jiménez, M.J.: Software for P systems. In: [23], chap. 17, pp. 437–454. Oxford University Press Inc. (2010)
8. Forgy, C.L.: Rete: A Fast Algorithm for the Many Pattern/Many Object Pattern Match Problem Expert Systems. IEEE Computer Society Press, Los Alamitos (1990)
9. García-Quismondo, M., Gutiérrez-Escudero, R., Pérez-Hurtado, I., Pérez-Jiménez, M.J., Riscos-Núñez, A.: An overview of P-lingua 2.0. In: Păun, G., Pérez-Jiménez, M.J., Riscos-Núñez, A., Rozenberg, G., Salomaa, A. (eds.) WMC 2009. LNCS, vol. 5957, pp. 264–288. Springer, Heidelberg (2010)
10. Graciani, C., Gutiérrez-Naranjo, M.Á., Pérez-Hurtado, I., Riscos-Núñez, A., Romero-Jiménez, Á.: A Rete-based algorithm for rule selection in P systems. Int. J. Unconventional Comput. 9(5–6), 367–384 (2013)
11. Gupta, A., Forgy, C., Newell, A., Wedig, R.: Parallel algorithms and architectures for rule-based systems. SIGARCH Comput. Archit. News 14(2), 28–37 (1986)
12. Gutiérrez-Naranjo, M.Á., Pérez-Jiménez, M.J., Riscos-Núñez, A.: Available membrane computing software. In: Ciobanu, G., et al. (eds.) Applications of Membrane Computing. Natural Computing Series, pp. 411–436. Springer, Heidelberg (2006)
13. Kuo, S., Moldovan, D.: The state of the art in parallel production systems. J. Parallel Distrib. Comput. 15(1), 1–26 (1992)
14. Macías–Ramos, L.F., Pérez–Hurtado, I., García–Quismondo, M., Valencia–Cabrera, L., Pérez–Jiménez, M.J., Riscos–Núñez, A.: A P–Lingua based simulator for spiking neural P systems. In: Gheorghe, M., Păun, Gh., Rozenberg, G., Salomaa, A., Verlan, S. (eds.) CMC 2011. LNCS, vol. 7184, pp. 257–281. Springer, Heidelberg (2012)
15. Martínez-del Amor, M.A., García-Quismondo, M., Macías-Ramos, L.F., Valencia-Cabrera, L., Riscos-Núñez, A., Pérez-Jiménez, M.J.: Simulating P systems on GPU devices: a survey. Fundamenta Informaticae 136, 269–284 (2015)
16. Martínez-del-Amor, M.A., et al.: DCBA: simulating population dynamics P systems with proportional object distribution. In: Csuhaj-Varjú, E., Gheorghe, M., Rozenberg, G., Salomaa, A., Vaszil, G. (eds.) CMC 2012. LNCS, vol. 7762, pp. 257–276. Springer, Heidelberg (2013)
17. Martínez-del-Amor, M.A., Pérez-Hurtado, I., Gastalver-Rubio, A., Elster, A.C., Pérez-Jiménez, M.J.: Population dynamics P systems on CUDA. In: Gilbert, D., Heiner, M. (eds.) CMSB 2012. LNCS, vol. 7605, pp. 247–266. Springer, Heidelberg (2012)
18. Martínez-del Amor, M.A., Pérez-Hurtado, I., Pérez-Jiménez, M.J., Riscos-Núñez, A.: A P-Lingua based simulator for tissue P systems. J. Log. Algebr. Program. 79(6), 374–382 (2010)
19. Miranker, D.P.: TREAT: a better match algorithm for AI production systems. In: Proceedings of the National Conference on Artificial Intelligence, pp. 42–47. American Association for Artificial Intelligence, August 1987
20. Nguyen, V., Kearney, D., Gioiosa, G.: An extensible, maintainable and elegant approach to hardware source code generation in reconfig-P. J. Log. Algebr. Program. 79(6), 383–396 (2010)
21. Peña-Cantillana, F., Díaz-Pernil, D., Berciano, A., Gutiérrez-Naranjo, M.A.: A parallel implementation of the thresholding problem by using tissue-like P systems. In: Real, P., Diaz-Pernil, D., Molina-Abril, H., Berciano, A., Kropatsch, W. (eds.) CAIP 2011, Part II. LNCS, vol. 6855, pp. 277–284. Springer, Heidelberg (2011)

22. Peña-Cantillana, F., Díaz-Pernil, D., Christinal, H.A., Gutiérrez-Naranjo, M.A.: Implementation on CUDA of the smoothing problem with tissue-like P systems. Int. J. Nat. Comput. Res. **2**(3), 25–34 (2011)
23. Păun, G., Rozenberg, G., Salomaa, A.: The Oxford Handbook of Membrane Computing. Oxford University Press Inc., New York (2010)
24. Wright, I., Marshall, J.: The execution kernel of RC++: RETE*: a faster RETE with TREAT as a special case. Int. J. Intell. Games Simul. **2**(1), 36–48 (2003)
25. The P systems webpage. http://ppage.psystems.eu/
26. The P–Lingua web site. http://www.p-lingua.org/wiki
27. The PMCGPU project site. http://sourceforge.net/projects/pmcgpu/

Automatic Translation of MP$^+$V Systems to Register Machines

Ricardo Henrique Gracini Guiraldelli[✉] and Vincenzo Manca

University of Verona, Strada Le Grazie, 15, 37134 Verona, Italy
{ricardo.guiraldelli,vincenzo.manca}@univr.it

Abstract. The present work proposes a translation of MP systems into register machines. The already proved universality of MP grammars [6] and the very simple subclass derived from it are used, in here, to present a specification of the metabolic computational paradigm of MP grammars at low (register) level, which is a first step toward a circuit-based implementation of these systems.

1 Introduction

Metabolic P (MP) systems have been evolving since its conception from a modelling language for biological systems using the nature inspired P system [11] to a computational framework for diverse mathematical activities, such as arithmetical operations [10] or regression of temporal series [13]. Consequently, questions concerning the computational power of MP systems have driven the research to some correspondent models [3,12] without a complete equivalence to Turing machines or more powerful devices [5,19].

From the synthetic and systems biology perspective, on the other hand, there is a rise on the number of methods seeking to import to those fields already established methodologies in engineering, in a kind of *computer-aided biology*. Component modelling [17], hardware design [7,16] and compiler techniques [1] are some of them. Although well-intentioned, these suggestions are reinterpretations of engineering practices and result to be alien, at times difficult, languages to the biological community.

Trying to unify both standpoints (discrete metabolic computing framework and formal design of systems and synthetic biology), the present work closes the cycle (started with [6]) of MP system as a universal computational model of discrete and deterministic metabolic computing, providing the means to convert a rule based system coded as a particular MP system (Definition 9) into an equivalent register machine description as well as formally describe the core algorithms implemented in our compiler software under development[1]; hence, a bidirectional bridge between computational and mathematical modelling and chemical and biological worlds is built and, as a consequence, also a base to develop new tools that connect them.

---

[1] The current version of the software (command-line application) may be downloaded at http://ricardo.guiraldelli.com/resources/software/compiler/regtomp.zip.

© Springer International Publishing Switzerland 2015
G. Rozenberg et al. (Eds.): CMC 2015, LNCS 9504, pp. 185–199, 2015.
DOI: 10.1007/978-3-319-28475-0_13

To introduce our mechanism of translation between models, the present paper is divided as follows: Sect. 2 introduces the concept of *register machine* and specifies the one used as target modelling language in the text; then, there is a review on classical MP systems followed by the presentation of the MP$^+$ class of systems, our reference model. Section 4 scrutinize the details of the translation between MP$^+$V systems and register machine. Finally, we make final remarks on the Sect. 5.

2   Register Machine

The literature enumerates several Turing-powerful models of computation [9], each one suitable for different context and applications given their own particularities. For the case in which the circumstance requires a great proximity to the bare-metal real computers, the *register machine* is one the most convenient models to be used.

A register machine is defined by a finite set R of registers, a finite set O of operations over the registers and a program P, an indexed sequence of applied operations. Each of the registers $r \in R$ has infinite capacity, storing numbers of arbitrary length and precision (in our case, any number $n \in \mathbb{N}$) [14]. The set of operations must, at least, provide the features to define and reproduce recursive functions [9], free access to resources (memory units or program instructions) as the unconstrained head of the Turing machine, a signalization of end of computation and be restricted to the set $\mathbb{N}$. Therefore, the set O can be defined using four operations: *zero, successor, decrements or jump* and *halt* [14]. Nevertheless, we have chosen to embrace both the standard and the extended[2] Shepherdson's and Sturgis' register machine models [18], both more appropriate for the development and understanding of the present work.

Definition 1 (Standard Register Machine). *A (standard) register machine $\mathcal{R}$ is a computational device defined as*

$$\mathcal{R} = (R, O, P)$$

where:

1. $R = \{R_1, R_2, \ldots, R_m\}$ *is a finite set of infinite capacity registers, with $m \in \mathbb{N}$;*
2. $O = \{\texttt{INC}, \texttt{DEC}, \texttt{JNZ}, \texttt{HALT}\}$ *is the set of operations;*
3. $P = (I_1, I_2, \ldots, I_n)$ *is the program, with $n \in \mathbb{N}$.*

The execution of the program P always start at the first instruction I_1 and proceeds sequentially (unless for programmed execution re-route).

---

[2] The original model of what we call Shepherdson's and Sturgis' extended register machine model [18] does not contain the JNZ instruction: it is introduced later and is shown that both JMP and JZ can be rewritten in terms of JNZ [18].

Definition 2 (Extended Register Machine). *An extended register machine* $\mathcal{R}$ *is a standard register machine as in Definition 1 with the set of operations* O *redefined as*

$$O = \{\texttt{INC}, \texttt{DEC}, \texttt{CLR}, \texttt{JMP}, \texttt{JZ}, \texttt{JNZ}, \texttt{HALT}\}$$

The concept of *instruction* of a register machine $\mathcal{R}$ (as referenced in Definition 1) is simply a convenient notation to name the operations in O over addressed registers $R_i \in R$ or other instructions; the behaviour of those mentioned so far is described in Definition 3.

Definition 3 (Instructions). *Let the content of register* R_i *be equal to* x. *Then, the definition of the instructions in the set* I *derived from the operations in* O *for the register machine* $\mathcal{R}$ *is:*

1. $\texttt{INC}(\texttt{R}_\texttt{i}) \equiv R_i \leftarrow x + 1$
2. $\texttt{DEC}(\texttt{R}_\texttt{i}) \equiv \begin{cases} R_i \leftarrow x - 1 & , \text{ if } x > 0 \\ R_i \leftarrow 0 & , \text{ otherwise} \end{cases}$
3. $\texttt{CLR}(\texttt{R}_\texttt{i}) \equiv R_i \leftarrow 0$
4. $\texttt{JMP}(\texttt{I}_\texttt{j})$ *change the execution flow of* $\mathcal{R}$, *setting* I_j *as the next instruction to be executed;*
5. $\texttt{JZ}(\texttt{R}_\texttt{i}, \texttt{I}_\texttt{j})$ *change the execution flow of* $\mathcal{R}$, *setting* I_j *as the next instruction to be executed case* $x = 0$; *otherwise, the execution flow keeps sequential;*
6. $\texttt{JNZ}(\texttt{R}_\texttt{i}, \texttt{I}_\texttt{j})$ *change the execution flow of* $\mathcal{R}$, *setting* I_j *as the next instruction to be executed case* $x > 0$; *otherwise, the execution flow keeps sequential;*
7. $\texttt{HALT}$ *ends the computation of* $\mathcal{R}$.

We also define three subprograms[3], CPY, ADD and SUB, to simplify some of the algorithms included in this text. CPY simply copy the contents of the origin register R_1 to the destination one, R_2, overwriting its values; the other two algorithms represent respectively the arithmetical operations of addition and subtraction and allow the destination register (R_3 in the Algorithms 2 and 3) to be one of the terms of the operation (R_1 or R_2), a desired property that also contributes for the conciseness of the codes in the Sect. 4.

The above definitions of register machine specify a very simple and powerful computation model very close to the real implementation of hardware architecture and can be translated to a series of other models, such as software instructions, digital circuits or metabolic systems [6], serving as an useful intermediate language.

---

[3] The algorithms use a kind of exponential notation to represent repetitions of commands, notation originally defined by Shepherdson and Sturgis [18]. They also make use of special registers, R_α and R_β, which are simply auxiliary registers to store values of intermediary operations. In fact, all the registers with greek-letter indexes, in the present work, are auxiliary registers. More details on them will be given in Sect. 4.

Algorithm 1. $\text{CPY}(R_1, R_2)$ subprogram, where $R_2 \leftarrow R_1$

```
1   CLR(R_α)
2   CLR(R_2)
3   {INC(R_α), INC(R_2)}^{R_1}
4   {INC(R_1)}^{R_α}
```

Algorithm 2. $\text{ADD}(R_1, R_2, R_3)$ subprogram, where $R_3 \leftarrow R_1 + R_2$

```
1   CLR(R_α)
2   CLR(R_β)
3   CPY(R_1, R_α)
4   {INC(R_α), INC(R_β)}^{R_2}
5   {INC(R_2)}^{R_β}
6   CPY(R_α, R_3)
```

3   Metabolic P Systems

Metabolic P (for short, MP) systems are a particular type of formalism inside the class of membrane computing. Originally, it has been developed inspired by the purposes of P systems but specialized to the modelling of biological dynamics [11] (particularly, *metabolic* ones).

Concerning its features, MP systems inherit the basic structures of its super-class [15] (membrane structure, multisets of objects and rules), but also possess those of discrete dynamical systems [8] such as *discrete step of execution, parallel execution of all of their rules* and *feedback-like update of their state variables*. The elements and the influence of both perspectives mentioned above can be seen in the formal (and modular) definition of the MP systems [10] given below.

Definition 4 (MP grammar). *An MP grammar G is a generative grammar for time series defined as*

$$G = (M, R, I, \Phi)$$

where:

1. *$M = \{x_1, x_2, \ldots, x_n\}$ the finite set of substances (variables or metabolites), and $n \in \mathbb{N}$ the number of substances.*
2. *$R = \{\alpha_j \rightarrow \beta_j : 1 \leq j \leq m\}$ the set of rules (or reactions), with α_j and β_j multisets over M, and $m \in \mathbb{N}$ the number of reactions.*

Algorithm 3. $\text{SUB}(R_1, R_2, R_3)$ subprogram, where $R_3 \leftarrow R_1 - R_2$

```
1   CLR(R_α)
2   CLR(R_β)
3   CPY(R_1, R_α)
4   {JZ(R_α, 5), DEC(R_α), INC(R_β)}^{R_2}
5   {INC(R_2)}^{R_β}
6   CPY(R_α, R_3)
```

3. $I = (x_1[0], x_2[0], \ldots, x_n[0])$ *is the vector of initial values of the substances or the metabolic state at initial step (step zero or t_0).*

4. $\Phi = \{\varphi_1, \varphi_2, \ldots, \varphi_m\}$ *is a set of functions (also called regulators or fluxes), in which every $\varphi_j : \mathbb{R}^n \mapsto \mathbb{R}$, for $1 \leq j \leq m$, is associated with a rule $r_j \in R$.*

The above, static definition of MP grammar encompasses all its composing elements as well as all membrane computing features: the membrane structure represented by the grammar G itself, the multisets defined by the metabolites M and their initial states I and the rules through the sets R and Φ. And although the set of fluxes Φ also indicates features of dynamical systems, it is essential to define the recurrent computational process of the state variables (*i.e.*, metabolites quantities) in order to give MP systems a dynamical behaviour.

Definition 5 (Stoichiometric Matrix). *Given an MP grammar $G = (M, R, I, \Phi)$, let $r_i \in R$ be an MP rule of the form $\alpha_i \to \beta_i$ as in Definition 4.*

The operator $\text{mult}^+(x_j, r_i)$ retrieves the multiplicity of the metabolite x_j in the right-side of the rule (i.e., in β_i). Its counterpart $\text{mult}^-(x_j, r_i)$ operates similarly, but over the multiset α_i.

Then, a stoichiometric matrix $\mathbb{A}$ for the MP grammar G has each of its elements defined by

$$a_{p,q} = \text{mult}^+(x_p, r_q) - \text{mult}^-(x_p, r_q)$$

for $1 \leq p \leq |M|$ and $1 \leq q \leq |R|$.

Definition 6 (Equational Metabolic Algorithm (EMA)). *At a given time $t_i \in \mathbb{N}$, let $\varphi_j(t_i)$ be the computed value of the flux φ_j at time t_i and $U[t_i] = (\varphi_1(t_i), \varphi_2(t_i), \ldots, \varphi_m(t_i))^\mathsf{T}$ the vector of all fluxes' values at that step.*

The vector of substance variation at step t_i, $\Delta[t_i]$, is defined by the equation

$$\Delta[t_i] = \mathbb{A} \times U[t_i]$$

and the so-called Equational Metabolic Algorithm, which computes the value of any substance in the future time step t_{i+1}, is computed through the following recurrent equation

$$X[t_{i+1}] = X[t_i] + \Delta[t_i]$$

Definition 7 (MP system). *An MP system $\mathcal{M}$ is a discrete dynamical system defined*[4] *as*

$$\mathcal{M} = (G, \tau)$$

with

---

[4] This definition of MP system is a simplification over the one presented in [10]: the concepts of *number ν of conventional mole* and *vector μ of mole masses* are useful in some circumstances, but not essential—specially in the context of the present work.

1. G being an MP grammar following the Definition 4;
2. $\tau \in \mathbb{R}$, the period (amount of time) of a computational step;

Hence, a static MP grammar becomes an MP (dynamical) system through the existence of a procedure to compute its future states (Definition 6) and an association with a time scale (Definition 7).

3.1   The MP$^+$ Class of Systems

There is a (sub)class of MP systems, introduced in [6], called *positively controlled MP systems* (or, for short, MP$^+$) which restricts the quantities of MP substances to the infimum of zero. With such attribute, this kind of system is suitable for correspondences with biological systems, in which quantities are represented in the set $\mathbb{N}$ or $\mathbb{R}^+$, and is enough to become a Turing-powerful model equivalent to register machine [6].

Definition 8 (MP$^+$ Grammar). *An MP$^+$ grammar $G' = (M, R, I', \Phi')$ is a derivation from a standard MP grammar $G = (M, R, I, \Phi)$ if its vector of initial values for substances I' has all components greater than or equal to zero, the set of consuming fluxes of the metabolite x defined as $\Phi'^-_x = \{\varphi'_j : \mathrm{mult}^-(x, r_j) > 0, \forall r_j \in R\}$, and G' respects the following restrictions at every computational step t_i:*

1. $\forall \varphi \in \Phi : \varphi'(t_i) = \begin{cases} \varphi(t_i), & \text{if } \varphi(t_i) \geq 0 \\ 0, & \text{otherwise} \end{cases}$;

2. $\displaystyle\sum_{\varphi' \in \Phi'^-_x} \varphi'(t_i) \leq x(t_i);$ *otherwise* $\varphi'(t_i) = 0, \forall \varphi' \in \Phi'^-_x$ *at the execution step* t_i.

From the procedures to transform a register machine into a MP$^+$ system [6] arises, as a pattern, a very simple and deterministic class which we call MP$^+$V (MP positively controlled grammar with variable gap regulators).

Definition 9 (MP$^+$ Grammar). *An MP$^+$V grammar $G = (M, R, I, \Phi)$ is a MP$^+$ one in which:*

1. $\forall r \in R$ *and* $v', v'' \in M$, r *must have one of the following shapes:*
    (a) $\emptyset \to v''$;
    (b) $v' \to \emptyset$; *or*
    (c) $v' \to v''$;
2. $\forall \varphi \in \Phi$ *and* $m', m'' \in M$, *the flux has either the form* $\varphi = m'$ *or* $\varphi = m' - m''$.

4   Translation of MP$^+$V Systems into Register Machine Programs

From the equivalence result between MP systems and Turing machines [6], it is easy to realize that any given algorithm $\mathcal{A}$ represented in register machine notation, which we may conveniently call $\mathcal{A}_R$, can also be expressed in MP terms (or, simply, as $\mathcal{A}_M$). From this equivalence also derives the transformation on the other way round, i.e. $\mathcal{T}_M : \mathcal{A}_M \mapsto \mathcal{A}_R$, translating any MP algorithm into a register machine one. In fact, $\mathcal{T}_M$ is the present focus of this work.

To simplify its definition, we are going to restrict the input MP system to the MP$^+$V class, without loss of generality (Sect. 3). This class of systems is chosen because:

1. it is the output from the transformation $\mathcal{T}_R : \mathcal{A}_R \mapsto \mathcal{A}_M$ [6];
2. all of its fluxes $\varphi \in \Phi$ are functions of the type $\mathbb{N} \mapsto \mathbb{N}$, meaning the operations of MP$^+$V systems are performed over the set $\mathbb{N}$ of number as those in the register machine; and,
3. it presents a reduced set of rules with only two types of fluxes: single variable or subtraction of two variables.

Although $\mathcal{T}_M$ may sound a trivial inverse transformation of $\mathcal{T}_R$, its definition poses challenges that require a proper treatment in order to provide a correct and total transformation of every $\mathcal{A}_M$ into $\mathcal{A}_R$. Hence, we dedicate the remainder of this section to describe and give mathematical treatment for all of them.

4.1   The Caveats of MP$^+$V

The MP$^+$V systems have two intrinsic properties nonexistent in most of the computational formalisms (including the register machines) that require attentive study before any attempt to define a translation procedure to those systems. These properties are the *unordered, parallel application of the rules* and the *positive control* property.

Inherited from P systems, the parallel application of the MP$^+$V rules has a meaning in the metabolic systems since it describes different contexts regulated by chemical rules independent among each other, inside the cell fluid and behaving under the Brownian rules.

This parallelism of the rules is converted to sequential steps through the establishment of a *block of execution* (such as those present in program languages) in which all the rules and its fluxes are computed for all the variables over auxiliary values, as if the variable values were frozen while the block is being computed. Figure 1 explains the process.

The positive control, on the other side, is a system's property which requires the variable values to be greater than or equal the sum of all its consuming fluxes; this restriction, though to not allow negative quantities of metabolites, is not completely satisfied by the subtraction in $\mathbb{N}$ and must be implemented as a special routine when translating MP$^+$V to register machine according to Definition 8.

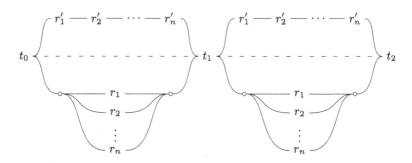

Fig. 1. Graphical representation of the block of execution. The upper part of the dashed line represents the sequential application of MP rules, while the lower part stands for the parallel application of MP rules in the system. Two computational steps are depicted in the figure, t_0–t_1 and t_1–t_2.

4.2   The MP$^+$V Rules

The MP$^+$V systems, as a result of the $\mathcal{A}_R \mapsto \mathcal{A}_M$ translation procedure [6], generates simply four kinds of MP rules that add quantity to a variable V_1 (*i.e.*, $\emptyset \to V_1$), remove quantity from it ($V_1 \to \emptyset$), transfer quantity to another variable V_2 (in the form of the rule $V_1 \to V_2$) or, halts the computation ($V_1 \to HALT$), which requires the additional, special purpose metabolite $HALT$ to signalize the end of the procedure[5]. All of them may be combined solely with fluxes controlled by a single referenced variable (*e.g.* $\varphi = V_1$) or a subtraction of two variables ($\varphi = V_1 - V_2$).

The translation procedures of $\mathcal{T}_M$ for each of the above MP rules resemble inverse versions of those in $\mathcal{T}_R$ [6]. Nonetheless, additional operations are added in order to provide the correct behavior for any inputted MP$^+$V system, not only those outputted from a $\mathcal{T}_R$ transformation.

The strictly increasing MP rule, the one of the form $\emptyset \to V_1 : \varphi$, simply add the value of $\varphi(t)$ (at time t) to the variable V_1; as a recurrent expression, it may be expressed as $V_1[t + 1] = V_1[t] + \varphi(t)$. In the context of the extended register machine, with R_{V_1} as the register address of the variable V_1, R_φ as the one for $\varphi(t)$ and R_{aux} the address for an auxiliary variable, we have the translation of strictly increasing MP rule as Algorithm 4.

Algorithm 4. Strictly increasing MP rule as Register Machine code.

1   `ADD(`$R_{V_1}, R_\varphi, R_{aux}$`)`
2   `CPY(`R_{aux}, R_{V_1}`)`

---

[5] In order to differentiate the two "halts" in this paper, `HALT` represents the halting instruction in register machines while $HALT$ the metabolite in MP$^+$V systems.

Similarly, the strictly decreasing MP rule $V_1 \rightarrow \emptyset : \varphi$ is mathematically represented as $V_1[t+1] = V_1[t] - \varphi(t)$ and produces a translation code of the form of Algorithm 5.

Algorithm 5. Strictly decreasing MP rule as Register Machine code.

```
1   SUB(R_{V_1}, R_{\varphi}, R_{aux})
2   CPY(R_{aux}, R_{V_1})
```

The transfer MP rule, $V_1 \rightarrow V_2 : \varphi$, can be seen as a composition of both previous rules according to I/O MP systems [10]; hence, it is not a single recurrent equation, but two of them (Eq. 1). Consequently, as can be seen in Algorithm 6, the register machine subprogram for its transformation is simply a concatenation of the previous Algorithms 4 and 5.

$$\begin{cases} V_1[t+1] = V_1[t] - \varphi(t) \\ V_2[t+1] = V_2[t] + \varphi(t) \end{cases} \tag{1}$$

Algorithm 6. Transfer MP rule as Register Machine code.

```
1   SUB(R_{V_1}, R_{\varphi}, R_{aux})
2   CPY(R_{aux}, R_{V_1})
3   ADD(R_{V_2}, R_{\varphi}, R_{aux})
4   CPY(R_{aux}, R_{V_2})
```

Finally, the halting rule $V_1 \rightarrow HALT : \varphi$ simply signalizes the end of the computation when the quantity of the $HALT$ variable is greater than zero. Hence, the produced code verifies if there is a halting situation (and halts if there is), otherwise updates the quantity of V_1 and halts the execution.

Algorithm 7. Halting MP rule as Register Machine code.

```
1   JNZ(R_{HALT}, 3)
2   JMP(4)
3   HALT
4   SUB(R_{V_1}, R_{\varphi}, R_{aux})
5   CPY(R_{aux}, R_{V_1})
6   ADD(R_{HALT}, R_{\varphi}, R_{aux})
7   CPY(R_{aux}, R_{HALT})
```

As already discussed and graphically shown in Fig. 1, one computational step of MP$^+$V systems is expanded in several register machine instructions that also include a framework of operations reflecting properties of MP$^+$V nonexistent in the addressed architecture. These additional operations are, now, studied in details.

4.3   Surroundings of MP⁺V Steps

Translating the rules of MP⁺V systems to register machine subprograms is just one of the parts to correct transform one system into another. As can be seen in Fig. 2 (and previously discussed in Sect. 4.1), it is necessary to define (i) a sequential, *block of computational* referent to the execution of a step in the MP⁺V dynamics; (ii) guards for the variables to isolate the computation of the future value (*i.e.*, $V[t+1]$) with the actual value $V[t]$; (iii) evaluation of the *positive control* property; and, finally, (iv) the recurrent call of the dynamical system.

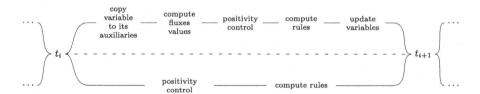

Fig. 2. Representation of a computation step MP⁺V systems (lower part) and its equivalent register machine (upper part).

The sequential block of computation is nothing more than simple concatenation of the aforementioned subprograms (ii) and (iii); it is the upper arc in Fig. 2 which, in a sequential way, process all the required procedures for the computation of a single MP⁺V step as a register machine.

The guards, by the other hand, are specialized pieces of code that keep the variables unchanged during the sequential execution of the MP⁺V step; as can be seen in Fig. 2, they represent all the surplus of operations nonexistent in the MP⁺V track: copy of the values of variables into auxiliary registers, computation of fluxes with assignment to particular registers and update of the variables value after computational step.

It is necessary to freeze the values of the variables, and rely on auxiliary register copies of them during a computational step, because rules and fluxes may reference the quantity of the variable V at time t_i (*i.e.* $V[t_i]$), not an intermediary and already changed value $V[t_{i+\epsilon}]$, with $t_i < t_{i+\epsilon} < t_{i+1}$, that solely exists in the sequential (or register machine) context: changes on variables quantities must occur uniquely in the end of the computational step, in accordance to the behaviour of dynamical systems; in-between, all operations must occur over auxiliary variables.

A similar pattern arises for the fluxes values. Fluxes must be updated at every MP⁺V step and their values must be promptly available for the re-computation of the variable quantities according to the application of the rules. Moreover, fluxes values are subject to the positivity control (Definition 8) which, in case of nonsatisfiability of the property, sets the appropriate fluxes to zero; hence, instead of performing computations of fluxes and their verification at each rule application, it is enough to calculate their values once in the step of computation and, then, consult them in their respective dedicated registers.

All these guards demand simplistic algorithms: the copy and update of variables rely on the CPY instruction, while the fluxes, depending of their nature, either on the CPY or the subtraction subprogram SUB.

Algorithm 8. Copy variable to its auxiliary register.

1   CPY($R_V, R_{V_{aux}}$)

Algorithm 9. Update variable with its auxiliary register value.

1   CPY($R_{V_{aux}}, R_V$)

Algorithm 10. Update the flux value.

if $\varphi = V$ **then**
   1   CPY(R_V, R_φ)
else   ▷ Hence, $\varphi = V_1 - V_2$
   1   SUB($R_{V_1}, R_{V_2}, R_\varphi$)
end if

The translation of the *positivity control* property to the register machine specification is, however, slightly more intricate: while in the MP$^+$V systems it is enough to be stated as a system's property, in the register machine it must be ensured by actually coding both constraints in Definition 8.

The first of them is a statement, in mathematical terms, that any flux φ is a function with co-domain equals to the natural set of numbers $\mathbb{N}$, an easily satisfied requirement since the values of the registers (and, hence, variables) are restricted to $\mathbb{N}$ by the register machine definition (Definition 1) and the fluxes are restricted to monomials or subtraction of variables. As we have already seen, the SUB subprogram has an intrinsic mechanism to guarantee no value goes below zero (Sect. 2).

Conversely, the other constraint requires a special subprogram to satisfy its conditions. It sets to zero all consuming fluxes for a certain variable V if the sum of them are greater than the actual available quantity of V. In mathematical terms, if Φ_V^- is the set of consuming fluxes of V, $\sum_{\varphi \in \Phi_V^-} \varphi(t_i) \leq V[t_i]$ at time t_i;

otherwise $\forall \varphi \in \Phi_V^-, \varphi(t_i) = 0$. Since the compiler knows both the variable V and the consuming fluxes $\Phi_V^- = \{\varphi_1, \varphi_2, \ldots, \varphi_k\}$ (with $k = |\Phi_V^-|$), the generated

Algorithm 11. Positivity control algorithm.

1	$\mathbf{CLR}(R_{sum})$
2	$\mathbf{ADD}(R_{\varphi_1}, R_{sum}, R_{sum})$
3	$\mathbf{ADD}(R_{\varphi_1}, R_{sum}, R_{sum})$
4	$\mathbf{ADD}(R_{\varphi_2}, R_{sum}, R_{sum})$
$\vdots$	
k+1	$\mathbf{ADD}(R_{\varphi_k}, R_{sum}, R_{sum})$
k+2	$\mathbf{CPY}(R_V, R_{comparator})$
k+3	$\mathbf{JZ}(R_{sum}, 2 \cdot k + 8)$
k+4	$\mathbf{JZ}(R_{comparator}, k + 8)$
k+5	$\mathbf{DEC}(R_{sum})$
k+6	$\mathbf{DEC}(R_{comparator})$
k+7	$\mathbf{JMP}(k + 3)$
k+8	$\mathbf{CLR}(R_{\varphi_1})$
k+9	$\mathbf{CLR}(R_{\varphi_2})$
$\vdots$	
2·k+7	$\mathbf{CLR}(R_{\varphi_k})$

subprogram does not have to seek for this information and, for each variable, can have the form of Algorithm 11.

The explicit references to the fluxes in Algorithm 11 in both computation of the sum (lines 2 to $k+1$) and the invalidation of the fluxes (lines $k+8$ to $2 \cdot k+7$) makes positivity control property the biggest contributor for the line of codes in the equivalent register machine version of a MP$^+$V system.

Finally, we must ensure the execution of the recurrent computation (Definition 6) of the MP$^+$V system in the $\mathcal{T}_M$ transformation. From examples such as Goniometricus or Sirius [10], we know that some MP systems work as generators for infinite series and signals, indefinitely computing values without an explicit procedure for stopping them; in contrast, functions such as $\max(R_1, R_2)$ implemented in [6] converges to a particular fixed-point (halt) state which signalizes the end of the calculation process of the system [6]. The differentiation between them, nonetheless, relies solely in the existence of a variable $HALT$ in the latter system, as well as a strictly increasing or transfer rule which increments the value of $HALT$. Hence, in terms of register machine, these systems diverge in the existence of a R_{HALT} register and an instruction to stop the execution when $R_{HALT} \neq 0$.

As can be seen in the upper part of Fig. 2, all the register machine code generated by the transformation $\mathcal{T}_M : \mathcal{A}_M \mapsto \mathcal{A}_R$ is enclosed inside two sequential steps t_i and t_{i+1}, except by the recurrent call of the dynamical system. In fact, all the computation performed by the equivalent register machine (*i.e.*, all the algorithms seen so far) is, actually, the computation of a single MP$^+$V step. The purpose of the recurrent call is, then, to recall the computation procedures up to the moment $R_{HALT} \neq 0$; to achieve it, the procedure verifies the state of the R_{HALT} before step reckoning and chooses if the program should be halt (a jump

Algorithm 12. Loop control of the dynamical systems that halts.

1	JNZ(R_{HALT}, ℓ)
	$\vdots$
ℓ-1	JMP(1)
ℓ	HALT

Algorithm 13. Complete translation procedure from MP$^+$V system to register machine

while $R_{HALT} = 0$ **do**
    for all variable $v \in M$ **do**   ▷ copy variables to auxiliaries
        $R_{v'} \leftarrow R_v$
    end for
    for all flux $\varphi \in \Phi$ **do**   ▷ compute fluxes
        $R_\varphi \leftarrow \varphi(t_i)$
    end for
    for all variable $v \in M$ **do**   ▷ positivity control property
        for all flux $\varphi_v^- \in \Phi_v^-$ **do**
            $R_{sum} \leftarrow R_{sum} + R_{\varphi_v^-}$
        end for
        if $R_{sum} > v$ **then**
            for all flux $\varphi_v^- \in \Phi_v^-$ **do**
                $R_{\varphi_v^-} \leftarrow 0$
            end for
        end if
    end for
    for all rule r **do**   ▷ compute rules
        if r is of the form $\emptyset \rightarrow v : \varphi$ **then**
            $R_{v'} \leftarrow R_{v'} + \varphi$
        else if r is of the form $v \rightarrow \emptyset : \varphi$ **then**
            $R_{v'} \leftarrow R_{v'} - \varphi$
        else   ▷ hence, it must be of the form $v_1 \rightarrow v_2 : \varphi$
            $R_{v_1'} \leftarrow R_{v_1'} + \varphi$
            $R_{v_2'} \leftarrow R_{v_2'} - \varphi$
        end if
    end for
    for all variable $v \in M$ **do**   ▷ update variables
        $R_v \leftarrow R_{v'}$
    end for
end while

to the last line of the program, ℓ in Algorithm 12, where a HALT is always present) or continue with normal execution; in case of the latter, the penultimate line of the program ($\ell - 1$) redirects the execution back to the first line. In algorithm terms:

Finally, the pseudo-code produced by the transformation is represented in Algorithm 13.

5   Conclusion

There were no doubts of the possibility to translate MP systems to register machine or any other Turing-powerful formalism: the discrete and deterministic characteristics of these metabolic systems are exactly those that guarantee the feasibility of this translation. The novelty, on the other hand, relies in the direct transformation of modelling languages with completely different paradigms: from the metabolic, parallel and centered on pair of substances transformations to a computational and globally oriented sequence of instructions standpoint; from MP systems to von Neumann architecture.

It is worth to note that it is not the target language (here the register machine, but equivalently for hardware description or programming ones), but the idea of an **algorithmic transformation between models** that permits the effortless and automatic translation of metabolic systems into either pieces of software (*e.g.*, for simulation purposes), hardware (such as [4,7,16]), visual representations (automata) or any other common use case for exogenous model transformation [2].

At last, the availability of the bidirectional translation and equivalence between MP^+V systems and register machines open the way for implementation of hardware circuits based on metabolic (MP) systems.

References

1. Beal, J., Lu, T., Weiss, R.: Automatic compilation from high-level biologically-oriented programming language to genetic regulatory networks. PLoS One **6**(8), e22490 (2011)
2. Brambilla, M., Cabot, J., Wimmer, M.: Model-Driven Software Engineering in Practice. Synthesis Lectures on Software Engineering, vol. 1, pp. 1–182. Morgan & Claypool, San Rafael (2012)
3. Castellini, A., Franco, G., Manca, V.: Hybrid functional Petri nets as MP systems. Nat. Comput. **9**, 61–81 (2010)
4. Fernandez, L., Martinez, V.J., Arroyo, F., Mingo, L.F.: A hardware circuit for selecting active rules in transition P systems. In: Seventh International Symposium on Symbolic and Numeric Algorithms for Scientific Computing (SYNASC 2005), p. 4. IEEE (2005)
5. Gheorghe, M., Stannett, M.: Membrane system models for super-turing paradigms. Nat. Comput. **11**(2), 253–259 (2012)
6. Gracini Guiraldelli, R.H., Manca, V.: The Computational Universality of Metabolic Computing (2015). arxiv.org/abs/1505.02420
7. Gravitz, L.: Cell on a Chip (2009). http://www.technologyreview.com/news/414622/cell-on-a-chip/
8. Hinrichsen, D., Pritchard, A.J.: Mathematical Systems Theory I: Modelling, State Space Analysis, Stability and Robustness, Texts in Applied Mathematics, vol. 48. Springer, Heidelberg (2005)
9. Lewis, H., Papadimitriou, C.: Elements of the Theory of Computation, 2nd edn. Prentice-Hall, Upper Saddle River (1997)
10. Manca, V.: Infobiotics: Information in Biotic Systems. Emergence, Complexity and Computation, vol. 3. Springer, Heidelberg (2013)

11. Manca, V., Bianco, L., Fontana, F.: Evolution and oscillation in P systems: applications to biological phenomena. In: Mauri, G., Păun, G., Pérez-Jímenez, M.J., Rozenberg, G., Salomaa, A. (eds.) WMC 2004. LNCS, vol. 3365, pp. 63–84. Springer, Heidelberg (2005)
12. Manca, V., Lombardo, R.: Computing with multi-membranes. In: Gheorghe, M., Păun, G., Rozenberg, G., Salomaa, A., Verlan, S. (eds.) CMC 2011. LNCS, vol. 7184, pp. 282–299. Springer, Heidelberg (2012)
13. Manca, V., Marchetti, L.: Solving dynamical inverse problems by means of metabolic P systems. Biosystems **109**(1), 78–86 (2012)
14. Minsky, M.: Computation: Finite and Infinite Machines, 1st edn. Prentice Hall, Englewood Cliffs (1967)
15. Păun, G.: A quick introduction to membrane computing. J. Logic Algebraic Program. **79**, 291–294 (2010)
16. Sarpeshkar, R.: Ultra-Low Power Bioelectronics: Fundamentals, Biomedical Applications, and Bio-Inspired Systems, 1st edn. Cambridge University Press, Cambridge (2010)
17. Sarpeshkar, R.: Analog synthetic biology. Philos. Trans. A Math. Phys. Eng. Sci. **372**(2012), 20130110 (2014)
18. Shepherdson, J.C., Sturgis, H.E.: Computability of recursive functions. J. ACM **10**, 217–255 (1963)
19. Siegelmann, H.T., Fishman, S.: Analog computation with dynamical systems. Physica D **120**(1–2), 214–235 (1998)

On the Communication Complexity
of the Vertex Cover Problem
and 3-Satisfiability Problem in ECP Systems

Nestine Hope S. Hernandez, Richelle Ann B. Juayong$^{(\boxtimes)}$, Sherlyne L. Francia,
Denise Alyssa A. Francisco, and Henry N. Adorna

Algorithms and Complexity Laboratory, Department of Computer Science,
University of the Philippines Diliman, Diliman, 1101 Quezon City, Philippines
{rbjuayong,slfrancia,dafrancisco}@up.edu.ph,
{nshernandez,hnadorna}@dcs.upd.edu.ph

Abstract. In this paper, the communication complexity of non-confluent solutions for Vertex Cover Problem (VCP) and 3-Satisfiability Problem (3SP) in Evolution-Communication P systems (ECP) are analyzed. We use dynamical communication measures suggested by previous literature in our analysis. Solutions are constructed in several modes of operation: when communication is prioritized over evolution (CPE), when evolution is prioritized over communication (EPC) and when no priority is imposed (CME). VCP and 3SP are problems that have already been problems of interest for works that investigate communication complexity in an ECP system variant called Evolution-Communication P system with Energy (ECPe system). In this paper, we are interested in employing the technique used in ECPe system, this time for solutions in ECP system.

Keywords: Membrane computing · Evolution-communication P systems · Communication complexity · Vertex cover problem · 3-satisfiability problem

1 Introduction

Membrane computing, as proposed by Gheorghe Păun, is a compartmentalized and distributed model of computing inspired by living cells [12]. These so-called P systems are often composed of several regions, each enclosed by a membrane, working together to perform a computation. Hence, communication among these membranes plays an essential role for the functioning of P systems.

However, the communication complexity of P systems is a less addressed issue in the field of membrane computing (this has been included as research topic in [13]). The authors in [1] tackled this concern, and presented the Evolution-Communication P systems with energy (ECPe systems) alongside dynamical complexity measures. In ECPe systems, energy objects e were introduced to

© Springer International Publishing Switzerland 2015
G. Rozenberg et al. (Eds.): CMC 2015, LNCS 9504, pp. 200–214, 2015.
DOI: 10.1007/978-3-319-28475-0_14

Evolution-Communication P systems (ECP) to aid in gauging the communication complexity of a system. The special objects e were used as a form of payment whenever an object is communicated. Initial investigation of ECPe system used three modes of operation: one has priority on evolution (EPC), another has priority on communication (CPE), and the other does not impose priority on either evolution or communication (CME). These modes were originally defined in [3] for ECP systems.

The dynamical measures presented in [1] were applied in [8] for analyzing the communication complexity of some decision problems solved in ECPe systems operating in CME mode. The problems tackled are NP-hard problems: the Vertex Cover Problem (VCP) and the 3-Satisfiability problem (3SP). These problems have already been solved [6,10,11] in other P system models, e.g. P systems with active membranes, where polynomial time solutions are traded-off with exponential workspace. While the solutions in these previous literatures are confluent, the ECPe system solutions presented in [8] are non-confluent; this means that whenever an instance of the problem is associated with a **yes**, there is a computation in the P system solution that outputs a **yes**. Otherwise, all computations in the P system solution outputs a **no**. Non-confluent solutions to VCP and 3SP in other modes, specifically CPE and EPC, were presented in [5].

In this paper, we present non-confluent solutions to VCP and 3SP, this time, in ECP systems. This model is introduced and shown to be computationally-complete in [3] (with additional completeness proofs in [2]). We are interested in exploring the communication resources when previous solutions are adapted in the original model, i.e. if we remove the object e requirement imposed during communication. Thus, the solutions in this paper follow a similar pattern as in previous solutions working in ECPe systems. In analyzing the communication resources used in computations, we used a slight modification of the dynamical measures given in previous works (e.g. in [1,8]).

2   Preliminaries

Before we proceed, we assume that readers are familiar with the fundamentals of formal language theory and membrane computing [12,14]. We start with a formal definition of the problems used in our study. We take the definitions of a graph, vertex cover, Vertex Cover Problem, Boolean formula and 3-Satisfiability Problem from [8].

A graph is defined as an ordered pair (V, E) where V is the set of vertices and the set of edges $E \subseteq V \times V$. Figure 1 is a graph where $V = \{1, 2, 3, 4\}$ and $E = \{(1, 2), (2, 3), (3, 4)\}$. A vertex cover VC_k where $1 \leq k \leq |V|$ is a set of vertices with size less than or equal to k where for all edges $(i, j) \in E$, $i \in VC_k$ or $j \in VC_k$.

Definition 1. _Vertex Cover Problem (VCP)_ _Given a graph_ $G = (V, E)$ _and a positive integer_ k _where_ $1 \leq k \leq |V|$, _is there a vertex cover_ VC_k?

A Boolean formula ϕ_X where X is a set of variables $x_1, x_2 \ldots x_p$ in conjunctive normal form (CNF) is a conjunction, denoted by $C_1 \wedge C_2 \wedge \ldots \wedge C_m$ where

Fig. 1. An example of a graph

$m \in \mathbb{Z}^+$, of propositional clauses C_i which are a disjunction of literals y_{i_j} defined as $C_i = (y_{i_1} \vee y_{i_2} \vee \ldots \vee y_{i_n})$ where $n \in \mathbb{Z}^+$ and $y_{i_j} \in X \cup \{\overline{x} | x \in X\}, 1 \leq j \leq n$. The notation $\overline{x}$ implies a negation.

In a k-CNF Boolean formula, each clause is a disjunction of exactly k variables. A Boolean formula is said to be satisfiable if there exists a truth value (1 as true, 0 as false) assignment for all variables on which the formula evaluates to true.

Definition 2. *3 Satisfiability Problem (3SP)* *Given a 3-CNF Boolean formula ϕ_X over a set of variables X, is ϕ_X satisfiable?*

We now give the formal definition of the main model used in this study. We define an Evolution-Communication P system (ECP system) similar to [3] as follows:

Definition 3. *An ECP system (without energy) is a construct of the form $\Pi = (O, \mu, w_1, \ldots, w_m, R_1, R'_1, \ldots, R_m, R'_m, h_{output})$ where m is the total number of membranes; O is the alphabet of objects; μ is a hierarchical membrane structure (a rooted tree) of degree m, bijectively labelled from 1 to m, and the interior of each membrane defines a region h ($1 \leq h \leq m$); the environment is referred as region 0; w_h is the initial multiset over (O^* in region h ($1 \leq h \leq m$); R_h is the set of evolution rules in region h; Each rule has the form $u \to v$ where $u \in O^+$, $v \in O^*$. R'_h are sets of communication rules in membrane h; There are two types of communication rules: symport and antiport. A symport rule takes one of the following form: (u, in) or (u, out), where $u \in O^+$. An antiport rule takes the form $(u, out; v, in)$ where $u, v \in O^+$. $h_{output} \in \{0, 1, \ldots, m\}$ is the output region.*

The model used in our P systems consist of the usual P system features, i.e. a hierarchical membrane structure; each membrane encloses a region that contains a multiset of objects; objects can be evolved or communicated through a set of rules. We represent a hierarchical membrane structure through a string of matching square brackets with labels. If membrane j is immediately contained in membrane h, i.e. $[\ldots[\ ]_j]_h$, h is referred as parent of j (denoted by $parent(j)$). Consequently, j is a *child membrane* of h. This is denoted by $j \in children(h)$ where $children(h)$ is the set of all child membranes of h. Suppose a region consists of a multiset w, we use the term 'copy of a' to refer to an instance of object a present in multiset w. We use the evolution rules associated with each region in order to evolve copies of objects, while communication rules associated with each membrane are used to communicate copies of objects across membranes.

A set of evolution rules R_h is associated with each region h. To describe how each evolution rule is executed, we refer to Definition 3 to recall the form followed by each rule in R_h. When applying a rule of this type, multiset u transforms into a multiset v in the next time step. This is similar to the multiset-rewriting rule for TP systems [12]. However, the multiset produced always stays in the same region. Each membrane h ($1 \leq h \leq m$) has a set of communication rules; each communication rule can either be a symport or an antiport rule. A symport rule can be of the form (u, in) or (u, out), where $u \in O^+$. By using this rule, the multiset u are transported inside (denoted by in) or outside (denoted by out) the membrane where the rule is defined. An antiport rule is of the form $(u, out; v, in)$ where $u, v \in O^+$. By using this rule, a multiset u in the region immediately outside the membrane where the rule is declared, and a multiset v inside the region bounded by the membrane should exist. When such rule is applied, multisets u and v are swapped in the different regions, respectively. As can be observed, the format for communication rules are adapted from rules used in another model called P systems with symport and antiport [12].

In the model presented, rules are applied in a non-deterministic and maximally parallel manner, starting from the initial multiset in each region. Non-determinism implies that at a certain step, if there are more than two rules that can be applied to a copy of an object, the system non-deterministically chooses the rule to be applied for each copy. Maximally parallel means that there are no further rules applicable to copies that are not used in any rule. A configuration C of a P system describes the state of a P system, i.e. the membrane structure and the content of regions. The process of applying all applicable rules in a current configuration, thus obtaining a new configuration is called a transition. A computation is a (finite or infinite) sequence of configurations such that: (a) the first term is the initial configuration of the system; (b) for each $n \geq 2$, the n-th configuration of the sequence is obtained from the previous configuration in one transition step; and (c) if the sequence is finite then the last term is a halting configuration (a configuration where no rule of the system is applicable to it). Computation succeeds when the system halts. If the computation doesn't halt, computation fails because the system did not produce any output.

It can be observed that in ECP system, evolution rules are distinguished from communication rules. Thus, following non-determinism, a copy of an object may either be communicated or evolved. In [3], aside from this usual mode of operation, they also investigated ECP systems where some priority is imposed over rules. The resulting three modes are explicitly stated in the next definition:

Definition 4. *We define three modes of operation for a given ECP system:*

- **CPE mode** *(communication has priority over evolution) - if there is a communication rule that can be applied in any membrane in the system, then only communication rules are applied on that step and no evolution rule can be performed.*

- **CME** mode *(communication and evolution rules are mixed) - there is no priority over evolution or communication rule.*
- **EPC** mode *(evolution has priority over communication) - if there is an evolution rule that can be applied in any membrane in the system, then only evolution rules are applied on that step and no evolution rule can be performed.*

To further illustrate these modes of operation, suppose in a computation step of an ECP system, we can apply an evolution rule r_1 and a communication rule r_2. In the CME mode, both rules are applied to proceed to the next configuration. However, in CPE mode, only rule r_2 is applied. In EPC mode, only rule r_1 is applied.

3 On Communication Complexity of Problems Solved in ECP Systems

We slightly modified the definitions in [8] to define communication complexity classes for problems solved in ECP systems.

3.1 Solving Hard Problems in ECP Systems

We first define a recognizer ECP system used in solving decision problems as adapted from [15].

Definition 5. *A recognizer ECP system is an ECP system Π whose alphabet contains two distinct objects **yes** and **no**. Every computation of Π is halting and during each computation, exactly one of the objects **yes**, **no** is sent out from the skin to signal acceptance or rejection. If all the computations of Π agree on the result, then Π is said to be confluent; if this is not necessarily the case, then it is said to be non-confluent and the global result is acceptance if and only if there exists an accepting computation.*

Based on [15], a decision problem can be represented as a *pair* $Y = (I_Y, \theta_Y)$ *where I_Y is a language over a finite alphabet and θ_Y is a total Boolean function over I_Y.* In the next definition, a family of recognizer ECP systems is used to solve a decision problem. A family of recognizer ECP systems $\Pi(n)$ is a set of ECP systems that takes a parameter n to construct each system.

Definition 6. *A family $\Pi(n), n \in \mathbb{N}$, of ECP systems, solves a problem (I_Y, θ_Y) if there exists a pair (cod, s) over I_Y such that for each instance $u \in I_Y$:*

(i) $n = s(u) \in \mathbb{N}$ and $cod(u)$ is an input multiset of the system $\Pi(n)$
(ii) there exists an accepting computation of $\Pi(n)$ with input $cod(u)$ if and only if $\theta_Y(u) = 1$.

3.2   Some Dynamical Communication Measures and Communication Complexity Class

We start with the definition of some dynamical communication measures originally defined in [1] for a variant of ECP systems called Evolution-Communication P systems with Energy (ECPe systems).

$$ComN(C_i \Rightarrow C_{i+1}) = \begin{cases} 1 \text{ if a communication rule is used} \\ \quad \text{in this transition,} \\ 0 \text{ otherwise} \end{cases}$$

$$ComR(C_i \Rightarrow C_{i+1}) = \text{the number of communication rules}$$
$$\text{used in this transition}$$

Another dynamical measure used in [1] employs special object e (so-called *energy*) as cost for every communicated object. Such form of cost is of importance when defining the weight of every communication (or $ComW$). Since ECP systems do not employ energy, we modified the communication weight used in this study, we denote it by $ComW'$.

$$ComW'(C_i \Rightarrow C_{i+1}) = \text{the sum of application of all communication rules}$$
$$\text{used in this transition.}$$

These measures can be extended for computations. Specifically, for $ComX \in \{ComN, ComR, ComW'\}$ and a halting computation $\delta : C_0 \Rightarrow C_1 \Rightarrow \cdots \Rightarrow C_h$:

$$ComX(\delta) = \sum_{i=0}^{h-1} ComX(C_i \Rightarrow C_{i+1})$$

We use the measures above to define communication complexity classes for ECP systems and for problems solved in ECP systems.

Definition 7. *Let $Y = (I_Y, \theta_Y)$ be a decision problem, $\Pi(n), n \in \mathbb{N}$, be a family of recognizer ECP systems solving Y with a pair (cod, s) over I_Y. For each instance $u \in I_Y$:*

$$ComX(u, \Pi(n)) = \quad min\{ComX(\delta) \mid \delta \; : \; C_0 \Rightarrow C_1 \Rightarrow \cdots \Rightarrow C_h \text{ in } \Pi(n)$$
$$\text{with } n = s(u) \text{ and } cod(u) \text{ is an input multiset in } \Pi(n)\},$$

where $X \in \{N, R, W'\}$. To analyze the communication resources used by $\Pi(n)$ in solving problem $Y, ComX(Y, \Pi(n))$ is defined as:

$$ComX(Y, \Pi(n)) = \quad max\{ComX(u, \Pi(n)) \mid u \in I_Y\}.$$

Definition 8. *Let $F_{mode}ComX$ where $X \in \{N, R, W'\}$ and $mode \in \{CPE, CME, EPC\}$. Decision problem $Y = (I_Y, \theta_Y) \in F_{mode}ComX(k)$ if and only if:*

(i) There exists a family $\Pi(n), n \in \mathbb{N}$, of confluent recognizer ECP systems that operates in mode and decides Y

(ii) $ComX(Y, \Pi(n)) = k$.

The analogous complexity classes for non-confluent recognizer ECP systems are $NF_{mode}ComX$ where $X \in \{N, R, W'\}$ and mode $\in \{CPE, CME, EPC\}$.

We say that $Y \in F_{mode}ComNRW'(p, q, r)$ if and only if $Y \in F_{mode}ComN(p)$, $Y \in F_{mode}ComR(q)$ and $Y \in F_{mode}ComW'(r)$. We use $NF_{mode}ComNRW'$ for non-confluent recognizer ECP systems.

4   On ECP Solutions to VCP

From [8], the Vertex Cover Problem (VCP) can be represented by a pair $VCP = (I_{VCP}, \theta_{VCP})$ where $I_{VCP} = \{w_{(G,k)} \mid w_{(G,k)}$ is a string representing a graph G and a positive integer $k\}$. The Boolean function $\theta_{VCP}(w_{(G,k)}) = 1$ whenever there is a vertex cover VC_k in the graph G; otherwise, $\theta_{VCP}(w_{(G,k)}) = 0$. In the succeeding VCP solutions, we will be using the same encoding as in [8]: The pair (cod, s) for every instance $w_{G,k}$ over I_{VCP} have $s(w_{G,k}) = |V_G|$ (which is also the parameter input for the family of ECP system solving VCP) and $cod(w_{G,k})$ as an input multiset in region 0 consisting of A_{ij} for every $(i, j) \in E_G$, k copies of object c, and $|E_G| - k$ copies of object d.

The solutions for VCP stated in the paper follow the pattern of the solution presented in [5, 8]. This implies that computations in every ECP solution for VCP follow four consecutive phases namely: setup phase, finding a candidate solution, verifying the candidate solution and output phase. During the setup phase, an end-vertex is selected for each of the edges. In the next phase, a candidate vertex cover is determined. The validity of the candidate vertex cover is examined in the succeeding phase. Finally, in the output phase, a **yes** or **no** is sent to the environment depending on whether the examined vertex cover is valid or not.

Theorem 1. $VCP \in NF_{CPE}ComNRW'(6, 2k + 4, |E_G| + 2k + 3)$ where E_G represents the set of edges.

Proof. To prove the above theorem, we define a family of ECP systems operating in CPE mode as $\Pi(n)$ where $n = s(w_{(G,k)}) = |V_G|$:

$$\Pi(n) = (O, [_0[_1]_1[_2]_2]_0, w_0, \emptyset, \emptyset, R_0, R_0', R_1, R_1', R_2, R_2', 0),$$

- $O = \{A_{ij}, v_i, i, \underline{i} \mid 1 \le i < j \le n\} \cup \{c, c', d, \textbf{no}, \textbf{yes}\} \cup \{\#_0, \#_1, \#_2, \#_3\}$
- $w_0 = v_1 v_2 \ldots v_n \#_0 cod(w_{(G,k)})$
- $R_0 = \{A_{ij} \rightarrow i, A_{ij} \rightarrow j \mid 1 \le i < j \le n\} \cup \{\#_3 \rightarrow \textbf{no}\}$
- $R_0' = \{(\textbf{yes}, out), (\textbf{no}, out)\}$
- $R_1 = \{v_i \rightarrow \underline{i}^{n-1} \mid 1 \le i \le n\} \cup \{c \rightarrow c'\}$
- $R_1' = \{(v_i, in; c', out), (i, in; \underline{i}, out) \mid 1 \le i \le n\} \cup \{(c, in)\}$
- $R_2 = \{\#_0 \rightarrow \#_1, \#_1 \rightarrow \#_2, \#_2 \rightarrow \#_3, \#_3 \rightarrow \textbf{yes}\}$
- $R_2' = \{(i, in; \#_3, out) \mid 1 \le i \le n\} \cup \{(\#_0, in), (\textbf{yes}, out), (\textbf{no}, out)\}$

Table 1. Communication Resources for VCP solution in CPE mode. N refers to the number of communication steps, R refers to the number of communication rules and W' refers to the sum of application of all communication rules

	N	R	W'
Setup	1	2	$k+1$
Finding a candidate	1	k	k
Validation	1	at most k	at most $|E_G|$ (if candidate is valid)
Output	2	2	2

The computation of the ECP system in CPE mode solving the VCP problem is as follows: the setup phase is composed of two steps. In the initial step, k copies of object c are transported to region 1 and $\#_0$ is transported to region 2. Since no communication can occur in the next step, evolution rules are applied. The evolution rules applied are used to evolve each A_{ij} to either i or j and each c to c'. Also, $\#_0$ evolves to $\#_1$. The next time step signals the phase of finding a candidate solution. There are k rules of the form $(v_i, in; c', out)$ that are used in this step to select a candidate vertex cover.

In the next step signaling the validation phase, no communication can be applied. Instead, select evolution rules are applied to evolve all v_i's into $n-1$ number of $\underline{i}$ objects. Simultaneously in region 2, $\#_1$ will evolve to $\#_2$. In the next step, the system can use some communication rules. Specifically, the communication rules of the form $(i, in; \underline{i}, out)$ may be used up to $|E_G|$ number of times depending on whether the candidate vertex cover is valid or not. If the chosen vertex cover is valid, the rule will be used $|E_G|$ times because all the edges will be covered. The next step involves an evolution rule that changes $\#_2$ to $\#_3$. This step signals the last phase, i.e. the output phase. When $\#_3$ already exists in region 2, two scenarios may occur. If the chosen vertex cover is invalid, the communication rule $(i, in; \#_3, out)$ will be used. Otherwise, $\#_3$ will evolve to **yes**. Note that although the rule $\#_3 \rightarrow$ **yes** may also be applicable in the case of an invalid candidate vertex cover, the rule will not be applied because the mode used in the system prioritizes communication over evolution. Afterwards, if the chosen vertex cover is invalid, the next step makes use of rule $\#_3 \rightarrow$ **no** in region 0. Otherwise, the object **yes** will be transported from region 2 to region 0. In the last step, either a **yes** or a **no** occurs in the outermost region. Thus in the last step, one of these objects is sent to the environment.

Table 1 summarizes the communication resources used per phase.

For the succeeding theorems in this section, we only give a sketch of their proofs.

Theorem 2. $VCP \in NF_{CME}ComNRW'(6, 2k+5, |E_G|+2k+4)$ *where* E_G *represents the set of edges.*

Proof. To prove Theorem 2, we define a family of ECP systems operating in CME mode as $\Pi(n)$ where $n = s(w_{(G,k)}) = |V_G|$:

$$\Pi(n) = (O, [_0[_1]_1[_2]_2]_0, w_0, \emptyset, \emptyset, R_0, R_0', R_1, R_1', R_2, R_2', 0),$$

- $O = \{A_{ij}, v_i, i, \underline{i} \mid 1 \le i < j \le n\} \cup \{c, c', d, \mathbf{no}, \mathbf{yes}\} \cup \{\#_0, \#_1, \#_2, \#_3, \#_4, \#_5, \#_6, \alpha_0, \alpha_1, \alpha_2, \alpha_3, \alpha_4\}$
- $w_0 = v_1 v_2 \ldots v_n \#_0 \alpha_0 cod(w_{(G,k)})$
- $R_0 = \{A_{ij} \to i, A_{ij} \to j \mid 1 \le i < j \le n\}$
  $\cup \{\#_0 \to \#_1, \#_1 \to \#_2, \#_2 \to \#_3, \#_3 \to \#_4, \#_4 \to \#_5, \#_5 \to \#_6\}$
- $R'_0 = \{(\mathbf{yes}, out), (\mathbf{no}, out)\}$
- $R_1 = \{c \to c'\} \cup \{v_i \to \underline{i}^{n-1} \mid 1 \le i \le n\}$
- $R'_1 = \{(c, in)\} \cup \{(v_i, in; c', out), (i, in; \underline{i}, out) \mid 1 \le i \le n\}$
- $R_2 = \{\alpha_0 \to \alpha_1, \alpha_1 \to \alpha_2, \alpha_2 \to \alpha_3, \alpha_3 \to \alpha_4\} \cup \{\#_6 \to \mathbf{yes}\}$
  $\cup \{i \to \mathbf{no} \mid 1 \le i \le n\}$
- $R'_2 = \{(\alpha_0, in), (\#_6, in; \alpha_4, out), (i, in; \alpha_4, out)\} \cup \{(\mathbf{yes}, out), (\mathbf{no}, out)\}$

Table 2 summarizes the communication resources used per phase.

Table 2. Communication Resources for VCP solution in CME mode. N refers to the number of communication steps, R refers to the number of communication rules and W' refers to the sum of application of all communication rules

	N	R	W'
Setup and finding a candidate	2	$k + 2$	$2k + 1$
Validation	1	at most k	at most $|E_G|$ (if candidate is valid)
Output	3	3	3

Theorem 3. $VCP \in NF_{EPC}ComNRW'(7, 2k + 8, |E_G| + 2k + 7)$ where E_G represents the set of edges.

Proof. To prove Theorem 3, we define a family of ECP systems operating in EPC mode as $\Pi(n)$ where $n = s(w_{(G,k)}) = |V_G|$:

$$\Pi(n) = (O, [_0[_1]_1[_2]_2]_0, w_0, \emptyset, \emptyset, R_0, R'_0, R_1, R'_1, R_2, R'_2, 0),$$

- $O = \{A_{ij}, v_i, i, \underline{i} \mid 1 \le i < j \le n\} \cup \{c, c', d, \mathbf{no}, \mathbf{yes}\} \cup \{\#_0, \#_1, \#_2, \alpha_0, \alpha_1, \Omega\}$
- $w_0 = v_1 v_2 \ldots v_n \#_0 cod(w_{(G,k)})$
- $R_0 = \{A_{ij} \to i, A_{ij} \to j \mid 1 \le i < j \le n\} \cup \{\#_1 \to \#_2, \alpha_0 \to \alpha_1\}$
- $R'_0 = \{(\mathbf{yes}, out), (\mathbf{no}, out)\}$
- $R_1 = \{c \to c'\} \cup \{v_i \to \underline{i}^{n-1} \mid 1 \le i \le n\}$
- $R'_1 = \{(c, in)\} \cup \{(v_i, in; c', out), (i, in; \underline{i}, out) \mid 1 \le i \le n\}$
- $R_2 = \{\#_0 \to \#_1, \#_2 \to \alpha_0 \Omega\} \cup \{\alpha_1 \to \mathbf{yes}\} \cup \{i \to \mathbf{no} \mid 1 \le i \le n\}$
- $R'_2 = \{(\#_0, in), (\#_1, out), (\#_2, in)\} \cup \{(\alpha_0, out), (\alpha_1, in; \Omega, out)\}$
  $\cup \{(i, in; \Omega, out) \mid 1 \le i \le n\} \cup \{(\mathbf{yes}, out), (\mathbf{no}, out)\}$

Table 3 summarizes the communication resources used per phase.

Table 3. Communication Resources for VCP solution in EPC mode. N refers to the number of communication steps, R refers to the number of communication rules and W' refers to the sum of application of all communication rules

	N	R	W'
Setup	1	2	$k+1$
Finding a candidate	1	$k+1$	$k+1$
Validation	1	at most $k+1$	at most $|E_G|+1$ (if candidate is valid)
Output	at most 4 (if candidate is valid)	at most 4 (if candidate is valid)	at most 4 (if candidate is valid)

5   On ECP Solutions to 3SP

In [8], the 3-Satisfiability Problem (3SP) can be represented by a pair $3SP = (I_{3SP}, \phi_{3SP})$ where $I_{3SP} = \{w_{\phi_X} \mid w_{\phi_X}$ is a string representing a 3-CNF Boolean formula $\phi_X\}$. The $\theta_{3SP}(w_{\phi_X}) = 1$ evaluates to 1 if ϕ_X is satisfiable; otherwise, $\theta_{3SP}(w_{\phi_X}) = 0$. In the succeeding 3SP solutions, we will be using the same encoding as in [8]: The pair (cod, s) associated with the ECP system for every instance w_{ϕ_X} over I_{ϕ_X} has size $s(w_{\phi_X})$ as the number of clauses for the Boolean formula ϕ_X. The encoding $cod(w_{\phi_X})$ is an input multiset in region 0. This encoding consists of $A_{i_1 i_2 i_3, q}$ for $1 \leq q \leq n$ where if $C_q = y_{i_1, q} \vee y_{i_2, q} \vee y_{i_3, q}$, then

$$i_l = \begin{cases} d \text{ if } y_{i_l, q} = x_d \\ \hat{d} \text{ if } y_{i_l, q} = \overline{x}_d \end{cases}$$

for $l = \{1, 2, 3\}$, where $x_d \in \{x_1, x_2, \ldots, x_n\}$.

As in solutions in VCP, solution in 3SP for the succeeding theorems follow the pattern of the solutions presented in [5,8]. Computations in every ECP solution for 3SP also follow four phases: setup phase, finding a candidate solution, verifying the candidate solution and output phase. During the setup phase and finding a candidate solution, objects representing each clause is sent to a target region whereas the variables involved are assigned a truth value. The validation phase determines whether all clauses are satisfied by the chosen truth assignment. Finally, in the output phase, a **yes** or **no** is sent to the environment depending on whether the examined truth assignment is valid or not.

Theorem 4. $3SP \in NF_{CPE}ComNRW'(6, 2n+4, 3n+3)$ where n is the number of clauses for the input 3-CNF Boolean formula.

Proof. To prove the above theorem, we define a family of ECP systems operating in CPE mode as $\Pi(n)$, $n = s(w_{\phi_X})$:

$$\Pi(n) = (O, [_0[_1]_1]_0, w_0, \emptyset, \emptyset, R_0, R'_0, R_1, R'_1, 0),$$

- $O = \{x_d, 0_d, 1_d, d, \hat{d} \mid 1 \leq d \leq 3n\} \cup \{A_{i_1 i_2 i_3, q} \mid 1 \leq q \leq n \text{ and } i_r \in \bigcup_{d=1}^{3n} \{d, \hat{d}\}, \forall r \in \{1, 2, 3\}\} \cup \{c, \#_0, \#_1, \#_2, \#_3, \alpha_2, \beta, \mathbf{no}, \mathbf{yes}\}$

- $w_0 = x_1 x_2 \ldots x_{3n} \#_0 cod(w_{\phi x})$

- $R_0 = \{x_d \to 0_d^n, x_d \to 1_d^n, d \to c, \hat{d} \to c \mid 1 \leq d \leq 3n\} \cup \{\#_0 \to \#_1, \#_2 \to \#_3, \#_1 \to \#_2 \alpha_2\}$

- $R_0' = \{(\mathbf{yes}, out), (\mathbf{no}, out)\}$

- $R_1 = \{\alpha_2 \to \alpha_3, \alpha_3 \to \mathbf{yes}, \#_3 \to \mathbf{no}\} \cup \{A_{i_1 i_2 i_3, q} \to i_1, A_{i_1 i_2 i_3, q} \to i_2, A_{i_1 i_2 i_3, q} \to i_3 \mid 1 \leq q \leq n \text{ and } i_r \in \bigcup_{d=1}^{3n} \{d, \hat{d}\}, \forall r \in \{1, 2, 3\}\} \cup \{0_d \to \beta, 1_d \to \beta \mid 1 \leq d \leq 3n\}$

- $R_1' = \{(A_{i_1 i_2 i_3, q}, in) \mid 1 \leq q \leq n \text{ and } i_r \in \bigcup_{d=1}^{3n} \{d, \hat{d}\}, \forall r \in \{1, 2, 3\}\} \cup \{(0_d, in; \hat{d}, out), (1_d, in; d, out), (\#_3, in; d, out), (\#_3, in; \hat{d}, out) \mid 1 \leq d \leq 3n\} \cup \{(c, in; \beta, out), (\#_3, in; \mathbf{yes}, out), (c, in; \mathbf{no}, out)\} \cup \{(\alpha_2, in)\}$

Computation proceeds as follows: Initially, since communication rules are prioritized, the first step is to send the objects $A_{i_1 i_2 i_3, q}$ (for $1 \leq q \leq n$), representing each clause in the formula, to region 1 using the rule $(A_{i_1 i_2 i_3, q}, in)$. In the next step, the assignment of truth value for each variable is done by non-deterministic application of any of the evolution rules $x_d \to 0_d^n$ or $x_d \to 1_d^n$ for each object x_d. In region 1, a literal contained in the clause is non-deterministically chosen to represent each clause through application of the rules having any of the following forms: $A_{i_1 i_2 i_3, q} \to i_1, A_{i_1 i_2 i_3, q} \to i_2$, and $A_{i_1 i_2 i_3, q} \to i_3$. At the same time, $\#_0$ evolves to $\#_1$.

The next step signals the validation step: objects representing variables in region 1 are exchanged with their corresponding truth values in region 0 through the rules $(0_d, in; \hat{d}, out)$ and/or $(1_d, in; d, out)$. When no copy of d or $\hat{d}$ remains in region 1, it means that all clauses are satisfied by the candidate variable assignment. In the next step, object $\#_1$ becomes $\#_2$ while also producing α_2. All copies of d are evolved to c and all copies of 0_d and 1_d are evolved to β. Object α_2 enters region 1 in the succeeding step, at the same time, every copy of β in region 1 is swapped with a copy of c in region 0. The objects $\#_2$ and α_2 then evolve to $\#_3$ and α_3, respectively.

If all the clauses are validated, no communication rule can be applied at this time step. Thus, α_3 in region 1 transforms into a **yes**. In the opposite case, object $\#_3$ is communicated through membrane 1 with the use of the rule $(\#_3, in; d, out)$ or $(\#_3, in; \hat{d}, out)$. If the object **yes** is in region 1, it will be sent to region 0 and to the environment in two steps. This implies that computation halts after two steps. If this is not the case, $\#_3$ evolves to a **no**. Then **no** will be sent to region 0 and eventually to the environment. Computation halts afterwards.

Table 4 summarizes the communication resources used per phase.

For the succeeding theorems in this section, we only give a sketch of their proofs.

Table 4. Communication Resources for 3SP solution in CPE mode. N refers to the number of communication steps, R refers to the number of communication rules and W' refers to the sum of application of all communication rules

	N	R	W'
Setup and finding a candidate solution	1	n	n
Validation and Output	at most 5 (if candidate is not valid)	at most $n+4$	at most $2n+3$ (if candidate is valid)

Theorem 5. $3SP \in NF_{CME}ComNRW'(5, 2n+4, 3n+3)$ where n is the number of clauses for the input 3-CNF Boolean formula.

Proof. To prove this theorem, we define a family of ECP systems operating in CME mode as $\Pi(n)$, $n = s(w_{\phi x})$.

$$\Pi(n) = (O, [_0[_1]_1]_0, w_0, \emptyset, \emptyset, R_0, R_0', R_1, R_1', 0),$$

- $O = \{x_d, 0_d, 1_d, d, \hat{d} \mid 1 \leq d \leq 3n\} \cup \{A_{i_1 i_2 i_3, q} \mid 1 \leq q \leq n \text{ and } i_r \in \bigcup_{d=1}^{3n} \{d, \hat{d}\}, \forall r \in \{1, 2, 3\}\} \cup \{c, \#_0, \#_1, \#_2, \#_3, \#_4, \alpha_0, \alpha_1, \alpha_2, \alpha_3, \beta, \textbf{no}, \textbf{yes}\}$
- $w_0 = x_1 x_2 \ldots x_{3n} \#_0 \alpha_0 cod(w_{\phi x})$
- $R_0 = \{x_d \rightarrow 0_d^n, x_d \rightarrow 1_d^n, d \rightarrow c, \hat{d} \rightarrow c \mid 1 \leq d \leq 3n\} \cup \{\#_0 \rightarrow \#_1, \#_1 \rightarrow \#_2, \#_2 \rightarrow \#_3, \#_3 \rightarrow \#_4\}$
- $R_0' = \{(\textbf{yes}, out), (\textbf{no}, out)\}$
- $R_1 = \{A_{i_1 i_2 i_3, q} \rightarrow i_1, A_{i_1 i_2 i_3, q} \rightarrow i_2, A_{i_1 i_2 i_3, q} \rightarrow i_3 \mid 1 \leq q \leq n \text{ and } i_r \in \bigcup_{d=1}^{3n} \{d, \hat{d}\}, \forall r \in \{1, 2, 3\}\} \cup \{0_d \rightarrow \beta, 1_d \rightarrow \beta \mid 1 \leq d \leq 3n\} \cup \{\alpha_0 \rightarrow \alpha_1, \alpha_1 \rightarrow \alpha_2, \alpha_2 \rightarrow \alpha_3, \alpha_3 \rightarrow \textbf{yes}, \#_4 \rightarrow \textbf{no}\}$
- $R_1' = \{(A_{i_1 i_2 i_3, q}, in) \mid 1 \leq q \leq n \text{ and } i_r \in \bigcup_{d=1}^{3n} \{d, \hat{d}\}, \forall r \in \{1, 2, 3\}\} \cup \{(0_d, in; \hat{d}, out), (1_d, in; d, out), (\#_4, in; d, out), (\#_4, in; \hat{d}, out) \mid 1 \leq d \leq 3n\} \cup \{(c, in; \beta, out), (\#_4, in; \textbf{yes}, out), (c, in; \textbf{no}, out), (\alpha_0, in)\}$

Table 5 below summarizes the communication resources used per phase.

Theorem 6. $3SP \in NF_{EPC}ComNRW'(5, 2n+4, 3n+3)$ where n is the number of clauses for the input 3-CNF Boolean formula.

Proof. To prove the above theorem, we define a family of ECP systems operating in EPC mode $\Pi(n)$.

$$\Pi(n) = (O, [_0[_1]_1]_0, w_0, \emptyset, \emptyset, R_0, R_0', R_1, R_1', 0),$$

- $O = \{x_d, 0_d, 1_d, d, \hat{d} \mid 1 \leq d \leq 3n\} \cup \{A_{i_1 i_2 i_3, q} \mid 1 \leq q \leq n \text{ and } i_r \in \bigcup_{d=1}^{3n} \{d, \hat{d}\}, \forall r \in \{1, 2, 3\}\} \cup \{c, \#_0, \#_1, \#_2, \#_3, \alpha_0, \alpha_1, \alpha_2, \beta, \textbf{no}, \textbf{yes}\}$

Table 5. Communication Resources for 3SP solution in CME mode. N refers to the number of communication steps, R refers to the number of communication rules and W′ refers to the sum of application of all communication rules

	N	R	W′
Setup and finding a candidate solution	1	$n+1$	$n+1$
Validation and Output	4	at most $n+3$	at most 2n+2 (if candidate is valid)

Table 6. Communication Resources for 3SP solution in EPC mode. N refers to the number of communication steps, R refers to the number of communication rules and W′ refers to the sum of application of all communication rules

	N	R	W′
Setup and finding a candidate solution	1	$n+1$	$n+1$
Validation and Output	4	at most $n+3$	at most 2n+2 (if candidate is valid)

- $w_0 = x_1 x_2 \ldots x_{3n} \#_0 \alpha_0 cod(w_{\phi x})$
- $R_0 = \{x_d \to 0_d^n, x_d \to 1_d^n, d \to c, \hat{d} \to c \mid 1 \leq d \leq 3n\} \cup \{\#_0 \to \#_1, \#_2 \to \#_3, \alpha_1 \to \alpha_2\}$
- $R_0' = \{(\mathbf{yes}, out), (\mathbf{no}, out)\}$
- $R_1 = \{\alpha_0 \to \alpha_1, \alpha_2 \to \alpha_3, \alpha_3 \to \mathbf{yes}, \#_1 \to \#_2, \#_3 \to \mathbf{no}\} \cup \{A_{i_1 i_2 i_3, q} \to i_1, A_{i_1 i_2 i_3, q} \to i_2, A_{i_1 i_2 i_3, q} \to i_3 \mid 1 \leq q \leq n \text{ and } i_r \in \bigcup_{d=1}^{3n} \{d, \hat{d}\}, \forall r \in \{1, 2, 3\}\} \cup \{0_d \to \beta, 1_d \to \beta \mid 1 \leq d \leq 3n\}$
- $R_1' = \{(A_{i_1 i_2 i_3, q}, in) \mid 1 \leq q \leq n \text{ and } i_r \in \bigcup_{d=1}^{3n} \{d, \hat{d}\}, \forall r \in \{1, 2, 3\}\} \cup \{(0_d, in; \hat{d}, out), (1_d, in; d, out), (\#_3, in; d, out), (\#_3, in; \hat{d}, out) \mid 1 \leq d \leq 3n\} \cup \{(c, in; \beta, out), (\#_3, in; \mathbf{yes}, out), (c, in; \mathbf{no}, out)\} \cup \{(\#_1, in), (\#_2, out)\} \cup \{(\alpha_0, in), (\alpha_1, out), (\alpha_2, in)\}$

Table 6 summarizes the communication resources used per phase.

6   Conclusion

The following are the summary of the results for non-confluent solution of VCP and 3SP in ECP system:

a. $VCP \in NF_{CPE}ComNRW'(6, 2k + 4, |E_G| + 2k + 3)$,
b. $VCP \in NF_{CME}ComNRW'(6, 2k + 5, |E_G| + 2k + 4)$,
c. $VCP \in NF_{EPC}ComNRW'(7, 2k + 8, |E_G| + 2k + 7)$, where E_G represents the set of edges, and k is the input positive integer k.

d. $3SP \in NF_{CPE}ComNRW'(6, 2n+4, 3n+3)$,

e. $3SP \in NF_{CME}ComNRW'(5, 2n+4, 3n+3)$,

f. $3SP \in NF_{EPC}ComNRW'(5, 2n+4, 3n+3)$ where n is the number of clauses for the input 3-CNF Boolean formula.

From the results for VCP, it can be observed that in all modes, there is a linear increase in the resources from the value $ComN$ to $ComR$ to $ComW'$. The result show a similar pattern as in [5,8] although we would like to emphasize that the third measure $(ComW')$ is different in previous work which makes use of the concept of energy to impose a form of payment for every communicated object. The results for VCP also seem to show increase of 'difficulty' in terms of communication resources from CPE to CME to EPC (an observation similar to that in [1]).

There is also a similarity in the results for 3SP in our current work and those presented in [5,8]. However, we can observe that in these previous works, the number of membranes utilized are linear to the number of clauses in the input formula. This is in contrast to our work where we only require two membranes. This seems to suggest that, for 3SP, it is more 'difficult' to devise non-confluent solutions in ECPe systems than in ECP system. In our future works, we aim to further investigate this issue by using Sevilla carpets [4,7], as suggested in [9], to provide a detailed comparison of the communication resources used for VCP and 3SP solutions in both ECPe systems and ECP systems operating in different modes.

We end our paper with some open problems: can we have a non-confluent solution in ECP system that can minimize the resources used in this paper (e.g. a constant ComR or a linear ComW' for VCP)? What about a comparison of communication resources for confluent and deterministic solutions?

Acknowledgments. N. Hernandez and R. Juayong would like to thank the DOST PCIEERD for the HRIDD HRDP grants I-15-1006-19 and I-15-0715-21, respectively. N. Hernandez is supported by the UPAA San Francisco & Mely & Rick Ray foundation professorial chair. R. Juayong is supported by the DOST-ERDT Scholarship Program. H. Adorna is funded by a DOST-ERDT research grant and the Semirara Mining Corporation professorial chair of the UP Diliman, College of Engineering.

References

1. Adorna, H., Păun, G., Pérez-Jiménez, M.J.: On communication complexity in evolution-communication P systems. Rom. J. Inf. Sci. Technol. **13**(2), 113–130 (2010)
2. Alhazov, A.: Communication in Membrane Systems with Symbol Objects. Ph.D. thesis, Universitat Rovira I Virgili (2006)
3. Cavaliere, M.: Evolution–communication P systems. In: Păun, G., Rozenberg, G., Salomaa, A., Zandron, C. (eds.) WMC 2002. LNCS, vol. 2597, pp. 134–145. Springer, Heidelberg (2003)

4. Ciobanu, G., Păun, G., Stefanescu, G.: Sevilla carpets associated with P systems. In: Proceedings of the Brainstorming Week on Membrane Computing, Tarragona, Spain, pp. 135–140 (2003)
5. Francia, S., Francisco, D., Juayong, R., Adorna, H.: On communication complexity of some hard problems in ECPe systems with priority. Philippine Comput. J. 9(2), 14–25 (2014)
6. Gazdag, Z.: Solving SAT by P systems with active membranes in linear time in the number of variables. In: Alhazov, A., Cojocaru, S., Gheorghe, M., Rogozhin, Y., Rozenberg, G., Salomaa, A. (eds.) CMC 2013. LNCS, vol. 8340, pp. 189–205. Springer, Heidelberg (2014)
7. Gutiérrez-Naranjo, M.A., Pérez-Jímenez, M.J., Riscos-Núñez, A.: On descriptive complexity of P systems. In: Mauri, G., Păun, G., Jesús Pérez-Jímenez, M., Rozenberg, G., Salomaa, A. (eds.) WMC 2004. LNCS, vol. 3365, pp. 320–330. Springer, Heidelberg (2005)
8. Hernandez, N.H.S., Juayong, R.A.B., Adorna, H.N.: On communication complexity of some hard problems in ECPe systems. In: Alhazov, A., Cojocaru, S., Gheorghe, M., Rogozhin, Y., Rozenberg, G., Salomaa, A. (eds.) CMC 2013. LNCS, vol. 8340, pp. 206–224. Springer, Heidelberg (2014)
9. Juayong, R., Adorna, H.: Communication complexity of evolution-communication P systems with energy and Sevilla carpet. Philippine Comput. J. 6(1), 34–40 (2010)
10. Lu, C., Zhang, X.: Solving vertex cover problem by means of tissue P systems with cell separation. Int. J. Comput. Commun. Control 5(4), 540–550 (2010)
11. Pan, L., Alhazov, A.: Solving HPP and SAT by P systems with active membranes and separation rules. Acta Informatica 43(2), 131–145 (2006)
12. Păun, G.: Membrane Computing. Springer-Verlag, Heidelberg (2002)
13. Păun, G.: Further open problems in membrane computing. In: Păun, G. (eds.) Proceedings of the Second Brainstorming Week on Membrane Computing, Sevilla, February 2004, Technical report, Research Group on Natural Computing, Sevilla University, Spain (2004)
14. Păun, G.: Introduction to membrane computing. In: Ciobanu, G., P ăun, G., Pérez-Jiménez, M.J. (eds.) Applications of Membrane Computing, pp. 1–42. Springer, Heidelberg (2006)
15. Pérez–Jiménez, M.J.: A computational complexity theory in membrane computing. In: Păun, G., Pérez-Jiménez, M.J., Riscos-Núñez, A., Rozenberg, G., Salomaa, A. (eds.) WMC 2009. LNCS, vol. 5957, pp. 125–148. Springer, Heidelberg (2010)

Membrane Computing Meets Temperature: A Thermoreceptor Model as Molecular Slide Rule with Evolutionary Potential

Thomas Hinze[1,2]([✉]), Korcan Kirkici[3], Patricia Sauer[1],
Peter Sauer[1], and Jörn Behre[4]

[1] Institute of Computer Science and Information and Media Technology,
Brandenburg University of Technology, Postfach 10 13 44, 03013 Cottbus, Germany
{thomas.hinze,schulpat,peter.sauer}@b-tu.de
[2] Friedrich Schiller University Jena, Ernst-Abbe-Platz 1–4, 07743 Jena, Germany
[3] Center for Information Services and High Performance Computing,
Dresden University of Technology, 01062 Dresden, Germany
korcan.kirkici@mailbox.tu-dresden.de
[4] Theoretical Systems Biology, Institute of Food Research,
Norwich Research Park, Colney Lane, Norwich NR4 7UA, UK
joern.behre@ifr.ac.uk

Abstract. Temperature represents an elementary environmental stimulus crucial for survival and fitness of organisms. Molecular membrane-based mechanisms for temperature sensing and behavioral response seem to be among the oldest principles of biological information processing. It is believed that some *archaea* – early microbes prior to bacteria and eukaryotes – developed *thermoreceptors*. In addition, they were able to maintain a *circadian clock*, a biochemical oscillatory system whose periodicity reflects a daily rhythm. Both features on their own, but especially their combination, gives raise for effective evolutionary advantage. Along with the notion of applied systems biology, we explore capabilities of resulting reaction models by exploitation of deterministic P modules and their dynamical coupling by means of simulation studies. Our findings indicate that a minimalistic circadian clock equipped with a chemical temperature sensor enables robust and practicable entrainment to an external daily temperature rhythm induced by the sun in contrast to a clock variant without thermoreceptor. Having a more adaptable circadian clock, *archaea* comprise better preconditions to populate larger oceanic regions from the equator towards the poles. From a modelling point of view, we incorporate the global quantity temperature and its effect on reaction velocity according to Arrhenius' equation into the framework of deterministic P modules.

1 Introduction and Background

Systems biology as a highly interdisciplinary field of research aims at achieving a detailed understanding of living organisms at a molecular level [19]. Having in mind that a single biological cell is typically composed of 10^8 up to 10^9 molecules,

© Springer International Publishing Switzerland 2015
G. Rozenberg et al. (Eds.): CMC 2015, LNCS 9504, pp. 215–235, 2015.
DOI: 10.1007/978-3-319-28475-0_15

it becomes obvious that coping with the tremendous number of possible molecular interactions and reactions turns out to be a challenging and interminable task even for unicellular organisms. A promising clue to tackle this challenge comes from engineering: Here, complex systems are mostly constructed from a small set of modular functional units in a hierarchical manner. Minimised and well-defined interfaces between these units imply a sparse scheme of interactions mainly organised in local clusters in which each unit communicates with a small number of other units. Due to this reduction of inherent complexity, the function of resulting systems can be understood more or less easily, even if the total number of elementary components in the entire system is high. Systems biology might benefit from engineering. To this end, a complex molecular system under study should be divided into its underlying functional units. Along with this identification process, the interface structure and potential multi-modular components become visible [9]. For a "minimal" unicellular life form whose genome comprises a magnitude of only 500 genes, these attempts succeeded in a first stage [5] while many other organisms revealed relevant parts of its function. This line of research also sheds light on an outstanding aspect: Tracing the potential progress of biological evolution in its early phase. There is some evidence that several molecular functional units have been widely conserved for more than 2 billion years [7]. A fascinating example in this context are molecular thermoreceptors able to sense environmental temperature.

From today's scientific perspective, our planet earth came into existence 4.6 billion years ago [7]. It is supposed that the potential origin of life on earth dates back around 3.8 billion years initiated by self-replicable strands composed of ribonucleic acid (RNA). After complementing RNA by more stable deoxyribonucleic acid (DNA) along with usage of proteins and the biochemical mechanism of transcription and translation based on genetic information, biological cells could have emerged able to reproduce by cell division. Mineral-rich oceanic water heated by submarine volcanic activity and surrounded by fine pored rocks and geological formations might have provided advantageous preconditions for long-term maintenance and survival of cell populations. The process of early cellular evolution could have resulted in the unicellular prokaryotic life form of *archaea* about 2.5 billion years ago. *Archaea* are seen as ancestor of subsequent biological domains like bacteria and eukaryotes. Possibly, *archaea* competitively succeeded since they combine a minimalistic molecular equipment with an astonishing flexibility in coping with environmental conditions. Nowadays, *archaea* can be found widespread at numerous places, even inside the human body. Most impressively, some *archaea* populate extreme regions, physically hostile to life. For instance, thermophilic exemplars grow at a temperature of $130°C$ when deep-sea water under enlarged pressure is still liquid. Others seem to prefer high environmental acid concentrations (pH ≈ 0) while alkaliphilic forms resist pH up to 10.

Prepared to spend their life by "swimming" in aqueous conditions, most forms of *archaea* possess flagella which allows a moderately controlled movement by chemotaxis. Sensory capabilities exist, but in a rudimentary state. To our best knowledge, there are no photoreceptors and no further sensors for light.

This means that *archaea* probably cannot detect sunlight directly which in turn might be dangerous: High-energy radiation induced by the sun is able to penetrate water up to several metres. Due to the lack of any atmospheric protection on earth at that primeval era, this radiation can cause life-threatening damages of DNA and other complex molecular structures. In consequence, the easiest survival strategy would consist in avoidance of water near the surface and preference to stay in deeper regions instead. Unfortunately, submarine CO_2 in heated water and organic substances, both needed for survival, are typically located near the surface in sufficient concentration. Despite this contradictory terms, there is some evidence that *archaea* succeeded in populating large areas of the oceans on earth around 2 billion years ago [27].

The crucial clue to overcome this obstacle could be exploitation of *temperature* signals. The temporal course of temperature follows the brightness and intensity of sunlight with a short delay. During the darkness of night with low influence of radiation, a stay near the water surface for resorption prevents from damages while persisting within a region of deeper water during the day enables protection. Organisms able to act in this manner come with an evolutionary advantage over those who do not. Studies show that the temperature of oceanic water from surface up to 2 m depth varies between approximately 3°C and 1°C according to the daily rhythm of sunlight [6]. Within equatorial lines of latitude, this effect is stronger than northwards and southwards since the periodical intensity of sunlight reaches its maximum here. Close to the poles, daily variations of sea surface temperature are negligible.

For response to daily variations of water temperature, a molecular thermoreceptor would fit which is able to reliably convert environmental temperature into a chemical signal suitable for further processing. Indeed, *archaea* organisms contain such sensorial units within their outer cell membrane.

Temperature Reception

Molecular thermoreception found in *archaea* is based on presence of movable electrically charged particles, especially *cations* (positively charged). This complements the observation that a majority of complex intracellular molecules exhibits a negative electrical charge such as RNA, DNA, and most proteins. Hence, the cell as a whole acts as a negative electrical potential surrounded by free or loosely bound cations like calcium (Ca^{2+}), natrium (Na^+), or potassium (K^+). Originated from environmental minerals, they reside at the outer face of the cell membrane.

An archaean thermoreceptor is made of an *ion channel*, a large protein placed throughout the outer cell membrane, see Fig. 1. An ion channel allows a group of ions to pass together into the cell driven by an electrochemical gradient [7]. To this end, the channel temporarily opens by deblocking a molecular gate. This gate, formed by an amino acid chain as a part of the underlying large protein, is controlled by electrical forces between the opposite ends of the channel. Whenever the resulting voltage difference exceeds a certain threshold, the molecular gate becomes open, and a group of ions quickly runs into the cell inducing a

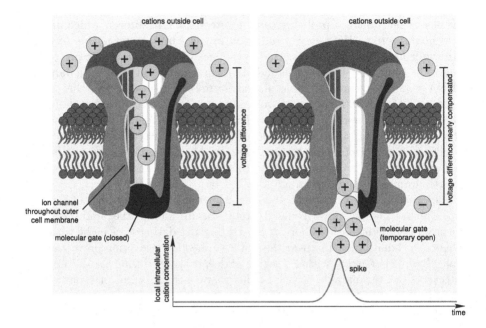

Fig. 1. Schematic representation of an ion channel and its functional principle. Cations (+) accumulate at the outer face of the cell membrane (**left**). After their amount has reached a certain threshold, the voltage difference with respect to the negatively charged inner part of the cell (−) induces an electrical force which in turn temporarily opens a molecular gate. A group of cations passes this gate together which results in a spiking signal (**right**). Afterwards, the voltage difference is nearly compensated and the molecular gate becomes closed again.

spike-shaped electrical signal. Afterwards, the voltage difference between the opposite ends of the channel is nearly compensated which implies closing the gate by adjusting the corresponding amino acid chain. It takes some time until enough cations accumulate at the outer end of the ion channel in order to open the gate again. Finally, the ion channel exhibits a spiking oscillatory behaviour over time regarding the concentration course of entering cations. Inside the cell, these cations propagate through the cytosol initiating wave patterns and triggering downstream processes [29]. In this connection, cations can either cycle within the cell or bind to other substances and become released into the environment leaving the cell.

Beneficially, the permeability of ion channels acting as thermoreceptors is sensitive to environmental temperature. Along with increasing temperature, the required electrical force to open the molecular gate becomes diminished [27]. This leads to a higher frequency (or shorter periodicity, respectively) of the spiking oscillation, see Fig. 2. From a systems biology point of view, a thermoreceptor based on an ion channel primarily performs a frequency encoding of the input temperature signal comparable with frequency modulation in engineering.

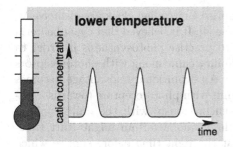 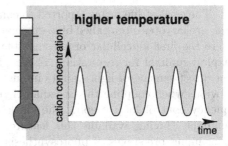

Fig. 2. Signalling scheme of a thermoreceptor based on an ion channel by frequency encoding of environmental temperature within physiological range (warm sensor).

In more detail, thermoreceptors found in *archaea* were identified as so-called *transient receptor potential* (TRP) channels [25]. In its original form, a TRP channel acts as a warm sensor meaning that higher temperature implies a higher spiking frequency and vice versa within a physiological range. The transfer curve mapping temperature into frequency resembles a logarithmic relationship.

The fundamental principle of molecular temperature sensing via TRP channels seems to be highly conserved throughout biological evolution. In the course of time, distinct variants of thermoreceptors emerged whose function is more selective to specific cations and whose physiological ranges slightly differ. It was reported that TRP receptors in the bacterium *Escherichia coli* can sense changes in temperature for thermotaxis [22]. Moreover, the motional intensity of flagella is directly controlled by environmental temperature which permits the bacterium to find an optimal survival strategy [23]. Interestingly, the temperature-dependent impulsive motion reaches its maximum in water between approximately 30°C and 40°C. The fruit fly *drosophila melanogaster* utilises TRP channels embedded in its skin as part of the nervous system in order to sense temperature [1]. In a similar way, the human body is provided with environmental temperature signals perceived by neural bursts [20].

Circadian Clock

Circadian rhythms embody an interesting biological phenomenon that can be seen as a widespread property of life. The coordination of biological activities into *daily cycles* provides an important advantage for the fitness of diverse organisms [28]. Based on a self-sustained biochemical oscillation, a circadian rhythm is characterised by a period in accordance with a full rotation of earth. To this end, a circadian clock is able to be entrained. This property allows a gradual reset of the underlying oscillatory system for adjustment by exposure to external stimuli like daily variations of brightness or daytime-nighttime temperature cycles. Under constant environmental conditions, the synchronism of the clock gets lost but the endogenous oscillation persists with slightly modified periodicity which runs the clock a bit faster or slower.

The earliest life forms reported to comprise a circadian clock are *cyanobacteria*, prokaryotes often called blue-green algae [4]. It is believed that cyanobacteria were the first unicellular organisms able to practise photosynthesis in order to exploit sunlight for respiration. This capability came along with photoreceptors for direct sensing of light and its intensity. An evolutionary advantage becomes obvious when coupling the circadian rhythm with photoreceptors towards a frequency control loop keeping the clock synchronously with the daily cycle of sunlight. Having available this feature, the cyanobacterium might start time-consuming pre-stages of photosynthesis at the right time before sunrise which facilitates a more comprehensive utilisation of sunlight.

In contrast to cyanobacteria, *archaea* probably lack any light-sensitive receptor and any potential of photosynthesis. Nevertheless, a circadian clock could be a useful attribute since it could help to optimally organise the day into phases of respiration and phases of regeneration and protection against harmful radiation. Possibly, circadian clocks turn out to be much older than those proved in cyanobacteria. Indeed, *archaea* could have developed early forms of a circadian clock around 2 billion years ago [4, 18]. A diurnally entrained anticipatory behaviour in *archaea* became also evident [30]. Although there is to our best knowledge no comprehensive experimental proof for existence of a circadian clock in *archaea*, the fascinating question arises: what if?

Combining Circadian Clock with Thermoreceptor

This paper is inspired by the idea to hypothesise about the importance of thermoreception for development and dissemination of life forms on earth during an early phase of biological evolution. Presence of an effective molecular thermoreceptor emphasises the conjecture that circadian clocks could have come into existence long before availability of photosensors just by exploiting daily variations of the sea-water temperature course for synchronisation. A reliable circadian rhythm is supposed to be helpful for *archaea* to populate large regions of oceans worldwide. An inherent clock supports division of each day into phases of dedicated activities in concert with regularly cycling environmental needs. An improved adaptability to environmental conditions in turn could be a crucial factor for an elongated life span in which a higher amount of cell divisions might occur. For sure, this line of argumentation remains rather speculative but it follows a conclusive chain of causes and effects.

In the following section, we familiarise the reader with mathematical and denotational prerequisites necessary for fine-grained description and simulation of coupled reaction systems. To this end, we extend the concept of *deterministic P modules* – introduced in [12] and refined in [14] – by a global component reflecting temperature and by reaction-specific components quantifying activation energy and reactivity in compliance with parameters in *Arrhenius' equation*. Section 3 is dedicated to a thermoreceptor model which mimics an ion channel together with intracellular signal transduction and a decoding mechanism converting the produced spiking frequency into a steady concentration value. Therefor, chemical modules for some numerical operations are employed like an integrator, a smoothing cascade, a subtractor, and a multiplier, all of them based on [11]. The model comes along with simulation studies revealing the overall capability of the entire information processing unit. Section 4 is focused on evolving an effective circadian clock model able to be entrained exclusively by environmental temperature. We start from a minimalistic model without thermoreceptor but comprising all other features of a frequency control system following the principle of a phase locked loop [11]. Astonishingly, this sensorless clock model is entrainable to daily temperature rhythms if and only if the amplitude of temperature variation is permanently kept below approximately 0.3°C. Although insufficient, it gives potential for evolutionary improvement. For this purpose, we combine the sensorless circadian clock model with our thermoreceptor model to achieve a temperature-entrainable clock within a reasonable physiological range between 0 and about 40°C. Final remarks summarise main findings in a broader context for further work.

2   Extending Deterministic P Modules by Temperature and Activation Energy

For description of the temporal behaviour of chemical reaction networks we consider substrate concentrations over time presuming homogeneity in reaction space. General *mass-action kinetics* [19] formulates reaction system's dynamics subject to production and consumption rates v_p and v_c of each substrate S in order to continuously change its concentration by $\frac{d\,[S]}{d\,t} = v_p - v_c$. A reaction system with a total number of n substrates and r reactions

$$a_{1,1}S_1 + a_{2,1}S_2 + \ldots + a_{n,1}S_n \xrightarrow{k_1} b_{1,1}S_1 + b_{2,1}S_2 + \ldots + b_{n,1}S_n$$

$$a_{1,2}S_1 + a_{2,2}S_2 + \ldots + a_{n,2}S_n \xrightarrow{k_2} b_{1,2}S_1 + b_{2,2}S_2 + \ldots + b_{n,2}S_n$$

$$\vdots$$

$$a_{1,r}S_1 + a_{2,r}S_2 + \ldots + a_{n,r}S_n \xrightarrow{k_r} b_{1,r}S_1 + b_{2,r}S_2 + \ldots + b_{n,r}S_n$$

employs stoichiometric factors $a_{i,j} \in \mathbb{N}$ (reactants), $b_{i,j} \in \mathbb{N}$ (products) and kinetic parameters $k_j \in \mathbb{R}_{>0}$ assigned to each reaction quantifying its velocity ($\mathbb{N}$: natural numbers, $\mathbb{R}_{>0}$: positive real numbers). The corresponding ordinary differential equations (ODEs) read:

$$[\dot{S_i}] = \frac{d\,[S_i]}{d\,t} = \sum_{h=1}^{r} \left(k_h \cdot (b_{i,h} - a_{i,h}) \cdot \prod_{l=1}^{n} [S_l]^{a_{l,h}} \right) \quad \text{with} \quad i = 1, \ldots, n$$

In order to obtain a concrete trajectory, all initial concentrations $[S_i](0) \in \mathbb{R}_{\geq 0}$, $i = 1, \ldots, n$ are allowed to be set according to the relevance for the system.

The kinetic parameter k_j captures for each reaction $j \in \{1, \ldots, r\}$ its dependency on environmental *temperature* T, *activation energy* $E_j(T)$, and sensitivity to spatial orientation of colliding molecules $A_j(T)$. The corresponding law is expressed by the *Arrhenius equation*:

$$k_j = A_j(T) \cdot e^{-\frac{E_j(T)}{R \cdot T}}$$

Here, the Kelvin-scaled temperature $T \in \mathbb{R}_{>0}$ acts as global quantity for the entire reaction system. Temperature subsumes the average kinetic energy of reactive molecules within the underlying system. Following the notion of a collision-based reaction model, a reaction occurs if and only if colliding substrate molecules comprise enough kinetic and free energy in order to exceed the required activation energy $E_j(T)$. Typical activation energies span a range from approximately 30 up to around 100 $\frac{kJ}{mol}$. Particularly in biochemistry, catalysts can reduce impractically high activation energies into a feasible guidance value of around 67 $\frac{kJ}{mol}$ [10]. The activation energy of a reaction commonly appears to be almost constant but it might be slightly subject to environmental temperature. For instance, chemical core oscillators found in circadian clocks are able to vary its activation energy along with temperature changes in order to keep constant k_j. In this way, reaction velocity is almost independent of temperature. So, the resulting clock pace cannot be perturbed by temperature within a physiological range [26]. Temperature compensation of circadian clocks by adjustment of activation energy is essential to maintain its function. We reflect this aspect by describing activation energy as a function subject to T. Furthermore, the Arrhenius equation contains the pre-exponential factor $A_j(T)$ whose value constitutes a possible sensitivity of the reaction to spatial orientation of colliding substrate molecules. By abstracting from the submolecular substrate structure and handled as a system global constant in sufficient approximation, $A_j(T)$ provides a parameter suitable for calibration in order to achieve a complete and consistent overall parameter setting throughout the reaction system. Finally, $R = 8.3144621 \frac{J}{K \cdot mol}$ denotes the gas constant.

When taking environmental temperature T as an input value in terms of performing a computation it turns out that we obtain a chemical counterpart of a *slide rule*. Here, numerical multiplication becomes reduced to addition on a logarithmic scale according to the law: $\log(x \cdot y) = \log(x) + \log(y)$ Chemically spoken, an amplification (multiplication) of reaction velocity can be reached by increase (addition) of temperature. In practical biochemistry, this is covered by the Q_{10} law which means that a reaction runs twice up to three times faster when temperature is increased by $10\,K$.

Within the sphere of membrane systems, the general framework of *deterministic P modules* [12] captures a mathematical specification of the temporal behaviour of a predictable system in its course of involved signals. Here, the system is specified by an underlying reaction system of coupled first-order ordinary differential equations according to mass-action reaction kinetics in addition with complementary functions for expression of Arrhenius equations, activation energies, and pre-exponential factors. A numerical solver supplements the deterministic P module in order to trace all signals (chemical concentrations and temperature) over time. Simultaneously, discretised signal values (each chemical concentration mapped into total amount of molecular species) are provided following the multiset-based notion of a P system [24]. We enrich each deterministic P module with an additional temperature signal T as part of the list of input signal identifiers. Hence, we consider a deterministic P module by a triple

$$< \text{module name} >= (\downarrow, \uparrow, \square)$$

where $\downarrow = (T, I_1, \ldots, I_i)$ indicates a finite enumerative list of input signal identifiers, $\uparrow = (O_1, \ldots, O_o)$ a finite enumerative list of output signal identifiers, and $\square$ the underlying system specification processing the input signals and producing the output signals with or without usage of auxiliary inherent signals not mentioned in the P module's input-output interface. Each signal is assumed to represent a real-valued temporal course, hence a specific function $\sigma : \mathbb{R}_{\geq 0} \longrightarrow \mathbb{R}$.

The system specification given in $\square$ can be exclusively composed of arithmetic equations in an explicit manner. Often, the specification is described implicitly instead, for instance resulting in ordinary differential equations (ODEs). Here, the deterministic P module makes use of a numerical ODE solver, preferably *Runge-Kutta* methods. For technical details, we refer the reader to [3]. In brief, the ODE system becomes adaptively discretised in progression of simulation time. For each point in time considered so far, the absolute number of molecules for each species derived from the concentration is estimated and temporarily stored. The process of numerical ODE solution in conjunction with determination of absolute molecule numbers for discrete points in time can be perceived in terms of running a membrane system as introduced in [24]. For in-silico simulation, we utilise the *Complex Pathway Simulator* (Copasi) [16] and *Matrix Laboratory* (MatLab) [21].

In line with the intention of systems biology stating that a complex (bio)chemical system is composed of functional units, so-called modules, we seize the formalism of *P meta framework* introduced in [12]. A P meta framework is able to describe a dynamical assembly of deterministic P modules towards more complex systems following the idea of a controlled evolutionary program. A P meta framework is a construct

$$\Pi_{\pi\uparrow\downarrow} = (M, P)$$

where M denotes a finite *multiset* of deterministic P modules with finite cardinality while the finite set P keeps the evolutionary program composed by a number of *instructions* affecting the interplay of underlying modules in M.

When initiating $\Pi_{\pi\uparrow\downarrow}$, a corresponding directed graph $G = (V, E)$ is created that formalises the current *connectivity structure* of interacting deterministic P modules. All available modules on their own instantiate the nodes of G. There are no connections between them before executing the program P:

$$V := \{m[i] \mid m \in \text{supp}(M) \ \wedge \ i \in \{1, \ldots, M(m)\}\} \qquad E := \emptyset$$

Indexing of all instances (copies) $m[i]$ constituted from a module m allows a unique identification necessary for an appropriate matching of nodes addressed by program instructions.

Directed edges between nodes of G symbolise the connectivity of module instances. Let $a = (a_\downarrow, a_\uparrow, a_\square) \in \text{supp}(M)$ and $b = (b_\downarrow, b_\uparrow, b_\square) \in \text{supp}(M)$ be two module instances derived from M. An edge $(a, b, R_{a \to b}) \in E$ denotes a connection from a to b where dedicated output species of a act as input species of b. To this end, each edge comes with a binary relation $R_{a \to b} \subseteq a_\uparrow \times b_\downarrow$ in which the mapping of a's output species onto b's input is given. $R_{a \to b}$ is handled in an injective manner since one output species is allowed to cover several downstream input species, but each input species must be supplied by at most one upstream output species. Formally, we require: $\forall x, z \in X$ and $\forall y \in Y : (x, y) \in R \land (z, y) \in R \Rightarrow x = z$ where $R \subseteq X \times Y$ stands for $R_{a \to b}$.

Attention must be paid to the composition of deterministic P modules to keep signal semantics and quantitative signal values along with signal identifiers consistent when migrating from one module to another.

The instructions of the evolutionary program P capture the dynamics of our P meta framework $\Pi_{\pi \uparrow \downarrow}$ in (re-)assembly of its module instances. The underlying graph G becomes updated whenever an instruction from P is executed. To bring the individual instructions into a temporal order, we assume a global clock whose progression is expressed by a non-negative real-valued variable t marking points in time. We arrange two types of instructions called $\texttt{ModuleConnect}$ and $\texttt{ModuleDisconnect}$. A time stamp t opens each instruction. Let $a = (a_\downarrow, a_\uparrow, a_\square) \in \text{supp}(M)$ and $b = (b_\downarrow, b_\uparrow, b_\square) \in \text{supp}(M)$ be two module instances derived from M:

$t : \texttt{ModuleConnect}(a \to b, R_{a \to b})$	connects some or all of module a's output species to represent b's input species by sharing species identifiers according to the injective binary relation $R_{a \to b} \subseteq a_\uparrow \times b_\downarrow$. Edge update scheme: $E := E \cup \{(a, b, R_{a \to b})\}$
$t : \texttt{ModuleDisconnect}(a \leftrightarrow b)$	completely disconnects modules a and b by annihilating all cross-modular species sharings. This comes along with removing $R_{a \to b}$ as well as $R_{b \to a}$, respectively. Edge update scheme: $E := E \setminus \{(a, b, R_{a \to b})\} \setminus \{(b, a, R_{b \to a})\}$

Several instructions in P might occur simultaneously if they are *effectively independent* from each other. This is the case if and only if all resulting permutations of sequences, in which instructions marked by the same time stamp t can be executed, lead to equivalent graphs G. We employ a P meta framework $\Pi_{\pi \uparrow \downarrow} = (M, P)$ for composition and analysis of a thermoreceptor model and its incorporation into a circadian clock model. Further examples of the P meta framework are given in [13,14].

3 Thermoreceptor Model Emulating Ion Channel, Frequency Modulation, Transduction, and Decoding

The spiking oscillatory behaviour of ion channels mimicking a temperature sensor results from a *positive feedback loop* within the underlying reaction scheme [15]. In more detail, the oscillation is driven by a controlled interplay between *calcium ions* (Ca^{2+}) and *inositol trisphosphate* (IP3), a secondary messenger hormone mainly available close to the cell membrane. We assume presence of a certain initial amount of IP3 which is required to modify the ion-channel forming protein for toggling between "open" and "closed" state by its spatial conformation. Accumulating calcium ions at the outer end of the channel need to reach a notable concentration in order to interact (pass) the ion channel.

During passage, a self-amplifying effect occurs (positive feedback) which attracts more and more available calcium ions to enter the cell. This self-amplification is restricted to be maintained for a short duration. Afterwards, there is no adequate supply of further calcium ions which in turn stalls the self-amplification. When attempting to formalise the spiking processing scheme, we noticed its high similarity to the *Brusselator*, an abstract model for spiking oscillations based on a positive feedback loop [2,31]. The Brusselator is composed of four abstract reactions: (1) $A \xrightarrow{k_1} D$; (2) $C + 2D \xrightarrow{k_2} 3D$; (3) $B + D \xrightarrow{k_3} C$; (4) $D \xrightarrow{k_4} W$. Figure 3 illustrates this reaction scheme by a hypergraph. The model is equipped with two supplier species A and B. A corresponds to IP3 and B symbolises calcium ions outside the cell. D can be seen as the permeability of the ion channel in a way that a high value $[D]$ stands for a closed channel while a low value marks the opened channel. W refers to a "waste" species collecting an excess of $[D]$ in order to delimit the maximum impermeability of the ion channel. Finally, calcium ions inside the cell are identified by species C whose concentration course $[C](t)$ over time forms the oscillatory output.

In its signalling function, the Brusselator generates limit-cycle oscillations which implies a high oscillatory stability along with extensive robustness against perturbations. In order to ensure an endogenous oscillatory behaviour, initial concentrations of species A, B, C, and D need to be set >0 to be attracted by the limit cycle. From numerous empirical simulation studies it became evident that a harmonised choice of kinetic parameter values k_1 up to k_4 takes care for widemost spread of undamped oscillatory region with respect to the kinetic parameter. Thus, we utilise a common mass-action parameter k inside the Brusselator by setting $k = k_1 = k_2 = k_3 = k_4$. Figure 3, lower left part, shows the resulting behaviour. Examining a range from $k = 10^{-100} \dots 10^{+100}$, we consistently observe a stable spiking oscillation whose period lengths reversely vary from a magnitude of 10^{+100} s up to 10^{-100} s.

For preparation of the Brusselator model to act as temperature sensor, a calibration is required by adjustment of relevant free parameters. To this end, we refer to [17] stating a spiking period length of about 100 ms for temperature sensitive ion channels at 20°C (293.15 K). Along with the common activation energy $E(T) = 67\,000\,\frac{J}{mol}$, this setting entails $Act(T) = 2.0149 \cdot 10^{14}$ as pre-exponential

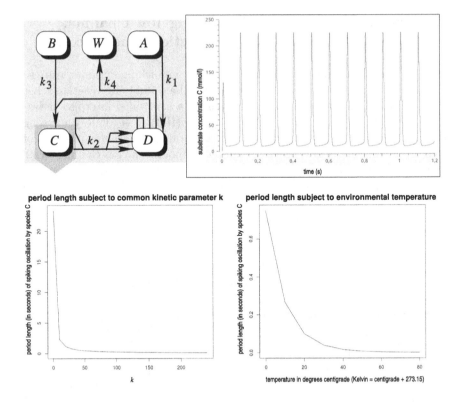

Fig. 3. Ion channel model based on Brusselator. Spiking oscillatory output: concentration course of C over time **(upper part, right)**. Initial concentrations: $[B](0) = 3, [A](0) = 1, [C](0) = 0.5, [D](0) = 0.5, [W](0) = 0$. Common mass-action parameter setting: $k = k_1 = k_2 = k_3 = k_4$. Transfer curve for calibration **(lower part, left)**. Oscillator calibrated to exhibit period length of 100 ms at temperature of 20°C obtained with $T = 293.15, E(T) = 67000, A(T) = 2.0149 \cdot 10^{14}, k = 232$. Period length subject to temperature most significantly within range $0 \dots 40$°C **(lower part, right)**

factor. The large value indicates a low interdependency on the spatial orientation of involved substrate molecules according to expectations of a non-selective ion channel. The lower right part of Fig. 3 depicts the Brusselator thermosensing transfer curve by exhibiting period length subject to temperature. Sensitivity is most significant between $0 \dots 40$°C which coincides with typical oceanic water temperatures near the surface.

Formally, the deterministic P module of the thermosensor reads:

$$\text{thermosensor} = ((T), ([C]), \Box) \quad \text{with}$$
$$\Box : [\dot{A}] = -k(T)[A], \quad [\dot{B}] = -k(T)[B][D], \quad [\dot{W}] = k(T)[D],$$
$$[\dot{C}] = k(T)[B][D] - k(T)[C][D]^2,$$
$$[\dot{D}] = -k(T)[B][D] + k(T)[C][D]^2 + k(T)[A] - k(T)[D],$$

$$k(T) = Act(T) \cdot e^{-\frac{E(T)}{R \cdot T}},$$

$$[A](0) = 1, [B](0) = 3, [C](0) = 0.5, [D](0) = 0.5, [W](0) = 0,$$

$$Act(T) = 2.0149 \cdot 10^{14}, E(T) = 67\,000, R = 8.31446$$

Since the thermosensor maps environmental temperature into a correspond-ing periodicity, it carries out a chemical counterpart of *frequency modulation* known from engineering. This concept for signal encoding is characterised by an outstanding robustness against perturbations, especially in comparison to signals managed in a purely analogous manner. By spatio-temporal waves of calcium ions (and/or additional further cations), the frequency-encoded temper-ature signal passes the cytosol (transduction) and finally reaches parts of the cell in charge of exploitation and response. An effective evaluation of a frequency-based oscillatory signal requires different processing stages in order to obtain a corresponding steady-state species concentration whose value can initiate and trigger subsequent intracellular processes in response.

A simple and reliable way to decode a frequency signal consists in utilisa-tion of a numerical *integrator*. For a predefined sliding time span, the oscillating input becomes consecutively accumulated. A high number of spikes within the time span induces a larger sum signal than a lower number of spikes within the same time span. In order to build a numerical integrator from chemical reactions, we define a reaction cascade to be passed by the oscillatory signal. Each reac-tion within this cascade produces a short delay (offset) in signal transduction. Furthermore, the original spiking waveform is successively transformed into an almost sinusoidal shape. By summation of the signal courses present at the indi-vidual nodes of the cascade, a numerical integration appears. Attention must be paid to an appropriate chemical integrator setup. The number of nodes within the cascade estimates the numerical precision of the output sum signal. A low number $(2 \ldots 4)$ seems to be improperly while a high number is implausible in terms of an evolutionary origination. In our sample setup, we employ six nodes, see Fig. 4. Kinetic parameters within the cascade need to be balanced in order to produce a sufficient signal offset on the one hand and keeping away on the other hand from obtaining a simple average signal from partially overlapping waves interfering to each other. We achieved practicable results by setting cas-cade kinetic parameters k_I around 10 times higher than k in the Brusselator. Reactions involved in summation should run at least at the same velocity as k_I. As output of the numerical integrator, the species concentration $[K]$ over time decodes temperature in a first approximation.

integrator $= ((T, [C]), ([K]), \square)$ with

$$\square : [\dot{I}_1] = k_C(T)[C] - k_{I,1}(T)[I_2] + k_{I,7}(T)[I_1],$$

$$[\dot{I}_j] = k_{I,j-1}(T)[I_{j-1}] - k_{I,j+1}(T)[I_{j+1}] \quad j = 2, \ldots, 5,$$

$$[\dot{I}_6] = k_{I,5}(T)[I_5],$$

$$[\dot{K}] = \left(\sum_{j=1}^{6} k_{I,7}(T)[I_j]\right) - k_{I,8}(T)[K],$$

$$k_{I,m}(T) = Act_m(T) \cdot e^{-\frac{E(T)}{R \cdot T}} \quad m = 1,\dots 8,$$

$$[I_p](0) = 0 \quad p = 1,\dots,6, [K](0) = 0,$$

$$Act_r(T) = 2.0571 \cdot 10^{15} \quad r = 1,\dots,5,$$

$$Act_7(T) = 2.02 \cdot 10^{14}, Act_8(T) = 2.02 \cdot 10^{14},$$

$$E(T) = 67\,000, R = 8.31446$$

After an initial transient phase, $[K]$ tends to oscillate between a minimal and a maximal value in low frequency due to the nature of the underlying input oscillation. A subsequent module called *smoother* acts in terms of a moving average element by forming a chemical low-pass filter as described in [11]. Within the smoother, we organise descending k_S values $k \cdot 10^{-2}$, $k \cdot 10^{-3}$, and $k \cdot 10^{-4}$ within the three-stage cascade. Species concentration $[X_1]$ over time provides the resulting smoothed signal value. When passing through the relevant temperature range it turns out that the corresponding steady $[X_1]$ values span a range starting away from zero. For instance, we realise 124.45.

$$\text{smoother} = ((T,[K]),([X_1]),\square) \quad \text{with}$$

$$\square : [\dot{L}] = k_{S,1}(T)[K]^2 - k_{S,2}(T)[M],$$

$$[\dot{M}] = k_{S,2}(T)[M] - k_{S,3}(T)[X_1],$$

$$[\dot{X_1}] = k_{S,3}(T)[X_1],$$

$$k_{S,m}(T) = Act_m(T) \cdot e^{-\frac{E(T)}{R \cdot T}} \quad m = 1,\dots,3,$$

$$Act_1(T) = 2.0149 \cdot 10^{12}, Act_2(T) = 2.0149 \cdot 10^{11},$$

$$Act_3(T) = 2.0149 \cdot 10^{10}, E(T) = 67\,000, R = 8.31446$$

Hence, the closing part of signal processing is dedicated to perform a final mapping into a species concentration ranging from 0 up to – lets say – 10 (arbitrarily chosen). To this end, we equip the thermoreceptor model with a *subtractor* (calculates $[S] := [X_1] \dot{-} [X_2]$) and a *multiplicator* ($[Y] := [F] \cdot [S]$). Both arithmetic P modules were introduced in [11] and incorporated into the final model whose topology and composition in a modular manner is shown in Fig. 4. Its lower left part depicts the overall transfer curve of species concentration $[Y]$ subject to environmental temperature T. In accordance with the delimited sliding time span of the numerical integrator, $[Y]$ converges towards an upper bound. Having all individual modules at hand (one copy of each), the corresponding P meta framework reads:

$$\Pi_{\text{thermoreceptor}} = (M,P) \quad \text{with}$$

$$M = \{(\text{thermosensor},1),(\text{integrator},1),(\text{smoother},1),$$

$$(\text{subtractor},1),(\text{multiplicator},1)\}$$

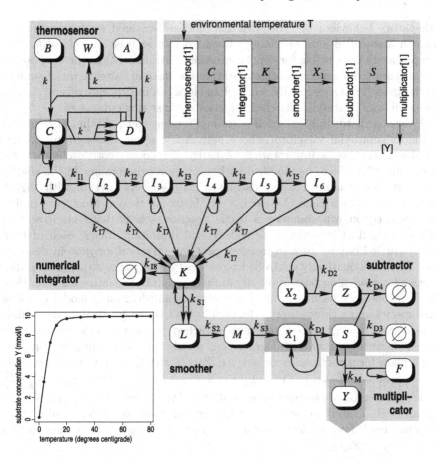

Fig. 4. Entire thermoreceptor model based on five subsequent modules: thermosensor (frequency encoder), numerical integrator (frequency decoder) with downstream smoother, subtractor ($[X_2](0) = 124.45$), and multiplicator ($[F](0) = 49.68$). Transfer curve maps input temperature T into species concentration $[Y]$.

$$P = \{0 : \texttt{ModuleConnect}(\text{thermosensor}[1] \rightarrow \text{integrator}[1], \{(C, C)\}),$$
$$0 : \texttt{ModuleConnect}(\text{integrator}[1] \rightarrow \text{smoother}[1], \{(K, K)\}),$$
$$0 : \texttt{ModuleConnect}(\text{smoother}[1] \rightarrow \text{subtractor}[1], \{(X_1, X_1)\}),$$
$$0 : \texttt{ModuleConnect}(\text{subtractor}[1] \rightarrow \text{multiplicator}[1], \{(S, S)\})\}$$

4   Evolving Temperature Entrainable Circadian Clock Model

It is believed that there are diverse evolutionary origins of circadian clocks what emphasises its importance for survival and fitness of organisms to exhibit an anticipatory behaviour [4]. All circadian clocks discovered up to now have in common a so-called *core oscillator* embedded into at least one *global feedback* loop primarily responsible for synchronisation (entrainment) of the core oscillator's rhythm to an external oscillatory stimulus like daily alterations of sunlight and darkness [28]. Occasionally, a circadian clock can incorporate several coupled core oscillators to stabilise its clock function against single damages.

A core oscillator induces a self-sustained (endogenous) rhythm of sinusoidal or almost sinusoidal waveform whose periodicity accomodates to an external stimulus indicating a full rotation of earth. To do so, core oscillator's frequency must be able to be modified within an appropriate range. In the absence of an external stimulus, a core oscillator maintains its rhythm with slightly varied period which runs the clock a bit faster or slower. Most core oscillators currently known comprise a cyclic reaction scheme with negative feedback composed of subsequent activating and inhibiting stages, each of them mainly carried out by gene expression, protein activation, or protein deactivation. These enzymatically controlled processes typically necessitate a saturation kinetics for modelling because of the limited amount of reactive enzyme. Here, *Goodwin-type* core oscillators [8] provide an established meta-model based on three species and a three-stage cycle. Oscillation frequency is mainly determined by velocities of degradation reactions attached to each species. When utilising enzymatically controlled degradation, we obtain a deterministic P module of the plain form core_oscillator $= ((), ([Z]), \square)$ with $\square$ containing three ODEs
$$[\dot{X}] = \frac{a}{b+K_1[Z]^2} - \frac{k_2[X]}{K_2+[X]}; \quad [\dot{Y}] = k_3[X] - k_5[Y] - \frac{k_4[Y]}{K_4+[Y]}; \quad [\dot{Z}] = k_5[Y] - \frac{k_6[Z]}{K_6+[Z]}$$
to formalise a Goodwin-type core oscillator. Parameters a, b, K_1, K_2, K_4, and K_6, all $\in \mathbb{R}_{>0}$, need to be set or fitted for the concrete system under study. The same holds for the kinetic parameters k_2 up to k_6 and initial concentrations $[X](0), [Y](0), [Z](0)$.

In [14], we introduced a minimalistic model of a circadian clock based on *deterministic P modules* equipped with a Goodwin-type core oscillator as central part of a chemical frequency control system representing a *phase locked loop* (PLL), see upper part of Fig. 5. The global feedback consists of a signal comparator (arithmetic multiplicator), a low-pass filter (reaction cascade) and a scaler for preparation of the tuning signal which in turn regulates core oscillator's frequency. In its original form, the PLL model releases the concentration course $[Z](t)$ over time as output signal adapted to $[E](t)$ that is handled as external oscillatory stimulus. For instance, $[E](t)$ could result from an upstream photo cascade converting the intensity of environmental light into a corresponding chemical concentration value.

Now, we are going to explore the minimalistic PLL circadian clock model concerning its entrainability exclusively by environmental temperature T. Additionally, we assume that there is no mechanism of temperature compensation within the circadian clock model under study. Temperature compensation neutralises the effect of varying environmental temperature to the clock pace in which higher temperature accelerates chemical reactions towards a faster rhythm and lower temperature vice versa. Mechanisms of temperature compensation by variation

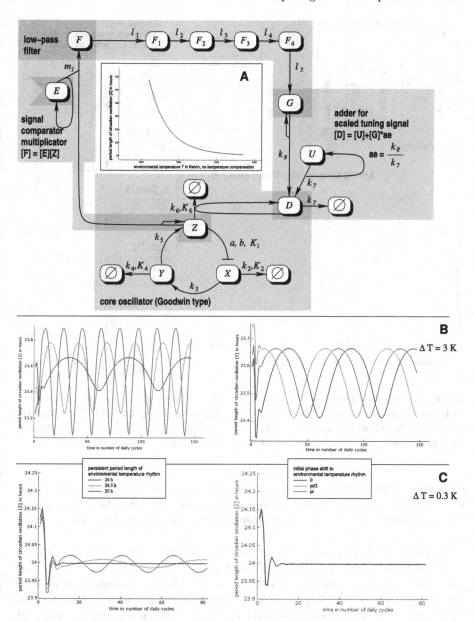

Fig. 5. Sensorless PLL-based circadian clock model with Goodwin-type core oscillator, low-pass filter, and scaler. Temperature exclusively handled via Arrhenius terms attached to the reactions. Constant concentrations: $[E](t) = 5, [U](t) = 1$. Temperature-independent kinetic parameterisation: $a = 6, b = 0.6, K_1 = 1, K_2 = 0.2, K_4 = 0.2, K_6 = 1.44$. Kinetic reference values at $T = 293.15$ K: $k_2 = 3.4, k_3 = 0.3, k_4 = 2.2, k_5 = 0.1, k_6 = 1.3, k_7 = 1000, k_8 = 100, l_1 = l_2 = l_3 = 0.108, l_4 = 3600, l_5 = 180, m_1 = 100$. Initial concentrations: $[Z](0) = 5$, all unmentioned species: 0. Studies **A**: oscillatory region, **B** and **C**: entrainability to external temperature rhythms, see text.

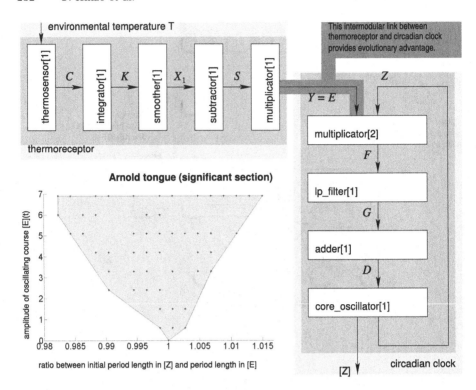

Fig. 6. Modular framework of PLL-based circadian clock model exclusively entrainable by temperature sensed using thermoreceptor (**upper and right part**). Deterministic P modules share common species to interact according to connectivity interface. Arnold tongue silhouettes significant section of entrainment region (**lower left part**).

of activation energy became apparent when life forms left the oceanic water and were exposed to comparatively strong changes in environmental temperature. Early submarine life forms like *archaea* could rarely benefit from temperature compensation.

Initially, we re-formulate the entire PLL model by interacting deterministic P modules including consideration of temperature. To this end, we need to refine all underlying kinetic parameters following Arrhenius' equation. Assuming all involved values k_i, l_i, m_i from [14] to be valid for 20°C (293.15 K) and $67\,000 \frac{J}{mol}$ activation energy, the corresponding pre-exponential factor arises for each individual reaction. Having the entire parameter setting at hand, we conduct different simulation studies.

Our first study intends to learn more about the influence of temperature onto the free running circadian clock. For this purpose, we disconnect the external stimulus by setting $[E](t)$ to the constant value 5 which represents the medium or average number of the former oscillation in [14]. The study is aimed at localisation of the stable oscillatory region subject to temporally constant environmental temperature. Part **A** of Fig. 5 shows resulting period lengths. It reveals that there is a minimum temperature of nearly 12°C (285.1 K) which marks the lower oscillatory limit. At 20°C (293.15 K), we obtain a period length of 24 h according to parameter calibration. Along with increasing temperature, period length of $[Z](t)$ becomes hyperbolically shortened. Around 62°C (335 K), the stable limit cycle oscillation turns into a pre-stage of deterministic chaos by poly-frequential behaviour. At this upper limit, period length had been reduced to less than one hour.

Now, we exploratively analyse entrainability of the sensorless PLL circadian clock model to an external oscillatory temperature stimulus inspired by daily variations of oceanic water temperature near the surface. We keep constant $[E](t) = 5$. Temperature is reflected exclusively by Arrhenius terms attached to the reactions. There is no dedicated temperature receptor or sensor. We start with amplitude of $\Delta T = 3$ K by sinusoidally oscillating environmental temperature between 18.5 and 21.5°C. Part **B** of Fig. 5 illustrates the resulting poor entrainability to both, slightly modified period length (left) and initial phase shift (right). In all cases, the circadian clock runs in a long-term poly-frequential manner unable to adjust a synchronous frequency. Since the PLL tries to "catch" external stimulus' frequency by accelerating its core oscillator due to an increasing error (difference) signal $[D](t)$, resulting period lengths decline into a range below 24 h. In subsequent studies, we successively decreased the amplitude ΔT. At 0.3 K (and below), we notice entrainability, see part **C**. This is due to the moderate growth of the error signal which prevents the core oscillator from excessive acceleration. Entrainability to various period lengths becomes worse with increasing deviation (left) while initial phase shifts have been reliably eliminated, even for an almost antiphasic scenario (initial phase shift $\phi = \pi$ or 12 h, respectively).

Finally, we combine the sensorless PLL circadian clock model with the thermoreceptor model from Sect. 3. Temporal concentration course of thermoreceptor output species Y acts as external stimulus E now connecting both modules by this shared species. For the entire framework of interacting deterministic P modules, we were able to confirm extensive entrainability. It turns out that there is no qualitative discrepancy between entrainment by light (managed via photo cascade, [14]) and entrainment by temperature (sensed via thermoreceptor). It seems that both concepts are equivalent regarding the entrainment power when considering region of entrainability. Entrainment by temperature tends to synchronise a bit slower than entrainment by light (time to synchronisation prolongated up to approx. 20 %) due to the inherent latency in signal processing caused by the thermoreceptor. Figure 6 depicts connectivity of all involved modules along with the summarising *Arnold tongue*. For numerous ratios between initial period lengths in $[Z]$ (internal oscillator) and $[E]$ (external oscillator) and for varying amplitudes of $[E]$, each black cross marks entrainability (signal synchronisation) proved by simulation. The highlighted tongue-shaped silhouette indicates the overall region of entrainability which coincides with typical daily changes in oceanic surface water temperature.

5 Conclusions

This paper is inspired by the hypothesis that effective circadian clocks could have been emerged without evolution of photoreceptors and lightsensors merely by exploitation of daily temperature cycles. By consistent utilisation and combination of modules following the notion of systems biology, we consolidate an imagination of functional simplicity and hence evolvability of underlying reaction schemes. The concept of deterministic P modules along with their assembly and combination towards complex models opens a wide field of applications within explorative elucidation using *grey boxes*, hypothetical but plausible chemical units successively replaced by its biological counterparts. Simulation studies were carried out using MatLab except those for transfer curve for Brusselator calibration whose data were obtained by Copasi due to its larger domain of numerical values. Sources are available from the first author upon request.

References

1. Barbagallo, B., Garrity, P.A.: Temperature sensation in Drosophila. Curr. Opin. Neurobiol. **34**, 8–13 (2015)
2. Belousov, B.P.: A periodic reaction and its mechanism. Compilation Abstr. Radiat. Med. **145**, 147 (1959)
3. Butcher, J.C.: Numerical Methods for Ordinary Differential Equations. Wiley, Chichester (2008)
4. Dvornyk, V., Vinogradova, O., Nevo, E.: Origin and evolution of circadian clock genes in prokaryotes. PNAS **100**(5), 2495–2500 (2003)
5. Gibson, D.G., Glass, J.I., Lartigue, C., et al.: Creation of a bacterial cell controlled by a chemically synthesized genome. Science **329**, 52–56 (2010)
6. Gierloff-Emden, H.-G.: Lehrbuch der allgemeinen Geographie. deGruyter, New York (1979)
7. Glaser, R.: Biophysics. An Introduction. Springer, Heidelberg (2012)
8. Goodwin, B.C.: Oscillatory behaviour in enzymatic control processes. Adv. Enzyme Regul. **3**, 425–438 (1965)
9. Hartwell, L.H., Hopfield, J.J., Leibler, S., Murray, A.W.: From molecular to modular cell biology. Nature **402**, 47–52 (1999)
10. Heiland, I., Bodenstein, C., Hinze, T., Weisheit, O., Ebenhöh, O., Mittag, M., Schuster, S.: Modeling temperature entrainment of circadian clocks using the Arrhenius equation and a reconstructed model from Chlamydomonas reinhardtii. J. Biol. Phys. **38**, 449–464 (2012)
11. Hinze, T., Bodenstein, C., Schau, B., Heiland, I., Schuster, S.: Chemical analog computers for clock frequency control based on P modules. In: Gheorghe, M., Păun, G., Rozenberg, G., Salomaa, A., Verlan, S. (eds.) CMC 2011. LNCS, vol. 7184, pp. 182–202. Springer, Heidelberg (2012)
12. Hinze, T., Schell, B., Schumann, M., Bodenstein, C.: Maintenance of chronobiological information by P system mediated assembly of control units for oscillatory waveforms and frequency. In: Csuhaj-Varjú, E., Gheorghe, M., Rozenberg, G., Salomaa, A., Vaszil, G. (eds.) CMC 2012. LNCS, vol. 7762, pp. 208–227. Springer, Heidelberg (2013)

13. Hinze, T.: Unraveling oscillating structures by means of P systems. In: Gheorghe, M., et al. (eds.) Research Frontiers of Membrane Computing: Open Problems and Research Topics. Int. J. Found. Comput. Sci. **24**(5), 547–623 (2013)
14. Hinze, T., et al.: Membrane systems and tools combining dynamical structures with reaction kinetics for applications in chronobiology. In: Frisco, P., Gheorghe, M., Perez-Jimenez, M.J. (eds.) Applications of Membrane Computing in Systems and Synthetic Biology. Series Emergence, Complexity, and Computation, vol. 7, pp. 133–173. Springer, Heidelberg (2014)
15. Harootunian, A.T., Kao, J.P.Y., Paranjape, S., Tsien, R.Y.: Generation of calcium oscillations in fibroblasts by positive feedback between calcium and IP_3. Science **251**, 75–78 (1991)
16. Hoops, S., Sahle, S., Gauges, R., Lee, C., Pahle, J., Simus, N., Singhal, M., Xu, L., Mendes, P., Kummer, U.: COPASI-a COmplex PAthway SImulator. Bioinformatics **22**(24), 3067–3074 (2006)
17. Izhikevich, E.M.: Simple model of spiking neurons. IEEE Trans. Neural Networks **14**(6), 1569–1572 (2003)
18. Johnson, C.H., Golden, S.S., Ishiura, M., Kondo, T.: Circadian clocks in prokaryotes. Mol. Microbiol. **21**(1), 5–11 (1996)
19. Klipp, E., Herwig, R., Kowald, A., Wierling, C., Lehrach, H.: Systems Biology in Practice. Wiley, Chichester (2008)
20. Lumpkin, E.A., Caterina, M.J.: Mechanisms of sensory transduction in the skin. Nature **445**, 858–865 (2007)
21. Lynch, S.: Dynamical Systems with Applications Using MatLab. Birkhäuser, Basel (2004)
22. Nishiyama, S., Ohno, S., Ohta, N., Inoue, Y., Fukuoka, H., Ishijima, A., Kawagishi, I.: Thermosensing function of the Echerichia coli redox sensor Aer. J. Bacteriol. **192**(6), 1740–1743 (2010)
23. Paster, E., Ryu, W.S.: The thermal impulse response of Escherichia coli. PNAS **105**(14), 5373–5377 (2008)
24. Păun, G.: Membrane Computing: An Introduction. Springer, Heidelberg (2002)
25. Romanovsky, A.A.: Thermoregulation: some concepts have changed. Functional architecture of the thermoregulatory system. Am. J. Physiol. Regul. Integr. Comp. Physiol. **292**, R37–R46 (2007)
26. Ruoff, P.: Introducing temperature-compensation in any reaction kinetic oscillator model. J. Interdiscipl. Cycle Res. **23**(2), 92–99 (1992)
27. Sengupta, P., Garrity, P.: Sensing temperature. Curr. Biol. **23**(8), R304 (2012)
28. Sharma, V.K., Joshi, A.: Clocks, genes, and evolution. The evolution of circadian organization. In: Kumar, V. (ed.) Biological Rhythms, pp. 5–23. Springer, Heidelberg (2002)
29. Viana, F., Pena, E., Belmonte, C.: Specificity of cold thermotransduction is determined by differential ionic channel expression. Nat. Neurosci. **5**(3), 254–260 (2002)
30. Whitehead, K., Pan, M., Masumura, K., Bonneau, R., Baliga, N.S.: Diurnally entrained anticipatory behavior in archaea. PLoS One **4**(5), e5485 (2009)
31. Zhabotinsky, A.M.: Periodic processes of malonic acid oxidation in a liquid phase. Biofizika **9**, 306–311 (1964)

A Solution of Horn-SAT with P Systems Using Antimatter

Gábor Kolonits[(✉)]

Department of Algorithms and their Applications, Faculty of Informatics,
Eötvös Loránd University, Budapest, Hungary
kolomax@inf.elte.hu

Abstract. In this paper we prove that uniform families of P systems with active membranes and using antimatter characterize the complexity class **P** when polarizations, dissolution rules and membrane division rules are not used. This means that the use of antimatter significantly increases the computational power of these systems having the above restrictions, since it is known that without the use of antimatter and using reasonably weak uniformity conditions they have very limited computational power only.

1 Introduction

The idea of generalizing the notion of spikes and anti-spikes from spiking neural P systems was first proposed in [9]. The use of *objects* and *anti-objects* (also called *matter* and *antimatter*, resp.) in various classes of P systems provides new research lines in Membrane Computing. Since an object a and its anti-object pair $\bar{a}$ can not stay together in a compartment, it is supposed that a rule of the form $a\bar{a} \to \lambda$ is applied to remove these objects regardless to the possible application of other kinds of rules. This means that these rules (which are also called *annihilation rules*) have priorities over the other types of rules. This phenomenon can significantly increase the computation power of those membrane systems where anti-matter and annihilation rules are used (see e.g. [1–3]).

Recently, it was shown in [3] that using antimatter and annihilation rules in P systems with active membranes without polarizations, without dissolution and with division of elementary and non-elementary membranes increases the power of these systems significantly: while without antimatter these systems can only solve problems in the complexity class **P** [6], with antimatter they are capable to solve **NP**-complete problems too.

In this paper we show that antimatter and annihilation rules increase the power also of those P systems which do not employ membrane division rules. Namely, we show that (**L,L**)-uniform families of P systems with active membranes, without polarizations, dissolution and division of membranes, but with antimatter and annihilation rules characterize the complexity class **P**. Here **L** denotes the class of functions computable by Turing machines using logarithmic space. The lower bound on the power of these P systems is shown by presenting

ⓒ Springer International Publishing Switzerland 2015
G. Rozenberg et al. (Eds.): CMC 2015, LNCS 9504, pp. 236–250, 2015.
DOI: 10.1007/978-3-319-28475-0_16

a solution of the **P**-complete Horn-SAT problem (where the task is to decide if a Horn-formula is satisfiable or not). Since it is known that these P systems without antimatter and using strict uniformity conditions have very limited computational power only (see e.g. Theorem 10 in [7]), our result shows that the use of antimatter significantly increases the computational power of these P systems.

The paper is organized as follows. In the next section the necessary notions concerning the investigated P systems are introduced. In Sect. 3 the main result of the paper is proved. Finally, in Sect. 4 some concluding remarks are given.

2   Preliminaries

First, we recall some basic concepts used later. Nevertheless, we assume that the reader is familiar with Membrane Computing techniques (for a detailed description, see e.g. [10]).

Propositional Formulas

Let $Var = \{X_1, X_2, X_3, \ldots\}$ be a countable set of *propositional variables* (*variables*, to be short), and, for every $n \in \mathbb{N}$, where $\mathbb{N}$ denotes the set of natural numbers, let $Var_n := \{X_1, \ldots, X_n\}$. An *interpretation of the variables in* Var_n (or just an *interpretation* if Var_n is clear from the context) is a function $\mathcal{I} : Var_n \to \{true, false\}$.

The variables and their negations are called *literals*. A literal l is called a *positive* (resp. *negative*) *literal*, if $l = X$ (resp. $l = \neg X$), for some $X \in Var$. A *clause* C is a disjunction of finitely many pairwise different literals satisfying the condition that there is no $X \in Var$ such that both X and $\neg X$ occur in C. A *formula in conjunctive normal form* (CNF) is a conjunction of finitely many clauses. We can treat formulas in CNF as finite sets of clauses, where the clauses are finite sets of literals. A *Horn formula* is a formula φ in CNF satisfying that every clause in φ contains at most one positive literal. A clause containing a single positive literal is called a *unit clause*. A formula φ in CNF over variables in Var_n, for some $n \in \mathbb{N}$, is satisfiable, if there is an interpretation under which φ evaluates to *true*. Notice that a formula φ in CNF is satisfiable, only if there is an interpretation I such that, for every clause of φ of the form $\{X\}$, $\mathcal{I}(X) = true$.

Recognizer P Systems

A *P system* is a construct of the form $\Pi = (\Gamma, H, \mu, w_1, \ldots, w_m, R)$, where $m \geq 1$ is the *initial degree* of the system; Γ is the *working alphabet of objects*; H is a finite set of *labels* of the membranes; μ is a *membrane structure* consisting of m membranes and labeled with elements of H; $w_1, \ldots, w_m \subseteq \Gamma^*$ are the *initial multisets of objects* placed in the m regions of μ; and R is a finite set of *developmental rules*.

A *P system with input* is a tuple (Π, Σ, i_0), where Π is a P system with working alphabet Γ; Σ is an (input) alphabet strictly contained in Γ; the initial multisets are over $\Gamma \backslash \Sigma$; and i_0 is the label of a distinguished (input) membrane.

We say that Π is a *recognizer P system* [11,12] if Π is a P system with input alphabet Σ and working alphabet Γ; Γ has two designated objects *yes* and *no*; every computation of Π halts and sends out to the environment the same object which is either *yes* or *no*, and this object is sent out in the last step of the computation. The input of Π is a word $w \in \Sigma^*$, whose corresponding multiset is added to the system by placing it into the input membrane i_0 in the initial configuration.

P Systems with Active Membranes Using Antimatter

In this paper we investigate recognizer P systems with active membranes [8]. In fact we will consider such a variant of these systems where the polarizations of the membranes, dissolution rules and membrane division rules are not used. On the other hand, the use of antimatter and annihilation rules are allowed. We denote the class of these P systems by $\mathcal{AM}^0_{-d,-e,+antPri}$, where $-d$ (resp. $-e$) denotes that dissolution (resp. membrane division) rules are not allowed, and $+antPri$ indicates that the use of antimatter and annihilation rules with priority are allowed. The rules of P systems of type $\mathcal{AM}^0_{-d,-e,+antPri}$ are formally defined as follows:

(a) $[a \rightarrow v]_h$, for $h \in H$, $a \in \Gamma$, $v \in \Gamma^*$ (*object evolution rules*, associated with membranes and depending on the label of the membranes, but not directly involving the membranes, in the sense that the membranes are neither taking part in the application of these rules nor are they modified by them)

(b) $a[\ ]_h \rightarrow [b]_h$, for $h \in H$, $a,b \in \Gamma$ (*send-in communication rules*, sending an object into a membrane, the object being maybe modified during this process)

(c) $[a]_h \rightarrow [\ ]_h b$, for $h \in H$, $a,b \in \Gamma$ (*send-out communication rules*; an object is sent out of the membrane, the object being maybe modified during this process)

(d) $[a\bar{a} \rightarrow \lambda]_h$ for $h \in H$, $a,\bar{a} \in \Gamma$ (*annihilation rules*, associated with a membrane labeled by h: the pair of objects $a,\bar{a} \in \Gamma$, belonging simultaneously to this membrane, disappears by the use of this rule).

As it is usual in membrane computing, a P system with active membranes using antimatter works in the *maximally parallel* manner:

– In one step, any object of a membrane that can evolve must evolve, but one object can be used by only one rule in (a)–(d).
– If an object can be used with two or more different rules, then one of these rules is non-deterministically chosen. The only exception is when an annihilation rule can be applied, since, by physical inspiration, these rules have priority over all of the other types of rules (see also [3]).
– When some rules in (b) or (c) can be applied to a certain membrane, then one of them must be applied, but a membrane can be the subject of only one of these rules during each step.

Uniform Families of P Systems

We will solve the Horn-SAT problem with a uniform family of P systems. Since this problem is in the complexity class **P**, we should use such a uniform family where the members of the family and the encoding of the Horn formulas can be constructed with reasonably weak Turing machines. According to the widely believed hypothesis that Turing machines using logarithmic space are strictly weaker than Turing machines using polynomial time, we will use logarithmic space uniform families of P systems. The definition of uniformity presented below follows the notion of uniformity used in [13]. Let **E** and **F** be classes of computable functions. A family $\mathbf{\Pi} = (\Pi(i))_{i \in \mathbb{N}}$ of recognizer P systems is called **(E,F)**-*uniform* if and only if (i) there is a function $f \in \mathbf{F}$ such that, for every $n \in \mathbb{N}$, $\Pi(n) = f(1^n)$ (i.e., mapping the unary encoding of each natural number to an encoding of the P system processing all the inputs of length n); (ii) there is a function $e \in \mathbf{E}$ that maps every word $x \in \Sigma^*$ with length n to a multiset $e(x) = w_x$ over the input alphabet of $\Pi(n)$.

An **(E, F)**-uniform family of P systems $\mathbf{\Pi} = (\Pi(i))_{i \in \mathbb{N}}$ *decides a language* $L \subseteq \Sigma^*$ if, for every word $x \in \Sigma^*$ with length n, when $\Pi(n)$ is started with w_x in its input membrane, it sends out to the environment *yes* if and only if $x \in L$. In general, **E** and **F** are well known complexity classes such as **P** or **L**, however in our work we use only **(L, L)**-uniform families of P systems. The class of problems decidable in polynomial time by **(E, F)**-uniform families of P systems of type $\mathcal{F}$ is denoted by $(\mathbf{E}, \mathbf{F}) - \mathbf{PMC}_{\mathcal{F}}$.

We say that $\Pi(n)$ *works in time* $t(n)$ $(t : \mathbb{N} \to \mathbb{N})$ if $\Pi(n)$ halts in at most $t(n)$ steps, for every input multiset in its input membrane.

3 The Main Result

Here we prove that the computational power of P systems of type $\mathcal{AM}^0_{-d,-e,+antPri}$ characterizes the complexity class **P**.

3.1 Solving Horn-SAT

In this subsection we give a family of P systems of type $\mathcal{AM}^0_{-d,-e,+antPri}$ to solve the **P**-complete Horn-SAT problem. This problem is the following one: *Given a Horn formula φ, decide if φ is satisfiable.*

We are going to implement the following algorithm HS, which is a simple modification of the well-known algorithm based on unit-propagation (see e.g. [4]), to solve Horn-SAT. We decided to use an outer **For** cycle instead of **While**, in order to avoid a more complicated implementation. Let $\varphi = H_1 \wedge \cdots \wedge H_m$ be a Horn formula over the variables in Var_n.

procedure Horn-SAT
input: φ
$\varphi' := \varphi$
For $i = 1 \ldots n$ do
    $R := \{H \in \varphi' \mid H \text{is a unit clause in } \varphi's$
    Foreach H in R **do**
        Foreach clause C in φ' **do**
            $C' := Reduce(C, H)$
            Replace C in φ' with C'
If φ' contains an empty clause **then return** $false$
else return $true$

function $Reduce(C, H)$
If C contains $\neg X$, for some $X \in H$ **then return** $C \backslash \{\neg X\}$
else return C

Intuitively, the above algorithm works as follows on an input formula φ. HS does an n-times iterated loop, where in every iteration step, it chooses the unit clauses of φ' (which, at the beginning, equals to φ). Clearly, if an interpretation satisfies φ', then it must assign $true$ to the variables occurring in these clauses. Then HS removes all the corresponding negative literals from the clauses of φ', since these negative literals cannot be $true$ in a satisfying interpretation. Then we get a formula, that is satisfiable if and only if φ is satisfiable. For example, $(X \vee \neg Y \vee \neg Z \vee \neg U) \wedge Y \wedge Z$ is satisfiable if and only if $X \vee \neg U$ is satisfiable, and such satisfying interpretations must assign $true$ to Y and Z. If at the end of the cycle φ' contains an empty clause, then it means that φ cannot be satisfied. Otherwise it can be. In the following example we show the working of the algorithm:

Example 1. $\varphi = X \wedge (\neg X \vee Y) \wedge (\neg Y)$
    $\varphi' := \varphi$
  1. $R = \{X\}$
    • For $X \in R$:
        - For $P \in \varphi'$:
            Reduce X (from φ') with X (from R); the solution is X
            Replace X in φ' with X
        - For $\neg X \vee Y \in \varphi'$:
            Reduce $\neg X \vee Y$ with X; the solution is Y
            Replace $\neg X \vee Y$ in φ' with Y
        - For $\neg Y \in \varphi'$:
            Reduce $\neg Y$ with X; the solution is $\neg Y$
            Replace $\neg Y$ in φ' with $\neg Y$
    • $\varphi' = \{X, Y, \neg Y\}$
  2. $R = \{X, Y\}$
    • For $X \in R$:
        $\ldots$
    • For $Y \in R$:

- For $X \in \varphi'$:
  Reduce X with Y; the solution is X
  Replace X in φ' with X
- For $Y \in \varphi'$:
  Reduce Y (from φ') with Y (from R); the solution is Y
  Replace Y in φ' with Y
- For $\neg Y \in \varphi'$:
  Reduce $\neg Y$ with Y; the solution is $\square$
  Replace $\neg Y$ in φ with $\square$

• $\varphi' = \{X, Y, \square\}$

Since φ' contains $\square$, the algorithm returns *false*

In this example the formula contains two literals (namely X and Y), so the algorithm will take a two rounded loop. In the first round it detects the only one unit clause, X, and removes its negated appearances from the clauses (namely it replaces $\neg X \lor Y$ with Y). In the second round there are two unit clauses, X and Y. The algorithm performs the necessary reduction(s), so $\square$ (i.e., the empty clause) appears in φ'. Then the algorithm gives the correct answer: the formula is unsatisfiable.

The P System. Here we present a family of P systems that implements the algorithm HS. We will use the following encoding of a Horn formula $\varphi = H_1 \land \cdots \land H_m$ over the variables in Var_n. The encoding of φ, denoted by $cod(\varphi)$, is a multiset over the alphabet $\{x_{i,j,k} \mid 1 \leq i \leq n, 1 \leq j \leq m, 0 \leq k \leq 1\}$, where $x_{i,j,1}$ (resp. $x_{i,j,0}$) represents the fact that x_i (resp. $\neg x_i$) occurs in H_j (notice that since barred objects usually denote antimatter, we cannot use $\bar{x}_{i,j}$ to represent negated variables).

Let us consider an appropriate pairing function $\langle \, , \, \rangle$ from $\mathbb{N} \times \mathbb{N}$ to $\mathbb{N}$. We construct a P system $\Pi(\langle n, m \rangle)$ processing φ, when $cod(\varphi)$ is supplied in its input membrane. The family presented here is:

$$\Pi = \{(\Pi(\langle n, m \rangle), \Sigma(\langle n, m \rangle), i(\langle n, m \rangle)) \mid (n, m) \in \mathbb{N}^2\},$$

where the input alphabet is $\Sigma(\langle n, m \rangle) = \{x_{i,j,k} \mid 1 \leq i \leq n, 1 \leq j \leq m, 0 \leq k \leq 1\}$, the input membrane is $i(\langle n, m \rangle) = 0$, and the P system

$$\Pi(\langle n, m \rangle) = (\Gamma(\langle n, m \rangle), H(\langle n, m \rangle), \mu, w_0, w_1, \ldots, w_m, R(\langle n, m \rangle))$$

is defined as follows:

- Working alphabet: $\Gamma(\langle n, m \rangle) = \Sigma(\langle n, m \rangle) \cup$

$\{x_{i,j,k}^{(p,q)}, y_i^{(p,q)} \mid 1 \leq i \leq n, 1 \leq j \leq m, 0 \leq k \leq 1, 0 \leq p \leq n-1, 1 \leq q \leq n\} \cup$

$\{x_{i,k}, x_{i,k}^{(q)} \mid 1 \leq i \leq n, 0 \leq k \leq 1, 0 \leq q \leq n-1\} \cup$

$\{x'^{(q)}_{i,k}, \bar{x}'^{(0)}_{i,k} \mid 1 \leq i \leq n, 0 \leq k \leq 1, 0 \leq q \leq n+2\} \cup$

$$\{y_i, \bar{y}_i, \bar{y}_i^{(0,n-i+1)}, \bar{x}_{i,0} \mid 1 \leq i \leq n\}\cup$$

$$\{y_i^{(q)}, z_i^{(q)} \mid 1 \leq i \leq n, \, 0 \leq q \leq n-1\}\cup$$

$$\{d^{(s)} \mid 0 \leq s \leq n^2 + 5n + 2\}\cup$$

$$\{e^{(t)} \mid 0 \leq t \leq n^2 + 5n + 4\}\cup$$

$$\{no, \, \bar{n}o, \, yes, \, y\bar{e}s, \, no_{out}, \, \bar{n}o_{out}, \, no_{kill}\}$$

- The set of labels: $H = \{SKIN, 0, 1, \ldots, m\}$
- The membrane structure: $\mu = [[[\ ]_1[\ ]_2 \ldots [\ ]_m]_0]_{SKIN}$
- The initial multisets: $w_{SKIN} = \emptyset$, $w_0 = \{e^{(0)}\}$, $w_1 = w_2 = \cdots = w_m = \{d^{(0)}\}$
- The set of rules R consists of the following subsets of rules:

(1) $[x_{i,j,k} \to x_{i,j,k}^{(i-1,n)}]_0$ $(1 \leq i \leq n, 1 \leq j \leq m, 0 \leq k \leq 1)$,

$[x_{i,j,k}^{(p,q)} \to x_{i,j,k}^{(p-1,q-1)}]_0$ $(1 \leq i \leq n, 1 \leq j \leq m, 0 \leq k \leq 1, 1 \leq p \leq n-1, 2 \leq q \leq n)$,

$x_{i,j,k}^{(0,n-i+1)}[\ ]_j \to [x_{i,k}^{(n-i)}]_j$ $(1 \leq i \leq n, 1 \leq j \leq m, 0 \leq k \leq 1)$,

$[x_{i,k}^{(q)} \to x_{i,k}^{(q-1)}]_j$ $(1 \leq i \leq n, 1 \leq j \leq m, 0 \leq k \leq 1, 1 \leq q \leq n-1)$,

$[x_{i,k}^{(0)} \to x_{i,k}]_j$ $(1 \leq i \leq n, 1 \leq j \leq m, 0 \leq k \leq 1)$.

(These rules are used to collect all the literals of a clause into the corresponding membrane; this is done in a synchronized way, i.e., the object that represents the first literal of the corresponding clause goes into the membrane at first.)

(2) (a) $[x_{i,1} \to x'^{(0)}_{i,1} y_i \bar{n}o]_j$, $[x_{i,0} \to x'^{(0)}_{i,0} \bar{y}_1 \bar{y}_2 \ldots \bar{y}_n \bar{n}o]_j$,

$[y_i \bar{y}_i \to \lambda]_j$, $[\bar{y}_i \to \lambda]_j$, $[y_i]_j \to [\ ]_j y_i$ $(1 \leq i \leq n, 1 \leq j \leq m)$.

(These rules are used to find those inner membranes which contain one positive literal and no negative literals; the last rule in this group sends out these literals to membrane 0.)

(b) $[y_i \to (y_i^{(i-1,n)} z_i^{(i-1)})^m]_0$ $(1 \leq i \leq n)$,

$[y_i^{(p,q)} \to y_i^{(p-1,q-1)}]_0$ $(1 \leq i \leq n, 1 \leq p \leq n-1, 2 \leq q \leq n)$,

$y_i^{(0,n-i+1)}[\ ]_j \to [y_i^{(n-i)}]_j$ $(1 \leq i \leq n, 1 \leq j \leq m)$,

$[y_i^{(q)} \to y_i^{(q-1)}]_j$ $(1 \leq i \leq n, 1 \leq j \leq m, 1 \leq q \leq n-1)$,

$[y_i^{(0)} \to \bar{x}_{i,0}]_j$ $(1 \leq i \leq n, 1 \leq j \leq m)$.

(These rules are used to create copies of the positive literals and send them into every inner membrane.)

(c) $[z_i^{(p)} \rightarrow z_i^{(p-1)}]_0$, $[z_i^{(0)} \rightarrow \bar{y}_i^{(0,n-i+1)}]_0$ $(1 \le i \le n, 1 \le p \le n-1)$,

$[\bar{y}_i^{(0,n-i+1)} y_i^{(0,n-i+1)} \rightarrow \lambda]_0$ $(1 \le i \le n)$.

(With these rules the system can remove certain superfluous copies of the positive literals occurring in the skin.)

(d) $[x'^{(q)}_{i,k} \rightarrow x'^{(q+1)}_{i,k}]_j$ $(1 \le i \le n, 1 \le j \le m, 0 \le q \le n+1, 0 \le k \le 1)$,

$[x'^{(n+2)}_{i,k} \rightarrow x_{i,k}]_j$ $(1 \le i \le n, 1 \le j \le m, 0 \le k \le 1)$,

$[x_{i,0} \bar{x}_{i,0} \rightarrow \lambda]_j$, $[\bar{x}_{i,0} \rightarrow \lambda]_j$ $(1 \le i \le n, 1 \le j \le m)$.

(These rules are used to remove those objects from the inner membranes that represent such negative literals that occur together with their positive pairs; in other words, these rules are responsible for simulating the function calls $reduce(C, H)$ in HS.)

(3) $[d^{(s)} \rightarrow d^{(s+1)}]_j$ $(1 \le j \le m, 0 \le s \le n^2 + 5n + 1)$,

$[d^{(n^2+5n+2)} \rightarrow no\, \bar{x}'^{(0)}_{1,0} \cdots \bar{x}'^{(0)}_{n,0}\, \bar{x}'^{(0)}_{1,1} \cdots \bar{x}'^{(0)}_{n,1}\, \bar{y}_1 \cdots \bar{y}_n]_j$ $(1 \le j \le m)$,

$[x'^{(0)}_{i,k}\, \bar{x}'^{(0)}_{i,k} \rightarrow \lambda]_j$, $[\bar{x}'^{(0)}_{i,k} \rightarrow \lambda]_j$ $(1 \le i \le n, 1 \le j \le m, 0 \le k \le 1)$,

(These rules are responsible for finishing the computation after simulating n iterations of the loop in HS.)

(4) $[no\, \bar{no} \rightarrow \lambda]_j$, $[no]_j \rightarrow [\,]_j no$, $[\bar{no} \rightarrow \lambda]_j$ $(1 \le j \le m)$,

$[no \rightarrow no_{out}\, \bar{yes}]_0$, $[no_{out}]_0 \rightarrow [\,]_0 no$, $[yes\, \bar{yes} \rightarrow \lambda]_0$,

$[e^{(t)} \rightarrow e^{(t+1)}]_0$ $(0 \le t \le n^2 + 5n + 3)$,

$[e^{(n^2+5n+4)} \rightarrow no_{kill}^{m-1}\, yes]_0$, $[yes]_0 \rightarrow [\,]_0 yes$, $[no_{kill} \rightarrow \bar{no}_{out}]_0$, $[\bar{no}_{out} \rightarrow \lambda]_0$, $[no]_{SKIN} \rightarrow [\,]_{SKIN} no$, $[yes]_{SKIN} \rightarrow [\,]_{SKIN} yes$.

(These rules generate the correct answer and send it out to the environment.)

A Short Overview of the Computation. Assume that the P system $\Pi(\langle n, m \rangle)$ is started with $cod(\varphi)$ in its input membrane, where $\varphi = H_1 \wedge \ldots \wedge H_m$ is a Horn formula over the variables in Var_n. The work of $\Pi(\langle n, m \rangle)$ on φ can be divided into the following stages.

Collection of the objects representing a clause. The objects of the form $x_{i,j,k}$, for some $j \in \{1, \ldots, m\}$, represent the jth clause of φ. First these objects are sent to the membrane with label j. In this way $\Pi(\langle n, m \rangle)$ collects all the literals of a clause into a corresponding membrane (this is done by rules (1) in R). In order to synchronize the collection of these literals, the objects of the form $x_{i,j,k}$ are assigned with two counters (first rule in (1)). At the beginning, the first counter is set to $i - 1$ and the second one to n. These counters will decrease at every step of $\Pi(\langle n, m \rangle)$. (Notice that in this stage of the computation this synchronization could be solved with only one counter, but later we will need two counters in a similar situation and thus, in order to unify the notations, we decided to use two counters already here).

When the first counter p in an object $x_{i,j,k}^{(p,q)}$ reaches 0, then this object enters into the jth membrane and "drops" its second index j and its first counter, as these components are not needed any more (thus the corresponding objects in membrane j have the form $x_{i,k}^{(p)}$, see the third rule in (1)). Now the remaining counter of these objects keep decreasing step by step, and at that time when this counter reaches 0, the membrane j contains all the literals that represent the corresponding clause of φ' (which equals to φ at this point). From now on the counter in the upper index is not needed, and the objects evolve to the form $x_{i,k}$ (last rule in (1)). This part of the computation takes $n + 2$ steps. The initial configuration of the P system solving the formula in Example 1 and its configuration after collecting the literals into the corresponding membranes can be seen in Figs. 1 and 2., respectively.

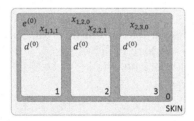

Fig. 1. The initial configuration of the system solving φ in Example 1

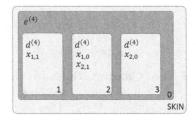

Fig. 2. The configuration after collecting the literals into the corresponding membranes

Implementation of the n-times iterated loop of HS. In this stage $\Pi(\langle n, m \rangle)$ first selects the unit clauses. To do so, every object $x_{i,1}$ (notice that such an object represents a positive literal) creates two objects y_i and $x'^{(0)}_{i,1}$ (first rule in (2a)). The primed object will be transformed back to $x_{i,1}$ after $n + 3$ steps in order to be able to start the simulation of the next iteration of the loop (first two rules in (2d)). It also creates the anti-object $\bar{n}o$, but this object will be used only when the last iteration of the loop is done. If this is not the case, then this object disappears after one step.

Meanwhile, every object of the form $x_{i,0}$ (notice that such an object represents a negative literal) in an inner membrane j creates a multiset $\{\bar{y}_l \mid l \in \{1, \ldots, m\}\}$ of anti-objects. Moreover, $x_{i,0}$ creates an object $x'^{(0)}_{i,0}$ and an anti-object $\bar{n}o$ too (second rule in (2a)). At this point the multiset content of the membrane with label j satisfies one of the following four possibilities:

1. It contains y_i and none of the anti-objects $\bar{y}_l$ ($l \in \{1, \ldots, m\}$) (i.e., the jth clause consists of a single positive literal). In this case y_i is sent out to the outer membrane (fifth rule in (2a)).
2. It contains y_i and all of the anti-objects $\bar{y}_l$ ($l \in \{1, \ldots, m\}$) (i.e., the jth clause consists of a positive and at least one negative literal). In this case the corresponding anti-object will annihilate y_i and the other anti-objects will disappear (third and fourth rules in (2a)).
3. It contains all of the anti-objects $\bar{y}_l$ ($l \in \{1, \ldots, m\}$) and does not contain any y_i (i.e., the jth clause contains no positive literals). In this case the anti-objects will disappear without applying any annihilation rule.
4. It does not contain neither the object y_i nor the anti-objects $\bar{y}_l$ ($l \in \{1, \ldots, m\}$) (i.e., the jth clause contains no literals). In this case the membrane is ready to produce the objects which will be used to send out *no* to the environment.

According to the above discussion, at this point of the computation the following holds. There is an object y_i ($i \in \{1, \ldots, n\}$) in the outer membrane if and only if the jth clause of φ' (for some $j \in \{1, \ldots, m\}$) consists of one positive literal (so it is a unit clause). Clearly, it can happen that more than one copy of y_i occur in the outer membrane (this happens when at least two different clauses of φ' equal to $\{X_i\}$).

The system should send every positive literal in the outer membrane to every inner membrane in order to be able to simulate the function calls $reduce(C, H)$ performed by Algorithm *HS*. For this purpose, every object y_i in the outer membrane creates m copies of itself by applying the first rule in (2b). These new copies are assigned with two counters. Clearly, if there are more than one copy of y_i in the outer membrane before the application of this rule, then more than m copies are produced. But the system works correctly only if exactly m copies are used in the computation. Therefore, the first rule in (2b) also introduces m copies of z_i, each assigned with a counter. These objects will eliminate the superfluous copies of y_i.

The counters in the copies of y_i (i.e., p and q in the objects of the form $y_i^{(p,q)}$) are decreased step by step (second rule in (2b)). Using these counters the system can send the copies of y_i to every inner membrane in a synchronized way (i.e., first the copies of y_1 can enter to the inner membranes, then the copies of y_2, and so on). The counter q of an object $y_i^{(q)}$ keeps decreasing in the inner membranes until it reaches 0 (fourth rules in (2b)). When this happens, $y_i^{(0)}$ introduces $\bar{x}_{i,0}$ (last rule in (2b)) which will annihilate the corresponding objects representing negative literals in the inner membranes (third rule in (2d)). In this way all the function calls $reduce(C, H)$ of HS in the current iteration step are simulated (notice that while usually the **Foreach** command is implemented in a sequential way, $\Pi(\langle n, m \rangle)$ will do the inner **Foreach** in parallel).

As we have discussed before, the extra copies of an object y_i in the outer membrane are eliminated by using the objects $z_i^{(q)}$ introduced by the first rule in (2b). Using their counters, these objects become proper anti-objects at the right moment and annihilate these superfluous copies of y_i (see rules in (2c)). The simulation of one iteration takes $n + 4$ steps. The configurations implementing the first round of the loop in Example 1 can be seen in Fig. 3.

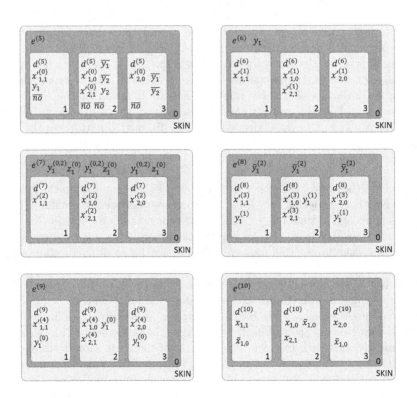

Fig. 3. The configurations implementing the first round of the loop in Example 1

Sending out the correct answer to the environment. After simulating n iterations of the loop in Algorithm HS, the system must stop the evolution of objects $x'_{i,k}$. For this purpose it uses a counter object $d^{(0)}$ in every inner membrane. This object, after $n^2 + 5n + 2$ evolution steps, introduces such anti-objects, that will annihilate the objects $x'^{(0)}_{i,k}$. At this step also an object no is introduced (see the rules in (3)). Now, after the simulation of the n-times iterated loop of HS (one step before the last evolution of object d) we have the following two possibilities.

Case 1. There is an inner membrane not containing any object of the form $x_{i,k}$. Then no anti-object $\bar{n}o$ is produced in this membrane. In this case the earlier produced no goes out to the outer membrane (second rule in (4)). In the outer membrane objects no evolve to no_{out}, one no_{out} goes out to the SKIN, and the rest of them are annihilated by anti-objects $\bar{n}o_{out}$ (first, fourth and fifth rules in (4), resp.). These anti-objects $\bar{n}o_{out}$ are produced by a properly timed counter object e (using the seventh, eighth, and eleventh rules in (4)). In this case the object yes (which is also produced during the evolution of e) is annihilated too (sixth rule in (4)). Thus, in this case one no goes out to the environment and the computation halts.

Case 2. Every inner membrane contains an object of the form $x_{i,k}$. Then no object no goes out to the outer membrane and no anti-object $\bar{y}es$ can be produced. Therefore the object yes (which is produced after the evolution of object e) is not annihilated. Thus yes goes out to SKIN, and then to the environment and the computation halts.

Using the above discussion we can see that $\Pi(\langle n, m \rangle)$ decides correctly the satisfiability of φ. Moreover, it works in quadratic time in n.

The (L,L)-uniformity of Π. As it is discussed earlier, in solutions of problems in **P** via uniform families of P systems we should use reasonably weak uniformity conditions. Therefore, to solve Horn-SAT we used an $(\mathbf{L}, \mathbf{L})$-uniform family of P systems. This can be seen as follows. For an instance φ of *Horn-SAT*, the multiset $cod(\varphi)$ can be computed by a Turing machine that reads the clauses of φ and needs to store only the number of the current clause in binary form on its tapes. This can be done using $\mathcal{O}(log(m))$ space. Moreover, as in our P systems the working alphabet Γ, the set of labels H, and the rule set R have size $\mathcal{O}(n^3 \cdot m)$ (the indexes of their elements are in ranges $1 \ldots n$ and $1 \ldots m$, respectively) and every rule in R has size $\mathcal{O}(n + m)$, there is a deterministic Turing machine that can enumerate the elements of Γ, H, and R using $\mathcal{O}(log(n) + log(m))$ space. This, together with the statement about the correctness and the running time of the presented family of P systems and using the fact that Horn-SAT is **P**-complete under log-space reduction implies the following theorem:

Theorem 1. $\mathbf{P} \subseteq (\mathbf{L}, \mathbf{L}) - \mathbf{PMC}_{\mathcal{AM}^0_{-d, -e, +antPri}}$

3.2 P Upper Bound

Here we show that $(\mathbf{L}, \mathbf{L}) - \mathbf{PMC}_{\mathcal{AM}^0_{-d, -e, +antPri}} \subseteq \mathbf{P}$. Let $\mathbf{\Pi} = (\Pi(n))_{n \in \mathbb{N}}$ be an $(\mathbf{L}, \mathbf{L})$-uniform family of P systems of type $\mathcal{AM}^0_{-d, -e, +antPri}$ and assume that the P systems in $\mathbf{\Pi}$ work in polynomial time in n. Let $p(n)$ be a polynomial such that the computation steps of a P system $\Pi(n) \in \mathbf{\Pi}$ are upper bounded by $p(n)$.

Let us consider now a P system $\Pi(n) \in \mathbf{\Pi}$ with an input multiset I in its input membrane (notice that the size of I is polynomially bounded in n). Since $\Pi(n)$ is a recognizer P system, all of its computations on I halt and yield the same answer. Thus, it is enough to simulate one particular halting computation of $\Pi(n)$ to find out its answer when it is started with input I. Therefore, we introduce weak priorities on the rules of type $(a) - (c)$ (clearly, by definition, annihilation rules have priority all over the rest of the rules): evolution rules have priority over the communication rules and send-in communication rules have priority over send-out communication rules. Moreover, if there are two different rules with the same type and having the same left hand side, then we assume that $\Pi(n)$ applies that rule which occurs earlier in the representation of $\Pi(n)$.

Assume that $C = C_1, \ldots, C_l$ is a halting computation of $\Pi(n)$ on I which satisfies the above introduced priorities. We describe an algorithm A that simulates the computation C using polynomial time in n. The input of A is the representation of $\Pi(n)$ together with an input multiset I. Since $\mathbf{\Pi}$ is an $(\mathbf{L}, \mathbf{L})$-uniform family of P systems, it follows that the size of the initial configuration of $\Pi(n)$ with I is upper-bounded by a polynomial $s(n)$.

Since $\Pi(n)$ does not use membrane division and dissolution rules, the number of membranes in the configurations in C is the same as that in C_1. Furthermore, the multiset content of a membrane M in a configuration C_i ($i \in \{1, \ldots, l\}$) can be represented in binary form using $O(p(n) \cdot \log n)$ bits (notice that the maximal number of objects in a configuration is bounded by $2^{p(n)} \cdot s(n)$, i.e., it is exponential in n). Thus, the configuration C_i can be represented by A using $O(p(n) \cdot \log n)$ space. Therefore, to simulate a computation step of $\Pi(n)$, A needs to go through the representation of the current configuration of Π and apply the rules to the objects in the configuration. This clearly can be done by A using polynomial time in n.

Since $\Pi(n)$ halts in $p(n)$ steps, it follows that the simulation of the whole computation takes polynomial time in n. Thus we have the following result:

Theorem 2. $(\mathbf{L}, \mathbf{L}) - \mathbf{PMC}_{\mathcal{AM}^0_{-d, -e, +antPri}} \subseteq \mathbf{P}$

This, together with Theorem 1 implies

Corollary 1. $(\mathbf{L}, \mathbf{L}) - \mathbf{PMC}_{\mathcal{AM}^0_{-d, -e, +antPri}} = \mathbf{P}$

4   Conclusions

It is known that P systems with active membranes that do not employ polarizations, dissolution and membrane division rules - so the usual ways of "communication" between objects are restricted - cannot significantly exceed the computational power of the systems that are used to construct them (see e.g. [7]). By using antimatter and annihilation rules in these systems, a new method of sending information between membranes in a controlled way is introduced. In this way, these systems are capable to exceed these bounds. However, this new method of exchanging information between membranes is not enough to solve computationally hard problems.

The **P** lower bound in our result came from proving that the **P**-complete Horn-SAT problem can be solved by a corresponding family of P systems in polynomial time. Although there are classical algorithms that solve Horn-SAT in polynomial time, the efficiency of the P systems can be seen in our solution too: while classical algorithms have running time that depends also on the number of clauses of the formula, the running time of our P systems depends only on the number of variables of the formula.

It is known that P systems with active membranes, without polarizations, without dissolution rules, with nonelementary membrane division rules, and endowed with antimatter and annihilation rules can solve **NP**-complete problems [3]. From our result it follows that if we remove from these systems the possibility of membrane division, then they can solve only problems in **P**. It is an interesting question what is the exact power of those variants where elementary membrane division rules are allowed but nonelementary membrane division rules not.

Acknowledgements. The author gratefully acknowledges the helpful suggestions and comments of the anonymous referees.

References

1. Alhazov, A., Aman, B., Freund, R.: P systems with anti-matter. In: Gheorghe, M., Rozenberg, G., Salomaa, A., Sosík, P., Zandron, C. (eds.) CMC 2014. LNCS, vol. 8961, pp. 66–85. Springer, Heidelberg (2014)
2. Alhazov, A., Aman, B., Freund, R., Păun, G.: Matter and anti-matter in membrane systems. In: Jürgensen, H., Karhumäki, J., Okhotin, A. (eds.) DCFS 2014. LNCS, vol. 8614, pp. 65–76. Springer, Heidelberg (2014)
3. Díaz-Pernil, D., Peña-Cantillana, F., Alhazov, A., Freund, R., Gutiérrez-Naranjo, M.A.: Antimatter as a frontier of tractability in membrane computing. Fundamenta Informaticae **134**, 83–96 (2014)
4. Dowling, W., Gallier, J.: Linear-time algorithms for testing the satisfiability of propositional Horn formulae. J. Logic Program. **3**, 267–284 (1984)
5. Freund, R., Păun, G., Rozenberg, G., Salomaa, A. (eds.): Membrane Computing. LNCS, vol. 3850. Springer, Heidelberg (2006). Revised Selected and Invited Papers
6. Gutiérrez-Naranjo, M.A., Pérez-Jiménez, M.J., Riscos-Núñez, A., Romero-Campero, F.J.: On the power of dissolution in P systems with active membranes. In: Freund et al. [5], pp. 224–240
7. Murphy, N., Woods, D.: The computational complexity of uniformity and semi-uniformity in membrane systems. In: Martínez-del-Amor, M.A., Orejuela-Pinedo, E.F., Păun, G., Pérez-Hurtado, I., Riscos-Núñez, A. (eds.) Seventh Brainstorming Week on Membrane Computing, vol. II, pp. 73–84. Fénix Editora, Sevilla (2009)

8. Păun, G.: P systems with active membranes: attacking NP-complete problems. J. Automata Lang. Comb. **6**(1), 75–90 (2001)
9. Păun, G.: Four (somewhat nonstandard) research topics. In: Maccías-Ramos, L.F., del Amor, M.A.M., Păun, G., Riscos-Núñez, A., Valencia-Cabrera, L. (eds.) Twelfth Brainstorming Week on Membrane Computing, pp. 305–309. Fénix Editora, Sevilla, Spain (2014)
10. Păun, G., Rozenberg, G., Salomaa, A. (eds.): The Oxford Handbook of Membrane Computing. Oxford University Press, Oxford (2010)
11. Pérez-Jiménez, M.J., Romero-Jiménez, A., Sancho-Caparrini, F.: A polynomial complexity class in P systems using membrane division. In: Csuhaj-Varjú, E., Kintala, C., Wotschke, D., Vaszil, G. (eds.) Proceeding of the 5th Workshop on Descriptional Complexity of Formal Systems, DCFS 2003, pp. 284–294 (2003)
12. Pérez-Jiménez, M.J., Romero-Jiménez, Á., Sancho-Caparrini, F.: A polynomial complexity class in P systems using membrane division. J. Automata Lang. Comb. **11**(4), 423–434 (2006)
13. Porreca, A.E., Leporati, A., Mauri, G., Zandron, C.: Sublinear-space P systems with active membranes. In: Csuhaj-Varjú, E., Gheorghe, M., Rozenberg, G., Salomaa, A., Vaszil, G. (eds.) CMC 2012. LNCS, vol. 7762, pp. 342–357. Springer, Heidelberg (2013)

Tissue P Systems Can be Simulated Efficiently with Counting Oracles

Alberto Leporati, Luca Manzoni, Giancarlo Mauri, Antonio E. Porreca, and Claudio Zandron[✉]

Dipartimento di Informatica, Sistemistica e Comunicazione, Università degli Studi di Milano-Bicocca, Viale Sarca 336/14, 20126 Milano, Italy {leporati,luca.manzoni,mauri,porreca,zandron}@disco.unimib.it

Abstract. We prove that polynomial-time tissue P systems with cell division or cell separation can be simulated efficiently by Turing machines with oracles for counting problems. This shows that the corresponding complexity classes are included in $\mathbf{P}^{\#\mathbf{P}}$, thus improving, under standard complexity theory assumptions, the previously known upper bound **PSPACE**.

1 Introduction

Tissue P systems [4] are known to solve **NP**-complete (and **coNP**-complete) problems in polynomial time when cell division [9] or cell separation rules [6] are available in addition to the standard, context-sensitive communication rules. In terms of complexity classes, this is denoted by $\mathbf{NP} \cup \mathbf{coNP} \subseteq \mathbf{PMC}_{\mathcal{TDC}}$ and $\mathbf{NP} \cup \mathbf{coNP} \subseteq \mathbf{PMC}_{\mathcal{TSC}}$, respectively. Division and separation rules allow the creation of exponentially many cells in polynomial time; the difference is that division replicates the contents of the original cell, while separation distributes such contents between the resulting cells according to the nature of the objects.

The previously known upper bound to the classes of problems solved in polynomial time by tissue P systems with cell division [11] or separation [10] is **PSPACE**, a class of problems also solved by P systems with active membranes [1]. Unlike these, tissue P systems lack a complex hierarchical membrane structure, a limitation they share with P systems with elementary active membranes, where membranes containing further membranes cannot divide; the problems solved by the latter are known to be bounded by $\mathbf{P}^{\#\mathbf{P}}$ [3], a class conjecturally smaller than **PSPACE**.

In this paper we show that the $\mathbf{P}^{\#\mathbf{P}}$ upper bound also applies to tissue P systems with cell division or cell separation; we describe a simulation that runs in polynomial time by delegating the communication between regions to an oracle for a counting problem.

This work was partially supported by Università degli Studi di Milano-Bicocca, FA 2013: "Complessità computazionale in modelli di calcolo bioispirati: Sistemi a membrane e sistemi di reazioni".

2   Basic Notions

We begin by recalling the definition of tissue P systems with division and separation rules; for a more detailed introduction on multiset processing and tissue P systems, we refer the reader to the original paper [4].

Definition 1. *A* tissue P system *is a structure* $\Pi = (\Gamma, E, w_1, \ldots, w_d, R)$, *where:*

- Γ *is an alphabet, i.e., a finite non-empty set of symbols, usually called* objects;
- $E \subseteq \Gamma$ *is the alphabet of objects initially located in the external environment, in* infinitely *many copies;*
- $d \geq 1$ *is the* degree *of the system, i.e., the initial number of cells;*
- $w_1, \ldots, w_d$ *are* finite *multisets over* Γ, *describing the initial contents of the* d *cells; here* $1, \ldots, d$ *are* labels *identifying the cells of the P systems, and* 0 *is the label of the external environment;*
- R *is a finite set of rules.*

The rules of R are of the following types:

(a) *Communication rules*, denoted in this paper by $[u]_h \leftrightarrow [v]_k$ and in the literature by $(h, u/v, k)$, where h and k are distinct labels (including the environment), and u and v are multisets over Γ (at least one of them nonempty): these rules are applicable if there exists a region with label h containing u as a submultiset and a region k containing v as a submultiset; the effect of the rule is to exchange u and v between the two regions. If $h = 0$ (resp., $k = 0$) then u (resp., v) must contain at least an object from $\Gamma - E$, i.e., an object with finite multiplicity[1]. In this paper we consider a rule $[u]_h \leftrightarrow [v]_k$ and its syntactic reverse $[v]_k \leftrightarrow [u]_h$ to be the same rule.
(b) *Division rules*, of the form $[a]_h \rightarrow [b]_h\ [c]_h$, where $h \neq 0$ is a cell label and $a, b, c \in \Gamma$: these rules can be applied to a cell with label h containing at least one copy of a; the effect of the rule is to divide the cell into two cells, both with label h; the object a is replaced in the two cells by b and c, respectively, while the rest of the original multiset contained in h is replicated in both cells.
(c) *Separation rules*, of the form $[a]_h \rightarrow [\Gamma_1]_h\ [\Gamma_2]_h$, where $h \neq 0$ is a cell label, $a \in \Gamma$, and $\{\Gamma_1, \Gamma_2\}$ is a partition of Γ: these rules can be applied to a cell with label h containing at least one copy of a; the effect of the rule is to separate the cell into two cells, both with label h; the object a is consumed, while the objects from Γ_1 in the original multiset contained in h are placed inside one of the cells, and those from Γ_2 in the other. All separation rules in R must share the same partition $\{\Gamma_1, \Gamma_2\}$ of Γ.

---

[1] Since communication rules are applied in a maximally parallel way, this restriction avoids the situation where infinitely many objects from the environment simultaneously enter a cell.

A *tissue P system with cell division* only uses communication and division rules, while a *tissue P system with cell separation* only uses communication and separation rules.

A *configuration* C of a tissue P system consists of a multiset over $\Gamma - E$ describing the objects appearing with finite multiplicity in the environment, and a multiset of pairs (h, w), where h is a cell label and w a finite multiset over Γ, describing the cells. A *computation step* changes the current configuration according to the following set of principles:

- Each object can be subject to at most one rule, and each cell can be subject to *any number* of communication rules or, *alternatively*, a *single* division or separation rule.
- The application of rules is *maximally parallel*: each region is subject to a maximal multiset of rules (i.e., no further rule can be applied).
- When several conflicting rules can be applied at the same time, a nondeterministic choice is performed; this implies that, in general, multiple possible configurations can be reached after a computation step.

A *halting computation* $C = (C_0, \ldots, C_k)$ of the tissue P system Π is a finite sequence of configurations, where C_0 is the initial configuration, every C_{i+1} is reachable from C_i via a single computation step, and no rules are applicable in C_k.

Tissue P systems can be used as language *recognisers* by employing two distinguished objects *yes* and *no*: we assume that all computations are halting, and that either *yes* or object *no* (but not both) is released into the environment, and only in the last computation step, in order to signal acceptance or rejection, respectively. If all computations starting from the same initial configuration are accepting, or all are rejecting, the tissue P system is said to be *confluent*.

In order to solve decision problems (i.e., decide languages), we use *families* of recogniser tissue P systems $\boldsymbol{\Pi} = \{\Pi_x : x \in \Sigma^*\}$. Each input x is associated with a tissue P system Π_x that decides the membership of x in the language $L \subseteq \Sigma^*$ by accepting or rejecting. The mapping $x \mapsto \Pi_x$ must be efficiently computable for inputs of any length, as discussed in detail in [5].

Definition 2. *A family of tissue P systems* $\boldsymbol{\Pi} = \{\Pi_x : x \in \Sigma^*\}$ *is said to be (polynomial-time) uniform if the mapping* $x \mapsto \Pi_x$ *can be computed by two polynomial-time deterministic Turing machines E and F as follows:*

- $F(1^n) = \Pi_n$, *where n is the length of the input x and* Π_n *is a common tissue P system for all inputs of length n, with a distinguished input cell.*
- $E(x) = w_x$, *where* w_x *is a multiset encoding the specific input x.*
- *Finally,* Π_x *is simply* Π_n *with* w_x *added to its input cell.*

On the other hand, the family $\boldsymbol{\Pi}$ *is said to be (polynomial-time) semi-uniform if there exists a single deterministic polynomial-time Turing machine H such that* $H(x) = \Pi_x$ *for each* $x \in \Sigma^*$.

Any explicit encoding of Π_x is allowed as output of the construction, as long as the number of cells and objects represented by it does not exceed the length of the whole description, and the rules are listed one by one. This is also called a permissible encoding [5].

The class of problems solved by uniform (resp., semi-uniform) families of confluent tissue P systems with cell division is denoted by $\mathbf{PMC}_{\mathcal{TDC}}$ (resp., $\mathbf{PMC}^\star_{\mathcal{TDC}}$); the corresponding classes for tissue P systems with separation are $\mathbf{PMC}_{\mathcal{TSC}}$ and $\mathbf{PMC}^\star_{\mathcal{TSC}}$. The inclusions $\mathbf{PMC}_{\mathcal{TDC}} \subseteq \mathbf{PMC}^\star_{\mathcal{TDC}}$ and $\mathbf{PMC}_{\mathcal{TSC}} \subseteq \mathbf{PMC}^\star_{\mathcal{TSC}}$ hold by definition, since uniformity is a special case of semi-uniformity.

Finally, we recall the definitions of the complexity classes $\#\mathbf{P}$ and $\mathbf{P}^{\#\mathbf{P}}$ [7].

Definition 3. *The complexity class $\#\mathbf{P}$ consists of all the functions $f \colon \Sigma^\star \to \mathbb{N}$, also called* counting problems, *with the following property: there exists a polynomial time nondeterministic Turing machine N such that, for each $x \in \Sigma^\star$, the number of accepting computations of N on input x is exactly $f(x)$.*

Definition 4. *The complexity class $\mathbf{P}^{\#\mathbf{P}}$ consists of all decision problems solvable in polynomial time by deterministic Turing machines with oracles for $\#\mathbf{P}$ functions. These are Turing machines M^f, with $f \in \#\mathbf{P}$, having a distinguished oracle tape and a* query state *such that, when M^f enters the query state, the string x on the oracle tape is replaced in one step with the binary encoding of $f(x)$.*

3   Simulating Tissue P Systems

When simulating a tissue P system, we can limit ourselves to explicitly storing the configuration of the external environment (i.e., its multiset of objects), since this is where the result objects *yes* and *no* ultimately appear. This configuration can be stored in polynomial space by keeping track of the multiplicities of the objects in binary, with a special marker for those appearing with infinite multiplicity.

This is possible as long as we have a way to update this configuration even when not storing the configurations of the cells; this requires computing the multisets of objects communicated from or to the environment at each computation step. We are going to prove that such task can be performed in polynomial time by querying a $\#\mathbf{P}$ oracle, by adapting the proof of an analogous result for P systems with elementary active membranes [3].

The query we would ideally ask is "How much does the multiplicity of object a in the environment of Π change at time step t?"; however, we only know how to answer this query by simulating an entire computation of the tissue P system in polynomial space [11]. In order to try to reduce its complexity, we break it down into multiple queries with additional inputs describing the history of the computation up to the previous time step, and partially including the simulation of the current step. These extra inputs are computed using the answers to previous queries.

First of all, we need a way to distinguish multiple cells having the same label. Since cell division can create at most 2^t cells with the same label after t computation steps, we assume that each of these has a unique identifier in the range $[0, 2^t)$; we do not require the identifiers to be contiguous, or that a cell keep the same identifier during each step of the computation.

Since we are only dealing with confluent tissue P systems in this paper, we can also make assumptions on how the rules to be applied during each step must be chosen. Without loss of generality, we give a *linear priority* to the rules, giving higher priority to communication rules, and applying a division (or separation) rule in a cell only when no communication occurs. Within the two groups of rules (communication versus division and separation), we fix an arbitrary total ordering. In particular, each communication rule is applied as many times as possible before applying any of those with lower priority.

We can now define a table associating each communication rule $[u]_h \leftrightarrow [v]_k$ with the set of identifiers of cells with labels h and k applying it at time t. Since describing arbitrary subsets of identifiers would require exponential space, we exploit once again the confluence assumption, and stipulate that each rule must be applied as many times as possible by all copies of h (resp., k) whose identifier belongs to a range of the form $[0, M_h)$ (resp., $[0, M_k)$) for some upper bound M_h (resp., M_k), where *zero* is an allowable number of applications. This corresponds to establishing another priority, over cells sharing the same label, given by the numerical ordering of the identifiers.

Definition 5. *A* communication table *for a tissue P system Π is a function $T: R \times \mathbb{N} \to \mathbb{N}^4$ such that, for $r = [u]_h \leftrightarrow [v]_k$ and $t \in \mathbb{N}$,*

$$T[r, t] = (M_h, \Delta_h, M_k, \Delta_k)$$

denotes that the cells with label h where rule r is applied at time t are those having identifiers in the range $[0, M_h]$; in particular, the rule is applied as many times as possible for identifiers strictly lower than M_h, and Δ_h times (a nonmaximal number of times) for identifier M_h. The values M_k and Δ_k, symmetrically, denote the instances of cell k where r is applied.

A procedure for computing a communication table for a tissue P system is described later, as a portion of Algorithm 1.

Example 1. Consider the configuration in Fig. 1 of a tissue P system Π after two computation steps, with three instances of cell h (having identifiers 0, 2, and 3) and two instances of cell k (with identifiers 0 and 2), and consider the following two communication rules:

$$r_1 = [aa]_h \leftrightarrow [b]_k \qquad r_2 = [c]_h \leftrightarrow [d]_k$$

By giving priority to r_1 over r_2, and to lower identifiers over higher ones, we determine a unique way to apply the rules: rule r_1 is applied three times between h_0 and k_2, and once between h_2 and k_2, while rule r_2 is applied once between h_2 and k_0, and once between h_3 and k_0. Notice that k_0 applies r_1 zero times, which

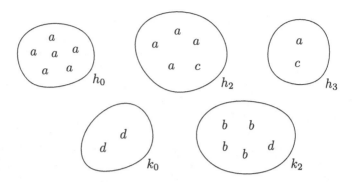

Fig. 1. Configuration of a tissue P system Π after two computation steps. The subscripts of the cell labels represent the identifiers of the corresponding cell.

happens to be maximal in this case (since k_0 does not contain any copy of b). Thus, the smallest ranges of identifiers for h where r_1 and r_2 are applied *maximally* are $[0,2)$ and $[0,4)$, respectively, while those for k are $[0,3)$ and $[0,1)$, respectively. Furthermore, h_2 applies r_1 one extra time. Thus, according to the reasoning above, the communication table for Π has $T[r_1, 2] = (2, 1, 3, 0)$ and $T[r_2, 2] = (4, 0, 1, 0)$.

Notice that a communication table for the first t steps of Π can be stored in polynomial space with respect to t and the length of the description of Π.

Let us now focus on the simulation of tissue P systems with division only, and let us formulate a query that allows us to perform this task without simulating the individual cells.

Query Q. *Given a tissue P system with division $\Pi = (\Gamma, E, w_1, \ldots, w_d, R)$, a time step t in unary notation, a communication rule $r = [u]_h \leftrightarrow [v]_k$, and a communication table T for Π, with entries $T[\rho, \tau]$ filled for all $\tau < t$ and for $\tau = t$ if ρ has priority over r, how many times is rule r applied at time t by cells with label h, assuming the availability of enough copies of v in cells with label k?*

An oracle for query Q allows us to simulate tissue P systems with cell division with a polynomial slowdown.

Lemma 1. $\mathbf{PMC}^\star_{\mathcal{TDC}} \subseteq \mathbf{P}^Q$

Proof. Let $L \in \mathbf{PMC}^\star_{\mathcal{TDC}}$ be a language, and let $\boldsymbol{\Pi} = \{\Pi_x : x \in \Sigma^\star\}$ be a semi-uniform family of tissue P systems with division deciding L in polynomial time. Algorithm 1 describes how each Π_x can be constructed and simulated, given the input string x, by a deterministic Turing machine with an oracle for Q.

In line 1 we obtain the description of Π_x by simulating the machine providing the semi-uniformity construction for $\boldsymbol{\Pi}$ on input x. This, by definition, can be carried out in polynomial time with respect to the length of x.

1	construct $\Pi_x = (\Gamma, E, w_1, \ldots, w_d, R)$ from x
2	**for** each time step t **do**
3	**for** each rule $r = [u]_h \leftrightarrow [v]_k \in R$ in priority order **do**
4	$T[r,t] := (2^t, 0, 2^t, 0)$
5	**repeat**
6	$p :=$ no. of applications of $[u]_h \leftrightarrow [v]_k$ in h at time t according to T
7	$q :=$ no. of applications of $[u]_h \leftrightarrow [v]_k$ in k at time t according to T
8	update $T[r,t]$ by binary search
9	**until** $p = q$
10	**for** each rule $r = [u]_h \leftrightarrow [v]_0$ **do**
11	$p :=$ no. of applications of r in h at time t according to T
12	remove p instances of v and add p instances of u to the environment
13	**if** *yes* or *no* appear in the environment **then**
14	**accept** or **reject** accordingly

Algorithm 1. Simulation of semi-uniform families of tissue P systems with cell division.

The loop of lines 2–14 is executed for each simulated time step t, hence, by hypothesis, a polynomial number of times. Inside this loop, the algorithm iterates across all communication rules $r = [u]_h \leftrightarrow [v]_k$ of Π in priority order (lines 3–9) in order to fill the corresponding entry $T[r,t]$ of the communication table.

We begin (line 4) by assuming that all existing copies of h, i.e., the full range of identifiers $[0, 2^t)$, are allowed to apply rule r, as if there were enough copies of multiset v among the copies of k; we make the same assumption for k. We then ask the oracle for Q how many times rule r is applied in cells with label h (line 6) and k (line 7) under those assumptions; call p and q those two numbers of applications. If $p \neq q$, then the number of copies of u in cells with label h differs from the number of copies of v in cells with label k; for the simulation to be consistent with the current configuration of Π, we need to ensure that $p = q$. Suppose, for the sake of example, that $p < q$. Then, we reduce the range of cells with label k by repeatedly adjusting the corresponding value M_k and re-evaluating q with further queries. By performing a binary search (line 8), we can find in polynomial time ($\log 2^t$ iterations) the smallest range $[0, M_k)$ of identifiers maximising the value of q, with the constraint $q \leq p$. The difference $p-q$ is finally recorded as Δ_k, the number of times r must be applied by the cell having label k and identifier M_k. (The argument is symmetric if the initial values of p and q are such that $p > q$.) This querying procedure is performed even if $h = 0$ or $k = 0$, i.e., one of them is the label of the environment.

The loop of lines 10–12 updates the configuration of the environment that we explicitly store, by asking the oracle the final number of applications of rules involving the environment, and adjusting the environment multiset accordingly. Notice that the rules not involving the environment are not simulated, since the

```
1    id := 0
2    for each time step τ ∈ {0, . . . , t} do
3         newid := 2 × id
4         newmultiset := ∅
5         for each rule ρ = [u]_h ↔ [v]_k in priority order do
6              (M_h, Δ_h, M_k, Δ_k) := T[ρ, τ]
7              if id < M_h then
8                   remove as many copies of u as possible from multiset
9                   add the same number of copies of v to newmultiset
10             else if id = M_h then
11                  remove Δ_h copies of u from multiset
12                  add the same number of copies of v to newmultiset
13        if a rule [a]_h → [b_0]_h [b_1]_h is applicable then
14             nondeterministically guess a bit i
15             newid := newid + i
16             remove a from multiset
17             add b_i to newmultiset
18        id := newid
19        multiset := multiset ∪ newmultiset
20   accept as many times as the no. of applications of r in step t
```

Algorithm 2. Nondeterministic simulation of the cells having label h, with computation of the number of applications of communication rule r at time t.

configurations of the cells are not stored by Algorithm 1. In lines 13 and 14 the computation is halted when one of the result objects *yes* or *no* finally appears.

Since the number of queries needed, as well as the number of bookkeeping operations, is polynomially bounded, the simulation can be performed in $\mathbf{P}^Q$.   □

In order to give a more precise upper bound of the complexity of simulating tissue P systems, we can now analyse query Q in detail, proving that it can be answered in polynomial time by a counting machine.

Lemma 2. *Query Q is in #$\mathbf{P}$*

Proof. Given a query Q with parameters Π, t, r, and T, Algorithm 2 describes a nondeterministic procedure for the parallel simulation of all cells of Π having label h, where each computation actually simulates a single cell. This algorithm manages the identifiers of the cells as follows: the identifier of the unique copy of cell h in the initial configuration is 0 (line 1); if the identifier of a copy of h at time τ is id, then in the next time step (line 18) the identifier is $2 \times id$ (line 3); if, furthermore, the cell divides, then the new copy, simulated by the computation where $i = 1$, has identifier $2 \times id + 1$ (line 15). This identifier schema is essentially identical to the one proposed by Sosík and Cienciala [11], and satisfies the two requirements described above: uniqueness among cells with the same label, and range $[0, 2^t)$ after t steps.

The algorithm simulates sequentially all steps up to t (line 2). In line 4 it initialises an empty multiset *newmultiset* to collect the objects entering the cell via communication rules, or rewritten via division rules; since the rules are simulated sequentially, we employ this auxiliary multiset (in addition to the actual content of the cell, named *multiset* in the pseudocode) in order to avoid applying more than one rule to each object.

The loop of lines 5–12 iterates across all communication rules ρ involving h (on either side of the rule). In line 6 we read the values corresponding to the ranges of identifiers for cell labels h and k where rule ρ is applied in the current time step. If the identifier of the cell being simulated belongs to the range $[0, M_h)$, then we apply rule ρ as many times as possible (lines 7–9). On the other hand, if the identifier is exactly M_h, we only apply the rule Δ_h times (line 10–12). The rule is not applied if the identifier is strictly greater than M_h.

If a division rule is applicable in the cell (this, in particular, requires that no communication rule was applied previously), then we apply the first one in priority order (line 13). This consists in nondeterministically choosing which of the two resulting cells the current computation will continue to simulate (line 14) and updating the identifier and contents of the selected cell (lines 15–17). Notice that this establishes a bijection between computations of the algorithm and instances of cell h.

We can then update the values of id and add to *multiset* the objects that appeared inside the current copy of cell h during the computation step just simulated (lines 18 and 19).

After having simulated t steps, we can check the number of times m that input rule r was applied in the cell during the last step. The algorithm can now "fork" m accepting computations[2] (line 20). This value contributes to the total number of accepting computations of the algorithm, which will then correspond to the number of applications of rule r at time t, as required.   □

By combining Lemmata 1 and 2 we finally obtain our main result.

Theorem 1. $\mathbf{PMC}_{\mathcal{TDC}} \subseteq \mathbf{PMC}^\star_{\mathcal{TDC}} \subseteq \mathbf{P}^{\#\mathbf{P}}$ □

3.1   Tissue P Systems with Separation

Simulating separation rules $[a]_h \rightarrow [\Gamma_0]_h [\Gamma_1]_h$ instead of (or in addition to) division rules only requires a slight change to lines 13 and 17 of Algorithm 2. After having nondeterministically chosen which of the two resulting cells to simulate (bit i), we need to update *multiset* by removing the objects in Γ_{1-i}. Since this can also be performed in polynomial time, query Q remains in $\#\mathbf{P}$ and, as a consequence, the simulation of tissue P systems with separation has the same complexity.

Theorem 2. $\mathbf{PMC}_{\mathcal{TSC}} \subseteq \mathbf{PMC}^\star_{\mathcal{TSC}} \subseteq \mathbf{P}^{\#\mathbf{P}}$ □

---

[2] This can be performed in polynomial time even if m is exponential, as it suffices to guess $\Theta(\log m)$ nondeterministic bits.

4   Conclusions

We have proved a $\mathbf{P}^{\#\mathbf{P}}$ upper bound to the class of problems solvable in polynomial time by uniform or semi-uniform families of tissue P systems using division or separation rules. The simulation of tissue P systems we provided is also relatively robust with respect to the addition of features; for instance, it can be easily adapted to accommodate charges, evolution and dissolution rules from P systems with active membranes [3].

This is the same upper bound that holds [3] for P systems with active membranes where division can only be applied to elementary membranes (i.e., not containing further membranes). These two variants of P systems share the inability to create the complex nested structures of dividing membranes (such as exponentially large full binary trees) that allow unrestricted P systems with active membranes to solve **PSPACE**-complete problems in polynomial time [1]. It would be interesting to understand if it is possible to formalise this intuitive reasoning and link such membrane structure "complexity" with the ability of P systems to solve problems in polynomial time.

We do not know yet whether the $\mathbf{P}^{\#\mathbf{P}}$ upper bound is tight, or whether it can be lowered. Based on analogous results for P systems with active membranes [2], we conjecture that $\mathbf{P}^{\#\mathbf{P}}$ is indeed a precise characterisation of the problems solvable by general tissue P systems with division or separation; however, tissue P systems with maximum communication rule length (i.e., number of objects appearing in a communication rule) bounded by a small constant might prove to be weaker. It would be particularly interesting to analyse the borderline case of tissue P systems with division having rules of length at most 2, or those with separation having rules of length at most 3, which is the minimum necessary to solve classically intractable problems [8].

References

1. Alhazov, A., Martín-Vide, C., Pan, L.: Solving a PSPACE-complete problem by recognizing P systems with restricted active membranes. Fundamenta Informaticae **58**(2), 67–77 (2003)
2. Leporati, A., Manzoni, L., Mauri, G., Porreca, A.E., Zandron, C.: Membrane division, oracles, and the counting hierarchy. Fundamenta Informaticae **138**(1–2), 97–111 (2015)
3. Leporati, A., Manzoni, L., Mauri, G., Porreca, A.E., Zandron, C.: Simulating elementary active membranes with an application to the P conjecture. In: Gheorghe, M., Rozenberg, G., Salomaa, A., Sosík, P., Zandron, C. (eds.) CMC 2014. LNCS, vol. 8961, pp. 284–299. Springer, Heidelberg (2014)
4. Martín-Vide, C., Păun, G., Pazos, J., Rodríguez-Patón, A.: Tissue P systems. Theoret. Comput. Sci. **296**(2), 295–326 (2003)
5. Murphy, N., Woods, D.: The computational power of membrane systems under tight uniformity conditions. Nat. Comput. **10**(1), 613–632 (2011)
6. Pan, L., Pérez-Jiménez, M.J.: Computational complexity of tissue-like P systems. J. Complex. **26**(3), 296–315 (2010)

7. Papadimitriou, C.H.: Computational Complexity. Addison-Wesley, Reading, Massachussets (1993)
8. Pérez-Jiménez, M.J.: The P versus NP problem from the membrane computing view. Eur. Rev. **22**(01), 18–33 (2014)
9. Păun, G., Pérez-Jiménez, M.J., Riscos Núñez, A.: Tissue P systems with cell division. Int. J. Comput. Commun. Control **3**(3), 295–303 (2008)
10. Sosík, P., Cienciala, L.: Computational power of cell separation in tissue P systems. Inf. Sci. **279**, 805–815 (2014)
11. Sosík, P., Cienciala, L.: A limitation of cell division in tissue P systems by PSPACE. J. Comput. Syst. Sci. **81**(2), 473–484 (2015)

Simulating FRSN P Systems with Real Numbers in P-Lingua on sequential and CUDA platforms

Luis F. Macías-Ramos$^{(\boxtimes)}$, Miguel A. Martínez-del-Amor,
and Mario J. Pérez-Jiménez

Research Group on Natural Computing,
Department of Computer Science and Artificial Intelligence,
University of Sevilla, Avda. Reina Mercedes s/n., 41012 Sevilla, Spain
{lfmaciasr,mdelamor,marper}@us.es

Abstract. Fuzzy Reasoning Spiking Neural P systems (FRSN P systems, for short) is a variant of Spiking Neural P systems incorporating fuzzy logic elements that make it suitable to model fuzzy diagnosis knowledge and reasoning required for fault diagnosis applications. In this sense, several FRSN P system variants have been proposed, dealing with real numbers, trapezoidal numbers, weights, etc. The model incorporating real numbers was the first introduced [13], presenting promising applications in the field of fault diagnosis of electrical systems. For this variant, a matrix-based algorithm was provided which, when executed on parallel computing platforms, fully exploits the model maximally parallel capacities. In this paper we introduce a **P-Lingua** framework extension to parse and simulate FRSN P systems with real numbers. Two simulators, implementing a variant of the original matrix-based simulation algorithm, are provided: a sequential one (written in Java), intended to run on traditional CPUs, and a parallel one, intended to run on **CUDA**-enabled devices.

Keywords: Membrane Computing · P systems · Spiking Neural P systems · Fuzzy Reasoning Spiking Neural P systems · Fault diagnosis · Fuzzy knowledge · Fuzzy reasoning · P-Lingua · Java · CUDA

1 Introduction

Membrane computing is a branch of natural computing, which takes inspiration from the structure and functioning of living cells to provide parallel and distributed computational models, called membrane systems or P systems.

P systems were first introduced in [15], and many variants were subsequently developed, which can be divided into three categories: cell-like systems, inspired by the hierarchical membrane structure of eukaryotic cells [15]; tissue-like systems, inspired by the way in which cells organize and communicate within a net-like structure in tissues [8]; and neural-like systems, inspired by the way in

© Springer International Publishing Switzerland 2015
G. Rozenberg et al. (Eds.): CMC 2015, LNCS 9504, pp. 262–276, 2015.
DOI: 10.1007/978-3-319-28475-0_18

which the neurons in the brain exchange information by means of the propagation of spikes [5]. Models belonging to this last variant are collectively called Spiking Neural P systems (SN P systems, for short).

An SN P system consists of a set of neurons placed as nodes of a directed graph (called the *synapse graph*). Each neuron contains a number of copies of a single object type, the *spike*. Rules are assigned to neurons to control the way information flows between connected neurons. Two kinds of rules are considered: firing/spiking rules and forgetting rules. By applying a firing/spiking rule, some spikes are consumed and new spikes are produced. Produced spikes are sent to all neurons linked to the neuron executing the rule. By applying a forgetting rule, spikes are removed from neurons. SN P systems usually work in synchronous mode, where a global clock is assumed. In each time unit, for each neuron, only one of the applicable rules is non-deterministically selected to be executed. Execution of rules takes place in parallel amongst all neurons of the system.

SN P systems have become really popular within the Membrane Computing community and extensive work has been conducted to study their properties and produce new variants. For instance, it has been proved that these systems are computational complete (equivalent in power to Turing machines) when considered as number computing devices [5], used as language generators [2,3], or to compute functions [14]. Different kinds of asynchronous "working modes" have been also addressed [12,16,17]. In what concerns to produce new variants of the model, this has involved incorporating new elements such as weights [19], anti-spikes [9], extended rules [16], budding and division rules [10] and astrocytes [1,7,11], among other examples.

In [13] a new SN P systems variant, called FRSN P systems, was introduced, incorporating fuzzy logic elements. The motivation of this variant was to bring together desirable features (understandable, dynamical, synchronized, non-linear, non-deterministic, able to handle incomplete and uncertain information) to model diagnosis knowledge and reasoning in the field of fault diagnosis. To accomplish this, new ingredients were added to extend original SN P systems: three types of neurons (proposition neurons, AND-type and OR-type rule neurons), fuzzy truth values (modelled by means of real numbers) and a new firing mechanism. Also, a matrix-based algorithm was provided, suitable to be executed on parallel computing platforms, and thus able to fully exploit the model maximally parallel capacities. Applications of this new model have been related to fault diagnosis on electrical systems so far [13,21]. Variants have also appeared since the model introduction, for instance dealing with trapezoidal numbers [22,23] and weights [20], with applications to power systems fault diagnosis.

Due to the promising applications of FRSN P systems, it becomes interesting to provide the corresponding simulators, thus favouring research on this model within Membrane Computing community as well as in applied fields. In this paper we introduce support for FRSN P systems with real numbers into P-Lingua [4,28] framework. P-Lingua consist of a general programming language for P systems called P-Lingua itself and a Java [26] based open source library called pLinguaCore. In particular, P-Lingua language provides a common syntax for specifying P systems variants, with pLinguaCore provides both parsers and simulators for such variants. The notable variety of supported models (see [28] for a list of related publications) contributed to make P-Lingua widely used among members of the Membrane Computing community, turning its specification language into *a sort of standard*.

Developing FRSN P systems support has involved designing a specific parser (since with respect to P-Lingua, FRSN P systems are considered a "separated" variant of SN P systems), a simulation algorithm (which is a variation of the one introduced in [13]) and the corresponding simulators. The provided simulation algorithm is a matrix-based one. As such is susceptible to being executed on parallel platforms, specially intended to work in simultaneously with hundreds to millions of data stored in matrices. In this way, it can take advantage of the corresponding execution speedup. Indeed, GPUs have been successfully used to accelerate well-known linear algebra libraries, such as MKL BLAS and LAPACK. Specifically, NVIDIA GPUs are able to execute scientific applications through CUDA [6], harnessing the highly parallel architecture within them (featuring up to 3000 computing cores). In this sense, CUDA offers special linear algebra libraries such as cuBLAS and CULA tools, delivering up to 17× of speedups for some applications [24]. Therefore, along with a Java sequential simulator, a parallel one has been developed intended to be able to run on the majority of CUDA-compatible [24] devices. This last simulator works by means of a JAVA-CUDA binding provided by the open source JCUDA [27] library, available for Windows, Linux, MacOS and other operating systems.

This paper is structured as follows. Section 2 is devoted to recall the basic ingredients of FRSN P systems with real numbers. In Sect. 3, a P-Lingua syntax for such variant is introduced. Section 4 is devoted to simulation aspects: the new matrix-based simulation algorithm is introduced, and invoking the sequential and parallel simulators is discussed. Also, compatibility and performance of the parallel simulator is addressed. Section 5 covers conclusions and future work.

2   Fuzzy Reasoning Spiking Neural P Systems with Real Numbers

In what follows, we recall FRSN P systems with real numbers, which constitute an extension of SN P systems. As new ingredients, three types of neurons (proposition neurons, AND-type and OR-type rule neurons), and elements from the fuzzy logic such as fuzzy truth values are incorporated, as well as a new firing mechanism defined after such fuzzy logic elements. FRSN P systems with real numbers can model and visualize fuzzy production rules in a diagnosis knowledge base due to their graphical nature. Combination of neuron's new firing mechanism and fuzzy logic ensures to automatically accomplish dynamic fuzzy reasoning. FRSN P systems with real numbers can be defined as follows (an extensive description of this model can be found at [13]):

Definition 1. *A FRSN P system Π with real numbers of degree (l, q, n, k), with $l, k \geq 1$, $q \geq 0$ and $n \geq l+q+1$, is a tuple of the form $(A, \sigma_1, \ldots, \sigma_{n+k}, syn, I, O)$, where*

(1) $A = \{a\}$ is the singleton alphabet (the object a is called spike);
(2) $\sigma_1, \ldots, \sigma_{n+k}$ are neurons, of the form $\sigma_i = (\alpha_i, \tau_i, r_i)$, $1 \leq i \leq n + k$, where
 (⋆) $\alpha_i \in [0,1]$ and it is called the (potential) value of spike contained in neuron σ_i (also called pulse value);
 (⋆) $\tau_i \in [0,1]$ is the truth value associated with neuron σ_i;
 (⋆) r_i is a firing/spiking rule contained in neuron σ_i, of the form $E/a^\alpha \rightarrow a^\beta$, where $\alpha, \beta \in [0,1]$.
(3) $syn \subseteq \{1, \ldots, n + k\} \times \{1, \ldots, n + k\}$ with $i \neq j$ for all $(i, j) \in syn$, $1 \leq i, j \leq n + k$ (synapses between neurons);
(4) $I = \{\sigma_1, \ldots, \sigma_l\}$ is the set of the input neurons that verifies the following: for each $\sigma \in I$, $indegree(\sigma) = 0$.
(5) $O = \{\sigma_{l+q+1}, \ldots, \sigma_n\}$ is the set of the output neurons that verifies the following: for each $\sigma \in O$, $outdegree(\sigma) = 0$.
(6) Neurons $\sigma_{l+1}, \ldots, \sigma_{l+q}$ are called internal neurons.

FRSN P systems with real numbers constitute an extension of SN P systems in the following way (we refer to [13] for more details):

– There are two types of neurons: proposition neurons (associated with propositions in a fuzzy knowledge base) and rule neurons (associated with fuzzy production rules with AND/OR-type antecedent part). Specifically, system Π has n proposition neurons $\sigma_1, \ldots, \sigma_n$ and k rule neurons $\sigma_{n+1}, \ldots, \sigma_{n+k}$. Rule neurons are classified into two classes: AND-type rule neuron and OR-type rule neuron.

$$\underbrace{\overbrace{\underbrace{\sigma_1, \ldots, \sigma_l}_{input\ neurons}, \underbrace{\sigma_{l+1}, \ldots, \sigma_{l+q}}_{internal\ neurons}, \underbrace{\sigma_{l+q+1}, \ldots, \sigma_n}_{output\ neurons}}^{proposition\ neurons}, \overbrace{\sigma_{n+1}, \ldots, \sigma_{n+k}}^{rule\ neurons}}$$

– Content of neuron σ_i is denoted by a fuzzy truth value $\alpha_i \in [0,1]$ which can be interpreted as the (potential) value of spike from the view point of biological neurons. For a neuron σ_i, if $\alpha_i > 0$, we say the neuron contains a spike with (potential) value α_i; otherwise, the neuron contains no spike.
– Given that each neuron is associated with either a fuzzy proposition or a fuzzy production rule, the value $\tau_i \in [0,1]$ will be used to express the truth value of the fuzzy proposition or confidence factor of the fuzzy production rule.
– Each neuron σ_i contains only one firing/spiking rule r_i, which has the form $E/a^\alpha \rightarrow a^\beta$, where $E = a^n$ and $n \in \mathbb{N}$ is the number of input synapses from other neurons to the neuron. The condition $E = a^n$ indicates that if σ_i receives n spikes the firing/spiking rule can be applied; otherwise, the rule is not enabled. When the number of spikes received by a neuron is less than n, value of the spikes received will be updated according to logical AND or OR operations.

– The firing mechanism of neurons can be described as follows. For neuron σ_i, if its firing rule $E/a^\alpha \to a^\beta$ can be applied, this means that its pulse value $\alpha > 0$ is consumed, the neuron fires, and then it produces a spike with value β: all neurons σ_j with $(i, j) \in syn$ will immediately receive the spike. Each kind of neurons use different ways to handle both α and β.

It is worth pointing out that fuzzy production rules of a fuzzy diagnosis knowledge base can be mapped into a FRSN P system model (again, we refer the reader to [13] for more details).

3   P–Lingua Syntax for FRSN P Systems with Real Numbers

In what follows we discuss an extension of the P-Lingua syntax to specify FRSN P systems with real numbers. Let us stress the fact that, with respect to P-Lingua, this variant is considered as separate model from SN P systems.

Definition of P system model

In order to define a FRSN P systems with real numbers, the first line of the P-Lingua file should be as follows:

$$\boxed{\texttt{@model<fuzzy\_psystems>}}.$$

Main module specification

In P-Lingua, instructions are organized into modules, except for global variables definitions, that are placed outside any module. At least a module is required, which is called `main`, at is the entry point to the P-Lingua model specification. The syntax to define this module is the following:

$$\boxed{\texttt{def main \{ /* instructions are placed here */ \}}},$$

Specification of the fuzzy variant

In order to specify the kind of FRSNPS, the following sentence must be written (it has to be the first sentence in the model specification):

$$\boxed{\texttt{@fvariant = v;}},$$

where `v` is a positive integer specifying the variant. In the case of FRSN P systems with real numbers, `v` must set to 1, hence `@fvariant = 1;`.

Specification of the sequential/parallel execution (experimental)

If the model is to be simulated on a `CUDA` parallel platform, the following sentence must be written below the `@fvariant` sentence:

$$\boxed{\texttt{@parallel;}}.$$

If this sentence is not included, a sequential simulation is performed. This way of specifying the sequential/parallel execution is experimental, and may change in future versions of P-Lingua.

Specification of proposition neurons

In order to specify the proposition neurons present in the system, the following sentence must be written:

$$\boxed{\texttt{@mu = p1,...,pi,...,pn;}}\,,$$

where `pi` is the label of the ith proposition neuron.

Specification of input proposition neurons

In order to specify the input proposition neurons present in the system, the following sentence must be written:

$$\boxed{\texttt{@min = pi1,...,piq,...,pis;}}\,,$$

where `piq` is the label of the qth input proposition neuron, and must correspond to a proposition neuron defined in the `@mu` instruction.

Specification of output proposition neurons

In order to specify the output proposition neurons present in the system, the following sentence must be written:

$$\boxed{\texttt{@mout = po1,...,pow,...,pod;}}\,,$$

where `pow` is the label of the wth output proposition neuron, and must correspond to a proposition neuron defined in the `@mu` instruction.

Specification of rule neurons

In order to specify the rule neurons present in the system, the following sentence must be written: $\boxed{\texttt{@frule(...);}}$. This sentence format depends on the kind of fuzzy production rule being modelled. The following cases are possible:

- Simple rules of the form R_i : IF p_j THEN p_k (CF $= \tau_i$) are written as

$$\boxed{\texttt{@frule(Ri,taui,pj,pk);}}.$$

- Type-1 composite rules (AND rules) of the form R_i : IF p_1 AND p_2 AND ... AND p_{k-1} THEN p_k (CF $= \tau_i$) are written as

$$\boxed{\texttt{@frule(Ri,taui,@fand(p1,p2,...,pk-1),pk);}}.$$

- Type-2 composite rules of the form R_i : IF p_1 THEN p_2 AND p_3 AND ... AND p_k (CF $= \tau_i$) are written as

$$\boxed{\texttt{@frule(Ri,taui,p1,(p2,p3,...,pk));}}.$$

- Type-3 composite rules (OR rules) of the form R_i : IF p_1 OR p_2 OR ... OR p_{k-1} THEN p_k (CF $= \tau_i$) are written as

$$\boxed{\texttt{@frule(Ri,taui,@for(p1,p2,...,pk-1),pk);}}.$$

Next we illustrate the syntax presented above with the specification the FRSN P systems with real numbers exemplified in [13].

```
@model<fuzzy_psystems>

def main()
{
@fvariant = 1;
@parallel;

@mu = p1,p2,p3,p4,p5,p6,p7,p8,p9,p10,p11,p12,p13,p14;

@fpin = (p1,0.8),(p2,0.2),(p3,0.8),(p4,0.8),(p5,0.9),
(p6,0.8),(p7,0.2),(p8,0.9),(p9,0.1),(p10,0.2);

@fpout = p11,p12,p13,p14;

@frule(r1,0.8,@fand(p1,p2),p11);
@frule(r2,0.8,@fand(p3,p4,p5,p6),p12);
@frule(r3,0.8,@fand(p5,p7,p8,p9),p13);
@frule(r4,0.8,@fand(p4,p5,p10),p14);
}
```

In this example, a parallel simulation is performed.

4   Simulating FRSN P Systems with Real Numbers

In this Section we present a matrix-based simulation algorithm for simulating FRSN P systems with real numbers (a modified version from the one shown in [13]) and we discuss on simulation of such systems into P-Lingua framework. Two simulators are provided, a sequential one (written in Java), intended to run on traditional CPUs, and a parallel one, able to be executed on CUDA-enabled GPUs. This last simulator works by means of a JAVA-CUDA binding provided by the open source JCUDA library, available for Windows, Linux, MacOS and other operating systems.

4.1   Simulation Algorithm

In what follows, we introduce a simulation algorithm for FRSN P systems with real numbers. In general, simulation algorithms capture semantics of the simulated models, reproducing one or many of the associated computations. In the case of FRSN P systems with real numbers, since these systems are deterministic (and thus confluent), providing an algorithm reproducing a single computation is enough. The algorithm that we are presenting is a revised version of the one introduced in [13], which re-defines the matrix-based functions and operations as well as provides an alternative way to compute fuzzy truth values for rule neurons. As it is a matrix-based algorithm, it is specially suitable to run on parallel platforms such a CUDA systems.

Before presenting the simulation algorithm, let us introduce some required notations, operations and functions, which closely follows from [13].

Let $\Pi = (A, \sigma_1, \ldots, \sigma_{n+k}, syn, I, O)$ be a FRSN P system with real numbers modelling all fuzzy production rules in a fuzzy knowledge base. Then, we can consider the following:

1. The set of neurons $\sigma = (\sigma_1, \ldots, \sigma_{n+k})$, composed of n proposition neurons and k rule neurons;
2. The set of n proposition neurons $\sigma_p = (\sigma_{p1}, \ldots, \sigma_{pn})$;
3. The set of k rule neurons $\sigma_r = (\sigma_{r1}, \ldots, \sigma_{rk})$, with each of them being either an AND-type or OR-type rule neuron;
4. The set $I = \{\sigma_{p_{i1}}, \ldots, \sigma_{p_{is}}\}$, of input proposition neurons, corresponding to fuzzy proposition neurons which fuzzy truth values are known;
5. The set $O = \{\sigma_{r_{o1}}, \ldots, \sigma_{r_{od}}\}$, of output proposition neurons, corresponding to fuzzy proposition neurons which fuzzy truth values are unknown and to be determined;

Let us consider the following vector and matrix notations:

1. $U = (u_{i,j})_{n \times k}$ is a binary matrix, where $u_{i,j} \in \{0, 1\}$, defined as follows:

$$u_{i,j} = \begin{cases} 1 \text{ if there is a directed arc from } \sigma_{pi} \text{ to } \sigma_{rj}; \\ 0 \text{ otherwise}; \end{cases}$$

2. $V = (v_{i,j})_{n \times k}$ is a binary matrix, where $v_{i,j} \in \{0, 1\}$, defined as follows:

$$v_{i,j} = \begin{cases} 1 \text{ if there is a directed arc from } \sigma_{rj} \text{ to } \sigma_{pi}; \\ 0 \text{ otherwise}; \end{cases}$$

3. $\Lambda = diag(\tau_{r1}, \ldots, \tau_{rk})$ is a diagonal real matrix, where τ_{rj} represents the confidence factor of the jth production rule, which is associated with rule neuron σ_{rj};
4. $H_1 = diag(h_1, \ldots, h_k)$ is a diagonal binary matrix, defined as follows:

$$h_j = \begin{cases} 1 \text{ if the } j\text{th rule neuron } \sigma_{rj} \text{ is an AND-type neuron}; \\ 0 \text{ otherwise}; \end{cases}$$

5. $H_2 = diag(h_1, \ldots, h_k)$ is a diagonal binary matrix, defined as follows:

$$h_j = \begin{cases} 1 \text{ if the } j\text{th rule neuron } \sigma_{rj} \text{ is an OR-type neuron}; \\ 0 \text{ otherwise}; \end{cases}$$

6. $\alpha_p = (\alpha_{p1}, \ldots, \alpha_{pn})^T$ is a truth value vector, where $\alpha_{pi} \in [0, 1]$ represents the truth value of ith proposition neuron σ_{pi};
7. $\alpha_r = (\alpha_{r1}, \ldots, \alpha_{rk})^T$ is a truth value vector, where $\alpha_{rj} \in [0, 1]$ represents the truth value of jth rule neuron σ_{rj};
8. $a_p = (a_{p1}, \ldots, a_{pn})^T$ is an integer vector, where a_{pi} represents the number of spikes received by the ith proposition neuron σ_{pi};

9. $a_r = (a_{r1}, \ldots, a_{rk})^T$ is an integer vector, where a_{rj} represents the number of spikes received by the jth rule neuron σ_{rj};

10. $\lambda_p = (\lambda_{p1}, \ldots, \lambda_{pn})^T$ is an integer vector, where λ_{pi} represents the number of spikes required to fire the ith proposition neuron σ_{pi};

11. $\lambda_r = (\lambda_{r1}, \ldots, \lambda_{rk})^T$ is an integer vector, where λ_{rj} represents the number of spikes required to fire the jth rule neuron σ_{rj};

12. $\beta_p = (\beta_{p1}, \ldots, \beta_{pn})^T$ is a truth value vector, where $\beta_{pi} \in [0, 1]$ represents the truth value exported by the ith proposition neuron σ_{pi} after firing;

13. $\beta_r = (\beta_{r1}, \ldots, \beta_{rk})^T$ is a truth value vector, where $\beta_{rj} \in [0, 1]$ represents the truth value exported by the jth rule neuron σ_{rj} after firing;

14. $b_p = (b_{p1}, \ldots, b_{pn})^T$ is an integer vector, where $b_{pi} \in \{0, 1\}$ represents the number of spikes exported by the ith proposition neuron σ_{pi} after firing;

15. $b_r = (b_{r1}, \ldots, b_{rk})^T$ is an integer vector, where $b_{rj} \in \{0, 1\}$ represents the number of spikes exported by the jth rule neuron σ_{rj} after firing;

16. $o_p = (o_{p1}, \ldots, o_{pn})^T$ is a binary vector, where $o_{pi} \in \{0, 1\}$, defined as follows:

$$o_{pi} = \begin{cases} 1 \text{ if } outdegree(\sigma_{pi}) > 0; \\ 0 \text{ otherwise;} \end{cases}$$

17. $o_r = (o_{r1}, \ldots, o_{rk})^T$ is a binary vector, where $o_{rj} \in \{0, 1\}$, defined as follows:

$$o_{rj} = \begin{cases} 1 \text{ if } outdegree(\sigma_{rj}) > 0; \\ 0 \text{ otherwise;} \end{cases}$$

Let us consider the following matrix functions:

1. diag: $D = diag(b)$, where $D = (d_{i,j})$ is a $f \times f$ diagonal real matrix and $b = (b_1, \ldots, b_f)$ a real vector, such that

$$d_{i,j} = \begin{cases} b_i \text{ if } i = j \\ 0 \text{ if } i \neq j \end{cases}, 1 \leq i, j \leq f;$$

2. fire: $\beta = fire(\alpha, a, \lambda, o)$, where $\beta = (\beta_1, \ldots, \beta_f)^T, \alpha = (\alpha_1, \ldots, \alpha_f)^T, a = (a_1, \ldots, a_f)^T, \lambda = (\lambda_1, \ldots, \lambda_f)^T, o = (o_1, \ldots, o_f)^T$, such that

$$\beta_i = \begin{cases} 0 \text{ if } a_i < \lambda_i \\ \alpha_i \text{ if } a_i = \lambda_i \wedge o_i = 0 \\ 0 \text{ if } a_i = \lambda_i \wedge o_i = 1 \end{cases}, 1 \leq i \leq f;$$

3. update: $\beta = update(\alpha, a, \lambda, o)$, where $\beta = (\beta_1, \ldots, \beta_f)^T, \alpha = (\alpha_1, \ldots, \alpha_f)^T, a = (a_1, \ldots, a_f)^T, \lambda = (\lambda_1, \ldots, \lambda_f)^T, o = (o_1, \ldots, o_f)^T$, such that

$$\beta_i = \begin{cases} 0 \text{ if } a_i = 0 \\ \alpha_i \text{ if } 0 < a_i < \lambda_i \\ 0 \text{ if } a_i = \lambda_i \wedge o_i = 0 \\ \alpha_i \text{ if } a_i = \lambda_i \wedge o_i = 1 \end{cases}, 1 \leq i \leq f;$$

Let us consider the following matrix operations:

1. $\oplus : C = A \oplus B$, where A, B, C are $f \times g$ matrices whose elements are non-negative real numbers, such that

$$c_{i,j} = \begin{cases} 0 & \text{if } a_{i,j} = 0 \wedge b_{i,j} = 0 \\ b_i & \text{if } a_{i,j} = 0 \wedge b_{i,j} > 0 \\ a_i & \text{if } a_{i,j} > 0 \wedge b_{i,j} = 0 \\ max\{a_{i,j}, b_{i,j}\} & \text{if } a_{i,j} > 0 \wedge b_{i,j} > 0 \end{cases}, 1 \leq i \leq f, 1 \leq j \leq g;$$

2. $\ominus : C = A \ominus B$, where A, B, C are $f \times g$ matrices whose elements are non-negative real numbers, such that

$$c_{i,j} = \begin{cases} 0 & \text{if } a_{i,j} = 0 \wedge b_{i,j} = 0 \\ b_i & \text{if } a_{i,j} = 0 \wedge b_{i,j} > 0 \\ a_i & \text{if } a_{i,j} > 0 \wedge b_{i,j} = 0 \\ min\{a_{i,j}, b_{i,j}\} & \text{if } a_{i,j} > 0 \wedge b_{i,j} > 0 \end{cases}, 1 \leq i \leq f, 1 \leq j \leq g;$$

3. $\otimes : C = A \otimes B$, where A, B, C are $f \times g, g \times h, f \times h$, matrices respectively, whose elements are non-negative real numbers, such that

$$S_{i,j} = \{a_{i,l} \cdot b_{l,j}, 1 \leq l \leq g\} \setminus \{0\}, 1 \leq i \leq f, 1 \leq j \leq h;$$

$$c_{i,j} = \begin{cases} 0 & \text{if } |S_{i,j}| = 0 \\ max\, S_{i,j} & \text{if } |S_{i,j}| > 0 \end{cases}, 1 \leq i \leq f, 1 \leq j \leq h;$$

4. $\odot : C = A \odot B$, where A, B, C are $f \times g, g \times h, f \times h$, matrices respectively, whose elements are non-negative real numbers, such that

$$S_{i,j} = \{a_{i,l} \cdot b_{l,j}, 1 \leq l \leq g\} \setminus \{0\}, 1 \leq i \leq f, 1 \leq j \leq h;$$

$$c_{i,j} = \begin{cases} 0 & \text{if } |S_{i,j}| = 0 \\ min\, S_{i,j} & \text{if } |S_{i,j}| > 0 \end{cases}, 1 \leq i \leq f, 1 \leq j \leq h;$$

Finally, we introduce the matrix-based simulation algorithm for FRSN P systems with real numbers.

FRSN P systems with real numbers simulation algorithm

- INPUT:
  - $U, V, \Lambda, H_1, H_2, \lambda_p, \lambda_r$;
  - $\alpha_p^0 = (\alpha_{p1}^0, \dots, \alpha_{pn}^0)$, with $\alpha_{pi}^0 = \begin{cases} \tau_{pi} & \text{if } \sigma_{pi} \in I, \tau_{pi} \text{ is the CF of } \sigma_{pi}; \\ 0 & \text{otherwise}; \end{cases}$
  - $a_p^0 = (a_{p1}^0, \dots, a_{pn}^0)$, with $a_{pi}^0 = \begin{cases} 1 & \text{if} \sigma_{pi} \in I; \\ 0 & \text{otherwise}; \end{cases}$
- OUTPUT:
  - $\alpha_{pout} = (\alpha_{pi_1}, \dots, \alpha_{pi_s})^T$, the vector containing the fuzzy truth values of proposition neurons in O.

Step 1. Let $\alpha_r^0 = (0, \ldots, 0)^T, a_r^0 = (0, \ldots, 0)^T$.

Step 2. Let $t = 0$.

Step 3. Do:
(1) Prepare firing of proposition neurons.
* $\beta_p^t = fire(\alpha_p^t, a_p^t, \lambda_p, o_p)$.
* $b_p^t = fire(1, a_p^t, \lambda_p, o_p)$.
* $\alpha_p^t = update(\alpha_p^t, a_p^t, \lambda_p, o_p)$.
* $a_p^t = update(a_p^t, a_p^t, \lambda_p, o_p)$.
* $B_p^t = diag(b_p^t)$.
(2) Prepare firing of rule neurons.
* $\beta_r^t = fire(\alpha_r^t, a_r^t, \lambda_r, o_r)$.
* $b_r^t = fire(1, a_r^t, \lambda_r, o_r)$.
* $\alpha_r^t = update(\alpha_r^t, a_r^t, \lambda_r, o_r)$.
* $a_r^t = update(a_r^t, a_r^t, \lambda_r, o_r)$.
* $B_r^t = diag(b_p^t)$.
(3) Update truth values and received spikes for proposition neurons.
* $\alpha_p^{t+1} = \alpha_p^t \oplus \left((V \cdot B_r^t) \otimes \beta_r^t \right)$.
* $a_p^{t+1} = a_p^t + \left((V \cdot B_r^t) \cdot b_r^t \right)$.
(4) Update truth values and received spikes for rule neurons.
* $\alpha_r^{t+1} = H_1 \cdot \left[\alpha_r^t \ominus \left((B_p^t \cdot U)^T \odot \beta_p^t \right) \right] + H_2 \cdot \left[\alpha_r^t \oplus \left((B_p^t \cdot U)^T \otimes \beta_p^t \right) \right]$.
* $a_r^{t+1} = a_r^t + \left((B_p^t \cdot U)^T \cdot b_p^t \right)$.

Step 4. Check termination condition. If the following conditions hold:
(a) $a_r^{t+1} = (0, 0, \ldots, 0)^T$;
(b) $a_p = (a_{p1}, \ldots, a_{pn})^T$, with: $a_{pi} = \begin{cases} 1 \text{ if } o_{pi} = 1 \\ 0 \text{ otherwise} \end{cases}, 1 \leq i \leq n$;
then HALT, otherwise go to Step 3.

4.2   P-Lingua Simulators for FRSN P Systems with Real Numbers

In [4], a Java library called pLinguaCore was presented, with this package being released under GPL [25] license. The library provides parsers to handle input files, built-in simulators to generate P system computations and is able to export several output file formats that represent P systems. In what follows, we detail how to invoke the brand new built-in simulators for FRSN P systems with real numbers. Two simulators are provided, a sequential one (written in Java), running on traditional CPUs, and a parallel one, able to run on CUDA-enabled devices. The parallel simulator uses a CUDA kernel in which threads compute the results of the different matrix-based operations executed in the simulation algorithm described above. This paper version of pLinguaCore library can be found at www.p-lingua.org/mecosim/.

Invoking the Sequential Simulator. Invoking the sequential simulator requires for the system to host a Java runtime environment properly installed and configured. The Java runtime can be found at https://java.com/es/download/. Also, the following directory structure must be created:

```
plingua/
├── plinguacore.jar
└── input.pli
```

The **plingua** directory contains all the required files to run the simulation. Files description follows:

- **plinguacore.jar** file hosts the **pLinguaCore** library.
- **input.pli** file hosts the FRSN P systems with real numbers model to simulate.

Once the files are ready, to invoke the simulator a system console must be opened and the following command has to be executed from the **plingua** directory:

```
java -jar plinguacore.jar plingua_sim -pli input.pli -o output.txt
```

This will produce an output file named **output.txt** in **plingua** directory where information about the parser process and the generated computation is stored.

Invoking the Parallel Simulator. Invoking the parallel simulator requires for the system to host both a Java runtime environment and a CUDA-enabled GPU device, with the corresponding NVIDIA driver with CUDA support and the CUDA Toolkit properly installed and configured. The NVIDIA software can be found at https://developer.nvidia.com/cuda-downloads. In order to interface the Java pLinguaCore library with the CUDA platform, a JAVA-CUDA binding is required, which is provided by the JCUDA library. In the present paper, version 0.6.5 of such library is used, as well as version 0.0.4 of JCudaUtils library, which contains a series of utility methods used by JCUDA library. Both of them can be found at http://www.jcuda.org/. Also, the following directory structure must be created:

```
plingua/
├── plinguacore.jar
├── input.pli
├── kernelReal.cu
├── jcudaUtils-0.0.4.jar
└── jcuda-0.6.5/
    └── *** jcuda-0.6.5 library files ***
```

The **plingua** directory contains all the required files to run the simulation. Files description follows:

- `plinguacore.jar` file hosts the pLinguaCore library.
- `input.pli` file hosts the FRSN P systems with real numbers model to simulate.
- `kernelReal.cu` file hosts the CUDA kernel corresponding to the parallel implementation.
- `jcudaUtils-0.0.4.jar` file hosts JCudaUtils library.
- `jcuda-0.6.5` folder hosts the contents of the zip file corresponding to the 0.6.5 version of JCUDA library.

Once the files are ready, to invoke the simulator a system console must be opened and the following command has to be executed from the `plingua` directory:

```
java -Djava.library.path=jcuda/
-cp"pLinguaCore.jar;jcudaUtils-0.0.4.jar;jcuda/jcuda-0.6.5.jar"
org.gcn.plinguacore.applications.AppMain
plingua_sim -pli input.pli -o output.txt
```

This will produce an output file named `output.txt` in `plingua` directory where information about the parser process and the generated computation is stored. Note: the `-cp` parameter uses the symbol ";" as element separator in Windows platforms. Other platforms use different separators. For example, Unix platforms use the symbol ":".

Parallel Simulator CUDA Compatibility and Performance Considerations. When developing the parallel simulator, the main goal was to make it able to handle arbitrary matrix size instances and to run on the majority of CUDA-compatible devices. This has involved making conservative choices in the implementation. A standard *block size* equal to 256 (16*16) has been chosen and the *tiling/memory coalescing* optimization technique has been applied, which requires a relatively low amount of *shared memory* for blocks (see [6] for more details). Fixing matrix size instances and minimum requirements for the CUDA-compatible device would enable implementing more complex optimization techniques, such as *loop unrolling, data prefetching and thread granularity* as well as a fine grained performance analysis. The appropriate combinations of performance tuning techniques can make tremendous difference in the performance achieved by the simulator; however the programming efforts to manually search through these combinations is quite large [6]. Automation tools to reduce such efforts such as CUDA-lite [18] and others become indispensable.

5   Conclusions and Future Work

In this paper we introduce P-Lingua framework support for a new P system variant, specifically FRSN P systems with real numbers, which incorporate fuzzy logic elements into SN P systems. The motivation of this variant is to produce a framework bringing together desirable features (understandable, dynamical, synchronized, non-linear, non-deterministic, able to handle incomplete and uncertain information) to model diagnosis knowledge and reasoning in the field of fault diagnosis. Applications of this variant are very promising, which are related to fault diagnosis of electrical systems [13,21]. In consequence, providing the corresponding P-Lingua support favours the research on this model within Membrane Computing community as well as in applied fields. Developing such support has involved designing a specific parser (since with respect to P-Lingua, FRSN P systems are considered a "separated" variant of SN P systems), a simulation algorithm (which is a variant of the one introduced in [13]) and the corresponding simulators. As the provided simulation algorithm is a matrix-based one, which can take advantage of parallel computing platforms, along with a Java sequential simulator, a parallel one has been developed intended to be able to run on the majority of CUDA-compatible devices.

As open research lines, we can identify addressing others FRSN P systems variants, dealing with trapezoidal numbers, weights, etc. and considering the implementation of more complex optimization techniques, possibly assisted by automation optimization tools.

Acknowledgements. This work was supported by Project TIN2012-37434 of the Ministerio de Economía y Competitividad of Spain, cofinanced by FEDER funds. The authors also acknowledge the support of the GPU Research Center program granted by NVIDIA to the University of Seville.

References

1. Binder, A., Freund, R., Oswald, M., Vock, L.: Extended spiking neural P systems with excitatory and inhibitory astrocytes. In: Proceedings of the 8th Conference on 8th WSEAS International Conference on Evolutionary Computing, EC 2007, vol. 8, pp. 320–325. World Scientific and Engineering Academy and Society (WSEAS), Stevens Point, Wisconsin, USA (2007)
2. Chen, H., Freund, R., Ionescu, M., Păun, G., Pérez-Jiménez, M.J.: On string languages generated by spiking neural P systems. Fundam. Inform. 75(1–4), 141–162 (2007)
3. Chen, H., Ionescu, M., Ishdorj, T.O., Păun, A., Păun, G., Pérez-Jiménez, M.J.: Spiking neural P systems with extended rules: universality and languages. Nat. Comput. 7(2), 147–166 (2008)
4. García-Quismondo, M., Gutiérrez-Escudero, R., del Amor, M.A.M., Orejuela-Pinedo, E.F., Pérez-Hurtado, I.: P-lingua 2.0: a software framework for cell-like P systems. Int. J. Comput. Commun. Control 4, 234–243 (2009)
5. Ionescu, M., Păun, G., Yokomori, T.: Spiking neural P systems. Fundam. Inf. 71, 279–308 (2006)
6. Kirk, D.B., Hwu, WmW: Programming Massively Parallel Processors: A Hands-on Approach, 1st edn. Morgan Kaufmann Publishers Inc., San Francisco (2010)
7. Macías-Ramos, L.F., Pérez-Jiménez, M.J.: Spiking neural P systems with functional astrocytes. In: Csuhaj-Varjú, E., Gheorghe, M., Rozenberg, G., Salomaa, A., Vaszil, G. (eds.) CMC 2012. LNCS, vol. 7762, pp. 228–242. Springer, Heidelberg (2013)

8. Martín-Vide, C., Păun, G., Pazos, J., Rodríguez-Patón, A.: Tissue P systems. Theor. Comput. Sci. **296**(2), 295–326 (2003)
9. Pan, L., Păun, G.: Spiking neural P systems with anti-spikes. Int. J. Comput. Commun. Control **4**, 273–282 (2009)
10. Pan, L., Păun, G., Pérez-Jiménez, M.J.: Spiking neural P systems with neuron division and budding. Sci. China Inf. Sci. **54**(8), 1596–1607 (2011)
11. Pan, L., Wang, J., Hoogeboom, H.J.: Asynchronous extended spiking neural P systems with astrocytes. In: Gheorghe, M., Păun, G., Rozenberg, G., Salomaa, A., Verlan, S. (eds.) CMC 2011. LNCS, vol. 7184, pp. 243–256. Springer, Heidelberg (2012)
12. Pan, L., Wang, J., Hoogeboom, H.J.: Limited asynchronous spiking neural P systems. Fundam. Inform. **110**(1–4), 271–293 (2011)
13. Peng, H., Wang, J., Pérez-Jiménez, M.J., Wang, H., Shao, J., Wang, T.: Fuzzy reasoning spiking neural P system for fault diagnosis. Inf. Sci. **235**, 106–116 (2013)
14. Păun, A., Păun, G.: Small universal spiking neural P systems. Biosystems **90**(1), 48–60 (2007)
15. Păun, G.: Computing with membranes. J. Comput. Syst. Sci. **61**, 108–143 (1998)
16. Păun, G., Rozenberg, G., Salomaa, A.: The Oxford Handbook of Membrane Computing. Oxford University Press Inc, New York (2010)
17. Song, T., Pan, L., Păun, G.: Asynchronous spiking neural P systems with local synchronization. Inf. Sci. **219**, 197–207 (2013)
18. Ueng, S.-Z., Lathara, M., Baghsorkhi, S.S., Hwu, W.W.: CUDA-Lite: reducing GPU programming complexity. In: Amaral, J.N. (ed.) LCPC 2008. LNCS, vol. 5335, pp. 1–15. Springer, Heidelberg (2008)
19. Wang, J., Hoogeboom, H.J., Pan, L., Păun, G., Pérez-Jiménez, M.J.: Spiking neural P systems with weights. Neural Comput. **22**(10), 2615–2646 (2010)
20. Wang, T., Zhang, G., Pérez-Jiménez, M.J.: Application of weighted fuzzy reasoning spiking neural P systems to fault diagnosis in traction power supply systems of high-speed railways. In: Twelfth Brainstorming Week on Membrane Computing (BWMC2014), pp. 329–350 (2014)
21. Wang, T., Zhang, G., Pérez-Jiménez, M.J.: Fault diagnosis models for electric locomotive systems based on fuzzy reasoning spiking neural P systems. In: Gheorghe, M., Rozenberg, G., Salomaa, A., Sosík, P., Zandron, C. (eds.) CMC 2014. LNCS, vol. 8961, pp. 385–395. Springer, Heidelberg (2014)
22. Wang, T., Zhang, G., Rong, H., Pérez-Jiménez, M.J.: Application of fuzzy reasoning spiking neural P systems to fault diagnosis. Int. J. Comput. Commun. Control **9**, 720–733 (2014)
23. Wang, T., Zhang, G., Zhao, J., He, Z., Wang, J., Pérez-Jiménez, M.: Fault diagnosis of electric power systems based on fuzzy reasoning spiking neural P systems. IEEE Trans. Power Syst. **30**(3), 1182–1194 (2015)
24. Web-page: The CUDA Website. https://developer.nvidia.com/cuda-zone
25. Web-page: The GNU GPL Website. http://www.gnu.org/copyleft/gpl.html
26. Web-page: The Java Website. https://www.java.com/
27. Web-page: The JCUDA Website. http://www.jcuda.org/
28. Web-page: The P-Lingua Website. http://www.p-lingua.org/

Pictures and Chomsky Languages in Array P System

Williams Sureshkumar, Kalpana Mahalingam, and Raghavan Rama[(✉)]

Department of Mathematics, Indian Institute of Technology,
Madras, Chennai 600036, India
wisureshkumariit@gmail.com, {kmahalingam,ramar}@iitm.ac.in

Abstract. A new array P system called 8-directional array P system is defined in this paper. The regulated evolution of this new model is capable of generating interesting pictures in its accepting mode of evolution. The relationship between the family of regulating languages of 8-directional array P system and the family of λ-free regular, context-free, context-sensitive languages is investigated. In the case of RE, the simulation result requires λ-labeled rules.

Keywords: 8-directional array P system · Regulating string · Dependability · Chomsky languages · RE

1 Introduction

A P system is a new computing model abstracting the biological happening in membranes. Hence the system is also called *membrane system*. This computing model now has several variants [1]. Most P systems variants are computationally universal exhibiting the power of the systems.

Recently, there were several research papers on array P systems. The arrays considered in [2] are set to evolve in a P system to generate various pictures. In [3] the authors set a collection of pictures made up of symbols to evolve using array rules mostly of isotonic type. The key idea was the construction of array language by means of halting P system. Hence it is clear to look for the nature of P systems which have well defined halting configurations. In [4] the authors looked at the regulating string associated with a computation of a P system with multi set of objects. In [5] the authors looked at the regulating evolution of an isotonic array P system where the evolution rules were either regular isotonic or context-free isotonic as defined in [6]. The authors in this paper also introduce a new type of isotonic rule called *restricted monotonic* type which is different from the array rules used in [3]. Some of the interesting P systems which use arrays as data structures can be seen in [7,8].

In this paper we introduce a new array model called *8-directional array P system*. The interpretation and manipulation of the data structure 'string' will

This work was funded by the Project No: MAT/15-16/046/DSTX/KALP, Department of Science and Technology, Government of India.

G. Rozenberg et al. (Eds.): CMC 2015, LNCS 9504, pp. 277–289, 2015.
DOI: 10.1007/978-3-319-28475-0_19

be like 'turtle-like' graphs with possibilities to turn in multiples of 45 degrees. This array P system naturally can be seen to produce several interesting arrays of both rectangular and non rectangular type. We are interested in looking at the evolution of this P system in a regulating manner.

In Sect. 2, we define 8-directional array grammar and 8-directional array P system ($8dAPS$). In Sect. 3, we define labeled 8-directional array P system in accepting mode ($L8dAPS^a$). We illustrate the model with interesting examples which are capable of generating pictures. In Sect. 4, we present the main results. Section 5 presents concluding remarks.

2   8-Directional Array P Systems

In this section we give two definitions: an 8-directional array grammar and another an 8-directional array P system.

Definition 1. *An 8-directional array grammar is defined as a quadruple $G = (N, T, P, S)$, where*

1. *N is a finite non-empty set of symbols called non-terminals.*
2. *T is a finite non-empty set of symbols called terminals such that it is disjoint from N i.e. $N \cap T = \emptyset$.*
3. *P is a finite non-empty set of θ-rotation rules of the form*

$$A \to \beta^\theta$$

or

$$\alpha^\theta \to \beta^\theta, \quad 2 \le |\alpha| \le |\beta|,$$

where $A \in N$, $\beta \in (N \cup T)^+$, α contains exactly one non-terminal symbol and all other symbols in α are terminals, $\theta \in \left\{0, \frac{\pi}{4}, \frac{\pi}{2}, \frac{3\pi}{4}, \pi, \frac{5\pi}{4}, \frac{3\pi}{2}, \frac{7\pi}{4}\right\}$. While applying the former type of rule, A is rewritten by α in the direction of θ such that the leftmost symbol of α is placed in the position of A. For the later type of rule, β is rewritten by α in the direction of θ such that the first symbol of β is placed in the position of the first symbol of α.
4. *$S \in N$ is the start symbol.*

Remark 1. For the rules of the form $A \to \beta^\theta$, the symbols following A are to be shifted by $|\beta - 1|$ positions in the direction of θ. For the rules $\alpha^\theta \to \beta^\theta$ the symbols following α are to be shifted by $|\beta| - |\alpha|$ positions in the direction of θ.

Example 1. If $A \to (aAB)^{\frac{\pi}{4}}$ means while applying the rule to any array of the form $\alpha A \beta$, the resultant array will be

$$
\begin{array}{ccc}
 & B & \\
 & A & \\
\alpha & a & \beta
\end{array}
$$

In the above array, apply the rule $(aA)^{\frac{\pi}{4}} \rightarrow (bcdE)^{\frac{\pi}{4}}$, the resultant array will be

$$
\begin{array}{cccc}
 & & B & \\
 & E & & \\
 & d & & \\
 & c & & \\
\alpha & b & \beta &
\end{array}
$$

Definition 2. *An 8-directional Array P System (8dAPS) of degree $m(\geq 1)$ is a construct $\Pi = (V, T, \mu, I_1, \ldots, I_m, (R_1, \rho_1), \ldots, (R_m, \rho_m), i_o)$, where V is the total alphabet, $T \subseteq V$ is the terminal alphabet, μ is a membrane structure with m membranes labeled in a one-to-one manner with $1, 2, \ldots, m$; $I_1, \ldots, I_m$ are finite sets of arrays over V associated with the m regions of μ; $R_1, \ldots, R_m$ are finite sets of θ-rotation rules over V associated with the m regions of μ; $\rho_1, \ldots, \rho_m$ are partial order relations over $R_1, \ldots, R_m$. The rules in R_i are of the form $A \rightarrow \alpha^\theta$ (tar), or $\alpha^\theta \rightarrow \beta^\theta$ (tar), $2 \leq |\alpha| \leq |\beta|$, where tar indicates the target location of the output array obtained by applying such rules. The tar can be here, out or in. Here $A \in (V \backslash T)$, α contains exactly one non-terminal symbol and all other symbols in α are terminals, $\beta \in V^+$ and $\theta \in \left\{0, \frac{\pi}{4}, \frac{\pi}{2}, \frac{3\pi}{4}, \pi, \frac{5\pi}{4}, \frac{3\pi}{2}, \frac{7\pi}{4}\right\}$. There can be more than one rule with A or α on its left hand side. The array produced by using this rule will go to the membrane indicated by tar; finally, i_o is the output membrane.*

We start from an initial configuration of the system and proceed iteratively, by transition steps performed by using the θ-rotation rules in parallel, to all arrays that can be rewritten, obeying the priority relations, and collecting the terminal arrays generated in a designated membrane, the output one.

Note that each array is processed by one rule only, the parallelism refers here to processing simultaneously all available arrays by all applicable θ-rotation rules. If several rules can be applied to an array, may be in several places each, then we take only one rule and only one possible location to apply it and consider the obtained array as the next form of the object described by the array. It is important to have in mind the fact that the evolution of the arrays is not independent of each other, but interrelated in two ways: (1) if we have priorities, a rule r_1 applicable to an array $\mathcal{A}$ can forbid the use of another rule, r_2, for rewriting another array, $\mathcal{B}$, which is present at that time in the same membrane; after applying the rule r_1, if r_1 is not applicable to $\mathcal{B}$ or to the array $\mathcal{A}'$ obtained from $\mathcal{A}$ by using r_1, then it is possible that the rule r_2 can now be applied to $\mathcal{B}$; (2) even without priorities, if an array $\mathcal{A}$ can be rewritten for ever, in the same membrane or on an itinerary through several membranes, and this cannot be avoided, then all arrays are lost, because the computation never stops, irrespective of the arrays collected in the output membrane and which cannot evolve further.

A computation is successful only if it stops, a configuration is reached where no rule can be applied to the existing arrays. The result of a halting computation consists of the arrays composed only of symbols from T (terminal symbols) placed in the membrane with label i_o in the halting configuration.

3   Labeled $8dAPS$ in Accepting Mode and Pictures

In this section we introduce labeled $8dAPS$ in accepting mode. We illustrate the model with a few interesting examples which halt always on pictures.

Definition 3. *A Labeled 8-directional Array P System in accepting mode (L8dAPS^a) Π of degree $m(\geq 1)$ is a construct $\Pi = (V, T, \mu, I_1, \ldots, I_m, (R_1, \rho_1), \ldots, (R_m, \rho_m), i_o, lab, F)$, where $V, T, \mu, I_1, \ldots, I_m, R_1, \ldots, R_m, \rho_1, \ldots, \rho_m, i_o$ are same as in definition 2, lab is a finite set of alphabet, which are used for labeling the rules and F is the set of final configurations. Let $R = \bigcup_{i=1}^m R_i$. Here we assign a label to every rule in R where the labels are chosen from a finite alphabet lab or the labels can be λ (empty label). Define a function $f : R \to lab \cup \{\lambda\}$ called a labeling function that assign a label to each rule in R. Noting that more than one rule may have the same label, but the same rule in different membranes cannot be assigned different labels. We extend the labeling for a label sequence $S = l_1\, l_2\, \ldots\, l_k \in R^*$ as follows: $f(\lambda) = \lambda$ and $f(l_1\, l_2\, \ldots\, l_k) = f(l_1)f(l_2 \ldots l_k)$. A transition $C \xRightarrow{b} C'$ between two successive configurations uses only rules with the same label b and rules labeled with λ. If at least one rule has a label $b \in lab$ then the transition is called λ-restricted transition. If we allow all rules with λ label then the transition is called λ-unrestricted transition (or λ-transition).*

A regulating string of input symbols (over *lab*) is said to be accepted if all its symbols are consumed and Π reaches a configuration in the set F. The set of all regulating strings accepted in this way by computations in a $L8dAPS^a$ Π is denoted by $L_\lambda^a 8dAP(\Pi)$. The subscript indicates the fact that λ-steps (all rules applied in one step can have λ label) are permitted. When only steps where at least one rule with a non-empty label is used, the accepting language is denoted by $L^a 8dAP(\Pi)$. The family of languages $L^a 8dAP(\Pi)$ associated with $L8dAPS^a$ with at most m membranes, working in accepting mode is denoted by $L^a 8dAP_m$. In the unrestricted case, the corresponding language family is denoted by $L_\lambda^a 8dAP_m$. If the number of membranes is unbounded, then the subscript m is replaced with $\star$.

We now give some interesting examples. In Examples 2 and 4 the regulating languages are regular, Example 3 has context-sensitive regulating language. From these examples one can see that the halting configuration set can contain both rectangular and non rectangular arrays.

Example 2. In this example the $L8dAPS^a$ Π_1, while accepting the regular regulating language, it halts on pictures of stars in its final configuration set F. The $L8dAPS^a$ Π_1 with three membranes is given as,

$$\Pi_1 = \left(\left\{ A, B, C, D, x \right\}, \left\{ x \right\}, [_1 [_2]_2 [_3]_3]_1, I_1, I_2, I_3, R_1, R_2, R_3, 3, \left\{ a \right\}, F \right),$$

where $I_2 = \left\{ A \right\}$, $I_1 = I_3 = \phi$ and $R_1 = \Big\{ (1)\ a : B \to (Cx)^0, in_2,\ (2)\ a : D \to$

$$(Ax)^\pi, in_2 \ , \ (3) \ a: D \rightarrow (xx)^\pi, in_3 \Bigg\},$$

$$R_2 = \Bigg\{ (4) \ a: A \rightarrow (Bx)^{\frac{\pi}{2}}, out \ , \ (5) \ a: C \rightarrow (Dx)^{\frac{3\pi}{2}}, out \ \Bigg\}, \ R_3 = \phi.$$

The set of final configurations is $F = \Bigg\{ \left(\phi, \phi, \begin{smallmatrix} x \\ x \ x \ x \\ x \end{smallmatrix} \right), \left(\phi, \phi, \begin{smallmatrix} x \\ x \ x \ x \ x \ x \\ x \end{smallmatrix} \right), \ldots \Bigg\}.$

The working of $L^a 8dAPS^a$ Π_1 with three membranes is as follows:

We start the configuration with axiom A in region 2, by applying the rule 4 which is the only possible choice. The resulting array is sent to region 1 and rule 1 is applied sending the array back to region 2. Then rule 5 is applied in region 2 and the array $\begin{smallmatrix} x \\ D \ x \\ x \end{smallmatrix}$. Now we have two choices, either rule 2 or rule 3 is applicable. Application of rule 2 will result in the array $\begin{smallmatrix} x \\ x \ A \ x \\ x \end{smallmatrix}$ and the entire process is repeated. Application rule 3 will terminate the configuration resulting in arrays in F. The above process will lead to the regulating language $L^a 8dAP(\Pi_1) = \{ a^{4n} : n \geq 1 \}.$

Example 3. Consider the $L8dAPS^a$ Π_2 with two membranes, while accepting the context-sensitive regulating language, it halts on an array in the set of picture configurations F given below. $L8dAPS^a$ Π_2 is given as,

$\Pi_2 = \left(\{ A, 0 \}, \{ 0 \}, [_1 [_2]_2]_1, I_1, I_2, R_1, R_2, 2, \{ a, b, c \}, F \right)$, where $I_1 = \{ A \}$,

$I_2 = \phi$ and $R_1 = \Bigg\{ (1) \ a: A \rightarrow (0A)^{\frac{\pi}{4}}, ((2) \ b: A \rightarrow (0A)^{\frac{7\pi}{4}}, (3) \ c: A \rightarrow$

$$(0A)^\pi, in_2 \Bigg\}$$

$$R_2 = \Bigg\{ (4) \ c: (0A0)^0 \rightarrow (000)^0 \ > \ (5) \ c: A \rightarrow (0A)^\pi \Bigg\}.$$

The set of final configurations is

$$F = \Bigg\{ \left(\phi, \begin{smallmatrix} & 0 & \\ & 0 \ 0 & \\ 0 \ 0 \ 0 \ 0 \ 0 & \end{smallmatrix} \right), \left(\phi, \begin{smallmatrix} & 0 & \\ & 0 \ 0 & \\ 0 & & 0 \\ 0 \ 0 \ 0 \ 0 \ 0 \ 0 \ 0 & \end{smallmatrix} \right), \ldots \Bigg\}.$$

The working of $L8dAPS^a$ Π_2 with two membranes is as follows: For any $n \geq 2$, application of rule 1, n times and rule 2, n times followed by rule 3 once will expel the array to region 2. In region 2, apply $(2n-2)$ times rule 5. Finally apply rule 4 one time, the system halts on an array in F. The corresponding regulating language accepted by Π_2 is $L^a 8dAP(\Pi_2) = \left\{ a^n b^n c^{2n} : n \geq 2 \right\}$.

Example 4. Consider the $L8dAPS^a$ Π_4 with two membranes, it accepts the regular regulating language and halts on an array in the given set of picture of a ladder in its final configuration F given below. $L8dAPS^a$ Π_4 is given as,

$$\Pi_4 = \left(\left\{ A, B, C, \star \right\}, \left\{ \star \right\}, [_1[_2]_2]_1, I_1, I_2, R_1, R_2, 2, \left\{ a, b, c \right\}, F \right), \text{ where}$$

$I_1 = \left\{ A \right\}$, $I_2 = \phi$ and

$$R_1 = \left\{ (1)\ a\ :\ A\ \rightarrow\ (B \star C)^0,\ (2)\ b\ :\ B\ \rightarrow\ (\star \star \star A)^{\frac{3\pi}{2}},\ (3)\ c\ :\ C\ \rightarrow \right.$$

$$\left. (\star \star \star)^{\frac{3\pi}{2}}, in_2 \right\}$$

$$R_2 = \left\{ (4)\ a\ :\ A\ \rightarrow\ (\star \star \star)^0,\ (5)\ a\ :\ A\ \rightarrow\ (B \star C)^0, out \right\}.$$

The set of final configurations is

$$F = \left\{ \left(\phi, \begin{array}{ccc} \star & \star & \star \\ \star & & \star \\ \star & & \star \\ \star & \star & \star \end{array} \right),\ \left(\phi, \begin{array}{ccc} \star & \star & \star \\ \star & & \star \\ \star & \star & \star \\ \star & & \star \\ \star & & \star \\ \star & \star & \star \end{array} \right), \ldots \right\}$$

The working of $L8dAPS^a$ Π_4 with two membranes is as follows: Starting with the axiom A in region 1, apply the rules 1, 2 and 3 in order to expel the array to region 2. In region 2, apply the rule 5 to send back the array to region 1. For halting apply rule 4 instead of rule 5. Repeating the above process will lead to an array in F. The corresponding regulating language accepted by Π_4 is $L^a 8dAP(\Pi_4) = \left\{ (abc)^n a : n \geq 1 \right\}$.

4   Main Results

In this section, we investigate the relationship between the family of regulating languages of 8-directional array P systems in acceptance mode (λ-restricted) and the family of λ-free regular, context-free, context-sensitive languages. The simulation of recursively enumerable languages is done via λ-unrestricted $L8dAPS^a$.

Notation: For any family $\mathcal{P}$ of languages, $\mathcal{P} \backslash \{\lambda\}$ means the family of λ-free languages.

Theorem 1. $(REG \backslash \{\lambda\}) \subseteq L^a 8dAP_1$.

Proof. Let $L \in (REG \backslash \{\lambda\})$ and let $D = (Q, \Sigma, \delta, p_0, F_D)$ be a deterministic finite automaton accepting L. Let n be the number of states in D. Rename the states as $q_i, 1 \leq i \leq n$, such that $q_1 = p_0$ and the transition rules are changed accordingly. Let $D' = (Q', \Sigma, \delta', q_1, F'_D)$ be the modified DFA. Using D' we construct a $L8dAPS^a$ Π_5 with one membrane accepting $L(D')$ as follows:

$$\Pi_5 = \left(Q' \cup \{x\}, \{x\}, [_1]_1, I_1, R_1, 1, \Sigma, F \right), \text{ where}$$

$R_1 = \left\{ a : q_i \rightarrow (q_j)^0 : (q_i, a, q_j) \in \delta' \right\} \cup \left\{ a : q_i \rightarrow (x)^0 : (q_i, a, q_f) \in \delta', q_f \in F'_D \right\}$ and $I_1 = \{ x\ q_1 \}$. The final configuration $F = \left\{ \left(x\ x \right) \right\}$

The $L8dAPS^a$ Π_5 constructed above works as follows: The $L8dAPS^a$ starts with an array $x\ q_1$ where q_1 corresponds to the start symbol of the DFA in the membrane. When the system uses the rule $a : q_i \rightarrow q_j$, it simulates the application of the rule $(q_i, a, q_j) \in \delta'$ by the DFA, i.e. if the current symbol is a and the system contains the object q_i, then the current input symbol a is consumed, and the object q_i, gets replaced by the object q_j (note that, at any instance, the $L8dAPS^a$ contains only a single element from Q' in the array). The system accepts the input string when the input is completely read and the corresponding configuration in F is reached. The membrane contains the array $\left(x\ x \right)$ which is from F. □

Remark 2. One can show that the context-free language $L = \left\{ a^n b^n : n \geq 1 \right\}$ can be accepted by an $8dAPS$. The following $8dAPS$ Π can accept L.

$\Pi = \left(\left\{ A, B, 0, \star \right\}, \left\{ 0, \star \right\}, [_1[_2]_2]_1, I_1, I_2, R_1, R_2, 2, \left\{ a, b \right\}, F \right)$, where $I_1 = \left\{ A \right\}$, $I_2 = \phi$ and $R_1 = \left\{ (1)\ a : A \rightarrow (0A)^0, (2)\ a : A \rightarrow (B)^0, in_2 \right\}$,

$$R_2 = \left\{ (3)\ b : (0B)^0 \rightarrow (B\star)^0 > (4)\ b : B \rightarrow (\star)^0 \right\}.$$

The set of final configurations is $F = \left\{ \left(\phi, \star^n \right) : n \geq 1 \right\}$.

Hence we can deduce the following:

Proposition 1. $L^a 8dAP_\star - REG \neq \emptyset$.

Remark 3. We conclude from Proposition 1 and Theorem 1 that $(REG\backslash\{\lambda\}) \subset L^a 8dAP_\star$. We proceed further to see whether $(CF\backslash\{\lambda\}) \subseteq L^a 8dAP_\star$ which we prove in the following theorem.

Theorem 2. $(CF\backslash\{\lambda\}) \subseteq L^a 8dAP_1$.

Proof. Let L be a context-free language. Then let $G = (N, T, P, S)$ be a context-free grammar in *Greibach* normal form generating L. Let n be the number of non-terminals in N. Now rename the non-terminals in N as $A_i, 1 \leq i \leq n$, such that $A_1 = S$ and also modify the rules with this renamed non-terminals. Let $G_1 = (N', T, P', A_1)$ be the grammar thus modified. Now, we construct a $L8dAPS^a$ Π_7 with one membrane for G_1 is as follows:

$\Pi_7 = \left(N' \cup \{\star\}, \{\star\}, [_1]_1, I_1, R_1, 1, T, F \right)$, where $I_1 = \{A_1\}$ and

$$R_1 = \left\{ a : A_i \to \star y \; : A_i \to ay \in P' \right\} \cup \left\{ a : A_i \to \star \; : A_i \to a \in P' \right\}$$

The final configuration $F = \left\{ (\star \star \cdots \star \star) \; : \; \text{number of } \star's \; = \; |w|, w \in L^a 8dAP(\Pi_7) \right\}$.

Initially, the $L8dAPS^a$ Π_7 starts with an axiom A_1, the start symbol of G_1. Now, we can apply either a rule $a : A_1 \to \star y$ corresponds to $A_1 \to ay$ or the rule $a : A_1 \to \star$ corresponds to $A_1 \to a$. If we apply the latter rule, then the system halts on the final configuration $\{(\star)\}$, the corresponding regulated string accepted by Π_7 is a. Suppose, we choose the former rule, A_1 is replaced with $\star y$, y is a string of non-terminals. We adopt the same procedure to the leftmost non-terminal in the array. Once we choose the rule $a : A_i \to \star$, then the leftmost non-terminal in the array is replaced by $\star$. Now, the leftmost symbol in the array is not a non-terminal, so we prefer the non-terminal next to $\star$. Again for this non-terminal we have two possibilities, either we can apply the rule $a : A_i \to \star y$ or the rule $a : A_i \to \star$. If we proceed in this way, and finally apply the only possible rule $A_i \to \star$ to rewrite remaining non-terminals in the array as $\star$'s, the system halts on the final configuration $\left\{ (\star \star \cdots \star \star) \; : \; \text{number of } \star's = |w|, w \in L^a 8dAP(\Pi_7) \right\}$. Note that what ever w may be, such that $|w| = n$, the halting array is of the form $\overbrace{\star \star \cdots \star \star}^{n}$. The regulated string is obtained by consuming a label of the rule in each step.   □

Remark 4. The context-sensitive language $\{a^n b^n c^n : n \geq 1\}$ can be accepted by an $8dAPS$ which gives the following proposition.

Proposition 2. $L^a 8dAP_\star - CF \neq \emptyset$.

Next in the hierarchy we look for CSL.

Theorem 3. $CS - L^a 8dAP_\star \neq \emptyset$.

Proof. For the proof of this theorem we give a context-sensitive language which can not be in any $L^a 8dAP_\star$. $L = \{a^{2^n} : n \geq 0\}$ is a context-sensitive language. Since L is over one letter alphabet and we intend to use no λ-rule, all the rules in the $L8dAPS^a$ must be an a-rule. Let $(\alpha)^\theta \to \beta_k^\theta$ be a θ-rotation rule such that α contains exactly one non-terminal (with zero or more number of terminals) and β_k contains exactly k non-terminals (with zero or more number of terminals). Suppose we assume that there exits a $L8dAPS^a$ Π_8 with m membranes that accepts L and halts on a configuration in F, where F is the set of final configurations. The nonexistence of such a system is shown for $m = 1$ first. The argument for m membrane P system will be identical to this. The reason is that in both situations we need infinite number of rules in the membrane system to build L. Let $\mathcal{A}_1, \mathcal{A}_2, \ldots, \mathcal{A}_n$ be the arrays in the initial configuration of Π_8.

We recall that the successful halting computation means the system must halt as well as the arrays remaining in the output membrane are terminal arrays (composed of only terminals).

In the following steps we actually look for rules in the membrane to build L recursively.

1. In order to accept a regulating string a, whose length is one, the system must go up to one step (transition). Therefore, each array $\mathcal{A}_1, \mathcal{A}_2, \ldots, \mathcal{A}_n$ in $\varPi_8$ must contain at most one non-terminal (no restriction on terminals). To reach the successful halting computation, we must apply one or more rules of type $a : \alpha^\theta \to \beta_0^\theta$. Note that we have introduced at least one new rule to accept the regulated string a.

2. By (1) above we know that each array $\mathcal{A}_1, \mathcal{A}_2, \ldots, \mathcal{A}_n$ contains at most one non-terminal. To accept regulating string a^2, the system must go up to two steps (transitions). In order to do this, at least to one of the array, we need to apply the rule of type $a : \alpha^\theta \to \beta_1^\theta$, which is a new rule. This rule may be recursive (repeat any number of times) or non-recursive (apply one time). If the rule is recursive, then it also accepts the strings $a^3, a^5, a^6, \ldots \notin L$. Suppose, it is non-recursive, we can apply it once, followed by an existing rule of type $\alpha^\theta \to \beta_0^\theta$ to halt the computation. Hence, to accept a^2, we have introduced a new rule of type $\alpha^\theta \to \beta_1^\theta$.

3. Similarly, in order to accept a^4, the system must go up to 4 steps. At least for one of the arrays we need to apply the rules in a way that there is no recursion. In all the possible cases, if any of the rule is recursive, it leads to the generation of a regulating string not in L. Therefore, the only possibility is non-recursive rules. In all the cases, we can see at least one new rule is required to accept a^4.

So, to accept each string in $L = \{a^{2^n} : n \geq 0\}$, we need to introduce at least one a-rule in each step. Since L is infinite, the number of a-rules required to accept L is also infinite.

Now we give the argumentative proof similar to the above to show that there does not exist any $L8dAPS^a$ to accept L. Suppose we assume that there is one such $L8dAPS^a$ $\varPi_8$ with m membranes. If at least in any one of the m membrane contain a recursive a-rule then, it leads to an infinite loop or the system accepts a string not in L. On the other hand, if the system contains only non recursive a-rules then, the number of a-rules must be infinite, which is a contradiction. Hence the theorem. $\qquad\Box$

Theorem 4. $L^a 8dAP_\star \subset CS$.

Proof. We show how $L8dAPS^a$ will be recognized by a linear bounded automaton. In order to do this, we simulate a computation of a $L8dAPS^a$ by remembering the number of symbols in the arrays and their corresponding shapes after the acceptance of each symbol in the regulating string. We then show that the total number of symbols in the arrays is bounded by the length of the regulating string.

Consider a regulating language L of a $L8dAPS^a$ Π_9 with m membranes and let p be the total number of rules in these m membranes. Let $w = b_1 b_2 \ldots b_l$, $l \geq 1$ be a regulating string in L. Let $\mathcal{A}_1, \mathcal{A}_2, \ldots, \mathcal{A}_n$ be the arrays in the m membranes of Π_9 in the initial configuration . We build a multi-track non-deterministic LBA B which simulates Π_9. In order for B to simulate Π_9, it has to keep track the symbols in the arrays and their shapes after accepting each symbol in the regulating string. So B has a track assigned to every rule of Π_9, a track for each pixel-symbol triple $(X, (x, y), i) \in V \times \mathbb{Z}^2 \times \{1, 2, \ldots, n\}$ and a track for each triple $(X, \mathcal{A}_i, j) \in V \times \{\mathcal{A}_1, \mathcal{A}_2, \ldots, \mathcal{A}_n\} \times \{0, 1, 2, \ldots\}$.

The array $\mathcal{A}_i$ plotted in the plane $Z = i$ is as follows: one of the symbols of the array $\mathcal{A}_i$ is plotted at $((0, 0), i)$, the origin of the plane $Z = i$. Fix this symbol, and place the other symbols of the array as follows: a symbol left to it is plotted at $((-1, 0), i)$; a symbol right to it is plotted at $((1, 0), i)$; a symbol above to it is plotted at $((0, 1), i)$; a symbol below to it is plotted at $((0, -1), i)$; a symbol 45 degree angle to it, is plotted at $((1, 1), i)$; a symbol 135 degree angle to it, is plotted at $((-1, 1), i)$; a symbol 225 degree angle to it, is plotted at $((-1, -1), i)$; a symbol 315 degree angle to it, is plotted at $((1, -1), i)$. In general, if the fixed symbol is in the position $((x, y), i)$, then a symbol left to it, is plotted at $((x - 1, y), i)$; a symbol right to it, is plotted at $((x + 1, y), i)$; a symbol above to it, is plotted at $((x, y + 1), i)$; a symbol below to it, is plotted at $((x, y - 1), i)$; a symbol 45 degree angle to it, is plotted at $((x + 1, y + 1), i)$; a symbol 135 degree angle to it, is plotted at $((x - 1, y + 1), i)$; a symbol 225 degree angle to it, is plotted at $((x - 1, y - 1), i)$; a symbol 315 degree angle to it, is plotted at $((x + 1, y - 1), i)$. If any symbol of the array remains, then change the fixed symbol and repeat the same procedure till all the symbols in the array are plotted.

B keeps track of the configuration of Π_9 by writing a positive integer 1 on each track assigned to the symbol-pixel triple $(X, (x, y), i)$, the symbol X being plotted in the pixel (x, y) of the plane $Z = i$. And also writing a positive integer on each track assigned to the symbol-configuration triple $(X, \mathcal{A}_i, j)$, denoting the number of symbols X in the array $\mathcal{A}_i$ at the configuration j. Then for each triple $(X, (x, y), i)$, B examines the chosen rule set and plots the symbols X in the pixel (x, y) of the plane $Z = i$ by the procedure mentioned above, increasing the number on the track $(X, \mathcal{A}_i, j)$ accordingly. We can see that in any step of the computation, the tracks contain integers bounded by the number of symbols inside Π_9 during the corresponding computation step. The shape of the arrays also preserved.

The number of symbols in the arrays in a configuration C during a computation step is bounded by $S(i)$, where i is the number of symbols generated. Then the space used by B to record the configurations and to calculate the configuration change of Π_9 is bounded by $t \times log_b(S(i))$, where b denotes the base of the track alphabet and t denotes the number of tracks used. Finally, B checks whether any more rules can be applied. If not, and also if it reaches the configuration in F (set of final configurations), it accepts the regulating string w, otherwise it rejects. So the number of symbols in the arrays present in the system is bounded by the input length and hence the accepted language is context-sensitive language.   □

Theorem 5. $L_\lambda^a 8dAP_\star = RE$.

Proof. The inclusion $L_\lambda^a 8dAP_\star \subseteq RE$ follows from Church-Turing hypothesis.

For the proof of the inclusion $RE \subseteq L_\lambda^a 8dAP_\star$, it is enough to prove that $RE \subseteq L_\lambda^a 8dAP_1$, since $L_\lambda^a 8dAP_1 \subseteq L_\lambda^a 8dAP_\star$.

Let $H = \{a_1, a_2, \ldots, a_k\}$ and let $L \subseteq H^*$ be a recursively enumerable language. Let $e : H \mapsto \{1^1, 1^2, 1^3, \ldots, 1^k\}$ such that $e(a_i) = 1^i$, $1 \le i \le k$. The encoding for a string $w = a_i a_j \ldots a_l$, $a_i, a_j, \ldots, a_l \in H$ is as follows: $e(w) = 0e(a_i)0e(a_j)0\ldots 0e(a_l)0$.

For any L, there exists a Turing machine $M = (K, \{0, 1\}, \Gamma, \delta, q_0, F')$ which halts after processing the input i_0 placed in its input tape if and only if $i_0 = e(w)$ for some $w \in L$. So it is sufficient to show how to simulate the encoding $e(w)$, and simulate the transitions of the Turing machine with a $L8dAPS^a$. The transitions of the Turing machine are simulated by a $L8dAPS^a$ is as follows:

- The transition $\delta(q, a) = (p, b, R)$ is simulated by the θ-rotation rule $(q\ a\ c)^0 \rightarrow (b\ p\ c)^0$, where c is some non-blank symbol.
- The transition $\delta(q, a) = (p, b, L)$ is simulated by the θ-rotation rule $(c\ q\ a)^0 \rightarrow (p\ c\ b)^0$, where c is some non-blank symbol.

We construct a $L8dAPS^a$ $\Pi' = \left(V, T, [_1]_1, I_1, R_1, 1, H, F\right)$, where $V = \{q_0, q_1, \ldots, q_k, 0, 1, x\}$, $T = \{0, 1, x\}$, $I_1 = \{q_0\ 0\ e(a_i)\ 0\ e(a_j)\ 0\ \ldots\ 0\ e(a_l)\ 0\ 0\}$, $R_1 = \{a_i : (q_0\ 0\ 1)^0 \rightarrow (0\ q_i\ 1)^0 : a_i \in H,\ 1 \le i \le k\} \cup$ set of all θ-rotation rules corresponding to the transitions of the Turing machine M which are labeled with λ. The set of final configurations is $F = \left\{\left(e(w)x\right) : w \in L\right\}$.

The $L8dAPS^a$ Π' performs the following operations.

1. For $1 \le i \le k$, and the symbol $a_i \in H$, the rule $(q_0\ 0\ 1)^0 \rightarrow (0\ q_i\ 1)^0$, labeled with a_i is used which introduce the symbol q_i, it is the symbol used in the first transition for generating the encoding in Step 2.
2. Perform the computation $e(au) = 0e(a)e(u)$, $u \in H^+$, $a \in H$. Assume that the encoding of w is represented by encoding of each symbol of u padded by 0 on both ends. The simulation of au is performed by the following subprogram.
   $\delta(q_i, 1) = (q_{i-1}, 1, R)$, $i = i,\ i-1,\ i-2, \ldots,\ 3,\ 2$.
   $\delta(q_1, 1) = (q_0, 1, R)$
   The transitions of the sub-program can be simulated by the θ-rotation rules as shown in the beginning of the proof, and these rules are assigned with label λ.
3. Repeat the Steps 1 and 2 non-deterministically until the last symbol of the regulated string w gets over.

4. The output array remains in the system is $\left\{ \left(e(w)x \right) \ : \ w \in L \right\}$, which is the final configuration. The array reduced in the system is equal to $e(w)x$ for some $w \in H^+$. We now start to simulate the working of the Turing machine M in recognizing the string $e(w)$. If the Turing machine halts, by introducing the following transitions:

$\delta(q_0, 0) = (0, x, R)$

and the corresponding θ-rotation rule is labeled with λ then $w \in L$, otherwise the machine goes into an infinite loop.

So, we can see that the computation halts after accepting a string w if and only if $w \in L$. $\qquad\qquad\qquad\qquad\qquad\qquad\qquad\qquad\qquad\qquad\qquad\qquad\qquad\qquad\qquad$ $\square$

5 Concluding Remarks

In this paper we introduced a new array P system called 8-directional array P system ($8dAPS$) and regulating $8dAPS$. The data structure 'string' is interpreted as 'turtle-like' graphs with a possibilities to turn in multiples of 45 degrees. This P system-based fractal description model can be used to construct several interesting pictures. The regulating evolution of this model makes the system more interesting. The regulating languages are from Chomsky hierarchy. We also understand the halting nature of this P system by means of 'dependability'. By dependability we mean to study the halting nature or halting configurations of P system via string over the labels of the rules. We know that in our model every rule is labeled and strings over the label set lead the application of the rules. Such strings decide the strategy of movements in the parallel distributed computing model, P system. Hence the study becomes significant. The main difference between grammar rewriting system of describing some space filling curves like 'Koch curve' and our recursive 8-directional array P system is that, we do not re-scale the template. If we are able to record some where in the system the shrinking effect, then our $8dAPS$ can generate almost all curves like 'Koch curve', Peano curve etc. One can also extend the study to understand more about space filling curves which have important role in antenna designing.

References

1. Păun, G., Rozenberg, G., Salomaa, A. (eds.): The Oxford Handbook of Membrane Computing. Oxford University Press, Oxford (2010)
2. Rama, R., Krishna, S.N., Krithivasan, K.: P Systems with picture Objects. Acta Cybern. **55**(1), 53–74 (2001)
3. Ceterchi, R., Mutyam, M., Păun, G., Subramanian, K.G.: Array-rewriting P systems. Nat. Comput. **2**, 229–249 (2003)
4. Krithivasan, K., Păun, G., Ramanujan, A.: On controlled P systems. Fundamenta Informaticae **131**(3–4), 451–464 (2014)
5. Rama, R., Sureshkumar, W.: Regulating a distributed computing model via chomsky hierarchy. J. Math. Stat. Oper. Res. **3**(1), 21–29 (2015)

6. Rosenfeld, A.: Isotonic grammars, parallel grammars, and picture grammars. Machine Intelligence VI. American Elsevier, New York (1971)
7. Freund, R.: Array grammars. Technical report 15/00, Research Group on Mathematical Linguistics, Rovira i Virgili University, Tarragona, p. 164 (2000)
8. Krithivasan, K., Anindya, D.: Terminal weighted grammars and picture description. Comput. Vis. Graph. Image Process. **30**, 13–31 (1985)

Sorting Using Spiking Neural P Systems with Anti-spikes and Rules on Synapses

Venkata Padmavati Metta[1]([☒]) and Alica Kelemenová[2]

[1] Bhilai Institute of Technology, Durg, India
vmetta@gmail.com
[2] Institute of Computer Science and Research Institute of the IT4Innovations Centre of Excellence, Silesian University in Opava, Opava, Czech Republic
alice.kelemenova@fpf.slu.cz

Abstract. This paper introduces and makes use of spiking neural P systems with anti-spikes and rules on synapses to sort integers. Here we discuss two types of sorting, bead sort and bitonic sort to sort integers.

1 Introduction

Spiking neural P systems (in short, SN P systems) introduced in [10] are parallel and distributed computing models which abstract the way neurons communicate by means of electrical impulses of identical shape, called spikes. There exist many variants of spiking neural P systems. However, in some cases, the difference in these variants are not with the actual structural features but with execution semantics like maximal, sequential, asynchronous, exhaustive etc. Some of them have special concepts like extended rules [1], astrocytes [7], anti-spikes [13], neuron division and budding [14], rules on the synapses [17] etc. We refer to the respective chapter of [15] for general information in this area, and to the membrane computing website from [18] for details.

Here we introduce the hybrid model of SN P systems combining the features of anti-spikes with rules on the synapses and name them as spiking neural P systems with anti-spikes and rules on synapses (in short, SN PA systems with rules on synapses). So these systems make use of two types of objects called spikes (a) and anti-spikes $(\bar{a})$. The use of anti-spikes not only simplify the complexity of the rules but also allow to include negative numbers in computing.

In standard SN P systems the rules reside inside neurons and upon firing the spikes emitted by the neurons are sent to all neighbouring neurons through their outgoing synapses. Instead of rules inside neurons, here we have rules on the synapses. At any step, when the number of spikes/anti-spikes present in a given neuron is satisfied by a rule on a synapse leaving from that neuron, the rule is enabled and upon firing a spike/an anti-spike is sent to the neuron at the end of the synapse. As expected, the SN PA systems with rules on synapses are able to compute all Turing computable sets of numbers.

Sorting is one of the most frequent operations in many applications, and parallel algorithms for sorting have been studied since the beginning of parallel computing. P systems are used to simulate various sorting algorithms [2,3].

© Springer International Publishing Switzerland 2015
G. Rozenberg et al. (Eds.): CMC 2015, LNCS 9504, pp. 290–303, 2015.
DOI: 10.1007/978-3-319-28475-0_20

Batcher's bitonic sorting network [6] was one of the first methods proposed. The method is simulated to sort non-negative integers using P systems [3] and SN P systems [8]. In this paper we simulate the bitonic sorting network using SN PA systems with rules on synapses to sort integers.

Another natural parallel sorting algorithm for sorting non-negative integers is bead sort [5]. This algorithm was also simulated using P systems in [4]. Ionescu and Sburlan in [11] used SN P system to sort n non-negative integers, and the model consisted of 3 layers of n neurons each. The first layer was made up of input neurons which in the initial configuration contained the input values codified as numbers of spikes. At each time unit these neurons sent one spike each to the second layer. This layer decanted the spikes to the third layer, where the output neurons were located. After a number of steps equal to the maximum value of the n numbers, the ith output neuron received the ith smallest value, codified as number of spikes, sorting thus in ascending order. In a way, the idea of the algorithm is the same as that of bead sort. The model makes use of $3n$ neurons, $(3n^2 + n)/2$ synapses and $n^2 + n$ rules. The time complexity of the algorithm is $O(M)$ where M is the maximum of the n numbers. In this paper we use SN PA systems with rules on synapses to simulate the algorithm and observe that this model makes use of $2n + 2$ neurons, $4n$ synapses and $n^2 + 3n$ rules to sort n integers, which is comparatively less complex than the system in [11].

2   Prerequisites

We assume the reader to be familiar with formal language theory and membrane computing. The reader can find details about them in [15, 16] etc.

For an alphabet V, V^* is the free monoid generated by V with respect to the concatenation operation and the identity λ (the empty string); the set of all non-empty strings over V, that is, $V^* - \{\lambda\}$, is denoted by V^+. When $V = \{a\}$ is a singleton, then we write a^* and a^+ instead of $\{a\}^*$ and $\{a\}^+$.

A regular expression over an alphabet V is defined as: (i) λ and each $a \in V$ is a regular expression, (ii) if E_1, E_2 are regular expressions over V, then $(E_1)(E_2)$, $(E_1) \cup (E_2)$, and $(E_1)^+$ are regular expressions over V, and (iii) nothing else is a regular expression over V. With each expression E we associate a language $L(E)$, defined in the following way: (i) $L(\lambda) = \{\lambda\}$ and $L(a) = \{a\}$, for all $a \in V$, (ii) $L((E_1) \cup (E_2)) = L(E_1) \cup L(E_2)$, $L((E_1)(E_2)) = L(E_1)L(E_2)$, and $L((E_1)^+) = L(E_1)^+$, for all regular expressions E_1, E_2 over V.

We now introduce spiking neural P systems with anti-spikes and rules on synapses.

2.1   Spiking Neural P Systems with Anti-spikes and Rules on Synapses

A spiking neural P system with anti-spikes and rules on synapses, of degree $m \geq 1$, is a construct

$$\Pi = (O, \sigma_1, \sigma_2, \sigma_3, \ldots, \sigma_m, syn, IN, OUT), \text{ where}$$

1. $O = \{a, \bar{a}\}$ is a binary alphabet; a is called *spike* and $\bar{a}$ is called an *anti-spike*.
2. $\sigma_1, \sigma_2, \sigma_3, \ldots, \sigma_m$ are neurons of the form $\sigma_i = (n_i)$ with $1 \leq i \leq m$ where n_i is the number of spikes or anti-spikes contained in the neuron σ_i and if $n_i > 0$ then the neuron is having n_i spikes and if $n_i < 0$ then the neuron is having $\mid n_i \mid$ anti-spikes;
3. *syn* is the set of synapses; each element in *syn* is a pair of the form $((i, j), R(i, j))$, where (i, j) indicates that there is a synapse connecting neurons σ_i and σ_j, with $i, j \in \{1, 2, \ldots, m\}$, $i \neq j$, and $R(i, j)$ is a finite set of rules of the following two forms:
   (i) $E/b^r \rightarrow b'$ where $b, b' \in \{a, \bar{a}\}$, $r \geq 1$ and E is a regular expression over b;
   (ii) $b^s \rightarrow \lambda$ for some $s \geq 1$, with the restriction that $b^s \notin L(E)$ for any rule $E/b^r \rightarrow b'$ of type (i) from $R(i, j)$;
   There are four categories of spiking rules identified by $(b, b') \in \{(a, a), (a, \bar{a}), (\bar{a}, a), (\bar{a}, \bar{a})\}$.
4. *IN*, *OUT* $\subseteq \{1, 2, 3, \ldots, m\}$ are the set of input and output neurons respectively.

A rule $E/b^r \rightarrow b' \in R(i, j)$ with $b, b' \in \{a, \bar{a}\}$ is applied as follows. If the neuron σ_i contains number of bs equal to c, and $b^c \in L(E)$, $c \geq r$, then the rule can *fire*, and upon application, r spikes of kind bs are consumed (thus only $c - r$ remain in σ_i) and a b' is released, which will immediately exit the neuron. The spike/anti-spike emitted by neuron σ_i will pass immediately to all neurons σ_j such that $E/b^r \rightarrow b' \in R(i, j)$. This means that the transmission of spike/anti-spike takes no waiting time (since the rules do not specify a time delay), the spike/anti-spike will be available in neuron σ_j in the next step. There is an additional restriction that a and $\bar{a}$ cannot stay together, they annihilate each other. If a neuron has either objects a or objects $\bar{a}$, and further objects of either type (maybe both) arrive from other neurons, such that we end with a^q and $\bar{a}^s$ inside, then immediately an annihilation rule $a\bar{a} \rightarrow \lambda$ (which is implicit in each neuron), is applied in a maximal manner, so that either a^{q-s} or $(\bar{a})^{s-q}$ remain for the next step, provided that $q \geq s$ or $s \geq q$, respectively. This mutual annihilation of spikes and anti-spikes takes no waiting time and the annihilation rule has priority over spiking and forgetting rules, so each neuron always contains either only spikes or anti-spikes. If we have a rule $E/b^r \rightarrow b'$ with $L(E) = \{b^r\}$, then we write it in the simplified form as $b^r \rightarrow b'$ and call it pure. The rules of the form $b^s \rightarrow \lambda \in R(i, j)$ are called forgetting rules. If the neuron contains exactly s number of bs, then the forgetting rule $b^s \rightarrow \lambda$ can be applied removing s number of bs from the neuron immediately.

The *configuration* of the system is described by $\mathcal{C} = \langle \beta_1, \beta_2, \ldots, \beta_m \rangle$, where β_i is the number of spikes/anti-spikes present in neuron σ_i. At any moment, if $\beta_i > 0$, it means that there are β_i spikes in neuron σ_i; if $\beta_i < 0$, it indicates that neuron σ_i contains $\mid \beta_i \mid$ anti-spikes. The initial configuration is $\mathcal{C}_0 = \langle n_1, n_2, \ldots, n_m \rangle$.

As usual in SN P systems, a global clock is assumed, marking the time for all neurons and synapses. In each time unit, if a synapse (i, j) can use one of its rules, then a rule from $R(i, j)$ must be used. It is possible that there is more than one rule that can be used on a synapse at some moment, since two firing rules, $E_1/b^c \rightarrow b'$ and $E_2/\hat{b}^r \rightarrow \hat{b}'$ may have $L(E_1) \cap L(E_2) \neq \emptyset$ where $\{b, b', \hat{b}, \hat{b}'\} \in \{a, \overline{a}\}$. In this case, the synapse will non-deterministically choose one of the enabled rules to be used.

The system works sequentially on each synapse (at most one rule from each set $R(i, j)$ can be used), and in parallel at the level of the system (if a synapse has at least one rule enabled, then it has to use a rule).

A delicate problem appears when several synapses starting from the same neuron have rules which can be applied. We work here with the restriction that all rules which are applied consume the same number of spikes from the given neuron. Let us assume that the applied rules on the synapses leaving from σ_i are of the form $E_u/b^c \rightarrow b'$ then c number of bs are removed from σ_i (and not a multiple of c, according to the number of applied rules). Of course, this restriction can be replaced by another strategy: various rules can consume various numbers of spikes and the sum of these numbers of spikes is removed from the neuron.

Using the rules in this way, we pass from one configuration of the system to another configuration; such a step is called a transition. For two configurations $\mathcal{C}$ and $\mathcal{C}'$ of Π we denote by $\mathcal{C} \Longrightarrow \mathcal{C}'$, if there is a direct transition from $\mathcal{C}$ to $\mathcal{C}'$ in Π.

A computation of Π is a finite or infinite sequence of transitions starting from the initial configuration, and every configuration appearing in such a sequence is called reachable. A computation halts if it reaches a configuration where no rule can be used. With any halting computation, we associate a number of spikes/anti-spikes appearing in the output neurons which encode the vector of integer numbers as the output of the system. When both the input and output neurons are considered, the system can be used as a transducer. Henceforth in the paper, SN P systems with anti-spikes and rules on synapses are used as transducers and are referred to as SN PA systems.

3   Bitonic Sorting Network

This section describes a variant of a sorting network called bitonic network that has a fast sorting or ordering capability. A sorting network can be used as a multiple-input, multiple-output switching network. Other applications of sorting networks are as a switching network with buffering, a multi-access memory, a multi-access content-addressable memory, and as a multiprocessor. The advantage of bitonic networks is the flexibility (one network can accommodate input lists of various lengths) and the modularity (a large network can be split up into several identical modules).

The basic component of a bitonic sorting network is a comparator. A comparator is a device with two inputs x and y and two outputs l and h. For an increasing comparator, $l = min(x, y)$ and $h = max(x, y)$; for a decreasing comparator $l = max(x, y)$ and $h = min(x, y)$. Figure 1 gives the schematic representation of the two types of comparators. As two elements enter the input wires of the comparator, they are compared and, if necessary, exchanged before

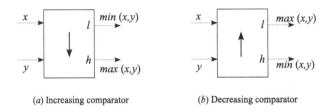

(a) Increasing comparator   (b) Decreasing comparator

Fig. 1. A schematic representation of comparators

they go to the output wires. We denote an increasing comparator by $\downarrow$ and a decreasing comparator by $\uparrow$.

The key operation of the bitonic sorting network is the rearrangement of a bitonic sequence into a sorted sequence. A bitonic sequence is a sequence of elements $< a_0, a_1, \ldots, a_{n-1} >$ with the property that either (1) there exists an index i, $0 \leq i \leq n - 1$, such that $< a_0, \ldots, a_i >$ is monotonically increasing and $< a_{i+1}, \ldots, a_{n-1} >$ is monotonically decreasing, or (2) there exists a cyclic shift of indices so that (1) is satisfied. For example, $< 1, 2, 4, 7, 6, 0 >$ is a bitonic sequence, because it first increases and then decreases.

We present a method to rearrange a bitonic sequence to obtain a monotonically increasing sequence. Let $S =< a_0, a_1, \ldots, a_{n-1} >$ be a bitonic sequence such that $a_0 \leq a_1 \leq, \ldots, \leq a_{n/2-1}$ and $a_{n/2} \geq a_{n/2+1} \geq, \ldots, \geq a_{n-1}$. Consider the following subsequences of S:

$S_1 =< min(a_0, a_{n/2}), min(a_1, a_{n/2+1}), \ldots, min(a_{n/2-1}, a_{n-1}) >$
$S_2 =< max(a_0, a_{n/2}), max(a_1, a_{n/2+1}), \ldots, max(a_{n/2-1}, a_{n-1}) >$.

The sequences S_1 and S_2 are bitonic sequences. Furthermore, every element of the first sequence is smaller than every element of the second sequence. Thus, we have reduced the initial problem of rearranging a bitonic sequence of size n to that of rearranging two smaller bitonic sequences and concatenating the results. We refer to the operation of splitting a bitonic sequence S of size n into the two bitonic sequences S_1 and S_2 as a *bitonic split*. Although in obtaining S_1 and S_2 we assumed that the original sequence had increasing and decreasing sequences of the same length, the bitonic split operation also holds for any bitonic sequence.

We can recursively obtain shorter bitonic sequences using bitonic split for each of the bitonic subsequences until we obtain subsequences of size one. At that point, the output is sorted in monotonically increasing order. Since after each bitonic split operation the size of the problem is halved, the number of splits required to rearrange the bitonic sequence into a sorted sequence is $log\ n$. The procedure of sorting a bitonic sequence using a series of bitonic splits is called *bitonic merge*.

So the key components of a bitonic sorting network are the bitonic splitters and the bitonic mergers. The splitter of size n takes as input a bitonic sequence of length n and partitions it in two bitonic sequences of equal length. A bitonic merger of size n consists of a splitter of size n and of two mergers of size $n/2$, of

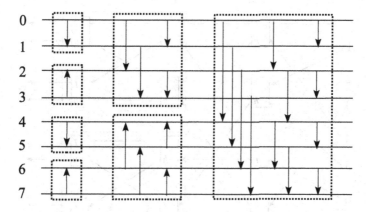

Fig. 2. A bitonic sorting network for $n = 8$. The network can be partitioned into three stages, each has bitonic mergers of size 2, 4, and 8 respectively.

opposite direction. It accepts as input a bitonic sequence and sorts it in ascending or descending order (direction).

Figure 2 illustrates a typical bitonic sorting network for sorting $n = 8$ numbers in ascending order. The input wires are numbered $0, 1, \ldots, n - 1$. The network can be partitioned into three stages, each has bitonic mergers of size 2, 4, and 8 respectively. Each stage has column of comparators drawn separately. The network takes an unsorted sequence of size 8 and outputs it in ascending order.

Let us now see how this network works. The first stage groups the list into $n/2$ bitonic sequences of length two. A sequence of two elements x and y forms a bitonic sequence, since either $x \leq y$, in which case the bitonic sequence has x and y in the increasing part and no elements in the decreasing part, or $x \geq y$, in which case the bitonic sequence has x and y in the decreasing part and no elements in the increasing part. Hence, any unsorted sequence of elements is a concatenation of bitonic sequences of size two. It merges the adjacent bitonic sequences in increasing and decreasing order to get bitonic sequences of size four.

So each stage of the network shown in Fig. 2 merges adjacent bitonic sequences in increasing and decreasing order. According to the definition of a bitonic sequence, the sequence obtained by concatenating the increasing and decreasing sequences is bitonic. Hence, the output of each stage in the network in Fig. 2 is a concatenation of bitonic sequences that are twice as long as those at the input. By merging larger and larger bitonic sequences, we eventually obtain a bitonic sequence of size n. Merging this sequence sorts the input. We refer to the algorithm embodied in this method as bitonic sort and the network as a bitonic sorting network. The first three stages of the network are shown in Fig. 2. The last stage of Fig. 2 is shown explicitly in Fig. 3.

A network can also be represented as a directed acyclic graph [9].

Definition 1 (Network). *A network T of size n is a directed acyclic graph such that:*

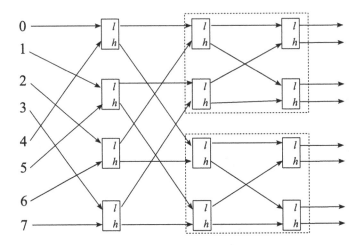

Fig. 3. Biotonic merger of size 8 represented as a graph

1. *there are n nodes, called input terminals, with in-degree 0 and out-degree 1, labeled from 0 to n − 1;*
2. *there are n nodes, called output terminals, with in-degree 1 and out-degree 0, labeled from 0 to n − 1;*
3. *all the remaining nodes u, representing comparators, have in-degree and out-degree 2.*

Figure 3 represents the bitonic merger under the above formalism. We define the depth of a node u of network T, $d(u)$, as the length of the longest path in T from an input node to u. The depth of network T, $d(T)$, is the maximum depth of a node of in-degree and out-degree 2 in T.

The last stage of an n-element bitonic sorting network contains a bitonic merging network with n inputs. This has a depth of $log\ n$. The other stages perform a complete sort of $n/2$ elements. Hence, the depth, $d(T)$, of the network in Fig. 2 is given by $\Theta(log^2 n)$.

The arcs of a network can be partitioned in n arc-disjoint paths, each joining an input node to an output node. Such a partition yields a line-representation of T, as in [12].

4   Bitonic Sorting of Integers Using SN PA Systems with Rules on the Synapses

We note that the above representation is a theoretical model which indicates the comparisons between input values. However, in the context of SN PA systems with rules on synapses, this model has a straightforward implementation. We encode the positive numbers as the number of spikes, negative numbers as the number of anti-spikes and zero with the symbol λ. Each wire is now represented by a synapse between two neurons, and each value x travels between two neurons as x spikes/anti-spikes, one spike/anti-spike per time unit. Comparators are implemented by a set of neurons which send the minimum and the maximum (as number of spikes/anti-spikes) through designated synapses. Once these two ingredients are at hand, we proceed to construct an SN PA system in the same way the original sorting network was constructed.

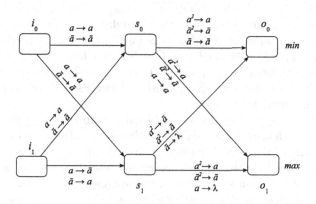

(*a*) Increasing comparator

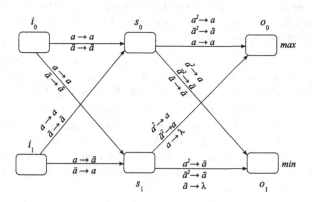

(*b*) Decreasing comparator

Fig. 4. SN PA with rules on synapses as comparator of integers

In this section we are concerned only with comparators of two elements, hence with SN PA systems which sort two numbers (for brevity called SN PA comparators). In Fig. 4(*a*) we give an ascending comparator, and in Fig. 4(*b*) we give a descending comparator. Consider the SN PA system modeling an ascending comparator in Fig. 4(*a*) and the numbers x and y to be sorted. In order to be able to use these SN PA systems with rules on synapses as building blocks of a bitonic sorting network, we assume that instead of loading the numbers

x and y as spikes/anti-spikes in i_0 and i_1 in the initial configuration, they are fed one by one to these input neurons by another neuron. At each step they instantaneously send one spike/anti-spike to both s_0 and s_1. Here there are two cases. The first case is if both the values are non-negative (negative) then as long as both the neurons i_0 and i_1 are sending their spikes (anti-spikes) in each step of the computation, only s_0 has two spikes (two anti-spikes) and thus sending a spike (an anti-spike) to both the output neurons o_0 and o_1. During these steps neuron s_1 remains empty because of the annihilation of spike and anti-spike it receives. After one input neuron has consumed all its spikes (anti-spikes), the minimum (maximum) is obtained in o_0 (o_1). There will be only one input neuron to send spikes (anti-spikes) to s_0 and s_1. In this case also, the outgoing synapse from s_1 forgets its spike (anti-spike), and s_0 forwards it to o_1 (o_0), where the maximum (minimum) is obtained.

The other case is if one value is non-negative and the other one is negative then as long as both i_0 and i_1 are sending their spikes/anti-spikes, only s_1 has two spikes or two anti-spikes and thus sending an anti-spike to neuron o_0 and a spike to neuron o_1 (since negative values are always less than non-negative values). During these steps neuron s_0 remains empty because of the annihilation of spike and anti-spike it receives. After one input neuron has consumed its spikes (anti-spikes), the maximum (minimum) value is obtained in o_1 (o_0). There will be only one input neuron to send anti-spikes (spikes) to s_0 and s_1. In this case, the outgoing synapse from s_1 forgets its spikes (anti-spikes), and s_0 sends them to o_0 (o_1), where the minimum (maximum) is obtained Now we prove the composition lemma for SN PA increasing comparators.

Lemma 1. *(Composition lemma for increasing comparator). Suppose that in each time unit from t_0 until $t_0 + (|x| - 1)$ neuron i_0 receives one spike/anti-spike and that in a rest it does not receive any spike/anti-spike. Analogously, suppose that in each time unit from t_0 to $t_0 + (|y| - 1)$ neuron i_1 receives one spike/anti-spike, and that in a rest it does not receive any spike/anti-spike. Then neurons o_0 and o_1 either or both receive spike/anti-spike only for time moments from $t_0 + 2$ until $t_0 + 2 + (max(|x|, |y|) - 1)$ and at time moment $t_0 + 2 + max(|x|, |y|)$, the minimum and maximum of x and y codified as number of spikes/anti-spikes are stored in o_0 and o_1 respectively.*

Proof. Consider the time moment t, with $t_0 \leq t \leq t_0 + (min(|x|, |y|) - 1)$. Both neurons i_0 and i_1 receive spikes/anti-spikes and in turn send them through the synapses by the rules. One of the neurons s_0 and s_1 has spikes/anti-spikes depending on the values of x and y, neuron s_0 or s_1 sends one spike/anti-spike to both of the neurons o_0 and o_1. Therefore at time moment $t + 2$ neurons o_0 and o_1 receive their first spike/anti-spike each. This continues till the step $t_0 + 2 + (min(|x|, |y|) - 1)$. From time moment $t_0 + min(|x|, |y|)$ onward, only one neuron of i_0 and i_1 sends spikes/anti-spikes, hence the rules on the outgoing synapses of s_0 and s_1 prevent one of o_0 and o_1 from receiving other spikes/anti-spikes. The first part of the claim is proved.

At each time moment t, with $t_0 + min(x, y) \leq t \leq t_0 + (max(x, y) - 1)$, one of the neurons o_0 and o_1 receives one spike/anti-spike at moment $t + 2$. After time moment $t_0 + max(|x|, |y|)$ there are no other spikes/anti-spikes enters into the system, hence from time moment $t_0 + 2 + max(|x|, |y|)$ onward there will be no other spikes entering neurons o_0 and o_1. The minimum and maximum of x and y codified as number of spikes/anti-spikes are stored in o_0 and o_1, respectively. A similar lemma is valid in the case of a SN PA decreasing comparator.

Assume that we are given a network T as a graph, and that we have a line representation of it (i.e., a set of n arc-disjoint path linking input terminals with output terminals). Hence, we extend Definition 1, by labeling edges, apart from input and output terminals. For every path that begins with input terminal labeled i, we label all its edges with i. More formally, we have the following definition.

Definition 2 (**Edge labeling**). *Given a graph T as in Definition 1 representing a sorting network, and a line-representation of T, we attach to each edge $e \in E(T)$ that belongs to a path in the line representation of T beginning with i, label $l(e) = l(i)$ (supposing that i is labeled with $l(i)$).*

For example, in Fig. 3, we have a labeled bitonic merger. A SN PA system modeling a sorting network given as a graph is obtained in the following way. For each input terminal node l we have a corresponding input neuron i_l. For each comparator (ascending / descending) we have the s- and o-neurons of a SN PA comparator (ascending / descending). For each edge of the graph between two comparators we have synapses between corresponding SN PA comparators. The output terminal nodes are the o-neurons of the last SN PA comparators.

More formally, we construct and label the SN PA system in the following recursive way.

1. for each input terminal node l we have a corresponding input neuron $i_l = i_{l,1}$, $0 \le l \le n - 1$;
2. for each comparator at depth $1 \le k \le d(T)$ with incident edges labeled with l and j, $l < j$, we add the s- and o-neurons of a SN PA comparator, connected in the previously specified way. With the notations in Fig. 4, let s_0 and s_1, and o_0 and o_1 be the s-, and o-neurons, respectively, just added. We add synapses between the following pairs of neurons: $((i_{l,k}, s_0), \{a \to a, \overline{a} \to \overline{a}\})$, $((i_{l,k}, s_1), \{a \to a, \overline{a} \to \overline{a}\})$, $((i_{j,k}, s_0), \{a \to a, \overline{a} \to \overline{a}\})$, $((i_{j,k}, s_1), \{a \to \overline{a}, \overline{a} \to a\})$. Additionally, if $k < d(T)$, we label o_0 with $o_{l,k} = i_{l,k+1}$, and o_1 with $o_{j,k} = i_{j,k+1}$; else we label o_0 with $o_{l,k} = o_l$, and o_1 with $o_{j,k} = o_j$.

As an example, Fig. 5 depicts an SN PA system with rules on synapses which models the bitonic merger of size 8.

Theorem 1. *For any SN PA ascending comparator at depth k corresponding to a comparator with incident edges $l < j$ which carry values x and y, respectively, we have that*

1. *in each time moment from $2(k-1)$ until $2(k-1) + |x|$ neuron $i_{l,k}$ receives one spike;*

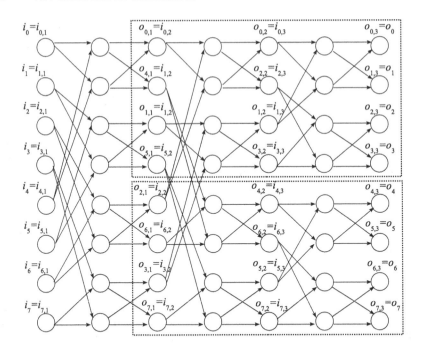

Fig. 5. SN PA system modelling the bitonic merger of size 8

2. *in each time moment from $2(k-1)$ until $2(k-1)+|y|$ neuron $i_{j,k}$ receives one spike.*
3. *in each time moment from $2k$ until $2k+min(|x|,|y|)$ both the neurons $o_{l,k}$ and $o_{j,k}$ receive one spike/anti-spike*
4. *in each time moment from $2k+min(|x|,|y|)+1$ until $2k+max(|x|,|y|)$ either of the neurons $o_{l,k}$ and $o_{j,k}$ receives one spike/anti-spike*

Proof. We prove the claim by induction on k. When $k=1$ we are at time moment $t=0$. We have explained previously that the behaviour of the system when the spikes/anti-spikes are loaded initially in the input neurons is identical to when they are fed one by one to these neurons. Claims 3 and 4 are true from Lemma 1 and $t_0 = 0$. We now suppose that the claim is true for k, with $1 \leq k < log\ n$, and prove it for $k+1$. From claims 3 and 4 of the induction hypothesis, we know that both the neurons $o_{l,k} = i_{l,k+1}$, $o_{j,k} = i_{j,k+1}$ receive one spike/anti-spike from $2k$ until $2k + min(|x|,|y|)$, where $min(|x|,|y|)$ is the number of spikes/anti-spikes carried by both the wires l and j before the comparator at depth $k+1$. After that, only one of the neurons $o_{l,k} = i_{l,k+1}$, $o_{j,k} = i_{j,k+1}$ receives one spike/spikes from $2k + min(|x|,|y|) + 1$ until $2k + max(|x|,|y|)$, where $max(|x|,|y|) - min(|x|,|y|)$ is the number of spikes/anti-spikes carried by wire l or j before the comparator at depth $k+1$. After the step $2k + max(|x|,|y|)$, the minimum $u = min(x,y)$ is stored $o_{l,k}$ and $v = max(x,y)$ is stored $o_{j,k}$. This proves claims 1 and 2. If we take $t_0 = 2k$, $x = u$, and $y = v$ in Lemma 1, we have that claims 3 and 4 are true.

5   Bead Sorting of Integers Using SN PA Systems with Rules on the Synapses

Here we design an SN PA system Π_s with rules on synapses that can sort n integers in ascending order. This model drastically decreases the complexity in terms of the number of neurons and synapses. We encode the positive numbers as the number of spikes, negative numbers as the number of anti-spikes and zero with the symbol λ.

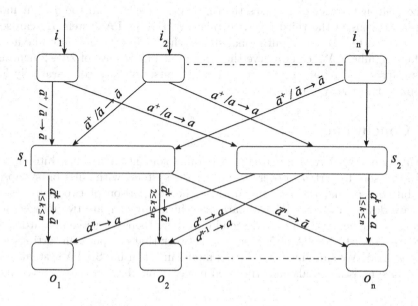

Fig. 6. SN PA system with rules on synapses Π_s for sorting integers

The SN PA system Π_s shown in Fig. 6 has n input neurons, n output neurons and two intermediate neurons (labeled s_1 and s_2). The input is stored in the first line of the system (hence in the neurons labeled i_1, i_2, ..., i_n) encoded in the form of number spikes/anti-spikes. Each input neuron has two synapses, one to neuron s_1 and the other to neuron s_2. At each step, each input neuron until not empty, sends an anti-spike to s_1 if it contains a negative number encoded in the form of number of anti-spikes. If the input neuron contains spikes (i.e., it represents a positive number), then it sends a spike to neuron s_2. So all the input neurons in the first layer of the structure Π_s are having the same type of synapses $((i_l, s_1), \{\bar{a}^+/\bar{a} \to \bar{a}\})$ and $((i_l, s_2), \{a^+/a \to a\})$ where $1 \leq l \leq n$. In the second layer the negative and non-negative integers are filtered. Let the number of negative numbers in list be m with $0 \leq m \leq n$. The number of anti-spikes neuron s_1 receives in the first step corresponds to the number of negative numbers in the original unsorted list. So, in the first step of the computation, neuron s_1 receives m anti-spikes which means that there are m number of negative integers and

$n - m$ non-negative integers in the unsorted list. The neuron s_1 sorts the m negative numbers in ascending order and stores them in the first m left most neurons of the third layer. Similarly neuron s_2 sorts the positive numbers and stores them in the rightmost neurons of the third layer.

Intermediate neurons s_1 and s_2 have outgoing synapses to all neurons in the third layer of the system. Depending upon the number of anti-spikes the neuron s_1 receives, it sends an anti-spike to one or more output neurons. At any step during computation, if neuron s_1 has p anti-spikes, then in the next step, it sends an anti-spike to all the p left most output neurons in the third layer. Similarly if the neuron s_2 receives q spikes then it sends a spike to all the q right most output neurons in the third layer. In this way, the SN PA system Π_s can sort n integers in $O(|M|)$ computational steps, where M is the absolute maximum of the n numbers. We can observe that this model makes use of $2n + 2$ neurons, $4n$ synapses and $n^2 + 3n$ rules to sort n integers, which is comparatively less complex than the system in [11].

6   Conclusion

In this paper we have simulated two parallel sorting algorithms, bitonic sort and bead sort to sort n integers using SN PA systems with rules on synapses. For bitonic sorting, the key operation is the comparison of two elements, so we have designed the SN PA comparators which can compare two integers and arrange them in ascending or descending order. Using these comparators, we have designed the SN PA bitonic sorting network that can perform sorting of an integer array. We simplified the sorting model in [11] using SN PA systems with rules on synapses and also incorporated negative numbers in the unsorted list.

Acknowledgements. Alica Kelemenová was supported by European Regional Development Fund in the IT4Innovations Centre of Excellence project (CZ.1.05/1.1.00/02.0070) and Silesian University in Opava project SGS/24/2013.

References

1. Alhazov, A., Freund, R., Oswald, M., Slavkovik, M.: Extended spiking neural P systems. In: Hoogeboom, H.J., Păun, G., Rozenberg, G., Salomaa, A. (eds.) WMC 2006. LNCS, vol. 4361, pp. 123–134. Springer, Heidelberg (2006)
2. Alhazov, A., Sburlan, D.: Static sorting P systems. In: Ciobanu, G., Păun, Gh., Pérez-Jiménez, M.J. (eds.) Applications of Membrane Computing. NCS, pp. 215–252. Springer, Heidelberg (2005)
3. Ardelean, I.I., Ceterchi, R., Tomescu, A.I.: Sorting with P systems: a biological perspective. Rom. J. Inf. Sci. Technol. **11**(3), 243–252 (2008)
4. Arulanandham, J.J.: Implementing bead-sort with P systems. In: Calude, C.S., Dinneen, M.J., Peper, F. (eds.) UMC 2002. LNCS, vol. 2509, p. 115. Springer, Heidelberg (2002)
5. Arulanandham, J.J., Calude, C.S., Dinneen, M.J.: Bead-sort: a natural sorting algorithm. Bull. Eur. Assoc. Theor. Comput. Sci. **76**, 153–162 (2002)

6. Batcher, K.E.: Sorting networks and their applications. In: AFIPS Springer Joint Computer Conference, pp. 307–314 (1968)
7. Binder, A., Freund, R., Oswald, M., Vock, L.: Extended spiking neural P systems with excitatory and inhibitory astrocytes. In: Aggarwal, A., Yager, R., Sandberg, I. W., (eds.) 8th WSEAS International Conference on Evolutionary Computing (EC 2007), pp. 320–325 (2007)
8. Ceterchi, R., Tomescu, A.I.: Implementing sorting networks with spiking neural P systems. Fundamenta Informaticae **87**(1), 35–48 (2008)
9. Dowd, M., Perl, Y., Saks, M., Rudolph, L.: The balanced sorting network. In: Second Annual ACM Symposium on Principles of Distributed Computing, pp. 161–172 (1983)
10. Ionescu, M., Păun, Gh., Yokomori, T.: Spiking neural P systems. Fundamenta Informaticae 71, 279–308 (2006)
11. Ionescu, M., Sburlan, D.: Some applications of spiking neural P systems. J. Comput. Inform. **27**, 515–528 (2008)
12. Knuth, D.E.: The Art of Computer Programming. Sorting and Searching. Addison Wesley Longman, Redwood City (1998)
13. Pan, L., Păun, Gh.: Spiking neural P systems with anti-spikes. Int. J. Comput. Commun. Control **4**(3), 273–282 (2009)
14. Pan, L., Păun, Gh., Pérez-Jiménez, M.J.: Spiking neural P systems with neuron division and budding. Sci. China Inf. Sci. **54**(8), 1596–1607 (2011)
15. Păun, Gh., Rozenberg, G., Salomaa, A. (eds.): Handbook of Membrane Computing, vol. 3, 2nd edn. Oxford University Press, New York (2010)
16. Rozenberg, G., Salomaa, A. (eds.): Handbook of Formal Languages. Springer, Berlin (1998)
17. Song, T., Pan, L., Păun, Gh.: Spiking neural P systems with rules on synapses. Theor. Comput. Sci. **529**, 82–95 (2014)
18. The P System Web Page. http://ppage.psystems.eu

Regulating Rule Application with Membrane Boundaries in P Systems

Tamás Mihálydeák and György Vaszil[(⊠)]

Department of Computer Science, Faculty of Informatics,
University of Debrecen, Kassai út 26, Debrecen 4028, Hungary
{mihalydeak.tamas,vaszil.gyorgy}@inf.unideb.hu

Abstract. Recently a new framework based on multiset approximation spaces were introduced for modeling the abstract notion of "closeness to membranes" in P systems. In real biotic/chemical interactions, however, objects not only have to be close enough to membranes, so that they are able to pass through them, but they also need to be in an unstable state, in a state where they are ready to engage into any type of interactions at all. In order to develop these ideas, we employ multiset approximation spaces for the description of stability and instability. We also demonstrate how the applicability and the use of reaction rules can be regulated during computations using the notion of membrane boundaries. An important feature of this type of regulation is the fact that it does not rely on the maximal parallel way of rule application, therefore it can be used to enhance the computational power of systems with asynchronous, sequential, or any other type of derivation modes. As an example, we show how P systems can generate any recursively enumerable set of numbers independently of the applied derivation mode, which is interesting, since without membrane boundaries asynchronous or sequential systems generate the Parikh sets of matrix languages only.

Keywords: Asynchronous P systems · Approximation spaces · Potential energy · Stable states

1 Introduction

Considering membrane systems with communication rules only (which are powerful means of interaction, see [2,8,12] for example), one might argue that real biotic/chemical interactions represented by these rules in P systems may take place only in the vicinity of membranes delimiting the regions. At first glance, vicinity is a spatial concept, but in order to avoid attributing location information to the objects, an abstract concept of "closeness to membranes" was formulated in [3] based on the theory of rough sets.

Rough set theory, Pawlak's classical theory of set approximations [6,7] gives a plausible opportunity to model boundary zones around sets in an abstract way. In P systems, however, regions are associated not with sets, but with multisets

© Springer International Publishing Switzerland 2015
G. Rozenberg et al. (Eds.): CMC 2015, LNCS 9504, pp. 304–320, 2015.
DOI: 10.1007/978-3-319-28475-0_21

of objects, thus in [3], the notion of multiset approximation space was introduced as a generalization of set approximation for multisets. P systems with membrane boundaries were also defined in [3] as an application of the multiset approximation framework. These systems have a two-component structure: (1) a (communicating) P system, and (2) a multiset approximation space which determines how the boundaries of the regions of the P system are computed. They were successfully used for the definition of membrane boundaries, some of their properties were further investigated in [1,4].

Using the multiset approximation technique, however, not only the abstract notion of closeness around membranes can be specified, but also the issue of stability can be addressed. This is the subject of the present paper.

Biotic/chemical processes are in the center of the motivation base of membrane computing, together with important aspects, such as robustness, stability, equilibrium, or periodicity. In order to explain the changes in natural processes, stored energy is a very useful notion. Stored energy is called potential because it has the "potential" to do work. In Nature, the lower the potential energy of a system, the more stable it is. Moreover, natural systems left to themselves attempt to reach the configuration with the lowest potential energy possible (under a given set of constraints). We might say that any change of the system configuration takes place because the system "wishes" to reach a more stable state, as if changes would resolve the unstabilities which are present.

In biotic/chemical processes there are many "small" coherent units (such as molecules, for example) which represent stability in the sense that they are less likely to engage into interactions than the others. In what follows, we will use the above described multiset approximation framework for the representation of this kind of "stability" in P systems by presenting a notion of membrane boundaries based on the concept of chemical or biological stability.

Moreover, as a further application of the concept, will also show how to generate membrane boundaries in such a way that they can be used to regulate the application of rules during computations. We will show how to implement the possibility of "appearance checking" of objects without relying on the maximal parallelism of rule application (as it is usually the case in P systems theory), thus, we will be able to use this technique also in asynchronous or sequential systems. As an initial result, we present a theorem showing that recursively enumerable sets of numbers can be generated by systems with one membrane using any type of rule application, which is interesting since systems without membrane boundaries in the asynchronous or sequential rule application modes can only generate Parikh sets of matrix languages (see Chapter 5 of [11]) which is a strict subclass of the class of recursively enumerable languages.

2   Preliminaries

Let U be a finite nonempty set. A *multiset* M, or an *mset* M for short, over U is a mapping $M : U \to \mathbb{N}$, where $\mathbb{N}$ is the set of natural numbers. If $M(a) \neq 0$, it is said that a belongs to M, otherwise a does not belong to M. The set $supp(M) = \{a \in U \mid M(a) \neq 0\}$ is called the *support* of M. The mset M is the *empty mset*, denoted by $\emptyset$, if $supp(M) = \emptyset$. A finite multiset M over an alphabet U can be represented by all permutations of a string $x = a_1^{M(a_1)} a_2^{M(a_2)} \ldots a_n^{M(a_n)} \in U^*$ where $a_j \in U$, $M(a_j) \neq 0$, $1 \leq j \leq n$. The size of a finite multiset M, represented by $x \in U^*$ is defined as $\sum_{a \in U} |x|_a$, where $|x|_a$ denotes the number of occurrences of $a \in U$ in x. We note that if no confusion arises, we also use the customary set notation for denoting multisets, and we denote the set of finite multisets over U by U^*. Let $n \in \mathbb{N}$ be a positive integer, we say that $a \in^n M$ $(a \in U)$ if $M(a) = n$, and $M_1 \sqsubseteq M_2$, if $M_1(a) \leq M_2(a)$ for all $a \in U$.

We describe the generalizations of the basic set–theoretical operations for multisets as follows. Let $M, M_1, M_2 \in U^*$ be msets over U. The *intersection* of two msets, $M_1 \sqcap M_2$ is defined as $(M_1 \sqcap M_2)(a) = \min\{M_1(a), M_2(a)\}$ for all $a \in U$. The *set–type union* of two msets, $M_1 \sqcup M_2$ is defined by $(M_1 \sqcup M_2)(a) = \max\{M_1(a), M_2(a)\}$ for all $a \in U$, with $\bigsqcup \emptyset = \emptyset$ by definition. The operation of *multiset addition* is defined by $(M_1 \oplus M_2)(a) = M_1(a) + M_2(a)$ for all $a \in U$. For any $n \in \mathbb{N}$, *n-times addition* of M, denoted by $\oplus_n M$, is given by the following inductive definition:

1. $\oplus_0 M = \emptyset$;
2. $\oplus_1 M = M$;
3. $\oplus_{n+1} M = \oplus_n M \oplus M$.

We will use the term *many-times addition*, if n is not specified. We also define *multiset subtraction* by $(M_1 \ominus M_2)(a) = \max\{M_1(a) - M_2(a), 0\}$ for all $a \in U$. Using the notion of n-times addition, the *n-times inclusion* relation can be defined for any $n \in \mathbb{N}$ as follows: $M_1 \sqsubseteq^n M_2$, if $\oplus_n M_1 \sqsubseteq M_2$ but $\oplus_{n+1} M_1 \not\sqsubseteq M_2$. We also denote by U^n the set of all msets M over U such that $M(a) \leq n$ for all $a \in U$.

Now we define the basic notions of P systems which were introduced in [9]. For more information, see the monograph [10] and the handbook [11]. A P system is a structure of hierarchically embedded membranes, each having a label and enclosing a region containing a multiset of objects and possibly other membranes. The out-most membrane which is unique and usually labeled with 1, is called the skin membrane. The membrane structure is denoted by a sequence of matching parentheses where the matching pairs have the same label as the membranes they represent. If membrane i contains membrane j, and there is no other membrane k, such that k contains j and i contains k then we say that membrane i is the parent membrane of j.

The evolution of the contents of the regions of a P system is described by rules associated to the regions. In the following we concentrate on communication rules called symport or antiport rules.

Configurations of the system are represented by the multisets of objects present inside the regions. The application of a collection of rules takes the system from one configurations to another, a series of configurations corresponds to a computation.

The end of the computation is defined by halting: A P system halts when no more rules can be applied in any of the regions, and the result is the number of objects in an elementary membrane labeled as output.

Definition 1. *A P system with symport/antiport of degree $n \geq 1$ is a construct*

$$\Pi = (V, \mu, w_1, \ldots, w_n, R_1, \ldots, R_n, out)$$

where

- *V is an alphabet of objects,*
- *μ is a membrane structure of n membranes,*
- *$w_i \in V^*$, $1 \leq i \leq n$, are the initial contents of the n regions,*
- *R_i, $1 \leq i \leq n$, are the sets of symport/antiport rules associated to the regions,*
- *$out \in \{1, \ldots, n\}$ is the label of an elementary membrane, the output membrane.*

The n-tuple of finite multisets of objects present in the n regions of the P system Π describes a *configuration* of Π; $(w_1, \ldots, w_n) \in (V^*)^n$ is the initial configuration.

The P systems changes its configurations by applying its rules simultaneously in the regions. A symport rule is of the form (x, in) or $(x, out), x \in V^*$. If such a rule is present in a region i, then the objects of the multiset x must enter from the parent region or must leave to the parent region, respectively. An antiport rule is of the form $(x, in; y, out), x, y \in V^*$, in this case, objects of x enter from the parent region and in the same step, objects of y leave to the parent region.

There are several rule application modes which can be considered. If the rules are applied in the *maximal parallel* manner, then as many rules are applied in each region as possible. In the *minimal parallel* mode, any number of rules can be applied, but at least one rule has to be applied in all those regions where there are applicable rules. If the rules are applied *asynchronously*, then any number of rules can be applied without any restriction, in the *sequential* mode, just one rule is applied in the whole system in each step. More information on these rule application modes can be found in Chapter 5 of the handbook [11].

3 Multiset Approximation Spaces

A multiset approximation space is defined over a finite alphabet U, and denoted by $\mathsf{MAS}(U)$. It has four basic constituents:

- *Domain* — a set of finite multisets over U whose members are approximated. If the multiset approximation space is associated to a membrane system, the contents of the regions belong to the domain.
- *Base system* — a set of msets from the domain serving as the basis for the approximation process. Its members are called *base msets*.
- The set of *definable msets* derived from base msets. They are possible approximations of the members of the domain. It is reasonable to define the approximation space in such a way that the base msets and the empty mset are definable. In approximation spaces associated to membrane systems, we will assume that the set of definable msets is obtained as the set of unions of the many-times additions of the base msets.

– *Approximation functions* — determining the lower and upper approximations and the boundaries of the msets of the domain.

Now we present the formal definition of the above listed components of a so called Pawlakian mset approximation space.

Definition 2. *The ordered 6–tuple* $\mathsf{MAS}(U) = \langle U^*, \mathfrak{B}, \mathfrak{D}_\mathfrak{B}, \mathsf{l}, \mathsf{u}, \mathsf{b} \rangle$ *is a Pawlakian mset approximation space over U with the domain U^* if*

1. U *is a nonempty set.*
2. $\mathfrak{B} \subseteq U^*$ *and if $B \in \mathfrak{B}$, then $B \neq \emptyset$. $\mathfrak{B}$ is called the* base system, *its members are the* base msets.
3. $\mathfrak{D}_\mathfrak{B} \subseteq U^*$ *is the set of* definable msets, *an extension of $\mathfrak{B}$ such that*
    (a) $\emptyset \in \mathfrak{D}_\mathfrak{B}$;
    (b) $\mathfrak{B} \subseteq \mathfrak{D}_\mathfrak{B}$;
    (c) *if $\mathfrak{B}^\oplus = \{\oplus_n B \mid B \in \mathfrak{B}, \ n = 1, 2, \dots\}$ and $\mathfrak{B}' \subseteq \mathfrak{B}^\oplus$, then $\bigsqcup \mathfrak{B}' \in \mathfrak{D}_\mathfrak{B}$.*
4. *The* approximation functions $\mathsf{l}, \mathsf{u}, \mathsf{b} : U^* \to U^*$ *representing the lower, upper approximations and the boundaries of an mset $M \in U^*$, respectively, are defined as*
    (a) $\mathsf{l}(M) = \bigsqcup\{\oplus_n B \mid n \in \mathbb{N}^+, B \in \mathfrak{B} \text{ and } B \sqsubseteq^n M\}$,
    (b) $\mathsf{b}(M) = \bigsqcup\{\oplus_n B \mid B \in \mathfrak{B}, B \not\sqsubseteq M, \ B \sqcap M \neq \emptyset \text{ and } B \sqcap M \sqsubseteq^n M\}$,
    (c) $\mathsf{u}(M) = \mathsf{l}(M) \sqcup \mathsf{b}(M)$.
    (When the approximation functions $\mathsf{l}, \mathsf{u}, \mathsf{b}$ are defined as above, they are called generalized Pawlakian.)

To clarify the above defined notion of multiset approximation space, we present the following example.

Example 1. Let $\mathsf{MAS} = \langle V^*, \mathfrak{B}, \mathfrak{D}_\mathfrak{B}, \mathsf{l}, \mathsf{u}, \mathsf{b} \rangle$ be an mset approximation space with $V = \{a, b, c, d, e, f\}$, and a set of base msets (the base system)

$$\mathfrak{B} = \{a^2 b, abcdef, ac, b^3 cd^2, b^3 d^2, b^3 d^2 f, c, f^2, f^4\}.$$

Now, according to the above definition, the set of definable msets $\mathfrak{D}_\mathfrak{B}$ can be obtained as follows:

– $\emptyset \in \mathfrak{D}_\mathfrak{B}$,
– $\mathfrak{B}^\oplus = \{a^2 b, a^4 b^2, a^6 b^3, \dots,$
    $abcdef, a^2 b^2 c^2 d^2 e^2 f^2, a^3 b^3 c^3 d^3 e^3 f^3, \dots,$
    $ac, a^2 c^2, a^3 c^3, \dots,$
    $b^3 cd^2, b^6 c^2 d^4, b^9 c^3 d^6, \dots,$
    $b^3 d^2, b^6 d^4, b^9 d^6, \dots,$
    $b^3 d^2 f, b^6 d^4 f^2, b^9 d^6 f^3, \dots,$
    $c, c^2, c^3 \dots, e^3, e^6, e^9, \dots,$
    $f^2, f^4, f^6, \dots\}$,
– for any $\mathfrak{B}' \subseteq \mathfrak{B}^\oplus$, $\bigsqcup \mathfrak{B}' \in \mathfrak{D}_\mathfrak{B}$.

Let M be the multiset $M = \{a, \underbrace{b, \ldots, b}_{11}, c, c, c, \underbrace{d, \ldots, d}_{9}\} = ab^{11}c^3d^9$, and let us compute boundary of M. According to Definition 2, the boundary is computed as

$$\mathsf{b}(ab^{11}c^3d^9) = \bigsqcup \{\oplus_n B \mid B \in \mathfrak{B}, B \not\sqsubseteq ab^{11}c^3d^9, B \sqcap ab^{11}c^3d^9 \neq \emptyset$$
$$\text{and } B \sqcap ab^{11}c^3d^9 \sqsubseteq^n ab^{11}c^3d^9\}.$$

Thus, we need all elements B of the base system $\mathfrak{B}$ which are not submultisets of M, but have nonempty intersections with M. These are

$$\{a^2b, \; abcdef, \; b^3d^2f\} = \{B_1, B_2, B_3\} \subseteq \mathfrak{B}.$$

Now we need to find for each B_i the numbers n_i, such that $B_i \sqcap M \sqsubseteq^{n_i} M$. We obtain

- $(a^2b \sqcap ab^{11}c^3d^9) = ab \sqsubseteq^1 ab^{11}c^3d^9$, thus, $n_1 = 1$,
- $(abcdef \sqcap ab^{11}c^3d^9) = abcd \sqsubseteq^1 ab^{11}c^3d^9$, thus $n_2 = 1$,
- $(b^3d^2f \sqcap ab^{11}c^3d^9) = b^3d^2 \sqsubseteq^3 ab^{11}c^3d^9$, thus $n_3 = 3$.

Now we can compute the boundary as

$$\mathsf{b}(M) = \bigsqcup \{\oplus_{n_i} B_i \mid 1 \leq i \leq 3\},$$

that is

$$\mathsf{b}(ab^{11}c^3d^9) = \bigsqcup \{\oplus_1 a^2b, \oplus_1 abcdef, \oplus_3 b^3d^2f\},$$

which means that

$$\mathsf{b}(ab^{11}c^3d^9) = \oplus_1 a^2b \sqcup \oplus_1 abcdef \sqcup \oplus_3 b^3d^2f$$
$$= a^2b \sqcup abcdef \sqcup b^9d^6f^3$$
$$= a^2b^9cd^6f^3.$$

4 Multiset Approximation Spaces in Membrane Computing

If the P system $\Pi = (V, \mu, w_1, w_2, \ldots, w_m, R_1, R_2, \ldots, R_m, out)$ is given, let $\mathsf{MAS}(\Pi) = \langle V^*, \mathfrak{B}, \mathfrak{D}_\mathfrak{B}, \mathsf{l}, \mathsf{u}, \mathsf{b} \rangle$ be a Pawlakian mset approximation space called the *joint membrane approximation space of the P system* Π. Note that in such a joint membrane approximation space, the definitions of $\mathsf{l}, \mathsf{u}, \mathsf{b}$ are given and the alphabet V is fixed, but depending on the choice of $\mathfrak{B}$, we can obtain different definable sets $\mathfrak{D}_\mathfrak{B}$, and different approximation spaces for a given Π.

Having given a membrane system Π and its joint membrane approximation space $\mathsf{MAS}(\Pi)$, we can define the boundaries of the regions $w_1, w_2, \ldots, w_m$ as msets with the help of approximation functions $\mathsf{l}, \mathsf{u}, \mathsf{b}$. But the general notion of mset boundaries given earlier cannot be used here, because membrane boundaries have to follow the given membrane structure μ. In the case of the skin region, the Pawlakian boundary $b(w_1)$ can be defined using the upper approximation $u(w_1)$ without any complications, since the environment is assumed to contain any object in an arbitrary number of copies. For $i = 2, \ldots, m$, however, the contents of the parent regions also have to be taken into consideration: those objects of the base msets making up the membrane boundary, which are not inside the membrane, have to be elements of the parent region. Thus, the Pawlakian boundaries have to be adjusted to the membrane structure and the contents of the regions by the function bnd. Note that $b(w_1) = \text{bnd}(w_1)$, but $b(w_i) \neq \text{bnd}(w_i)$ $(i = 2, \ldots, m)$ in general. Moreover, membrane boundaries $\text{bnd}(w_i)$ $(i = 1, \ldots, m)$ are split into two parts, inside and outside membrane boundaries.

Before presenting the formal definitions, we illustrate the considerations above with the following example.

Example 2. Let $\mathsf{MAS} = \langle V^*, \mathfrak{B}, \mathfrak{D}_\mathfrak{B}, \mathsf{l}, \mathsf{u}, \mathsf{b} \rangle$ be the mset approximation space from Example 1 associated to the P system $\Pi = (V, [\ [\ ]_2\ ]_1, w_1, w_2, R_1, R_2, out)$ where $w_1 = ef^2$ and w_2 is the multiset from Example 1, thus $w_2 = ab^{11}c^3d^9$.

When computing the boundary of $w_2 = ab^{11}c^3d^9$, we need to take into account that the parent region does not contain the objects in arbitrary number of copies. Considering the base sets which have nonempty intersections with w_2, we obtain the following.

- Although $(a^2b \sqcap ab^{11}c^3d^9) = ab$, there is no a in the parent region $w_1 = ef^2$, so a^2b cannot lie in the boundary of the two regions, it cannot be taken into account when computing the boundary (that is, $n_1 = 0$ using the notation of Example 1);
- $(abcdef \sqcap ab^{11}c^3d^9) = abcd \sqsubseteq^1 ab^{11}c^3d^9$ and $ef \sqsubseteq ef^2$, so $abcdef$ is taken into account when computing the boundary ($n_2 = 1$ using the notation of Example 1);
- $(b^3d^2f \sqcap ab^{11}c^3d^9) = b^3d^2$ and $f \sqsubseteq^2 ef^2$, so b^3d^2f is considered for the boundary ($n_3 = 2$ using the notation of Example 1).

Thus, the boundary of the contents of the second region $w_2 = b^{11}c^3d^9$ is computed as

$$\text{bnd}(ab^{11}c^3d^9) = \bigsqcup\{\oplus_0 a^2b, \oplus_1 abcdef, \oplus_2 b^3d^2f\},$$

which means that

$$\text{bnd}(ab^{11}c^3d^9) = \oplus_0 a^2b \oplus_1 abcdef \sqcup \oplus_2 b^3d^2f$$
$$= \emptyset \sqcup abcdef \sqcup b^6d^4f^2 = ab^7cd^5ef^2.$$

These considerations are formalized in the following definition.

Definition 3. *Let* $\Pi = \langle V, \mu, w_1, w_2, \ldots, w_m, R_1, R_2, \ldots, R_m \rangle$ *be a P system and* $\mathsf{MAS}(\Pi) = \langle V^*, \mathfrak{B}, \mathfrak{D}_\mathfrak{B}, \mathsf{l}, \mathsf{u}, \mathsf{b} \rangle$ *be its joint membrane approximation space. If* $B \in \mathfrak{B}$ *and* $i = 1, 2, \ldots, m$, *let*

$$N(B, i) = \begin{cases} 0, & \text{if } B \sqsubseteq w_i \text{ or } B \sqcap w_i = \emptyset; \\ n, & \text{if } i = 1 \text{ and } B \sqcap w_1 \sqsubseteq^n w_1; \\ \min\{k, n \mid B \sqcap w_i \sqsubseteq^k w_i, \text{ and } B \ominus w_i \sqsubseteq^n w_{\text{parent}(i)}\}, & \text{otherwise.} \end{cases}$$

Then, for $i = 1, \ldots, m$,

$$\mathsf{bnd}(w_i) = \bigsqcup \{ \oplus_{N(B,i)} B \mid B \in \mathfrak{B} \};$$
$$\mathsf{bnd}^{\mathsf{out}}(w_i) = \mathsf{bnd}(w_i) \ominus w_i;$$
$$\mathsf{bnd}^{\mathsf{in}}(w_i) = \mathsf{bnd}(w_i) \ominus \mathsf{bnd}^{\mathsf{out}}(w_i).$$

The functions bnd, $\mathsf{bnd}^{\mathsf{out}}$ and $\mathsf{bnd}^{\mathsf{in}}$ represent *membrane boundaries, outside* and *inside membrane boundaries*, respectively.

Example 3. Consider the MAS $= \langle V^*, \mathfrak{B}, \mathfrak{D}_{\mathfrak{B}}, \mathsf{I}, \mathsf{u}, \mathsf{b} \rangle$ associated to the P system $\Pi = (V, [\,[\,]_2\,]_1, w_1, w_2, R_1, R_2, out)$ with $w_1 = ef^2$, $w_2 = ab^{11}c^3d^9$ from Example 2.

Considering the base system $\mathfrak{B}$ (see Example 1), we have $N(B,2) = 0$ for almost all the base sets from $\mathfrak{B}$, except for $B \in \{a^2b, abcdef, b^3d^2f\}$.

Now $N(a^2b, 2) = \min\{k, n\}$, where

$$(a^2b \sqcap ab^{11}c^3d^9) \sqsubseteq^k ab^{11}c^3d^9, \text{ and } (a^2b \ominus ab^{11}c^3d^9) \sqsubseteq^n w_1 = ef^2,$$

thus, $N(a^2b, 2) = \min\{1, 0\} = 0$.

Similarly, $N(abcdef, 2) = \min\{k, n\}$, where

$$(abcdef \sqcap ab^{11}c^3d^9) \sqsubseteq^k ab^{11}c^3d^9, \text{ and } (abcdef \ominus ab^{11}c^3d^9) \sqsubseteq^n w_1 = ef^2,$$

thus, $N(abcdef, 2) = \min\{1, 1\} = 1$, and $N(b^3d^2f, 2) = \min\{k, n\}$, where

$$(b^3d^2f \sqcap ab^{11}c^3d^9) \sqsubseteq^k ab^{11}c^3d^9, \text{ and } (b^3d^2f \ominus ab^{11}c^3d^9) \sqsubseteq^n w_1 = ef^2,$$

thus, $N(abcdef, 2) = \min\{3, 2\} = 2$.

Now we obtain the boundary of the second region $w_2 = ab^{11}c^3d^9$ as

$$\mathsf{bnd}(w_2) = \bigsqcup \{ \oplus_{N(B,2)} B \mid B \in \mathfrak{B} \} = \{ \oplus_0 a^2 b \} \sqcup \{ \oplus_1 abcdef \} \sqcup \{ \oplus_2 b^3 d^2 f \}$$
$$= abcdef \sqcup b^6 d^4 f^2$$
$$= ab^7 cd^5 ef^2.$$

When computing the boundary of the first region, $w_1 = ef^2$, we have $N(B,1) = 0$ for all $B \in \mathfrak{B}$ where $B \neq abcdef$, so we need to determine $N(abcdef, 1) = n$ where

$$(abcdef \sqcap ef^2) \sqsubseteq^n ef^2,$$

which means that $N(abcdef, 1) = 1$, therefore

$$\mathsf{bnd}(w_1) = \bigsqcup \{ \oplus_{N(B,1)} B \mid B \in \mathfrak{B} \} = \{ \oplus_1 abcdef \}$$
$$= abcdef.$$

The inside and outside boundaries are obtained as follows.

$$\mathsf{bnd}^{\mathsf{out}}(w_2) = \mathsf{bnd}(w_2) \ominus w_2 = ab^7 cd^5 ef^2 \ominus ab^{11}c^3d^9 = ef^2;$$
$$\mathsf{bnd}^{\mathsf{in}}(w_2) = \mathsf{bnd}(w_2) \ominus \mathsf{bnd}^{\mathsf{out}}(w_2) = ab^7 cd^5 ef^2 \ominus ef^2 = ab^7 cd^5.$$

and

$$\mathsf{bnd^{out}}(w_1) = \mathsf{bnd}(w_1) \ominus w_1 = abcdef \ominus ef^2 = abcd;$$
$$\mathsf{bnd^{in}}(w_1) = \mathsf{bnd}(w_1) \ominus \mathsf{bnd^{out}}(w_1) = abcdef \ominus abcd = ef.$$

Using membrane boundaries, the following constraints for rule executions are prescribed: a rule $r \in R_i$ of a membrane i ($i = 1, \ldots, m$) has to work only in the membrane boundary of its region. More precisely,

- a symport rule (u, in) is executed only in the case when $u \sqsubseteq \mathsf{bnd^{out}}(w_i)$;
- a symport rule (u, out) is executed only in the case when $u \sqsubseteq \mathsf{bnd^{in}}(w_i)$;
- an antiport rule $(u, in; v, out)$ is executed only in the case when $u \sqsubseteq \mathsf{bnd^{out}}(w_i)$ and $v \sqsubseteq \mathsf{bnd^{in}}(w_i)$.

In [1,3,4], the authors presented examples and showed how the given notion of membrane boundaries work in a P system.

5   Chemical Stability and the Notion of Membrane Boundaries

In the present paper we continue to develop the above described framework, we employ membrane boundaries for the description of the notion of chemical stability. In this section, we provide an informal background to our considerations.

In the following, within the scope of the proposed framework, the question of stability of P systems will be focused in our study. The notion of stability appears in P systems trivially, since if one asks when a membrane computation process stops, then the answer can be the following: when it reaches a stable state i.e. when there is no rule which can execute. This means that in systems which are able to perform some computation, the initial state is not stable: there are some rules which can work. If the whole computation process is considered, it can be viewed as a transition form an unstable state to a stable one, but here we would also like to consider the individual computation steps. What we are looking for, is a refined notion of stability which is able to capture how the computational steps themselves lead to more and more stable states, how they are executed by "resolving" some of the unstabilities of the system which are present.

In a joint membrane approximation space $\mathsf{MAS}(\Pi)$, each base mset can be considered as stable or coherent unit i.e. consisting of objects which together form a coherent unit. Hence, base msets can be taken as the representation of compounds whose potential energy is lower than the potential energy of their parts. Therefore, they represent a more stable state of their constituent objects, and the objects have lower (potential) energy together as they would have separately.

Membrane boundaries are collections of base msets. A very important aspect of these base msets is that all of them are split into two parts by the membranes: They have nonempty intersections with the regions inside and also outside, these form the inner and outer parts of the boundaries. In both parts, bisected base msets are not stable from the energetic point of view. In other words, they are in "excited states", i.e., they have higher energy as they would have together as a coherent unit, namely, a base mset. As it was mentioned earlier, a natural system, left to itself, attempts to reach the configuration with the possible lowest energy. Accordingly, base msets bisected by membranes are ready for moving towards the stable states of lower potential energy. However, they can reach these states only in the case if the adequate objects are able to pass through the membranes.

The movements of objects through membranes are regulated by communication rules restricted to membrane boundaries. Consequently, a base mset split into two parts can only reach a state with lower potential energy, i.e., a more stable state, if the communication rules make it possible that the objects form a base mset again. If this happens, the (re)combined base mset may wholly get inside/outside the region. (Then, at the same time, it is removed from the membrane boundary as well, i.e., after each computation step in the framework, boundaries have to be recalculated.)

6   A Notion of Membrane Boundaries Based on Chemical Stability

We would like to emphasize here again that our definition of membrane boundaries does not rely on the notion of space (the notion of physical "closeness"), it is also possible to consider the notion of stability as its intuitive background. Boundaries relying on base msets answer the following questions in each computational step: how is a communication rule activated, or in other words, why do some communication rules execute and others do not? The answer is related to the notion of stability: the executed rules make direct steps to reach a more stable state, that is, they try to eliminate some of the unstabilities present.

If we look at the notion of boundaries from this point of view, there is a problem that we need to solve: We need to take into consideration the stability of a region and the stability of its parent. Membrane boundaries can only contain objects that are neither elements of the stable parts of the region, nor of the stable part of its parent.

In order to take these considerations into account, we will define the boundaries in the following way. First, the lower approximation of the regions is computed, and those objects which are not elements of the lower approximation are considered unstable. The unstable objects are able to take part in reactions, thus, they may become part of the boundary of the region. If unstable objects on the two sides of one membrane can form one of the base msets together, then there is a certain attraction among them towards each other as they could constitute a stable complex together, thus, this is the situation when they are considered to be on the boundary.

Let $\Pi = (V, \mu, w_1, \ldots, w_m, R_1, \ldots, R_m, out)$ be a P system and $\mathsf{MAS}(\Pi) = \langle V^*, \mathfrak{B}, \mathfrak{D}_{\mathfrak{B}}, \mathsf{l}, \mathsf{u}, \mathsf{b} \rangle$ be its joint membrane approximation space. We define the (inner) unstable parts of regions as the elements which do not belong to their lower approximations.

For $1 \leq i \leq m$, let

$$\mathsf{UNS^{in}}(i) = w_i \ominus \mathsf{l}(w_i).$$

We also need the notion of the "outer" unstable part of a region, which is just the inner unstable part of its parent. (As the objects are assumed to be present in any number of copies in the environment, the skin region has no outer unstable part.) Thus, for $i \neq 1$, let

$$\mathsf{UNS^{out}}(i) = w_{\mathsf{parent}(i)} \ominus \mathsf{l}(w_{\mathsf{parent}(i)})(= \mathsf{UNS^{in}}(parent(i))).$$

Let us define for all $B \in \mathfrak{B}$ and $1 \leq i \leq m$ the numbers $K(B, i), K'(B, i)$, $L(B, i)$ and $L'(B, i)$ as follows.

If $B \sqcap \mathsf{UNS^{in}}(i) = \emptyset$ or $B \sqsubseteq \mathsf{UNS^{in}}(i)$, then $L(B, i)$ and $K(B, i)$ are undefined, otherwise let

1. $L(B, i) = l$ where $B \sqcap \mathsf{UNS^{in}}(i) \sqsubseteq^l \mathsf{UNS^{in}}(i)$ for $1 \leq i \leq m$;
2. $K(B, 1) = L(B, 1)$;
3. $K(B, i) = k$ where $B \ominus (B \sqcap \mathsf{UNS^{in}}(i)) \sqsubseteq^k \mathsf{UNS^{out}}(i)$ for $2 \leq i \leq m$.

Similarly, if $B \sqcap \mathsf{UNS^{out}}(i) = \emptyset$ or $B \sqsubseteq \mathsf{UNS^{out}}(i)$, then $L'(B, i)$ and $K'(B, i)$ are undefined, otherwise let

1. $L'(B, 1) = L(B, 1)$;
2. $L'(B, i) = l'$ where $B \ominus (B \sqcap \mathsf{UNS^{out}}(i)) \sqsubseteq^{l'} \mathsf{UNS^{in}}(i)$ for $2 \leq i \leq m$;
3. $K'(B, 1) = K(B, 1)$;
4. $K'(B, i) = k'$ where $B \sqcap \mathsf{UNS^{out}}(i) \sqsubseteq^{k'} \mathsf{UNS^{out}}(i)$ for $2 \leq i \leq m$.

Before continuing, let us consider the following example.

Example 4. Let us suppose that $\mathsf{MAS} = \langle V^*, \mathfrak{B}, \mathfrak{D}_\mathfrak{B}, \mathsf{l}, \mathsf{u}, \mathsf{b} \rangle$ is an mset approximation space with $V = \{a, b, c\}$ and $\mathfrak{B} = \{aaab, cc\}$, associated to the P system $\Pi = (V, [\,[\,]_2\,]_1, w_1, w_2, R_1, R_2, out)$ where $w_1 = aabc^6$ and $w_2 = a^{12}c^4$. The unstable parts of the regions of Π are obtained as follows.

$$\mathsf{UNS^{in}}(1) = w_1 \ominus \mathsf{l}(w_1) = aabc^6 \ominus c^6 = aab,$$
$$\mathsf{UNS^{in}}(2) = w_2 \ominus \mathsf{l}(w_2) = a^{12}c^4 \ominus c^4 = a^{12},$$

the multiset $\mathsf{UNS^{out}}(1)$ is undefined, and

$$\mathsf{UNS^{out}}(2) = \mathsf{UNS^{in}}(1) = aab.$$

Now, the only $B \in \mathfrak{B}$ such that it has a nonempty intersection with the unstable parts of the regions is $B = aaab$. We can calculate the numbers $K(B, i), K'(B, i), L(B, i)$ and $L'(B, i)$ in the following way.

1. $L(aaab, 1) = 1$ since $(aaab \sqcap aab) \sqsubseteq^1 aab$;
2. $K(aaab, 1) = L(aaab, 1) = 1$;
3. $L(aaab, 2) = 4$ since $(aaab \sqcap a^{12}) \sqsubseteq^4 a^{12}$; and

4. $K(aaab, 2) = 1$ since $aaab \ominus (aaab \sqcap a^{12}) \sqsubseteq^1 aab$.

Similarly, $L'(B, i)$ and $K'(B, i)$ are calculated as

1. $L'(aaab, 1) = L(aaab, 1) = 1$;
2. $L'(aaab, 2) = 12$ since $aaab \ominus (aaab \sqcap aab) \sqsubseteq^{12} a^{12}$;
3. $K'(aaab, 1) = K(aaab, 1) = 1$; and
4. $K'(aaab, 2) = 1$ since $aaab \sqcap aab \sqsubseteq^1 aab$.

The following definition gives the new notions of boundaries based on the stability of regions and their parents (inside and outside boundaries, as well).

Definition 4. *Let* $\Pi = (V, \mu, w_1, w_2, \ldots, w_m, R_1, R_2, \ldots, R_m)$ *be a P system and* $\mathsf{MAS}(\Pi) = \langle V^*, \mathfrak{B}, \mathfrak{D}_{\mathfrak{B}}, \mathsf{l}, \mathsf{u}, \mathsf{b} \rangle$ *be its joint membrane approximation space. If* $B \in \mathfrak{B}$ *and* $i = 1, 2, \ldots, m$, *then let us define* $\mathsf{Min}(B, i)$ *and* $\mathsf{Min}'(B, i)$.

1. *Let* $B \in \mathfrak{B}$ *and* i, $1 \leq i \leq m$, *such that* $K(B, i)$ *and* $L(B, i)$ *are defined, and let*
$$\mathsf{Min}(B, i) = \min\{K(B, i), L(B, i)\}.$$
   Otherwise let $\mathsf{Min}(B, i) = 0$.
2. *Let* $B \in \mathfrak{B}$ *and* i, $1 \leq i \leq m$, *such that* $K'(B, i)$ *and* $L'(B, i)$ *are defined, and let*
$$\mathsf{Min}'(B, i) = \min\{K'(B, i), L'(B, i)\}.$$
   Otherwise let $\mathsf{Min}'(B, i) = 0$.

Now for $1 \leq i \leq m$, *we have*

- $\mathsf{bnd}^{from\ in}_{stable}(w_i) = \bigsqcup\{\oplus_{\mathsf{Min}(B,i)} B \mid B \in \mathfrak{B}\}$,
- $\mathsf{bnd}^{from\ out}_{stable}(w_i) = \bigsqcup\{\oplus_{\mathsf{Min}'(B,i)} B \mid B \in \mathfrak{B}\}$,

and finally, the boundary and its inner and outer parts are given as

- $\mathsf{bnd}_{stable}(w_i) = \mathsf{bnd}^{from\ in}_{stable}(w_i) \sqcup \mathsf{bnd}^{from\ out}_{stable}(w_i)$, *and*
- $\mathsf{bnd}^{in}_{stable}(w_i) = \mathsf{bnd}_{stable}(w_i) \sqcap \mathsf{UNS}^{in}(i)$ *for* $1 \leq i \leq m$,
- $\mathsf{bnd}^{out}_{stable}(w_1) = \mathsf{bnd}_{stable}(w_1) \ominus \mathsf{bnd}^{in}_{stable}(w_1)$,
- $\mathsf{bnd}^{out}_{stable}(w_i) = \mathsf{bnd}_{stable}(w_i) \sqcap \mathsf{UNS}^{out}(i)$, *for* $2 \leq i \leq m$.

Example 5. Let $\mathsf{MAS} = \langle V^*, \mathfrak{B}, \mathfrak{D}_{\mathfrak{B}}, \mathsf{l}, \mathsf{u}, \mathsf{b} \rangle$ be the mset approximation space and $\Pi = (V, [\ [\ ]_2\ ]_1, w_1, w_2, R_1, R_2, out)$ be the P system from Example 4, thus, $V = \{a, b, c\}$, $\mathfrak{B} = \{aaab, cc\}$, $w_1 = aabc^6$ and $w_2 = a^{12}c^4$.

Since $cc \in \mathfrak{B}$ does not have a nonempty intersection with any of the unstable parts of any of the regions, $\mathsf{Min}(B, i)$ and $\mathsf{Min}'(B, i)$ are only defined for $B = aaab$, $i = 1, 2$:

$$\mathsf{Min}(aaab, 1) = \min\{1, 1\} = 1, \quad \mathsf{Min}(aaab, 2) = \min\{4, 1\} = 1,$$
$$\mathsf{Min}'(aaab, 1) = \min\{1, 1\} = 1, \quad \mathsf{Min}'(aaab, 2) = \min\{12, 1\} = 1.$$

Now, for any i, $1 \leq i \leq 2$

$$\mathsf{bnd}^{from\ in}_{stable}(w_i) = \mathsf{bnd}^{from\ out}_{stable}(w_i) = \bigsqcup\{\oplus_1 aaab\} = aaab,$$

so the boundary and its inner and outer parts are given as

- $\mathsf{bnd}_{\mathsf{stable}}(w_1) = aaab \sqcup aaab = aaab,$
- $\mathsf{bnd}^{\mathsf{in}}_{\mathsf{stable}}(w_1) = aaab \sqcap \mathsf{UNS}^{\mathsf{in}}(1) = aaab \sqcap aab = aab,$
- $\mathsf{bnd}^{\mathsf{out}}_{\mathsf{stable}}(w_1) = aaab \ominus aab = a,$

and

- $\mathsf{bnd}_{\mathsf{stable}}(w_2) = aaab \sqcup aaab = aaab,$
- $\mathsf{bnd}^{\mathsf{in}}_{\mathsf{stable}}(w_2) = aaab \sqcap \mathsf{UNS}^{\mathsf{in}}(2) = aaab \sqcap a^{12} = aaa,$
- $\mathsf{bnd}^{\mathsf{out}}_{\mathsf{stable}}(w_2) = aaab \sqcap \mathsf{UNS}^{\mathsf{out}}(2) = aaab \sqcap aab = aab.$

7 Regulating Rule Application in Asynchronous P Systems

Now we demonstrate how the boundaries $\mathsf{bnd}^{\mathsf{in}}_{\mathsf{stable}}$ and $\mathsf{bnd}^{\mathsf{out}}_{\mathsf{stable}}$ can be used to regulate the applicability of symport/antiport rules in membrane computations. We show how we can give the base sets of $\mathfrak{B}$ in such a way that a certain rule is only applicable when a given object is not present in the region. This boundary based method is interesting, because we can implement a kind of "appearance checking" feature in such a way that it does not rely on the maximal parallelism of rule application. Thus, it allows us to use it in asynchronous or sequential systems. As an initial result, we present a theorem showing that recursively enumerable sets of numbers can be generated by systems with one membrane using any type of rule application. This result is interesting, because systems without membrane boundaries can only generate a strict subclass of the class of recursively enumerable languages, namely the Parikh sets of matrix languages with asynchronous or sequential rule application (see [11], Chapter 5).

The proof of our theorem relies on the notion of register machines, so we briefly review this concept first (more information can be found in [5]). A register machine consists of a given number of registers each of which can hold an arbitrarily large non-negative integer number, and a set of labeled instructions which specify how the numbers stored in registers can be manipulated.

Formally, it is a construct $M = (m, H, l_0, l_h, R)$, where m is the number of registers, H is the set of instruction labels, l_0 is the start label, l_h is the halting label, and R is the set of instructions; each label from H labels only one instruction from R. There are several types of instructions which can be used. For $l_i, l_j, l_k \in H$ and $r \in \{1, \ldots, m\}$ we have

- $l_i : (\mathsf{nADD}(r), l_j, l_k)$ - *nondeterministic add*: Add 1 to register r and then go to one of the instructions with labels l_j or l_k, nondeterministically chosen.
- $l_i : (\mathsf{SUB}(r), l_j, l_k)$ - *zero check and subtract*: If register r is non-empty, then subtract 1 from it and go to the instruction with label l_j, otherwise go to the instruction with label l_k.
- $l_h : \mathsf{HALT}$ - *halt*: Stop the machine.

A register machine M computes a set $N(M)$ of numbers in the following way: It starts with empty registers by executing the instruction with label l_0 and proceeds by applying instructions as indicated by the labels (and made possible by the contents of the registers). If the halt instruction is reached, then the number stored at that time in register 1 is said to be computed by M. Because of the nondeterminism in choosing the continuation of the computation in the case of nADD instructions, $N(M)$ can be an infinite set.

Note that register machines can be defined with a deterministic variant of the nADD instructions, $l_i : (\text{ADD}(r), l_j)$, as deterministic computing devices which compute some function of an input value placed initially in an input register. It is known (see, e.g., [5]) that in this way they can compute all functions which are Turing computable. We made the add instruction nondeterministic in order to obtain a device which generates sets of numbers starting from a unique initial configuration. As any recursively enumerable set can be obtained as the range of a Turing computable function on the set of non-negative integers, this way we can generate any recursively enumerable set of numbers.

Theorem 1. *All recursively enumerable sets of natural numbers can be generated by a symport/antiport P system with membrane boundaries having one membrane and using minimal parallel, sequential, or asynchronous rule application.*

Proof. We show how the computations of a register machine can be simulated by a P system where the applicability of the rules are regulated by the generated membrane boundaries. Let $M = (m, H, l_0, l_h, R)$ be a register machine as above, and let us assume, without the loss of generality, that besides the output register, all registers are empty when the halt instruction is executed.

Let $\Pi_M = (V, [\ ]_1, w_1, R_1)$ be a P system as follows.

$$V = \{t_{i,j} \mid l_i, l_j \in H\} \cup \{a_i \mid 1 \leq i \leq m\} \cup \{t_{ini}, t_h, b, c, d\},$$

$$w_1 = t_{ini},$$

$$\begin{aligned}
R_1 = \{&(t_{ini}, out; t_{0,i}, in), (t_{ini}, out; t_{0,j}, in) \mid l_0 : (\text{nADD}(r), l_i, l_j) \in R \text{ or} \\
&l_0 : (\text{SUB}(r), l_i, l_j) \in R\} \cup \\
&\{(t_{i,j}, out; a_r t_{j,X}, in), (t_{i,k}, out; a_r t_{k,X}, in) \mid l_i : (\text{nADD}(r), l_j, l_k) \in R, \\
&l_X \in H\} \cup \\
&\{(a_r t_{i,j}, out; t_{j,X}, in), (t_{i,k}, out; t_{k,X}, in) \mid l_i : (\text{SUB}(r), l_j, l_k) \in R, \\
&l_X \in H\} \cup \\
&\{(t_{h,X}, out; t_h, in) \mid l_X \in H\} \cup \{(c, out; c, in), (t_h cd, out)\}.
\end{aligned}$$

The membrane approximation space $\text{MAS}(\Pi_M) = \langle V^*, \mathfrak{B}, \mathfrak{D}_\mathfrak{B}, \mathsf{l}, \mathsf{u}, \mathsf{b} \rangle$ associated to Π_M is defined by the base multisets (we use the string notation for multisets, as before)

$$\begin{aligned}
\mathfrak{B} = \{&cc, t_h b\} \cup \{a_r b, a_r d \mid 1 \leq r \leq m\} \cup \{t_{h,X} t_h \mid X \in H\} \cup \\
&\{t_{i,j} t_{j,X} \mid l_i, l_j, l_X \in H\} \cup \{t_{i,k} a_r \mid l_i : (\text{SUB}(r), l_j, l_k) \in R\} \cup \\
&\{a_i^n db \mid 1 \leq i \leq m, \ n \geq 1\} \cup \{t_{ini} t_{0,X} \mid l_X \in H\}.
\end{aligned}$$

Note that the set of base msets is infinite, it contains a multiset $a_i^n db$ for all $1 \leq i \leq m$ and $n \geq 1$.

To see how the register machine M is simulated by Π_M, consider the following. Π_M starts in the initial configuration

$$(t_{ini}cd).$$

The msets $t_{ini}t_{0,X}$ are in $\mathfrak{B}$ for all $l_X \in H$, but there is no object $t_{0,X}$ inside the first region, so t_{ini} is element of the unstable part $\mathsf{UNS}^{in}(1)$ of the first (and only) region, and as there is an unlimited supply of $t_{0,X}$ in the environment, it is also element of the boundary $\mathsf{bnd}^{in}_{stable}(1)$ while $t_{0,X}$ for all $l_X \in H$ are in $\mathsf{bnd}^{out}_{stable}(1)$. This means that a rule $(t_{ini}, out; t_{0,X}, in)$ can be used resulting in the configuration

$$(t_{0,X}d) \text{ for some } l_X \in H.$$

This configuration corresponds to the situation when M is going to execute the instruction l_0 which will be followed by instruction l_X.

To look at the simulation in a more general way, note that configurations

$$(a_1^{n_1} a_2^{n_2} \ldots a_m^{n_m} t_{i,X} d)$$

of Π correspond to the configurations of M in such a way, that n_i, the number of occurrences of object a_i, $1 \leq i \leq m$, is the value stored in the ith register, and the next executed instruction l_i will be followed by l_X.

(1) If $l_X \neq l_k$ for some $l_i : (\mathtt{SUB}(r), l_j, l_k)$, then $t_{i,X}$ is again the element of the unstable part of the region, moreover, it is in $\mathsf{bnd}^{in}_{stable}(1)$ while $t_{X,Y}$ for all $l_X, l_Y \in H$ are in $\mathsf{bnd}^{out}_{stable}(1)$ (because $t_{i,X}t_{X,Y} \in \mathfrak{B}$), so the rule simulating the instruction l_i can be executed.

Let us suppose that $l_X = l_j$ for some instruction $l_i : (\mathtt{nADD}(r), l_j, l_k)$ or $l_i : (\mathtt{nADD}(r), l_k, l_j)$. In this case, the number of a_r objects inside the region should be increased by one. Since the only base msets containing a_rs are $a_r^n db$ for $n \geq 1$, and b is not present inside the region, there are either no a_rs, or they are the elements of $\mathsf{UNS}^{in}(1)$. Moreover, since $a_r^n db \in \mathfrak{B}$ for all $n \geq 1$, there is an unlimited supply of a_r in the outside boundary $\mathsf{bnd}^{out}_{stable}(w_1)$. Thus, a rule $(t_{i,j}, out; a_r t_{j,X}, in)$ increasing the number of a_rs inside the system and introducing the transition symbol $t_{j,X}$ for some $l_X \in H$ can be used.

If $l_X = l_j$ for an instruction $l_i : (\mathtt{SUB}(r), l_j, l_k)$, then the number of a_r objects inside the region should be decreased by one. Since $a_r db \in \mathfrak{B}$ and b is not inside the system, if there are a_r symbols inside, then they are in the inner boundary $\mathsf{bnd}^{in}_{stable}(w_1)$. This means that the rule $(a_r t_{i,j}, out; t_{j,X}, in)$ simulating the decrement instruction can be used.

(2) If $l_X = l_k$ for some $l_i : (\mathtt{SUB}(r), l_j, l_k)$, then there should be no a_r present inside the system. As $t_{i,k}$ is an element of the boundary only if no a_r is present (because $a_r t_{i,k}$ is a base mset, so if there are a_rs inside, then $t_{i,k}$ does not become part of the unstable region of the membrane) the computation can only continue, if this requirement is satisfied.

To summarize the above considerations, we can conclude that a configuration

$$(a_1^{n_1} a_2^{n_2} \dots a_m^{n_m} t_{i,X} d)$$

is changed to

$$(a_1^{n_1'} a_2^{n_2'} \dots a_m^{n_m'} t_{X,Y} d)$$

such that the numbers of occurrences n_i' of a_i, $1 \leq i \leq m$ correspond to the counter contents after executing the instruction labeled by l_i.

If at some point of the functioning of Π_M, the object $t_{h,X}$ is introduced for some $l_X \in H$, then the execution of the halting instruction should follow. This is possible, since $t_{h,X}$ is part of the inner, and t_h is part of the outer boundary, so after the use of the rule $(t_{h,X}, out; t_h, in)$ we have t_h inside the system, which is again an element of the inner boundary, since $t_h b \in \mathfrak{B}$. Thus, the rule $(t_h cd, out)$ can be used (c is also in the boundary, because of $cc \in \mathfrak{B}$, just as is d, because of $a_i^n db \in \mathfrak{B}$) ending the computation by stopping the "infinite loop" implemented by the rule $(c, out; c, in)$. This infinite loop prevents the halting of the system in the case of a computation which does not correspond to a computation of the simulated register machine M.

8   Conclusion

We have introduced a notion of boundaries in membrane systems which is based on the concept of chemical stability: The base msets of the multiset approximation space represent stable complexes, the objects which are in a low energy state together, a state where they are not likely to engage into any type of interaction, or chemical reaction.

We have also demonstrated how this new notion of membrane boundaries can be employed to control the application of rules, or more precisely, the availability of objects for interaction: objects can only be the subject of rule application if they are on the boundary of the region that contains them. As an initial result, we used this technique to implement "appearance checking" (or zero checking) in such a way which does not rely on the maximal parallel way of rule application, thus, membrane systems with boundaries can simulate register machines also when using any type of "non-maximal-parallel" or asynchronous rule application. This is an interesting result since these types of systems without membrane boundaries can only generate the Parikh sets of matrix languages, which is a strict subclass of the class of recursively enumerable languages (see [11], Chapter 5 for more details).

References

1. Csajbók, Z.E.H., Mihálydeák, T.: Maximal parallelism in membrane systems with generated membrane boundaries. In: Beckmann, A., Csuhaj-Varjú, E., Meer, K. (eds.) CiE 2014. LNCS, vol. 8493, pp. 103–112. Springer, Heidelberg (2014)
2. Freund, R., Păun, A.: Membrane systems with symport/antiport rules: universality results. In: Păun, G., Rozenberg, G., Salomaa, A., Zandron, C. (eds.) WMC 2002. LNCS, vol. 2597. Springer, Heidelberg (2003)
3. Mihálydeák, T., Csajbók, Z.E.H.: Membranes with boundaries. In: Csuhaj-Varjú, E., Gheorghe, M., Rozenberg, G., Salomaa, A., Vaszil, G. (eds.) CMC 2012. LNCS, vol. 7762, pp. 277–294. Springer, Heidelberg (2013)
4. Mihálydeák, T., Csajbók, Z.E.H., Takács, P.: Communication rules controlled by generated membrane boundaries. In: Alhazov, A., Cojocaru, S., Gheorghe, M., Rogozhin, Y., Rozenberg, G., Salomaa, A. (eds.) CMC 2013. LNCS, vol. 8340, pp. 265–279. Springer, Heidelberg (2014)
5. Minsky, M.: Computation - Finite and Infinite Machines. Prentice Hall, Englewood Cliffs (1967)
6. Pawlak, Z.: Rough sets. Int. J. Comput. Inf. Sci. 11(5), 341–356 (1982)
7. Pawlak, Z.: Rough Sets: Theoretical Aspects of Reasoning about Data. Kluwer Academic Publishers, Dordrecht (1991)
8. Păun, A., Păun, G.: The power of communication: P systems with symport/antiport. New Gener. Comput. 20(3), 295–305 (2002)
9. Păun, G.: Computing with membranes. J. Comput. Syst. Sci. 61(1), 108–143 (2000)
10. Păun, G.: Membrane Computing: An Introduction. Springer, Berlin (2002)
11. Păun, G., Rozenberg, G., Salomaa, A. (eds.): Oxford Handbooks. Oxford University Press Inc., New York (2010)
12. Sosík, P.: P systems versus register machines: two universality proofs. In: Păun, G., Zandron, C. (eds.) Pre-Proceedings of Workshop on Membrane Computing (WMC-CdeA2002), pp. 371–382. Romania, Curtea de Argeş (2002)

Structured Grid Algorithms Modelled with Complex Objects

Radu Nicolescu[(✉)]

Department of Computer Science, University of Auckland,
Private Bag 92019, Auckland, New Zealand
r.nicolescu@auckland.ac.nz

Abstract. We present a simple membrane computing model for a typical structured grid algorithm: a parallel and distributed seeded region growing algorithm for gray images. With a proper granularity, the system can be efficiently mapped to a distributed Actor system, possibly a cloud-based Actor system. The image pixels are partitioned in rectangular sub-images, which are modeled as complex cells and evolve via inter-cell parallelism. Pixels inside a cell are modeled as sub-cellular objects and evolve via intra-cell parallelism. The presented model is synchronous, but can be further extended to an asynchronous version. Each cell can be efficiently implemented on a multi-core or many-core architecture and cells can communicate their boundary data via messages.

Keywords: Membrane computing · P systems · Inter-cell parallelism · Intra-cell parallelism · Prolog terms · Complex objects · Generic rules · Image processing · Seeded region growing · Parallel and concurrent models · Synchronous and asynchronous models · Termination detection · Message-based · Actor model · Computation and communication patterns · The 13 Berkeley dwarfs

1 Introduction

We have previously used complex objects to successfully model problems in a wide variety of domains: image processing and computer vision [12,13,17,18]; graph theory [11,22]; distributed algorithms [6,9,10,21,23,29]; high-level P systems programming [19,20]; numerical P systems [19,20]; NP-complete problems [19,20,23].

In this paper, we choose another fundamental image processing task: *seeded region growing* of gray images. Specifically, we model the massively parallel algorithm presented by Braünl et al. [5]. This algorithm is typical for a wide range of parallel algorithms, collectively forming the *structured grid dwarf* – one of the *13 Berkeley dwarfs* [3].

The image pixels are partitioned in *rectangular blocks*, which are modeled as *complex cells* and evolve via *inter-cell parallelism*. Pixels inside a cell are modeled as *sub-cellular objects* and evolve via *intra-cell parallelism*. Cells can

© Springer International Publishing Switzerland 2015
G. Rozenberg et al. (Eds.): CMC 2015, LNCS 9504, pp. 321–337, 2015.
DOI: 10.1007/978-3-319-28475-0_22

communicate their boundary data via *messages*, as in the Actor model [2,14]. The model presented here is *synchronous*, but can be further extended to an *asynchronous* version.

Further, although not detailed here (for lack of space), we provide a couple of direct emulations of this model in the Actors framework, using, first, (i) the single system F#'s mailbox processor library [28]; and, next, (ii) its research cloud-based extension Orleans [4,7]. Each cell/actor can be efficiently implemented on a multi-core or many-core architecture.

We are aware of only a few previous papers studying membrane computing models for real-life complex image processing tasks. We remark an interesting series of papers on membrane models for image thinning algorithms: (i) Reina-Molina et al. [27] propose a traditional tissue system; (ii) Reina-Molina and Díaz-Pernil [26] discuss a similar tissue based system; (iii) Peña-Cantillana et al. [24] discuss a related cellular model, mapped on the CUDA platform; (iv) Díaz-Pernil et al. [8] propose a spiking neural model, also mapped on the CUDA platform; (v) Nicolescu [17] proposes several models based on complex objects: two multi-cells systems, based on 1:1 mappings between pixels and cells; and a single-cell system, based on a 1:1 mapping between pixels and sub-cellular objects.

This experiment reinforces our earlier conjecture [17] that, given a good support for pattern matching, the translation from complex objects to Actors can be largely automatised, not only for similar image processing tasks, but for many other parallel applications, for both synchronous and asynchronous cases.

As in other similar papers, here we do *not* cover two important issues: the initialisation and the termination detection of distributed algorithms. In fact, we are not aware of many membrane computing studies on the distributed termination detection, which could be quite complex in the asynchronous setting.

For example, Nicolescu and Wu [23] and Wu [30] have recently studied a systematic approach to distributed termination detection for diffusing (single source) algorithms, but more studies are needed on non-diffusing (multiple source) algorithms such as this (especially for scenarios when a master control node cannot be easily incorporated). For the P systems model considered in this paper, we just follow the standard theoretical definition that the whole system "magically" stops when none of its cells can further evolve.

Because of space constraints, for the rest of the paper, we assume some basic familiarity with:

- The basic *region growing* concepts. Section 2 presents a bird's eye view; for further details see the monograph of Braünl et al. [5].
- The *structured grid* pattern in *parallel processing*. Section 3 presents a bird's eye view; for further details see the classical Berkeley papers on the 13 parallel dwarfs topic, e.g. [1,3].
- The *Actor* model in *functional programming*, e.g. as discussed in Sime's monograph [28].

- The basic definitions used in traditional *tissue-like transition P systems*, including state based rules, weak priority, promoters and inhibitors, e.g. as discussed in the membrane computing handbook [25].
- The membrane extensions collectively known as *complex objects*, proposed by Nicolescu et al. [17,19,20,23], i.e. *complex objects, generic rules*, and *"micro-surgeries"* on inner nested sub-cellular objects. However, to ensure some degree of self-containment, these extensions are reviewed in Sect. 4.

2   Background: Seeded Region Growing

Like other segmentation methods [5], *region growing* wants to simplify an image by evidencing large connected sets of pixels with similar characteristics, which probably belong to the same objects. More technically, the ideal goal of region growing is a partition of an image A into regions R_i, such that:

1. $A = \bigcup R_i$, the regions cover the entire image
2. Each region, R_i, is connected (over the 4 or 8 neighbourhood)
3. $R_i \cap R_j = \emptyset, i \neq j$, regions are disjoint (of course)
4. All pixels of a region, R_i, satisfy a specific condition $P(R_i)$
5. $\neg P(R_i \cup R_j), i \neq j$, pixels of the union of any two regions do not satisfy the given condition P

Often, the condition P can simply require that the gray values of pixels are not too far apart – i.e. their difference is less than a given *threshold*.

Typically, region growing works bottom-up, in a sequence of *steps*. It starts from a set of *seeds* which define the *initial regions*. At each step, each region may *grow* by annexing adjacent pixels which verify the given condition P; these pixels may have been unallocated, but may also be taken from less suitable regions (which means that some regions may also shrink or shift in the image space).

The condition P is further specialized. Each region has a *value*, equal to the pixel value of its initial seed. Besides the pixel intensity, each node holds a copy of the region *value* and an unique *label* (ID). A region can claim a pixel if the difference between the region *value* and that pixel *intensity* is less than the given *threshold*. The process ends when no more changes are possible.

For our study, we select the region growing algorithm described by Bräunl et al. [5]. As in this monograph, we assume that the seeds and the threshold have already been selected, e.g. either by their gray intensity or by an arithmetic progression on the image axes – for example, pixels are seeds if their coordinates are divisible by a given number (e.g. 8). However, we side note that selecting the best seeds and threshold is another interesting and complex problem.

Conflicting claims, when two regions attempt to annex the same pixel, are arbitrarily resolved by allocating unique labels (IDs) to each seed and region, and giving priority to the region with the highest label. This ensures that the algorithm is highly parallelisable and the resulting solution is unique (but the result is biased in favour of higher numbered regions).

While practically validating our P membrane model, we noticed that this simple algorithm does *not* necessarily fulfills its theoretical ideal goals:

– The algorithm may violate item (1): the resulting region may *not* cover the whole image, as some pixels may remain unallocated. While theoretically annoying, this is acceptable, as it makes sense in practical cases.
– More problematic, but still acceptable practically, the algorithm may also violate item (2): a region may split and become *unconnected*, after some of its pixels are annexed by another higher-priority region.

It should be interesting to design and investigate more advanced versions of this algorithm, which are less biased and theoretically correct, but still retaining a high parallelisation potential — however, this is an open problem, outside the scope of this paper.

Figures 1, 2, 3 and 4 illustrate a small artificial test image (8 × 8). The following parameters were used: (i) the 4 neighborhood; (ii) the threshold was 80; (iii) seeds were defined as pixels with coordinates divisible by 3.

Figure 3 shows the regions which have started to form after the first step: there were 22 changes and, in particular, the initial singleton region 55 (with value 200) has extended to its N, S and W neighbours (with pixel intensities 200, 200, 180, respectively).

The final results of Fig. 4 highlights the above mentioned issues: (i) some of the pixels remain unallocated – region label 0; (ii) region 52 ended disconnected into four areas – also seen on Fig. 1b as medium gray shades below the dark region.

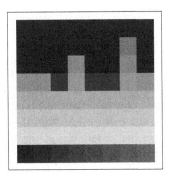

(a) Test image – 8 × 8 pixels with deep zoom

(b) Regions resulting from our implementation – deep zoom

Fig. 1. Test which includes "pathological" cases (parameters in the text)

Figure 5 show a practical result of this algorithm. The left Fig. 5a shows a photo of a night-time lightning. The right Fig. 5b shows the resulting regions, after applying our implementation, where (i) we used the 4 neighborhood; (ii) the

10	10	10	130	160	180	200	10
10	10	10	130	160	180	200	20
10	10	10	30	160	180	200	30
10	10	120	140	160	180	200	40
10	10	10	30	160	180	200	50
10	10	10	30	160	180	200	60
10	100	120	140	160	180	200	70
10	10	10	130	160	180	200	80

1	0	0	4	0	0	7	0
0	0	0	0	0	0	0	0
0	0	0	0	0	0	0	0
25	0	0	28	0	0	31	0
0	0	0	0	0	0	0	0
0	0	0	0	0	0	0	0
49	0	0	52	0	0	55	0
0	0	0	0	0	0	0	0

(a) Pixel *intensities*   (b) Seeds and initial region *labels*

Fig. 2. Initial test image and its 9 seeds (initial regions)

10	10	10	130	130	200	200	10
10	10	10	130	160	180	200	20
10	10	10	30	160	180	200	30
10	10	140	140	140	200	200	40
10	10	10	30	160	180	200	50
10	10	10	30	160	180	200	60
10	100	140	140	140	200	200	70
10	10	10	140	160	180	200	80

1	1	0	4	4	7	7	0
1	0	0	4	0	0	7	0
25	0	0	0	0	0	31	0
25	25	28	28	28	31	31	0
25	0	0	0	0	0	31	0
49	0	0	0	0	0	55	0
49	0	52	52	52	55	55	0
49	0	0	52	0	0	55	0

(a) Region *values* after step #1   (b) Region *labels* after step #1

Fig. 3. Regions after step #1

10	10	10	140	200	200	200	10
10	10	10	140	200	200	200	20
10	10	10	10	200	200	200	30
10	10	140	200	200	200	200	40
10	10	10	10	200	200	200	50
10	10	10	10	200	200	200	60
10	140	140	200	200	200	200	70
10	10	10	140	200	200	200	80

49	49	49	52	55	55	55	0
49	49	49	52	55	55	55	0
49	49	49	49	55	55	55	0
49	49	52	55	55	55	55	0
49	49	49	49	55	55	55	0
49	49	49	49	55	55	55	0
49	52	52	55	55	55	55	0
49	49	49	52	55	55	55	0

(a) Final region *values*   (b) Final region *labels*

Fig. 4. Final 3 regions (49, 52, 55) of the test image

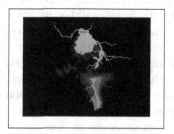

(a) Original lightning image from wikipedia – 457 × 334 pixels

(b) Regions resulting from our implementation

Fig. 5. Region growing – lightning picture (parameters indicated in the text)

threshold was 80; (iii) seeds were defined as the union of pixels with maximum intensity (255 = white) and pixels with coordinates divisible by 4.

Like all algorithms from the structured grid class, this algorithm has a high parallelisation potential and can be straightforwardly adapted for many-core processors such as GPUs. In this paper, we are looking at modeling and implementing it in a combined parallel+distributed way, where the distributed nodes can be systems on a given network, but also cloud-based nodes.

3   Background: Structured Grid Dwarf

In the simplest form of the *structured grid* [1,3], the data is arranged in the nodes of a rectangular 2D grid of nodes (e.g. 2D arrays) and is processed in a sequence of steps (phases). Each step computes new values, which only depend on the current values of a node and its adjacent grid neighbours.

Typically, this local neighbourhood consists of the four horizontally and vertically adjacent nodes – symbolically denoted as N, E, S, W – as shown in Fig. 6a. In some scenarious, the neighbourhood may also include the four diagonally adjacent nodes – symbolically denoted as NE, SE, SW, NW – however, here we do not follow this possible extension. The basic system works synchronously and, typically, the new values become accessible to the neighbours only after all nodes have completed their step.

On an uniprocessor system, each step requires a full sweep over the whole grid. On a typical many-core system (e.g. GPU based), each node is mapped to its own "thread" and all threads evolve in lock-step. On a multi-core system, the grid can be partitioned among available cores, and, for each step, each core sweeps over its allocated region and then post-step synchronisations are required.

Like the multi-core solution, a distributed solution starts with a partition – typically rectangular – and its sub-grids are allocated among available systems, as shown in Fig. 6b. Each of these systems can independently be an uni-core, a many-core or a multi-core system, thus the final solution may combine the benefits of parallel and distributed computing.

However, the problem is a bit more complex, as border nodes from one system need data from neighboring systems. This problem can be solved via "ghost" nodes, i.e. copies of border nodes of adjacent systems. In the simplest case, the ghost nodes are aligned in one node wide rows and columns and are considered read-only for the current sub-grid (essentially a one-way buffer), as their next step values depend on data which is only available in the neighbouring systems.

Of course, these ghost nodes must be timely updated after each global step, via post-step messages between systems – these updates can be performed via high-level messages exchanged by a distributed or even cloud-based Actor system, such as Orleans [4,7]. Thus, this algorithmic pattern is theoretically synchronous, but its practical implementations need to cope with these typically asynchronous messages exchanged between systems.

More flexible or more efficient systems can be designed by using (i) larger ghost areas combined with less frequent messages and/or (ii) more complex logic that allows some of the inner nodes to independently progress a few steps ahead, without requiring synchronizations. These are interesting questions which however are out of the scope of this paper.

As it should now be apparent, the structured grid pattern is a good match for the selected region growing algorithm. And, as we will show in Sect. 5, both are decently modelled by membrane systems with complex objects.

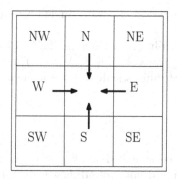

(a) Computing new values in the 4 neighbourhood

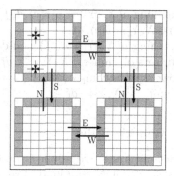

(b) Distributed grid with ghost nodes (gray), local computing (short arrows) and cloning messages (long thick arrows)

Fig. 6. Structured grid – bird's eye view

4   Membrane Computing with Complex Objects

For self-containment, we recall a few non-standard details of our complex-objects framework. For a fuller picture, the reader is advised to check our earlier paper on parallel thinning with complex objects [17].

4.1   Complex Objects

Complex objects play the roles of cellular micro-compartments or substructures, such as organelles, vesicles or cytoophidium assemblies ("snakes"), which are embedded in cells or travel between cells, but without having the full processing power of a complete cell. In our proposal, complex objects represent structured data that have no own processing power: they are acted upon by the rules of their enclosing cells.

Technically, our *complex objects*, are Prolog-like *first-order terms*, recursively built from *multisets* of atoms and variables, but *extended* over *multisets* (*bags*). *Atoms* are typically denoted by lower case letters, such as a, b, c. *Variables* are typically denoted by uppercase letters, such as X, Y, Z.

Unification. All terms (ground or not) can be (asymmetrically) *matched* against *ground* terms, using an ad-hoc version of *pattern matching*, more precisely, a *one-way first-order syntactic unification*, where an atom can only match another copy of itself, and a variable can match any bag of ground terms (including the empty bag, λ). This may create a combinatorial *non-determinism*, when a combination of two or more variables are matched against the same bag, in which case an arbitrary matching is chosen. For example:

- Matching $a(X, eY) = a(b(c), def)$ deterministically creates a single set of unifiers: $X, Y = b(c), df$.
- Matching $a(XY) = a(df)$ non-deterministically creates one of the following four sets of unifiers: $X, Y = \lambda, df$; $X, Y = df, \lambda$; $X, Y = d, f$; $X, Y = f, d$.
- However, matching $a(XY, Y) = a(def, e)$ deterministically creates a single set of unifiers: $X, Y = df, e$.

4.2   Generic Rules

By default, rules are applied top-down, in the so-called *weak priority* order. *Rules* may contain *any* kind of terms, ground and not-ground; however, in this proposal, *cells* can only contain *ground* terms.

Pattern Matching. Rules are matched against cell contents using the above discussed *pattern matching*, which involves the rule's left-hand side, promoters and inhibitors. Moreover, the matching is *valid* only if, after substituting variables by their values, the rule's right-hand side contains ground terms only (so *no* free variables are injected in the cell or sent to its neighbours), as illustrated by the following sample scenario:

- The cell's *current content* includes the *ground term*:
  $n(l^{10}, n(l^{20}, f(l^{30}), f(l^{40})), f(l^{50}))$
- The following *rewriting rule* is considered:
  $n(X, n(Y, Y_1, Y_2), f(Z)) \rightarrow v(X)\, n(Y, Y_1, Y_2)\, v(Z)$
- Our pattern matching determines the following *unifiers*:
  $X = l^{10}$, $Y = l^{20}$, $Y_1 = l^{30}$, $Y_2 = l^{40}$, $Z = l^{50}$.
- This is a *valid* matching and, after *substitutions*, the rule's *right-hand* side gives the *new content*:
  $v(l^{10})\, n(l^{20}, f(l^{30}), f(l^{40}))\, v(l^{50})$

Generic Rules Format. More generally, we consider rules of the following *generic* format, which defines templates involving variables (here we present a simplified version, enough to cover all scenarios used in this paper):

---

current-state objects... $\rightarrow_\alpha$ target-state in-objects... (out-objects)$_\delta$...

| promoters... $\neg$ inhibitors...

Where:

- *States* are complex objects (which can be *matched*, as previously described).
- All *objects*, *promoters* and *inhibitors* are *bags of terms*, possibly containing *variables* (which are *matched* as previously described).
- *Out-objects* are sent, at the end of the step, to the cell's structural neighbours. These objects are enclosed in round parentheses which further indicate their destinations, above abbreviated as δ; the most usual scenarios include: (a) $\downarrow_i$ indicates that a is sent to child i (unicast), (a) $\uparrow_i$ indicates that a is sent to parent i (unicast), (a) $\downarrow_\forall$ indicates that a is sent to all children (broadcast), (a) $\uparrow_\forall$ indicates that a is sent to all parents (broadcast), (a) $\updownarrow_\forall$ indicates that a is sent to all neighbours (broadcast).
- Symbol $\alpha \in \{\text{min, max}\} \times \{\text{min, max}\}$, indicates a combined instantiation and rewriting mode, as further discussed below.

Example. To explain our combined instantiation and rewriting mode, let us consider a cell, σ, containing three counter-like complex objects, $c(c(a))$, $c(c(a))$, $c(c(c(a)))$, and the four possible instantiation$\otimes$rewriting modes of the following "decrementing" rule:

$$(\rho_\alpha) \ S_1 \ c(c(X)) \to_\alpha S_2 \ c(X), \text{where } \alpha \in \{\text{min,max}\} \times \{\text{min,max}\}.$$

1. If $\alpha = \text{min}\otimes\text{min}$, rule $\rho_{\text{min}\otimes\text{min}}$ nondeterministically generates and applies (in the min mode) *one* of the following two rule instances:

$$(\rho_1') \ S_1 \ c(c(a)) \to_{\text{min}} S_2 \ c(a) \quad \text{or}$$
$$(\rho_1'') \ S_1 \ c(c(c(a))) \to_{\text{min}} S_2 \ c(c(a)).$$

Using (ρ_1'), cell σ ends with counters $c(a)$, $c(c(a))$, $c(c(c(a)))$. Using (ρ_1''), cell σ ends with counters $c(c(a))$, $c(c(a))$, $c(c(a))$.

2. If $\alpha = \text{max}\otimes\text{min}$, rule $\rho_{\text{max}\otimes\text{min}}$ first generates and then applies (in the min mode) the following *two* rule instances:

$$(\rho_2') \ S_1 \ c(c(a)) \to_{\text{min}} S_2 \ c(a) \quad \text{and}$$
$$(\rho_2'') \ S_1 \ c(c(c(a))) \to_{\text{min}} S_2 \ c(c(a)).$$

Using (ρ_2') and (ρ_2''), cell σ ends with counters $c(a)$, $c(c(a))$, $c(c(a))$.

3. If $\alpha = \text{min}\otimes\text{max}$, rule $\rho_{\text{min}\otimes\text{max}}$ nondeterministically generates and applies (in the max mode) *one* of the following rule instances:

$$(\rho_3') \ S_1 \ c(c(a)) \to_{\text{max}} S_2 \ c(a) \quad \text{or}$$
$$(\rho_3'') \ S_1 \ c(c(c(a))) \to_{\text{max}} S_2 \ c(c(a)).$$

Using (ρ_3'), cell σ ends with counters $c(a)$, $c(a)$, $c(c(c(a)))$. Using (ρ_3''), cell σ ends with counters $c(c(a))$, $c(c(a))$, $c(c(a))$.

4. If $\alpha = \mathtt{max} \otimes \mathtt{max}$, rule $\rho_{\mathtt{min} \otimes \mathtt{max}}$ first generates and then applies (in the $\mathtt{max}$ mode) the following *two* rule instances:

$$(\rho_4')\quad S_1\ c(c(a))\ \rightarrow_{\mathtt{max}}\ S_2\ c(a)\quad \text{and}$$
$$(\rho_4'')\quad S_1\ c(c(c(a)))\ \rightarrow_{\mathtt{max}}\ S_2\ c(c(a)).$$

Using (ρ_4') and (ρ_4''), cell σ ends with counters $c(a)$, $c(a)$, $c(c(a))$.

The interpretation of $\mathtt{min} \otimes \mathtt{min}$, $\mathtt{min} \otimes \mathtt{max}$ and $\mathtt{max} \otimes \mathtt{max}$ modes is straightforward. While other interpretations could be considered, the mode $\mathtt{max} \otimes \mathtt{min}$ indicates that the generic rule is instantiated as *many* times as possible, without *superfluous* instances (i.e. without duplicates or instances which are not applicable) and each one of the instantiated rules is applied *once*, if possible.

If a rule does not contain any non-ground term, then it has only one possible instantiation: itself. Thus, in this case, the instantiation is an *idempotent* transformation, and the modes $\mathtt{min} \otimes \mathtt{min}$, $\mathtt{min} \otimes \mathtt{max}$, $\mathtt{max} \otimes \mathtt{min}$, $\mathtt{max} \otimes \mathtt{max}$ fall back onto traditional modes $\mathtt{min}$, $\mathtt{max}$, $\mathtt{min}$, $\mathtt{max}$, respectively.

Special Cases. Simple scenarios involving generic rules are sometimes semantically equivalent to loop-based sets of non-generic rules. For example, consider the rule

$$S_1\ a(I, J)\ \rightarrow_{\mathtt{max} \otimes \mathtt{min}}\ S_2\ b(I)\ c(J),$$

where I and J are guaranteed to only match integers in ranges $[1, n]$ and $[1, m]$, respectively. Under these assumptions, this rule is equivalent to the following set of non-generic rules:

$$S_1\ a(i, j)\ \rightarrow_{\mathtt{min}}\ S_2\ b(i)\ c(j),\ \forall i \in [1, n], j \in [1, m].$$

However, unification is a much more powerful concept, which cannot be generally reduced to simple loops.

Note. For all modes, the instantiations are *conceptually* created when rules are tested for applicability and are also *ephemeral*, i.e. they disappear at the end of the step. P system implementations are encouraged to directly apply high-level generic rules, if this is more efficient (it usually is); they may, but need not, start by transforming high-level rules into low-level rules, by way of instantiations.

Benefits. This kind of generic rules allows (i) a reasonably fast parsing and processing of subcomponents, and (ii) algorithm descriptions with *fixed size alphabets* and *fixed sized rulesets*, independent of the size of the problem and number of cells in the system (often impossible with only atomic symbols).

Synchronous vs Asynchronous. In our models, we do not make any syntactic difference between the synchronous and asynchronous scenarios; this is strictly a *runtime* assumption [16]. Any model is able to run in both the synchronous and asynchronous runtime "engines", albeit the results may differ.

In traditional *synchronous* P systems, all rules in a step take exactly *one* time unit and then all message exchanges (including loopback messages for in-objects) are performed at the end of the step, in *zero* time (i.e. instantaneously).

Alternatively, but logically equivalent, we consider that rules in a step are performed in *zero* time (i.e. instantaneously) and then all message exchanges are performed in exactly *one* time unit. This second interpretation is useful, because it allows us to interpret synchronous runs as special cases of asynchronous runs.

In the *asynchronous* scenario, we still consider that rules in a step are performed in *zero* time (i.e. instantaneously), but then each message may take *any* finite real time to arrive at the destination. Additionally, unless otherwise specified, we also assume that messages traveling on the same directed arc follow a *FIFO* rule, i.e. no fast message can overtake a slow progressing one. This definition closely emulates the standard definition used for asynchronous distributed algorithms [15].

Obviously, any algorithm that works correctly in the asynchronous mode will also work correctly in the synchronous mode, but the converse is *not* generally true: extra care may be needed to transform a correct synchronous algorithm into a correct asynchronous one; there are also general control layers, such as *synchronisers*, that can attempt to run a synchronous algorithm on an existing asynchronous runtime, but this does not always work [15].

5   Membrane Model

We model the distributed structured grid pattern illustrated in Fig. 6b with one cell for each sub-grid of the grid partition. Each cell contains a set of complex objects, representing the internal nodes of the corresponding sub-grid – including the ghost nodes.

In the basic theoretical scenario, like in many theoretical distributed algorithms of the *synchronous network model* [15], all cells work synchronously and exchange messages at the end of each logical step. Messages are sent along arcs which are labelled N, E, S and W, according to the usual conventions. Effectively, these messages clone the data of the border nodes into ghost nodes of neighbouring cells.

We use a slightly modified unary notation for all numerical data: coordinates, pixel intensities, region values, region labels. We use digit 1 as the tally symbol; e.g., multiset 1^3 represents number 3 and the empty multiset $\emptyset$ represents 0. Like other theoretical models, such as lambda calculus, we use a base 1 number representation. As our model uses only simple arithmetic operations, which can be very efficiently expressed by our complex rules (incrementations, decrementations, comparisons), this representation does not affect the runtime performance.

The threshold is described by a global complex object $t(h)$, a copy of this is present in each cell. Conceptually, we view each sub-grid as a 0-based 2D array, whose last coordinates are described by a cell-global complex tuple $d(x, y)$.

For example, $d(1^7, 1^7)$ can describe the size of any of the sub-grids of Fig. 6b, which all have 6×6 *proper* nodes and four groups of 6 *ghost* nodes – in this sample, the x and y coordinates run in the 0..7 inclusive interval. Note that *borders* are *proper* nodes, not *ghosts* – in this sample, borders have one of their coordinates (either x or y or both) 1 or 6.

Each internal node is represented as a complex tuple $n(x, y, p, v, r)$, where (i) x and y are its internal coordinates – zero or maximal x, y coordinates indicate ghost nodes, otherwise the node is proper; (ii) p is the pixel intensity; (iii) v is region value; (iv) r is the region label. Temporary copies have an additional component (v) c, a change flag, indicating whether the contents have been changed, 0 – no, 1 – yes.

Essentially, a cell updates all its proper nodes in parallel, where each node updates its state according to the states of its adjacent N, E, S and W nodes. Although the whole evolution could be described by a single (but quite complex) membrane step, we prefer a more straightforward ruleset, using a small but fixed number of membrane steps. Without loss of generality, adjacent nodes are successively considered in this order: 1–N, 2–E, 3–S, and 4–W.

We start by making temporary copies of all current tuples n, logically keeping these at the same coordinates, but resetting the change flag to 0 – the resulting tuples are called n_0:

$$s_0 \qquad \xrightarrow{\text{max} \otimes \text{min}} s_0\ n_0(X, Y, P, V, R, 0)$$
$$|\ n(X, Y, P, V, R)$$

Let us now consider the temporary tuple $n_0(x, y1, p, v, r, c)$ and its N neighbour's tuple $n(x, y, p', v', r')$. If $|p - v'| < h$ and $r < r'$, then this node can be claimed by its neighbour's region and we create another temporary tuple reflecting this, $n_1(x, y1, p, v', r', 1)$. Otherwise, the new tuple n_1 is just a copy of n_0. The following membrane rules model this conditional evolution as one transition step, from s_0 to s_1:

$$s_0\ n_0(X, Y1, P, V, R, \_) \qquad \xrightarrow{\text{max} \otimes \text{min}} s_1\ n_1(X, Y1, P, PG, R1R', 1)$$
$$|\ t(G1\_)\ n(X, Y, P', PG, R1R')$$

$$s_0\ n_0(X, Y1, V'G, V, R, \_) \qquad \xrightarrow{\text{max} \otimes \text{min}} s_1\ n_1(X, Y1, V'G, V', R1R', 1)$$
$$|\ t(G1\_)\ n(X, Y, P', V', R1R')$$

$$s_0\ n_0(X, Y1, P, V, R, C) \qquad \xrightarrow{\text{max} \otimes \text{min}} s_1\ n_1(X, Y1, P, V, R, 1)$$
$$|\ n(X, Y, P', V', R')$$

We repeat similar rules to check the other neighbours, E, S and W: we next check $n_1(x, y, p, v, r, c)$ against the E neighbour $n(x1, y, p', v', r', c')$, then $n_2(x, y, p, v, r, c)$ against the S neighbour $n(x, y1, p', v', r', c')$, and finally $n_3(x1, y, p, v, r, c)$ against the W neighbour $n(x, y, p', v', r', c')$. We end in state s_4, with a temporary tuple n_4.

We now replace the existing tuples n by the possibly modified tuples n_4 and then send the updated border nodes data to neighbouring cells. The following rules detail this update and the outgoing messages due for the N border, which are sent over the outgoing arc labelled N (the other border cases are not detailed, but follow the same pattern). Note the N border is defined by the coordinate $y = 1$.

$$s_4 \; n(X,Y,P,V,R) \; n_4(X,Y,P',V',R',C') \quad \rightarrow_{\max\otimes\min} \; s_5 \; n(X,Y,P',V',R',C')$$

$$s_5 \quad\quad\quad\quad\quad\quad\quad\quad\quad\quad\quad \rightarrow_{\max\otimes\min} \; s_6 \; g(X,1,P,V,R,C) \uparrow_N$$
$$\mid \; n(X,1,P,V,R,C)$$

$$s_5 \quad\quad\quad\quad\quad\quad\quad\quad\quad\quad\quad\quad\quad\quad \rightarrow_{\max\otimes\min} \; s_6$$

The next and final step of this mini-cycle is to reset all ghost cells to the received data, and then to loop back to the initial state s_0. Here we only detail the process of data received from the S neighbour. Note that data received from the N border of our S neighbour has $y = 1$. The system uses these to replace the S ghost line, which has Y equal to the maximum Y of this cell, as given by our dimension tuple d.

$$s_6 \; n(X,Y,\_,\_,\_,\_) \; g(X,1,P,V,R,C) \quad \rightarrow_{\max\otimes\min} \; s_0 \; n(X,Y,P,V,R,C)$$
$$\mid \; d(\_,Y)$$

...

$$s_6 \quad\quad\quad\quad\quad\quad\quad\quad\quad\quad\quad\quad\quad\quad \rightarrow_{\max\otimes\min} \; s_0$$

The theoretical system stops when there are no more changes, but practical implementations must find means that allow the cells to actively detect the termination. The simplest ad-hoc – but less than optimal – solution is to add a new node which has only one task: to centralize the state of each other node and notify the global termination when no cell can make further progress.

6   Evaluation

We evaluate our P systems with Complex Objects model (PCO) against the Parallaxis version (PAR), used in the original proposal [5].

In contrast with more traditional P systems, but like other models based on complex objects, PCO uses a *small fixed size ruleset* and runs in the *same number of rounds* as PAR. We believe that the results are encouraging, despite the fact that there is no totally objective (non-biased) way to directly compare two very different frameworks, such as PCO and PAR.

Program size

PCO has 11 rules (fixed size). PAR has 42 statements.

Runtime

Both algorithms take the same number of *rounds*. A PCO round takes 10 P steps. A PAR round takes 8 critical MOVE/SEND steps, a few other minor steps, plus a costly critical REDUCE macro-step – which itself may take $\log n^2$ more elementary steps.

Scalability

PAR runs on one single system only, which may be single-core, multi-core or a many-core massively parallel SIMD.

Without any changes, PCO scales from running on one single cell to a distributed grid of cells. In a practical implementation, each cell can be mapped to one computing node, where each node can independently be a single-core, multi-core or many-core system.

Asynchronous Support

As defined, PAR strictly requires a synchronous system. As presented here, PCO also runs on synchronous systems; however, it can be adapted to run on asynchronous systems.

Specifically, a local synchronizer logic [15] can be retrofitted into existing cells, by including step numbers in data and rules – these will inhibit any evolution until all required data is available (i.e. until receiving all step messages).

Termination

In both cases, the termination detection is laborious or solved by ad-hoc means. Despite running on one single system only, PAR ends each round with a costly REDUCE macro-step, which indicates the need for a further round.

As described here, PCO uses the *traditional definition* for P systems termination: the system stops when no more changes are globally possible. While mathematically appealing, this solution is hardly practical in the real world.

A clean shortcut is possible when PCO runs on one single cell (like PAR): the system could easily stop at state s_2, if there are no cell-wide changes, which is indicated by $c(0)$. For a grid-based implementation, state s_2 is good point to start a termination detection round, but this issue is not further discussed here.

This membrane model has been manually implemented, using F#, as functional Actor system. Conceptually, the implementation is a close match of the model and its performance is comparable to the performance of manually crafted more imperative implementations.

7   Conclusions

We discussed a membrane model for a fundamental image processing task: seeded region growing. Our proposed model is heavily based on our complex object extensions and compares favourably with the original high-level formalisation, in terms of size (fixed!), complexity (self-contained) and runtime performance (counting the number of steps). Our model can be straightforwardly mapped as a distributed Actor model and further implemented on physical parallel and distributed systems, including cloud distributed Actor systems.

Our experience suggests that similar modelling techniques can be applied to many other parallel algorithms which follow patterns similar to the structured grid of the Berkeley dwarf mine. Our exercise has also highlighted an extant open problem, previously unnoticed, in the original algorithm which inspired its starting base.

While typical image segmentation tasks may not require cloud-based implementations, other structured grid applications do require substantial processing power. For example, in medical image analysis, typical 3D images may contain n^3 voxels; $n = 500..2000$ and more, and many such images are involved in 4D (3D + time) dynamic sequences like cine heart images. Such volumes may require cloud processing. In principle, our approach seems extendable to multi-dimensional spaces, to offer directly executable models for such complex tasks.

Together with some of our previous results (which have resulted in a corrected and better refactored practical image processing implementation), these new results strengthen our positive views on the adequacy of our complex objects extensions for modelling real world parallel and distributed problems.

This exercise raises quite a few open questions, perhaps more interesting than the problem it solved (some of these were asked by the reviewers). Can we design better versions of the considered segmentation algorithm, which overcomes its limitations while still remaining highly parallelisable? Are there better ways to detect the termination of such non-diffusing distributed computations? What is the optimal width of the ghost areas and is it worth to allow a partial asynchrony (e.g. allowing some cells to make several operations ahead of receiving their post-step synchronisation messages)? Can we effectively develop crisp and efficient P systems models for structured grid tasks in n-dimensional spaces? How straightforward can other algorithms or patterns from Berkeley's dwarf mine be modelled via P systems with complex objects (or else, would this require additional extensions)?

Acknowledgments. We are deeply indebted to the anonymous reviewers for their valuable comments and suggestions.

References

1. The landscape of parallel computing research: A view from Berkeley, Revision as of 22:32 (2008). http://view.eecs.berkeley.edu/wiki/Dwarfs. Accessed 17 November 2008
2. Agha, G., Thati, P.: An algebraic theory of actors and its application to a simple object-based language. In: Owe, O., Krogdahl, S., Lyche, T. (eds.) From Object-Orientation to Formal Methods. LNCS, vol. 2635, pp. 26–57. Springer, Heidelberg (2004)
3. Asanovic, K., Bodik, R., Catanzaro, B.C., Gebis, J.J., Husbands, P., Keutzer, K., Patterson, D.A., Plishker, W.L., Shalf, J., Williams, S.W., Yelick, K.A.: The landscape of parallel computing research: A view from Berkeley. Tech. report UCB/EECS-2006-183, EECS Department, University of California, Berkeley, December 2006. http://www.eecs.berkeley.edu/Pubs/TechRpts/2006/EECS-2006-183.html

4. Bernstein, P.A., Bykov, S., Geller, A., Kliot, G., Thelin, J.: Orleans: Distributed virtual actors for programmability and scalability. Tech. report MSR-TR-2014-41, March 2014. http://research.microsoft.com/apps/pubs/default.aspx?id=210931
5. Braünl, T., Feyrer, S., Rapf, W., Reinhardt, M.: Parallel Image Processing. Springer, Heidelberg (2010). Reprint edition
6. Bălănescu, T., Nicolescu, R., Wu, H.: Asynchronous P systems. Int. J. Nat. Comput. Res. **2**(2), 1–18 (2011)
7. Bykov, S., Geller, A., Kliot, G., Larus, J., Pandya, R., Thelin, J.: Orleans: cloud computing for everyone. In: ACM Symposium on Cloud Computing (SOCC 2011). ACM, October 2011. http://research.microsoft.com/apps/pubs/default. aspx?id=153347
8. Díaz-Pernil, D., Peña-Cantillana, F., Gutiérrez-Naranjo, M.A.: A parallel algorithm for skeletonizing images by using spiking neural P systems. Neurocomputing
   - **115**, 81–91 (2013)
9. Dinneen, M.J., Kim, Y.-B., Nicolescu, R.: A faster P solution for the byzantine agreement problem. In: Gheorghe, M., Hinze, T., Păun, G., Rozenberg, G., Salomaa, A. (eds.) CMC 2010. LNCS, vol. 6501, pp. 175–197. Springer, Heidelberg (2010)
10. Dinneen, M.J., Kim, Y.B., Nicolescu, R.: P systems and the Byzantine agreement. J. Logic Algebraic Program. **79**(6), 334–349 (2010)
11. ElGindy, H., Nicolescu, R., Wu, H.: Fast distributed DFS solutions for edge-disjoint paths in digraphs. In: Csuhaj-Varjú, E., Gheorghe, M., Rozenberg, G., Salomaa, A., Vaszil, G. (eds.) CMC 2012. LNCS, vol. 7762, pp. 173–194. Springer, Heidelberg (2013)
12. Gimel'farb, G., Nicolescu, R., Ragavan, S.: P systems in stereo matching. In: Real, P., Diaz-Pernil, D., Molina-Abril, H., Berciano, A., Kropatsch, W. (eds.) CAIP 2011, Part II. LNCS, vol. 6855, pp. 285–292. Springer, Heidelberg (2011)
13. Gimel'farb, G., Nicolescu, R., Ragavan, S.: P system implementation of dynamic programming stereo. J. Math. Imag. Vis. **47**(1–2), 13–26 (2013). http://dx.doi.org/10.1007/s10851-012-0367-6
14. Hewitt, C.: Viewing control structures as patterns of passing messages. Artif. Intell. **8**(3), 323–364 (1977). http://www.sciencedirect.com/science/article/pii/0004370277900339
15. Lynch, N.A.: Distributed Algorithms. Morgan Kaufmann Publishers Inc., San Francisco (1996)
16. Nicolescu, R.: Parallel and distributed algorithms in P systems. In: Gheorghe, M., Păun, G., Rozenberg, G., Salomaa, A., Verlan, S. (eds.) CMC 2011. LNCS, vol. 7184, pp. 35–50. Springer, Heidelberg (2012)
17. Nicolescu, R.: Parallel thinning with complex objects and actors. In: Gheorghe, M., Rozenberg, G., Salomaa, A., Sosík, P., Zandron, C. (eds.) CMC 2014. LNCS, vol. 8961, pp. 330–354. Springer, Heidelberg (2014)
18. Nicolescu, R., Gimel'farb, G., Morris, J., Gong, R., Delmas, P.: Regularising ill-posed discrete optimisation: quests with P systems. Fundam. Inf. **131**(3–4), 465–483 (2014)
19. Nicolescu, R., Ipate, F., Wu, H.: Programming P systems with complex objects. In: Alhazov, A., Cojocaru, S., Gheorghe, M., Rogozhin, Y., Rozenberg, G., Salomaa, A. (eds.) CMC 2013. LNCS, vol. 8340, pp. 280–300. Springer, Heidelberg (2014)
20. Nicolescu, R., Ipate, F., Wu, H.: Towards high-level P systems programming using complex objects. In: Alhazov, A., Cojocaru, S., Gheorghe, M., Rogozhin, Y. (eds.) 14th International Conference on Membrane Computing, CMC 2014, Chişinău,

Moldova, 20–23 August 2013, Proceedings, pp. 255–276. Institute of Mathematics and Computer Science, Academy of Sciences of Moldova, Chișinău (2013)

21. Nicolescu, R., Wu, H.: BFS solution for disjoint paths in P systems. In: Calude, C.S., Kari, J., Petre, I., Rozenberg, G. (eds.) UC 2011. LNCS, vol. 6714, pp. 164–176. Springer, Heidelberg (2011)

22. Nicolescu, R., Wu, H.: New solutions for disjoint paths in P systems. Nat. Comput. **11**, 637–651 (2012). http://dx.doi.org/10.1007/s11047-012-9342-9

23. Nicolescu, R., Wu, H.: Complex objects for complex applications. Rom. J. Inf. Sci. Technol. **17**(1), 46–62 (2014)

24. Peña-Cantillana, F., Berciano, A., Díaz-Pernil, D., Gutiérrez-Naranjo, M.A.: Parallel skeletonizing of digital images by using cellular automata. In: Ferri, M., Frosini, P., Landi, C., Cerri, A., Di Fabio, B. (eds.) CTIC 2012. LNCS, vol. 7309, pp. 39–48. Springer, Heidelberg (2012)

25. Păun, G., Rozenberg, G., Salomaa, A.: The Oxford Handbook of Membrane Computing. Oxford University Press Inc., New York (2010)

26. Reina-Molina, R., Díaz-Pernil, D.: Bioinspired parallel 2D or 3D skeletonization. IMAGEN-A **3**(5), 41–44 (2013)

27. Reina-Molina, R., Díaz-Pernil, D., Gutiérrez-Naranjo, M.A.: Cell complexes and membrane computing for thinning 2D and 3D images. In: del Amor, M.A.M., Păun, G., Pérez-Hurtado, I., Romero-Campero, F.J. (eds.) Tenth Brainstorming Week on Membrane Computing. RGNC REPORT, vol. 1, pp. 91–110. Universidad de Sevilla (2012)

28. Syme, D., Granicz, A., Cisternino, A.: Expert F# 3.0, 3rd edn. Apress, Berkely (2012)

29. Wu, H.: Minimum spanning tree in P systems. In: Pan, L., Păun, G., Song, T. (eds.) Proceedings of the Asian Conference on Membrane Computing (ACMC2012), pp. 88–104. Huazhong University of Science and Technology, Wuhan (2012)

30. Wu, H.: Distributed Algorithms in P Systems. Ph.D. thesis, The University of Auckland, Auckland, New Zealand (2014)

Chemistry-Inspired Adaptive Stream Processing

Javier Rojas Balderrama, Matthieu Simonin, and Cédric Tedeschi[✉]

IRISA Laboratory, Inria / University of Rennes 1, Rennes, France
cedric.tedeschi@inria.fr

Abstract. Stream processing engines have appeared as the next generation of data processing systems, facing the needs for low-delay processing. While these systems have been widely studied recently, their ability to adapt their processing logics at run time upon the detection of some events calling for adaptation is still an open issue.

Chemistry-inspired models of computation have been shown to ease the specification of adaptive systems. In this paper, we argue that a higher-order chemical model can be used to specify such an adaptive SPE in a natural way. We also show how such programming abstractions can get enacted in a decentralised environment.

1 Introduction

In the quest to reducing data processing delays for demanding applications, industry is shifting from the traditional user-driven *store-and-process* approach to a system-driven *on-the-fly processing* approach. The reduction of processing delays is particularly crucial in domains such as social networking, where current trends need to be figured out quickly before they get outdated, environmental systems (e.g., climate and traffic), or military applications (e.g., missile or target detection).

This reduction of processing delays has led to a new generation of Stream Processing Engines (SPEs) addressing the processing of continuous streams of data, while minimizing the end-to-end processing delay. SPE tools and approaches [1,2,8,10,13] share a common ground in their programming model: the programmer needs to specify a set of *operators* every data item is supposed to traverse. The operators are combined in a directed acyclic graph (DAG). SPEs are closely related to the field of *workflow computing* in which the applications are specified as a DAG of tasks.

For many reasons, this workflow of operators processing an incoming continuous stream of data may have to be adapted at some point at run time. Imagine for instance a weather monitoring system based on a workflow W. In regular conditions of operation, W stays the same, and data sent from the set of sensors allowing to monitor the weather systematically follows the same path. Imagine further that, some particular pattern in the data is detected, meaning that a storm is coming. This calls for a different processing pipeline, specialised in emergency situations. In this state, W needs to be adapted to, say, W' in order to reflect this new processing pipeline. In other words, the program itself

© Springer International Publishing Switzerland 2015
G. Rozenberg et al. (Eds.): CMC 2015, LNCS 9504, pp. 338–352, 2015.
DOI: 10.1007/978-3-319-28475-0_23

needs to be changed at run time, upon the detection of some particular (possibly complex) event. This kind of adaptiveness cannot afford stopping and restarting the system as it would require too much time.

Chemistry-inspired models of computation have been shown to ease the specification of adaptive systems. In this paper, we argue that a higher-order chemical model can be used to specify such an adaptive SPE in a natural way. We also show how such programming abstractions can get enacted in a decentralised environment.

Section 2 presents related work. In Sect. 3, the basics of our programming model is introduced. In Sect. 4, the abstractions for the specification of adaptive workflows are presented and illustrated. In Sect. 5, our software prototype for decentralised workflow execution is briefly discussed, as well as how to include the support for the new concepts, and Sect. 6 concludes this work.

2   Related Work

There is a longstanding effort to provide suitable frameworks to the scientific community in order to design and enact workflows [16]. However, most of current solutions are not designed to handle stream processing. Moreover, workflow adaptiveness is rarely targeted in scientific workflows. In this section, we present some works describing analogous techniques and models.

In [11], authors propose a framework to compensate for the impedance mismatch between scientific workflows and continuous data streams. They also propose workflow semantics to incorporate stream in scientific workflows. They aim at extending the support for workflow execution in a way that satisfies the following requirements: preserve the workflow programming model for the user; make changes transparent to the workflow engine; and define workflow patterns to use them as new workflow semantics. In a similar way, the work in [19] addresses the lack of integrated support for data models to support emerging applications that are streaming oriented. They propose a scientific workflow framework supporting files, structured collections and data streams. Both approaches place the emphasis upon the programming model rather than the execution model. They clearly state the need for streaming support in scientific workflows for applications that responds to events in the environment at real time, but distributed execution and adaptiveness are not addressed in these works.

Most workflow manager systems ensure enactment flexibility at infrastructure level. Nevertheless, the work presented in [17] proposes an adaptive exception handling at definition level that is comparable to our programming abstractions defined for adaptiveness. The authors propose two patterns to manage the exception handling based on the Reference Nets-within-Nets formalism: propagation and replacement. In spite of mechanisms for dynamically adapting the workflow structure at run time, the resulting representation with their reference model suggests a complex workflow definition, where the original scenario and the alternative path are mixed (expressed in the same description artifact).

Our work envisages the workflow execution as an autonomous process evolving in time according to the requirements and dependencies without bounding to any preset constraint. A similar approach described by Verma et al. [18] proposes a workflow manager system inspired by P-Systems. Nevertheless, they are focused on the elasticity properties of their framework and the associated formalism. They do not cover features such as adaptiveness or stream processing support. In terms of architecture, our approach takes its roots in the work presented in [7]. Although there is an important evolution due to the adaptiveness introduction and the continuous data streams management detailed hereafter.

The idea of using chemical programming to enact workflows autonomously is not new [4,5,12]. These works, however, remain abstract, and only few clues are given concerning how to implement such approach, or if it would include centralised or decentralised settings. Again, they do not consider neither streams nor adaptiveness.

3 Preliminaries

In this paper, we rely on the Higher-Order Chemical Language (HOCL) [3].

3.1 HOCL

HOCL is a rule-based language. In HOCL, data is left unstructured in a multiset on which a set of rules is applied concurrently. The role of the programmer is to write this set of rules, which given a particular input multiset will output another multiset containing the results. In other words, the initial multiset of data, containing the input, is *re-written* by the rules, to produce the final multiset, containing the output. Such a programming approach allows users to concentrate on the problem to be solved without having to worry on some external constraints on data structures and control. Let us illustrate the expressiveness of HOCL through the classic *max* problem, which extracts the highest values from a multiset of values. In HOCL, the *max* problem is solved by the following program, given a particular input:

$$\textbf{let } \max = \textbf{ replace } x, y \textbf{ by } x \textbf{ if } x \geq y \textbf{ in } \langle 2, 3, 5, 8, 9, \max \rangle$$

The *max* rule consumes two integers x and y when $x \geq y$ and replaces them by x. Initially, several reactions are possible in the provided multiset (between symbols $<$ and $>$), *max* can use any couple of integers satisfying the condition: 2 and 3, 2 and 5, 8 and 9, etc. At run time, the rule will be applied in some order (unknown, and left to the interpreter's developer). Whatever the order is, the final content of the multiset will be $\langle 9 \rangle$.

Looking carefully, we observe that *max* is part of the program. HOCL provides the higher order: rules are first-class citizens in the multiset. In fact, *max* is present in the solution from the beginning to the end of the execution. Also, a rule can apply on other rules. For instance, removing *max* can be done by structuring the multiset and adding a rule in the initial program.

$$\textbf{let } \max = \textbf{ replace } x, y \textbf{ by } x \textbf{ if } x \geq y \textbf{ in}$$
$$\textbf{let } \text{clean} = \textbf{ replace} - \textbf{one } \langle \max, \omega \rangle \textbf{ by } \omega \textbf{ in } \langle \langle 2, 3, 5, 8, 9, \max \rangle, \text{clean} \rangle$$

The program has been restructured to put our initial program in an outer multiset containing it and a new *clean* rule which will extract the result from the inner multiset, and remove *max* at the same time. However, to be sure that the final (outer) multiset contains the correct result, we need to apply this new rule only when the execution of the inner multiset is completed. This is what the HOCL execution model assumes. Note that the latter rule is a **replace-one** rule. It is one-shot: it will disappear from the multiset once triggered (and completed). The ω symbol has a special connotation as it can match any molecule. In this case, it will match the result.

The chemical analogy is as follows: the multiset is a *solution* in which data *atoms* float and react according to *reaction* rules when they meet. In the following, we adopt the chemical vocabulary to designate artifacts of the programming model. Note that the terms *solution* and *multiset* can be used interchangeably. An atom can be either a simple one (such as a number or a string), or a structured one, such as a subsolution, denoted $\langle A_1, A_2, \ldots, A_n \rangle$, or a tuple denoted $A_1 : A_2 : \cdots : A_n$.

The previous example shows how the program's behaviour can change dynamically through the injection or removal of some rules. It also suggests that the multiset is a container for the state of the program, on which possibly distributed engines can apply rules.

For the sake of simplicity, in the following, we will use the notation $A \rightarrow B$ to simplify the specification of the n-shot rule **replace** A **by** B. A one-shot rule will be written $A \rightarrow_1 B$. Some of them can be named using the following syntax:

$$\text{RULENAME} : A \rightarrow B$$

Ordered collections are manipulated as lists using the following functions:

- `first(1)` returns the first element of the list `1`,
- `rest(1)` returns `1` deprived of its first element,
- `cons(e,1)` returns `1` with the element `e` added at its end, and
- `concat(11,12)` returns the concatenation of `11` and `12`,

Note that ω denotes any combination of atoms. It is used as a *wildcard molecule*, and `[]` denotes the empty list.

3.2 HOCL and P-Systems

Built on top of the principles of chemical programming, *membrane computing*, also called *P-systems*, relies on a structure of nested membranes [15]. The elements floating in them are called molecules. The membranes form a hierarchical structure, and the membrane containing another membranes is called its parent. An element can move from one membrane to another one which is either its parent or one of its child membranes. These movements between membranes can be used to model communications. In terms of execution model, and following a discrete-time approach, one of their primary objective is to consume as many molecules as possible at each step, in order to try to minimise the global execution time. This execution model constitutes a difference with the execution model of chemical computing where the actual level of parallelism is left to the engine implementor. Other peculiarities of HOCL compared to P-systems, is its ability to model sequential behaviours through *subsolutioning*, and the higher-order. Note however, that many flavours of execution models, especially regarding level of parallelism, have been discussed for P-systems in literature [14]. Let us finally mention the series of work about the MGS system, which is another good example of a series of work where rule-based programming has been investigated in conjunction with membrane systems [9].

4   Programming Abstractions for Workflows

4.1   Workflow Description

We now devise a set of abstractions based on HOCL to program adaptive workflows. Each service taking part in the workflow is represented as a subsolution, and each of these subsolutions will contain a set of atoms modeling queues storing incoming or result data. Let SRC be the set of sources of one given service. Each of these queues is a list ℓ tagged by the parametric keyword IN_i. Then, the set of queues can be written:

$$\{\text{IN}_i : \ell_{\text{IN}_i} \mid i \in \text{SRC}\}$$

Secondly, a service is equipped with a queue where to put the results of the computation. This queue is unique for each service and is tagged by RES:

$$\text{RES} : \ell_{\text{RES}}$$

Note that a service implementation (the actual binary program producing the output) needs to be specified. This will be simplified as a function name tagged by SRV in the following. To sum up, a service S having the set of sources SRC and the implementation "func" can be denoted as follows:

$$S : \langle \{\text{IN}_i : \ell_{\text{IN}_i} \mid i \in \text{SRC}\}, \text{RES} : \ell_{\text{RES}}, \text{SRV} : \text{"func"} \rangle$$

Let us now give an example of a workflow. Consider the workflow depicted in Fig. 1. It is given in its graphic form, on the left, and in its HOCL description form (i.e., the initial multiset) on the right. Each subsolution S_i acts as a container of the information related to a given service. IN and RES queues, as well as the actual service to be called, are specified within each service's subsolution. All S_i subsolutions act as *contexts*, and delimit the scope of atoms it contains. For instance, the $\text{IN} : \ell_{\text{IN}}$ atom is present in both S_1 and S_2 but they are two different atoms, representing two different input queues. Note that initially, all queues are empty, except for S_1 and S_2 that are the first services of the workflow and receive their input from the external world.

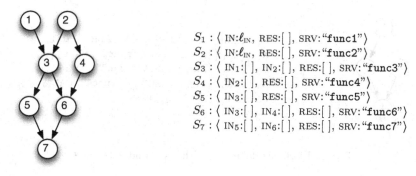

$S_1 : \langle$ IN:ℓ_{IN}, RES:[ ], SRV:"**func1**"$\rangle$
$S_2 : \langle$ IN:ℓ_{IN}, RES:[ ], SRV:"**func2**"$\rangle$
$S_3 : \langle$ IN$_1$:[ ], IN$_2$:[ ], RES:[ ], SRV:"**func3**"$\rangle$
$S_4 : \langle$ IN$_2$:[ ], RES:[ ], SRV:"**func4**"$\rangle$
$S_5 : \langle$ IN$_3$:[ ], RES:[ ], SRV:"**func5**"$\rangle$
$S_6 : \langle$ IN$_3$:[ ], IN$_4$:[ ], RES:[ ], SRV:"**func6**"$\rangle$
$S_7 : \langle$ IN$_5$:[ ], IN$_6$:[ ], RES:[ ], SRV:"**func7**"$\rangle$

Fig. 1. A workflow DAG and its HOCL description counterpart

4.2   Workflow Enactment

Let us now describe the set of rules needed to enact this workflow, in an HOCL interpreter. We actually need two types of rules. The first one, denoted CALL, is related to processing. In other words, it applies the operator specified in the atom tagged by the SRV keyword to the set of inputs. Each service's input consists in one element taken from each of the input queues, this represents the set of parameters for the **func-i** operator. For instance, the CALL$_{1,\emptyset}$ parametric rule to be put within S_1 is:

$$\text{IN} : \ell_{\text{IN}}, \text{RES} : \ell_{\text{RES}}, \text{SRV} : \text{``\textbf{func1}''}$$
$$\downarrow$$
$$\text{IN} : \text{rest}\,(\ell_{\text{IN}}), \text{RES} : \text{cons}\,(\textbf{func1}(\text{first}\,(\ell_{\text{IN}})), \ell_{\text{RES}}, \text{SRV} : \text{``\textbf{func1}''})$$

This operation takes its input in the head of the IN queue, and puts the result of the invocation of the service it encapsulates at the tail of the RES queue. This rule is specific to S_1. The equivalent for S_3, CALL$_{3,\{1,2\}}$ is the following—the only noticeable difference, compared to S_1 stands in the fact that one element is taken from both IN queues containing the results of S_1 and S_2, respectively.

$$\text{IN}_1 : \ell_{\text{IN}_1}, \text{IN}_2 : \ell_{\text{IN}_2}, \text{RES} : \ell_{\text{RES}}, \text{SRV} : \text{``\textbf{func3}''}$$
$$\downarrow$$
$$\text{IN}_1 : \text{rest}\,(\ell_{\text{IN}_1}), \text{IN}_2 : \text{rest}\,(\ell_{\text{IN}_2}), \text{RES} : \text{cons}\,(\textbf{func3}(\text{first}\,(\ell_{\text{IN}_1}), \text{first}\,(\ell_{\text{IN}_2})), \ell_{\text{RES}})$$

More generally, the CALL$_{i,\text{SRC}}$ rule can be seen as a parametric template, parametric by 1) i, the service identifier and 2) SRC, the set of identifiers of the sources of the service. Then, rule CALL$_{i,\text{SRC}}$ has the following general form:

$$\{\text{IN}_j : \ell_{\text{IN}_j} \mid j \in \text{SRC}\}, \text{RES} : \ell_{\text{RES}}, \text{SRV} : \textit{func} :: \textit{String}$$
$$\downarrow$$
$$\{\text{IN}_j : \text{rest}\,(\ell_{\text{IN}_j}) \mid j \in \text{SRC}\}, \text{RES} : \text{cons}\,(\textit{func}(\{\text{first}\,(\ell_{\text{IN}_j}) \mid j \in \text{SRC}\}), \ell_{\text{RES}})$$

The second type of rules, denoted PASS, enables the information transfer between services. Let us consider the transfer needed from S_1 to S_3. What is needed here is to model the transfer from S_1's queue RES to the queue IN$_1$ included in the S_3 subsolution:

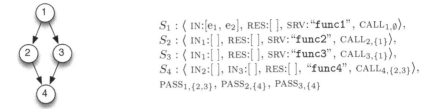

$S_1 : \langle$ IN:$[e_1, e_2]$, RES:$[\ ]$, SRV:"$\texttt{func1}$", $\text{CALL}_{1,\emptyset}\rangle$,
$S_2 : \langle$ IN$_1$:$[\ ]$, RES:$[\ ]$, SRV:"$\texttt{func2}$", $\text{CALL}_{2,\{1\}}\rangle$,
$S_3 : \langle$ IN$_1$:$[\ ]$, RES:$[\ ]$, SRV:"$\texttt{func3}$", $\text{CALL}_{3,\{1\}}\rangle$,
$S_4 : \langle$ IN$_2$:$[\ ]$, IN$_3$:$[\ ]$, RES:$[\ ]$, "$\texttt{func4}$", $\text{CALL}_{4,\{2,3\}}\rangle$,
$\text{PASS}_{1,\{2,3\}}$, $\text{PASS}_{2,\{4\}}$, $\text{PASS}_{3,\{4\}}$

Fig. 2. Workflow definition with CALL and PASS rules

$$S_1 : \langle \text{RES} : \ell_{\text{RES}}, \omega_1 \rangle, S_3 : \langle \text{IN}_1 : \ell_{\text{IN}_3}, \omega_3 \rangle$$
$$\downarrow$$
$$S_1 : \langle \text{RES} : [\ ], \omega_1 \rangle, S_3 : \langle \text{IN}_1 : \text{concat}\,(\ell_{\text{IN}_3}, \ell_{\text{RES}}), \omega_3 \rangle$$

Note that, while the CALL rule makes sense inside the subsolution of the service invoked, in the PASS rule, several subsolutions (source and destinations) are pertained by the action. Similarly, as for the rule modeling the information transfer from S_1, the rule for S_3 is as follows:

$$S_3 : \langle \text{RES} : \ell_{\text{RES}}, \omega_3 \rangle,$$
$$S_5 : \langle \text{IN}_3 : \ell_{\text{IN}_{5,3}}, \omega_5 \rangle, S_6 : \langle \text{IN}_3 : \ell_{\text{IN}_{6,3}}, \omega_6 \rangle$$
$$\downarrow$$
$$S_3 : \langle \text{RES} : [\ ], \omega_3 \rangle,$$
$$S_5 : \langle \text{IN}_3 : \text{concat}\,(\ell_{\text{IN}_{5,3}}, \ell_{\text{RES}}), \omega_5 \rangle, S_6 : \langle \text{IN}_3 : \text{concat}\,(\ell_{\text{IN}_{6,3}}, \ell_{\text{RES}}), \omega_6 \rangle$$

Each time this rule is invoked, it empties the result queues, and transfers all the elements that have been queued since the last application of this rule. More generally, the PASS rules are of the parametric form $\text{PASS}_{src,\text{DST}}$, the parameters being 1) src, the index of the source service, and 2) DST the set of destination services.

$$S_{src} : \langle \text{RES} : \ell_{\text{RES}}, \omega_{src} \rangle, \{S_i : \langle \text{IN}_{src} : \ell_{\text{IN}_{j,src}}, \omega_i \rangle \mid j \in \text{DST}\}$$
$$\downarrow$$
$$S_{src} : \langle \text{RES} : [\ ], \omega_{src} \rangle, \{S_i : \langle \text{IN}_{src} : \text{concat}\,(\ell_{\text{IN}_{j,src}}, \ell_{\text{RES}}), \omega_i \rangle \mid j \in \text{DST}\}$$

Let us simplify our example to illustrate a workflow execution. Our simplified workflow is given in Fig. 2 (left). As detailed above, enacting the workflow consists in adding the correct set of CALL and PASS rules at the right locations within the HOCL description to make it a runnable HOCL program. Then, that description is processed by an HOCL interpreter which actually executes the workflow.

The right part of Fig. 2 represents the HOCL program to be submitted to some HOCL interpreter acting as the workflow orchestrator and the initial state of the multiset. For the sake of clarity, we omit the explicit definitions of CALL and PASS rules, as their parameters are sufficient to get fully understood. Initially, only the IN queue of the initial service contains some data: the input data.[1] For this example, as illustrated in Fig. 2, we assume two inputs e_1 and e_2 have been sent to the workflow to be processed.

Initially, only the $CALL_{1,\emptyset}$ is enabled. Indeed, to get enabled, a CALL rule needs all the IN queues in the relevant services to be non-empty, which is only the case for S_1. The same applies for the PASS rules: they need the RES queue to be non-empty. So, in a finite time, $CALL_{1,\emptyset}$ is applied. This rule application encapsulates the invocation of the service, the collection of the results and the pushing of the results in the RES queue of S_1, resulting in the following updated solution (the unchanged part has been greyed out and rules removed for clarity):

S_1 : $\langle$ IN:$[e_2]$, RES:$[out_{e_1}]$, SRV:"func1"$\rangle$,
S_2 : $\langle$ IN$_1$:$[\,]$, RES:$[\,]$, SRV:"func2"$\rangle$,
S_3 : $\langle$ IN$_1$:$[\,]$, RES:$[\,]$, SRV:"func3"$\rangle$,
S_4 : $\langle$ IN$_2$:$[\,]$, IN$_3$:$[\,]$, RES:$[\,]$, SRV:"func4"$\rangle$

At this point, two rules are enabled, namely $CALL_{1,\emptyset}$ and $PASS_{1,\{2,3\}}$. In other words, it is possible to process e_2 as well as to transfer a first S_1 result to S_2 and S_3. We can verify that all other rules are disabled. Assuming both rules are applied, the resulting intermediate multiset is the following (again, unchanged lines/subsolutions have been greyed out):

S_1 : $\langle$ IN:$[\,]$, RES:$[out_{e_2}]$, SRV:"func1"$\rangle$,
S_2 : $\langle$ IN$_1$:$[out_{e_1}]$, RES:$[\,]$, SRV:"func2"$\rangle$,
S_3 : $\langle$ IN$_1$:$[out_{e_1}]$, RES:$[\,]$, SRV:"func3"$\rangle$,
S_4 : $\langle$ IN$_2$:$[\,]$, IN$_3$:$[\,]$, RES:$[\,]$, SRV:"func4"$\rangle$

Now, S_2 and S_3 can be called in parallel through the concurrent application of $CALL_{2,\{1\}}$ and $CALL_{3,\{1\}}$ rules, respectively ($PASS_{1,\{2,3\}}$ could also be triggered but the model does not enforce the application of all enabled rules), leading to the following multiset's state:

S_1 : $\langle$ IN:$[\,]$, RES:$[out_{e_2}]$, SRV:"func1"$\rangle$,
S_2 : $\langle$ IN$_1$:$[\,]$, RES:$[out_{e_{12}}]$, SRV:"func2"$\rangle$,
S_3 : $\langle$ IN$_1$:$[\,]$, RES:$[out_{e_{13}}]$, SRV:"func3"$\rangle$,
S_4 : $\langle$ IN$_2$:$[\,]$, IN$_3$:$[\,]$, RES:$[\,]$, SRV:"func4"$\rangle$

While the second result of S_1 is transferred to S_2 and S_3, results of S_2 and S_3 can also be sent to S_4. These actions are enabled through the concurrent application of $PASS_{1,\{2,3\}}$, $PASS_{2,\{4\}}$ and $PASS_{3,\{4\}}$ with the following outcome:

S_1 : $\langle$ IN:$[\,]$, RES:$[\,]$, SRV:"func1"$\rangle$,
S_2 : $\langle$ IN$_1$:$[out_{e_2}]$, RES:$[\,]$, SRV:"func2"$\rangle$,

---

[1] We assume, that after some time, data is sent to the workflow, filling the IN-tagged list in S_1 triggering the workflow.

$$S_3 : \langle \text{ IN}_1{:}[\text{out}_{e_2}], \text{ RES}{:}[\ ], \text{ SRV}{:}\text{``func3''} \rangle,$$
$$S_4 : \langle \text{ IN}_2{:}[\text{out}_{e_{12}}], \text{ IN}_3{:}[\text{out}_{e_{13}}], \text{ RES}{:}[\ ], \text{ SRV}{:}\text{``func4''} \rangle$$

We are now in a state where CALL rules can be applied, in S_2, S_3 and S_4. Assuming they are applied, the new multiset state is the following:

$$S_1 : \langle \text{ IN}{:}[\ ], \text{ RES}{:}[\ ], \text{ SRV}{:}\text{``func1''} \rangle,$$
$$S_2 : \langle \text{ IN}_1{:}[\ ], \text{ RES}{:}[\text{out}_{e_{22}}], \text{ SRV}{:}\text{``func2''} \rangle,$$
$$S_3 : \langle \text{ IN}_1{:}[\ ], \text{ RES}{:}[\text{out}_{e_{23}}], \text{ SRV}{:}\text{``func3''} \rangle,$$
$$S_4 : \langle \text{ IN}_2{:}[\ ], \text{ IN}_3{:}[\ ], \text{ RES}{:}[\text{out}_{e_{14}}], \text{ SRV}{:}\text{``func4''} \rangle$$

The remainder of the execution consists in (1) transferring the second set of results from the RES queues of S_2 and S_3 to the IN queues in S_4, and (2) invoking func4 on them, leading to the following final inert multiset (as long as no new data is injected in the IN queue of S_1).

$$S_1 : \langle \text{ IN}{:}[\ ], \text{ RES}{:}[\ ], \text{ SRV}{:}\text{``func1''} \rangle,$$
$$S_2 : \langle \text{ IN}_1{:}[\ ], \text{ RES}{:}[\ ], \text{ SRV}{:}\text{``func2''} \rangle,$$
$$S_3 : \langle \text{ IN}_1{:}[\ ], \text{ RES}{:}[\ ], \text{ SRV}{:}\text{``func3''} \rangle,$$
$$S_4 : \langle \text{ IN}_2{:}[\ ], \text{ IN}_3{:}[\ ], \text{ RES}{:}[\text{out}_{e_{14}}, \text{out}_{e_{24}}], \text{ SRV}{:}\text{``func4''} \rangle$$

The idea behind using parametric rules is that they can be easily constructed using the rule template and the parameters given by the user in its workflow description. The idea is not necessarily to let the user write the HOCL code directly, but to generate the HOCL code from the user's own description.

4.3   Adaptiveness

When workflow reconfiguration is needed, the set of atoms (data and rules) describing the workflow needs to get updated. Let us consider the adaptive workflow depicted in Fig. 3, along with its HOCL code.

As illustrated on the left of Fig. 3, an alternate workflow is specified by the services and links in dashed lines, to replace Service 3 in case adaptation is requested. More specifically, the two services $a1$ and $a2$ are to replace Service 3. The two last lines of the initial workflow specify these two services. Services $a1$ and $a2$ are initially *disabled* in the sense that no PASS rule transfers data into them. Note also the UPDATE_PASS and UPDATE_S5 (within S_5 subsolution) rules whose purpose is to *re-branch* the workflow upon adaptation.

The basic idea is to enable the additional services only if the adaptation is required (i.e., when the reason for adapting is satisfied). As discussed above, the need for adaptations can take several forms. For the sake of simplicity, we will assume that the execution monitoring system is simply made to inject some particular atom in the multiset, so as to trigger the adaptation. In our example, we will use the ADAPT atom keyword to reflect this. The execution monitoring

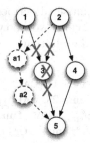

$S_1 : \langle$ IN:$[e_1, e_2]$, RES:$[\ ]$, SRV:"**func1**", CALL$_{1,\emptyset}\rangle$,
$S_2 : \langle$ IN:$[e_1, e_2]$, RES:$[\ ]$, SRV:"**func2**", CALL$_{2,\emptyset}\rangle$,
$S_3 : \langle$ IN$_1$:$[\ ]$, IN$_2$:$[\ ]$, RES:$[\ ]$, SRV:"**func3**", CALL$_{3,\{1,2\}}\rangle$,
$S_4 : \langle$ IN$_2$:$[\ ]$, RES:$[\ ]$, SRV:"**func4**", CALL$_{4,\{2\}}\rangle$,
$S_5 : \langle$ IN$_3$:$[\ ]$, IN$_4$:$[\ ]$, RES:$[\ ]$, SRV:"**func5**", CALL$_{5,\{3,4\}}$, UPDATE_$\mathcal{S}_5\rangle$,
PASS$_{1,\{3\}}$, PASS$_{2,\{3,4\}}$, PASS$_{3,\{5\}}$, PASS$_{4,\{5\}}$,

UPDATE_PASS,
$S_{a1} : \langle$ IN$_1$:$[\ ]$, RES:$[\ ]$, SRV:"**func-a1**", CALL$_{a1,\{1\}}\rangle$,
$S_{a2} : \langle$ IN$_{a1}$:$[\ ]$, RES:$[\ ]$, SRV:"**func-a2**", CALL$_{a2,\{a1\}}\rangle$

Fig. 3. An adaptive workflow, including its HOCL description

system will inject it where needed, namely, at the level of the multiset, and also inside the S_5 subsolution.

When the need for adaptation is declared, the multiset requires to get updated on-the-fly so as to enable services $a1$ and $a2$, and partially redirect the data flow accordingly. To modify the path of data some PASS rules need to be removed and replaced by PASS$_{1,\{a1\}}$, PASS$_{2,\{a1,4\}}$, PASS$_{a1,\{a2\}}$ and PASS$_{a2,\{5\}}$. The specific higher-order one-shot rule UPDATE_PASS, defined below, achieves this:

$$\text{ADAPT, PASS}_{1,\{3\}}, \text{ PASS}_{2,\{3,4\}}, \text{ PASS}_{3,\{5\}}$$
$$\downarrow_1$$
$$\text{PASS}_{1,\{a1\}}, \text{ PASS}_{2,\{a1,4\}}, \text{ PASS}_{a1,\{a2\}}, \text{ PASS}_{a2,\{5\}}$$

The other update to perform concerns the internals of S_5, the IN$_3$ queue needs to be removed and replaced by an IN$_{a2}$ queue, in order to satisfy the indices. The S_5 CALL rule needs to be updated accordingly from CALL$_{5,\{3,4\}}$ to CALL$_{5,\{a2,4\}}$, as specified by the UPDATE_$\mathcal{S}_5$ rule:

$$\text{ADAPT, IN}_3{:}\ell_{\text{IN}}, \text{ CALL}_{5,\{3,4\}}$$
$$\downarrow_1$$
$$\text{IN}_{a2}{:}[\ ], \text{ CALL}_{5,\{a2,4\}}$$

This rule is supposed to take place within the S_5 subsolution. These rules are initially present in the multiset, but it can react only if the ADAPT atoms have been injecting by the monitoring system. Let us review the execution of such an example. Initially, we have the multiset described in Fig. 3. The data traverses the graph similarly as for the previous workflow. At some point however, the monitoring system decides that the alternate workflow needs to be triggered, leading to the following multiset:

$$S_1 : \langle \text{ IN}:\ell_{\text{IN}_1}, \text{RES}:\ell_{\text{RES}_1}, \text{SRV}:\text{``func1''}, \text{CALL}_{1,\emptyset}\rangle,$$
$$S_2 : \langle \text{ IN}:\ell_{\text{IN}_2}, \text{RES}:\ell_{\text{RES}_2}, \text{SRV}:\text{``func2''}, \text{CALL}_{2,\emptyset}\rangle,$$
$$S_3 : \langle \text{ IN}_1:\ell_{\text{IN}_{31}}, \text{IN}_2:\ell_{\text{IN}_{32}}, \text{RES}:\ell_{\text{RES}_3}, \text{SRV}:\text{``func3''}, \text{CALL}_{3,\{1,2\}}\rangle,$$
$$S_4 : \langle \text{ IN}_2:\ell_{\text{IN}_{42}}, \text{RES}:\ell_{\text{RES}_4}, \text{SRV}:\text{``func4''}, \text{CALL}_{4,\{2\}}\rangle,$$
$$S_5 : \langle \text{ IN}_3:\ell_{\text{IN}_{53}}, \text{IN}_4:\ell_{\text{IN}_{54}}, \text{RES}:\ell_{\text{RES}_5}, \text{SRV}:\text{``func5''}, \text{CALL}_{5,\{3,4\}},$$
$$\text{UPDATE}_{S_5}, \text{ADAPT}\rangle,$$
$$\text{PASS}_{1,\{3\}}, \text{PASS}_{2,\{3,4\}}, \text{PASS}_{3,\{5\}}, \text{PASS}_{4,\{5\}},$$

$$\text{UPDATE\_PASS}, \text{ADAPT},$$
$$S_{a1} : \langle \text{ IN}_1:[\,], \text{RES}:[\,], \text{SRV}:\text{``func-a1''}, \text{CALL}_{a1,\{1\}}\rangle,$$
$$S_{a2} : \langle \text{ IN}_{a1}:[\,], \text{RES}:[\,], \text{SRV}:\text{``func-a2''}, \text{CALL}_{a2,\{a1\}}\rangle$$

At this point, due to the presence of ADAPT at both global and S_5 levels, the two UPDATE_* rules are triggered, leading to the following multiset, where PASS rules have been replaced and where S_5 has been updated—note that the UPDATE rules, one-shot, have been removed in the reactions:

$$S_1 : \langle \text{ IN}:\ell_{\text{IN}_1}, \text{RES}:\ell_{\text{RES}_1}, \text{SRV}:\text{``func1''}, \text{CALL}_{1,\emptyset}\rangle,$$
$$S_2 : \langle \text{ IN}:\ell_{\text{IN}_2}, \text{RES}:\ell_{\text{RES}_2}, \text{SRV}:\text{``func2''}, \text{CALL}_{2,\emptyset}\rangle,$$
$$S_3 : \langle \text{ IN}_1:\ell_{\text{IN}_{31}}, \text{IN}_2:\ell_{\text{IN}_{32}}, \text{RES}:\ell_{\text{RES}_3}, \text{SRV}:\text{``func3''}, \text{CALL}_{3,\{1,2\}}\rangle,$$
$$S_4 : \langle \text{ IN}_2:\ell_{\text{IN}_{42}}, \text{RES}:\ell_{\text{RES}_4}, \text{SRV}:\text{``func4''}, \text{CALL}_{4,\{2\}}\rangle,$$
$$S_5 : \langle \text{ IN}_{a2}:[\,], \text{IN}_4:\ell_{\text{IN}_{54}}, \text{RES}:\ell_{\text{RES}_5}, \text{SRV}:\text{``func5''}, \text{CALL}_{5,\{3,4\}}\rangle,$$
$$S_{a1} : \langle \text{ IN}_1:[\,], \text{RES}:[\,], \text{SRV}:\text{``func-a1''}, \text{CALL}_{a1,\{1\}}\rangle,$$
$$S_{a2} : \langle \text{ IN}_{a1}:[\,], \text{RES}:[\,], \text{SRV}:\text{``func-a2''}, \text{CALL}_{a2,\{a1\}}\rangle,$$
$$\text{PASS}_{1,\{a1\}}, \text{PASS}_{2,\{a1,4\}}, \text{PASS}_{a1,\{a2\}}, \text{PASS}_{a2,\{5\}}, \text{PASS}_{4,\{5\}}$$

As soon as it is updated, the new workflow is operational, new data flows being specified by the newly injected rules.

To sum up, two types of workflow-specific one-shot higher-order rules are needed to enhance the adaptation of the streaming workflow at run time: one to update the PASS rule and one to update the internals of the services whose sources have changed in the update. Again, these rules can be generated from a high-level description of the workflow provided by the user.

5   Architecture and Implementation

5.1   Decentralised Architecture

We plan to implement the programming abstractions presented above in Gin-Flow[2], a software initially developed in the context of service composition,

---

[2] http://ginflow.inria.fr.

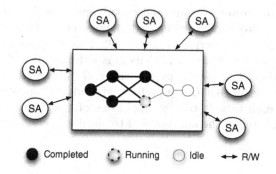

Fig. 4. Shared space-based coordination

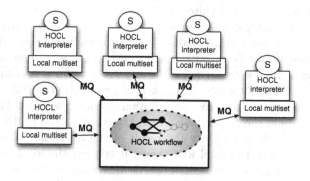

Fig. 5. Software prototype architecture

and whose architecture, implementation and experimentation has been recently detailed in [7]. These works intend to decentralise the execution of workflows and rely on a shared space to coordinate services involved in a composition. Specifically, it sits on the HOCL language to describe the service composition (*workflow* of services) and its enactment. In this architecture, services are encapsulated into agents communicating by reading and writing information in a shared data space.

The architectural model is depicted in Fig. 4. As detailed in [6], the shared space contains the description of the workflow. During enactment, each time the execution moves forward, this description is updated so as to reflect the execution progress. The service agents (SAs) are essentially workers that encapsulate the invocation of the services. This encapsulation includes an engine able to read, interpret and update the information contained in the shared space. For instance, when a SA completes the invocation of a service and collects the result, it pushes this information to the shared space, allowing another service agent, which was waiting for this result, to collect this result and use it as input to invoke its own service.

In the software prototype built and experimented in [7], each service agent taking part in the workflow is composed of three elements as shown in Fig. 5. The first element is the service to invoke (S), or a wrapper of an application representing the service. The second element is a storage place for a local partial copy of the multiset. This local copy acts as a cache of the service's subsolution. The third element is an HOCL interpreter that reads and updates the local copy of the multiset each time it tries to apply one of the rule in the subsolution. Communication between the multiset and the agents is done through the use of ActiveMQ.[3]

5.2   Decentralising the Adaptive Stream Processing Rules

Let us now review how the CALL, PASS and UPDATE rules can be implemented on top of this decentralised architecture.

Firstly, when CALL rules are applied, the service is called from the HOCL interpreter and the result is injected into the local multiset. Secondly, the PASS rule is supposed to act from outside subsolutions since it requires to match the atoms from several subsolutions. To avoid the need for a monitoring system having the global view of the system and keep the control decentralised[4], the PASS rules are modified to act within a subsolution. In other words, a $\text{PASS}_{i,\text{DST}}$ rule will be placed inside the S_i service and get triggered by the HOCL interpreter of the SA encapsulating S_i. Once the result of the invocation of some service is collected and put in the local RES queue, it triggers the local version of the PASS rule which sends a message to the destination, via the multiset. When the message is received in the multiset, it is automatically pushed to the right subsolution. For instance, the $\text{PASS}_{1,\{3\}}$ rule will be within the S_3 subsolution and look like this:

$$\text{RES} : \ell_{\text{RES}}, \omega_1$$
$$\downarrow$$
$$\text{RES} : [\ ], \texttt{transfer}(\ell_{\text{RES}}, S_3), \omega_1$$

The `transfer()` method sends a message to the multiset, which will update the state of the S_3 subsolution by adding ℓ_{RES} in its IN_1 queue and push it to the S_3 SA through ActiveMQ.

Finally, to make the UPDATE rule work in these decentralised settings, we need to slightly improve the program. We will first assume that each SA is equipped with a monitoring system able to inject the ADAPT atom within the local multiset managed by the SA. Then, we use that SA, upon the appearance of the ADAPT atom, to change the PASS rules to reflect the new dataflow. In fact, instead of only one UPDATE rule, we need one UPDATE_i rule for each service that requires to update its dataflow, and include it within each S_i subsolution:

$$\text{UPDATE}_1: \text{PASS}_{1,\{3\}} \rightarrow \text{PASS}_{1,\{a1\}}$$

---

[3] http://activemq.apache.org/.

[4] Each SA is allowed to store only its own description.

$$\text{UPDATE}_2: \text{PASS}_{2,\{3,4\}} \rightarrow \text{PASS}_{2,\{a1,4\}}$$
$$\text{UPDATE}_5: \text{IN}_3 : \ell_{\text{RES}} \rightarrow \text{IN}_{a1}$$

These three rules, initially absent from the multiset, will be injected by the SA who detected the failure in a manner similar to the PASS process. Assume that the ADAPT atom has been injected in the S_3 service. The following rule, put within the S_3 subsolution will make the UPDATE$_i$ rules appear in the relevant subsolutions, in a fashion similar to how the PASS rule transfers results:

$$\text{TRIGGER-ADAPT: ADAPT}$$
$$\downarrow$$
$$\texttt{transfer}(\text{UPDATE}_1, S_1), \texttt{transfer}(\text{UPDATE}_2, S_2), \texttt{transfer}(\text{UPDATE}_5, S_5)$$

As soon as the UPDATE$_i$ rule appears in the S_i subsolution, it is triggered by the HOCL interpreter of its SA encapsulating it. Every UPDATE$_i$ can be triggered concurrently, thus realising the update concurrently.

6 Conclusions

We have presented a set of abstractions using chemistry-inspired programming model for adaptive decentralised workflows supporting continuous dataflows. We have described the rules to define workflows, modify their behaviour when exceptions are raised, and ensure service invocation management with data streams. We also have shown the generic approach of services execution based on parametric rules. These rules enable a workflow enactment taking advantage of a distributed execution environment. The use of high-level definitions encompasses a concise and clear description of workflows delegating the complex instrumentation to the workflow engine. These definitions allow users to specify the workflow and its alternate paths at design time. Future work includes testing the framework with real use-cases and evolve towards better scheduling.

References

1. Abadi, D.J., Ahmad, Y., Balazinska, M., Çetintemel, U., Cherniack, M., Hwang, J., Lindner, W., Maskey, A., Rasin, A., Ryvkina, E., Tatbul, N., Xing, Y., Zdonik, S.B.: The design of the Borealis stream processing engine. In: Second Biennial Conference on Innovative Data Systems Research, Asilomar, CA (2005)
2. Apache Software Foundation: Apache Storm. https://storm.apache.org/
3. Banâtre, J.P., Fradet, P., Radenac, Y.: Generalised multisets for chemical programming. Math. Struct. Comput. Sci. **16**(4), 557–580 (2006)
4. Caeiro, M., Németh, Z., Priol, T.: A chemical model for dynamic workflow coordination. In: The 19th Euromicro International Conference on Parallel, Distributed and network-based Processing. Ayia Napa, Cyprus, February 2011
5. Di Napoli, C., Giordano, M., Németh, Z., Tonellotto, N.: Adaptive instantiation of service workflows using a chemical approach. In: The 16th International Euro-Par Conference on Parallel Processing, Ischia, Italy (2010)

6. Fernández, H., Priol, T., Tedeschi, C.: Decentralized approach for execution of composite web services using the chemical paradigm. In: The 8th IEEE International Conference on Web Services, Miami, FL, July 2010

7. Fernández, H., Tedeschi, C., Priol, T.: Rule-driven service coordination middleware for scientific applications. Future Gener. Comput. Syst. **35**, 1–13 (2014)

8. Gedik, B., Andrade, H., Wu, K., Yu, P.S., Doo, M.: SPADE: the system S declarative stream processing engine. In: The ACM SIGMOD International Conference on Management of Data, Vancouver, Canada, June 2008

9. Giavitto, J., Michel, O.: MGS: a rule-based programming language for complex objects and collections. Electronic Notes Theoretical Computer Science, 59(4), 286–304 (2001). http://dx.doi.org/10.1016/S1571-0661(04)00293-2

10. Gulisano, V., Jiménez-Peris, R., Patiño-Martínez, M., Soriente, C., Valduriez, P.: StreamCloud: an elastic and scalable data streaming system. IEEE Trans. Parallel Distrib. Syst. **23**(12), 2351–2365 (2012)

11. Herath, C., Plale, B.: Streamflow programming model for data streaming in scientific workflows. In: The 10th IEEE/ACM International Conference on Cluster, Cloud and Grid Computing, Melbourne, Australia, May 2010

12. Németh, Z., Pérez, C., Priol, T.: Workflow enactment based on a chemical methaphor. In: The 3rd IEEE International Conference on Software Engineering and Formal Methods, Koblenz, Germany, September 2005

13. Neumeyer, L., Robbins, B., Nair, A., Kesari, A.: S4: distributed stream computing platform. In: The 13th IEEE International Conference on Data Mining Workshops, Sydney, Australia, December 2010

14. Paun, G., Rozenberg, G., Salomaa, A.: The Oxford Handbook of Membrane Computing. Oxford University Press Inc, New York, NY, USA (2010)

15. Păun, G.: Computing with membranes. J. Comput. Syst. Sci. **61**(1), 108–143 (2000)

16. Taylor, I.J., Deelman, E., Gannon, D.B., Shields, M. (eds.): Workflows for e-Science. Springer, London (2007)

17. Tolosana-Calasanz, R., Bañares, J.A., Rana, O.F., Álvarez, P., Ezpeleta, J., Hoheisel, A.: Adaptive exception handling for scientific workflows. Concurr. Comput. Pract. Experience **22**(5), 617–642 (2010)

18. Verma, R., Ahmed, T., Srivastava, A.: Expressing workflow and workflow enactment using P systems. In: The 15th International Conference on Membrane Computing. Prague, Czech Republic, August 2014

19. Zinn, D., Hart, Q., McPhillips, T., Ludäscher, B., Simmhan, Y., Giakkoupis, M., Prasanna, V.K.: Towards reliable, performant workflows for streaming-applications on cloud platforms. In: The 11th IEEE/ACM International Conference on Cluster, Cloud and Grid Computing, Newport Beach, CA, May 2011

Computing Partial Recursive Functions by Virus Machines

Álvaro Romero-Jiménez[(⊠)], Luis Valencia-Cabrera,
Agustín Riscos-Núñez, and Mario J. Pérez-Jiménez

Research Group on Natural Computing,
Department of Computer Science and Artificial Intelligence,
Universidad de Sevilla, Avda. Reina Mercedes S/n, 41012 Seville, Spain
{romero.alvaro,lvalencia,ariscosn,marper}@us.es

Abstract. Virus Machines are a computational paradigm inspired by the manner in which viruses replicate and transmit from one host cell to another. This paradigm provides non-deterministic sequential devices. Non-restricted Virus Machines are unbounded Virus Machines, in the sense that no restriction on the number of hosts, the number of instructions and the number of viruses contained in any host along any computation is placed on them. The computational completeness of these machines has been obtained by simulating register machines. In this paper, Virus Machines as function computing devices are considered. Then, the universality of non-restricted virus machines is proved by showing that they can compute all partial recursive functions.

1 Introduction

A new computational paradigm inspired by the replications and transmissions of viruses was introduced in [1]. The computational devices in this paradigm are called *Virus Machines* and they consist of several processing units, called *hosts*, connected to each other by *transmission channels*. A host can be viewed as a group of cells (being part of a colony, organism, system, organ or tissue). Each cell in the group will contain at most one virus, but we will not take into account the number of cells in the group, we will only focus on the number of viruses that are present in some of the cells of that group (not every cell in the group does necessarily hold a virus). Only one type of viruses is considered. Channels allow viruses to be transmitted from one host to another or to the environment of the system. Each channel has a natural number (the *weight* of the channel) associated with it, indicating the number of copies of the virus that will be generated and transmitted from an original one (i.e., one virus may replicate, generating a number of copies to be transmitted to the target host group of cells). Each transmission channel is closed by default and it can be opened by a control instruction unit. Specifically, there is an *instruction-channel control network* that allows opening a channel by means of an activated instruction. In that moment, the opened channel allows a virus (only one virus) to replicate

© Springer International Publishing Switzerland 2015
G. Rozenberg et al. (Eds.): CMC 2015, LNCS 9504, pp. 353–368, 2015.
DOI: 10.1007/978-3-319-28475-0_24

and transmit through it. Instructions are activated individually according to a protocol given by an *instruction transfer network*, so that only one instruction is enabled in each computation step. That is, an instruction activation signal is transferred to the network to activate instructions in sequence.

In this work, Virus Machines as computing function devices are introduced. For this purpose, we deal with Virus Machines having input hosts, allowing us to introduce some additional numbers of viruses (encoding the information) in certain distinguished hosts as an input to the Virus Machine. The universality of non-restricted Virus Machines (Virus Machines where there is no restriction on the number of hosts, the number of instructions and the number of viruses contained in any host along any computation) working in the computing mode is proved by showing that they can compute all partial recursive functions.

This paper is structured as follows. First, some preliminaries are briefly introduced in order to make the work self-contained. Then, in Sect. 3, we formally define the computing model of virus machines. Section 4 is devoted to discuss the power of non-restricted Virus Machines, and their computational completeness (via computing partial recursive functions) is stated. Finally, in Sect. 5 the main conclusions of this work are summarized and some suggestions for possible lines of future research are outlined.

2   Preliminaries

In this section some basic concepts needed throughout this paper are introduced, thus making it self-contained.

2.1   Sets and Functions

In this paper $\mathbb{Z}$ denotes the set of integer numbers, $\mathbb{Z}_{>0}$ the set of positive integers, and $\mathbb{N} = \mathbb{Z}_{\geq 0}$ the set of non-negative integers or natural numbers.

A function from a set A to a set B is a subset of $A \times B$ such that every element of A is related through f with at most one element of B. The domain of f, $\text{dom}(f)$, is the subset of A consisting of all the elements for which f is defined. If $\text{dom}(f) = A$ we say that the function is total, and denote it by $f : A \rightarrow B$. Otherwise, we say that the function is partial, and denote it by $f : A \dashrightarrow B$.

2.2   Graphs

An *undirected graph* G is a pair (V, E), where V is a finite set and E is a subset of $\{\{x, y\} \mid x \in V, y \in V, x \neq y\}$. The set V is called the *vertex set* of G, and its elements are called *vertices*. The set E is called the *edge set* of G, and its elements are called *edges*. If $e = \{x, y\} \in E$ is an edge of G, then we say that edge e is incident on vertices x and y. In an undirected graph, the *degree* of a vertex x is the number of edges incident on it. A *bipartite graph* G is an undirected graph (V, E) in which V can be partitioned into two sets V_1, V_2 such that $\{u, v\} \in E$

implies either $u \in V_1$ and $v \in V_2$ or $u \in V_2$ and $v \in V_1$; that is, all edges are arranged between the two sets V_1 and V_2 (see [3] for details).

A *directed graph* G is a pair (V, E), where V is a finite set and E is a subset of $V \times V$. The set V is called the vertex set of G, and its elements are called vertices. The set E is called the *arc set* of G, and its elements are called *arcs*. In a directed graph, the *out-degree* of a vertex is the number of arcs leaving it, and the *in-degree* of a vertex is the number of arcs entering it.

3   Virus Machines

In what follows we formally define the syntax of the Virus Machines (see [1] for more details).

Definition 1. *A* Virus Machine *Π of degree (p, q), with $p \geq 1, q \geq 1$, is a tuple $(\Gamma, H, I, D_H, D_I, G_C, n_1, \ldots, n_p, i_{\text{start}}, h_{\text{out}})$, where:*

- *$\Gamma = \{v\}$ is the singleton alphabet;*
- *$H = \{h_1, \ldots, h_p\}$ and $I = \{i_1, \ldots, i_q\}$ are ordered sets such that $v \notin H \cup I$ and $H \cap I = \emptyset$;*
- *$D_H = (H \cup \{h_{\text{out}}\}, E_H, w_H)$ is a weighted directed graph, verifying that $E_H \subseteq H \times (H \cup \{h_{\text{out}}\})$, $(h, h) \notin E_H$ for each $h \in H$, out-degree$(h_{\text{out}}) = 0$, and w_H is a mapping from E_H to $\mathbb{Z}_{>0}$;*
- *$D_I = (I, E_I, w_I)$ is a weighted directed graph, where $E_I \subseteq I \times I$, w_I is a mapping from E_I to $\mathbb{Z}_{>0}$ and, for each vertex $i_j \in I$, the out-degree of i_j is less than or equal to 2;*
- *$G_C = (V_C, E_C)$ is an undirected bipartite graph, where $V_C = I \cup E_H$, being $\{I, E_H\}$ the partition associated with it (i.e., all edges go between the two sets I and E_H). In addition, for each vertex $i_j \in I$, the degree of i_j in G_C is less than or equal to 1;*
- *$n_j \in \mathbb{N}$ $(1 \leq j \leq p)$ and $i_{\text{start}} \in I$;*
- *$h_{\text{out}} \notin I \cup \{v\}$ and h_{out} is denoted by h_0 in the case that $h_{\text{out}} \notin H$.*

A Virus Machine $\Pi = (\Gamma, H, I, D_H, D_I, G_C, n_1, \ldots, n_p, i_{\text{start}}, h_{\text{out}})$ of degree (p, q) can be viewed as an ordered set of p *hosts* labelled with $h_1, \ldots, h_p$ (where each host h_j, $1 \leq j \leq p$, initially contains exactly n_j *viruses* –copies of the symbol v–), and an ordered set of q *control instruction units* labelled with $i_1, \ldots, i_q$. Symbol h_{out} represents the *output region* of the system (we use the term *region* to refer to host h_{out} in the case that $h_{\text{out}} \in H$ and to refer to the environment in the case that $h_{\text{out}} = h_0$). Arcs $(h_s, h_{s'})$ from D_H represent *transmission channels* through which viruses can travel from host h_s to $h_{s'}$.

Each channel is *closed* by default, and so it remains until it is opened by a control instruction (which is attached to the channel by means of an edge in graph G_C) when that instruction is *activated*. Furthermore, each channel $(h_s, h_{s'})$ is assigned with a positive integer weight, denoted by $w_{s,s'}$, which indicates the number of viruses that will be transmitted/replicated to the receiving host of the channel.

Arcs $(i_j, i_{j'})$ from D_I represent *instruction transfer paths*, and they have a weight, denoted by $w_{j,j'}$, associated with it. Finally, the undirected bipartite graph G_C represents the *instruction-channel network* by which an edge $\{i_j, (h_s, h_{s'})\}$ indicates a control relationship between instruction i_j and channel $(h_s, h_{s'})$: when instruction i_j is activated, the channel $(h_s, h_{s'})$ is opened.

A *configuration* $\mathcal{C}_t$ of a Virus Machine at an instant t is described by a tuple $(a_{1,t}, \ldots, a_{p,t}, u_t, e_t)$, where $a_{1,t}, \ldots, a_{p,t}$ and e_t are non-negative integers and $u_t \in I \cup \{\#\}$, with $\# \notin \{v\} \cup H \cup \{h_0\} \cup I$. The meaning is the following: at instant t the host h_s of the system contains exactly $a_{s,t}$ viruses, the output region h_{out} contains exactly e_t viruses and, if $u_t \in I$, then the control instruction unit u_t will be activated at step $t + 1$. Otherwise, if $u_t = \#$, then no further instruction will be activated. The *initial configuration* of the system is the configuration $\mathcal{C}_0 = (n_1, \ldots, n_p, i_{\text{start}}, 0)$.

A configuration $\mathcal{C}_t = (a_{1,t}, \ldots, a_{p,t}, u_t, e_t)$ is a *halting configuration* if and only if u_t is the object $\#$. A non-halting configuration $\mathcal{C}_t = (a_{1,t}, \ldots, a_{p,t}, u_t, e_t)$ yields configuration $\mathcal{C}_{t+1} = (a_{1,t+1}, \ldots, a_{p,t+1}, u_{t+1}, e_{t+1})$ in one *transition step*, denoted by $\mathcal{C}_t \Rightarrow_\Pi \mathcal{C}_{t+1}$, if we can pass from $\mathcal{C}_t$ to $\mathcal{C}_{t+1}$ as follows:

1. First, given that $\mathcal{C}_t$ is a non-halting configuration, we have $u_t \in I$. So the control instruction unit u_t is activated.
2. Let us assume that instruction u_t is attached to channel $(h_s, h_{s'})$. Then this channel will be opened and:
   - If $a_{s,t} \geq 1$, then a virus (only one virus) is consumed from host h_s and $w_{s,s'}$ copies of v are produced in host $h_{s'}$ (if $s' \neq out$) or in the output region h_{out}.
   - If $a_{s,t} = 0$, then there is no transmission of viruses.
3. Let us assume that instruction u_t is not attached to any channel $(h_s, h_{s'})$. Then there is no transmission of viruses.
4. Object $u_{t+1} \in I \cup \{\#\}$ is obtained as follows:
   - Let us suppose that out-degree$(u_t) = 2$, that is, there are two different instructions $u_{t'}$ and $u_{t''}$ such that $(u_t, u_{t'}) \in E_I$ and $(u_t, u_{t''}) \in E_I$.
     - If instruction u_t is attached to a channel $(h_s, h_{s'})$ and $a_{s,t} \geq 1$ then u_{t+1} is the instruction corresponding to the *highest* weight path.
     - If instruction u_t is attached to a channel $(h_s, h_{s'})$ and $a_{s,t} = 0$ then u_{t+1} is the instruction corresponding to the *lowest* weight path.
     - If both weights are equal or if instruction u_t is not attached to a channel, then the next instruction u_{t+1} is either $u_{t'}$ or $u_{t''}$, selected in a non-deterministic way.
   - If out-degree$(u_t) = 1$ then the system behaves deterministically and u_{t+1} is the instruction that verifies $(u_t, u_{t+1}) \in E_I$.
   - If out-degree$(u_t) = 0$ then u_{t+1} is object $\#$ and configuration $\mathcal{C}_{t+1}$ is a halting configuration.

A *computation* of a Virus Machine Π is a (finite or infinite) sequence of configurations such that: (a) the first element is the initial configuration $\mathcal{C}_0$ of the system; (b) for each $n \geq 1$, the n-th element of the sequence is obtained from the previous element in one transition step; and (c) if the sequence is finite (called *halting computation*) then the last element is a halting configuration. All the computations start from the initial configuration and proceed as stated above; only halting computations give a result, which is encoded in the contents of the output region for the halting configuration.

Definition 2. *A Virus Machine Π with input of degree (p, q, r), $p \geq 1$, $q \geq 1$, $r \geq 1$, is a tuple $(\Gamma, H, H_r, I, D_H, D_I, G_C, n_1, \ldots, n_p, i_{start}, h_{out})$, where:*

- *$(\Gamma, H, I, D_H, D_I, G_C, n_1, \ldots, n_p, i_{start}, h_{out})$ represents a Virus Machine of degree (p, q).*
- *$H_r = \{h_{j_1}, \ldots, h_{j_r}\} \subseteq H$ is the ordered set of r input hosts and $h_{out} \notin H_r$.*

The *initial configuration* of Π with input $(\alpha_1, \ldots, \alpha_r)$ is the configuration $(m_1, \ldots, m_p, i_{start}, 0)$, where $m_j = n_j + \alpha_j$, if $j \in \{j_1, \ldots, j_r\}$, and $m_j = n_j$ otherwise. Therefore, in a Virus Machine with input we have an initial configuration associated with each $(\alpha_1, \ldots, \alpha_r) \in \mathbb{N}^r$. A computation of a Virus Machine Π with input $(\alpha_1, \ldots, \alpha_r)$, denoted by $\Pi + (\alpha_1, \ldots, \alpha_r)$, starts with the initial configuration $(m_1, \ldots, m_p, i_{start}, 0)$ and proceeds as stated above.

In this paper we work with Virus Machines working in the *computing mode*. That is, the result of a computation of a Virus Machine Π with input $(\alpha_1, \ldots, \alpha_r)$ is the total number n of viruses sent to the output region during the computation. We say that number n is *computed* by the Virus Machine $\Pi + (\alpha_1, \ldots, \alpha_r)$. We denote by $N(\Pi + (\alpha_1, \ldots, \alpha_r))$ the set of all natural numbers computed by $\Pi + (\alpha_1, \ldots, \alpha_r)$.

Throughout this paper, due to technical reasons, we consider $h_{out} \in H$, that is, the output region of a Virus Machine will be a host.

3.1   Virus Machines as Function Computing Devices

Virus Machines can work in several modes. In this section we introduce a particular kind of virus machines working in the computing mode providing function computing devices.

Definition 3. *Let $f : \mathbb{N}^k \dashrightarrow \mathbb{N}$ be a partial function. We say that f is computable by a Virus Machine Π with k input hosts working in the computing mode if the following holds: for each $(x_1, \ldots, x_k) \in \mathbb{N}^k$,*

- *If $(x_1, \ldots, x_k) \in \mathrm{dom}(f)$ and $f(x_1, \ldots, x_k) = z$, then every computation $\Pi + (x_1, \ldots, x_k)$ is a halting computation with output z.*
- *If $(x_1, \ldots, x_k) \notin \mathrm{dom}(f)$, then every computation $\Pi + (x_1, \ldots, x_k)$ is a non-halting computation.*

The concept of computation of a subset of $\mathbb{N}^k$ is introduced below, via function computing Virus Machines.

Definition 4. *Let $A \subseteq \mathbb{N}^k$ be a set of k-tuples of natural numbers. We say that A is computed by a Virus Machine Π with k input hosts working in the computing mode if Π computes the partial characteristic function $\mathcal{C}_A^*$ of A, defined as follows:*

$$\mathcal{C}_A^*(x_1, \ldots, x_k) = \begin{cases} 1, & if \ (x_1, \ldots, x_k) \in A \\ undefined, & otherwise \end{cases}$$

4 The Universality of Non-restricted Virus Machines

A *non-restricted Virus Machine* is a Virus Machine such that there is no restriction on the number of hosts, the number of instructions and the number of viruses contained in any host along any computation.

For each $p, q, n \geq 1$, we denote by $NVM(p, q, n)$ the family of all subsets of $\mathbb{N}$ computed by Virus Machines with at most p hosts, q instructions, and all hosts having at most n viruses at any instant of each computation. If one of the numbers p, q, n is not bounded, then it is replaced with $*$. In particular, $NVM(*, *, *)$ denotes the family of all subsets of natural numbers computed by non-restricted Virus Machines.

4.1 Computing Partial Recursive Functions by Virus Machines

In this section, the computational completeness of non-restricted Virus Machines working in the computing mode is established. Specifically, we prove that they can compute all partial recursive functions. Indeed, we will design non-restricted Virus Machines that:

1. Compute the *basic or initial functions*: constant zero function, successor function and projection functions.
2. Compute the *composition* of functions, from Virus Machines computing the functions to be composed.
3. Compute the *primitive recursion* of functions, from Virus Machines computing the functions that participate in the recursion.
4. Compute the *unbounded minimization* of functions, from a Virus Machine computing the function to be minimized.

4.2 Modules

In order to ease the design of the Virus Machines computing any partial recursive function, the construction of such Virus Machines will be made in a modular manner. A *module* can be seen as a Virus Machine without output host, with the initial instruction marked as the *in* instruction and with at least one instruction marked as an *out* instruction. The *out* instructions must have outdegree less than two, so that they can still be connected to another instruction. This way, a module m_1 can be plugged in before another module m_2 or Virus Machine instruction i by simply connecting the *out* instructions of m_1 with the *in* instruction of m_2 or with the instruction i.

The layout of a module must be carefully design to avoid conflicts with other modules and to allow the module to be executed any number of times. To achieve the first condition, we will consider that all the hosts (with the only exception of those belonging to the parameters of the module) and instructions of a module are individualized for that module, being distinct from the ones of any other module or Virus Machine. The second condition is met if we ensure that, after the execution of the module, all its hosts except its parameters contain the same number of viruses as before the execution.

In this paper we consider two types of modules: action modules and predicate modules. For the action modules we require all of its *out* instructions to be connected to the *in* instruction of the following module, or to the following instruction of the Virus Machine. For the predicate modules we consider its *out* instructions to be divided in two subsets: the *out* instructions representing a *yes* answer and the *out* instructions representing a *no* answer of the predicate. For each of these subsets, all of its instructions have to be connected to the same module *in* instruction or Virus Machine instruction.

The library of modules used in this paper consists of the following modules (we name the action modules as verbs and the predicate modules as questions):

- EMPTY(h): action module that sets to zero the number of viruses in host h.
  To implement this module we only need to introduce an internal host h', initially with zero viruses, and associate with the channel from h to h' an action that transfers all the viruses from h. Note that host h' may end with a nonzero number of viruses, but this does not prevent the module to be reused, because h' plays a passive role.

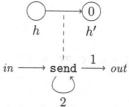

- ADD(h_1, h_2): action module that adds to host h_2 the number of viruses in host h_1, without modifying the number of viruses in h_1.
  This module is implemented as follows:

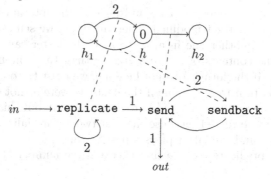

This way, the module starts by transferring one by one all the viruses from h_1 to h, duplicating them along the way. Then it sends, again and again, one virus from h to h_2 and another one from h to h_1, until there are no more viruses left. It is clear then that when the module ends, the host h_1 retains its initial number of viruses, the host h is empty (thus allowing the module to be reused), and the host h_2 has a number of viruses equal to the sum of the initial number of viruses in h_1 and h_2.

– COPY(h_1, h_2): action module that sets the number of viruses in h_2 the same as in h_1, without modifying the number of viruses in h_1.
This module is implemented by the following concatenation of modules:

$$in \rightarrow \text{EMPTY}(h_2) \rightarrow \text{ADD}(h_1, h_2) \rightarrow out$$

That is, we first get rid of all the viruses from h_2, and then add the viruses from h_1, so h_2 ends with the same number of viruses as h_1. Also observe that the module ADD(h_1, h_2) does not modify the number of viruses in h_1, what will be important later.

– SET(h, n): action module that sets to n the number of viruses in host h. This module is implemented simply by introducing an internal host h' with initial number of viruses n and using the module COPY(h', h).

– AREEQUAL?(h_1, h_2): predicate module that checks if the number of viruses in hosts h_1 and h_2 coincides.
This module is implemented as follows, where h_1', h_2' and h are new internal hosts:

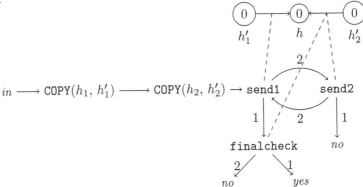

We first copy the contents of h_1 and h_2 into the internal hosts h_1' and h_2', so that they do not get modified. Then, in turns, we send one virus from h_1' to h and then another one from h_2' to h. If the latter can not be done, this is because the contents of h_1 were greater than the contents of h_2 and the answer is no. If the former can not be done, we must try once more to send a virus from h_2' to h to determine if the contents were or not equal.
Notice that the contents of h_1', h_2' and h get modified, but this does not prevent the module to be reused, because the first two get initialized by the first two COPY modules and the latter plays a passive role.

– ISZERO?(h): predicate module that checks if the number of viruses in host h is zero.

This module is simply implemented by introducing an empty internal host h' and using the module AREEQUAL?(h, h').

Finally, notice that we can consider any Virus Machine Π as an action module without parameters, where the initial instruction is the *in* instruction and any instruction with out-degree zero is an *out* instruction. The only problem is that Π would be a module of one use, because it is not guaranteed that the contents of its hosts are the same before and after execution. If we wanted to reuse it, we would need to set Π to its initial state, by means of the following module:

- RESTART(Π): action module that sets the number of viruses of each host h_i of Π to its initial contents n_i.
  This module is implemented by the following concatenation of modules:

$$in \to \text{SET}(h_1, n_1) \to \cdots \to \text{SET}(h_p, n_p) \to out$$

where $h_1, \ldots, h_p$ are the hosts of Π and $n_1, \ldots, n_p$ are their initial contents.

4.3   Basic or Initial Functions

We begin by describing function computing Virus Machines that allow us to compute the basic functions.

- The *constant zero function*, $\mathcal{O} : \mathbb{N} \to \mathbb{N}$, defined by $\mathcal{O}(x) = 0$, for every $x \in \mathbb{N}$, can be computed by the following virus machine $\Pi_{\mathcal{O}}$ with input working in the computing mode:
  - The hosts are $H_{\mathcal{O}} = \{h, h_{\text{zero}}\}$, each of them initially empty.
  - The input host is h and the output host is h_{zero}.
  - The initial and only instruction is halt.
  - Each of the three graphs $D_{H_{\mathcal{O}}}$, $D_{I_{\mathcal{O}}}$ and $G_{C_{\mathcal{O}}}$ determining the functioning of the machine has an empty set of edges.
  This way, for any input the Virus Machine $\Pi_{\mathcal{O}}$ halts in the very first step, and the output host h_{zero} remains empty. So the output of this machine is always zero.
- The *successor function*, $\mathcal{S} : \mathbb{N} \to \mathbb{N}$, defined by $\mathcal{S}(x) = x + 1$, for every $x \in \mathbb{N}$, can be computed by the following virus machine $\Pi_{\mathcal{S}}$ with input working in the computing mode:
  - The hosts are $H_{\mathcal{S}} = \{h, h_{\text{one}}\}$, together with the internal hosts of the module ADD(h, h_{one}).
  - The initial contents are zero for the host h and one for the host h_{one}, together with the initial contents of the internal hosts of the module ADD(h, h_{one}).
  - The input host is h and the output host is h_{one}.
  - The instructions are $I_{\mathcal{S}} = \{\text{halt}\}$, together with the instructions of the module ADD(h, h_{one}).
  - The initial instruction is the *in* instruction of the module ADD(h, h_{one}).

- The functioning of the Virus Machine is given by the following sequence, which determines the graphs D_{H_S}, D_{I_S} and G_{C_S}:

$$\text{ADD}(h, h_{\text{one}}) \to \texttt{halt}$$

This way, for any input the Virus Machine Π_S adds it from h to h_{one} and halts. Since host h_{one} contained one virus, the output of this machine is equal to the input plus one, as required.

– The *projection functions*, $\Pi_i^m : \mathbb{N}^m \to \mathbb{N}$, with $m \geq 1$ and $1 \leq i \leq m$, defined by $\Pi_i^m(x_1, \ldots, x_m) = x_i$, for every $(x_1, \ldots, x_m) \in \mathbb{N}^m$, can be computed by the following Virus Machine $\Pi_{\Pi_i^m}$ with input working in the computing mode:
  - The hosts are $H_{\Pi_i^m} = \{h_1, \ldots, h_m, h_{\text{out}}\}$, together with the internal hosts of the module $\text{COPY}(h_i, h_{\text{out}})$.
  - The initial contents are zero for the hosts $h_1, \ldots, h_m, h_{\text{out}}$, together with the initial contents of the internal hosts of the module $\text{COPY}(h_i, h_{\text{out}})$.
  - The input hosts are $h_1, \ldots, h_m$ and the output host is h_{out}.
  - The instructions are $I_{\Pi_i^m} = \{\texttt{halt}\}$, together with the instructions of the module $\text{COPY}(h_i, h_{\text{out}})$.
  - The initial instruction is the *in* instruction of the module $\text{COPY}(h_i, h_{\text{out}})$.
  - The functioning of the Virus Machine is given by the following sequence, which determines the graphs $D_{H_{\Pi_i^m}}$, $D_{I_{\Pi_i^m}}$ and $G_{C_{\Pi_i^m}}$:

$$\text{COPY}(h_i, h_{\text{out}}) \to \texttt{halt}$$

This way, for any input the Virus Machine $\Pi_{\Pi_i^m}$ copies the i-th component from h_i to h_{out} and halts, so the output of the machine is that component.

4.4   Composition of Functions

We show now how the composition of functions can be simulated by Virus Machines with input working in the computing mode.

Definition 5. *Let $f : \mathbb{N}^m \dashrightarrow \mathbb{N}$ and $g_1 : \mathbb{N}^n \dashrightarrow \mathbb{N}, \ldots, g_m : \mathbb{N}^n \dashrightarrow \mathbb{N}$. Then, the composition of f with g_1 to g_m, denoted $C(f; g_1, \ldots, g_m)$, is a partial function from $\mathbb{N}^n$ to $\mathbb{N}$ defined as follows:*

$$C(f; g_1, \ldots, g_m)(x_1, \ldots, x_n) = f(g_1(x_1, \ldots, x_n), \ldots, g_m(x_1, \ldots, x_n))$$

for each $(x_1, \ldots, x_n) \in \mathbb{N}^n$.

Let $\Pi_f, \Pi_{g_1}, \ldots, \Pi_{g_m}$ be Virus Machines with input, computing the functions $f, g_1, \ldots, g_m$, respectively. Let us assume that for each $x \in \{f, g_1, \ldots, g_m\}$ the elements of the Virus Machine Π_x are the following:

– The hosts are $H_x = \{h_1^x, \ldots, h_{p_x}^x\}$.
– The initial contents of the hosts are $n_1^x, \ldots, n_{p_x}^x$.
– The input hosts are $h_1^f, \ldots, h_m^f$ and $h_1^x, \ldots, h_n^x$ for $x \in \{g_1, \ldots, g_m\}$.
– The output host is h_{out}^x.

- The instructions are $I_x = \{i_1^x, \ldots, i_{q_x}^x\}$.
- The initial instruction is i_{start}^x.
- The functioning of the Virus Machine is determined by the directed graphs D_{H_x}, D_{I_x} and the bipartite graph G_{C_x}.

Then, the composition of f with $g_1, \ldots, g_m$ can be computed by the following Virus Machine $\Pi_{C(f;g_1,\ldots,g_m)}$ with input:

- The hosts are $H = \{h_1, \ldots, h_n\} \cup H_f \cup H_{g_1} \cup \cdots \cup H_{g_m}$, together with the internal hosts of the modules.
- The initial contents of the hosts are

$$(0, \ldots, 0, n_1^f, \ldots, n_{p_f}^f, n_1^{g_1}, \ldots, n_{p_{g_1}}^{g_1}, \ldots, n_1^{g_m}, \ldots, n_{p_{g_m}}^{g_m})$$

together with the initial contents of the internal hosts of the modules.
- The input hosts are $\{h_1, \ldots, h_n\}$.
- The output host is h_{out}^f.
- The instructions are $I_f \cup I_{g_1} \cup \cdots \cup I_{g_m} \cup \{\texttt{halt}\}$, together with the individualized instructions of the modules.
- The initial instruction is the *in* instruction of the first module.
- The functioning of the Virus Machine is given by the following sequence of concatenated modules, which determines the graphs D_H, D_I and G_C:

  1. First we simulate the introduction of the input into the input hosts of Π_{g_1}. Recall that the module $\texttt{ADD}(h_1, h_2)$ does not change the content of host h_1.
  $$\texttt{ADD}(h_1, h_1^{g_1}) \rightarrow \cdots \rightarrow \texttt{ADD}(h_n, h_n^{g_1}) \rightarrow$$

  2. We do the same for the machines $\Pi_{g_2}, \ldots, \Pi_{g_m}$.
  $$\rightarrow \texttt{ADD}(h_1, h_1^{g_2}) \rightarrow \cdots \rightarrow \texttt{ADD}(h_n, h_n^{g_2}) \rightarrow$$
  $$\vdots$$
  $$\rightarrow \texttt{ADD}(h_1, h_1^{g_m}) \rightarrow \cdots \rightarrow \texttt{ADD}(h_n, h_n^{g_m}) \rightarrow$$

  3. Now we can simulate the functions $g_1, \ldots, g_m$ over the received input.
  $$\rightarrow \Pi_{g_1} \rightarrow \ldots \rightarrow \Pi_{g_m} \rightarrow$$

  4. Finally, we introduce the outputs of the previous simulations as input for Π_f, simulate f and finish the execution.
  $$\rightarrow \texttt{ADD}(h_{out}^{g_1}, h_1^f) \rightarrow \cdots \rightarrow \texttt{ADD}(h_{out}^{g_m}, h_m^f) \rightarrow \Pi_f \rightarrow \texttt{halt}$$

4.5 Primitive Recursion of Functions

We show now how the primitive recursion of functions can be simulated by Virus Machines with input working in the computing mode.

Definition 6. *Let $f : \mathbb{N}^m \dashrightarrow \mathbb{N}$ and $g : \mathbb{N}^{m+2} \dashrightarrow \mathbb{N}$. Then, the function obtained by primitive recursion from f and g, denoted $Rec(f; g)$, is a partial function from $\mathbb{N}^{m+1}$ to $\mathbb{N}$ defined as follows:*

$$Rec(f; g)(x_1, \ldots, x_m, x_{m+1}) = \begin{cases} f(x_1, \ldots, x_m), & \text{if } x_{m+1} = 0 \\ g(x_1, \ldots, x_m, x_{m+1}, y), & \text{otherwise} \end{cases}$$

where $y = Rec(f; g)(x_1, \ldots, x_m, x_{m+1} - 1)$

for each $(x_1, \ldots, x_m, x_{m+1}) \in \mathbb{N}^{m+1}$.

Let Π_f and Π_g be Virus Machines with input, computing the functions f and g, respectively. Let us suppose that for each function $x \in \{f, g\}$ the elements of the virus machine Π_x are the following:

- The hosts are $H_x = \{h_1^x, \ldots, h_{p_x}^x\}$.
- The initial contents of the hosts are $(n_1^x, \ldots, n_{p_x}^x)$.
- The input hosts are $h_1^f, \ldots, h_m^f$ and $h_1^g, \ldots, h_{m+2}^g$.
- The output host is h_{out}^x.
- The instructions are $I_x = \{i_1^x, \ldots, i_{q_x}^x\}$.
- The initial instruction is i_{start}^x.
- The functioning of the Virus Machine is determined by the directed graphs D_{H_x}, D_{I_x} and the bipartite graph G_{C_x}.

Then, the function $Rec(f; g)$ can be computed by the following Virus Machine with input $\Pi_{Rec(f;g)}$:

- The hosts are $H = \{h_1, \ldots, h_{m+1}, h', h_{\text{one}}, h_{\text{out}}, h_{\text{out}}'\} \cup H_f \cup H_g$, together with the internal hosts of the modules.
- The initial contents of the hosts are $0, \ldots, 0, 0, 1, 0, 0, n_1^f, \ldots, n_{p_f}^f, n_1^g, \ldots, n_{p_g}^g$, together with the initial contents of the internal hosts of the modules.
- The input hosts are $\{h_1, \ldots, h_{m+1}\}$.
- The output host is h_{out}.
- The instructions are $I_f \cup I_g \cup \{\texttt{halt}\}$, together with the individualized instructions of the modules.
- The initial instruction is the *in* instruction of the first module.
- The functioning of the Virus Machine is given by the following sequence of concatenated modules, which determines the graphs D_H, D_I and G_C:
  1. Observe that to compute the function $Rec(f; g)$ we have to repeatedly compute the function g as many times as indicated by the $(m + 1)$-th argument, except for the first time in which the function f has to be computed instead.
  2. First we simulate the introduction of the input for the function f into the input hosts of Π_f.

$$\texttt{ADD}(h_1, h_1^f) \to \cdots \to \texttt{ADD}(h_m, h_m^f) \to$$

3. We now simulate the function f over its input and copy the result to h_{out} and h'_{out}. This is because if we are done, then the result has to be in h_{out}, but if we are not done, we must pass this result as the last argument to g. However, h_{out} is required to have out-degree zero, so we take the result from h'_{out} instead.

$$\rightarrow \Pi_f \rightarrow \text{COPY}(h^f_{out}, h_{out}) \rightarrow \text{COPY}(h^f_{out}, h'_{out}) \rightarrow$$

4. We check if we are done, in which case stop the execution.

$$\rightarrow \text{AREEQUAL?}(h_{m+1}, h') \overset{yes}{\hookrightarrow} \text{halt}$$
$$\downarrow no$$

5. If we are not done, one computation of g has to be simulated. For that, the $(m+1)$-th argument of g is updated by adding 1 to it and the appropriate input is introduced into the input hosts of Π_g. The input for the last argument is the result of the previous computation, that we will ensure is always within host h'_{out}.

$$\overset{no}{\rightarrow} \text{ADD}(h_{one}, h') \rightarrow \text{ADD}(h_1, h^g_1) \rightarrow \cdots \rightarrow \text{ADD}(h_m, h^g_m) \rightarrow$$
$$\text{ADD}(h', h^g_{m+1}) \rightarrow \text{ADD}(h'_{out}, h^g_{m+2}) \rightarrow$$

6. We simulate the function g and copy the result to both hosts h_{out} and h'_{out}. Before continuing to step 4, the machine Π_g has to be restarted to its initial state, so that it can be used to simulate again the function g, if necessary.

$$\rightarrow \Pi_g \rightarrow \text{COPY}(h^g_{out}, h_{out}) \rightarrow \text{COPY}(h^g_{out}, h'_{out}) \rightarrow$$
$$\text{RESTART}(\Pi_g) \rightarrow \text{back to step 4}$$

4.6   Unbounded Minimization of Functions

We show now how the unbounded minimization of functions can be simulated by Virus Machines with input working in the computing mode.

Definition 7. *Let* $f : \mathbb{N}^{m+1} \dashrightarrow \mathbb{N}$*. Then, the function obtained by unbounded minimization from* f*, denoted* $Min(f)$*, is a partial function from* $\mathbb{N}^m$ *to* $\mathbb{N}$ *defined as follows:*

$$Min(f)(x_1, \ldots, x_m) = \begin{cases} y_{x_1, \ldots, x_m}, & \text{if it exists} \\ \text{undefined}, & \text{otherwise} \end{cases}$$

where

$$y_{x_1, \ldots, x_m} = \min\{y \in \mathbb{N} \mid \forall z < y \left(f \text{ is defined over } (x_1, \ldots, x_m, z) \right) \wedge$$
$$f(x_1, \ldots, x_m, y) = 0\}$$

for each $(x_1, \ldots, x_m) \in \mathbb{N}^m$.

Let Π_f be a Virus Machine with input, computing the function f. Let us suppose that the elements of the Virus Machine Π_f are the following:

- The hosts are $H_f = \{h_1^f, \ldots, h_{p_f}^f\}$.
- The initial contents of the hosts are $n_1^f, \ldots, n_{p_f}^f$.
- The input hosts are $h_1^f, \ldots, h_{m+1}^f$.
- The output host is h_{out}^f.
- The instructions are $I_f = \{i_1^f, \ldots, i_{q_f}^f\}$.
- The initial instruction is i_{start}^f.
- The functioning of the Virus Machine is determined by the directed graphs D_{H_f}, D_{I_f} and the bipartite graph G_{C_f}.

Then, the function $Min(f)$ can be computed by the following Virus Machine with input $\Pi_{Min(f)}$:

- The hosts are $H = \{h_1, \ldots, h_m, h_{m+1}, h_{\text{one}}, h_{\text{out}}\} \cup H_f$, together with the internal hosts of the modules.
- The initial contents of the hosts are $0, \ldots, 0, 0, 1, 0, n_1^f, \ldots, n_{p_f}^f$, together with the initial contents of the internal hosts of the modules.
- The input hosts are $\{h_1, \ldots, h_m\}$.
- The output host is h_{out}.
- The instructions are $I_f \cup \{\texttt{halt}\}$, together with the individualized instructions of the modules.
- The initial instruction is the in instruction of the first module.
- The functioning of the Virus Machine is given by the following sequence of concatenated modules, which determines the graphs D_H, D_I and G_C:
  1. Observe that to compute the function $Min(f)$ we have to repeatedly compute the function f until we obtain a zero result.
  2. First we simulate the introduction of the input for the function f into the input hosts of Π_f.

$$\texttt{ADD}(h_1, h_1^f) \to \cdots \to \texttt{ADD}(h_{m+1}, h_{m+1}^f) \to$$

  3. We now simulate the function f over its input and check if the result is or not zero.

$$\to \Pi_f \to \texttt{ISZERO?}(h_{\text{out}}^f) \overset{yes}{\to}$$
$$\downarrow no$$

  4. In the case that the result obtained is zero, we copy the last argument to the output host and stop the execution.

$$\overset{yes}{\to} \texttt{COPY}(h_{m+1}, h_{\text{out}}) \to \texttt{halt}$$

  5. Otherwise, we add one to the last argument, restart the machine Π_f so that it can be used again to simulate f, and go back to step 2.

$$\overset{no}{\to} \texttt{ADD}(h_{one}, h_{m+1}) \to \texttt{RESTART}(\Pi_f) \to \text{back to step 2}$$

4.7   Main Result

Taking into account that the class of partial recursive functions coincides with the least class that contains the basic functions and is closed under composition, primitive recursion and unbounded minimization (see [2]), it is guaranteed that it is possible to construct virus machines that compute any partial recursive function. Then, we have the following result.

Theorem 1. *The family $NVM(*, *, *)$ equals to the family of all the recursively enumerable sets of natural numbers.*

5   Conclusions and Future Work

Virus Machines are a bio-inspired computational paradigm based on the transmissions and replications of viruses [1]. The computational completeness of Virus Machines having no restriction on the number of hosts, the number of instructions and the number of viruses contained in any host along any computation has been established by simulating register machines. However, when an upper bound on the number of viruses present in any host during a computation is set, the computational power of these systems decreases; in fact, a characterization of semi-linear sets of numbers is obtained [1].

The semantics of the model makes it easy to construct specific Virus Machines by assembling small components that carry out a part of the task to be solved. It is then convenient to develop a library of modules solving common problems such as comparisons or arithmetic operations between contents of hosts.

In this paper, Virus Machines able to compute partial functions on natural numbers are introduced. The universality of non-restricted Virus Machines is then proved by showing that they can compute all partial recursive functions.

In [5] Virus Machines working in the generating mode are considered, and it is shown how they can generate any diophantine set, providing, via the MRDP theorem, another proof of the universality of this model of computation. What is interesting is that the structure of the design of these systems has served as inspiration to defined a parallel variant of Virus Machines having several independent instruction transfer networks. It could be interesting to explore other means of introducing parallelism, such as considering more than one type of viruses or allowing more than one virus to be transmitted when a channel is opened.

To study the computational efficiency of this model of computation, for example to analyze if the parallel variants of Virus Machines represent an improvement over the sequential one, a computational complexity theory is required. This way, the resources needed to solve (hard) problems can be rigorously measured.

Acknowledgments. This work was supported by Project TIN2012-37434 of the Ministerio de Economía y Competitividad of Spain, cofinanced by FEDER funds.

References

1. Chen, X., Valencia-Cabrera, L., Pérez-Jiménez, M.J., Wang, B., Zeng, X.: Computing with viruses. Int. J. Bioinspired Comput. (2015, submitted)
2. Cohen, D.E.: Computability and Logic. Ellis Horwood, Chichester (1987)
3. Cormen, T.H., Leiserson, C.E., Rivest, R.L.: An Introduction to Algorithms. The MIT Press, Cambridge, Massachussets (1994)
4. Dimmock, N.J., Easton, A.J., Leppard, K.: Introduction to Modern Virology. Blackwell Publishing, Malden (USA) (2007)
5. Romero-Jiménez, Á., Valencia-Cabrera, L., Pérez-Jiménez, M.J.: Sequential and parallel generation of diophantine sets by virus machines. J. Comput. Theor. Nanosci. (2015, submitted)
6. Rozenberg, G., Bäck, T., Kok, J.N.: Handbook of Natural Computing, 1st edn. Springer, Heidelberg (2012)

About Models Derived from Colonies

Šárka Vavrečková, Luděk Cienciala, and Lucie Ciencialová[✉]

Institute of Computer Science and Research Institute of the IT4Innovations
Centre of Excellence, Silesian University, Opava, Czech Republic
{sarka.vavreckova,lucie.ciencialova,ludek.cienciala}@fpf.slu.cz

Abstract. There are many different theoretical computational models,
where mutually independent agents interfere in a shared environment or
they interact with it directly.

In our paper we focus on three models which originate from
colonies – the first of them, eco-colonies, are grammar systems with very
simple agents parallely modifying the shared environment, where the
environment is also evolved by environmental rules (0L scheme). The
second model are P colonies with agents and unordered environment
without its own development, and the third model are eco-P colonies
with a self-developing environment. We compare these three models in
meaning of structure, the way of computation and computational power.

1 Introduction

Eco-colonies were introduced in [16] as extension of colonies [8] – grammar
systems with very simple grammars (components, agents) acting together in
an environment. Eco-colonies extend this concept with environment evolution.
In eco-colonies the evolution of the environment is determined by Lindenmayer
scheme without interaction – 0L scheme (see e.g. [13,15]).

Agents according to their rules process symbols in the environment, the
remaining symbols are processed by the environment. An agent can process
only one particular symbol (in each step it scans the environment, this element
is called the start symbol). Action rules of the given agent specify the strings,
to which the agent can overwrite one occurrence of its start symbol found in the
environment. The important limitation is that the agent is unable to generate
its own start symbol.

In the source [16] two modes of derivation in eco-colony are defined – weakly
parallel wp and strongly parallel sp. In both cases the agents work in parallel,
in wp mode only agents which can find its start symbol in the environment
can work, in sp mode all agents must work otherwise computation ends. Weak
parallelism was defined in a lot of manners (they are more or less equivalent), in
this paper we use the definition published in [12].

L. Ciencialová—This work was partially supported by the European Regional Development Fund in the IT4Innovations Centre of Excellence project (CZ.1.05/1.1.00/-
02.0070), and by SGS/24/2013 and SGS/6/2014.

© Springer International Publishing Switzerland 2015
G. Rozenberg et al. (Eds.): CMC 2015, LNCS 9504, pp. 369–386, 2015.
DOI: 10.1007/978-3-319-28475-0_25

P colonies were introduced in [11] as formal models of a computing device combining properties of membrane systems and above mentioned distributed systems of formal grammars called colonies. The concept is inspired by the structure and functioning of a community of living organisms in a shared environment (for more information consult [14]).

Eco-P colonies are extended concept of P colonies, where the evolution of the environment is based on 0L scheme and agents use different type of programs from programs in P colonies. Reader can find more information in [1].

Sufficient information about options and possibilities of using membrane systems, P colonies and other models is available on web page http://ppage.psystems.eu/.

The eco-colonies and P colonies come from the same concept of colonies. It seems to be interesting question how different are the models. In this paper we focus on comparability of the environment in eco-colonies and P colonies (and eco-P colonies respectively). In the first section we remind notations and definitions, we also show the main properties of the given three systems. The second section is devoted to relationship of eco-colonies and P colonies, and in the third section we compare eco-colonies and eco-P colonies.

2   Preliminaries

Throughout the paper we assume the reader to be familiar with the basics of the formal language theory and membrane computing. For further details we refer to [7,14].

For an alphabet Σ, the set of all words over Σ (including the empty word, ε), is denoted by Σ^*. We denote the length of a word $w \in \Sigma^*$ by $|w|$ and the number of occurrences of a symbol $a \in \Sigma$ in w by $|w|_a$.

A multiset of objects M is a pair $M = (V, f)$, where V is an arbitrary (not necessarily finite) set of objects and f is a mapping $f: V \to N$; f assigns to each object in V its multiplicity in M. The set of all multisets over the set of objects V is denoted by V°. The set V' is called the support of M and denoted by $supp(M)$ if $f(x) \neq 0$ holds for all $x \in V'$. The cardinality of M, denoted by $|M|$, is defined as $|M| = \sum_{a \in V} f(a)$. Any multiset of objects M with the set of objects $V' = \{a_1, \ldots a_n\}$ can be represented as a string w over alphabet V' with $|w|_{a_i} = f(a_i)$; $1 \leq i \leq n$. Obviously, all words obtained from w by permuting the letters can also represent the same multiset M, and ε represents the empty multiset.

Let $x \in \Sigma^*$ be an arbitrary string. The number of occurrences of symbols from Σ in a string x is denoted by $|x|$. For a language $L \subseteq \Sigma^*$ the set $length(L) = \{|x| \mid x \in L\}$ is called the length set of L. For a family of languages FL we denote the family of length sets of languages in FL by NFL.

2.1   Eco-Colonies

We start this subsection with definition of eco-colony, the derivation step and language generated by eco-colony.

Definition 1 (0L eco-colony). *An 0L eco-colony of degree* n, $n \geq 1$, *is an* $(n+2)$-*tuple* $\Sigma = (E, w_0, A_1, A_2, \ldots, A_n)$, *where*

- $E = (V, P)$ *is 0L scheme, where*
  - V *is a nonempty alphabet,*
  - $P \subseteq V \times V^*$ *is a finite set of 0L rewriting rules over* V,
- $w_0 \in V^*$ *is the axiom,*
- $A_i = (S_i, F_i)$ *is the* i-*th agent,* $1 \leq i \leq n$, *where*
  - $S_i \in V$ *is the start symbol of the agent,*
  - $F_i \subseteq (V - \{S_i\})^*$ *is a finite set of action rules of the agent (the language of the agent).*

Derivation step in eco-colony is weakly parallel (*wp* for short), when every agent which can work must work. An agent can work if its start symbol is in the environment and any other agent does not occupy selected occurrence of the symbol. One agent can rewrite only one occurrence of its start symbol in one step of derivation. In one step the i-th agent finds its start symbol S_i and it rewrites S_i to one of strings in the set F_i. Symbols in the environment, which are not processed by any agent, are changed according to evolving rules of the environment.

Definition 2. *We define a weakly competitive parallel derivation step in an eco-colony* $\Sigma = (E, w_0, A_1, A_2, \ldots, A_n)$ *as the relation* $\overset{wp}{\Rightarrow}$ *and we say that* α *directly derives* β *in wp mode of derivation (written as* $\alpha \overset{wp}{\Rightarrow} \beta$) *if*

- $\alpha = v_0 S_{i_1} v_1 S_{i_2} v_2 \ldots v_{r-1} S_{i_r} v_r$, $r > 0$,
- $\beta = v_0' f_{i_1} v_1' f_{i_2} v_2' \ldots v_{r-1}' f_{i_r} v_r'$
  for $A_{i_k} = (S_{i_k}, F_{i_k})$, $f_{i_k} \in F_{i_k}$, $1 \leq k \leq r$,
- $\{i_1, \ldots, i_r\} \subseteq \{1, \ldots, n\}$, $i_k \neq i_m$ *for all* $k \neq m$, $1 \leq k, m \leq r$,
- *we denote* t_S *the number of agents with the start symbol* S *for all symbols* $S \in V$; *then*

$$\sum_{\substack{j=1 \\ S_{i_j}=S}}^{r} |\alpha|_{S_{i_j}} = \min\left(|\alpha|_S, t_S\right) \qquad (1)$$

The left side of the equation gives the number of agents with the start symbol S *which work in the given derivation step, the right side of the equation gives the number of agents with start symbol* S *which can process their start symbol in the string* α *(all agents which can work – their start symbol is in the environment and some of the occurrences of this symbol is not occupied by any other agent – they must work),*

- $v_k \Rightarrow v_k'$, $v_k \in V^*$, $0 \leq k \leq r$ *is the derivation step of the scheme* E.

The computation ends when no agent can find its start symbol in the environment. For the relation $\overset{wp}{\Rightarrow}$ we denote by $\overset{wp}{\Rightarrow}^*$ the reflexive and transitive closure.

Table 1. Summary of properties of eco-colonies

Property of	0L eco-colony
Environment $E = (V, P)$	Dynamic, of type 0L, state is a string
Agents $A = (S, F)$	Are stateless, they can process one specific symbol in the environment, they can rewrite it to a string
Action rules	$S \rightarrow f_1 \mid f_2 \mid \cdots \mid f_k,$ $f_j \in F, \ F \subseteq (V - S)^*$
Priority	Agents have priority over the environment
Activity of agents	Parallel
Output	String – state of the environment

Definition 3. *Let $\Sigma = (E, w_0, A_1, A_2, \ldots, A_n)$ be an eco-colony. The language generated by Σ using the derivation mode wp is*

$$L(\Sigma, wp) = \left\{ w \in V^* \mid w_0 \overset{wp}{\Longrightarrow}{}^* w \right\}$$

We use $0EC_{wp}$ for the class of languages generated by 0L eco-colonies with the wp mode of derivation.

As regards, for the generative power of 0L eco-colonies we find out the following: $0EC_{wp} \subset RE$, but $0EC_{wp}$ and the class of context-free languages (CF) are incomparable.

$0EC_{wp}$ and the class of $0L$ languages are incomparable – 0L eco-colonies are not able to generate $L_1 = \left\{ a^{2^n} \mid n \geq 0 \right\}$ because of the fact that agents cannot generate their own start symbols, and this language is 0L. Contrarily, the language of the 0L eco-colony $\Sigma = (E, a^3, A)$ where $E = (\{a\}, \{a \rightarrow aa\})$ and $A = (a, \{\varepsilon\})$ is not 0L. This language is infinite and the lengths of the words are members of the following sequence: $a_0 = 3$, $a_{n+1} = 2 \cdot (a_n - 1)$ (Table 1).

2.2 P Colonies

We briefly recall the notion of P colonies. A P colony consists of agents and an environment. Both the agents and the environment contain objects. With each agent a set of programs is associated. There are two types of rules in the programs. The rules of the first type, called the evolution rules, are of the form $a \rightarrow b$. It means that the object a inside the agent is rewritten (evolved) to the object b. The rules of the second type, called the communication rules, are of the form $c \leftrightarrow d$. When the communication rule is performed, the object c inside the agent and the object d outside the agent swap their places. Thus after execution of the rule, the object d appears inside the agent and the object c is placed outside the agent.

In [9] the set of programs was extended by the checking rules. These rules give the opportunity to the agents to opt between two possibilities. The rules are of the form r_1/r_2. If the checking rule is performed, then the rule r_1 has higher priority to be executed over the rule r_2. It means that the agent checks whether the rule r_1 is applicable. If the rule can be executed, then the agent is compulsory to use it. If the rule r_1 cannot be applied, then the agent uses the rule r_2.

Definition 4. *The P colony of the capacity k is a construct*
$$\Pi = (A, e, f, V_E, B_1, \ldots, B_n), \text{ where}$$

- *A is the alphabet of the colony, its elements are called objects,*
- *$e \in A$ is the basic object of the colony,*
- *$f \in A$ is the final object of the colony,*
- *V_E is a multiset over $A - \{e\}$,*
- *B_i, $1 \leq i \leq n$, are agents, each agent is a construct $B_i = (O_i, P_i)$, where*
  - *O_i is a multiset over A, it determines the initial state (content) of the agent, $|O_i| = k$,*
  - *$P_i = \{p_{i,1}, \ldots, p_{i,k_i}\}$ is a finite multiset of programs, where each program contains exactly k rules, which are in one of the following forms each:*
    - *$a \to b$, called the evolution rule,*
    - *$c \leftrightarrow d$, called the communication rule,*
    - *r_1/r_2, called the checking rule; r_1, r_2 are the evolution rules or the communication rules.*

A initial configuration of the P colony is an $(n+1)$-tuple of strings of objects present in the P colony at the beginning of the computation. It is given by the multiset O_i for $1 \leq i \leq n$ and by the set V_E. Formally, a configuration of the P colony Π is given by $(w_1, \ldots, w_n, w_E)$, where $|w_i| = k$, $1 \leq i \leq n$, w_i represents all the objects placed inside the i-th agent, and $w_E \in (A - \{e\})^\circ$ represents all the objects in the environment different from the object e.

In the paper the parallel model of P colonies will be studied. In each step of the parallel computation every agent tries to find one usable program. If the number of applicable programs are higher than one, then the agent chooses one of its rules nondeterministically. In one step of the computation the maximal possible number of agents are active.

A configuration is halting if the set of program labels P satisfying the conditions above is the empty set. A set of all possible halting configurations is denoted by H. A halting computation can be associated with the result of the computation. It is given by the number of copies of the special symbol f present in the environment. The set of numbers computed by a P colony Π is defined as

$$N(\Pi) = \{|v_E|_f \mid (w_1, \ldots, w_n, V_E) \Rightarrow^* (v_1, \ldots, v_n, v_E) \in H\},$$

where $(w_1, \ldots, w_n, V_E)$ is the initial configuration, $(v_1, \ldots, v_n, v_E)$ is a halting configuration, and $\Rightarrow^*$ denotes the reflexive and transitive closure of $\Rightarrow$.

Let Π be a P colony $\Pi = (A, e, f, {}_*v_E, B_1, \ldots, B_n)$, the maximal number of programs associated with the agents is called the height. The degree is the number of agents in P colony Π. The third parameter characterizing a P colony is the capacity describing the number of the objects inside each of the agents (Table 2).

Table 2. Summary of proprieties of P colonies

Property of	P colony
Environment V_E	Static, state is multiset of objects
Agents $B = (O, P)$	Have their state, they are equipped by rules allowing communication with environment
Rules in programs	$-a \to b$, $a \in O$ (rewriting, evolution)
	$-c \leftrightarrow d$, $c \in O$, $d \in V_E$ (communication)
	$-p_1/p_2$, where p_1, p_2 are evolution and communication rules (checking)
Priority	Agents have higher priority, environment has no rules
Action of agents	Sequential or *parallel*
Output	Number – the number of objects f present in the environment

Let us use the following notations:
$NPCOL_{par}(c, n, h)$ for the family of all sets of numbers computed by the P colonies working in parallel, using no checking rules and with:

- the capacity at most c,
- the degree at most n and
- the height at most h.

If the checking rules are allowed, the family of all sets of numbers computed by P colonies is denoted by $NPCOL_{par}K$. If the P colonies are restricted, we use notation $NPCOL_{par}R$ and $NPCOL_{par}KR$, respectively.

The P colonies with capacity two are computationally complete.

- $NPCOL_{par}KR(2, *, 5) = NRE$ in [5,11],
- $NPCOL_{par}R(2, *, 5) = NRE$ in [6],
- $NPCOL_{par}K(2, *, 4) = NRE$ in [5],
- $NPCOL_{par}KR(2, 1, *) = NRE$ in [6],
- $NPCOL_{par}R(2, 2, *) = NRE$ in [2].

The following results are stated for the P colonies with capacity one – there is only one object inside each agent and each program contains only one rule.

- $NPCOL_{par}K(1, *, 7) = NRE$ in [2],
- $NPCOL_{par}K(1, 4, *) = NRE$ in [2],
- $NPCOL_{par}(1, 6, *) = NRE$ in [4].

2.3   Eco-P Colonies

In [3] were introduced new types of programs for P colonies with two objects inside each agent. The first of them are deletion programs — $\langle a_{in}; bc \to d \rangle$, using this program the agent consumes one object (a) from the environment and transforms two objects (b, c) inside the agent into the new one (d). The second type are insertion programs, the insertion program is of the form $\langle a_{out}; b \rightarrow cd \rangle$. By executing it the agent sends to the environment one object (a) and from the second object (b) the agent generates two new objects (c, d).

The environment of P colonies is static and it can be changed only by activity of agents. Eco-P colonies are constructed as a natural extension of P colonies with the environment dynamically evolving independently of agents. The mechanism of evolution in the environment is based on $0L$ scheme. $0L$ scheme is a pair (Σ, P), where Σ is the alphabet of $0L$ scheme and P is the set of context free rules, it fulfills the following condition $\forall a \in \Sigma \ \exists \alpha \in \Sigma^*$ such that $(a \rightarrow \alpha) \in P$. For $w_1, w_2 \in \Sigma^*$ we write $w_1 \Rightarrow w_2$ if $w_1 = a_1 a_1 \ldots a_n$, $w_2 = \alpha_2 \alpha_2 \ldots \alpha_n$, for $a_i \rightarrow \alpha_i \in P$, $1 \leq i \leq n$.

Definition 5. *The eco-P colony is a structure*
$$\Pi = (A, e, f, V_E, D_E, B_1, \ldots, B_n), \text{ where}$$
- *A is the alphabet of the eco-P colony, its elements are called objects,*
- *e is the basic (environmental) object of the eco-P colony, $e \in A$,*
- *f is the final object of the eco-P colony, $f \in A$,*
- *V_E is the initial content of the environment, $V_E \in (A - \{e\})^*$,*
- *D_E is $0L$ scheme (A, P_E), where P_E is the set of context-free rules,*
- *B_i, $1 \leq i \leq n$, are the agents, every agent is the structure $B_i = (O_i, P_i)$, where O_i is the multiset over A, it defines the initial state (content) of the agent B_i and $|O_i| = 2$, and $P_i = \{p_{i,1}, \ldots, p_{i,k_i}\}$ is the finite set of programs of two types:*
  - *(1) generating $\langle a \rightarrow bc, d \text{ out} \rangle$ – this program is applicable if agent contains objects a and d. Object a is used for generating new content of the agent and object d is sent into the environment.*
  - *(2) consuming $\langle ab \rightarrow c, d \text{ in} \rangle$ – this program is applicable if the agent contains objects a and b. These objects are evolved to one new object c and the agent imports object d from the environment.*

*Every agent has only one type of programs. The agent with generating programs is called **sender** and the agent with consuming programs is called **consumer**.*

The computation of eco-P colonies is maximally parallel. The configuration of eco-P colony is final when no agent can find applicable program. The result of computation is the number of objects f placed in the environment in a final configuration. Because of nondeterminism we can associate with eco-P colony Π the set of natural numbers $N(\Pi)$.

We denote $NEPCOL_{x,y,z}(n, h)$ the family of the sets computing by eco-P colonies such that:

- x can be one two symbols: s, c. s — if there is an agent sender, c — if there is an agent consumer in eco-P colony,
- $y = passive$ if the rules of $0L$ scheme are of the type $a \rightarrow a$ only,

Table 3. Summary of properties of eco-P colonies

Property of	Eco-P colony
Environment	Dynamic, state is multiset of objects, it can evolve because of 0L scheme
Agents $B = (O, P)$	Have state, two types of rules (programs), depending on their state they can change the state of the environment
Rules	$-\langle a \to bc, d\ out\rangle,\ a, d \in O$ (generating)
	$-\langle ab \to c, d\ in\rangle,\ a, b \in O,\ d \in V_E$ (consuming)
Priority	Agents have higher priority over actions of the environment
Action of the agents	Parallel
Output	Number – the number of objects f present in the environment

- $y = active$ if the set of rules of 0L scheme contains at least one rule of another type than $a \to a$,
- $z = ini$ if the environment or agents contain objects different from e, otherwise we eliminate this notation,
- the degree of eco-P colony is at most n and
- the height is at most h.

The eco-P colonies with two agents (senders and consumers) with passive environment are computationally complete. If the environment is active, the eco-P colony can be computationally complete with two agents consumers and initial content of the environment different from e.

- $NEPCOL_{sc,passive}(2, *) = NRE$,
- $NEPCOL_{c,active,ini}(2, *) = NRE$ in [1] (Table 3).

3   Eco-Colonies vs. P Colonies

First we will analyse the notion of environment in eco-colonies and P colonies. In both cases the agents act in the shared environment. But it is everything in what they are similar. In eco-colonies the environment is changing dynamically, in P colonies it is static. Moreover, the general concept of the environment is discrepant – the environment of eco-colony is a string with 0L scheme assigned to it to determine its evolution, P colony's environment is formed as a multiset of objects in which we do not consider any order of objects.

The P colony agent's rules are very simple. By using one rule the agent can process only one object. A rule of agent in eco-colony can generate a string, its elements are bound to their order and they are inserted into specific, precisely determined place in the environment.

What is the extent to which we can compare, assimilate and eventually simulate the activities of agents in the environment of eco-colonies and P colonies?

Disregarding the differences in understanding of environment and the result of computation (string vs. number), we find similarity, and the basis for the simulation of the following: Let $\Sigma = (E, w_0, A_1, \ldots, A_n)$ be an eco-colony, with

- static environment $E = (V, P)$, P contains only rules of type $a \to a$, $\forall a \in V$,
- the agents $A_i = (S_i, F_i)$, $1 \leq i \leq n$, they have restricted possibilities, they can generate only the strings with length 1: $F_i = \{f_{i,1}, \ldots, f_{i,r_i}\}$, $f_{i,j} \in (V - S_i)$, $1 \leq j \leq r_i$.

We construct P colony $\Pi(\Sigma)$:

- the agents B_i are created according to agents A_i to obtain similar activity,
- we add two more agents to check whether there are any objects corresponding to the agents from eco-colony in the environment; in negative case they cause halting,
- capacity of the P colony is 1,
- there are $n + 6$ consecutive steps of computation corresponding to one step of derivation in eco-colony,
- every agent B_i has r_i programs to evolve object $f_{i,j}$, $1 \leq j \leq r_i$, and $2 * r_i$ programs to exchange this object with S_i (corresponding to agent A_i) from the environment,
- the initial content of the environment is similar to the initial state of the given eco-colony, the initial content of an agent B_i corresponding to an agent $A_i = (S_i, F_i)$ is $S_i \in V$.

The whole conversion process is described in Algorithm 1.

Let us outline how the use of a rule $S_i \to f_{i,j}$ by an agent A_i from the eco-colony will be simulated by execution of programs of the corresponding agent B_i in the P colony.

The agent B_{n+1} checks whether there is any object S_i in the environment. It is done from checking of presence S_1 to checking of presence S_n. In every step of checking, if it finds some S_i (the i-th agent consumes the object S_i) it puts object h_i to the environment and waits for appearance of an object a in the environment. If there is no processable object S_i in the environment, the agent B_{n+1} puts the object T_1 to the environment. This object can stop activity of the agent B_1.

Let us go through simulation of one derivation step in the eco-colony. It starts in the initial configuration – the content of the environment corresponds to the initial state of the eco-colony, the initial content of the agents $B_1, \ldots, B_n$ correspond to the start symbols of appropriate agents of the eco-colony.

The programs associated with the agents $B_1, B_2, \ldots, B_n$ rely on the action rules of the corresponding agents from the eco-colony.

Algorithm 1. Eco-colony $\rightarrow$ P colony

Input : $\Sigma = (E, w_0, A_1, \ldots, A_n)$
  Environment $E = (V, P)$, static;
  Agents $A_i = (S_i, F_i)$, $F_i = \{f_{i,1}, \ldots, f_{i,r_i}\}$,
  $f_{i,j} \in (V - S_i)$, $1 \le j \le r_i$;
  Initial configuration $- w_0 \in V^*$, $|w_0| = d$;
Output: $\Pi(\Sigma) = (A, e, f, V_E, B_1, \ldots, B_{n+2})$ with capacity $k = 1$
  agents $B_i = (O_i, P_i)$,
  initial configuration $- (V_E, O_1, \ldots, O_n)$,
Environment:
$\quad|\quad$ Alphabet: $A = V \cup \{a, e, h, 2, 3, 4, 5, \ldots, n + 4\} \cup \{T_i \mid 1 \le i \le n + 1\}$
$\quad|\quad$ $V_E = \bigcup_{1 \le j \le d} a_j$, where $w_0 = a_1, \ldots, a_d$
end

Agents: $B_i = (O_i, P_i)$, $1 \le i \le n$, $O_i = S_i$ (capacity is 1)
$\quad|\quad$ We construct P_i according to $F_i = \{f_{i,1}, \ldots, f_{i,r_i}\}$:
$\quad|\quad$ $P_i = \bigcup_{1 \le j \le r_i} \{p_{i,ja}, p_{i,jb}, p_{i,jc}\} \cup P_i'$, where
$\quad|\quad$ $P_i' = \{\langle S_i \rightarrow S_i' \rangle ; \langle S_i' \rightarrow 2 \rangle ; \langle 2 \rightarrow 3 \rangle ; \ldots ; \langle n + 3 \rightarrow n + 4 \rangle ; \}$ and
$\quad|\quad$ **for** j, $1 \le j \le r_i$ **do**
$\quad|\quad\quad|\quad$ $p_{i,ja} = \langle n + 4 \rightarrow f_{i,j} \rangle$;
$\quad|\quad\quad|\quad$ $p_{i,jb} = \langle f_{i,j} \leftrightarrow S_i \mathbin{/} f_{i,j} \rightarrow T_{i+1} \rangle$;
$\quad|\quad\quad|\quad$ $p_{i,jc} = \langle T_{i+1} \leftrightarrow T_i \mathbin{/} T_{i+1} \rightarrow S_i' \rangle$;
$\quad|\quad$ **end**
end

Agent: $B_{n+1} = (h, P_{n+1})$
$\quad|\quad$ $P_{n+1} = \{\langle a \rightarrow h \rangle ; \langle h \rightarrow h_1 \rangle ; \langle T_1 \leftrightarrow e \rangle ; \langle S_n \leftrightarrow a \rangle;$
$\quad|\quad$ $\langle h_n \leftrightarrow S_n \mathbin{/} h_n \rightarrow T_1 \rangle\} \cup \bigcup_{1 \le i \le n} \{p_{ia}, p_{ib}\}$
$\quad|\quad$ **for** i, $1 \le i \le n - 1$ **do**
$\quad|\quad\quad|\quad$ $p_{ia} = \langle h_i \leftrightarrow S_i \mathbin{/} h_i \rightarrow h_{i+1} \rangle$;
$\quad|\quad\quad|\quad$ $p_{ib} = \langle S_i \leftrightarrow a \rangle$;
$\quad|\quad$ **end**
end

Agent: $B_{n+2} = (e, P_{n+2})$
$\quad|\quad$ $P_{n+2} = \{\langle h_n \rightarrow a \rangle ; \langle a \leftrightarrow e \rangle ; \langle e \leftrightarrow T_{n+1} \rangle\} \cup \bigcup_{1 \le i \le n} \{p_{ia}, p_{ib}\}$
$\quad|\quad$ **for** i, $1 \le i \le n - 1$ **do**
$\quad|\quad\quad|\quad$ $p_{ia} = \langle e \leftrightarrow h_i \rangle$;
$\quad|\quad\quad|\quad$ $p_{ib} = \langle h_i \rightarrow h_{i+1} \rangle$;
$\quad|\quad$ **end**
end

Every simulation of use of an action rule starts with $n + 3$ steps of evolving content of the agent. In this phase the agents B_{n+1} and B_{n+2} need to check whether there is any object S_i in the environment. In $(n+4)$-th step the agent B_i rewrites the object $n+4$ to some $f_{i,j}$ – the object corresponding to a symbol generated by the agent A_i. If there is any S_i in the environment, the agent B_{n+1} consumes it and sends the object h_i to the environment. Appearance of the object h_i in the environment makes the program of the agent B_{n+2} applicable. The agent B_{n+2} consumes this object and after some "waiting" steps it puts the object a into the environment.

The "waiting" steps ensure that every simulated derivation step of the eco-colony takes the same number of steps of computation in the P colony. The agent B_{n+1} exchanges the object S_i for the object a and the agents $B_1, B_2, \ldots, B_n$ can trade "their" contents for the corresponding objects $S_1, \ldots S_n$ in case that these objects are placed in the environment. Let S_2 (resp. S_{n-1}) be an object present in the environment, $w \in A^*$. The two sequences of configurations for these two objects (see Table 4) show that the given computation takes the same number of steps for each agent corresponding to an agent of the eco-colony.

Table 4. Configurations of P colony during simulation of execution of the action rule of the agents B_2 or B_{n-1} in the case of presence at least one copy of the corresponding symbol S_2 or S_{n-1} in the environment

	env.	B_2	B_{n-1}	B_{n+1}	B_{n+2}
1.	wS_2S_{n-1}	S_2	S_{n-1}	h	e
2.	wS_2S_{n-1}	S_2'	S_{n-1}'	h_1	e
3.	wS_2S_{n-1}	2	2	h_2	e
4.	wh_2S_{n-1}	3	3	S_2	e
5.	wS_{n-1}	4	4	S_2	h_2
6.	wS_{n-1}	5	5	S_2	h_3
7.	wS_{n-1}	6	6	S_2	h_4
$\vdots$					
$(n+2).$	wS_{n-1}	$n+1$	$n+1$	S_2	h_{n-1}
$(n+3).$	wS_{n-1}	$n+2$	$n+2$	S_2	h_n
$(n+4).$	wS_{n-1}	$n+3$	$n+3$	S_2	a
$(n+5).$	$wS_{n-1}a$	$n+4$	$n+4$	S_2	e
$(n+6).$	wS_2S_{n-1}	$f_{2,j}$	$f_{n-1,k}$	a	e
$(n+7).$	$wf_{2,j}f_{n-1}$	S_2	S_{n-1}	h	e

	env.	B_{n-1}	B_{n+1}	B_{n+2}
1.	wS_{n-1}	S_{n-1}	h	e
2.	wS_{n-1}	S_{n-1}'	h_1	e
3.	wS_{n-1}	2	h_2	e
4.	wS_{n-1}	3	h_3	e
5.	wS_{n-1}	4	h_4	e
$\vdots$				
$n.$	wS_{n-1}	$n-1$	h_{n-1}	e
$(n+1).$	wh_{n-1}	n	S_{n-1}	e
$(n+2).$	w	$n+1$	S_{n-1}	h_{n-1}
$(n+3).$	w	$n+2$	S_{n-1}	h_n
$(n+4).$	w	$n+3$	S_{n-1}	a
$(n+5).$	wa	$n+4$	S_{n-1}	e
$(n+6).$	wS_{n-1}	$f_{n-1,j}$	a	e
$(n+7).$	$wf_{n-1,j}$	S_{n-1}	h	e

Two situations can arise in the next configuration – an object S_i is either present or absent in the environment. If there is at least one occurrence of the object S_i in the environment, the i-th agent can use a program with a communication rule $f_{i,j} \leftrightarrow S_i$. Otherwise the agent uses an evolution rule $f_{i,j} \to T_{i+1}$. Because of priority (the communication rule must be used if it is possible) we group these two rules into one checking program. In the following step the agent rewrites its content to S_i and continues with simulation of the next derivation step of the eco-colony. It does not hold if the object T_i appears in the environment. The object T_i signals that no agent can work and it is necessary to

Table 5. Configurations of P colony during simulation of execution of action rule of agent B_2, agent B_{n-1} cannot work because of absence "its" object S_{n-1} in the environment

	env.	B_2	B_{n-1}	B_{n+1}	B_{n+2}	
1.	wS_2	S_2	S_{n-1}	h	e	
2.	wS_2	S_2'	S_{n-1}'	h_1	e	
3.	wS_2	2	2	h_2	e	
4.	wh_2	3	3	S_2	e	
5.	w	4	4	S_2	h_2	
6.	w	5	5	S_2	h_3	
7.	w	6	6	S_2	h_4	
$\vdots$						
$(n+2)$.	w	$n+1$	$n+1$	S_{n-1}	h_{n-1}	
$(n+3)$.	w	$n+2$	$n+2$	S_2	h_n	
$(n+4)$.	w	$n+3$	$n+3$	S_2	a	
$(n+5)$.	wa	$n+4$	$n+4$	S_2	e	
$(n+6)$.	wS_2	$f_{2,j}$	$f_{n-1,k}$	a	e	
$(n+7)$.	$wf_{2,j}$	S_2	T_n	h	e	
$(n+8)$.	$wf_{2,j}$	S_2'	S_{n-1}'	h_1	e	– this configuration corresponds to the configuration 2.

stop computation. After consuming such object, the agent has no applicable program. While consuming the object T_i, $1 \leq i \leq n$, the agent B_i gives the halting object for the agent B_{i+1} into the environment except of object T_{n+1}, this one is consumed by the agent B_{n+2}.

The sample computation for the case when there is no object S_{n-1} corresponding with the agent A_{n-1} in the environment is shown in Table 5.

When there is no object S_i, $1 \leq i \leq n$, in the environment the computation is performed in the way that it is shown in Table 6.

The computation of the P colony begins with the objects corresponding to the axiom of the eco-colony in the environment. As shown above the previous agents correctly simulate the behaviour of the eco-colony, and the computation of the P colony stops if and only if the computation of the eco-colony halts.

According to the previous algorithm and description of simulation process we obtain the following theorem:

Theorem 1. *Let P colony $\Pi = (A, e, f, V_E, B_1, \ldots, B_{n+2})$ with capacity 1 be constructed from the eco-colony $\Sigma = (E, w_0, A_1, \ldots, A_n)$ where $A_i = (S_i, F_i)$, $1 \geq i \geq n$ and with $|f_{i,j}| \leq 1$ for all $f_{i,j} \in F_i$, $1 \geq i \geq n$ in accordance with Algorithm 1. If w_k is state of the environment in the eco-colony Σ after k derivation steps, $k \geq 0$, and w_k' is state of the environment of the P colony Π after $k \cdot (n+6)$ derivation steps, then $|w_k|_a = |w_k'|_a$ for all $a \in V$.*

In general, we can simulate the execution of the action rules $f_{i,j}$ with the length greater than one but we have to use a P colony with the capacity at least two to generate all symbols from the string.

Table 6. Configurations of P colony during preparing to end the computation

	env.	B_1	B_2	...	B_n	B_{n+1}	B_{n+2}
1.	w	S_1	S_2	...	S_n	h	e
2.	w	S_1'	S_2'	...	S_n'	h_1	e
3.	w	2	2	...	2	h_2	e
4.	w	3	3	...	3	h_3	e
$\vdots$							
$(n+1)$.	w	n	n	...	n	h_n	e
$(n+2)$.	w	$n+1$	$n+1$	...	$n+1$	T_1	e
$(n+3)$.	wT_1	$n+2$	$n+2$	...	$n+2$	e	e
$(n+4)$.	wT_1	$n+3$	$n+3$	...	$n+3$	e	e
$(n+5)$.	wT_1	$n+4$	$n+4$	...	$n+4$	e	e
$(n+6)$.	wT_1	f_{1,j_1}	f_{2,j_2}	...	f_{n,j_n}	e	e
$(n+7)$.	wT_1	T_2	T_3	...	T_{n+1}	e	e
$(n+8)$.	wT_2	T_1	S_2'	...	S_n'	e	e
$(n+9)$.	wT_2	T_1	2	...	2	e	e
$(n+10)$.	wT_2	T_1	3	...	3	e	e
$\vdots$							
$(n+15)$.	wT_2	T_1	$n+4$	...	$n+4$	e	e
$(n+16)$.	wT_2	T_1	f_{2,j_2}	...	f_{n,j_n}	e	e
$(n+17)$.	wT_2	T_1	T_3	...	T_{n+1}	e	e
$(n+18)$.	wT_3	T_1	T_2	...	S_n'	e	e
$\vdots$							
$(10n)$.	wT_{n+1}	T_1	T_2	...	T_n	e	e
$(10n+1)$.	w	T_1	T_2	...	T_n	e	T_{n+1}

4 Eco-Colonies vs. Eco-P Colonies

In accordance with the definitions above, a closer relationship between eco-colonies and eco-P colonies could be expected than in case of the previous comparison of eco-colonies and P colonies. In the both systems there is dynamic environment, the environmental changes depend not only on agents' activity.

Let $\Sigma = (E, w_0, A_1, \ldots, A_n)$ be an eco-colony with n agents where

- the environment $E = (V, P)$ is 0L scheme,
- the agents $A_i = (S_i, F_i)$, $1 \leq i \leq n$ generate the strings according to the action rules from $F_i = \{f_{i,1}, \ldots, f_{i,r_i}\}$, $f_{i,j} \in (V - S_i)^*$, $1 \leq j \leq r_i$.

We construct the eco-P colony $\Pi(\Sigma)$:

- the agents B_i are created by the agents A_i such that their activity will be similar to that of the agents in the environment of the eco-colony,
- one step of derivation in the eco-colony will be simulated in three steps of computation in the eco-P colony,

– every agent B_i has r_i triples of sets of programs, for each triple-step one of these sets will be chosen (the third program is the same in all sets so the agent B_i has $2 * r_i + 1$ programs),
– the initial content of the eco-P colony's environment V_E corresponds to the axiom w_0 in the eco-colony, and the initial content of an agent B_i based on the agent $A_i = (S_i, F_i)$ is $S_i X$.

Whole construction of the eco-P colony from the given eco-colony is described in Algorithm 2.

Algorithm 2. Eco-colony → eco-P colony

Input : $\Sigma = (E, w_0, A_1, \ldots, A_n)$
  environment $E = (V, P)$ is 0L scheme
  agents $A_i = (S_i, F_i)$,
  $F_i = \{f_{i,1}, \ldots, f_{i,r_i}\}$ $f_{i,j} \in (V - S_i)^*$, $1 \leq j \leq r_i$
  axiom $w_0 \in V^*$, $|w_0| = d$

Output: $\Pi(\Sigma) = (A, e, f, V_E, D_E, B_1, \ldots, B_n)$
  agents $B_i = (O_i, P_i)$,
  the initial configuration $(V_E, O_1, \ldots, O_n)$

Environment:

$A = V \cup \{e, f, X\} \cup \{a', a''; \ a \in V\} \cup \{[i, j]; \ 1 \leq i \leq n, 1 \leq j \leq r_i\};$
$V_E = \bigcup_{1 \leq j \leq d} a_j,$ where $w_0 = a_1, \ldots, a_d;$
$D_E = (A - \{X\}, P_E),$ where
$P_E = \{a \to a', \ a' \to a'', \ a'' \to \beta; \ \text{where} \ (a \to \beta) \in P_E\} \cup$
  $\cup \{f \to f\} \cup \{e \to e\} \cup \{[i, j] \to f_{i,j} ; \ 1 \leq i \leq n, \ f_{i,j} \in F_i\}$

end

Agents: $B_i = (O_i, P_i),$ $1 \leq i \leq n$

$O_i = S_i X$
P_i is constructed according to $F_i = \{f_{i,1}, \ldots, f_{i,r_i}\}$:
$P_i = \{p_{i,c} = \langle S_i \to S_i X, \ f \ out\rangle\} \cup \left(\bigcup_{1 \leq j \leq r_i} \{p_{i,ja}, p_{i,jb}\}\right),$ where

for j, $1 \leq j \leq r_i$ **do**
  $p_{i,ja} = \langle S_i X \to [i, j], \ S_i \ in\rangle$
  $p_{i,jb} = \langle S_i \to S_i f, \ [i, j] \ out\rangle$
end

end

One computation step of the eco-colony is simulated in three (sub)steps in the eco-P colony. We show that:

– in the first substep (from the given triple-step) only such agents B_i work whose objects S_i are present in the environment,
– in the second and third substep only those agents work, who worked in the first substep,
– the concept of priority of agents over the evolution of environment is kept.

We describe how the agents work and how the environment responds. Let us follow the action of an agent B_i, $1 \leq i \leq n$:

Substep 1. Only such agent who can find "free" object (which it can process) in the environment can work. The agent B_i nondeterministically chooses an action rule from F_i and consumes the object S_i from the environment simultaneously, by using a program $\langle S_i X \rightarrow [i,j], S_i \ in \rangle$ for some j, $1 \leq j \leq r_i$. The agent changes its content from $S_i X$ to $S_i[i,j]$.

But if the agent B_i does not find its object S_i in the environment, it cannot work in this triple-step because

- any programs of the type $p_{i,ja}$ (see Algorithm 2) are not applicable – there is no object S_i in the environment,
- any programs of the type $p_{i,jb}$ are not applicable – there is no object $[i,j]$ inside the agent,
- the program $p_{i,c}$ is not applicable – there is no object f inside the agent to be placed into the environment.

The rules of the type $a \rightarrow a'$ are used to evolve the environmentÀfter executing this substep there are only objects a', $a \in V$ in the environment.

Substep 2. Let the agent B_i worked in the previous substep. Its content is $S_i[i,j]$. There is only one applicable program $\langle S_i \rightarrow S_i f, [i,j] \ out \rangle$ for some index $j \in \{1,\ldots,r_i\}$ ($p_{i,ja}$ are not applicable because there is no object S_i in the environment, $p_{i,c}$ cannot be applied because there is no f inside the agent). The content of the agent changes to $S_i f$, the object $[i,j]$ is placed into the environment.

After execution of the substep 2 there are these objects in the environment: a'', $a \in V$ (e and f eventually) and $[i,j]$ produced by active agents.

Substep 3. The agent B_i is in the state $S_i f$. It has only one applicable program $\langle S_i \rightarrow S_i X, f \ out \rangle$. The content of the agent changes to $S_i X$ and the object f is placed into the environment.

The rules of the environment evolve it in the following way:

- the objects a'' are processed by the rules $a'' \rightarrow \beta$ (simulating execution using the 0L rules of the eco-colony),
- the objects $[i,j]$ are evolved using rules $[i,j] \rightarrow f_{i,j}$ (the environment cooperates on simulation activity of the agents A_i from the eco-colony).

The content of the environment is corresponding to the string in the eco-colony except the order of elements. Moreover there is one object f per active agent in the environment of the eco-P colony.

It is obvious that the process of computation in the eco-P colony corresponds to this one in the given eco-colony. The number of steps in computation in the eco-colony is tripled. Now we focus on halting in the eco-P colony. If no agent in the eco-colony can work (there are not any corresponding objects S_i), the computation in the eco-P colony enters analogical configuration – no agent B_i can apply any of its programs, and computation ends (Table 7).

Table 7. Content of the environment and agents in eco-P colony

Substeps:	first		second		third	
Object S_i is present in the environment:						
environment	$\alpha S_i \beta$	$\Rightarrow$	$\alpha' S_i \beta'$	$\Rightarrow$	$\alpha''[i,j]\beta''$	$\Rightarrow \quad \gamma f_{i,j} f \delta$
agent B_i	$S_i X$	$\Rightarrow$	$S_i[i,j]$	$\Rightarrow$	$S_i f$	$\Rightarrow \quad S_i X$
Object S_i is absent in the environment:						
environment	$\alpha\beta$	$\Rightarrow$	$\alpha'\beta'$	$\Rightarrow$	$\alpha''\beta''$	$\Rightarrow \quad \gamma\delta$
agent B_i	$S_i X$	$\Rightarrow$	$S_i X$	$\Rightarrow$	$S_i X$	$\Rightarrow \quad S_i X$

As the result of computation in the eco-P colony we can observe how many agents were working during whole computation (the number of occurrences of the object f at the end of computation placed in the environment).

From the previous algorithm and the description of simulation process we obtain the following theorem:

Theorem 2. *Let eco-P colony $\Pi = (A, e, f, V_E, D_E, B_1, \ldots, B_n)$ be constructed from the eco-colony $\Sigma = (E, w_0, A_1, \ldots, A_n)$ in accordance with Algorithm 2. If w_k is state of the environment in the eco-colony Σ after k derivation steps, $k \geq 0$, and w'_k is state of the environment of the P colony Π after $k \cdot 3$ derivation steps, then $|w_k|_a = |w'_k|_a$ for all $a \in V$.*

5 Conclusion

As pointed out in Introduction, the aim of this paper is not to compare the computational power of the discussed models, we dealt with comparison of activities of agents in their shared environment.

While agents of eco-colonies are (intentionally) very simple to construct, they have no internal status, they only affect the environment (moreover, they can not generate their own starting symbol), agents of P colonies and eco-P colonies are rather more *sophisticated* – they have their own internal state and they interact with the environment by using several types of rules. By contrast, agents in eco-colonies can generate various strings, different number of symbols than one as well, but agents in P colonies and eco-P colonies work with strictly specified number of symbols in each derivation step.

Eco-colonies and eco-P colonies share one important trait – their environment is able to self-develop.

In this paper we introduce two algorithms – the input of the both algorithms is an eco-colony (in the first case it is of the restricted form), the output is a P colony (Algorithm 1) or an eco-P colony emulating the actions of agents in the environment. The goal was to ensure similarity of environment changes synchronously with the original system as close as possible.

The first algorithm is more complicated – it is not possible to utilize self-developing environment, agents generate only symbols instead of strings, and one derivation step of an original (and restricted) eco-colony is simulated by $n+6$ steps of the constructed P colony. The main problem was to stop derivation of the constructed P colony in the step corresponding to the stopping step of the given eco-colony – it is the reason of adding the additional agents B_{n+1} and B_{n+2} and derivation lengthening.

In the second algorithm we were able to count on the possibility of development in the environment, we used it not merely for simulating the self-development of the environment itself but also to provide inserting variously long strings, in the given eco-colony inserted by agents. One derivation step of the original eco-colony is simulated by three derivation steps of the constructed eco-P colony.

We can undoubtedly say that eco-colonies are much more similar to eco-P colonies than to P colonies, and the above stated algorithms specify degree of this similarity respectively difference.

Acknowledgement. This work was partially supported by the European Regional Development Fund in the IT4Innovations Centre of Excellence project (CZ.1.05/-1.1.00/02.0070) and by SGS/24/2013 and SGS/6/2014.

References

1. Cienciala, L., Ciencialová, L.: P colonies and their extensions. In: Kelemen, J., Kelemenová, A. (eds.) Computation, Cooperation, and Life. LNCS, vol. 6610, pp. 158–169. Springer, Heidelberg (2011)
2. Cienciala, L., Ciencialová, L., Kelemenová, A.: On the number of agents in P colonies. In: Eleftherakis, G., Kefalas, P., Păun, Gh., Rozenberg, G., Salomaa, A. (eds.) WMC 2007. LNCS, vol. 4860, pp. 193–208. Springer, Heidelberg (2007)
3. Ciencialová, L., Cienciala, L., Csuhaj-Varjú, E., Kelemenová, A., György, V.: On very simple P colonies. In: Proceeding of the Seventh Brainstorming Week on Membrane Computing, vol. 1, pp. 97–108 (2009)
4. Ciencialová, L., Csuhaj-Varjú, E., Kelemenová, A., Vaszil, G.: Variants of P colonies with very simple cell structure. Int. J. Comput. Commun. Control IV **3**, 224–233 (2009)
5. Csuhaj-Varjú, E., Kelemen, J., Kelemenová, A., Păun, Gh., Vaszil, G.: Computing with cells in environment: P colonies. J. Multiple Valued Logic Soft Comput. **12**(3/4), 201 (2006)
6. Freund, R., Oswald, M.: P colonies working in the maximally parallel and in the sequential mode. In: Proceedings - Seventh International Symposium on Symbolic and Numeric Algorithms for Scientific Computing, SYNASC, pp. 419–426 (2005)
7. Hopcroft, J.E., Ullman, J.D. (eds.): Introduction to Automata Theory, Languages and Computation. Addison Wesley, Reading (1979)
8. Kelemen, J., Kelemenová, A.: A grammar-theoretic treatment of multiagent systems. Cybern. Syst. **23**(6), 621–633 (1992)
9. Kelemen, J., Kelemenová, A.: On P colonies, a biochemically inspired model of computation. In: Proceedings of the 6th International Symposium of Hungarian Researchers on Computational Intelligence, pp. 40–56 (2005)

10. Kelemen, J., Kelemenová, A. (eds.): Computation, Cooperation, and Life: Essays Dedicated to Gheorghe Păun on the Occasion of His 60th Birthday. LNCS, vol. 6610. Springer, Heidelberg (2011)

11. Kelemen, J., Kelemenová, A., Păun, Gh.: Preview of P colonies: a biochemically inspired computing model. In: Workshop and Tutorial Proceedings. Ninth International Conference on the Simulation and Synthesis of Living Systems (Alife IX), pp. 82–86, Boston, Mass (2004)

12. Kelemenová, A., Vavrečková, S.: Generative power of eco-colonies. In: Kelemen, J., Kelemenová, A. (eds.) Computation, Cooperation, and Life: Essays Dedicated to Gheorghe Păun on the Occasion of His 60th Birthday. LNCS, vol. 6610, pp. 107–121. Springer, Heidelberg (2011)

13. Lindenmayer, A.: Mathematical models for cellular interactions in development i. filaments with one-sided inputs. J. Theor. Bio. **18**(3), 280–299 (1968)

14. Păun, Gh., Rozenberg, G., Salomaa, A.: The Oxford Handbook of Membrane Computing. Oxford University Press Inc., New York (2010)

15. Rozenberg, G., Doucet, P.: On 0L-languages. Inf. Control **19**(4), 302–318 (1971)

16. Vavrečková, Š.: Eko-kolonie. Kognice a umělý život - sborník konference, pp. 601–612 (2005)

Author Index

Printed in the United States
By Bookmasters